W9-BRL-421

THE ARC DE TRIOMPHE.

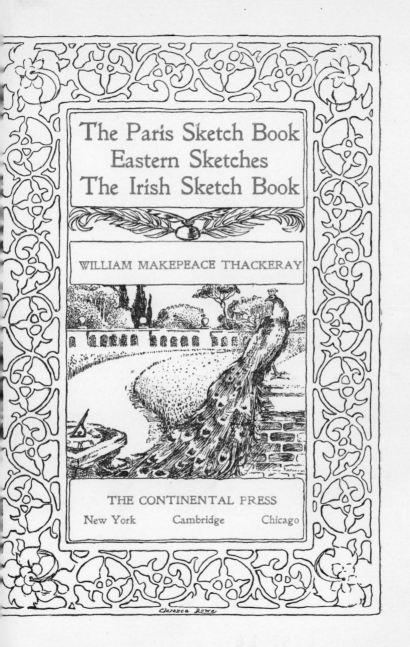

The Paris Sketch Book
Eastern Sketches
The Irish Sketch Book

WILLIAM MAKEPEACE THACKERAY

THE CONTINENTAL PRESS

New York   Cambridge   Chicago

Clarence Rowe

Press of
Braunworth & Co.
Bookbinders and Printers
Brooklyn, N. Y.

4257 16

828
T36.26
5386

CONTENTS.

THE PARIS SKETCH BOOK.

	PAGE
An Invasion of France	5
A Caution to Travellers	16
The Fêtes of July	32
On the French School of Painting	40
The Painter's Bargain	58
Cartouche	71
On some French Fashionable Novels	82
A Gambler's Death	102
Napoleon and his System	111
The Story of Mary Ancel	124
Beatrice Merger	142
Caricatures and Lithography in Paris	149
Little Poinsinet	175
The Devil's Wager	188
Madame Sand and the new Apocalypse	198
The Case of Peytel	221
Four Imitations of Béranger	248
French Dramas and Melodramas	258
Meditations at Versailles	276

CONTENTS.

EASTERN SKETCHES.

A JOURNEY FROM CORNHILL TO CAIRO.

CHAPTER		PAGE
	DEDICATION	293
	PREFACE	295
I.	VIGO. — Thoughts at Sea — Sight of Land — Vigo — Spanish Ground — Spanish Troops — Pasagero . . .	297
II.	LISBON — CADIZ. — Lisbon — The Belem Road — A School — Landscape — Palace of Necessidades — Cadiz — The Rock	303
III.	THE "LADY MARY WOOD." — British Lions — Travelling Friends — Bishop No. 2 — "Good-by, Bishop" — The Meek Lieutenant — "Lady Mary Wood" . . .	311
IV.	GIBRALTAR. — Mess-Room Gossip — Military Horticulture — "All's Well" — A Release — Gibraltar — Malta — Religion and Nobility — Malta Relics — The Lazaretto — Death in the Lazaretto	317
V.	ATHENS. — Reminiscences of τύπτω — The Peiræus — Landscape — Basileus — England for Ever! — Classic Remains — τύπτω again	328
VI.	SMYRNA — FIRST GLIMPSES OF THE EAST. — First Emotions — The Bazaar — A Bastinado — Women — The Caravan Bridge — Smyrna — The Whistler	336
VII.	CONSTANTINOPLE. — Caïques — Eothen's "Misseri" — A Turkish Bath — Constantinople — His Highness the Sultan — Ich möchte nicht der Sultan seyn — A Subject for a Ghazul — The Child-Murderer — Turkish Children — Modesty — The Seraglio — The Sultanas' Puffs — The Sublime Porte — The Schoolmaster in Constantinople	344
VIII.	RHODES. — Jew Pilgrims — Jew Bargaining — Relics of Chivalry — Mahometanism Bankrupt — A Dragoman — A Fine Day — Rhodes	363

CONTENTS.

CHAPTER | PAGE

IX. THE WHITE SQUALL 370

X. TELMESSUS — BEYROUT. — Telmessus — Halil Pasha — Beyrout — A Portrait — A Ball on Board — A Syrian Prince 373

XI. A DAY AND NIGHT IN SYRIA. — Landing at Jaffa — Jaffa — The Cadi of Jaffa — The Cadi's Divan — A Night-Scene at Jaffa — Syrian Night's Entertainments 380

XII. FROM JAFFA TO JERUSALEM. — A Cavalcade — Marching Order — A Tournament — Ramleh — Roadside Sketches — Rencontres — Abou Gosh — Night before Jerusalem 387

XIII. JERUSALEM. — A Pillar of the Church — Quarters — Jewish Pilgrims — Jerusalem Jews — English Service — Jewish History — The Church of the Sepulchre — The Porch of the Sepulchre — Greek and Latin Legends — The Church of the Sepulchre — Bethlehem — The Latin Convent — The American Consul — Subjects for Sketching — Departure — A Day's March — Ramleh 3ᴄ5

XIV. FROM JAFFA TO ALEXANDRIA. — Bill of Fare — From Jaffa to Alexandria 4ᶜ3

XV. TO CAIRO. — The Nile — First Sight of Cheops — The Ezbekieh — The Hôtel d'Orient — The Conqueror Waghorn — Architecture — The Chief of the Hag — A Street-Scene — Arnaoots — A Gracious Prince — The Screw-Propeller in Egypt — The "Rint" in Egypt — The Maligned Orient — "The Sex" — Subjects for Painters — Slaves — A Hyde Park Moslem — Glimpses of the Harem — An Eastern Acquaintance — An Egyptian Dinner — Life in the Desert — From the Top of the Pyramid — Groups for Landscape — Pigmies and Pyramids — Things to think of — Finis . . 418

CONTENTS.

THE IRISH SKETCH BOOK

OF 1842.

CHAPTER		PAGE
	Dedication	3
I.	A Summer Day in Dublin, or There and Thereabouts .	5
II.	A Country-house in Kildare — Sketches of an Irish Family and Farm	25
III.	From Carlow to Waterford	34
IV.	From Waterford to Cork	44
V.	Cork — The Agricultural Show — Father Mathew . . .	53
VI.	Cork — The Ursuline Convent	61
VII.	Cork	68
VIII.	From Cork to Bantry; with an Account of the City of Skibbereen	80
IX.	Rainy Days at Glengariff	90
X.	From Glengariff to Killarney	96
XI.	Killarney — Stag-hunting on the Lake	104
XII.	Killarney — The Races — Muckross	109
XIII.	Tralee — Listowel — Tarbert	118
XIV.	Limerick	123
XV.	Galway — "Kilroy's Hotel" — Galway Nights' Entertainments — First Night: An Evening with Captain Freeny	135
XVI.	More Rain in Galway — A Walk there — And the Second Galway Night's Entertainment	153

CONTENTS.

CHAPTER		PAGE
XVII.	From Galway to Ballinahinch	175
XVIII.	Roundstone Petty Sessions	186
XIX.	Clifden to Westport	190
XX.	Westport	196
XXI.	The Pattern at Croaghpatrick	200
XXII.	From Westport to Ballinasloe	205
XXIII.	Ballinasloe to Dublin	209
XXIV.	Two Days in Wicklow	213
XXV.	Country Meetings in Kildare — Meath — Drogheda	229
XXVI.	Dundalk	242
XXVII.	Newry, Armagh, Belfast — From Dundalk to Newry	255
XXVIII.	Belfast to the Causeway	266
XXIX.	The Giant's Causeway — Coleraine — Portrush	275
XXX.	Peg of Limavaddy	285
XXXI.	Templemoyle — Derry	289
XXXII.	Dublin at Last	301

CHARACTER SKETCHES.

Captain Rook and Mr. Pigeon		315
The Fashionable Authoress		332
The Artists		345

THE PARIS SKETCH BOOK

DEDICATORY LETTER

TO

M. ARETZ, TAILOR, Etc.

27, RUE RICHELIEU, PARIS.

Sir, — It becomes every man in his station to acknowledge and praise virtue wheresoever he may find it, and to point it out for the admiration and example of his fellow-men.

Some months since, when you presented to the writer of these pages a small account for coats and pantaloons manufactured by you, and when you were met by a statement from your creditor, that an immediate settlement of your bill would be extremely inconvenient to him; your reply was, "Mon Dieu. Sir, let not that annoy you; if you want money, as a gentleman often does in a strange country, I have a thousand-franc note at my house which is quite at your service."

History or experience, Sir, makes us acquainted with so few actions that can be compared to yours, — an offer like this from a stranger and a tailor seems to me so astonishing, — that you must pardon me for thus making your virtue public, and acquainting the English nation with your merit and your name. Let me add, Sir, that you live on the first floor; that your clothes and fit are excellent, and your charges moderate and just; and, as a humble tribute of my admiration, permit me to lay these volumes at your feet.

Your obliged, faithful servant,

M. A. TITMARSH.

ADVERTISEMENT TO THE FIRST EDITION.

ABOUT half of the sketches in these volumes have already appeared in print, in various periodical works. A part of the text of one tale, and the plots of two others, have been borrowed from French originals; the other stories, which are, in the main, true, have been written upon facts and characters that came within the Author's observation during a residence in Paris.

As the remaining papers relate to public events which occurred during the same period, or to Parisian Art and Literature, he has ventured to give his publication the title which it bears.

LONDON, July 1, 1840.

AN INVASION OF FRANCE.

"Cæsar venit in Galliam summâ diligentiâ."

ABOUT twelve o'clock, just as the bell of the packet is tolling a farewell to London Bridge, and warning off the blackguard-boys with the newspapers, who have been shoving *Times*, *Herald*, *Penny Paul-Pry*, *Penny Satirist*, *Flare-up*, and other abominations, into your face — just as the bell has tolled, and the Jews, strangers, people-taking-leave-of-their-families, and blackguard-boys aforesaid, are making a rush for the narrow plank which conducts from the paddle-box of the "Emerald" steamboat unto the quay — you perceive, staggering down Thames Street, those two hackney-coaches, for the arrival of which you have been praying, trembling, hoping, despairing, swearing — sw—, I beg your pardon, I believe the word is not used in polite company — and transpiring, for the last half-hour. Yes, at last, the two coaches draw near, and from thence an awful number of trunks, children, carpet-bags, nursery-maids, hat-boxes, band-boxes, bonnet-boxes, desks, cloaks, and an affectionate wife, are discharged on the quay.

"Elizabeth, take care of Miss Jane," screams that worthy woman, who has been for a fortnight employed in getting this tremendous body of troops and baggage into marching order. "Hicks! Hicks! for heaven's sake mind the babies!" — "George — Edward, sir, if you go near that porter with the trunk, he will tumble down and kill you, you naughty boy! — My love, *do* take the cloaks and umbrellas, and give a hand to Fanny and Lucy; and I wish you would speak to the hackney-coachmen, dear, they want fifteen shillings, and count the packages, love — twenty-seven packages, — and bring little Flo; where's little Flo? — Flo! Flo!" — (Flo comes sneaking in;

she has been speaking a few parting words to a one-eyed terrier, that sneaks off similarly, landward.)

As when the hawk menaces the hen-roost, in like manner, when such a danger as a voyage menaces a mother, she becomes suddenly endowed with a ferocious presence of mind, and bristling up and screaming in the front of her brood, and in the face of circumstances, succeeds, by her courage, in putting her enemy to flight; in like manner you will always, I think, find your wife (if that lady be good for twopence) shrill, eager, and ill-humored, before, and during a great family move of this nature. Well, the swindling hackney-coachmen are paid, the mother leading on her regiment of little ones, and supported by her auxiliary nurse-maids, are safe in the cabin; — you have counted twenty-six of the twenty-seven parcels, and have them on board, and that horrid man on the paddle-box, who, for twenty minutes past, has been roaring out, NOW, SIR! — says, *now, sir*, no more.

I never yet knew how a steamer began to move, being always too busy among the trunks and children, for the first half-hour, to mark any of the movements of the vessel. When these private arrangements are made, you find yourself opposite Greenwich (farewell, sweet, sweet whitebait!), and quiet begins to enter your soul. Your wife smiles for the first time these ten days; you pass by plantations of ship-masts, and forests of steam-chimneys; the sailors are singing on board the ships, the bargees salute you with oaths, grins, and phrases facetious and familiar; the man on the paddle-box roars, " Ease her, stop her!" which mysterious words a shrill voice from below repeats, and pipes out, " Ease her, stop her!" in echo; the deck is crowded with groups of figures, and the sun shines over all.

The sun shines over all, and the steward comes up to say, " Lunch, ladies and gentlemen! Will any lady or gentleman please to take anythink?" About a dozen do : boiled beef and pickles, and great red raw Cheshire cheese, tempt the epicure : little dumpy bottles of stout are produced, and fizz and bang about with a spirit one would never have looked for in individuals of their size and stature.

The decks have a strange look; the people on them, that is. Wives, elderly stout husbands, nurse-maids, and children predominate, of course, in English steamboats. Such may be considered as the distinctive marks of the English gentleman at three or four and forty: two or three of such groups have pitched their camps on the deck. Then there are a number of young men, of whom three or four have allowed their mous-

taches to *begin* to grow since last Friday; for they are going
" on the Continent," and they look, therefore, as if their upper
lips were smeared with snuff.

A *danseuse* from the opera is on her way to Paris. Followed
by her *bonne* and her little dog, she paces the deck, stepping
out, in the real dancer fashion, and ogling all around. How
happy the two young Englishmen are, who can speak French,
and make up to her : and how all criticise her points and paces !
Yonder is a group of young ladies, who are going to Paris to
learn how to be governesses : those two splendidly dressed ladies
are milliners from the Rue Richelieu, who have just brought
over, and disposed of, their cargo of Summer fashions. Here
sits the Rev. Mr. Snodgrass with his pupils, whom he is conducting to his establishment, near Boulogne, where, in addition
to a classical and mathematical education (washing included),
the young gentlemen have the benefit of learning French among
the French themselves. Accordingly, the young gentlemen are
locked up in a great rickety house, two miles from Boulogne
and never see a soul, except the French usher and the cook.

Some few French people are there already, preparing to be
ill — (I never shall forget a dreadful sight I once had in the
little dark, dirty, six-foot cabin of a Dover steamer. Four
gaunt Frenchmen, but for their pantaloons, in the costume of
Adam in Paradise, solemnly anointing themselves with some
charm against sea-sickness !) — a few Frenchmen are there, but
these, for the most part, and with a proper philosophy, go to the
fore-cabin of the ship, and you see them on the fore-deck (is that
the name for that part of the vessel which is in the region of the
bowsprit?) lowering in huge cloaks and caps ; snuffy, wretched,
pale, and wet ; and not jabbering now, as their wont is on shore.
I never could fancy the Mounseers formidable at sea.

There are, of course, many Jews on board. Who ever
travelled by steamboat, coach, diligence, eilwagen, vetturino,
mule-back, or sledge, without meeting some of the wandering
race ?

By the time these remarks have been made the steward is on
the deck again, and dinner is ready : and about two hours after
dinner comes tea ; and then there is brandy-and-water, which he
eagerly presses as a preventive against what may happen ; and
about this time you pass the Foreland, the wind blowing pretty
fresh ; and the groups on deck disappear, and your wife, giving you an alarmed look, descends, with her little ones, to the
ladies' cabin, and you see the steward and his boys issuing from
their den under the paddle-box, with each a heap of round tin

vases, like those which are called, I believe, in America, *expec-toratoons*, only these are larger.

. . . . . .

The wind blows, the water looks greener and more beautiful than ever — ridge by ridge of long white rock passes away. " That's Ramsgit," says the man at the helm ; and, presently, " That there's Deal — it's dreadful fallen off since the war ; " and " That's Dover, round that there pint, only you can't see it." And, in the meantime, the sun has plumped his hot face into the water, and the moon has shown hers as soon as ever his back is turned, and Mrs. — (the wife in general,) has brought up her children and self from the horrid cabin, in which she says it is impossible to breathe ; and the poor little wretches are, by the officious stewardess and smart steward (expecto-ratoonifer), accommodated with a heap of blankets, pillows, and mattresses, in the midst of which they crawl, as best they may, and from the heaving heap of which are, during the rest of the voyage, heard occasional faint cries, and sounds of puking woe !

Dear, dear Maria ! Is this the woman who, anon, braved the jeers and brutal wrath of swindling hackney-coachmen ; who repelled the insolence of haggling porters, with a scorn that brought down their demands at least eighteenpence ? Is this the woman at whose voice servants tremble ; at the sound of whose steps the nursery, ay, and mayhap the parlor, is in order ? Look at her now, prostrate, prostrate — no strength has she to speak, scarce power to push to her youngest one — her suffering, struggling Rosa, — to push to her the — the instrumentoon !

In the midst of all these throes and agonies, at which all the passengers, who have their own woes (you yourself — for how can you help *them ?* — you are on your back on a bench, and if you move all is up with you,) are looking on indifferent — one man there is who has been watching you with the utmost care, and bestowing on your helpless family the tenderness that a father denies them. He is a foreigner, and you have been con-versing with him, in the course of the morning, in French — which, he says, you speak remarkably well, like a native in fact, and then in English (which, after all, you find is more convenient). What can express your gratitude to this gentle-man for all his goodness towards your family and yourself — you talk to him, he has served under the Emperor, and is, for all that, sensible, modest, and well-informed. He speaks, in-deed, of his countrymen almost with contempt, and readily admits the superiority of a Briton, on the seas and elsewhere.

One loves to meet with such genuine liberality in a foreigner, and respects the man who can sacrifice vanity to truth. This distinguished foreigner has travelled much; he asks whither you are going? — where you stop? if you have a great quantity of luggage on board? — and laughs when he hears of the twenty-seven packages, and hopes you have some friend at the custom-house, who can spare you the monstrous trouble of unpacking that which has taken you weeks to put up. Nine, ten, eleven, the distinguished foreigner is ever at your side; you find him now, perhaps, (with characteristic ingratitude,) something of a bore, but, at least, he has been most tender to the children and their mamma. At last a Boulogne light comes in sight, (you see it over the bows of the vessel, when, having bobbed violently upwards, it sinks swiftly down,) Boulogne harbor is in sight, and the foreigner says, —

The distinguished foreigner says, says he — " Sare, eef you af no 'otel, I sall recommend you, milor, to ze 'Otel Betfort, in ze Quay, sare, close to the bathing-machines and custom-haoose. Good bets and fine garten, sare ; table-d'hôte, sare, à cinq heures ; breakfast, sare, in French or English style ; — I am the commissionaire, sare, and vill see to your loggish."

. . . Curse the fellow, for an impudent, swindling, sneaking French humbug ! — Your tone instantly changes, and you tell him to go about his business : but at twelve o'clock at night, when the voyage is over, and the custom-house business done, knowing not whither to go, with a wife and fourteen exhausted children, scarce able to stand, and longing for bed, you find yourself, somehow, in the Hôtel Bedford (and you can't be better), and smiling chambermaids carry off your children to snug beds ; while smart waiters produce for your honor — a cold fowl, say, and a salad, and a bottle of Bordeaux and Seltzer-water.

The morning comes — I don't know a pleasanter feeling than that of waking with the sun shining on objects quite new, and (although you have made the voyage a dozen times,) quite strange. Mrs. X. and you occupy a very light bed, which has a tall canopy of red " *percale ;* " the windows are smartly draped with cheap gaudy calicoes and muslins ; there are little mean strips of carpet about the tiled floor of the room, and yet all seems as gay and as comfortable as may be — the sun shines brighter than you have seen it for a year, the sky is a thousand times bluer, and what a cheery clatter of shrill quick French voices comes up from the court-yard under the windows ! Bells are jangling; a family, mayhap, is going to Paris, *en poste*, and wondrous is the jabber of the courier, the postilion, the inn-waiters, and the lookers-on. The landlord calls out for " Quatre biftecks aux pommes pour le trente-trois," — (O my country-men, I love your tastes and your ways!) — the chambermaid is laughing and says, " Finissez donc, Monsieur Pierre!" (what can they be about?) — a fat Englishman has opened his window violently, and says, " Dee dong, garsong, vooly voo me donny lo sho, ou vooly voo pah?" He has been ringing for half an hour — the last energetic appeal succeeds, and shortly he is enabled to descend to the coffee-room, where, with three hot rolls, grilled ham, cold fowl, and four boiled eggs, he makes what he calls his first *French* breakfast.

It is a strange, mongrel, merry place, this town of Boulogne; the little French fishermen's children are beautiful, and the little French soldiers, four feet high, red-breeched, with huge *pompons* on their caps, and brown faces, and clear sharp eyes, look, for all their littleness, far more military and more intelligent than the heavy louts one has seen swaggering about the garrison towns in England. Yonder go a crowd of bare-legged fishermen; there is the town idiot, mocking a woman who is screaming " Fleuve du Tage," at an inn-window, to a harp, and there are the little gamins mocking *him*. Lo! these seven young ladies, with red hair and green veils, they are from neighboring Albion, and going to bathe. Here comes three Englishmen, *habitués* evidently of the place, — dandy specimens of our countrymen: one wears a marine dress, another has a shooting dress, a third has a blouse and a pair of guiltless spurs — all have as much hair on the face as nature or art can supply, and all wear their hats very much on one side. Believe me, there is on the face of this world no scamp like an English one, no blackguard like one of these half-gentlemen, so mean, so low, so vulgar, — so ludicrously ignorant and conceited, so desperately heartless and depraved.

But why, my dear sir, get into a passion? — Take things coolly. As the poet has observed, " Those only is gentlemen who behave as sich ; " with such, then, consort, be they cobblers or dukes. Don't give us, cries the patriotic reader, any abuse of our fellow-countrymen (anybody else can do that), but rather continue in that good-humored, facetious, descriptive style with which your letter has commenced. — Your remark, sir, is perfectly just, and does honor to your head and excellent heart.

There is little need to give a description of the good town of Boulogne, which, haute and basse, with the new light-house and the new harbor, and the gas-lamps, and the manufactures, and the convents, and the number of English and French residents, and the pillar erected in honor of the grand *Armée d'Angleterre*, so called because it *didn't* go to England, have all been excellently described by the facetious Coglan, the learned Dr. Millingen, and by innumerable guide-books besides. A fine thing it is to hear the stout old Frenchmen of Napoleon's time argue how that audacious Corsican *would* have marched to London, after swallowing Nelson and all his gun-boats, but for *cette malheureuse guerre d'Espagne* and *cette glorieuse campagne d'Autriche*, which the gold of Pitt caused to be raised at the Emperor's tail, in order to call him off from the helpless country in his front. Some Frenchmen go farther still, and vow that in Spain they were never beaten at all; indeed, if you read in the *Biographie des Hommes du Jour*, article " Soult," you will fancy that, with the exception of the disaster at Vittoria, the campaigns in Spain and Portugal were a series of triumphs. Only, by looking at a map, it is observable that Vimeiro is a mortal long way from Toulouse, where, at the end of certain years of victories, we somehow find the honest Marshal. And what then? — he went to Toulouse for the purpose of beating the English there, to be sure; — a known fact, on which comment would be superfluous. However, we shall never get to Paris at this rate; let us break off further palaver, and away at once. . . .

(During this pause, the ingenious reader is kindly requested to pay his bill at the Hotel at Boulogne, to mount the Diligence of Laffitte, Caillard and Company, and to travel for twenty-five hours, amidst much jingling of harness-bells and screaming of postilions.)

.   .   .   .

The French milliner, who occupies one of the corners, begins to remove the greasy pieces of paper which have enveloped her locks during the journey. She withdraws the " Madras " of dubious hue which has bound her head for the last five-and-twenty hours, and replaces it by the black velvet bonnet, which, bobbing against your nose, has hung from the Diligence roof since your departure from Boulogne. The old lady in the opposite corner, who has been sucking bonbons, and smells dreadfully of anisette, arranges her little parcels in that immense basket of abominations which all old women carry in their laps. She rubs her mouth and eyes with her dusty cambric handkerchief, she ties up her nightcap into a little bundle, and replaces it by a more becoming head-piece, covered with withered artificial flowers, and crumpled tags of ribbon; she looks wistfully at the company for an instant, and then places her hand-kerchief before her mouth : — her eyes roll strangely about for an instant, and you hear a faint clattering noise : the old lady has been getting ready her teeth, which had lain in her basket among the bonbons, pins, oranges, pomatum, bits of cake, loz-enges, prayer-books, peppermint-water, copper money, and false hair — stowed away there during the voyage. The Jewish gentleman, who has been so attentive to the milliner during the journey, and is a traveller and bagman by profession, gathers together his various goods. The sallow-faced English lad, who has been drunk ever since we left Boulogne yesterday, and is coming to Paris to pursue the study of medicine, swears that he rejoices to leave the cursed Diligence, is sick of the infernal journey, and d—d glad that the d—d voyage is so nearly over. " *Enfin !* " says your neighbor, yawning, and inserting an elbow into the mouth of his right and left hand companion, " *nous voilà.*"

Nous Voilà ! — We are at Paris ! This must account for the removal of the milliner's curl-papers, and the fixing of the old lady's teeth. — Since the last *relais*, the Diligence has been travelling with extraordinary speed. The postilion cracks his terrible whip, and screams shrilly. The conductor blows in-cessantly on his horn, the bells of the harness, the bumping and ringing of the wheels and chains, and the clatter of the great hoofs of the heavy snorting Norman stallions, have wondrously increased within this, the last ten minutes ; and the Diligence, which has been proceeding hitherto at the rate of a league in an hour, now dashes gallantly forward, as if it would traverse at least six miles in the same space of time. Thus it is, when Sir Robert maketh a speech at Saint Stephen's — he useth his strength at the beginning, only, and the end. He gallopeth at the commencement ; in the middle he lingers ; at the close, again, he rouses the House, which has fallen asleep ; he crack-eth the whip of his satire ; he shouts the shout of his patriotism ; and, urging his eloquence to its roughest canter, awakens the sleepers, and inspires the weary, until men say, What a won-drous orator ! What a capital coach ! We will ride henceforth in it, and in no other !

But, behold us at Paris ! The Diligence has reached a rude-looking gate, or *grille*, flanked by two lodges ; the French Kings of old made their entry by this gate ; some of the hottest battles of the late revolution were fought before it. At pres-ent, it is blocked by carts and peasants, and a busy crowd of men, in green, examining the packages before they enter, probing the straw with long needles. It is the Barrier of St. Denis, and the green men are the customs'-men of the city of Paris. If you are a countryman, who would introduce a cow into the metropolis, the city demands twenty-four francs for such a privilege : if you have a hundredweight of tallow-candles, you must, previously, disburse three francs : if a drove of hogs, nine francs per whole hog : but upon these subjects Mr. Bulwer, Mrs. Trollope, and other writers, have already enlightened the public. In the present instance, after a momentary pause, one of the men in green mounts by the side of the conductor, and the ponderous vehicle pursues its journey.

The street which we enter, that of the Faubourg St. Denis, presents a strange contrast to the dark uniformity of a London street, where everything, in the dingy and smoky atmosphere, looks as though it were painted in India-ink — black houses, black passengers, and black sky. Here, on the contrary, is a thousand times more life and color. Before you, shining in the sun, is a long glistening line of *gutter*, — not a very pleasing object in a city, but in a picture invaluable. On each side are houses of all dimensions and hues ; some but of one story ; some as high as the tower of Babel. From these the haberdashers (and this is their favorite street) flaunt long strips of gaudy calicoes, which give a strange air of rude gayety to the street. Milk-women, with a little crowd of gossips round each, are, at this early hour of morning, selling the chief material of the Parisian *café-au-lait*. Gay wine-shops, painted red, and smartly decorated with vines and gilded railings, are filled with workmen taking their morning's draught. That gloomy-looking prison on your right is a prison for women ; once it was a convent for Lazarists : a thousand unfortunate individuals of the softer sex now occupy that mansion : they bake, as we find in the guide-books, the bread of all the other prisons ; they mend and wash the shirts and stockings of all the other prisoners ; they make hooks-and-eyes and phosphorus-boxes, and they attend chapel every Sunday : — if occupation can help them, sure they have enough of it. Was it not a great stroke of the legislature to superintend the morals and linen at once, and thus keep these poor creatures continually mending? — But we have passed the prison long ago, and are at the Porte St. Denis itself.

There is only time to take a hasty glance as we pass : it commemorates some of the wonderful feats of arms of Ludovicus Magnus, and abounds in ponderous allegories — nymphs, and river-gods, and pyramids crowned with fleurs-de-lis ; Louis passing over the Rhine in triumph, and the Dutch Lion giving

up the ghost, in the year of our Lord 1672.   The Dutch Lion
revived, and overcame the man some years afterwards ; but of
this fact, singularly enough, the inscriptions make no mention.
Passing, then, *round* the gate, and not under it (after the general
custom, in respect of triumphal arches), you cross the boulevard,
which gives a glimpse of trees and sunshine, and gleaming
white buildings ; then, dashing down the Rue de Bourbon Ville-
neuve, a dirty street, which seems interminable, and the Rue
St. Eustache, the conductor gives a last blast on his horn, and
the great vehicle clatters into the court-yard, where the journey
is destined to conclude.

If there was a noise before of screaming postilions and
cracked horns, it was nothing to the Babel-like clatter which
greets us now.   We are in a great court, which Hajji Baba
would call the father of Diligences.   Half a dozen other coaches
arrive at the same minute — no light affairs, like your English
vehicles, but ponderous machines, containing fifteen passengers
inside, more in the cabriolet, and vast towers of luggage on the
roof : others are loading : the yard is filled with passengers
coming or departing ; — bustling porters and screaming *commissionaires.*   These latter seize you as you descend from your
place, — twenty cards are thrust into your hand, and as many
voices, jabbering with inconceivable swiftness, shriek into your
ear, " Dis way, sare ; are you for ze ' 'Otel of Rhin? ' ' *Hôtel de
l'Amirauté !* ' — ' Hotel Bristol,' sare ! — *Monsieur, ' l'Hôtel de
Lille ? '   Sacr-rrré 'nom de Dieu, laissez passer ce petit, Monsieur !*
Ow mosh loggish ave you, sare ? "

And now, if you are a stranger in Paris, listen to the words
of Titmarsh. — If you cannot speak a syllable of French, and
love English comfort, clean rooms, breakfasts, and waiters ; if
you would have plentiful dinners, and are not particular (as how
should you be ?) concerning wine ; if, in this foreign country,
you *will* have your English companions, your porter, your
friend, and your brandy-and-water — do not listen to any of
these commissioner fellows, but with your best English accent,
shout out boldly, " MEURICE ! " and straightway a man will
step forward to conduct you to the Rue de Rivoli.

Here you will find apartments at any price : a very neat
room, for instance, for three francs daily ; an English breakfast
of eternal boiled eggs, or grilled ham ; a nondescript dinner,
profuse but cold ; and a society which will rejoice your heart.
Here are young gentlemen from the universities ; young merchants on a lark ; large families of nine daughters, with fat
father and mother ; officers of dragoons, and lawyers' clerks.

The last time we dined at " Meurice's " we hobbed and nobbed
with no less a person than Mr. Moses, the celebrated bailiff of
Chancery Lane; Lord Brougham was on his right, and a clergyman's lady, with a train of white-haired girls, sat on his left,
wonderfully taken with the diamond rings of the fascinating
stranger!

It is, as you will perceive, an admirable way to see Paris,
especially if you spend your days reading the English papers
at Galignani's, as many of our foreign tourists do.

But all this is promiscuous, and not to the purpose.   If, — to
continue on the subject of hotel choosing, — if you love quiet,
heavy bills, and the best *table-d'hôte* in the city, go, O stranger!
to the " Hôtel des Princes;" it is close to the Boulevard, and
convenient for Frascati's.   The " Hôtel Mirabeau" possesses
scarcely less attraction; but of this you will find, in Mr. Bulwer's " Autobiography of Pelham," a faithful and complete
account.   " Lawson's Hotel " has likewise its merits, as also
the " Hôtel de Lille," which may be described as a " second
chop " Meurice.

If you are a poor student come to study the humanities, or
the pleasant art of amputation, cross the water forthwith, and
proceed to the " Hôtel Corneille," near the Odéon, or others of
its species; there are many where you can live royally (until
you economize by going into lodgings) on four francs a day;
and where, if by any strange chance you are desirous for a
while to get rid of your countrymen, you will find that they
scarcely ever penetrate.

But above all, O my countrymen! shun boarding-houses,
especially if you have ladies in your train; or ponder well, and
examine the characters of the keepers thereof, before you lead
your innocent daughters, and their mamma, into places so
dangerous.   In the first place, you have bad dinners; and,
secondly, bad company.   If you play cards, you are very likely
playing with a swindler; if you dance, you dance with a ——
person with whom you had better have nothing to do.

Note (which ladies are requested not to read). — In one of these establishments, daily advertised as most eligible for English, a friend of the
writer lived.   A lady, who had passed for some time as the wife of one of
the inmates, suddenly changed her husband and name, her original husband
remaining in the house, and saluting her by her new title.

A CAUTION TO TRAVELLERS.

A MILLION dangers and snares await the traveller, as soon as he issues out of that vast messagerie which we have just quitted: and as each man cannot do better than relate such events as have happened in the course of his own experience, and may keep the unwary from the path of danger, let us take this, the very earliest opportunity, of imparting to the public a little of the wisdom which we painfully have acquired.

And first, then, with regard to the city of Paris, it is to be remarked, that in that metropolis flourish a greater number of native and exotic swindlers than are to be found in any other European nursery. What young Englishman that visits it, but has not determined, in his heart, to have a little share of the gayeties that go on — just for once, just to see what they are like? How many, when the horrible gambling dens were open, did resist a sight of them? — nay, was not a young fellow rather flattered by a dinner invitation from the Salon, whither he went, fondly pretending that he should see "French society," in the persons of certain Dukes and Counts who used to frequent the place?

My friend Pogson is a young fellow, not much worse, although perhaps a little weaker and simpler than his neighbors; and coming to Paris with exactly the same notions that bring many others of the British youth to that capital, events befell him there, last winter, which are strictly true, and shall here be narrated, by way of warning to all.

Pog, it must be premised, is a city man, who travels in drugs for a couple of the best London houses, blows the flute, has an album, drives his own gig, and is considered, both on the road and in the metropolis, a remarkably nice, intelligent, thriving young man. Pogson's only fault is too great an attachment to the fair : — " the sex," as he says often " will be his ruin : " the fact is, that Pog never travels without a " Don Juan " under his driving-cushion, and is a pretty-looking young fellow enough.

Sam Pogson had occasion to visit Paris, last October ; and it was in that city that his love of the sex had liked to have cost him dear. He worked his way down to Dover ; placing, right and left, at the towns on his route, rhubarb, sodas, and other such delectable wares as his masters dealt in (" the sweetest sample of castor oil, smelt like a nosegay — went off like wildfire — hogshead and a half at Rochester, eight-and twenty gallons at Canterbury," and so on), and crossed to Calais, and thence voyaged to Paris in the coupé of the Diligence. He paid for two places, too, although a single man, and the reason shall now be made known.

Dining at the *table-d'hôte* at " Quillacq's " — it is the best inn on the Continent of Europe — our little traveller had the happiness to be placed next to a lady, who was, he saw at a glance, one of the extreme pink of the nobility. A large lady, in black satin, with eyes and hair as black as sloes, with gold chains, scent-bottles, sable tippet, worked pocket-handkerchief, and four twinkling rings on each of her plump white fingers. Her cheeks were as pink as the finest Chinese rouge could make them. Pog knew the article : he travelled in it. Her lips were as red as the ruby lip salve : she used the very best, that was clear.

She was a fine-looking woman, certainly (holding down her eyes, and talking perpetually of " *mes trente-deux ans* ") ; and Pogson, the wicked young dog, who professed not to care for young misses, saying they smelt so of bread-and-butter, declared, at once, that the lady was one of *his* beauties ; in fact, when he spoke to us about her, he said, " She's a slap-up thing, I tell you ; a reg'lar good one ; *one of my sort !* " And such was Pogson's credit in all commercial rooms, that one of *his* sort was considered to surpass all other sorts.

During dinner-time, Mr. Pogson was profoundly polite and attentive to the lady at his side, and kindly communicated to her, as is the way with the best-bred English on their first arrival " on the Continent," all his impressions regarding the sights and persons he had seen. Such remarks having been made during half an hour's ramble about the ramparts and town, and in the course of a walk down to the custom-house, and a confidential communication with the *commissionaire*, must be, doubtless, very valuable to Frenchmen in their own country ;

and the lady listened to Pogson's opinions : not only with benevolent attention, but actually, she said, with pleasure and
delight. Mr. Pogson said that there was no such thing as
good meat in France, and that's why they cooked their victuals
in this queer way ; he had seen many soldiers parading about
the place, and expressed a true Englishman's abhorrence of an
armed force ; not that he feared such fellows as these — little
whipper-snappers — our men would eat them. Hereupon the
lady admitted that our Guards were angels, but that Monsieur
must not be too hard upon the French ; " her father was a
General of the Emperor."

Pogson felt a tremendous respect for himself at the notion
that he was dining with a General's daughter, and instantly
ordered a bottle of champagne to keep up his consequence.

" Mrs. Bironn, ma'am," said he, for he had heard the waiter
call her by some such name, " if you *will* accept a glass of
champagne, ma'am, you'll do me, I'm sure, great *h*onor : they
say it's very good, and a precious sight cheaper than it is on
our side of the way, too — not that I care for money. Mrs.
Bironn, ma'am, your health, ma'am."

The lady smiled very graciously, and drank the wine.

" Har you any relation, ma'am, if I may make so bold ;
har you anyways connected with the family of our immortal
bard ? "

" Sir, I beg your pardon."

" Don't mention it, ma'am : but B*ironn* and *By*ron are hevi-
dently the same names, only you pronounce in the French way ;
and I thought you might be related to his lordship : his horigin,
ma'am, was of French extraction : " and here Pogson began to
repeat, —

> " Hare thy heyes like thy mother's, my fair child,
> Hada ! sole daughter of my 'ouse and 'art ? "

" Oh ! " said the lady, laughing, " you speak of *Lor*
Byron ? "

" Hauthor of ' Don Juan,' ' Child 'Arold,' and ' Cain, a
Mystery,' " said Pogson : — " I do ; and hearing the waiter
calling you Madam la Bironn, took the liberty of hasking
whether you were connected with his lordship ; that's hall : "
and my friend here grew dreadfully red, and began twiddling
his long ringlets in his fingers, and examining very eagerly the
contents of his plate.

" Oh, no : Madame la Baronne means Mistress Baroness ;
my husband was Baron, and I am Baroness."

"What! 'ave I the honor — I beg your pardon, ma'am — is your ladyship a Baroness, and I not know it? pray excuse me for calling you ma'am."

The Baroness smiled most graciously — with such a look as Juno cast upon unfortunate Jupiter when she wished to gain her wicked ends upon him — the Baroness smiled ; and, stealing her hand into a black velvet bag, drew from it an ivory card-case, and from the ivory card-case extracted a glazed card, printed in gold ; on it was engraved a coronet, and under the coronet the words

BARONNE DE FLORVAL-DELVAL,

NÉE DE MELVAL-NORVAL.

Rue Taitbout.

The grand Pitt diamond — the Queen's own star of the garter — a sample of otto-of-roses at a guinea a drop, would not be handled more curiously, or more respectfully, than this porcelain card of the Baroness. Trembling he put it into his little Russia-leather pocket-book : and when he ventured to look up, and saw the eyes of the Baroness de Florval-Delval, née de Melval-Norval, gazing upon him with friendly and serene glances, a thrill of pride tingled through Pogson's blood : he felt himself to be the very happiest fellow " on the Continent."

But Pogson did not, for some time, venture to resume that sprightly and elegant familiarity which generally forms the great charm of his conversation : he was too much frightened at the presence he was in, and contented himself by graceful and solemn bows, deep attention, and ejaculations of " Yes, my lady," and " No, your ladyship," for some minutes after the discovery had been made. Pogson piqued himself on his breeding : " I hate the aristocracy," he said, " but that's no reason why I shouldn't behave like a gentleman."

A surly, silent little gentleman, who had been the third at the ordinary, and would take no part either in the conversation or in Pogson's champagne, now took up his hat, and, grunting, left the room, when the happy bagman had the delight of a *tête-à-tête.* The Baroness did not appear inclined to move : it was cold ; a fire was comfortable, and she had ordered none in her apartment. Might Pogson give her one more glass of champagne, or would her ladyship prefer " something hot." Her ladyship

gravely said, she never took *anything* hot. "Some champagne,
then; a leetle drop?" She would! she would! O gods!
how Pogson's hand shook as he filled and offered her the
glass!

What took place during the rest of the evening had better be
described by Mr. Pogson himself, who has given us permission
to publish his letter.

"QUILLACQ'S HOTEL (*pronounced* KILLYAX), CALAIS.

"DEAR TIT, — I arrived at Cally, as they call it, this day, or, rather,
yesterday; for it is past midnight, as I sit thinking of a wonderful adventure that has just befallen me. A woman in course; that's always the case
with *me*, you know: but oh, Tit! if you *could* but see her! Of the first
family in France, the Florval-Delvals, beautiful as an angel, and no more
caring for money than I do for split peas.

"I'll tell you how it occurred. Everybody in France, you know, dines
at the ordinary — it's quite distangy to do so. There was only three of us
to-day, however, — the Baroness, me, and a gent, who never spoke a word;
and we didn't want him to, neither: do you mark that?

"You know my way with the women: champagne's the thing; make
'em drink, make 'em talk; — make 'em talk, make 'em do anything. So I
orders a bottle, as if for myself; and, 'Ma'am,' says I, 'will you take a
glass of Sham — just one?' Take it she did — for you know it's quite
distangy here: everybody dines at the *table de hôte*, and everybody accepts
everybody's wine. Bob Irons, who travels in linen on our circuit, told me
that he had made some slap-up acquaintances among the genteelest people
at Paris, nothing but by offering them Sham.

"Well, my Baroness takes one glass, two glasses, three glasses — the
old fellow goes — we have a deal of chat (she took me for a military man,
she said: is it not singular that so many people should?), and by ten o'clock
we had grown so intimate, that I had from her her whole history, knew
where she came from, and where she was going. Leave me alone with
'em: I can find out any woman's history in half an hour.

"And where do you think she *is* going? to Paris to be sure: she has
her seat in what they call the coopy (though you're not near so cooped in
it as in our coaches. I've been to the office and seen one of 'em). She has
her place in the coopy, and the coopy holds *three;* so what does Sam Pogson
do? — he goes and takes the other two. Ain't I up to a thing or two? Oh,
no, not the least; but I shall have her to myself the whole of the way.

"We shall be in the French metropolis the day after this reaches you:
please look out for a handsome lodging for me, and never mind the expense.
And I say, if you could, in her hearing, when you came down to the coach,
call me Captain Pogson, I wish you would — it sounds well travelling, you
know; and when she asked me if I was not an officer, I couldn't say no.
Adieu, then, my dear fellow, till Monday, and vive le joy, as they say.
The Baroness says I speak French charmingly, she talks English as well
as you or I.

                              "Your affectionate friend,
                                          "S. POGSON."

This letter reached us duly, in our garrets, and we engaged
such an apartment for Mr. Pogson, as beseemed a gentleman of

his rank in the world and the army. At the appointed hour, too, we repaired to the Diligence office, and there beheld the arrival of the machine which contained him and his lovely Baroness.

Those who have much frequented the society of gentlemen of his profession (and what more delightful?) must be aware, that, when all the rest of mankind look hideous, dirty, peevish, wretched, after a forty hours' coach-journey, a bagman appears as gay and spruce as when he started; having within himself a thousand little conveniences for the voyage, which common travellers neglect. Pogson had a little portable toilet, of which he had not failed to take advantage, and with his long, curling, flaxen hair, flowing under a seal-skin cap, with a gold tassel, with a blue and gold satin handkerchief, a crimson velvet waistcoat, a light green cut-away coat, a pair of barred brickdust-colored pantaloons, and a neat mackintosh, presented, altogether, as elegant and *distingué* an appearance as any one could desire. He had put on a clean collar at breakfast, and a pair of white kids as he entered the barrier, and looked, as he rushed into my arms, more like a man stepping out of a band-box, than one descending from a vehicle that has just performed one of the laziest, dullest, flattest, stalest, dirtiest journeys in Europe.

To my surprise, there were *two* ladies in the coach with my friend, and not *one*, as I had expected. One of these, a stout female, carrying sundry baskets, bags, umbrellas, and woman's wraps, was evidently a maid-servant: the other, in black, was Pogson's fair one, evidently. I could see a gleam of curl-papers over a sallow face, — of a dusky nightcap flapping over the curl-papers, — but these were hidden by a lace veil and a huge velvet bonnet, of which the crowning birds-of-paradise were evidently in a moulting state. She was encased in many shawls and wrappers; she put, hesitatingly, a pretty little foot out of the carriage — Pogson was by her side in an instant, and, gallantly putting one of his white kids round her waist, aided this interesting creature to descend. I saw, by her walk, that she was five-and-forty, and that my little Pogson was a lost man.

After some brief parley between them — in which it was charming to hear how my friend Samuel *would* speak, what he called French, to a lady who could not understand one syllable of his jargon — the mutual hackney-coaches drew up; Madame la Baronne waved to the Captain a graceful French curtsy. "*Ad*you!" said Samuel, and waved his lily hand. "*Adyou-addimang.*"

A brisk little gentleman, who had made the journey in the

same coach with Pogson, but had more modestly taken a seat
in the Imperial, here passed us, and greeted me with a "How
d'ye do?" He had shouldered his own little valise, and was
trudging off, scattering a cloud of *commissionaires*, who would
fain have spared him the trouble.

"Do you know that chap?" says Pogson; "surly fellow,
ain't he?"

"The kindest man in existence," answered I; "all the
world knows little Major British."

"He's a Major, is he? — why, that's the fellow that dined
with us at Killyax's; it's lucky I did not call myself Captain
before him, he mightn't have liked it, you know:" and then
Sam fell into a reverie; — what was the subject of his thoughts
soon appeared.

"Did you ever *see* such a foot and ankle?" said Sam, after
sitting for some time, regardless of the novelty of the scene,
his hands in his pockets, plunged in the deepest thought.

"*Isn't* she a slap-up woman, eh, now?" pursued he; and
began enumerating her attractions, as a horse-jockey would the
points of a favorite animal.

"You seem to have gone a pretty length already," said I,
"by promising to visit her to-morrow."

"A good length? — I believe you. Leave *me* alone for
that."

"But I thought you were only to be two in the *coupé*, you
wicked rogue."

"Two in the *coopy?* Oh! ah! yes, you know — why, that
is, I didn't know she had her maid with her (what an ass I was
to think of a noblewoman travelling without one!) and couldn't,
in course, refuse, when she asked me to let the maid in."

"Of course not."

"Couldn't, you know, as a man of *honor*; but I made up
for all that," said Pogson, winking slyly, and putting his hand
to his little bunch of a nose, in a very knowing way.

"You did, and how?"

"Why, you dog, I sat next to her; sat in the middle the
whole way, and my back's half broke, I can tell you:" and
thus, having depicted his happiness, we soon reached the inn
where this back-broken young man was to lodge during his stay
in Paris.

The next day at five we met; Mr. Pogson had seen his
Baroness, and described her lodgings, in his own expressive
way, as "slap-up." She had received him quite like an old
friend; treated him to *eau sucrée*, of which beverage he ex-

pressed himself a great admirer; and actually asked him to dine the next day. But there was a cloud over the ingenuous youth's brow, and I inquired still farther.

"Why," said he, with a sigh, " I thought she was a widow; and, hang it! who should come in but her husband the Baron : a big fellow, sir, with a blue coat, a red ribbing, and *such* a pair of mustachios ! "

"Well," said I, "he didn't turn you out, I suppose?"

"Oh, no! on the contrary, as kind as possible; his lordship said that he respected the English army ; asked me what corps I was in, — said he had fought in Spain against us, — and made me welcome."

"What could you want more?"

Mr. Pogson at this only whistled ; and if some very profound observer of human nature had been there to read into this little bagman's heart, it would, perhaps, have been manifest, that the appearance of a whiskered soldier of a husband had counteracted some plans that the young scoundrel was concocting.

I live up a hundred and thirty-seven steps in the remote quarter of the Luxembourg, and it is not to be expected that such a fashionable fellow as Sam Pogson, with his pockets full of money, and a new city to see, should be always wandering to my dull quarters ; so that, although he did not make his appearance for some time, he must not be accused of any lukewarmness of friendship on that score.

He was out, too, when I called at his hotel; but once, I had the good fortune to see him, with his hat curiously on one side, looking as pleased as Punch, and being driven, in an open cab, in the *Champs Elysées*. "That's *another* tip-top chap," said he, when we met, at length. "What do you think of an Earl's son, my boy? Honorable Tom Ringwood, son of the Earl of Cinqbars : what do you think of that, eh?"

I thought he was getting into very good society. Sam was a dashing fellow, and was always above his own line of life ; he had met Mr. Ringwood at the Baron's, and they'd been to the play together ; and the honorable gent, as Sam called him, had joked with him about being well to do *in a certain quarter ;* and he had had a game of billiards with the Baron, at the *Estaminy*, "a very distangy place, where you smoke," said Sam ; "quite select, and frequented by the tip-top nobility ; " and they were as thick as peas in a shell ; and they were to dine that day at Ringwood's, and sup, the next night, with the Baroness.

"I think the chaps down the road will stare," said Sam, "when they hear how I've been coming it." And stare, no doubt, they would ; for it is certain that very few commercial gentlemen have had Mr. Pogson's advantages.

The next morning we had made an arrangement to go out shopping together, and to purchase some articles of female gear, that Sam intended to bestow on his relations when he returned. Seven needle-books, for his sisters ; a gilt buckle, for his mamma ; a handsome French cashmere shawl and bonnet, for his aunt (the old lady keeps an inn in the Borough, and has plenty of money, and no heirs) ; and a toothpick case, for his father. Sam is a good fellow to all his relations, and as for his aunt, he adores her. Well, we were to go and make these purchases, and I arrived punctually at my time ; but Sam was stretched on a sofa, very pale and dismal.

I saw how it had been. — " A little too much of Mr. Ringwood's claret, I suppose ? "

He only gave a sickly stare.

" Where does the Honorable Tom live ? " says I.

" *Honorable !* " says Sam, with a hollow, horrid laugh ; " I tell you, Tit, he's no more Honorable than you are."

" What, an impostor ? "

" No, no ; not that. He is a real Honorable, only — "

" Oh, ho ! I smell a rat — a little jealous, eh ? "

" Jealousy be hanged ! I tell you he's a thief ; and the Baron's a thief ; and, hang me, if I think his wife is any better. Eight-and-thirty pounds he won of me before supper ; and made me drunk, and sent me home : — is *that* honorable ? How can I afford to lose forty pounds ? It's took me two years to save it up : — if my old aunt gets wind of it, she'll cut me off with a shilling : hang me ! " — and here Sam, in an agony, tore his fair hair.

While bewailing his lot in this lamentable strain, his bell was rung, which signal being answered by a surly " Come in," a tall, very fashionable gentleman, with a fur coat, and a fierce tuft to his chin, entered the room. " Pogson my buck, how goes it ? " said he, familiarly, and gave a stare at me : I was making for my hat.

" Don't go," said Sam, rather eagerly ; and I sat down again.

The Honorable Mr. Ringwood hummed and ha'd : and, at last, said he wished to speak to Mr. Pogson on business, in private, if possible.

" There's no secrets betwixt me and my friend," cried Sam.

Mr. Ringwood paused a little : — " An awkward business that of last night," at length exclaimed he.

"I believe it *was* an awkward business," said Sam, dryly.

"I really am very sorry for your losses."

"Thank you: and so am I, *I* can tell you," said Sam.

"You must mind, my good fellow, and not drink; for, when you drink, you *will* play high: by Gad, you led *us* in, and not we you."

"I dare say," answered Sam, with something of peevishness; "losses is losses: there's no use talking about 'em when they're over and paid."

"And paid?" here wonderingly spoke Mr. Ringwood; "why, my dear fel— what the deuce — has Florval been with you?"

"D— Florval!" growled Sam, "I've never set eyes on his face since last night; and never wish to see him again."

"Come, come, enough of this talk; how do you intend to settle the bills which you gave him last night?"

"Bills! what do you mean?"

"I mean, sir, these bills," said the Honorable Tom, produ-cing two out of his pocket-book, and looking as stern as a lion. "'I promise to pay, on demand, to the Baron de Florval, the sum of four hundred pounds. October 20, 1838.' 'Ten days after date I promise to pay the Baron de et cætera et cætera, one hundred and ninety-eight pounds. Samuel Pogson.' You didn't say what regiment you were in."

"WHAT!" shouted poor Sam, as from a dream, starting up and looking preternaturally pale and hideous.

"D— it, sir, you don't affect ignorance: you don't pretend not to remember that you signed these bills, for money lost in my rooms: money *lent* to you, by Madame de Florval, at your own request, and lost to her husband? You don't suppose, sir, that I shall be such an infernal idiot as to believe you, or such a coward as to put up with a mean subterfuge of this sort. Will you, or will you not, pay the money, sir?"

"I will not," said Sam, stoutly; "it's a d—d swin—"

Here Mr. Ringwood sprung up, clenching his riding-whip, and looking so fierce that Sam and I bounded back to the other end of the room. "Utter that word again, and, by heaven, I'll murder you!" shouted Mr. Ringwood, and looked as if he would, too: "once more, will you, or will you not, pay this money?"

"I can't," said Sam faintly.

"I'll call again, Captain Pogson," said Mr. Ringwood, "I'll call again in one hour; and, unless you come to some arrange-ment, you must meet my friend, the Baron de Florval, or I'll post you for a swindler and a coward." With this he went out: the door thundered to after him, and when the clink of his steps departing had subsided, I was enabled to look round at Pog. The poor little man had his elbows on the marble table, his head between his hands, and looked, as one has seen gentlemen look over a steam-vessel off Ramsgate, the wind blowing remarkably fresh : at last he fairly burst out crying.

"If Mrs. Pogson heard of this," said I, "what would become of the 'Three Tuns?'" (for I wished to give him a lesson). "If your Ma, who took you every Sunday to meeting, should know that her boy was paying attention to married women ; — if Drench, Glauber and Co., your employers, were to know that their confidential agent was a gambler, and unfit to be trusted with their money, how long do you think your connection would last with them, and who would afterwards employ you?"

To this poor Pog had not a word of answer ; but sat on his sofa whimpering so bitterly, that the sternest of moralists would have relented towards him, and would have been touched by the little wretch's tears. Everything, too, must be pleaded in excuse for this unfortunate bagman : who, if he wished to pass for a captain, had only done so because he had an intense respect and longing for rank : if he had made love to the Baroness, had only done so because he was given to understand by Lord Byron's "Don Juan" that making love was a very correct, natty thing : and if he had gambled, had only been induced to do so by the bright eyes and example of the Baron and the Baroness. O ye Barons and Baronesses of England ! if ye knew what a number of small commoners are daily occupied in studying your lives, and imitating your aristocratic ways, how careful would ye be of your morals, manners, and conversation !

My soul was filled, then, with a gentle yearning pity for Pogson, and revolved many plans for his rescue : none of these seeming to be practicable, at last we hit on the very wisest of all, and determined to apply for counsel to no less a person than Major British.

A blessing it is to be acquainted with my worthy friend, little Major British ; and heaven, sure, it was that put the Major into my head, when I heard of this awkward scrape of poor Pog's. The Major is on half-pay, and occupies a modest apartment *au quatrième*, in the very hotel which Pogson had patronized at my suggestion ; indeed, I had chosen it from Major British's own peculiar recommendation.

There is no better guide to follow than such a character as

the honest Major, of whom there are many likenesses now scattered over the Continent of Europe : men who love to live well, and are forced to live cheaply, and who find the English abroad a thousand times easier, merrier, and more hospitable than the same persons at home. I, for my part, never landed on Calais pier without feeling that a load of sorrows was left on the other side of the water ; and have always fancied that black care stepped on board the steamer, along with the custom-house officers at Gravesend, and accompanied one to yonder black louring towers of London — so busy, so dismal, and so vast.

British would have cut any foreigner's throat who ventured to say so much, but entertained, no doubt, private sentiments of this nature ; for he passed eight months of the year, regularly, abroad, with headquarters at Paris (the garrets before alluded to), and only went to England for the month's shooting, on the grounds of his old colonel, now an old lord, of whose acquaintance the Major was passably inclined to boast.

He loved and respected, like a good staunch Tory as he is, every one of the English nobility ; gave himself certain little airs of a man of fashion, that were by no means disagreeable ; and was, indeed, kindly regarded by such English aristocracy as he met, in his little annual tours among the German courts, in Italy or in Paris, where he never missed an ambassador's night : he retailed to us, who didn't go, but were delighted to know all that had taken place, accurate accounts of the dishes, the dresses, and the scandal which had there fallen under his observation.

He is, moreover, one of the most useful persons in society that can possibly be ; for besides being incorrigibly duelsome on his own account, he is, for others, the most acute and peaceable counsellor in the world, and has carried more friends through scrapes and prevented more deaths than any member of the Humane Society. British never bought a single step in the army, as is well known. In '14 he killed a celebrated French fire-eater, who had slain a young friend of his, and living, as he does, a great deal with young men of pleasure, and good old sober family people, he is loved by them both, and has as welcome a place made for him at a roaring bachelor's supper at the " Café Anglais," as at a staid dowager's dinner-table in the Faubourg St. Honoré. Such pleasant old boys are very profitable acquaintances, let me tell you ; and lucky is the young man who has one or two such friends in his list.

Hurrying on Pogson in his dress, I conducted him, panting, up to the Major's *quatrième*, where we were cheerfully bidden to come in. The little gentleman was in his travelling jacket, and occupied in painting, elegantly, one of those natty pairs of boots in which he daily promenaded the Boulevards. A couple of pairs of tough buff gloves had been undergoing some pipe-claying operation under his hands; no man stepped out so spick and span, with a hat so nicely brushed, with a stiff cravat tied so neatly under a fat little red face, with a blue frock-coat so scrupulously fitted to a punchy little person, as Major British, about whom we have written these two pages. He stared rather hardly at my companion, but gave me a kind shake of the hand, and we proceeded at once to business. "Major British," said I, "we want your advice in regard to an unpleasant affair which has just occurred to my friend Pogson."

"Pogson, take a chair."

"You must know, sir, that Mr. Pogson, coming from Calais the other day, encountered, in the diligence, a very handsome woman."

British winked at Pogson, who, wretched as he was, could not help feeling pleased.

"Mr. Pogson was not more pleased with this lovely creature than was she with him; for, it appears, she gave him her card, invited him to her house, where he has been constantly, and has been received with much kindness."

"I see," says British.

"Her husband the Baron——"

"*Now* it's coming," said the Major, with a grin: "her husband is jealous, I suppose, and there is a talk of the Bois de Boulogne: my dear sir, you can't refuse — can't refuse."

"It's not that," said Pogson, wagging his head passionately.

"Her husband the Baron seemed quite as much taken with Pogson as his lady was, and has introduced him to some very *distingué* friends of his own set. Last night one of the Baron's friends gave a party in honor of my friend Pogson, who lost forty-eight pounds at cards *before* he was made drunk, and heaven knows how much after."

"Not a shilling, by sacred heaven! — not a shilling!" yelled out Pogson. "After the supper I 'ad such an 'eadach', I couldn't do anything but fall asleep on the sofa."

"You 'ad such an 'eadach', sir," says British, sternly, who piques himself on his grammar and pronunciation, and scorns a cockney.

"Such a *h*-eadache, sir," replied Pogson, with much meekness.

"The unfortunate man is brought home at two o'clock, as tipsy as possible, dragged up stairs, senseless, to bed, and, on waking, receives a visit from his entertainer of the night before — a lord's son, Major, a tip-top fellow, — who brings a couple of bills that my friend Pogson is said to have signed."

"Well, my dear fellow, the thing's quite simple, — he must pay them."

"I can't pay them."

"He can't pay them," said we both in a breath: "Pogson is a commercial traveller, with thirty shillings a week, and how the deuce is he to pay five hundred pounds?"

"A bagman, sir! and what right has a bagman to gamble? Gentlemen gamble, sir; tradesmen, sir, have no business with the amusements of the gentry. What business had you with barons and lords' sons, sir? — serve you right, sir."

"Sir," says Pogson, with some dignity, "merit, and not birth, is the criterion of a man: I despise an hereditary aristocracy, and admire only Nature's gentlemen. For my part, I think that a British merch—"

"Hold your tongue, sir," bounced out the Major, "and don't lecture me; don't come to me, sir, with your slang about Nature's gentlemen — Nature's tomfools, sir! Did Nature open a cash account for you at a banker's, sir? Did Nature give you an education, sir? What do you mean by competing with people to whom Nature has given all these things? Stick to your bags, Mr. Pogson, and your bagmen, and leave barons and their like to their own ways."

"Yes, but, Major," here cried that faithful friend, who has always stood by Pogson; "they won't leave him alone."

"The honorable gent says I must fight if I don't pay," whimpered Sam.

"What! fight *you?* Do you mean that the honorable gent, as you call him, will go out with a bagman?"

"He doesn't know I'm a — I'm a commercial man," blushingly said Sam: "he fancies I'm a military gent."

The Major's gravity was quite upset at this absurd notion; and he laughed outrageously. "Why, the fact is, sir," said I, "that my friend Pogson, knowing the value of the title of Captain, and being complimented by the Baroness on his warlike appearance, said, boldly, he was in the army. He only assumed the rank in order to dazzle her weak imagination, never fancying that there was a husband, and a circle of friends, with whom he was afterwards to make an acquaintance; and then, you know, it was too late to withdraw."

" A pretty pickle you have put yourself in. Mr. Pogson, by making love to other men's wives, and calling yourself names," said the Major, who was restored to good humor. " And pray, who is the *h*onorable gent?"

" The Earl of Cinqbars' son," says Pogson, " the Honorable Tom Ringwood."

" I thought it was some such character; and the Baron is the Baron de Florval-Delval?"

" The very same."

" And his wife a black-haired woman, with a pretty foot and ankle; calls herself Athenais; and is always talking about her trente-deux ans? Why, sir, that woman was an actress on the Boulevard, when we were here in '15. She's no more his wife than I am. Delval's name is Chicot. The woman is always travelling between London and Paris: I saw she was hooking you at Calais; she has hooked ten men, in the course of the last two years, in this very way. She lent you money, didn't she?" " Yes." " And she leans on your shoulder, and whispers, 'Play half for me,' and somebody wins it, and the poor thing is as sorry as you are, and her husband storms and rages, and insists on double stakes; and she leans over your shoulder again, and tells every card in your hand to your adversary, and that's the way it's done, Mr. Pogson."

" I've been *'ad*, I see I 'ave," said Pogson, very humbly.

" Well, sir," said the Major, " in consideration, not of you, sir — for, give me leave to tell you, Mr. Pogson, that you are a pitiful little scoundrel — in consideration for my Lord Cinqbars, sir, with whom, I am proud to say, I am intimate," (the Major dearly loved a lord, and was, by his own showing, acquainted with half the peerage,) " I will aid you in this affair. Your cursed vanity, sir, and want of principle, has set you, in the first place, intriguing with other men's wives; and if you had been shot for your pains, a bullet would have only served you right, sir. You must go about as an impostor, sir, in society; and you pay richly for your swindling, sir, by being swindled yourself: but, as I think your punishment has been already pretty severe, I shall do my best, out of regard for my friend, Lord Cinqbars, to prevent the matter going any farther; and I recommend you to leave Paris without delay. Now let me wish you a good morning." — Wherewith British made a majestic bow, and began giving the last touch to his varnished boots.

We departed: poor Sam perfectly silent and chapfallen; and I meditating on the wisdom of the half-pay philosopher.

and wondering what means he would employ to rescue Pogson from his fate.

What these means were I know not; but Mr. Ringwood did *not* make his appearance at six; and, at eight, a letter arrived for " Mr. Pogson, commercial traveller," &c. &c. It was blank inside, but contained his two bills. Mr. Ringwood left town, almost immediately, for Vienna; nor did the Major explain the circumstances which caused his departure; but he muttered something about " knew some of his old tricks," " threatened police, and made him disgorge directly."

Mr. Ringwood is, as yet, young at his trade; and I have often thought it was very green of him to give up the bills to the Major, who, certainly, would never have pressed the matter before the police, out of respect for his friend, Lord Cinqbars.

THE FÊTES OF JULY.

IN A LETTER TO THE EDITOR OF THE "BUNGAY BEACON."

PARIS, July 30th, 1839.

WE have arrived here just in time for the fêtes of July. — You have read, no doubt, of that glorious revolution which took place here nine years ago, and which is now commemorated annually, in a pretty facetious manner, by gun-firing, student-processions, pole-climbing-for-silver-spoons, gold-watches and legs-of-mutton, monarchical orations, and what not, and sanctioned, moreover, by Chamber-of-Deputies, with a grant of a couple of hundred thousand francs to defray the expenses of all the crackers, gun-firings, and legs-of-mutton aforesaid. There is a new fountain in the Place Louis Quinze, otherwise called the Place Louis Seize, or else the Place de la Révolution, or else the Place de la Concorde (who can say why?) — which, I am told, is to run bad wine during certain hours to-morrow, and there *would* have been a review of the National Guards and the Line — only, since the Fieschi business, reviews are no joke, and so this latter part of the festivity has been discontinued.

Do you not laugh, O Pharos of Bungay, at the continuance of a humbug such as this? — at the humbugging anniversary of a humbug? The King of the Barricades is, next to the Emperor Nicholas, the most absolute Sovereign in Europe; yet there is not in the whole of this fair kingdom of France a single man who cares sixpence about him, or his dynasty: except, mayhap, a few hangers-on at the Château, who eat his dinners, and put their hands in his purse. The feeling of loyalty is as dead as old Charles the Tenth; the Chambers have been laughed at, the country has been laughed at, all the successive ministries have been laughed at (and you know who is the wag that has amused

PLACE DE LA CONCORDE.

himself with them all) ; and, behold, here come three days at the end of July, and cannons think it necessary to fire off, squibs and crackers to blaze and fizz, fountains to run wine, kings to make speeches, and subjects to crawl up greasy mâts-de-cocagne in token of gratitude and *réjouissance publique!* My dear sir, in their aptitude to swallow, to utter, to enact humbugs, these French people, from Majesty downwards, beat all the other nations of this earth. In looking at these men, their manners, dresses, opinions, politics, actions, history, it is impossible to preserve a grave countenance ; instead of having Carlyle to write a History of the French Revolution, I often think it should be handed over to Dickens or Theodore Hook : and oh ! where is the Rabelais to be the faithful historian of the last phase of the Revolution — the last glorious nine years of which we are now commemorating the last glorious three days?

I had made a vow not to say a syllable on the subject, although I have seen, with my neighbors, all the gingerbread stalls down the Champs Elysées, and some of the " catafalques " erected to the memory of the heroes of July, where the students and others, not connected personally with the victims, and not naving in the least profited by their deaths, come and weep ; but the grief shown on the first day is quite as absurd and fictitious as the joy exhibited on the last. The subject is one which admits of much wholesome reflection and food for mirth ; and, besides, is so richly treated by the French themselves, that it would be a sin and a shame to pass it over. Allow me to have the honor of translating, for your edification, an account of the first day's proceedings — it is mighty amusing, to my thinking.

"CELEBRATION OF THE DAYS OF JULY.

" To-day (Saturday), funeral ceremonies. in honor of the victims of July, were held in the various edifices consecrated to public worship.

" These edifices, with the exception of some churches (especially that of the Petits-Pères), were uniformly hung with black on the outside ; the hangings bore only this inscription : 27, 28, 29 July, 1830 — surrounded by a wreath of oak-leaves.

" In the interior of the Catholic churches, it had only been thought proper to dress *little catafalques*, as for burials of the third and fourth class. Very few clergy attended ; but a considerable number of the National Guard.

" The Synagogue of the Israelites was entirely hung with

black; and a great concourse of people attended. The service was performed with the greatest pomp.

"In the Protestant temples there was likewise a very full attendance: *apologetical discourses* on the Revolution of July were pronounced by the pastors.

"The absence of M. de Quélen (Archbishop of Paris), and of many members of the superior clergy, was remarked at Notre Dame.

"The civil authorities attended service in their several districts.

"The poles, ornamented with tri-colored flags, which formerly were placed on Notre Dame, were, it was remarked, suppressed. The flags on the Pont Neuf were, during the ceremony, only half-mast high, and covered with crape."

Et cætera, et cætera, et cætera.

"The tombs of the Louvre were covered with black hangings, and adorned with tri-colored flags. In front and in the middle was erected an expiatory monument of a pyramidical shape, and surmounted by a funeral vase.

"*These tombs were guarded by the* MUNICIPAL GUARD, THE TROOPS OF THE LINE, THE SERGENS DE VILLE (*town patrol*), AND A BRIGADE OF AGENTS OF POLICE IN PLAIN CLOTHES, under the orders of peace-officer Vassal.

"Between eleven and twelve o'clock, some young men, to the number of 400 or 500, assembled on the Place de la Bourse, one of them bearing a tri-colored banner with an inscription, ' To THE MANES OF JULY :' ranging themselves in order, they marched five abreast to the Marché des Innocens. On their arrival, the Municipal Guards of the Halle aux Draps, where the post had been doubled, issued out without arms, and the town-sergeants placed themselves before the market to prevent the entry of the procession. The young men passed in perfect order, and without saying a word — only lifting their hats as they defiled before the tombs. When they arrived at the Louvre they found the gates shut, and the garden evacuated. The troops were under arms, and formed in battalion.

"After the passage of the procession, the Garden was again open to the public."

And the evening and the morning were the first day.

There's nothing serious in mortality : is there, from the beginning of this account to the end thereof, aught but sheer, open, monstrous, undisguised humbug? I said, before, that you should have a history of these people by Dickens or Theodore Hook, but there is little need of professed wags ; — do not the men write their own tale with an admirable Sancho-like gravity and naïveté, which one could not desire improved? How good is that touch of sly indignation about the *little cata-falques!* how rich the contrast presented by the economy of the Catholics to the splendid disregard of expense exhibited by the devout Jews! and how touching the " *apologetical discourses* on the Revolution," delivered by the Protestant pastors! Fancy the profound affliction of the Gardes Municipaux, the Sergens de Ville, the police agents in plain clothes, and the troops with fixed bayonets, sobbing round the " expiatory monuments of a pyramidical shape, surmounted by funeral vases," and com-pelled, by sad duty, to fire into the public who might wish to indulge in the same woe! O " manes of July!" (the phrase is pretty and grammatical) why did you with sharp bullets break those Louvre windows? Why did you bayonet red-coated Swiss behind that fair white façade, and, braving cannon, musket, sabre, perspective guillotine, burst yonder bronze gates, rush through that peaceful picture-gallery, and hurl royalty, loyalty, and a thousand years of Kings, head-over-heels out of yonder Tuileries' windows?

It is, you will allow, a little difficult to say: — there is, however, *one* benefit that the country has gained (as for liberty of press, or person, diminished taxation, a juster representa-tion, who ever thinks of them?) — *one* benefit they have gained, or nearly — *abolition de la peine-de-mort pour délit politique:* no more wicked guillotining for revolutions. A Frenchman must have his revolution — it is his nature to knock down omnibuses in the street, and across them to fire at troops of the line — it is a sin to balk it. Did not the King send off Revolutionary Prince Napoleon in a coach-and-four? Did not the jury, before the face of God and Justice, proclaim Revolutionary Colonel Vaudrey not guilty? — One may hope, soon, that if a man shows decent courage and energy in half a dozen *émeutes,* he will get promotion and a premium.

I do not (although, perhaps, partial to the subject,) want to talk more nonsense than the occasion warrants, and will pray you to cast your eyes over the following anecdote, that is now going the round of the papers, and respects the commu-tation of the punishment of that wretched, fool-hardy Barbés, who, on his trial, seemed to invite the penalty which has just been remitted to him. You recollect the braggart's speech: " When the Indian falls into the power of the enemy, he knows the fate that awaits him, and submits his head to the knife: — *I* am the Indian!"

" Well — "

" M. Hugo was at the Opera on the night the sentence of the Court of Peers, condemning Barbés to death, was published. The great poet composed the following verses : —

> 'Par votre ange envolée, ainsi qu'une colombe,
> Par le royal enfant, doux et frêle roseau,
> Grace encore une fois ! Grace au nom de la tombe !
> Grace au nom du berçeau !'*

" M. Victor Hugo wrote the lines out instantly on a sheet of paper, which he folded, and simply despatched them to the King of the French by the penny-post.

" That truly is a noble voice, which can at all hours thus speak to the throne. Poetry, in old days, was called the language of the Gods — it is better named now — it is the language of the Kings.

" But the clemency of the King had anticipated the letter of the Poet. His Majesty had signed the commutation of Barbés, while the poet was still writing.

" Louis Philippe replied to the author of ' Ruy Blas ' most graciously, that he had already subscribed to a wish so noble, and that the verses had only confirmed his previous disposition to mercy."

Now in countries where fools most abound, did one ever read of more monstrous, palpable folly? In any country, save this, would a poet who chose to write four crack-brained verses, comparing an angel to a dove, and a little boy to a reed, and calling upon the chief magistrate, in the name of the angel, or dove (the Princess Mary), in her tomb, and the little infant in his cradle, to spare a criminal, have received a " gracious answer " to his nonsense? Would he have ever despatched the nonsense? and would any journalist have been silly enough to talk of " the noble voice that could thus speak to the throne," and the noble throne that could return such a noble answer to the noble voice? You get nothing done here gravely and decently. Tawdry stage tricks are played, and braggadocio claptraps uttered, on every occasion, however sacred or solemn : in the face of death, as by Barbés with his hideous Indian metaphor ; in the teeth of reason, as by M. Victor Hugo with

---

* Translated for the benefit of country gentlemen : —

> "By your angel flown away just like a dove,
> By the royal infant, that frail and tender reed,
> Pardon yet once more ! Pardon in the name of the tomb !
> Pardon in the name of the cradle ! "

his twopenny-post poetry ; and of justice, as by the King's absurd reply to this absurd demand ! Suppose the Count of Paris to be twenty times a reed, and the Princess Mary a host of angels, is that any reason why the law should not have its course? Justice is the God of our lower world, our great omnipresent guardian : as such it moves, or should move on majestic, awful, irresistible, having no passions — like a God : but, in the very midst of the path across which it is to pass, lo ! M. Victor Hugo trips forward, smirking, and says, O divine Justice ! I will trouble you to listen to the following trifling effusion of mine : —

Par votre ange envolée, ainsi qu'une," &c.

Awful Justice stops, and, bowing gravely, listens to M. Hugo's verses, and, with true French politeness, says, " Mon cher Monsieur, these verses are charming, *ravissans*, *délicieux*, and, coming from such a *célébrité littéraire* as yourself, shall meet with every possible attention — in fact, had I required anything to confirm my own previous opinions, this charming poem would have done so. Bon jour, mon cher Monsieur Hugo, au revoir ! " — and they part : — Justice taking off his hat and bowing, and the author of " Ruy Blas " quite convinced that he has been treating with him *d'égal en égal*. I can hardly bring my mind to fancy that anything is serious in France — it seems to be all rant, tinsel, and stage-play. Sham liberty, sham monarchy, sham glory, sham justice, — *où diable donc la vérité va-t-elle se nicher ?*

.   .   .   .

The last rocket of the fête of July has just mounted, exploded, made a portentous bang, and emitted a gorgeous show of blue lights, and then (like many reputations) disappeared totally : the hundredth gun on the Invalid terrace has uttered its last roar — and a great comfort it is for eyes and ears that the festival is over. We shall be able to go about our everyday business again, and not be hustled by the gendarmes or the crowd.

The sight which I have just come away from is as brilliant, happy, and beautiful as can be conceived ; and if you want to see French people to the greatest advantage, you should go to a festival like this, where their manners, and innocent gayety, show a very pleasing contrast to the coarse and vulgar hilarity which the same class would exhibit in our own country — at Epsom racecourse, for instance, or Greenwich Fair. The greatest noise that I heard was that of a company of jolly villagers

from a place in the neighborhood of Paris, who, as soon as the
fireworks were over, formed themselves into a line, three or
four abreast, and so marched singing home. As for the fire-
works, squibs and crackers are very hard to describe, and very
little was to be seen of them : to me, the prettiest sight was
the vast, orderly, happy crowd, the number of children, and the
extraordinary care and kindness of the parents towards these
little creatures. It does one good to see honest, heavy *épiciers*,
fathers of families, playing with them in the Tuileries, or, as
to-night, bearing them stoutly on their shoulders, through many
long hours, in order that the little ones too may have their share
of the fun. John Bull, I fear, is more selfish : he does not take
Mrs. Bull to the public-house ; but leaves her, for the most
part, to take care of the children at home.

The fête, then, is over ; the pompous black pyramid at the
Louvre is only a skeleton now ; all the flags have been miracu-
lously whisked away during the night, and the fine chandeliers
which glittered down the Champs Elysées for full half a mile,
have been consigned to their dens and darkness. Will they
ever be reproduced for other celebrations of the glorious 29th
of July ? — I think not ; the Government which vowed that there
should be no more persecutions of the press, was, on that very
29th, seizing a Legitimist paper, for some real or fancied offence
against it : it had seized, and was seizing daily, numbers of
persons merely suspected of being disaffected (and you may
fancy how liberty is understood, when some of these prisoners,
the other day, on coming to trial, were found guilty and sentenced to *one* day's imprisonment, after *thirty-six days' detention
on suspicion*). I think the Government which follows such a
system, cannot be very anxious about any farther revolutionary
fêtes, and that the Chamber may reasonably refuse to vote more
money for them. Why should men be so mighty proud of having, on a certain day, cut a certain number of their fellow-
countrymen's throats? The Guards and the Line employed this
time nine years did no more than those who cannonaded the
starving Lyonnese, or bayoneted the luckless inhabitants of
the Rue Transnounain : — they did but fulfil the soldier's honorable duty : — his superiors bid him kill and he killeth : — perhaps, had he gone to his work with a little more heart, the
result would have been different, and then — would the conquering party have been justified in annually rejoicing over the
conquered? Would we have thought Charles X. justified in
causing fireworks to be blazed, and concerts to be sung, and
speeches to be spouted, in commemoration of his victory over

his slaughtered countrymen? — I wish for my part they would allow the people to go about their business as on the other 362 days of the year, and leave the Champs Elysées free for the omnibuses to run, and the Tuileries in quiet, so that the nurse-maids might come as usual, and the newspapers be read for a halfpenny apiece.

Shall I trouble you with an account of the speculations of these latter, and the state of the parties which they represent? The complication is not a little curious, and may form, perhaps, a subject of graver disquisition. The July fêtes occupy, as you may imagine, a considerable part of their columns just now, and it is amusing to follow them one by one; to read Tweedledum's praise, and Tweedledee's indignation — to read, in the *Débats* how the King was received with shouts and loyal vivats — in the *Nation*, how not a tongue was wagged in his praise, but, on the instant of his departure, how the people called for the " Marseillaise " and applauded *that*. — But best say no more about the fête. The Legitimists were always in-dignant at it. The high Philippist party sneers at and despises it; the Republicans hate it: it seems a joke against *them*. Why continue it? — If there be anything sacred in the name and idea of loyalty, why renew this fête? It only shows how a rightful monarch was hurled from his throne, and a dexterous usurper stole his precious diadem. If there be anything noble in the memory of a day, when citizens, unused to war, rose against practised veterans, and, armed with the strength of their cause, overthrew them, why speak of it now? or renew the bitter recollections of the bootless struggle and victory? O Lafayette! O hero of two worlds! O accomplished Crom-well Grandison! you have to answer for more than any mor-tal man who has played a part in history: two republics and one monarchy does the world owe to you; and especially grateful should your country be to you. Did you not, in '90, make clear the path for honest Robespierre, and in '30, pre-pare the way for —

[The Editor of the *Bungay Beacon* would insert no more of this letter, which is, therefore, for ever lost to the public.]

ON THE FRENCH SCHOOL OF PAINTING:

WITH APPROPRIATE ANECDOTES, ILLUSTRATIONS, AND PHILOSOPHICAL DISQUISITIONS.

IN A LETTER TO MR. MACGILP, OF LONDON.

THE three collections of pictures at the Louvre, the Luxembourg, and the Ecole des Beaux Arts, contain a number of specimens of French art, since its commencement almost, and give the stranger a pretty fair opportunity to study and appreciate the school. The French list of painters contains some very good names — no very great ones, except Poussin (unless the admirers of Claude choose to rank him among great painters), — and I think the school was never in so flourishing a condition as it is at the present day. They say there are three thousand artists in this town alone : of these a handsome minority paint not merely tolerably, but well understand their business : draw the figure accurately ; sketch with cleverness ; and paint portraits, churches, or restaurateurs' shops, in a decent manner.

To account for a superiority over England — which, I think, as regards art, is incontestable — it must be remembered that the painter's trade, in France, is a very good one ; better appreciated, better understood, and, generally, far better paid than with us. There are a dozen excellent schools which a lad may enter here, and, under the eye of a practised master, learn the apprenticeship of his art at an expense of about ten pounds a year. In England there is no school except the Academy, unless the student can afford to pay a very large sum, and place himself under the tuition of some particular artist. Here, a young man, for his ten pounds, has all sorts of accessory instruction, models, &c. ; and has further, and for nothing, numberless incitements to study his profession which are not to be found in England : — the streets are filled with picture-shops, the people themselves are pictures walking about; the churches, theatres, eating-houses, concert-rooms are covered with pictures: Nature itself is inclined more kindly to him, for the sky is a thousand times more bright and beautiful, and the sun shines for the greater part of the year. Add to this, incitements more selfish, but quite as powerful: a French artist is paid very handsomely; for five hundred a year is much where all are poor; and has a rank in society rather above his merits than below them, being caressed by hosts and hostesses in places where titles are laughed at and a baron is thought of no more account than a banker's clerk.

The life of the young artist here is the easiest, merriest, dirtiest existence possible. He comes to Paris, probably at sixteen, from his province; his parents settle forty pounds a year on him, and pay his master; he establishes himself in the Pays Latin, or in the new quarter of Notre Dame de Lorette (which is quite peopled with painters); he arrives at his atelier at a tolerably early hour, and labors among a score of companions as merry and poor as himself. Each gentleman has his favorite tobacco-pipe; and the pictures are painted in the midst of a cloud of smoke, and a din of puns and choice French slang, and a roar of choruses, of which no one can form an idea who has not been present at such an assembly.

You see here every variety of *coiffure* that has ever been known. Some young men of genius have ringlets hanging over their shoulders — you may smell the tobacco with which they are scented across the street; some have straight locks, black, oily, and redundant; some have *toupets* in the famous Louis-Philippe fashion; some are cropped close; some have adopted the present mode — which he who would follow must, in order to do so, part his hair in the middle, grease it with grease, and gum it with gum, and iron it flat down over his ears; when arrived at the ears, you take the tongs and make a couple of ranges of curls close round the whole head, — such curls as you may see under a gilt three-cornered hat, and in her Britannic Majesty's coachman's state wig.

This is the last fashion. As for the beards, there is no end of them; all my friends the artists have beards who can raise them; and Nature, though she has rather stinted the bodies and limbs of the French nation, has been very liberal to them of hair, as you may see by the following specimen.* Fancy these heads and beards under all sorts of caps — Chinese caps, Mandarin caps, Greek skull-caps, English jockey-caps, Russian or

* This refers to an illustrated edition of the work.

Kuzzilbash caps, Middle-age caps (such as are called, in heraldry, caps of maintenance), Spanish nets, and striped worsted nightcaps. Fancy all the jackets you have ever seen, and you have before you, as well as pen can describe, the costumes of these indescribable Frenchmen.

In this company and costume the French student of art passes his days and acquires knowledge; how he passes his evenings, at what theatres, at what *guinguettes*, in company with what seducing little milliner, there is no need to say; but I knew one who pawned his coat to go to a carnival ball, and walked abroad very cheerfully in his blouse for six weeks, until he could redeem the absent garment.

These young men (together with the students of sciences) comport themselves towards the sober citizen pretty much as the German *bursch* towards the *philister*, or as the military man, during the empire, did to the *pékin :* — from the height of their poverty they look down upon him with the greatest imaginable scorn — a scorn, I think, by which the citizen seems dazzled, for his respect for the arts is intense. The case is very different in England, where a grocer's daughter would think she made a misalliance by marrying a painter, and where a literary man (in spite of all we can say against it) ranks below that class of gentry composed of the apothecary, the attorney, the wine-merchant, whose positions, in country towns at least, are so equivocal. As, for instance, my friend the Rev. James Asterisk, who has an undeniable pedigree, a paternal estate, and a living to boot, once dined in Warwickshire, in company with several squires and parsons of that enlightened county. Asterisk, as usual, made himself extraordinarily agreeable at dinner, and delighted all present with his learning and wit. "Who is that monstrous pleasant fellow?" said one of the squires. "Don't you know?" replied another. "It's Asterisk, the author of so-and-so, and a famous contributor to such and such a magazine." "Good heavens!" said the squire, quite horrified! "a literary man! I thought he had been a gentleman!"

Another instance : M. Guizot, when he was Minister here, had the grand hotel of the Ministry, and gave entertainments to all the great *de par le monde*, as Brantôme says, and entertained them in a proper ministerial magnificence. The splendid and beautiful Duchess of Dash was at one of his ministerial parties ; and went, a fortnight afterwards, as in duty bound, to pay her respects to M. Guizot. But it happened, in this fortnight, that M. Guizot was Minister no longer ; having given up his portfolio, and his grand hotel, to retire into private life, and to occupy his humble apartments in the house which he possesses, and of which he lets the greater portion. A friend of mine was present at one of the ex-Minister's *soirées*, where the Duchess of Dash made her appearance. He says the Duchess, at her entrance, seemed quite astounded, and examined the premises with a most curious wonder. Two or three shabby little rooms, with ordinary furniture, and a Minister *en retraite*, who lives by letting lodgings! In our country was ever such a thing heard of? No, thank heaven! and a Briton ought to be proud of the difference.

But to our muttons. This country is surely the paradise of painters and penny-a-liners; and when one reads of M. Horace Vernet at Rome, exceeding ambassadors at Rome by his magnificence, and leading such a life as Rubens or Titian did of old; when one sees M. Thiers's grand villa in the Rue St. George (a dozen years ago he was not even a penny-a-liner: no such luck); when one contemplates, in imagination, M. Gudin, the marine painter, too lame to walk through the picture-gallery of the Louvre, accommodated, therefore, with a wheel-chair, a privilege of princes only, and accompanied — nay, for what I know, actually trundled — down the gallery by majesty itself —who does not long to make one of the great nation, exchange his native tongue for the melodious jabber of France; or, at least, adopt it for his native country, like Marshal Saxe, Napoleon, and Anacharsis Clootz? Noble people! they made Tom Paine a deputy; and as for Tom Macaulay, they would make a *dynasty* of him.

Well, this being the case, no wonder there are so many painters in France; and here, at least, we are back to them. At the Ecole Royale des Beaux Arts, you see two or three hundred specimens of their performances; all the prize-men, since 1750, I think, being bound to leave their prize sketch or picture. Can anything good come out of the Royal Academy? is a question which has been considerably mooted in England (in the neighborhood of Suffolk Street especially). The hundreds of French samples are, I think, not very satisfactory. The subjects are almost all what are called classical: Orestes pursued by every variety of Furies; numbers of little wolf-sucking Romuluses; Hectors and Andromaches in a complication of parting embraces, and so forth; for it was the absurd maxim of our forefathers, that because these subjects had been the fashion twenty centuries ago, they must remain so in *sæcula sæculorum;* because to these lofty heights giants had scaled.

behold the race of pigmies must get upon stilts and jump at them likewise! and on the canvas, and in the theatre, the French frogs (excuse the pleasantry) were instructed to swell out and roar as much as possible like bulls.

What was the consequence, my dear friend? In trying to make themselves into bulls, the frogs make themselves into jackasses, as might be expected. For a hundred and ten years the classical humbug oppressed the nation; and you may see, in this gallery of the Beaux Arts, seventy years' specimens of the dulness which it engendered.

Now, as Nature made every man with a nose and eyes of his own, she gave him a character of his own too; and yet we, O foolish race! must try our very best to ape some one or two of our neighbors, whose ideas fit us no more than their breeches! It is the study of nature, surely, that profits us, and not of these imitations of her. A man, as a man, from a dustman up to Æschylus, is God's work, and good to read, as all works of Nature are: but the silly animal is never content; is ever trying to fit itself into another shape; wants to deny its own identity, and has not the courage to utter its own thoughts. Because Lord Byron was wicked, and quarrelled with the world; and found himself growing fat, and quarrelled with his victuals, and thus, naturally, grew ill-humored, did not half Europe grow ill-humored too? Did not every poet feel his young affections withered, and despair and darkness cast upon his soul? Because certain mighty men of old could make heroical statues and plays, must we not be told that there is no other beauty but classical beauty? — must not every little whipster of a French poet chalk you out plays, " Henriades," and such-like, and vow that here was the real thing, the undeniable Kalon?

The undeniable fiddlestick! For a hundred years, my dear sir, the world was humbugged by the so-called classical artists, as they now are by what is called the Christian art (of which anon); and it is curious to look at the pictorial traditions as here handed down. The consequence of them is, that scarce one of the classical pictures exhibited is worth much more than two-and-sixpence. Borrowed from statuary, in the first place, the color of the paintings seems, as much as possible, to participate in it; they are mostly of a misty, stony green, dismal hue, as if they had been painted in a world where no color was. In every picture, there are, of course, white mantles, white urns, white columns, white statues — those *obligé* accomplishments of the sublime. There are the endless straight noses, long eyes,

round chins, short upper lips, just as they are ruled down for
you in the drawing-books, as if the latter were the revelations
of beauty, issued by supreme authority, from which there was
no appeal? Why is the classical reign to endure? Why is
yonder simpering Venus de' Medicis to be our standard of
beauty, or the Greek tragedies to bound our notions of the
sublime? There was no reason why Agamemnon should set
the fashions, and remain ἄναξ ἀνδρῶν to eternity : and there is
a classical quotation, which you may have occasionally heard,
beginning *Vixere fortes*, &c., which, as it avers that there were
a great number of stout fellows before Agamemnon, may not
unreasonably induce us to conclude that similar heroes were to
succeed him. Shakspeare made a better man when his imagination moulded the mighty figure of Macbeth. And if you will
measure Satan by Prometheus, the blind old Puritan's work by
that of the fiery Grecian poet, does not Milton's angel surpass
Æschylus's — surpass him by " many a rood?"

In the same school of the Beaux Arts, where are to be found
such a number of pale imitations of the antique, Monsieur
Thiers (and he ought to be thanked for it) has caused to be
placed a full-sized copy of "The Last Judgment" of Michel
Angelo, and a number of casts from statues by the same
splendid hand. There *is* the sublime, if you please — a new
sublime — an original sublime — quite as sublime as the Greek
sublime. See yonder, in the midst of his angels, the Judge of
the world descending in glory ; and near him, beautiful and
gentle, and yet indescribably august and pure, the Virgin by
his side. There is the " Moses," the grandest figure that ever
was carved in stone. It has about it something frightfully
majestic, if one may so speak. In examining this, and the
astonishing picture of " The Judgment," or even a single figure
of it, the spectator's sense amounts almost to pain. I would
not like to be left in a room alone with the " Moses." How
did the artist live amongst them, and create them? How did
he suffer the painful labor of invention? One fancies that he
would have been scorched up, like Semele, by sights too tremendous for his vision to bear. One cannot imagine him, with our
small physical endowments and weaknesses, a man like ourselves.

As for the Ecole Royale des Beaux Arts, then, and all the
good its students have done, as students, it is stark naught.
When the men did anything, it was after they had left the
academy, and began thinking for themselves. There is only
one picture among the many hundreds that has, to my idea,
much merit (a charming composition of Homer singing, signe*

Jourdy) ; and the only good that the Academy has done by its pupils was to send them to Rome, where they might learn better things. At home, the intolerable, stupid classicalities, taught by men who, belonging to the least erudite country in Europe, were themselves, from their profession, the least learned among their countrymen, only weighed the pupils down, and cramped their hands, their eyes, and their imaginations ; drove them away from natural beauty, which, thank God, is fresh and attainable by us all, to-day, and yesterday, and to-morrow ; and sent them rambling after artificial grace, without the proper means of judging or attaining it.

A word for the building of the Palais des Beaux Arts. It is beautiful, and as well finished and convenient as beautiful. With its light and elegant fabric, its pretty fountain, its arch-way of the *Renaissance*, and fragments of sculpture, you can hardly see, on a fine day, a place more *riant* and pleasing.

Passing from thence up the picturesque Rue de Seine, let us walk to the Luxembourg, where bonnes, students, grisettes, and old gentlemen with pigtails, love to wander in the melancholy, quaint old gardens ; where the peers have a new and comfortable court of justice, to judge all the *émeutes* which are to take place ; and where, as everybody knows, is the picture-gallery of modern French artists, whom government thinks worthy of patronage.

A very great proportion of the pictures, as we see by the catalogue, are by the students whose works we have just been to visit at the Beaux Arts, and who, having performed their pilgrimage to Rome, have taken rank among the professors of the art. I don't know a more pleasing exhibition ; for there are not a dozen really bad pictures in the collection, some very good, and the rest showing great skill and smartness of execution.

In the same way, however, that it has been supposed that no man could be a great poet unless he wrote a very big poem, the tradition is kept up among the painters, and we have here a vast number of large canvases, with figures of the proper heroical length and nakedness. The anticlassicists did not arise in France until about 1827 ; and, in consequence, up to that period, we have here the old classical faith in full vigor. There is Brutus, having chopped his son's head off, with all the agony of a father, and then, calling for number two ; there is Æneas carrying off old Anchises ; there are Paris and Venus, as naked as two Hottentots, and many more such choice subjects from Lemprière.

But the chief specimens of the sublime are in the way of murders, with which the catalogue swarms. Here are a few extracts from it : —

7. Beaume, Chevalier de la Légion d'Honneur. "The Grand Dauphiness Dying.
18. Blondel, Chevalier de la, &c. "Zenobia found Dead."
36. Debay, Chevalier. "The Death of Lucretia."
38. Dejuinne. "The Death of Hector."
34. Court, Chevalier de la, &c. "The Death of Cæsar."
39, 40, 41. Delacroix, Chevalier. "Dante and Virgil in the Infernal Lake," "The Massacre of Scio," and "Medea going to Murder her Children."
43. Delaroche, Chevalier. "Joas taken from among the Dead."
44. "The Death of Queen Elizabeth."
45. "Edward V. and his Brother" (preparing for death).
50. "Hecuba going to be Sacrificed." Drolling, Chevalier.
51. Dubois. "Young Clovis found Dead."
56. Henry, Chevalier. "The Massacre of St. Bartholomew."
75. Guérin, Chevalier. "Cain, after the Death of Abel."
83. Jacquand. "Death of Adelaide de Comminges."
88. "The Death of Eudamidas."
93. "The Death of Hymetto."
103. "The Death of Philip of Austria." — And so on.

You see what woful subjects they take, and how profusely they are decorated with knighthood. They are like the Black Brunswickers, these painters, and ought to be called *Chevaliers de la Mort*. I don't know why the merriest people in the world should please themselves with such grim representations and varieties of murder, or why murder itself should be considered so eminently sublime and poetical. It is good at the end of a tragedy ; but, then, it is good because it is the end, and because, by the events foregone, the mind is prepared for it. But these men will have nothing but fifth acts ; and seem to skip, as unworthy, all the circumstances leading to them. This, however, is part of the scheme — the bloated, unnatural, stilted, spouting, sham sublime, that our teachers have believed and tried to pass off as real, and which your humble servant and other antihumbuggists should heartily, according to the strength that is in them, endeavor to pull down. What, for instance, could Monsieur Lafond care about the death of Eudamidas? What was Hecuba to Chevalier Drolling, or Chevalier Drolling to Hecuba? I would lay a wager that neither of them ever conjugated τύπτω, and that their school learning carried them not as far as the letter, but only to the game of taw. How were they to be inspired by such subjects? From having seen Talma and Mademoiselle Georges flaunting in sham Greek costumes, and having read up the articles Eudamidas, Hecuba, in the " Mythological Dictionary." What a classicism, inspired by rouge, gas-lamps, and a few lines in Lemprière, and copied, half from ancient statues, and half from a naked guardsman at one shilling and sixpence the hour!

Delacroix is a man of a very different genius, and his " Medea " is a genuine creation of a noble fancy. For most of the others, Mrs. Brownrigg, and her two female 'prentices, would have done as well as the desperate Colchian with her τέκνα φίλτατα. M. Delacroix has produced a number of rude, barbarous pictures; but there is the stamp of genius on all of them, — the great poetical *intention*, which is worth all your execution. Delaroche is another man of high merit; with not such a great *heart*, perhaps, as the other, but a fine and careful draughtsman, and an excellent arranger of his subject. " The Death of Elizabeth " is a raw young performance seemingly — not, at least, to my taste. The " Enfans d'Edouard " is renowned over Europe, and has appeared in a hundred different ways in print. It is properly pathetic and gloomy, and merits fully its high reputation. This painter rejoices in such subjects — in what Lord Portsmouth used to call " black jobs." He has killed Charles I. and Lady Jane Grey, and the Dukes of Guise, and I don't know whom besides. He is, at present, occupied with a vast work at the Beaux Arts, where the writer of this had the honor of seeing him, — a little, keen-looking man, some five feet in height. He wore, on this important occasion, a bandanna round his head, and was in the act of smoking a cigar.

Horace Vernet, whose beautiful daughter Delaroche married, is the king of French battle-painters — an amazingly rapid and dexterous draughtsman, who has Napoleon and all the campaigns by heart, and has painted the Grenadier Français under all sorts of attitudes. His pictures on such subjects are spirited, natural, and excellent; and he is so clever a man, that all he does is good to a certain degree. His " Judith " is somewhat violent, perhaps. His " Rebecca " most pleasing; and not the less so for a little pretty affectation of attitude and needless singularity of costume. " Raphael and Michael Angelo " is as clever a picture as can be — clever is just the word — the groups and drawing excellent, the coloring pleasantly bright and gaudy; and the French students study it incessantly; there are a dozen who copy it for one who copies Delacroix. His little scraps of wood-cuts, in the now publishing " Life of Napoleon," are perfect gems in their way, and the noble price paid for them not a penny more than he merits.

The picture, by Court, of "The Death of Cæsar," is remarkable for effect and excellent workmanship: and the head of Brutus (who looks like Armand Carrel) is full of energy. There are some beautiful heads of women, and some very good color in the picture. Jacquand's "Death of Adelaide de Comminges" is neither more nor less than beautiful. Adelaide had, it appears, a lover, who betook himself to a convent of Trappists. She followed him thither, disguised as a man, took the vows, and was not discovered by him till on her death-bed. The painter has told this story in a most pleasing and affecting manner: the picture is full of *onction* and melancholy grace. The objects, too, are capitally represented; and the tone and color very good. Decaisne's "Guardian Angel" is not so good in color, but is equally beautiful in expression and grace. A little child and a nurse are asleep: an angel watches the infant. You see women look very wistfully at this sweet picture; and what triumph would a painter have more?

We must not quit the Luxembourg without noticing the dashing sea-pieces of Gudin, and one or two landscapes by Giroux (the plain of Grasivaudan), and "The Prometheus" of Aligny. This is an imitation, perhaps; as is a noble picture of "Jesus Christ and the Children," by Flandrin: but the artists are imitating better models, at any rate; and one begins to perceive that the odious classical dynasty is no more. Poussin's magnificent "Polyphemus" (I only know a print of that marvellous composition) has, perhaps, suggested the first-named picture; and the latter has been inspired by a good enthusiastic study of the Roman schools.

Of this revolution, Monsieur Ingres has been one of the chief instruments. He was, before Horace Vernet, president of the French Academy at Rome, and is famous as a chief of a school. When he broke up his atelier here, to set out for his presidency, many of his pupils attended him faithfully some way on his journey; and some, with scarcely a penny in their pouches, walked through France and across the Alps, in a pious pilgrimage to Rome, being determined not to forsake their old master. Such an action was worthy of them, and of the high rank which their profession holds in France, where the honors to be acquired by art are only inferior to those which are gained in war. One reads of such peregrinations in old days, when the scholars of some great Italian painter followed him from Venice to Rome, or from Florence to Ferrara. In regard of Ingres's individual merit as a painter, the writer of this is not a fair judge, having seen but three pictures by him ; one being a *plafond* in the Louvre, which his disciples much admire.

Ingres stands between the Imperio-Davido-classical school of French art, and the namby-pamby mystical German school, which is for carrying us back to Cranach and Dürer, and which is making progress here.

For everything here finds imitation : the French have the genius of imitation and caricature. This absurd humbug, called the Christian or Catholic art, is sure to tickle our neighbors, and will be a favorite with them, when better known. My dear MacGilp, I do believe this to be a greater humbug than the humbug of David and Girodet, inasmuch as the latter was founded on Nature at least ; whereas the former is made up of silly affectations, and improvements upon Nature. Here, for instance, is Chevalier Ziegler's picture of "St. Luke painting the Virgin." St. Luke has a monk's dress on, embroidered, however, smartly round the sleeves. The Virgin sits in an immense yellow-ochre halo, with her son in her arms. She looks preternaturally solemn ; as does St. Luke, who is eying his paint-brush with an intense ominous mystical look. They call this Catholic art. There is nothing, my dear friend, more easy in life. First take your colors, and rub them down clean, — bright carmine, bright yellow, bright sienna, bright ultramarine, bright green. Make the costumes of your figures as much as possible like the costumes of the early part of the fifteenth century. Paint them in with the above colors ; and if on a gold ground, the more " Catholic " your art is. Dress your apostles like priests before the altar ; and remember to have a good commodity of crosiers, censers, and other such gimcracks, as you may see in the Catholic chapels, in Sutton Street and elsewhere. Deal in Virgins, and dress them like a burgomaster's wife by Cranach or Van Eyck. Give them all long twisted tails to their gowns, and proper angular draperies. Place all their heads on one side, with the eyes shut, and the proper solemn simper. At the back of the head, draw, and gild with gold-leaf, a halo or glory, of the exact shape of a cart-wheel : and you have the thing done. It is Catholic art *tout craché*, as Louis Philippe says. We have it still in England, handed down to us for four centuries, in the pictures on the cards, as the redoubtable king and queen of clubs. Look at them : you will see that the costumes and attitudes are precisely similar to those which figure in the catholicities of the school of Overbeck and Cornelius.

Before you take your cane at the door, look for one instant at the statue-room. Yonder is Jouffley's "Jeune Fille confiant son premier secret à Vénus." Charming, charming! It is from the exhibition of this year only; and I think the best sculpture in the gallery — pretty, fanciful, *naïve*; admirable in workmanship and imitation of Nature. I have seldom seen flesh better represented in marble. Examine, also, Jaley's "Pudeur," Jacquot's "Nymph," and Rude's "Boy with the Tortoise." These are not very exalted subjects, or what are called exalted, and do not go beyond simple, smiling beauty and nature. But what then? Are we gods, Miltons, Michel Angelos, that can leave earth when we please, and soar to heights immeasurable? No, my dear MacGilp; but the fools of academicians would fain make us so. Are you not, and half the painters in London, panting for an opportunity to show your genius in a great "historical picture?" O blind race! Have you wings? Not a feather: and yet you must be ever puffing, sweating up to the tops of rugged hills; and, arrived there, clapping and shaking your ragged elbows, and making as if you would fly! Come down, silly Dædalus; come down to the lowly places in which Nature ordered you to walk. The sweet flowers are springing there; the fat muttons are waiting there; the pleasant sun shines there; be content and humble, and take your share of the good cheer.

While we have been indulging in this discussion, the omnibus has gayly conducted us across the water; and *le garde qui veille a la porte du Louvre ne défend pas* our entry.

What a paradise this gallery is for French students, or foreigners who sojourn in the capital! It is hardly necessary to say that the brethren of the brush are not usually supplied by Fortune with any extraordinary wealth, or means of enjoying the luxuries with which Paris, more than any other city, abounds. But here they have a luxury which surpasses all others, and spend their days in a palace which all the money of all the Rothschilds could not buy. They sleep, perhaps, in a garret, and dine in a cellar; but no grandee in Europe has such a drawing-room. Kings' houses have, at best, but damask hangings, and gilt cornices. What are these to a wall covered with canvas by Paul Veronese, or a hundred yards of Rubens? Artists from England, who have a national gallery that resembles a moderate-sized gin-shop, who may not copy pictures, except under particular restrictions, and on rare and particular days, may revel here to their hearts' content. Here is a room half a mile long, with as many windows as Aladdin's palace, open from sunrise till evening, and free to all manners and all varieties of study : the only puzzle to the student is to select the one he shall begin upon, and keep his eyes away from the rest.

Fontaine's grand staircase, with its arches, and painted ceilings and shining Doric columns, leads directly to the gallery ; but it is thought too fine for working days, and is only opened for the public entrance on Sabbath. A little back stair (leading from a court, in which stand numerous bas-reliefs, and a solemn sphinx, of polished granite,) is the common entry for students and others, who, during the week, enter the gallery.

Hither have lately been transported a number of the works of French artists, which formerly covered the walls of the Luxembourg (death only entitles the French painter to a place in the Louvre) ; and let us confine ourselves to the Frenchmen only, for the space of this letter.

I have seen, in a fine private collection at St. Germain, one or two admirable single figures of David, full of life, truth, and gayety. The color is not good, but all the rest excellent ; and one of these so much-lauded pictures is the portrait of a washerwoman. " Pope Pius," at the Louvre, is as bad in color as remarkable for its vigor and look of life. The man had a genius for painting portraits and common life, but must attempt the heroic ; — failed signally ; and what is worse, carried a whole nation blundering after him. Had you told a Frenchman so, twenty years ago, he would have thrown the *démenti* in your teeth ; or, at least, laughed at you in scornful incredulity. They say of us that we don't know when we are beaten : they go a step further, and swear their defeats are victories. David was a part of the glory of the empire ; and one might as well have said then that " Romulus " was a bad picture, as that Toulouse was a lost battle. Old-fashioned people, who believe in the Emperor, believe in the Théâtre Français, and believe that Ducis improved upon Shakspeare, have the above opinion. Still, it is curious to remark, in this place, how art and literature become party matters, and political sects have their favorite painters and authors.

Nevertheless, Jacques Louis David is dead. He died about a year after his bodily demise in 1825. The romanticism killed him. Walter Scott, from his Castle of Abbotsford, sent out a troop of gallant young Scotch adventurers, merry outlaws, valiant knights, and savage Highlanders, who, with trunk hosen and buff jerkins, fierce two-handed swords, and harness on their back, did challenge, combat, and overcome the heroes and demi-gods of Greece and Rome. *Notre Dame à la rescousse!* Sir Brian de Bois Guilbert has borne Hector of Troy clear out of his saddle. Andromache may weep: but her spouse is beyond the reach of physic. See! Robin Hood twangs his bow, and the heathen gods fly, howling. *Montjoie Saint Denis!* down goes Ajax under the mace of Dunois; and yonder are Leonidas and Romulus begging their lives of Rob Roy Macgregor. Classicism is dead. Sir John Froissart has taken Dr. Lemprière by the nose, and reigns sovereign.

Of the great pictures of David the defunct, we need not, then, say much. Romulus is a mighty fine young fellow, no doubt; and if he has come out to battle stark naked (except a very handsome helmet), it is because the costume became him, and shows off his figure to advantage. But was there ever anything so absurd as this passion for the nude, which was followed by all the painters of the Davidian epoch? And how are we to suppose yonder straddle to be the true characteristic of the heroic and the sublime? Romulus stretches his legs as far as ever nature will allow; the Horatii, in receiving their swords, think proper to stretch their legs too, and to thrust forward their arms, thus, —

Romulus.   The Horatii.

Romulus's is in the exact action of a telegraph; and the Horatii are all in the position of the lunge. Is this the sublime? Mr. Angelo, of Bond Street, might admire the attitude; his name-sake, Michel, I don't think would.

The little picture of "Paris and Helen," one of the master's earliest, I believe, is likewise one of his best: the details are exquisitely painted. Helen looks needlessly sheepish, and Paris has a most odious ogle; but the limbs of the male figure are beautifully designed, and have not the green tone which you see in the later pictures of the master. What is the meaning of this green? Was it the fashion, or the varnish? Girodet's pictures are green; Gros's emperors and grenadiers have universally the jaundice. Gerard's "Psyche" has a most decided green-sickness; and I am at a loss, I confess, to account for the enthusiasm which this performance inspired on its first appearance before the public.

In the same room with it is Girodet's ghastly " Deluge," and Gericault's dismal " Medusa." Gericault died, they say, for want of fame. He was a man who possessed a considerable fortune of his own; but pined because no one in his day would purchase his pictures, and so acknowledge his talent. At present, a scrawl from his pencil brings an enormous price. All his works have a grand *cachet :* he never did anything mean. When he painted the " Raft of the Medusa," it is said he lived for a long time among the corpses which he painted, and that his studio was a second Morgue. If you have not seen the picture, you are familiar, probably, with Reynolds's admirable engraving of it. A huge black sea; a raft beating upon it; a horrid company of men dead, half dead, writhing and frantic with hideous hunger or hideous hope; and, far away, black, against a stormy sunset, a sail. The story is powerfully told, and has a legitimate tragic interest, so to speak, — deeper, because more natural, than Girodet's green " Deluge," for instance : or his livid " Orestes," or red-hot " Clytemnestra."

Seen from a distance the latter's " Deluge " has a certain awe-inspiring air with it. A slimy green man stands on a green rock, and clutches hold of a tree. On the green man's shoulders is his old father, in a green old age; to him hangs his wife, with a babe on her breast, and dangling at her hair, another child. In the water floats a corpse (a beautiful head); and a green sea and atmosphere envelops all this dismal group. The old father is represented with a bag of money in his hand; and the tree, which the man catches, is cracking, and just on the point of giving way. These two points were considered very fine by the critics : they are two such ghastly epigrams as continually disfigure French Tragedy. For this reason I have never been able to read Racine with pleasure, — the dialogue is so crammed with these lugubrious good things — melancholy antitheses — sparkling undertakers' wit; but this is heresy, and had better be spoken discreetly.

The gallery contains a vast number of Poussin's pictures; they put me in mind of the color of objects in dreams, — a strange, hazy, lurid hue. How noble are some of his landscapes! What a depth of solemn shadow is in yonder wood, near which, by the side of a black water, halts Diogenes. The air is thunder-laden, and breathes heavily. You hear ominous whispers in the vast forest gloom.

Near it is a landscape, by Carel Dujardin, I believe, conceived *in* quite a different mood, but exquisitely poetical too. A horse-man is riding up a hill, and giving money to a blowsy beggar-wench. *O matutini rores auræque salubres !* in what a wonderful way has the artist managed to create you out of a few bladders of paint and pots of varnish. You can see the matutinal dews twinkling in the grass, and feel the fresh, salubrious airs (" the breath of Nature blowing free," as the corn-law man sings) blow-ing free over the heath ; silvery vapors are rising up from the blue lowlands. You can tell the hour of the morning and the time of the year : you can do anything but describe it in words. As with regard to the Poussin above mentioned, one can never pass it without bearing away a certain pleasing, dreamy feeling of awe and musing ; the other landscape inspires the spectator infallibly with the most delightful briskness and cheerfulness of spirit. Herein lies the vast privilege of the landscape-painter : he does not address you with one fixed particular subject or ex-pression, but with a thousand never contemplated by himself, and which only arise out of occasion. You may always be look-ing at a natural landscape as at a fine pictorial imitation of one ; it seems eternally producing new thoughts in your bosom, as it does fresh beauties from its own. I cannot fancy more delight-ful, cheerful, silent companions for a man than half a dozen landscapes hung round his study. Portraits, on the contrary, and large pieces of figures, have a painful, fixed, staring look, which must jar upon the mind in many of its moods. Fancy living in a room with David's sans-culotte Leonidas staring per-petually in your face !

There is a little Watteau here, and a rare piece of fantastical brightness and gayety it is. What a delightful affectation about yonder ladies flirting their fans, and trailing about in their long brocades ! What splendid dandies are those, ever-smirking, turning out their toes, with broad blue ribbons to tie up their crooks and their pigtails, and wonderful gorgeous crimson satin breeches ! Yonder, in the midst of a golden atmosphere, rises a bevy of little round Cupids, bubbling up in clusters as out of a champagne-bottle, and melting away in air. There is, to be sure, a hidden analogy between liquors and pictures : the eye is deliciously tickled by these frisky Watteaus, and yields itself up to a light, smiling, gentlemanlike intoxication. Thus, were we inclined to pursue further this mighty subject, yonder landscape of Claude, — calm, fresh, delicate, yet full of flavor, — should be likened to a bottle of Château Margaux. And what is the Poussin before spoken of but Romanée Gelée ? — heavy, slug-gish, — the luscious odor almost sickens you ; a sultry sort of

drink; your limbs sink under it; you feel as if you had been
drinking hot blood.

An ordinary man would be whirled away in a fever, or would
hobble off this mortal stage in a premature gout-fit, if he too
early or too often indulged in such tremendous drink. I think
in my heart I am fonder of pretty third-rate pictures than of
your great thundering first-rates. Confess how many times you
have read Béranger, and how many Milton? If you go to the
" Star and Garter," don't you grow sick of that vast, luscious
landscape, and long for the sight of a couple of cows, or a
donkey, and a few yards of common? Donkeys, my dear Mac-
Gilp, since we have come to this subject, say not so ; Richmond
Hill for them. Milton they never grow tired of; and are as
familiar with Raphael as Bottom with exquisite Titania. Let
us thank heaven, my dear sir, for according to us the power to
taste and appreciate the pleasures of mediocrity. I have never
heard that we were great geniuses. Earthy are we, and of the
earth ; glimpses of the sublime are but rare to us; leave we
them to great geniuses, and to the donkeys ; and if it nothing
profit us *aërias tentâsse domos* along with them, let us thankfully
remain below, being merry and humble.

I have now only to mention the charming " Cruche Cassée "
of Greuze, which all the young ladies delight to copy ; and of
which the color (a thought too blue, perhaps) is marvellously
graceful and delicate. There are three more pictures by the
artist, containing exquisite female heads and color ; but they
have charms for French critics which are difficult to be discovered by English eyes ; and the pictures seem weak to me.
A very fine picture by Bon Bollongue, " Saint Benedict resusci-
tating a Child," deserves particular attention, and is superb in
vigor and richness of color. You must look, too, at the large,
noble, melancholy landscapes of Philippe de Champagne ; and
the two magnificent Italian pictures of Léopold Robert: they
are, perhaps, the very finest pictures that the French school has
produced, — as deep as Poussin, of a better color, and of a
wonderful minuteness and veracity in the representation of
objects.

Every one of Lesueur's church-pictures is worth examining
and admiring ; they are full of " unction " and pious mystical
grace. " Saint Scholastica " is divine ; and the " Taking down
from the Cross " as noble a composition as ever was seen ; I
care not by whom the other may be. There is more beauty,
and less affectation, about this picture than you will find in the
performances of many Italian masters, with high-sounding

names (out with it, and say RAPHAEL at once). I hate those simpering Madonnas. I declare that the "Jardinière" is a puking, smirking miss, with nothing heavenly about her. I vow that the "Saint Elizabeth" is a bad picture, — a bad composition, badly drawn, badly colored, in a bad imitation of Titian, — a piece of vile affectation. I say, that when Raphael painted this picture two years before his death, the spirit of painting had gone from out of him ; he was no longer inspired ; *it was time that he should die ! !*

There, — the murder is out ! My paper is filled to the brim, and there is no time to speak of Lesueur's "Crucifixion," which is odiously colored, to be sure ; but earnest, tender, simple, holy. But such things are most difficult to translate into words ; — one lays down the pen, and thinks and thinks. The figures appear, and take their places one by one : ranging themselves according to order, in light or in gloom, the colors are reflected duly in the little camera obscura of the brain, and the whole picture lies there complete ; but can you describe it? No, not if pens were fitch-brushes, and words were bladders of paint. With which, for the present, adieu.

Your faithful

M. A. T.

To MR. ROBERT MACGILP,
   NEWMAN STREET, LONDON.

THE PAINTER'S BARGAIN.

SIMON GAMBOUGE was the son of Solomon Gambouge; and
as all the world knows, both father and son were astonishingly
clever fellows at their profession. Solomon painted landscapes, which nobody bought; and Simon took a higher line,
and painted portraits to admiration, only nobody came to sit
to him.

As he was not gaining five pounds a year by his profession,
and had arrived at the age of twenty, at least, Simon determined to better himself by taking a wife, — a plan which a
number of other wise men adopt, in similar years and circumstances. So Simon prevailed upon a butcher's daughter (to
whom he owed considerably for cutlets) to quit the meat-shop
and follow him. Griskinissa — such was the fair creature's
name — " was as lovely a bit of mutton," her father said, " as
ever a man would wish to stick a knife into." She had sat
to the painter for all sorts of characters; and the curious who
possess any of Gambouge's pictures will see her as Venus,
Minerva, Madonna, and in numberless other characters: Portrait of a lady — Griskinissa; Sleeping Nymph — Griskinissa,
without a rag of clothes, lying in a forest; Maternal Solicitude
— Griskinissa again, with young Master Gambouge, who was
by this time the offspring of their affections.

The lady brought the painter a handsome little fortune of
a couple of hundred pounds; and as long as this sum lasted
no woman could be more lovely or loving. But want began
speedily to attack their little household; bakers' bills were unpaid; rent was due, and the reckless landlord gave no quarter;
and, to crown the whole, her father, unnatural butcher! suddenly stopped the supplies of mutton-chops; and swore that

his daughter, and the dauber, her husband, should have no more of his wares. At first they embraced tenderly, and, kissing and crying over their little infant, vowed to heaven that they would do without: but in the course of the evening Griskinissa grew peckish, and poor Simon pawned his best coat.

When this habit of pawning is discovered, it appears to the poor a kind of Eldorado. Gambouge and his wife were so delighted, that they, in the course of a month, made away with her gold chain, her great warming-pan, his best crimson plush inexpressibles, two wigs, a washhand basin and ewer, fire-irons, window-curtains, crockery, and arm-chairs. Griskinissa said, smiling, that she had found a second father in *her uncle*, — a base pun, which showed that her mind was corrupted, and that she was no longer the tender, simple Griskinissa of other days.

I am sorry to say that she had taken to drinking; she swallowed the warming-pan in the course of three days, and fuddled herself one whole evening with the crimson plush breeches.

Drinking is the devil — the father, that is to say, of all vices. Griskinissa's face and her mind grew ugly together; her good humor changed to bilious, bitter discontent; her pretty, fond epithets, to foul abuse and swearing; her tender blue eyes grew watery and blear, and the peach-color on her cheeks fled from its old habitation, and crowded up into her nose, where, with a number of pimples, it stuck fast. Add to this a dirty, draggle-tailed chintz; long, matted hair, wandering into her eyes, and over her lean shoulders, which were once so snowy, and you have the picture of drunkenness and Mrs. Simon Gambouge.

Poor Simon, who had been a gay, lively fellow enough in the days of his better fortune, was completely cast down by his present ill luck, and cowed by the ferocity of his wife. From morning till night the neighbors could hear this woman's tongue, and understand her doings; bellows went skimming across the room, chairs were flumped down on the floor, and poor Gambouge's oil and varnish pots went clattering through the windows, or down the stairs. The baby roared all day; and Simon sat pale and idle in a corner, taking a small sup at the brandy-bottle, when Mrs. Gambouge was out of the way.

One day, as he sat disconsolately at his easel, furbishing up a picture of his wife, in the character of Peace, which he had commenced a year before, he was more than ordinarily desperate, and cursed and swore in the most pathetic manner. "O miserable fate of genius!" cried he, "was I, a man of such

commanding talents, born for this? to be bullied by a fiend of a
wife ; to have my masterpieces neglected by the world, or sold
only for a few pieces? Cursed be the love which has misled
me ; cursed be the art which is unworthy of me ! Let me dig
or steal, let me sell myself as a soldier, or sell myself to the
Devil, I should not be more wretched than I am now ! "

"Quite the contrary," cried a small, cheery voice.

"What!" exclaimed Gambouge, trembling and surprised.
"Who's there? — where are you? — who are you?"

"You were just speaking of me," said the voice.

Gambouge held, in his left hand, his palette ; in his right, a
bladder of crimson lake, which he was about to squeeze out
upon the mahogany. "Where are you?" cried he again.

"S-q-u-e-e-z-e!" exclaimed the little voice.

Gambouge picked out the nail from the bladder, and gave
a squeeze ; when, as sure as I am living, a little imp spurted
out from the hole upon the palette, and began laughing in the
most singular and oily manner.

When first born he was little bigger than a tadpole ; then he
grew to be as big as a mouse ; then he arrived at the size of a
cat ; and then he jumped off the palette, and, turning head over
heels, asked the poor painter what he wanted with him.

.   .   .   .

The strange little animal twisted head over heels, and fixed
himself at last upon the top of Gambouge's easel, — smearing
out, with his heels, all the white and vermilion which had just
been laid on the allegoric portrait of Mrs. Gambouge.

"What!" exclaimed Simon, "is it the — "

"Exactly so ; talk of me, you know, and I am always at
hand : besides, I am not half so black as I am painted, as you
will see when you know me a little better."

"Upon my word," said the painter, "it is a very singular
surprise which you have given me. To tell truth, I did not
even believe in your existence."

The little imp put on a theatrical air, and, with one of Mr.
Macready's best looks, said, —

> "There are more things in heaven and earth, Gambogio,
> Than are dreamed of in your philosophy."

Gambouge, being a Frenchman, did not understand the
quotation, but felt somehow strangely and singularly interested
in the conversation of his new friend.

Diabolus continued : "You are a man of merit, and want
money ; you will starve on your merit ; you can only get money

from me. Come, my friend, how much is it? I ask the easiest interest in the world : old Mordecai, the usurer, has made you pay twice as heavily before now : nothing but the signature of a bond, which is a mere ceremony, and the transfer of an article which, in itself, is a supposition — a valueless, windy, uncertain property of yours, called, by some poet of your own, I think, an *animula, vagula, blandula* — bah! there is no use beating about the bush — I mean *a soul.* Come, let me have it ; you know you will sell it some other way, and not get such good pay for your bargain !" — and, having made this speech, the Devil pulled out from his fob a sheet as big as a double *Times,* only there was a different *stamp* in the corner.

It is useless and tedious to describe law documents : lawyers only love to read them ; and they have as good in Chitty as any that are to be found in the Devil's own ; so nobly have the apprentices emulated the skill of the master. Suffice it to say, that poor Gambouge read over the paper, and signed it. He was to have all he wished for seven years, and at the end of that time was to become the property of the —— ; 𝔓𝔯𝔬𝔟𝔦𝔡𝔢𝔡 that, during the course of the seven years, every single wish which he might form should be gratified by the other of the contracting parties ; otherwise the deed became null and non-avenue, and Gambouge should be left " to go to the —— his own way."

" You will never see me again," said Diabolus, in shaking hands with poor Simon, on whose fingers he left such a mark as is to be seen at this day — " never, at least, unless you want me ; for everything you ask will be performed in the most quiet and every-day manner : believe me, it is best and most gentlemanlike, and avoids anything like scandal. But if you set me about anything which is extraordinary, and out of the course of nature, as it were, come I must, you know ; and of this you are the best judge." So saying, Diabolus disappeared ; but whether up the chimney, through the keyhole, or by any other aperture or contrivance, nobody knows. Simon Gambouge was left in a fever of delight, as, heaven forgive me ! I believe many a worthy man would be, if he were allowed an opportunity to make a similar bargain.

"Heigho!" said Simon. "I wonder whether this be a reality or a dream. — I am sober, I know ; for who will give me credit for the means to be drunk? and as for sleeping, I'm too hungry for that. I wish I could see a capon and a bottle of white wine."

" MONSIEUR SIMON ! " cried a voice on the landing-place.

"C'est ici," quoth Gambouge, hastening to open the door. He did so; and lo! there was a *restaurateur's* boy at the door, supporting a tray, a tin-covered dish, and plates on the same; and, by its side, a tall amber-colored flask of Sauterne.

"I am the new boy, sir," exclaimed this youth, on entering; "but I believe this is the right door, and you asked for these things."

Simon grinned, and said, "Certainly, I did *ask for* these things." But such was the effect which his interview with the demon had had on his innocent mind, that he took them, although he knew that they were for old Simon, the Jew dandy, who was mad after an opera girl, and lived on the floor beneath.

"Go, my boy," he said; "it is good: call in a couple of hours, and remove the plates and glasses."

The little waiter trotted down stairs, and Simon sat greedily down to discuss the capon and the white wine. He bolted the legs, he devoured the wings, he cut every morsel of flesh from the breast; — seasoning his repast with pleasant draughts of wine, and caring nothing for the inevitable bill, which was to follow all.

"Ye gods!" said he, as he scraped away at the backbone, "what a dinner! what wine! — and how gayly served up too!" There were silver forks and spoons, and the remnants of the fowl were upon a silver dish. "Why, the money for this dish and these spoons," cried Simon, "would keep me and Mrs. G. for a month! I wish" — and here Simon whistled, and turned round to see that nobody was peeping — "I wish the plate were mine."

Oh, the horrid progress of the Devil! "Here they are," thought Simon to himself; "why should not I *take them?*" And take them he did. "Detection," said he, "is not so bad as starvation; and I would as soon live at the galleys as live with Madame Gambouge."

So Gambouge shovelled dish and spoons into the flap of his surtout, and ran down stairs as if the Devil were behind him — as, indeed, he was.

He immediately made for the house of his old friend the pawnbroker — that establishment which is called in France the Mont de Piété. "I am obliged to come to you again, my old friend," said Simon, "with some family plate, of which I beseech you to take care."

The pawnbroker smiled as he examined the goods. "I can give you nothing upon them," said he.

"What!" cried Simon; "not even the worth of the silver?"

"No; I could buy them at that price at the 'Café Morisot,'
Rue de la Verrerie, where, I suppose, you got them a little
cheaper." And, so saying, he showed to the guilt-stricken
Gambouge how the name of that coffee-house was inscribed
upon every one of the articles which he had wished to pawn.

The effects of conscience are dreadful indeed. Oh! how
fearful is retribution, how deep is despair, how bitter is remorse
for crime — *when crime is found out!* — otherwise, conscience
takes matters much more easily. Gambouge cursed his fate,
and swore henceforth to be virtuous.

"But, hark ye, my friend," continued the honest broker,
"there is no reason why, because I cannot lend upon these
things, I should not buy them : they will do to melt, if for no
other purpose. Will you have half the money? — speak, or I
peach."

Simon's resolves about virtue were dissipated instantaneously. "Give me half," he said, "and let me go. — What
scoundrels are these pawnbrokers!" ejaculated he, as he passed
out of the accursed shop, "seeking every wicked pretext to
rob the poor man of his hard-won gain."

When he had marched forwards for a street or two, Gambouge counted the money which he had received, and found
that he was in possession of no less than a hundred francs. It
was night, as he reckoned out his equivocal gains, and he
counted them at the light of a lamp. He looked up at the
lamp, in doubt as to the course he should next pursue : upon
it was inscribed the simple number, 152. "A gambling-
house," thought Gambouge. "I wish I had half the money
that is now on the table, up stairs."

He mounted, as many a rogue has done before him, and
found half a hundred persons busy at a table of *rouge et noir*.
Gambouge's five napoleons looked insignificant by the side of
the heaps which were around him ; but the effects of the wine, of
the theft, and of the detection by the pawnbroker, were upon
him, and he threw down his capital stoutly upon the 0 0.

It is a dangerous spot that 0 0, or double zero; but to
Simon it was more lucky than to the rest of the world. The
ball went spinning round — in "its predestined circle rolled,"
as Shelley has it, after Goethe — and plumped down at last in
the double zero. One hundred and thirty-five gold napoleons
(louis they were then) were counted out to the delighted painter.
"Oh, Diabolus!" cried he, "now it is that I begin to believe

in thee! Don't talk about merit," he cried; "talk about fortune. Tell me not about heroes for the future — tell me of *zeroes*." And down went twenty napoleons more upon the 0.

The Devil was certainly in the ball: round it twirled, and dropped into zero as naturally as a duck pops its head into a pond. Our friend received five hundred pounds for his stake; and the croupiers and lookers-on began to stare at him.

There were twelve thousand pounds on the table. Suffice it to say, that Simon won half, and retired from the Palais Royal with a thick bundle of bank-notes crammed into his dirty three-cornered hat. He had been but half an hour in the place, and he had won the revenues of a prince for half a year!

Gambouge, as soon as he felt that he was a capitalist, and that he had a stake in the country, discovered that he was an altered man. He repented of his foul deed, and his base purloining of the restaurateur's plate. "O honesty!" he cried, "how unworthy is an action like this of a man who has a property like mine!" So he went back to the pawnbroker with the gloomiest face imaginable. "My friend," said he, "I have sinned against all that I hold most sacred: I have forgotten my family and my religion. Here is thy money. In the name of heaven, restore me the plate which I have wrongfully sold thee!"

But the pawnbroker grinned, and said, "Nay, Mr. Gambouge, I will sell that plate for a thousand francs to you, or I never will sell it at all."

"Well," cried Gambouge, "thou art an inexorable ruffian, Troisboules; but I will give thee all I am worth." And here he produced a billet of five hundred francs. "Look," said he, "this money is all I own; it is the payment of two years' lodging. To raise it, I have toiled for many months; and, failing, I have been a criminal. O heaven! I *stole* that plate that I might pay my debt, and keep my dear wife from wandering houseless. But I cannot bear this load of ignominy — I cannot suffer the thought of this crime. I will go to the person to whom I did wrong, I will starve, I will confess; but I will, I *will* do right!"

The broker was alarmed. "Give me thy note," he cried; "here is the plate."

"Give me an acquittal first," cried Simon, almost brokenhearted; "sign me a paper, and the money is yours." So Troisboules wrote according to Gambouge's dictation: "Received, for thirteen ounces of plate, twenty pounds."

"Monster of iniquity!" cried the painter, "fiend of wickedness! thou art caught in thine own snares. Hast thou not sold me five pounds' worth of plate for twenty? Have I it not in my pocket? Art thou not a convicted dealer in stolen goods? Yield, scoundrel, yield thy money, or I will bring thee to justice!"

The frightened pawnbroker bullied and battled for a while; but he gave up his money at last, and the dispute ended. Thus it will be seen that Diabolus had rather a hard bargain in the wily Gambouge. He had taken a victim prisoner, but he had assuredly caught a Tartar. Simon now returned home, and, to do him justice, paid the bill for his dinner, and restored the plate.

.   .   .   .

And now I may add (and the reader should ponder upon this, as a profound picture of human life), that Gambouge, since he had grown rich, grew likewise abundantly moral. He was a most exemplary father. He fed the poor, and was loved by them. He scorned a base action. And I have no doubt that Mr. Thurtell, or the late lamented Mr. Greenacre, in similar circumstances, would have acted like the worthy Simon Gambouge.

There was but one blot upon his character — he hated Mrs. Gam. worse than ever. As he grew more benevolent, she grew more virulent: when he went to plays, she went to Bible societies, and *vice versâ:* in fact, she led him such a life as Xantippe led Socrates, or as that dog leads a cat in the same kitchen. With all his fortune — for, as may be supposed, Simon prospered in all worldly things — he was the most miserable dog in the whole city of Paris. Only in the point of drinking did he and Mrs. Simon agree; and for many years, and during a considerable number of hours in each day, he thus dissipated, partially, his domestic chagrin. O philosophy! we may talk of thee: but, except at the bottom of the wine-cup, where thou liest like truth in a well, where shall we find thee?

He lived so long, and in his worldly matters prospered so much, there was so little sign of devilment in the accomplishment of his wishes, and the increase of his prosperity, that Simon, at the end of six years, began to doubt whether he had made any such bargain at all, as that which we have described at the commencement of this history. He had grown, as we said, very pious and moral. He went regularly to mass, and had a confessor into the bargain. He resolved, therefore, to consult that reverend gentleman, and to lay before him the whole matter.

"I am inclined to think, holy sir," said Gambouge, after he had concluded his history, and shown how, in some miraculous way, all his desires were accomplished, "that, after all, this demon was no other than the creation of my own brain, heated by the effects of that bottle of wine, the cause of my crime and my prosperity."

The confessor agreed with him, and they walked out of church comfortably together, and entered afterwards a *café*, where they sat down to refresh themselves after the fatigues of their devotion.

A respectable old gentleman, with a number of orders at his buttonhole, presently entered the room, and sauntered up to the marble table, before which reposed Simon and his clerical friend. "Excuse me, gentlemen," he said, as he took a place opposite them, and began reading the papers of the day.

"Bah!" said he, at last, — "sont-ils grands ces journaux Anglais? Look, sir," he said, handing over an immense sheet of *The Times* to Mr. Gambouge, "was ever anything so monstrous?"

Gambouge smiled politely, and examined the proffered page. "It is enormous" he said; "but I do not read English."

"Nay," said the man with the orders, "look closer at it, Signor Gambouge; it is astonishing how easy the language is."

Wondering, Simon took a sheet of paper. He turned pale as he looked at it, and began to curse the ices and the waiter. "Come, M. l'Abbé," he said; "the heat and glare of this place are intolerable."

.   .   .   .

The stranger rose with them. "Au plaisir de vous revoir, mon cher monsieur," said he; "I do not mind speaking before the Abbé here, who will be my very good friend one of these days; but I thought it necessary to refresh your memory, concerning our little business transaction six years since; and could not exactly talk of it *at church*, as you may fancy."

Simon Gambouge had seen, in the double-sheeted *Times*, the paper signed by himself, which the little Devil had pulled out of his fob.

.   .   .   .

There was no doubt on the subject; and Simon, who had but a year to live, grew more pious, and more careful than ever. He had consultations with all the doctors of the Sorbonne and all the lawyers of the Palais. But his magnificence grew as wearisome to him as his poverty had been before ; and not one of the doctors whom he consulted could give him a pennyworth of consolation.

Then he grew outrageous in his demands upon the Devil, and put him to all sorts of absurd and ridiculous tasks ; but they were all punctually performed, until Simon could invent no new ones, and the Devil sat all day with his hands in his pockets doing nothing.

One day, Simon's confessor came bounding into the room, with the greatest glee. "My friend," said he, "I have it ! Eureka ! — I have found it. Send the Pope a hundred thousand crowns, build a new Jesuit college at Rome, give a hundred gold candlesticks to St. Peter's ; and tell his Holiness you will double all, if he will give you absolution ! "

Gambouge caught at the notion, and hurried off a courier to Rome *ventre à terre*. His Holiness agreed to the request of the petition, and sent him an absolution, written out with his own fist, and all in due form.

" Now," said he, " foul fiend, I defy you ! arise, Diabolus ! your contract is not worth a jot : the Pope has absolved me, and I am safe on the road to salvation." In a fervor of gratitude he clasped the hand of his confessor, and embraced him : tears of joy ran down the cheeks of these good men.

They heard an inordinate roar of laughter, and there was Diabolus sitting opposite to them, holding his sides, and lashing his tail about, as if he would have gone mad with glee.

" Why," said he, " what nonsense is this ! do you suppose I care about *that ?* " and he tossed the Pope's missive into a corner. " M. l'Abbé knows," he said, bowing and grinning, " that though the Pope's paper may pass current *here*, it is not worth twopence in our country. What do I care about the Pope's absolution? You might just as well be absolved by your under butler."

" Egad," said the Abbé, " the rogue is right — I quite forgot the fact, which he points out clearly enough."

" No, no, Gambouge," continued Diabolus, with horrid familiarity, " go thy ways, old fellow, that *cock won't fight.*" And he retired up the chimney, chuckling at his wit and his triumph. Gambouge heard his tail scuttling all the way up, as if he had been a sweeper by profession.

Simon was left in that condition of grief in which, according to the newspapers, cities and nations are found when a murder is committed, or a lord ill of the gout — a situation, we say, more easy to imagine than to describe.

To add to his woes, Mrs. Gambouge, who was now first made acquainted with his compact, and its probable consequences, raised such a storm about his ears, as made him wish almost that his seven years were expired. She screamed, she scolded, she swore, she wept, she went into such fits of hysterics, that poor Gambouge, who had completely knocked under to her, was worn out of his life. He was allowed no rest, night or day: he moped about his fine house, solitary and wretched, and cursed his stars that he ever had married the butcher's daughter.

It wanted six months of the time.

A sudden and desperate resolution seemed all at once to have taken possession of Simon Gambouge. He called his family and his friends together — he gave one of the greatest feasts that ever was known in the city of Paris — he gayly presided at one end of his table, while Mrs. Gam., splendidly arrayed, gave herself airs at the other extremity.

After dinner, using the customary formula, he called upon Diabolus to appear. The old ladies screamed, and hoped he would not appear naked ; the young ones tittered, and longed to see the monster : everybody was pale with expectation and affright.

A very quiet, gentlemanly man, neatly dressed in black, made his appearance, to the surprise of all present, and bowed all round to the company. " I will not show my *credentials*," he said, blushing, and pointing to his hoofs, which were cleverly hidden by his pumps and shoe-buckles, " unless the ladies absolutely wish it ; but I am the person you want, Mr. Gambouge ; pray tell me what is your will."

" You know," said that gentleman, in a stately and determined voice, " that you are bound to me, according to our agreement, for six months to come."

" I am," replied the new comer.

" You are to do all that I ask, whatsoever it may be, or you forfeit the bond which I gave you?"

" It is true."

" You declare this before the present company?"

" Upon my honor, as a gentleman," said Diabolus, bowing, and laying his hand upon his waistcoat.

A whisper of applause ran round the room : all were charmed with the bland manners of the fascinating stranger.

" My love," continued Gambouge, mildly addressing his

lady, " will you be so polite as to step this way? You know I must go soon, and I am anxious, before this noble company, to make a provision for one who, in sickness as in health, in poverty as in riches, has been my truest and fondest companion."

Gambouge mopped his eyes with his handkerchief — all the company did likewise. Diabolus sobbed audibly, and Mrs. Gambouge sidled up to her husband's side, and took him tenderly by the hand. " Simon !" said she, " is it true? and do you really love your Griskinissa?"

Simon continued solemnly : " Come hither, Diabolus ; you are bound to obey me in all things for the six months during which our contract has to run ; take, then, Griskinissa Gambouge, live alone with her for half a year, never leave her from morning till night, obey all her caprices, follow all her whims, and listen to all the abuse which falls from her infernal tongue. Do this, and I ask no more of you ; I will deliver myself up at the appointed time."

Not Lord G——, when flogged by Lord B——, in the House,— not Mr. Cartlitch, of Astley's Amphitheatre, in his most pathetic passages, could look more crestfallen, and howl more hideously, than Diabolus did now. " Take another year, Gambouge," screamed he ; " two more — ten more — a century ; roast me on Lawrence's gridiron, boil me in holy water, but don't ask that : don't, don't bid me live with Mrs. Gambouge !"

Simon smiled sternly. " I have said it," he cried ; " do this, or our contract is at an end."

The Devil, at this, grinned so horribly that every drop of beer in the house turned sour : he gnashed his teeth so frightfully that every person in the company wellnigh fainted with the cholic. He slapped down the great parchment upon the floor, trampled upon it madly, and lashed it with his hoofs and his tail : at last, spreading out a mighty pair of wings as wide as from here to Regent Street, he slapped Gambouge with his tail over one eye, and vanished, abruptly, through the keyhole.

.   .   .   .

Gambouge screamed with pain and started up. " You drunken, lazy scoundrel ! " cried a shrill and well-known voice, " you have been asleep these two hours : " and here he received another terrific box on the ear.

It was too true, he had fallen asleep at his work ; and the beautiful vision had been dispelled by the thumps of the tipsy Griskinissa. Nothing remained to corroborate his story, except the bladder of lake, and this was spirted all over his waistcoat and breeches.

"I wish," said the poor fellow, rubbing his tingling cheeks, "that dreams were true;" and he went to work again at his portrait.

.   .   .   .

My last accounts of Gambouge are, that he has left the arts, and is footman in a small family. Mrs. Gam. takes in washing; and it is said that her continual dealings with soap-suds and hot water have been the only things in life which have kept her from spontaneous combustion.

CARTOUCHE.

I HAVE been much interested with an account of the exploits of Monsieur Louis Dominic Cartouche, and as Newgate and the highways are so much the fashion with us in England, we may be allowed to look abroad for histories of a similar tendency. It is pleasant to find that virtue is cosmopolite, and may exist among wooden-shoed Papists as well as honest Church-of-England men.

Louis Dominic was born in a quarter of Paris called the Courtille, says the historian whose work lies before me ; — born in the Courtille, and in the year 1693. Another biographer asserts that he was born two years later, and in the Marais ; — of respectable parents, of course. Think of the talent that our two countries produced about this time : Marlborough, Villars, Mandrin, Turpin, Boileau, Dryden, Swift, Addison, Molière, Racine, Jack Sheppard, and Louis Cartouche, — all famous within the same twenty years, and fighting, writing, robbing *à l'envi !*

Well, Marlborough was no chicken when he began to show his genius ; Swift was but a dull, idle, college lad ; but if we read the histories of some other great men mentioned in the above list — I mean the thieves, especially — we shall find that they all commenced very early : they showed a passion for their art, as little Raphael did, or little Mozart ; and the history of Cartouche's knaveries begins almost with his breeches.

Dominic's parents sent him to school at the college of Clermont (now Louis le Grand) ; and although it has never been discovered that the Jesuits, who directed that seminary, advanced him much in classical or theological knowledge, Cartouche, in revenge, showed, by repeated instances, his own natural bent and genius, which no difficulties were strong enough to overcome. His first great action on record, although not successful in the end, and tinctured with the innocence of youth, is yet highly creditable to him. He made a general swoop of a hundred and twenty nightcaps belonging to his companions, and disposed of them to his satisfaction; but as it was discovered that of all the youths in the college of Clermont, he only was the possessor of a cap to sleep in, suspicion (which, alas! was confirmed) immediately fell upon him: and by this little piece of youthful *naïveté*, a scheme, prettily conceived and smartly performed, was rendered naught.

Cartouche had a wonderful love for good eating, and put all the apple-women and cooks, who came to supply the students, under contribution. Not always, however, desirous of robbing these, he used to deal with them, occasionally, on honest principles of barter; that is, whenever he could get hold of his schoolfellows' knives, books, rulers, or playthings, which he used fairly to exchange for tarts and gingerbread.

It seemed as if the presiding genius of evil was determined to patronize this young man; for before he had been long at college, and soon after he had, with the greatest difficulty, escaped from the nightcap scrape, an opportunity occurred by which he was enabled to gratify both his propensities at once, and not only to steal, but to steal sweetmeats. It happened that the principal of the college received some pots of Narbonne honey, which came under the eyes of Cartouche, and in which that young gentleman, as soon as ever he saw them, determined to put his fingers. The president of the college put aside his honey-pots in an apartment within his own; to which, except by the one door which led into the room which his reverence usually occupied, there was no outlet. There was no chimney in the room; and the windows looked into the court, where there was a porter at night, and where crowds passed by day. What was Cartouche to do? — have the honey he must.

Over this chamber, which contained what his soul longed after, and over the president's rooms, there ran a set of unoccupied garrets, into which the dexterous Cartouche penetrated. These were divided from the rooms below, according to the fashion of those days, by a set of large beams, which reached across the whole building, and across which rude planks were laid, which formed the ceiling of the lower story and the floor of the upper. Some of these planks did young Cartouche remove; and having descended by means of a rope, tied a couple of others to the neck of the honey-pots, climbed back again, and drew up his prey in safety. He then cunningly fixed the planks again in their old places, and retired to gorge himself upon his booty. And, now, see the punishment of avarice! Everybody knows that the brethren of the order of Jesus are bound by a vow to have no more than a certain small sum of money in their possession. The principal of the college of Clermont had amassed a larger sum, in defiance of this rule: and where do you think the old gentleman had hidden it? In the honey-pots! As Cartouche dug his spoon into one of them, he brought out, besides a quantity of golden honey, a couple of golden louis, which, with ninety-eight more of their fellows, were comfortably hidden in the pots. Little Dominic, who, before, had cut rather a poor figure among his fellow-students, now appeared in as fine clothes as any of them could boast of; and when asked by his parents, on going home, how he came by them, said that a young nobleman of his schoolfellows had taken a violent fancy to him, and made him a present of a couple of his suits. Cartouche the elder, good man, went to thank the young nobleman; but none such could be found, and young Cartouche disdained to give any explanation of his manner of gaining the money.

Here, again, we have to regret and remark the inadvertence of youth. Cartouche lost a hundred louis — for what? For a pot of honey not worth a couple of shillings. Had he fished out the pieces, and replaced the pots and the honey, he might have been safe, and a respectable citizen all his life after. The principal would not have dared to confess the loss of his money, and did not, openly; but he vowed vengeance against the stealer of his sweetmeat, and a rigid search was made. Cartouche, as usual, was fixed upon; and in the tick of his bed, lo! there were found a couple of empty honey-pots! From this scrape there is no knowing how he would have escaped, had not the president himself been a little anxious to hush the matter up; and accordingly, young Cartouche was made to disgorge the residue of his ill-gotten gold pieces, old Cartouche made up the deficiency, and his son was allowed to remain unpunished — until the next time.

This, you may fancy, was not very long in coming; and though history has not made us acquainted with the exact crime which Louis Dominic next committed, it must have been a serious one; for Cartouche, who had borne philosophically all the whippings and punishments which were administered to him at college, did not dare to face that one which his indignant father had in pickle for him. As he was coming home from school, on the first day after his crime, when he received permission to go abroad, one of his brothers, who was on the look-out for him, met him at a short distance from home, and told him what was in preparation; which so frightened this young thief, that he declined returning home altogether, and set out upon the wide world to shift for himself as he could.

Undoubted as his genius was, he had not arrived at the full exercise of it, and his gains were by no means equal to his appetite. In whatever professions he tried, — whether he joined the gipsies, which he did, — whether he picked pockets on the Pont Neuf, which occupation history attributes to him, — poor Cartouche was always hungry. Hungry and ragged, he wandered from one place and profession to another, and regretted the honey-pots at Clermont, and the comfortable soup and *bouilli* at home.

Cartouche had an uncle, a kind man, who was a merchant, and had dealings at Rouen. One day, walking on the quays of that city, this gentleman saw a very miserable, dirty, starving lad, who had just made a pounce upon some bones and turnip-peelings, that had been flung out on the quay, and was eating them as greedily as if they had been turkeys and truffles. The worthy man examined the lad a little closer. O heavens! it was their runaway prodigal — it was little Louis Dominic! The merchant was touched by his case; and forgetting the nightcaps, the honey-pots, and the rags and dirt of little Louis, took him to his arms, and kissed and hugged him with the tenderest affection. Louis kissed and hugged too, and blubbered a great deal: he was very repentant, as a man often is when he is hungry; and he went home with his uncle, and his peace was made; and his mother got him new clothes, and filled his belly, and for a while Louis was as good a son as might be.

But why attempt to balk the progress of genius? Louis's was not to be kept down. He was sixteen years of age by this time — a smart, lively young fellow, and, what is more, desperately enamored of a lovely washerwoman. To be successful in your love, as Louis knew, you must have something more than mere flames and sentiment; — a washer, or any other woman, cannot live upon sighs only; but must have new gowns and caps, and a necklace every now and then, and a few handkerchiefs and silk stockings, and a treat into the country or to the play. Now, how are all these things to be had without money? Cartouche saw at once that it was impossible; and as his father would give him none, he was obliged to look for it elsewhere. He took to his old courses, and lifted a purse here, and a watch there; and found, moreover, an accommodating gentleman, who took the wares off his hands.

This gentleman introduced him into a very select and agreeable society, in which Cartouche's merit began speedily to be recognized, and in which he learnt how pleasant it is in life to have friends to assist one, and how much may be done by a proper division of labor. M. Cartouche, in fact, formed part of a regular company or gang of gentlemen, who were associated together for the purpose of making war on the public and the law.

Cartouche had a lovely young sister, who was to be married to a rich young gentleman from the provinces. As is the fashion in France, the parents had arranged the match among themselves; and the young people had never met until just before the time appointed for the marriage, when the bridegroom came up to Paris with his title-deeds, and settlements, and money. Now there can hardly be found in history a finer instance of devotion than Cartouche now exhibited. He went to his captain, explained the matter to him, and actually, for the good of his country, as it were (the thieves might be called his country), sacrificed his sister's husband's property. Informations were taken, the house of the bridegroom was reconnoitred, and, one night, Cartouche, in company with some chosen friends, made his first visit to the house of his brother-in-law. All the people were gone to bed; and, doubtless, for fear of disturbing the porter, Cartouche and his companions spared him the trouble of opening the door, by ascending quietly at the window. They arrived at the room where the bridegroom kept his great chest, and set industriously to work, filing and picking the locks which defended the treasure.

The bridegroom slept in the next room; but however tenderly Cartouche and his workmen handled their tools, from fear of disturbing his slumbers, their benevolent design was disappointed, for awaken him they did; and quietly slipping out of bed, he came to a place where he had a complete view of all that was going on. He did not cry out, or frighten himself sillily; but, on the contrary, contented himself with watching the countenances of the robbers, so that he might recognize them on another occasion; and, though an avaricious man, he did not feel the slightest anxiety about his money-chest; for the fact is, he had removed all the cash and papers the day before.

As soon, however, as they had broken all the locks, and found the nothing which lay at the bottom of the chest, he shouted with such a loud voice, " Here, Thomas ! — John ! — officer ! — keep the gate, fire at the rascals ! " that they, incontinently taking fright, skipped nimbly out of window, and left the house free.

Cartouche, after this, did not care to meet his brother-in-law, but eschewed all those occasions on which the latter was to be present at his father's house. The evening before the marriage came ; and then his father insisted upon his appearance among the other relatives of the bride's and bridegroom's families, who were all to assemble and make merry. Cartouche was obliged to yield ; and brought with him one or two of his companions, who had been, by the way, present in the affair of the empty money-boxes ; and though he never fancied that there was any danger in meeting his brother-in-law, for he had no idea that he had been seen on the night of the attack, with a natural modesty, which did him really credit, he kept out of the young bridegroom's sight as much as he could, and showed no desire to be presented to him. At supper, however, as he was sneaking modestly down to a side-table, his father shouted after him, " Ho, Dominic, come hither, and sit opposite to your brother-in-law : " which Dominic did, his friends following. The bridegroom pledged him very gracefully in a bumper ; and was in the act of making him a pretty speech, on the honor of an alliance with such a family, and on the pleasures of brother-in-lawship in general, when, looking in his face — ye gods ! he saw the very man who had been filing at his money-chest a few nights ago ! By his side, too, sat a couple more of the gang. The poor fellow turned deadly pale and sick, and, setting his glass down, ran quickly out of the room, for he thought he was in company of a whole gang of robbers. And when he got home, he wrote a letter to the elder Cartouche, humbly declining any connection with his family.

Cartouche the elder, of course, angrily asked the reason of such an abrupt dissolution of the engagement ; and then, much to his horror, heard of his eldest son's doings. " You would not have me marry into such a family ? " said the ex-bridegroom. And old Cartouche, an honest old citizen, confessed, with a heavy heart, that he would not. What was he to do with the lad ? He did not like to ask for a *lettre de cachet*, and shut him up in the Bastile. He determined to give him a year's discipline at the monastery of St. Lazare.

But how to catch the young gentleman ? Old Cartouche

knew that, were he to tell his son of the scheme, the latter would never obey, and, therefore, he determined to be very cunning. He told Dominic that he was about to make a heavy bargain with the fathers, and should require a witness; so they stepped into a carriage together, and drove unsuspectingly to the Rue St. Denis. But, when they arrived near the convent, Cartouche saw several ominous figures gathering round the coach, and felt that his doom was sealed. However, he made as if he knew nothing of the conspiracy; and the carriage drew up, and his father descended, and, bidding him wait for a minute in the coach, promised to return to him. Cartouche looked out; on the other side of the way half a dozen men were posted, evidently with the intention of arresting him.

Cartouche now performed a great and celebrated stroke of genius, which, if he had not been professionally employed in the morning, he never could have executed. He had in his pocket a piece of linen, which he had laid hold of at the door of some shop, and from which he quickly tore three suitable stripes. One he tied round his head, after the fashion of a nightcap; a second round his waist, like an apron; and with the third he covered his hat, a round one, with a large brim. His coat and his periwig he left behind him in the carriage; and when he stepped out from it (which he did without asking the coachman to let down the steps), he bore exactly the appearance of a cook's boy carrying a dish; and with this he slipped through the exempts quite unsuspected, and bade adieu to the Lazarists and his honest father, who came out speedily to seek him, and was not a little annoyed to find only his coat and wig.

With that coat and wig, Cartouche left home, father, friends, conscience, remorse, society, behind him. He discovered (like a great number of other philosophers and poets, when they have committed rascally actions) that the world was all going wrong, and he quarrelled with it outright. One of the first stories told of the illustrious Cartouche, when he became professionally and openly a robber, redounds highly to his credit, and shows that he knew how to take advantage of the occasion, and how much he had improved in the course of a very few years' experience. His courage and ingenuity were vastly admired by his friends; so much so, that, one day, the captain of the band thought fit to compliment him, and vowed that when he (the captain) died, Cartouche should infallibly be called to the command-in-chief. This conversation, so flattering to Cartouche, was carried on between the two gentlemen as they were walking, one night, on the quays by the side of the Seine. Cartouche, when the captain made the last remark, blushingly protested against it, and pleaded his extreme youth as a reason why his comrades could never put entire trust in him. "Psha, man!" said the captain, "thy youth is in thy favor; thou wilt live only the longer to lead thy troops to victory. As for strength, bravery, and cunning, wert thou as old as Methuselah, thou couldst not be better provided than thou art now, at eighteen." What was the reply of Monsieur Cartouche? He answered, not by words, but by actions. Drawing his knife from his girdle, he instantly dug it into the captain's left side, as near his heart as possible; and then, seizing that imprudent commander, precipitated him violently into the waters of the Seine, to keep company with the gudgeons and river-gods. When he returned to the band, and recounted how the captain had basely attempted to assassinate him, and how he, on the contrary, had, by exertion of superior skill, overcome the captain, not one of the society believed a word of his history; but they elected him captain forthwith. I think his Excellency Don Rafael Maroto, the pacificator of Spain, is an amiable character, for whom history has not been written in vain.

Being arrived at this exalted position, there is no end of the feats which Cartouche performed; and his band reached to such a pitch of glory, that if there had been a hundred thousand, instead of a hundred of them, who knows but that a new and popular dynasty might not have been founded, and "Louis Dominic, premier Empereur des Français," might have performed innumerable glorious actions, and fixed himself in the hearts of his people, just as other monarchs have done, a hundred years after Cartouche's death.

A story similar to the above, and equally moral, is that of Cartouche, who, in company with two other gentlemen, robbed the *coche*, or packet-boat, from Melun, where they took a good quantity of booty, — making the passengers lie down on the decks, and rifling them at leisure. "This money will be but very little among three," whispered Cartouche to his neighbor, as the three conquerors were making merry over their gains; "if you were but to pull the trigger of your pistol in the neighborhood of your comrade's ear, perhaps it might go off, and then there would be but two of us to share." Strangely enough, as Cartouche said, the pistol *did* go off, and No. 3 perished. "Give him another ball," said Cartouche; and another was fired into him. But no sooner had Cartouche's comrade discharged both his pistols, than Cartouche himself, seized with a furious indignation, drew his: "Learn, monster," cried he, "not to be so greedy of gold, and perish, the victim of thy disloyalty and avarice!" So Cartouche slew the second robber; and there is no man in Europe who can say that the latter did not merit well his punishment.

I could fill volumes, and not mere sheets of paper, with tales of the triumphs of Cartouche and his band; how he robbed the Countess of O——, going to Dijon, in her coach, and how the Countess fell in love with him, and was faithful to him ever after; how, when the lieutenant of police offered a reward of a hundred pistoles to any man who would bring Cartouche before him, a noble Marquess, in a coach and six, drove up to the hotel of the police; and the noble Marquess, desiring to see Monsieur de la Reynie, on matters of the highest moment, alone, the latter introduced him into his private cabinet; and how, when there, the Marquess drew from his pocket a long, curiously shaped dagger: "Look at this, Monsieur de la Reynie," said he; "this dagger is poisoned!"

"Is it possible?" said M. de la Reynie.

"A prick of it would do for any man," said the Marquess.

"You don't say so!" said M. de la Reynie.

"I do, though; and, what is more," says the Marquess, in a terrible voice, "if you do not instantly lay yourself flat on the ground, with your face towards it, and your hands crossed over your back, or if you make the slightest noise or cry, I will stick this poisoned dagger between your ribs, as sure as my name is Cartouche?"

At the sound of this dreadful name, M. de la Reynie sunk incontinently down on his stomach, and submitted to be carefully gagged and corded; after which Monsieur Cartouche laid his hands upon all the money which was kept in the lieutenant's cabinet. Alas! and alas! many a stout bailiff, and many an honest fellow of a spy, went, for that day, without his pay and his victuals.

There is a story that Cartouche once took the diligence to Lille, and found in it a certain Abbé Potter, who was full of indignation against this monster of a Cartouche, and said that when he went back to Paris, which he proposed to do in about a fortnight, he should give the lieutenant of police some information, which would infallibly lead to the scoundrel's capture. But poor Potter was disappointed in his designs; for, before he could fulfil them, he was made the victim of Cartouche's cruelty.

A letter came to the lieutenant of police, to state that Cartouche had travelled to Lille, in company with the Abbé de Potter, of that town ; that, on the reverend gentleman's return towards Paris, Cartouche had waylaid him, murdered him, taken his papers, and would come to Paris himself, bearing the name and clothes of the unfortunate Abbé, by the Lille coach, on such a day.   The Lille coach arrived, was surrounded by police agents ; the monster Cartouche was there, sure enough, in the Abbé's guise.   He was seized, bound, flung into prison, brought out to be examined, and, on examination, found to be no other than the Abbé Potter himself !   It is pleasant to read thus of the relaxations of great men, and find them condescending to joke like the meanest of us.

Another diligence adventure is recounted of the famous Cartouche.   It happened that he met, in the coach, a young and lovely lady, clad in widow's weeds, and bound to Paris, with a couple of servants.   The poor thing was the widow of a rich old gentleman of Marseilles, and was going to the capital to arrange with her lawyers, and to settle her husband's will. The Count de Grinche (for so her fellow-passenger was called) was quite as candid as the pretty widow had been, and stated that he was a captain in the regiment of Nivernois ; that he was going to Paris to buy a colonelcy, which his relatives, the Duke de Bouillon, the Prince de Montmorency, the Commandeur de la Trémoille, with all their interest at court, could not fail to procure for him.   To be short, in the course of the four days' journey, the Count Louis Dominic de Grinche played his cards so well, that the poor little widow half forgot her late husband ; and her eyes glistened with tears as the Count kissed her hand at parting — at parting, he hoped, only for a few hours.

Day and night the insinuating Count followed her ; and when, at the end of a fortnight, and in the midst of a *tête-à-tête*, he plunged, one morning, suddenly on his knees, and said, " Leonora, do you love me? " the poor thing heaved the gentlest, tenderest, sweetest sigh in the world ; and, sinking her blushing head on his shoulder, whispered, "Oh, Dominic, je t'aime ! Ah ! " said she, " how noble is it of my Dominic to take me with the little I have, and he so rich a nobleman ! "   The fact is, the old Baron's titles and estates had passed away to his nephews ; his dowager was only left with three hundred thousand livres, in *rentes sur l'état* — a handsome sum, but nothing to compare to the rent-roll of Count Dominic, Count de la Grinche, Seigneur de la Haute Pigre, Baron de la Bigorne : he had estates and wealth which might authorize him to aspire to the hand of a duchess, at least.

The unfortunate widow never for a moment suspected the cruel trick that was about to be played on her; and, at the request of her affianced husband, sold out her money, and realized it in gold, to be made over to him on the day when the contract was to be signed. The day arrived; and, according to the custom in France, the relations of both parties attended. The widow's relatives, though respectable, were not of the first nobility, being chiefly persons of the *finance* or the *robe:* there was the president of the court of Arras, and his lady; a farmer-general; a judge of a court of Paris; and other such grave and respectable people. As for Monsieur le Comte de la Grinche, he was not bound for names; and, having the whole peerage to choose from, brought a host of Montmorencies, Créquis, De la Tours, and Guises at his back. His *homme d'affaires* brought his papers in a sack, and displayed the plans of his estates, and the titles of his glorious ancestry. The widow's lawyers had her money in sacks; and between the gold on the one side, and the parchments on the other, lay the contract which was to make the widow's three hundred thousand francs the property of the Count de Grinche. The Count de la Grinche was just about to sign; when the Marshal de Villars, stepping up to him, said, "Captain, do you know who the president of the court of Arras, yonder, is? It is old Manasseh, the fence, of Brussels. I pawned a gold watch to him, which I stole from Cadogan, when I was with Malbrook's army in Flanders."

Here the Duc de la Roche Guyon came forward, very much alarmed. "Run me through the body!" said his Grace, "but the comptroller-general's lady, there, is no other than that old hag of a Margoton who keeps the ——" Here the Duc de la Roche Guyon's voice fell.

Cartouche smiled graciously, and walked up to the table. He took up one of the widow's fifteen thousand gold pieces; — it was as pretty a bit of copper as you could wish to see. "My dear," said he politely, "there is some mistake here, and this business had better stop."

"Count!" gasped the poor widow.

"Count be hanged!" answered the bridegroom, sternly; "my name is CARTOUCHE!"

ON SOME FRENCH FASHIONABLE NOVELS.

WITH A PLEA FOR ROMANCES IN GENERAL.

THERE is an old story of a Spanish court painter, who, being pressed for money, and having received a piece of damask, which he was to wear in a state procession, pawned the damask, and appeared, at the show, dressed out in some very fine sheets of paper, which he had painted so as exactly to resemble silk. Nay, his coat looked so much richer than the doublets of all the rest, that the Emperor Charles, in whose honor the procession was given, remarked the painter, and so his deceit was found out.

I have often thought that, in respect of sham and real histories, a similar fact may be noticed; the sham story appearing a great deal more agreeable, life-like, and natural than the true one: and all who, from laziness as well as principle, are inclined to follow the easy and comfortable study of novels, may console themselves with the notion that they are studying matters quite as important as history, and that their favorite duodecimos are as instructive as the biggest quartos in the world.

If then, ladies, the big-wigs begin to sneer at the course of our studies, calling our darling romances foolish, trivial, noxious to the mind, enervators of intellect, fathers of idleness, and what not, let us at once take a high ground, and say, — Go you to your own employments, and to such dull studies as you fancy; go and bob for triangles, from the Pons Asinorum; go enjoy your dull black draughts of metaphysics; go fumble over history books, and dissert upon Herodotus and Livy; *our* histories are, perhaps, as true as yours; our drink is the brisk sparkling champagne drink, from the presses of Colburn, Bentley and Co.; our walks are over such sunshiny pleasure-grounds

as Scott and Shakspeare have laid out for us ; and if our dwellings are castles in the air, we find them excessively splendid
and commodious ; — be not you envious because you have no
wings to fly thither.   Let the big-wigs despise us ; such contempt of their neighbors is the custom of all barbarous tribes ;
— witness, the learned Chinese : Tippoo Sultaun declared that
there were not in all Europe ten thousand men : the Sklavonic
hordes, it is said, so entitled themselves from a word in their
jargon, which signifies " to speak ; " the ruffians imagining that
they had a monopoly of this agreeable faculty, and that all other
nations were dumb.

Not so : others may be *deaf ;* but the novelist has a loud,
eloquent, instructive language, though his enemies may despise
or deny it ever so much.   What is more, one could, perhaps,
meet the stoutest historian on his own ground, and argue with
him ; showing that sham histories were much truer than real
histories ; which are, in fact, mere contemptible catalogues of
names and places, that can have no moral effect upon the
reader.

As thus : —

Julius Cæsar beat Pompey, at Pharsalia.
The Duke of Marlborough beat Marshal Tallard at Blenheim.
The Constable of Bourbon beat Francis the First, at Pavia.

And what have we here? — so many names, simply.   Suppose
Pharsalia had been, at that mysterious period when names were
given, called Pavia ; and that Julius Cæsar's family name had
been John Churchill ; — the fact would have stood in history,
thus : —

" Pompey ran away from the Duke of Marlborough at Pavia."

And why not? — we should have been just as wise.   Or it might
be stated that —

" The tenth legion charged the French infantry at Blenheim ; and Cæsar,
writing home to his mamma, said, ' *Madame, tout est perdu fors l'honneur.*' "

What a contemptible science this is, then, about which quartos are written, and sixty-volumed Biographies Universelles,
and Lardner's Cabinet Cyclopædias, and the like ! the facts are
nothing in it, the names everything ; and a gentleman might
as well improve his mind by learning Walker's " Gazetteer,"
or getting by heart a fifty-years-old edition of the " Court
Guide."

Having thus disposed of the historians, let us come to the point in question — the novelists.

On the title-page of these volumes the reader has, doubtless, remarked, that among the pieces introduced, some are announced as "copies" and "compositions." Many of the histories have, accordingly, been neatly stolen from the collections of French authors (and mutilated, according to the old saying, so that their owners should not know them) and, for compositions, we intend to favor the public with some studies of French modern works, that have not as yet, we believe, attracted the notice of the English public.

Of such works there appear many hundreds yearly, as may be seen by the French catalogues ; but the writer has not so much to do with works political, philosophical, historical, metaphysical, scientifical, theological, as with those for which he has been putting forward a plea — novels, namely ; on which he has expended a great deal of time and study. And passing from novels in general to French novels, let us confess, with much humiliation, that we borrow from these stories a great deal more knowledge of French society than from our own personal observation we ever can hope to gain : for, let a gentleman who has dwelt two, four, or ten years in Paris (and has not gone thither for the purpose of making a book, when three weeks are sufficient — let an English gentleman say, at the end of any given period, how much he knows of French society, how many French houses he has entered, and how many French friends he has made ? — He has enjoyed, at the end of the year, say —

At the English Ambassador's, so many soirées.
At houses to which he has brought letters, so many tea-parties.
At Cafés, so many dinners.
At French private houses, say three dinners, and very lucky too.

He has, we say, seen an immense number of wax candles, cups of tea, glasses of orgeat, and French people, in best clothes, enjoying the same ; but intimacy there is none ; we see but the outsides of the people. Year by year we live in France, and grow gray, and see no more. We play écarté with Monsieur de Trêfle every night ; but what know we of the heart of the man — of the inward ways, thoughts, and customs of Trêfle? If we have good legs, and love the amusement, we dance with Countess Flicflac, Tuesdays and Thursdays, ever since the Peace ; and how far are we advanced in acquaintance with her since we first twirled her round a room? We know her velvet gown, and her diamonds (about three-fourths of them are sham, by the way) ; we know her smiles, and her simpers, and her rouge — but no more : she may turn into a kitchen wench at twelve on Thursday night, for aught we know ; her *voiture*, a pumpkin ; and her *gens*, so many rats : but the real, rougeless, *intime* Flicflac, we know not. This privilege is granted to no Englishman : we may understand the French language as well as Monsieur de Levizac, but never can penetrate into Flicflac's confidence : our ways are not her ways ; our manners of thinking, not hers : when we say a good thing, in the course of the night, we are wondrous lucky and pleased ; Flicflac will trill you off fifty in ten minutes, and wonder at the *bêtise* of the Briton, who has never a word to say. We are married, and have fourteen children, and would just as soon make love to the Pope of Rome as to any one but our own wife. If you do not make love to Flicflac, from the day after her marriage to the day she reaches sixty, she thinks you a fool. We won't play at écarté with Trêfle on Sunday nights ; and are seen walking, about one o'clock (accompanied by fourteen red-haired children, with fourteen gleaming prayer-books), away from the church. " Grand Dieu ! " cries Trêfle, " is that man mad? He won't play at cards on a Sunday ; he goes to church on a Sunday : he has fourteen children ! "

Was ever Frenchman known to do likewise? Pass we on to our argument. which is, that with our English notions and moral and physical constitution, it is quite impossible that we should become intimate with our brisk neighbors ; and when such authors as Lady Morgan and Mrs. Trollope, having frequented a certain number of tea-parties in the French capital, begin to prattle about French manners and men, — with all respect for the talents of those ladies, we do believe their information not to be worth a sixpence ; they speak to us not of men but of tea-parties. Tea-parties are the same all the world over ; with the exception that, with the French, there are more lights and prettier dresses ; and with us, a mighty deal more tea in the pot.

There is, however, a cheap and delightful way of travelling, that a man may perform in his easy-chair, without expense of passports or post-boys. On the wings of a novel, from the next circulating library, he sends his imagination a-gadding, and gains acquaintance with people and manners whom he could not hope otherwise to know. Twopence a volume bears us whithersoever we will ; — back to Ivanhoe and Cœur de

Lion, or to Waverley and the Young Pretender, along with Walter Scott; up the heights of fashion with the charming enchanters of the silver-fork school; or, better still, to the snug inn-parlor, or the jovial tap-room, with Mr. Pickwick and his faithful Sancho Weller. I am sure that a man who, a hundred years hence should sit down to write the history of our time, would do wrong to put that great contemporary history of "Pickwick" aside as a frivolous work. It contains true character under false names; and, like "Roderick Random," an inferior work, and "Tom Jones" (one that is immeasurably superior), gives us a better idea of the state and ways of the people than one could gather from any more pompous or authentic histories.

We have, therefore, introduced into these volumes one or two short reviews of French fiction writers, of particular classes, whose Paris sketches may give the reader some notion of manners in that capital. If not original, at least the drawings are accurate; for, as a Frenchman might have lived a thousand years in England, and never could have written "Pickwick," an Englishman cannot hope to give a good description of the inward thoughts and ways of his neighbors.

To a person inclined to study these, in that light and amusing fashion in which the novelist treats them, let us recommend the works of a new writer, Monsieur de Bernard, who has painted actual manners, without those monstrous and terrible exaggerations in which late French writers have indulged; and who, if he occasionally wounds the English sense of propriety (as what French man or woman alive will not?) does so more by slighting than by outraging it, as, with their labored descriptions of all sorts of imaginable wickedness, some of his brethren of the press have done. M. de Bernard's characters are men and women of genteel society — rascals enough, but living in no state of convulsive crimes; and we follow him in his lively, malicious account of their manners, without risk of lighting upon any such horrors as Balzac or Dumas has provided for us.

Let us give an instance: — it is from the amusing novel called "Les Ailes d'Icare," and contains what is to us quite a new picture of a French fashionable rogue. The fashions will change in a few years, and the rogue, of course, with them. Let us catch this delightful fellow ere he flies. It is impossible to sketch the character in a more sparkling, gentlemanlike way than M. de Bernard's; but such light things are very difficult of translation, and the sparkle sadly evaporates during the process of *decanting.*

A FRENCH FASHIONABLE LETTER.

" My dear Victor — It is six in the morning : I have just
come from the English Ambassador's ball, and as my plans for
the day do not admit of my sleeping, I write you a line ; for, at
this moment, saturated as I am with the enchantments of a
fairy night, all other pleasures would be too wearisome to keep
me awake, except that of conversing with you.   Indeed, were
I not to write to you now, when should I find the possibility of
doing so?   Time flies here with such a frightful rapidity, my
pleasures and my affairs whirl onwards together in such a tor-
rentuous galopade, that I am compelled to seize occasion by
the forelock ; for each moment has its imperious employ.   Do
not then accuse me of negligence : if my correspondence has not
always that regularity which I would fain give it, attribute the
fault solely to the whirlwind in which I live, and which carries
me hither and thither at its will.

" However, you are not the only person with whom I am
behindhand : I assure you, on the contrary, that you are one of
a very numerous and fashionable company, to whom, towards
the discharge of my debts, I propose to consecrate four hours
to-day.   I give you the preference to all the world, even to the
lovely Duchess of San Severino, a delicious Italian, whom, for
my special happiness, I met last summer at the Waters of Aix.
I have also a most important negotiation to conclude with one
of our Princes of Finance : but *n'importe*, I commence with
thee : friendship before love or money — friendship before
everything.   My despatches concluded, I am engaged to ride
with the Marquis de Grigneure, the Comte de Castijars, and
Lord Cobham, in order that we may recover, for a breakfast at
the Rocher de Cancale that Grigneure has lost, the appetite
which we all of us so cruelly abused last night at the Ambassador's gala.   On my honor, my dear fellow, everybody was of
a *caprice prestigieux* and a *comfortable mirobolant*.   Fancy, for
a banquet-hall, a royal orangery hung with white damask ; the
boxes of the shrubs transformed into so many sideboards ;
lights gleaming through the foliage ; and, for guests, the loveliest women and most brilliant cavaliers of Paris.   Orleans and
Nemours were there, dancing and eating like simple mortals.
In a word, Albion did the thing very handsomely, and I accord
it my esteem.

" Here I pause, to call for my valet-de-chambre, and call for
tea ; for my head is heavy, and I've no time for a headache.
In serving me, this rascal of a Frédéric has broken a cup, true

Japan, upon my honor — the rogue does nothing else. Yesterday, for instance, did he not thump me prodigiously, by letting fall a goblet, after Cellini, of which the carving alone cost me three hundred francs? I must positively put the wretch out of doors, to ensure the safety of my furniture ; and in consequence of this, Eneas, an audacious young negro, in whom wisdom hath not waited for years — Eneas, my groom, I say, will probably be elevated to the post of valet-de-chambre. But where was I? I think I was speaking to you of an oyster breakfast, to which, on our return from the Park (du Bois), a company of pleasant rakes are invited. After quitting Borel's, we propose to adjourn to the Barrière du Combat, where Lord Cobham proposes to try some bull-dogs, which he has brought over from England — one of these, O'Connell (Lord Cobham is a Tory,) has a face in which I place much confidence : I have a bet of ten louis with Castijars on the strength of it. After the fight, we shall make our accustomed appearance at the ' Café de Paris,' (the only place, by the way, where a man who respects himself may be seen,) — and then away with frocks and spurs, and on with our dress-coats for the rest of the evening. In the first place, I shall go doze for a couple of hours at the Opera, where my presence is indispensable ; for Coralie, a charming creature, passes this evening from the rank of the *rats* to that of the *tigers*, in a *pas-de-trois*, and our box patronizes her. After the Opera, I must show my face to two or three *salons* in the Faubourg St. Honoré ; and having thus performed my duties to the world of fashion, I return to the exercise of my rights as a member of the Carnival. At two o'clock all the world meets at the Théâtre Ventadour : lions and tigers — the whole of our menagerie will be present. Evoé ! off we go ! roaring and bounding Bacchanal and Saturnal ; 'tis agreed that we shall be everything that is low. To conclude, we sup with Castijars, the most ' furiously dishevelled ' orgy that ever was known."

.   .   .   .

The rest of the letter is on matters of finance, equally curious and instructive. But pause we for the present, to consider the fashionable part : and caricature as it is, we have an accurate picture of the actual French dandy. Bets, breakfasts, riding, dinners at the " Café de Paris," and delirious Carnival balls : the animal goes through all such frantic pleasures at the season that precedes Lent. He has a wondrous respect for English " gentlemen-sportsmen ; " he imitates their clubs — their love of horse-flesh : he calls his palefrenier a groom, wears blue birds's-eye neck-cloths, sports his pink out hunting, rides steeple-chases, and has his Jockey Club. The "tigers and lions" alluded to in the report have been borrowed from our own country, and a great compliment is it to Monsieur de Bernard, the writer of the above amusing sketch, that he has such a knowledge of English names and things, as to give a Tory lord the decent title of Lord Cobham, and to call his dog O'Connell. Paul de Kock calls an English nobleman, in one of his last novels, *Lord Boulingrog*, and appears vastly delighted at the verisimilitude of the title.

For the "*rugissements et bondissements, bacchanale et saturnale, galop infernal, ronde du sabbat tout le tremblement*," these words give a most clear, untranslatable idea of the Carnival ball. A sight more hideous can hardly strike a man's eye. I was present at one where the four thousand guests whirled screaming, reeling, roaring, out of the ball-room in the Rue St. Honoré, and tore down to the column in the Place Vendôme, round which they went shrieking their own music, twenty miles an hour, and so tore madly back again. Let a man go alone to such a place of amusement, and the sight for him is perfectly terrible : the horrid frantic gayety of the place puts him in mind more of the merriment of demons than of men : bang, bang, drums, trumpets, chairs, pistol-shots, pour out of the orchestra, which seems as mad as the dancers ; whiz, a whirlwind of paint and patches, all the costumes under the sun, all the ranks in the empire, all the he and she scoundrels of the capital, writhed and twisted together, rush by you ; if a man falls, woe be to him : two thousand screaming menads go trampling over his carcass : they have neither power nor will to stop.

A set of Malays drunk with bhang and running amuck, a company of howling dervishes, may possibly, in our own day, go through similar frantic vagaries ; but I doubt if any civilized European people but the French would permit and enjoy such scenes. Yet our neighbors see little shame in them ; and it is very true that men of all classes, high and low, here congregate and give themselves up to the disgusting worship of the genius of the place. — From the dandy of the Boulevard and the " Café Anglais," let us turn to the dandy of " Flicoteau's " and the Pays Latin — the Paris student, whose exploits among the grisettes are so celebrated, and whose fierce republicanism keeps gendarmes for ever on the alert. The following is M. de Bernard's description of him : —

" I became acquainted with Dambergeac when we were

students at the Ecole de Droit; we lived in the same Hotel on the Place du Panthéon. No doubt, madam, you have occasionally met little children dedicated to the Virgin, and, to this end, clothed in white raiment from head to foot: my friend, Dambergeac, had received a different consecration. His father, a great patriot of the Revolution, had determined that his son should bear into the world a sign of indelible republicanism; so, to the great displeasure of his godmother and the parish curate, Dambergeac was christened by the pagan name of Harmodius. It was a kind of moral tricolor-cockade, which the child was to bear through the vicissitudes of all the revolutions to come. Under such influences, my friend's character began to develop itself, and, fired by the example of his father, and by the warm atmosphere of his native place, Marseilles, he grew up to have an independent spirit, and a grand liberality of politics, which were at their height when first I made his acquaintance.

" He was then a young man of eighteen, with a tall, slim figure, a broad chest, and a flaming black eye, out of all which personal charms he knew how to draw the most advantage: and though his costume was such as Staub might probably have criticised, he had, nevertheless, a style peculiar to himself — to himself and the students, among whom he was the leader of the fashion. A tight black coat, buttoned up to the chin, across the chest, set off that part of his person; a low-crowned hat, with a voluminous rim, cast solemn shadows over a countenance bronzed by a southern sun: he wore, at one time, enormous flowing black locks, which he sacrificed pitilessly, however, and adopted a Brutus, as being more revolutionary: finally, he carried an enormous club, that was his code and digest: in like manner, De Retz used to carry a stiletto in his pocket by way of a breviary.

" Although of different ways of thinking in politics, certain sympathies of character and conduct united Dambergeac and myself, and we speedily became close friends. I don't think, in the whole course of his three years' residence, Dambergeac ever went through a single course of lectures. For the examinations, he trusted to luck, and to his own facility, which was prodigious: as for honors, he never aimed at them, but was content to do exactly as little as was necessary for him to gain his degree. In like manner he sedulously avoided those horrible circulating libraries, where daily are seen to congregate the ' reading men' of our schools. But, in revenge, there was not a milliner's shop, or a *lingère's*, in all our quartier Latin, which he did not industriously frequent, and of which he was not the oracle. Nay, it was said that his victories were not confined to the left bank of the Seine; reports did occasionally come to us of fabulous adventures by him accomplished in the far regions of the Rue de la Paix and the Boulevard Poissonnière. Such recitals were, for us less favored mortals, like tales of Bacchus conquering in the East; they excited our ambition, but not our jealousy; for the superiority of Harmodius was acknowledged by us all, and we never thought of a rivalry with him. No man ever cantered a hack through the Champs Elysées with such elegant assurance; no man ever made such a massacre of dolls at the shooting-gallery; or won you a rubber at billiards with more easy grace; or thundered out a couplet out of Béranger with such a roaring melodious bass. He was the monarch of the Prado in winter: in summer of the Chaumière and Mont Parnasse. Not a frequenter of those fashionable places of entertainment showed a more amiable *laisser-aller* in the dance — that peculiar dance at which gendarmes think proper to blush, and which squeamish society has banished from her salons. In a word, Harmodius was the prince of *mauvais sujets*, a youth with all the accomplishments of Göttingen and Jena, and all the eminent graces of his own country.

" Besides dissipation and gallantry, our friend had one other vast and absorbing occupation — politics, namely; in which he was as turbulent and enthusiastic as in pleasure. *La Patrie* was his idol, his heaven, his nightmare; by day he spouted, by night he dreamed, of his country. I have spoken to you of his coiffure à la Sylla; need I mention his pipe, his meerschaum pipe, of which General Foy's head was the bowl; his handkerchief with the Charte printed thereon; and his celebrated tricolor braces, which kept the rallying sign of his country ever close to his heart? Besides these outward and visible signs of sedition, he had inward and secret plans of revolution: he belonged to clubs, frequented associations, read the *Constitutionnel* (Liberals, in those days, swore by the *Constitutionnel*), harangued peers and deputies who had deserved well of their country; and if death happened to fall on such, and the *Constitutionnel* declared their merit, Harmodius was the very first to attend their obsequies, or to set his shoulder to their coffins.

" Such were his tastes and passions: his antipathies were not less lively. He detested three things: a Jesuit, a gendarme, and a claqueur at a theatre. At this period, missionaries were rife about Paris, and endeavored to re-illume the zeal of the faithful by public preachings in the churches. '*In-fâmes jesuites!*' would Harmodius exclaim, who, in the excess of his toleration, tolerated nothing; and, at the head of a band of philosophers like himself, would attend with scrupulous exactitude the meetings of the reverend gentlemen. But, instead of a contrite heart, Harmodius only brought the abomination of desolation into their sanctuary. A perpetual fire of fulminating balls would bang from under the feet of the faithful; odors of impure assafœtida would mingle with the fumes of the incense; and wicked drinking choruses would rise up along with the holy canticles, in hideous dissonance, reminding one of the old orgies under the reign of the Abbot of Unreason.

"His hatred of the gendarmes was equally ferocious: and as for the claqueurs, woe be to them when Harmodius was in the pit! They knew him, and trembled before him, like the earth before Alexander; and his famous war-cry, '*La Carte au chapeau!*' was so much dreaded, that the '*entrepreneurs de succès dramatiques*' demanded twice as much to *do* the Odéon Theatre (which we students and Harmodius frequented), as to applaud at any other place of amusement: and, indeed, their double pay was hardly gained; Harmodius taking care that they should earn the most of it under the benches."

This passage, with which we have taken some liberties, will give the reader a more lively idea of the reckless, jovial, turbulent Paris student, than any with which a foreigner could furnish him: the grisette is his heroine; and dear old Béranger, the cynic-epicurean, has celebrated him and her in the most delightful verses in the world. Of these we may have occasion to say a word or two anon. Meanwhile let us follow Monsieur de Bernard in his amusing descriptions of his countrymen somewhat farther; and, having seen how Dambergeac was a ferocious republican, being a bachelor, let us see how age, sense, and a little government pay — the great agent of conversions in France — nay, in England — has reduced him to be a pompous, quiet, loyal supporter of the juste milieu: his former portrait was that of the student, the present will stand for an admirable lively likeness of

THE SOUS-PRÉFET.

"Saying that I would wait for Dambergeac in his own study, I was introduced into that apartment, and saw around me the usual furniture of a man in his station. There was, in the middle of the room, a large bureau, surrounded by

orthodox arm-chairs ; and there were many shelves with boxes
duly ticketed ; there were a number of maps, and among them
a great one of the department over which Dambergeac ruled ;
and facing the windows, on a wooden pedestal, stood a plas-
ter-cast of the '*Roi des Français.*' Recollecting my friend's
former republicanism, I smiled at this piece of furniture ; but
before I had time to carry my observations any farther, a
heavy rolling sound of carriage-wheels, that caused the windows to rattle and seemed to shake the whole edifice of the
sub-prefecture, called my attention to the court without. Its
iron gates were flung open, and in rolled, with a great deal
of din, a chariot escorted by a brace of gendarmes, sword
in hand. A tall gentleman, with a cocked-hat and feathers,
wearing a blue and silver uniform coat, descended from the
vehicle ; and having, with much grave condescension, saluted
his escort, mounted the stair. A moment afterwards the door
of the study was opened, and I embraced my friend.

" After the first warmth and salutations, we began to examine each other with an equal curiosity, for eight years had
elapsed since we had last met.

" 'You are grown very thin and pale,' said Harmodius,
after a moment.

" ' In revenge I find you fat and rosy : if I am a walking
satire on celibacy, — you, at least, are a living panegyric on
marriage.'

" In fact a great change, and such an one as many people would call a change for the better, had taken place in my
friend : he had grown fat, and announced a decided disposition to become what French people call a *bel homme :* that is,
a very fat one. His complexion, bronzed before, was now
clear white and red : there were no more political allusions in
his hair, which was, on the contrary, neatly frizzed, and
brushed over the forehead, shell-shape. This head-dress,
joined to a thin pair of whiskers, cut crescent-wise from the
ear to the nose, gave my friend a regular bourgeois physiognomy, wax-doll-like : he looked a great deal too well ; and,
added to this, the solemnity of his prefectural costume, gave
his whole appearance a pompous well-fed look that by no
means pleased.

" ' I surprise you,' said I, 'in the midst of your splendor :
do you know that this costume and yonder attendants have
a look excessively awful and splendid ? You entered your
palace just now with the air of a pasha.'

" 'You see me in uniform in honor of Monseigneur the

Bishop, who has just made his diocesan visit, and whom I have just conducted to the limit of the *arrondissement*.'

" ' What! ' said I, ' you have gendarmes for guards, and dance attendance on bishops? There are no more janissaries and Jesuits, I suppose? ' The sub-prefect smiled.

" ' I assure you that my gendarmes are very worthy fellows ; and that among the gentlemen who compose our clergy there are some of the very best rank and talent : besides, my wife is niece to one of the vicars-general.'

" ' What have you done with that great Tasso beard that poor Armandine used to love so? '

" ' My wife does not like a beard ; and you know that what is permitted to a student is not very becoming to a magistrate.'

" I began to laugh. ' Harmodius and a magistrate ! — how shall I ever couple the two words together? But tell me, in your correspondences, your audiences, your sittings with village mayors and petty councils, how do you manage to remain awake? '

" ' In the commencement,' said Harmodius, gravely, ' it *was* very difficult ; and, in order to keep my eyes open, I used to stick pins into my legs : now, however, I am used to it ; and I'm sure I don't take more than fifty pinches of snuff at a sitting.'

" ' Ah! àpropos of snuff : you are near Spain here, and were always a famous smoker. Give me a cigar, — it will take away the musty odor of these piles of papers.'

" ' Impossible, my dear ; I don't smoke ; my wife cannot bear a cigar.'

" His wife ! thought I ; always his wife : and I remember Juliette, who really grew sick at the smell of a pipe, and Harmodius would smoke, until, at last, the poor thing grew to smoke herself, like a trooper. To compensate, however, as much as possible for the loss of my cigar, Dambergeac drew from his pocket an enormous gold snuff-box, on which figured the self-same head that I had before remarked in plaster, but this time surrounded with a ring of pretty princes and princesses, all nicely painted in miniature. As for the statue of Louis Philippe, that, in the cabinet of an official, is a thing of course ; but the snuff-box seemed to indicate a degree of sentimental and personal devotion, such as the old Royalists were only supposed to be guilty of.

" ' What! you are turned decided juste milieu? ' said I.

" ' I am a sous-préfet,' answered Harmodius.

" I had nothing to say, but held my tongue, wondering, not

at the change which had taken place in the habits, manners, and opinions of my friend, but at my own folly, which led me to fancy that I should find the student of '26 in the functionary of '34. At this moment a domestic appeared.

"'Madame is waiting for Monsieur,' said he: 'the last bell has gone, and mass beginning.'

"'Mass!' said I, bounding up from my chair. 'You at mass like a decent serious Christian, without crackers in your pocket, and bored keys to whistle through?' — The sous-préfet rose, his countenance was calm, and an indulgent smile played upon his lips, as he said, 'My arrondissement is very devout; and not to interfere with the belief of the population is the maxim of every wise politician: I have precise orders from Government on the point, too, and go to eleven o'clock mass every Sunday.'"

There is a great deal of curious matter for speculation in the accounts here so wittily given by M. de Bernard: but, perhaps, it is still more curious to think of what he has *not* written, and to judge of his characters, not so much by the words in which he describes them, as by the unconscious testimony that the words all together convey. In the first place, our author describes a swindler imitating the manners of a dandy; and many swindlers and dandies be there, doubtless, in London as well as in Paris. But there is about the present swindler, and about Monsieur Dambergeac the student, and Monsieur Dambergeac the sous-préfet, and his friend, a rich store of calm internal *debauch*, which does not, let us hope and pray, exist in England. Hearken to M. de Gustan, and his smirking whispers, about the Duchess of San Severino, who *pour son bonheur particulier*, &c. &c. Listen to Monsieur Dambergeac's friend's remonstrances concerning *pauvre Juliette* who grew sick at the smell of a pipe; to his *naïve* admiration at the fact that the sous-préfet goes to church: and we may set down, as axioms, that religion is so uncommon among the Parisians, as to awaken the surprise of all candid observers; that gallantry is so common as to create no remark, and to be considered as a matter of course. With us, at least, the converse of the proposition prevails: it is the man professing *ir*religion who would be remarked and reprehended in England; and, if the second-named vice exists, at any rate, it adopts the decency of secrecy and is not made patent and notorious to all the world. A French gentleman thinks no more of proclaiming that he has a mistress than that he has a tailor; and one lives the time of Boccaccio over again, in the thousand and one French novels which depict society in that country.

For instance, here are before us a few specimens (do not, madam, be alarmed, you can skip the sentence if you like,) to be found in as many admirable witty tales, by the before-lauded Monsieur de Bernard. He is more remarkable than any other French author, to our notion, for writing like a gentleman : there is ease, grace and *ton*, in his style, which, if we judge aright, cannot be discovered in Balzac, or Soulié, or Dumas. We have then — " Gerfaut," a novel : a lovely creature is married to a brave, haughty, Alsacian nobleman, who allows her to spend her winters at Paris, he remaining on his *terres*, cultivating, carousing, and hunting the boar. The lovely creature meets the fascinating Gerfaut at Paris ; instantly the latter makes love to her ; a duel takes place : baron killed ; wife throws herself out of window ; Gerfaut plunges into dissipation ; and so the tale ends.

Next : " La Femme de Quarante Ans," a capital tale, full of exquisite fun and sparkling satire : La femme de quarante ans has a husband and *three* lovers ; all of whom find out their mutual connection one starry night ; for the lady of forty is of a romantic poetical turn, and has given her three admirers *a star apiece ;* saying to one and the other, " Alphonse, when yon pale orb rises in heaven, think of me ; " " Isadore, when that bright planet sparkles in the sky, remember your Caroline," &c.

" Un Acte de Vertu," from which we have taken Dambergeac's history, contains him, the husband — a wife — and a brace of lovers ; and a great deal of fun takes place in the manner in which one lover supplants the other. — Pretty morals truly !

If we examine an author who rejoices in the aristocratic name of le Comte Horace de Viel-Castel, we find, though with infinitely less wit, exactly the same intrigues going on. A noble Count lives in the Faubourg St. Honoré, and has a noble Duchess for a mistress : he introduces her Grace to the Countess his wife. The Countess his wife, in order to *ramener* her lord to his conjugal duties, is counselled, by a friend, *to pretend to take a lover :* one is found, who, poor fellow ! takes the affair in earnest : climax — duel, death, despair, and what not? In the " Faubourg St. Germain," another novel by the same writer, which professes to describe the very pink of that society which Napoleon dreaded more than Russia, Prussia, and Austria, there is an old husband, of course ; a sentimental young

German nobleman, who falls in love with his wife ; and the moral of the piece lies in the showing up of the conduct of the lady, who is reprehended — not for deceiving her husband (poor devil!) — but for being a flirt, *and taking a second lover*, to the utter despair, confusion, and annihilation of the first.

Why, ye gods, do Frenchmen marry at all? Had Père Enfantin (who, it is said, has shaved his ambrosial beard, and is now a clerk in a banking-house) been allowed to carry out his chaste, just, dignified social scheme, what a deal of marital discomfort might have been avoided : — would it not be advisable that a great reformer and lawgiver of our own, Mr. Robert Owen, should be presented at the Tuileries, and there propound his scheme for the regeneration of France?

He might, perhaps, be spared, for our country is not yet sufficiently advanced to give such a philosopher fair play. In London, as yet, there are no blessed *Bureaux de Mariage*, where an old bachelor may have a charming young maiden — for his money ; or a widow of seventy may buy a gay young fellow of twenty, for a certain number of bank-billets. If *mariages de convenance* take place here (as they will wherever avarice, and poverty, and desire, and yearning after riches are to be found), at least, thank God, such unions are not arranged upon a regular organized *system :* there is a fiction of attachment with us, and there is a consolation in the deceit (" the homage," according to the old *mot* of Rochefoucauld, " which vice pays to virtue"; for the very falsehood shows that the virtue exists somewhere. We once heard a furious old French colonel inveighing against the chastity of English *demoiselles :* "Figurez-vous, sir," said he (he had been a prisoner in England), " that these women come down to dinner in low dresses, and walk out alone with the men!" — and, pray heaven, so may they walk, fancy-free in all sorts of maiden meditations, and suffer no more molestation than that young lady of whom Moore sings, and who (there must have been a famous lord-lieutenant in those days) walked through all Ireland, with rich and rare gems, beauty, and a gold ring on her stick, without meeting or thinking of harm.

Now, whether Monsieur de Viel-Castel has given a true picture of the Faubourg St. Germain, it is impossible for most foreigners to say ; but some of his descriptions will not fail to astonish the English reader ; and all are filled with that remarkable *naïf* contempt of the institution called marriage, which we have seen in M. de Bernard. The romantic young nobleman of Westphalia arrives at Paris, and is admitted into what a celebrated female author calls *la crème de la crème de la haute voloe* of Parisian society. He is a youth of about twenty years of age. " No passion had as yet come to move his heart, and give life to his faculties ; he was awaiting and fearing the moment of love ; calling for it, and yet trembling at its approach ; feeling in the depths of his soul, that that moment would create a mighty change in his being, and decide, perhaps, by its influence, the whole of his future life."

Is it not remarkable, that a young nobleman, with these ideas, should not pitch upon a *demoiselle*, or a widow, at least? but no, the rogue must have a married woman, bad luck to him ; and what his fate is to be, is thus recounted by our author, in the shape of

A FRENCH FASHIONABLE CONVERSATION.

" A lady, with a great deal of *esprit*, to whom forty years' experience of the great world had given a prodigious perspicacity of judgment, the Duchess of Chalux, arbitress of the opinion to be held on all new comers to the Faubourg Saint Germain, and of their destiny and reception in it ; — one of those women, in a word, who make or ruin a man, — said, in speaking of Gerard de Stolberg, whom she received at her own house, and met everywhere, ' This young German will never gain for himself the title of an exquisite, or a man of bonnes fortunes, among us. In spite of his calm and politeness, I think I can see in his character some rude and insurmountable difficulties, which time will only increase, and which will prevent him for ever from bending to the exigencies of either profession ; but, unless I very much deceive myself, he will, one day, be the hero of a veritable romance.'

" ' He, madame?' answered a young man, of fair complexion and fair hair, one of the most devoted slaves of the fashion : — ' He, Madame la Duchesse? why, the man is, at best, but an original, fished out of the Rhine : a dull, heavy creature, as much capable of understanding a woman's heart as I am of speaking bas-Breton.'

" ' Well, Monsieur de Belport, you will speak bas-Breton. Monsieur de Stolberg has not your admirable ease of manner, nor your facility of telling pretty nothings, nor your — in a word, that particular something which makes you the most recherché man of the Faubourg Saint Germain ; and even I avow to you that, were I still young, and a coquette, *and that I took it into my head to have a lover*, I would prefer you.'

"All this was said by the Duchess, with a certain air of raillery and such a mixture of earnest and malice, that Monsieur de Belport, piqued not a little, could not help saying, as he bowed profoundly before the Duchess's chair, 'And might I, madam, be permitted to ask the reason of this preference?'

"'O mon Dieu, oui,' said the Duchess, always in the same tone; 'because a lover like you would never think of carrying his attachment to the height of passion; and these passions, do you know, have frightened me all my life. One cannot retreat at will from the grasp of a passionate lover; one leaves behind one some fragment of one's moral *self*, or the best part of one's physical life. A passion, if it does not kill you, adds cruelly to your years; in a word, it is the very lowest possible taste. And now you understand why I should prefer you, M. de Belport — you who are reputed to be the leader of the fashion.'

"'Perfectly,' murmured the gentleman, piqued more and more.

"'Gerard de Stolberg *will* be passionate. I don't know what woman will please him, or will be pleased by him' (here the Duchess of Chalux spoke more gravely); 'but his love will be no play, I repeat it to you once more. All this astonishes you, because you, great leaders of the ton that you are, never fancy that a hero of romance should be found among your number. Gerard de Stolberg — but, look, here he comes!'

"M. de Belport rose, and quitted the Duchess, without believing in her prophecy; but he could not avoid smiling as he passed near the *hero of romance*.

"It was because M. de Stolberg had never, in all his life, been a hero of romance, or even an apprentice-hero of romance.

. . . .

"Gerard de Stolberg was not, as yet, initiated into the thousand secrets in the chronicle of the great world: he knew but superficially the society in which he lived; and, therefore, he devoted his evening to the gathering of all the information which he could acquire from the indiscreet conversations of the people about him. His whole man became ear and memory; so much was Stolberg convinced of the necessity of becoming a diligent student in this new school, where was taught the art of knowing and advancing in the great world. In the recess of a window he learned more on this one night than months of investigation would have taught him. The talk of a ball is more indiscreet than the confidential chatter of a company of idle women. No man present at a ball, whether listener or speaker, thinks he has a right to affect any indulgence for his companions, and the most learned in malice will always pass for the most witty.

" ' How ! ' said the Viscount de Mondragé : ' the Duchess of Rivesalte arrives alone to-night, without her inevitable Dormilly ! ' — And the Viscount, as he spoke, pointed towards a tall and slender young woman, who, gliding rather than walking, met the ladies by whom she passed, with a graceful and modest salute, and replied to the looks of the men *by brilliant veiled glances full of coquetry and attack.*

" ' Parbleu ! ' said an elegant personage standing near the Viscount de Mondragé, ' don't you see Dormilly ranged behind the Duchess, in quality of train-bearer, and hiding, under his long locks and his great screen of moustaches, the blushing consciousness of his good luck? — They call him *the fourth chapter* of the Duchess's memoirs. The little Marquise d'Alberas is ready to die out of spite ; but the best of the joke is, that she has only taken poor de Vendre for a lover in order to vent her spleen on him. Look at him against the chimney yonder ; if the Marchioness do not break at once with him by quitting him for somebody else, the poor fellow will turn an idiot.'

" ' Is he jealous? ' asked a young man, looking as if he did not know what jealousy was and as if he had no time to be jealous.

" ' Jealous ! the very incarnation of jealousy ; the second edition, revised, corrected, and considerably enlarged ; as jealous as poor Gressigny, who is dying of it.'

" ' What ! Gressigny too? why, 'tis growing quite into fashion : egad ! *I* must try and be jealous,' said Monsieur de Beauval. ' But see ! here comes the delicious Duchess of Bellefiore,' " &c. &c. &c.

.   .   .   .

Enough, enough : this kind of fashionable Parisian conversation, which is, says our author, " a prodigious labor of improvising," a " chef-d'œuvre," a " strange and singular thing, in which monotony is unknown," seems to be, if correctly reported, a " strange and singular thing " indeed ; but somewhat monotonous at least to an English reader, and " prodigious " only, if we may take leave to say so, for the wonderful rascality which all the conversationists betray. Miss Neverout and the Colonel, in Swift's famous dialogue, are a thousand times more entertaining and moral ; and, besides, we can laugh *at* those worthies as well as with them ; whereas the " prodigious " French wits are to us quite incomprehensible. Fancy a duchess as old as Lady —— herself, and who should begin to tell us "ot what she would do if ever she had a mind to take a lover;" and another duchess, with a fourth lover, tripping modestly among the ladies, and returning the gaze of the men by veiled glances, full of coquetry and attack! — Parbleu, if Monsieur de Viel-Castel should find himself among a society of French duchesses, and they should tear his eyes out, and send the fashionable Orpheus floating by the Seine, his slaughter might almost be considered as justifiable *Counticide.*

A GAMBLER'S DEATH.

ANYBODY who was at C—— school some twelve years since, must recollect Jack Attwood : he was the most dashing lad in the place, with more money in his pocket than belonged to the whole fifth form in which we were companions.

When he was about fifteen, Jack suddenly retreated from C——, and presently we heard that he had a commission in a cavalry regiment, and was to have a great fortune from his father, when that old gentleman should die. Jack himself came to confirm these stories a few months after, and paid a visit to his old school chums. He had laid aside his little school-jacket and inky corduroys, and now appeared in such a splendid military suit as won the respect of all of us. His hair was dripping with oil, his hands were covered with rings, he had a dusky down over his upper lip which looked not unlike a moustache, and a multiplicity of frogs and braiding on his surtout which would have sufficed to lace a field-marshal. When old Swishtail, the usher, passed in his seedy black coat and gaiters, Jack gave him such a look of contempt as set us all a-laughing : in fact it was his turn to laugh now ; for he used to roar very stoutly some months before, when Swishtail was in the custom of belaboring him with his great cane.

Jack's talk was all about the regiment and the fine fellows in it : how he had ridden a steeple-chase with Captain Boldero, and licked him at the last hedge ; and how he had very nearly fought a duel with Sir George Grig, about dancing with Lady Mary Slamken at a ball. " I soon made the baronet know what it was to deal with a man of the n—th," said Jack. " Dammee, sir, when I lugged out my barkers, and talked of fighting across the mess-room table, Grig turned as pale as a sheet, or as —— "

" Or as you used to do, Attwood, when Swishtail hauled you up," piped out little Hicks, the foundation-boy.

It was beneath Jack's dignity to thrash anybody, now, but a grown-up baronet ; so he let off little Hicks, and passed over the general titter which was raised at his expense. However, he entertained us with his histories about lords and ladies, and so-and-so " of ours," until we thought him one of the greatest men in his Majesty's service, and until the school-bell rung ; when, with a heavy heart, we got our books together, and marched in to be whacked by old Swishtail. I promise you he revenged himself on us for Jack's contempt of him. I got that day at least twenty cuts to my share, which ought to have belonged to Cornet Attwood, of the n—th dragoons.

When we came to think more coolly over our quondam schoolfellow's swaggering talk and manner, we were not quite so impressed by his merits as at his first appearance among us. We recollected how he used, in former times, to tell us great stories, which were so monstrously improbable that the smallest boy in the school would scout them ; how often we caught him tripping in facts, and how unblushingly he admitted his little errors in the score of veracity. He and I, though never great friends, had been close companions : I was Jack's form-fellow (we fought with amazing emulation for the *last* place in the class) ; but still I was rather hurt at the coolness of my old comrade, who had forgotten all our former intimacy, in his steeple-chases with Captain Boldero and his duel with Sir George Grig.

Nothing more was heard of Attwood for some years ; a tailor one day came down to C——, who had made clothes for Jack in his school-days, and furnished him with regimentals : he produced a long bill for one hundred and twenty pounds and upwards, and asked where news might be had of his customer. Jack was in India, with his regiment, shooting tigers and jackals, no doubt. Occasionally, from that distant country, some magnificent rumor would reach us of his proceedings. Once I heard that he had been called to a court-martial for unbecoming conduct ; another time, that he kept twenty horses, and won the gold plate at the Calcutta races. Presently, however, as the recollections of the fifth form wore away, Jack's image disappeared likewise, and I ceased to ask or think about my college chum.

A year since, as I was smoking my cigar in the " Estaminet du Grand Balcon," an excellent smoking-shop, where the tobacco is unexceptionable, and the Hollands of singular merit, a

dark-looking, thick-set man, in a greasy well-cut coat, with a
shabby hat, cocked on one side of his dirty face, took the place
opposite me, at the little marble table, and called for brandy. I
did not much admire the impudence or the appearance of my
friend, nor the fixed stare with which he chose to examine me.
At last, he thrust a great greasy hand across the table, and
said, " Titmarsh, do you forget your old friend Attwood?"

I confess my recognition of him was not so joyful as on the
day ten years earlier, when he had come, bedizened with lace
and gold rings, to see us at C—— school: a man in the tenth
part of a century learns a deal of worldly wisdom, and his hand,
which goes naturally forward to seize the gloved finger of a
millionnaire, or a milor, draws instinctively back from a dirty
fist, encompassed by a ragged wristband and a tattered cuff.
But Attwood was in nowise so backward; and the iron squeeze
with which he shook my passive paw, proved that he was either
very affectionate or very poor. You, my dear sir, who are
reading this history, know very well the great art of shaking
hands : recollect how you shook Lord Dash's hand the other
day, and how you shook *off* poor Blank, when he came to borrow five pounds of you.

However, the genial influence of the Hollands speedily dissipated anything like coolness between us ; and, in the course of
an hour's conversation, we became almost as intimate as when
we were suffering together under the ferule of old Swishtail.
Jack told me that he had quitted the army in disgust ; and that
his father, who was to leave him a fortune, had died ten thousand pounds in debt: he did not touch upon his own circumstances ; but I could read them in his elbows, which were
peeping through his old frock. He talked a great deal, however, of runs of luck, good and bad ; and related to me an
infallible plan for breaking all the play-banks in Europe — a
great number of old tricks ; — and a vast quantity of gin-punch
was consumed on the occasion ; so long, in fact, did our conversation continue, that, I confess it with shame, the sentiment,
or something stronger, quite got the better of me, and I have,
to this day, no sort of notion how our palaver concluded. —
Only, on the next morning, I did not possess a certain five-
pound note which on the previous evening was in my sketch-
book (by far the prettiest drawing by the way in the collection) ;
but there, instead, was a strip of paper, thus inscribed : —

I O U
Five Pounds. JOHN ATTWOOD,
Late of the N—th Dragoons.

I suppose Attwood borrowed the money, from this remarkable
and ceremonious acknowledgment on his part : had I been sober
I would just as soon have lent him the nose on my face ; for, in
my then circumstances, the note was of much more consequence
to me.

As I lay, cursing my ill fortune, and thinking how on earth
I should manage to subsist for the next two months, Attwood
burst into my little garret — his face strangely flushed — singing and shouting as if it had been the night before.   "Titmarsh," cried he, "you are my preserver! — my best friend !
Look here, and here, and here!"   And at every word Mr.
Attwood produced a handful of gold, or a glittering heap of
five-franc pieces, or a bundle of greasy, dusky bank-notes, more
beautiful than either silver or gold : — he had won thirteen
thousand francs after leaving me at midnight in my garret.
He separated my poor little all, of six pieces, from this shining
and imposing collection ; and the passion of envy entered my
soul : I felt far more anxious now than before, although starvation was then staring me in the face ; I hated Attwood for
cheating me out of all this wealth.   Poor fellow ! it had been
better for him had he never seen a shilling of it.

However, a grand breakfast at the Café Anglais dissipated
my chagrin ; and I will do my friend the justice to say, that he
nobly shared some portion of his good fortune with me.   As far
as the creature comforts were concerned I feasted as well as
he, and never was particular as to settling my share of the
reckoning.

Jack now changed his lodgings ; had cards, with Captain
Attwood engraved on them, and drove about a prancing cab-
horse, as tall as the giraffe at the Jardin des Plantes ; he had
as many frogs on his coat as in the old days, and frequented
all the flash restaurateurs' and boarding-houses of the capital.
Madame de Saint Laurent, and Madame la Baronne de Vaudrey, and Madame la Comtesse de Jonville, ladies of the highest
rank, who keep a *société choisie* and condescend to give dinners
at five-francs a head, vied with each other in their attentions to
Jack.   His was the wing of the fowl, and the largest portion
of the Charlotte-Russe ; his was the place at the écarté table,
where the Countess would ease him nightly of a few pieces,
declaring that he was the most charming cavalier, la fleur
d'Albion.   Jack's society, it may be seen, was not very select ;
nor, in truth, were his inclinations : he was a careless, dare-
devil, Macheath kind of fellow, who might be seen daily with a
wife on each arm.

It may be supposed that, with the life he led, his five hundred pounds of winnings would not last him long; nor did they; but, for some time, his luck never deserted him; and his cash, instead of growing lower, seemed always to maintain a certain level: he played every night.

Of course, such a humble fellow as I, could not hope for a continued acquaintance and intimacy with Attwood. He grew overbearing and cool, I thought; at any rate I did not admire my situation as his follower and dependant, and left his grand dinner for a certain ordinary, where I could partake of five capital dishes for ninepence. Occasionally, however, Attwood favored me with a visit, or gave me a drive behind his great cab-horse. He had formed a whole host of friends besides. There was Fips, the barrister; heaven knows what he was doing at Paris; and Gortz, the West Indian, who was there on the same business, and Flapper, a medical student, — all these three I met one night at Flapper's rooms, where Jack was invited, and a great " spread" was laid in honor of him.

Jack arrived rather late — he looked pale and agitated; and, though he ate no supper, he drank raw brandy in such a manner as made Flapper's eyes wink: the poor fellow had but three bottles, and Jack bade fair to swallow them all. However, the West Indian generously remedied the evil, and producing a napoleon, we speedily got the change for it in the shape of four bottles of champagne.

Our supper was uproariously harmonious; Fips sung the good " Old English Gentleman;" Jack the " British Grenadiers;" and your humble servant, when called upon, sang that beautiful ditty, " When the Bloom is on the Rye," in a manner that drew tears from every eye, except Flapper's, who was asleep, and Jack's, who was singing the " Bay of Biscay O," at the same time. Gortz and Fips were all the time lunging at each other with a pair of single-sticks, the barrister having a very strong notion that he was Richard the Third. At last Fips hit the West Indian such a blow across his sconce, that the other grew furious; he seized a champagne-bottle, which was, providentially, empty, and hurled it across the room at Fips: had that celebrated barrister not bowed his head at the moment, the Queen's Bench would have lost one of its most eloquent practitioners.

Fips stood as straight as he could; his cheek was pale with wrath. " M-m-ister Go-gortz," he said, " I always heard you were a blackguard; now I can pr-pr-peperove it. Flapper, your pistols! every ge-ge-genlmn knows what I mean."

Young Mr. Flapper had a small pair of pocket-pistols, which the tipsy barrister had suddenly remembered, and with which he proposed to sacrifice the West Indian. Gortz was nothing loth, but was quite as valorous as the lawyer.

Attwood, who, in spite of his potations, seemed the soberest man of the party, had much enjoyed the scene, until this sudden demand for the weapons. "Pshaw!" said he, eagerly, "don't give these men the means of murdering each other; sit down and let us have another song." But they would not be still; and Flapper forthwith produced his pistol-case, and opened it, in order that the duel might take place on the spot. There were no pistols there! "I beg your pardon," said Attwood, looking much confused; "I — I took the pistols home with me to clean them!"

I don't know what there was in his tone, or in the words, but we were sobered all of a sudden. Attwood was conscious of the singular effect produced by him, for he blushed, and endeavored to speak of other things, but we could not bring our spirits back to the mark again, and soon separated for the night. As we issued into the street Jack took me aside, and whispered, "Have you a napoleon, Titmarsh, in your purse?" Alas! I was not so rich. My reply was, that I was coming to Jack, only in the morning, to borrow a similar sum.

He did not make any reply, but turned away homeward: I never heard him speak another word.

.   .   .   .

Two mornings after (for none of our party met on the day succeeding the supper), I was awakened by my porter, who brought a pressing letter from Mr. Gortz : —

"DEAR T., — I wish you would come over here to breakfast. There's a row about Attwood. — Yours truly,
                                                    "SOLOMON GORTZ."

I immediately set forward to Gortz's; he lived in the Rue du Helder, a few doors from Attwood's new lodging. If the reader is curious to know the house in which the catastrophe of this history took place, he has but to march some twenty doors down from the Boulevard des Italiens, when he will see a fine door, with a naked Cupid shooting at him from the hall, and a Venus beckoning him up the stairs. On arriving at the West Indian's, at about mid-day (it was a Sunday morning), I found that gentleman in his dressing-gown, discussing, in the company of Mr Fips, a large plate of *bifteck aux pommes*.

"Here's a pretty row!" said Gortz, quoting from his letter; — "Attwood's off — have a bit of beefsteak?"

"What do you mean?" exclaimed I, adopting the familiar phraseology of my acquaintances: — "Attwood off? — has he cut his stick?"

"Not bad," said the feeling and elegant Fips — "not such a bad guess, my boy; but he has not exactly *cut his stick*."

"What then?"

"*Why, his throat.*" The man's mouth was full of bleeding beef as he uttered this gentlemanly witticism.

I wish I could say that I was myself in the least affected by the news. I did not joke about it like my friend Fips; this was more for propriety's sake than for feeling's: but for my old school acquaintance, the friend of my early days, the merry associate of the last few months, I own, with shame, that I had not a tear or a pang. In some German tale there is an account of a creature most beautiful and bewitching, whom all men admire and follow; but this charming and fantastic spirit only leads them, one by one, into ruin, and then leaves them. The novelist, who describes her beauty, says that his heroine is a fairy, and *has no heart*. I think the intimacy which is begotten over the wine-bottle, is a spirit of this nature; I never knew a good feeling come from it, or an honest friendship made by it; it only entices men and ruins them; it is only a phantom of friendship and feeling, called up by the delirious blood, and the wicked spells of the wine.

But to drop this strain of moralizing (in which the writer is not too anxious to proceed, for he cuts in it a most pitiful figure), we passed sundry criticisms upon poor Attwood's character, expressed our horror at his death — which sentiment was fully proved by Mr. Fips, who declared that the notion of it made him feel quite faint, and was obliged to drink a large glass of brandy; and, finally, we agreed that we would go and see the poor fellow's corpse, and witness, if necessary, his burial.

Flapper, who had joined us, was the first to propose this visit: he said he did not mind the fifteen francs which Jack owed him for billiards, but he was anxious to *get back his pistol*. Accordingly, we sallied forth, and speedily arrived at the hotel which Attwood inhabited still. He had occupied, for a time, very fine apartments in this house: and it was only on arriving there that day that we found he had been gradually driven from his magnificent suite of rooms *au premier*, to a little chamber in the fifth story: — we mounted, and found him. It was a little shabby room, with a few articles of rickety furniture, and a bed in an alcove; the light from the one window was falling full upon the bed and the body. Jack was dressed in a fine lawn shirt; he had kept it, poor fellow, *to die in;* for in all his drawers and cupboards there was not a single article of clothing; he had pawned everything by which he could raise a penny — desk, books, dressing-case, and clothes; and not a single halfpenny was found in his possession.*

He was lying as I have drawn him,† one hand on his breast, the other falling towards the ground. There was an expression of perfect calm on the face, and no mark of blood to stain the side towards the light. On the other side, however, there was a great pool of black blood, and in it the pistol; it looked more like a toy than a weapon to take away the life of this vigorous young man. In his forehead, at the side, was a small black wound; Jack's life had passed through it; it was little bigger than a mole.

. . . .

"Regardez un peu," said the landlady, "messieurs, il m'a gâté trois matelas, et il me doit quarante quatre francs."

This was all his epitaph: he had spoiled three mattresses, and owed the landlady four-and-forty francs. In the whole world there was not a soul to love him or lament him. We, his friends, were looking at his body more as an object of curiosity, watching it with a kind of interest with which one follows the fifth act of a tragedy, and leaving it with the same feeling with which one leaves the theatre when the play is over and the curtain is down.

Beside Jack's bed, on his little "table de nuit," lay the remains of his last meal, and an open letter, which we read. It was from one of his suspicious acquaintances of former days, and ran thus: —

"Où es tu, cher Jack? *why you not come and see me* — tu me dois de l'argent, entends tu? — un chapeau, une cachemire, *a box of the Play.* Viens demain soir, je t'attendrai *at eight o'clock*, Passage des Panoramas. *My Sir is at his country.*

"Adieu à demain.
"FIFINE.

"Samedi."

. . . .

* In order to account for these trivial details, the reader must be told that the story is, for the chief part, a fact; and that the little sketch in this page was *taken from nature.* The letter was likewise a copy from one found in the manner described.

† This refers to an illustrated edition of the work.

I shuddered as I walked through this very Passage des Panoramas, in the evening. The girl was there, pacing to and fro, and looking in the countenance of every passer-by, to recognize Attwood. "ADIEU À DEMAIN!" — there was a dreadful meaning in the words, which the writer of them little knew. "Adieu à demain!" — the morrow was come, and the soul of the poor suicide was now in the presence of God. I dare not think of his fate; for, except in the fact of his poverty and desperation, was he worse than any of us, his companions, who had shared his debauches, and marched with him up to the very brink of the grave?

There is but one more circumstance to relate regarding poor Jack — his burial; it was of a piece with his death.

He was nailed into a paltry coffin and buried, at the expense of the arrondissement, in a nook of the burial-place beyond the Barrière de l'Etoile. They buried him at six o'clock, of a bitter winter's morning, and it was with difficulty that an English clergyman could be found to read a service over his grave. The three men who have figured in this history acted as Jack's mourners; and as the ceremony was to take place so early in the morning, these men sat up the night through, *and were almost drunk* as they followed his coffin to its resting-place.

MORAL.

"When we turned out in our great-coats," said one of them afterwards, "reeking of cigars and brandy-and-water, d——e, sir, we quite frightened the old buck of a parson; he did not much like our company." After the ceremony was concluded, these gentlemen were very happy to get home to a warm and comfortable breakfast, and finished the day royally at Frascati's.

NAPOLEON AND HIS SYSTEM.

ON PRINCE LOUIS NAPOLEON'S WORK.

ANY person who recollects the history of the absurd out-break of Strasburg, in which Prince Louis Napoleon Bonaparte figured, three years ago, must remember that, however silly the revolt was, however foolish its pretext, however doubtful its aim, and inexperienced its leader, there was, nevertheless, a party, and a considerable one in France, that were not un-willing to lend the new projectors their aid. The troops who declared against the Prince, were, it was said, all but willing to declare for him; and it was certain that, in many of the regiments of the army, there existed a strong spirit of disaffec-tion, and an eager wish for the return of the imperial system and family.

As to the good that was to be derived from the change, that is another question. Why the Emperor of the French should be better than the King of the French, or the King of the French better than the King of France and Navarre, it is not our business to inquire; but all the three monarchs have no lack of supporters; republicanism has no lack of supporters; St. Simonianism was followed by a respectable body of admir-ers; Robespierrism has a select party of friends. If, in a country where so many quacks have had their day, Prince Louis Napoleon thought he might renew the imperial quackery, why should he not? It has recollections with it that must always be dear to a gallant nation; it has certain claptraps in its vocabulary that can never fail to inflame a vain, restless, grasping, disappointed one.

In the first place, and don't let us endeavor to disguise it, they hate us. Not all the protestations of friendship, not all the wisdom of Lord Palmerston, not all the diplomacy of our distinguished plenipotentiary, Mr. Henry Lytton Bulwer — and let us add, not all the benefit which both countries would derive from the alliance — can make it, in our times at least, permanent and cordial. They hate us. The Carlist organs revile us with a querulous fury that never sleeps ; the moderate party, if they admit the utility of our alliance, are continually pointing out our treachery, our insolence, and our monstrous infractions of it ; and for the Republicans, as sure as the morning comes, the columns of their journals thunder out volleys of fierce denunciations against our unfortunate country. They live by feeding the natural hatred against England, by keeping old wounds open, by recurring ceaselessly to the history of old quarrels, and as in these we, by God's help, by land and by sea, in old times and late, have had the uppermost, they perpetuate the shame and mortification of the losing party, the bitterness or past defeats, and the eager desire to avenge them. A party which knows how to *exploiter* this hatred will always be popular to a certain extent ; and the imperial scheme has this, at least, among its conditions.

Then there is the favorite claptrap of the "natural frontier." The Frenchman yearns to be bounded by the Rhine and the Alps ; and next follows the cry, "Let France take her place among nations, and direct, as she ought to do, the affairs of Europe." These are the two chief articles contained in the new imperial programme, if we may credit the journal which has been established to advocate the cause. A natural boundary — stand among the nations — popular development — Russian alliance, and a reduction of *la perfide Albion* to its proper insignificance. As yet we know little more of the plan : and yet such foundations are sufficient to build a party upon, and with such windy weapons a substantial Government is to be overthrown !

In order to give these doctrines, such as they are, a chance of finding favor with his countrymen, Prince Louis has the advantage of being able to refer to a former great professor of them — his uncle Napoleon. His attempt is at once pious and prudent ; it exalts the memory of the uncle, and furthers the interests of the nephew, who attempts to show what Napoleon's ideas really were ; what good had already resulted from the practice of them ; how cruelly they had been thwarted by foreign wars and difficulties ; and what vast benefits *would* have resulted from them ; ay, and (it is reasonable to conclude) might still, if the French nation would be wise enough to pitch upon a governor that would continue the interrupted scheme. It is, however, to be borne in mind that the Emperor Napoleon had certain arguments in favor of his opinions for the time being, which his nephew has not employed. On the 13th Vendemiaire, when General Bonaparte believed in the excellence of a Directory, it may be remembered that he aided his opinions by forty pieces of artillery, and by Colonel Murat at the head of his dragoons. There was no resisting such a philosopher; the Directory was established forthwith, and the sacred cause of the minority triumphed. In like manner, when the General was convinced of the weakness of the Directory, and saw fully the necessity of establishing a Consulate, what were his arguments? Moreau, Lannes, Murat, Berthier, Leclerc, Lefebvre — gentle apostles of the truth! — marched to St. Cloud, and there, with fixed bayonets, caused it to prevail. Error vanished in an instant. At once five hundred of its high-priests tumbled out of windows, and lo! three Consuls appeared to guide the destinies of France! How much more expeditious, reasonable, and clinching was this argument of the 18th Brumaire, than any one that can be found in any pamphlet! A fig for your duodecimos and octavos! Talk about points, there are none like those at the end of a bayonet; and the most powerful of styles is a good rattling " article" from a nine-pounder.

At least this is our interpretation of the manner in which were always propagated the *Idées Napoléoniennes*. Not such, however, is Prince Louis's belief; and, if you wish to go along with him in opinion, you will discover that a more liberal, peaceable, prudent Prince never existed : you will read that " the mission of Napoleon " was to be the " *testamentary executor of the revolution ;*" and the Prince should have added the legatee ; or, more justly still, as well as the *executor*, he should be called the *executioner*, and then his title would be complete. In Vendemiaire, the military Tartuffe, he threw aside the Revolution's natural heirs, and made her, as it were, *alter her will ;* on the 18th of Brumaire he strangled her, and on the 19th seized on her property, and kept it until force deprived him of it. Illustrations, to be sure, are no arguments, but the example is the Prince's, not ours.

In the Prince's eyes, then, his uncle is a god; of all monarchs, the most wise, upright, and merciful. Thirty years ago the opinion had millions of supporters ; while millions again were ready to avouch the exact contrary. It is curious to think of the former difference of opinion concerning Napoleon ; and, in reading his nephew's rapturous encomiums of him, one goes back to the days when we ourselves were as loud and mad in his dispraise. Who does not remember his own personal hatred and horror, twenty-five years ago, for the man whom we used to call the "bloody Corsican upstart and assassin?" What stories did we not believe of him?—what murders, rapes, robberies, not lay to his charge?—we who were living within a few miles of his territory, and might, by books and newspapers, be made as well acquainted with his merits or demerits as any of his own countrymen.

Then was the age when the *Idées Napoléoniennes* might have passed through many editions; for while we were thus outrageously bitter, our neighbors were as extravagantly attached to him by a strange infatuation—adored him like a god, whom we chose to consider as a fiend; and vowed that, under his government, their nation had attained its highest pitch of grandeur and glory. In revenge there existed in England (as is proved by a thousand authentic documents) a monster so hideous, a tyrant so ruthless and bloody, that the world's history cannot show his parallel. This ruffian's name was, during the early part of the French revolution, Pittetcobourg. Pittetcobourg's emissaries were in every corner of France; Pittetcobourg's gold chinked in the pockets of every traitor in Europe; it menaced the life of the godlike Robespierre; it drove into cellars and fits of delirium even the gentle philanthropist Marat; it fourteen times caused the dagger to be lifted against the bosom of the First Consul, Emperor, and King,—that first, great, glorious, irresistible, cowardly, contemptible, bloody hero and fiend, Bonaparte, before mentioned.

On our side of the Channel we have had leisure, long since, to re-consider our verdict against Napoleon; though, to be sure, we have not changed our opinion about Pittetcobourg. After five-and-thirty years all parties bear witness to his honesty, and speak with affectionate reverence of his patriotism, his genius, and his private virtue. In France, however, or, at least among certain parties in France, there has been no such modification of opinion. With the Republicans, Pittetcobourg is Pittetcobourg still,—crafty, bloody, seeking whom he may devour; and *perfide Albion* more perfidious than ever. This hatred is the point of union between the Republic and the Empire; it has been fostered ever since, and must be continued by Prince Louis, if he would hope to conciliate both parties.

With regard to the Emperor, then, Prince Louis erects to his memory as fine a monument as his wits can raise. One need not say that the imperial apologist's opinion should be received with the utmost caution; for a man who has such a hero for an uncle may naturally be proud of and partial to him; and when this nephew of the great man would be his heir likewise, and, bearing his name, step also into his imperial shoes, one may reasonably look for much affectionate panegyric. "The empire was the best of empires," cries the Prince; and possibly it was; undoubtedly, the Prince thinks it was; but he is the very last person who would convince a man with the proper suspicious impartiality.   One remembers a certain consultation of politicians which is recorded in the Spelling-book; and the opinion of that patriotic sage who avowed that, for a real blameless constitution, an impenetrable shield for liberty, and cheap defence of nations, there was nothing like leather.

Let us examine some of the Prince's article.   If we may be allowed humbly to express an opinion, his leather is not only quite insufficient for those vast public purposes for which he destines it, but is, moreover, and in itself, very *bad leather*.   The hides are poor, small, unsound slips of skin; or, to drop this cobbling metaphor, the style is not particularly brilliant, the facts not very startling, and, as for the conclusions, one may differ with almost every one of them.   Here is an extract from his first chapter, " on governments in general : " —

" I speak it with regret, I can see but two governments, at this day, which fulfil the mission that Providence has confided to them; they are the two colossi at the end of the world; one at the extremity of the old world, the other at the extremity of the new.   Whilst our old European centre is as a volcano, consuming itself in its crater, the two nations of the East and the West, march without hesitation, towards perfection; the one under the will of a single individual, the other under liberty.

" Providence has confided to the United States of North America the task of peopling and civilizing that immense territory which stretches from the Atlantic to the South Sea, and from the North Pole to the Equator.   The Government, which is only a simple administration, has only hitherto been called upon to put in practice the old adage, *Laissez faire, laissez passer*, in order to favor that irresistible instinct which pushes the people of America to the west.

" In Russia it is to the imperial dynasty that is owing all the vast progress which, in a century and a half, has rescued that empire from barbarism.   The imperial power must contend against all the ancient prejudices of our old Europe : it must centralize, as far as possible, all the powers of the state in the hands of one person, in order to destroy the abuses which the feudal and communal franchises have served to perpetuate. The last alone can hope to receive from it the improvements which it expects.

"But thou, France of Henry IV., of Louis XIV., of Carnot, of Napoleon — thou, who wert always for the west of Europe the source of progress, who possessest in thyself the two great pillars of empire, the genius for the arts of peace and the genius of war — hast thou no further mission to fulfil? Wilt thou never cease to waste thy force and energies in intestine struggles? No; such cannot be thy destiny: the day will soon come, when, to govern thee, it will be necessary to understand that thy part is to place in all treaties thy sword of Brennus on the side of civilization."

These are the conclusions of the Prince's remarks upon governments in general; and it must be supposed that the reader is very little wiser at the end than at the beginning. But two governments in the world fulfil their mission : the one government, which is no government; the other, which is a despotism. The duty of France is *in all treaties* to place her sword of Brennus in the scale of civilization. Without quarrelling with the somewhat confused language of the latter proposition, may we ask what, in heaven's name, is the meaning of all the three? What is this *épée de Brennus?* and how is France to use it? Where is the great source of political truth, from which, flowing pure, we trace American republicanism in one stream, Russian despotism in another? Vastly prosperous is the great republic, if you will: if dollars and cents constitute happiness, there is plenty for all : but can any one, who has read of the American doings in the late frontier troubles, and the daily disputes on the slave question, praise the *Government* of the States? — a Government which dares not punish homicide or arson performed before its very eyes, and which the pirates of Texas and the pirates of Canada can brave at their will? There is no government, but a prosperous anarchy ; as the Prince's other favorite government is a prosperous slavery. What, then, is to be the *épée de Brennus* government? Is it to be a mixture of the two? "Society," writes the Prince, axiomatically, "contains in itself two principles — the one of progress and immortality, the other of disease and disorganization." No doubt ; and as the one tends towards liberty, so the other is only to be cured by order : and then, with a singular felicity, Prince Louis picks us out a couple of governments, in one of which the common regulating power is as notoriously too weak, as it is in the other too strong, and talks

in rapturous terms of the manner in which they fulfil their
" providential mission ! "

From these considerations on things in general, the Prince
conducts us to Napoleon in particular, and enters largely into
a discussion of the merits of the imperial system. Our author
speaks of the Emperor's advent in the following grandiose
way : —

" Napoleon, on arriving at the public stage, saw that his
part was to be the *testamentary executor* of the Revolution.
The destructive fire of parties was extinct ; and when the Revolution, dying, but not vanquished, delegated to Napoleon the
accomplishment of her last will, she said to him, ' Establish
upon solid bases the principal result of my efforts. Unite
divided Frenchmen. Defeat feudal Europe that is leagued
against me. Cicatrize my wounds. Enlighten the nations.
Execute that in width, which I have had to perform in depth.
Be for Europe what I have been for France. And, even if
you must water the tree of civilization with your blood — if
you must see your projects misunderstood, and your sons without a country, wandering over the face of the earth, never
abandon the sacred cause of the French people. Insure its
triumph by all the means which genius can discover and humanity approve.'

" This grand mission Napoleon performed to the end. His
task was difficult. He had to place upon new principles a
society still boiling with hatred and revenge ; and to use, for
building up, the same instruments which had been employed
for pulling down.

" The common lot of every new truth that arises, is to
wound rather than to convince — rather than to gain prose-
lytes, to awaken fear. For, oppressed as it long has been, it
rushes forward with additional force ; having to encounter
obstacles, it is compelled to combat them, and overthrow them ;
until, at length, comprehended and adopted by the generality,
it becomes the basis of new social order.

" Liberty will follow the same march as the Christian religion. Armed with death from the ancient society of Rome, it
for a long while excited the hatred and fear of the people. At
last, by force of martyrdoms and persecutions, the religion of
Christ penetrated into the conscience and the soul ; it soon had
kings and armies at its orders, and Constantine and Charle-
magne bore it triumphant throughout Europe. Religion then
laid down her arms of war. It laid open to all the principles
of peace and order which it contained ; it became the prop of

Government, as it was the organizing element of society.
Thus will it be with liberty. In 1793 it frightened people and
sovereigns alike ; then, having clothed itself in a milder garb,
it insinuated itself everywhere in the train of our battalions. In
1815 all parties adopted its flag, and armed themselves with
its moral force — covered themselves with its colors. The
adoption was not sincere, and liberty was soon obliged to re-
assume its warlike accoutrements. With the contest their fears
returned. Let us hope that they will soon cease, and that liberty will soon resume her peaceful standards, to quit them no
more.

" The Emperor Napoleon contributed more than any one
else towards accelerating the reign of liberty, by saving the
moral influence of the revolution, and diminishing the fears
which it imposed. Without the Consulate and the Empire, the
revolution would have been only a grand drama, leaving grand
revolutions but no traces : the revolution would have been
drowned in the counter-revolution. The contrary, however,
was the case. Napoleon rooted the revolution in France, and
introduced, throughout Europe, the principal benefits of the
crisis of 1789. To use his own words, ' He purified the revolution, he confirmed kings, and ennobled people.' He purified the
revolution, in separating the truths which it contained from the
passions that, during its delirium, disfigured it. He ennobled
the people in giving them the consciousness of their force, and
those institutions which raise men in their own eyes. The
Emperor may be considered as the Messiah of the new ideas ;
for — and we must confess it — in the moments immediately
succeeding a social revolution, it is not so essential to put
rigidly into practice all the propositions resulting from the new
theory, but to become master of the regenerative genius, to
identify one's self with the sentiments of the people, and boldly
to direct them towards the desired point. To accomplish such
a task *your fibre should respond to that of the people*, as the Emperor said ; you should feel like it, your interests should be so
intimately raised with its own, that you should vanquish or fall
together."

Let us take breath after these big phrases, — grand round
figures of speech, — which, when put together, amount like
certain other combinations of round figures to exactly 0. We
shall not stop to argue the merits and demerits of Prince Louis's
notable comparison between the Christian religion and the
Imperial-revolutionary system. There are many blunders in
the above extract as we read it ; blundering metaphors, blunder-

ing arguments, and blundering assertions; but this is surely
the grandest blunder of all; and one wonders at the blindness
of the legislator and historian who can advance such a parallel.
And what are we to say of the legacy of the dying revolution
to Napoleon? Revolutions do not die, and, on their death-
beds, making fine speeches, hand over their property to young
officers of artillery. We have all read the history of his rise.
The constitution of the year III. was carried. Old men of the
Montagne, disguised royalists, Paris sections, *Pittetcobourg*,
above all, with his money-bags, thought that here was a fine
opportunity for a revolt, and opposed the new constitution in
arms: the new constitution had knowledge of a young officer
who would not hesitate to defend its cause, and who effectually
beat the majority. The tale may be found in every account of
the revolution, and the rest of his story need not be told. We
know every step that he took: we know how, by doses of
cannon-balls promptly administered, he cured the fever of the
sections — that fever which another camp-physician (Menou)
declined to prescribe for; we know how he abolished the Directory; and how the Consulship came; and then the Empire;
and then the disgrace, exile, and lonely death. Has not all
this been written by historians in all tongues? — by memoir-
writing pages, chamberlains, marshals, lackeys, secretaries,
contemporaries, and ladies of honor? Not a word of miracle
is there in all this narration; not a word of celestial missions,
or political Messiahs. From Napoleon's rise to his fall, the
bayonet marches alongside of him: now he points it at the
tails of the scampering " five hundred," — now he charges with
it across the bloody planks of Arcola — now he flies before it
over the fatal plain of Waterloo.

Unwilling, however, as he may be to grant that there are
any spots in the character of his hero's government, the Prince
is, nevertheless, obliged to allow that such existed; that the
Emperor's manner of rule was a little more abrupt and dicta-
torial than might possibly be agreeable. For this the Prince
has always an answer ready — it is the same poor one that
Napoleon uttered a million of times to his companions in
exile — the excuse of necessity. He *would* have been very
liberal, but that the people were not fit for it; or that the
cursed war prevented him — or any other reason why. His
first duty, however, says his apologist, was to form a general union of Frenchmen, and he set about his plan in this
wise: —

" Let us not forget, that all which Napoleon undertook, in

order to create a general fusion, he performed without re-
nouncing the principles of the revolution. He recalled the
émigrés, without touching upon the law by which their goods
had been confiscated and sold as public property. He re-
established the Catholic religion at the same time that he proclaimed the liberty of conscience, and endowed equally the
ministers of all sects. He caused himself to be consecrated by
the Sovereign Pontiff, without conceding to the Pope's demand
any of the liberties of the Gallican church. He married a
daughter of the Emperor of Austria, without abandoning any
of the rights of France to the conquests she had made. He re-
established noble titles, without attaching to them any privileges or prerogatives, and these titles were conferred on all
ranks, on all services, on all professions. Under the empire
all idea of caste was destroyed; no man ever thought of vaunt-
ing his pedigree — no man ever was asked how he was born,
but what he had done.

" The first quality of a people which aspires to liberal government, is respect to the law. Now, a law has no other power
than lies in the interest which each citizen has to defend or to
contravene it. In order to make a people respect the law, it
was necessary that it should be executed in the interest of all,
and should consecrate the principle of equality in all its exten-
sion. It was necessary to restore the *prestige* with which the
Government had been formerly invested, and to make the principles of the revolution take root in the public manners. At
the commencement of a new society, it is the legislator who
makes or corrects the manners; later, it is the manners which
make the law, or preserve it from age to age intact."

Some of these fusions are amusing. No man in the empire
was asked how he was born, but what he had done; and, accordingly, as a man's actions were sufficient to illustrate him,
the Emperor took care to make a host of new title-bearers,
princes, dukes, barons, and what not, whose rank has descended to their children. He married a princess of Austria;
but, for all that, did not abandon his conquests — perhaps not
actually; but he abandoned his allies, and, eventually, his whole
kingdom. Who does not recollect his answer to the Poles, at
the commencement of the Russian campaign? But for Napoleon's imperial father-in-law, Poland would have been a kingdom, and his race, perhaps, imperial still. Why was he to
fetch this princess out of Austria to make heirs for his throne?
Why did not the man of the people marry a girl of the people?
Why must he have a Pope to crown him — half a dozen kings

for brothers, and a bevy of aides-de-camp dressed out like so many mountebanks from Astley's, with dukes' coronets, and grand blue velvet marshals' bâtons? We have repeatedly his words for it. He wanted to create an aristocracy — another acknowledgment on his part of the Republican dilemma — another apology for the revolutionary blunder. To keep the republic within bounds, a despotism is necessary; to rally round the despotism, an aristocracy must be created; and for what have we been laboring all this while? for what have bastiles been battered down, and king's heads hurled, as a gage of battle, in the face of armed Europe? To have a Duke of Otranto instead of a Duke de la Tremouille, and Emperor Stork in place of King Log. O lame conclusion! Is the blessed revolution which is prophesied for us in England only to end in establishing a Prince Fergus O'Connor, or a Cardinal Wade, or a Duke Daniel Whittle Harvey? Great as those patriots are, we love them better under their simple family names, and scorn titles and coronets.

At present, in France, the delicate matter of titles seems to be better arranged, any gentleman, since the Revolution, being free to adopt any one he may fix upon ; and it appears that the Crown no longer confers any patents of nobility, but contents itself with saying, as in the case of M. de Pontois, the other day, " *Le Roi trouve convenable* that you take the title of," &c.

To execute the legacy of the revolution, then ; to fulfil his providential mission ; to keep his place, — in other words, for the simplest are always the best, — to keep his place, and to keep his Government in decent order, the Emperor was obliged to establish a military despotism, to re-establish honors and titles ; it was necessary, as the Prince confesses, to restore the old *prestige* of the Government, in order to make the people respect it ; and he adds — a truth which one hardly would expect from him, — " At the commencement of a new society, it is the legislator who makes and corrects the manners; later, it is the manners which preserve the laws." Of course, and here is the great risk that all revolutionizing people run — they must tend to despotism ; " they must personify themselves in a man," is the Prince's phrase ; and, according as is his temperament or disposition — according as he is a Cromwell, a Washington, or a Napoleon — the revolution becomes tyranny or freedom, prospers or falls.

Somewhere in the St. Helena memorials, Napoleon reports a message of his to the Pope. " Tell the Pope," he says to an archbishop, " to remember that I have six hundred thousand armed Frenchmen, *qui marcheront avec moi, pour moi, et comme moi.*" And this is the legacy of the revolution, the advancement of freedom! A hundred volumes of imperial special pleading will not avail against such a speech as this — one so insolent, and at the same time so humiliating, which gives unwittingly the whole of the Emperor's progress, strength, and weakness. The six hundred thousand armed Frenchmen were used up, and the whole fabric falls; the six hundred thousand are reduced to sixty thousand, and straightway all the rest of the fine imperial scheme vanishes: the miserable senate, so crawling and abject but now, becomes of a sudden endowed with a wondrous independence; the miserable sham nobles, sham empress, sham kings, dukes, princes, chamberlains, pack up their plumes and embroideries, pounce upon what money and plate they can lay their hands on, and when the allies appear before Paris, when for courage and manliness there is yet hope, when with fierce marches hastening to the relief of his capital, bursting through ranks upon ranks of the enemy, and crushing or scattering them from the path of his swift and victorious despair, the Emperor at last is at home, — where are the great dignitaries and the lieutenant-generals of the empire? Where is Maria Louisa, the Empress Eagle, with her little callow king of Rome? Is she going to defend her nest and her eaglet? Not she. Empress-queen, lieutenant-general, and court dignitaries, are off on the wings of all the winds — *profligati sunt,* they are away with the money-bags, and Louis Stanislas Xavier rolls into the palace of his fathers.

With regard to Napoleon's excellences as an administrator, a legislator, a constructor of public works, and a skilful financier, his nephew speaks with much diffuse praise, and few persons, we suppose, will be disposed to contradict him. Whether the Emperor composed his famous code, or borrowed it, is of little importance; but he established it, and made the law equal for every man in France except one. His vast public works and vaster wars were carried on without new loans or exorbitant taxes; it was only the blood and liberty of the people that were taxed, and we shall want a better advocate than Prince Louis to show us that these were not most unnecessarily and lavishly thrown away. As for the former and material improvements, it is not necessary to confess here that a despotic energy can effect such far more readily than a Government of which the strength is diffused in many conflicting parties. No doubt, if we could create a despotical governing machine, a steam autocrat, — passionless, untiring, and supreme, — we should advance further, and live more at ease than under any other form of government. Ministers might enjoy their pensions and follow their own devices; Lord John might compose histories or tragedies at his leisure, and Lord Palmerston, instead of racking his brains to write leading articles for Cupid, might crown his locks with flowers, and sing ἔρωτα μοῦνον, his natural Anacreontics; but alas! not so: if the despotic Government has its good side, Prince Louis Napoleon must acknowledge that it has its bad, and it is for this that the civilized world is compelled to substitute for it something more orderly and less capricious. Good as the Imperial Government might have been, it must be recollected, too, that since its first fall, both the Emperor and his admirer and would-be successor have had their chance of re-establishing it. "Fly from steeple to steeple" the eagles of the former did actually, and according to promise perch for a while on the towers of Notre Dame. We know the event: if the fate of war declared against the Emperor, the country declared against him too; and, with old Lafayette for a mouthpiece, the representatives of the nation did, in a neat speech, pronounce themselves in permanence, but spoke no more of the Emperor than if he had never been. Thereupon the Emperor proclaimed his son the Emperor Napoleon II. "L'Empereur est mort, vive l'Empereur!" shouted Prince Lucien. Psha! not a soul echoed the words: the play was played, and as for old Lafayette and his "permanent" representatives, a corporal with a hammer nailed up the door of their spouting-club, and once more Louis Stanislas Xavier rolled back to the bosom of his people.

In like manner Napoleon III. returned from exile, and made his appearance on the frontier. His eagle appeared at Strasburg, and from Strasburg advanced to the capital; but it arrived at Paris with a keeper, and in a post-chaise; whence, by the orders of the sovereign, it was removed to the American shores, and there magnanimously let loose. Who knows, however, how soon it may be on the wing again, and what a flight it will take?

THE STORY OF MARY ANCEL.

"Go, my nephew," said old Father Jacob to me, "and complete thy studies at Strasburg : Heaven surely hath ordained thee for the ministry in these times of trouble, and my excellent friend Schneider will work out the divine intention."

Schneider was an old college friend of uncle Jacob's, was a Benedictine monk, and a man famous for his learning ; as for me, I was at that time my uncle's chorister, clerk, and sacristan ; I swept the church, chanted the prayers with my shrill treble, and swung the great copper incense-pot on Sundays and feasts ; and I toiled over the Fathers for the other days of the week.

The old gentleman said that my progress was prodigious, and, without vanity, I believe he was right, for I then verily considered that praying was my vocation, and not fighting, as I have found since.

You would hardly conceive (said the Captain, swearing a great oath) how devout and how learned I was in those days ; I talked Latin faster than my own beautiful *patois* of Alsacian French ; I could utterly overthrow in argument every Protestant (heretics we called them) parson in the neighborhood, and there was a confounded sprinkling of these unbelievers in our part of the country. I prayed half a dozen times a day ; I fasted thrice in a week ; and, as for penance, I used to scourge my little sides, till they had no more feeling than a peg-top : such was the godly life I led at my uncle Jacob's in the village of Steinbach.

Our family had long dwelt in this place, and a large farm and a pleasant house were then in the possession of another uncle — uncle Edward. He was the youngest of the three sons of my grandfather; but Jacob, the elder, had shown a decided vocation for the church, from, I believe, the age of three, and now was by no means tired of it at sixty. My father, who was to have inherited the paternal property, was, as I hear, a terrible scamp and scapegrace, quarrelled with his family, and disappeared altogether, living and dying at Paris; so far we knew through my mother, who came, poor woman, with me, a child of six months, on her bosom, was refused all shelter by my grandfather, but was housed and kindly cared for by my good uncle Jacob.

Here she lived for about seven years, and the old gentleman, when she died, wept over her grave a great deal more than I did, who was then too young to mind anything but toys or sweetmeats.

During this time my grandfather was likewise carried off: he left, as I said, the property to his son Edward, with a small proviso in his will that something should be done for me, his grandson.

Edward was himself a widower, with one daughter, Mary, about three years older than I, and certainly she was the dearest little treasure with which Providence ever blessed a miserly father; by the time she was fifteen, five farmers, three lawyers, twelve Protestant parsons, and a lieutenant of Dragoons had made her offers : it must not be denied that she was an heiress as well as a beauty, which, perhaps, had something to do with the love of these gentlemen. However, Mary declared that she intended to live single, turned away her lovers one after another, and devoted herself to the care of her father.

Uncle Jacob was as fond of her as he was of any saint or martyr. As for me, at the mature age of twelve I had made a kind of divinity of her, and when we sang " Ave Maria " on Sundays I could not refrain from turning to her, where she knelt, blushing and praying and looking like an angel, as she was. Besides her beauty, Mary had a thousand good qualities; she could play better on the harpsichord, she could dance more lightly, she could make better pickles and puddings, than any girl in Alsace ; there was not a want or a fancy of the old hunks her father, or a wish of mine or my uncle's, that she would not gratify if she could ; as for herself, the sweet soul had neither wants nor wishes except to see us happy.

I could talk to you for a year of all the pretty kindnesses that she would do for me ; how, when she found me of early mornings among my books, her presence " would cast a light upon the day ; " how she used to smooth and fold my little surplice, and embroider me caps and gowns for high feast-days; how she used to bring flowers for the altar, and who could deck it so well as she? But sentiment does not come glibly from under a grizzled moustache, so I will drop it, if you please.

Amongst other favors she showed me, Mary used to be particularly fond of kissing me: it was a thing I did not so much value in those days, but I found that the more I grew alive to the extent of the benefit, the less she would condescend to confer it on me; till at last, when I was about fourteen, she discontinued it altogether, of her own wish at least; only sometimes I used to be rude, and take what she had now become so mighty unwilling to give.

I was engaged in a contest of this sort one day with Mary, when, just as I was about to carry off a kiss from her cheek, I was saluted with a staggering slap on my own, which was bestowed by uncle Edward, and sent me reeling some yards down the garden.

The old gentleman, whose tongue was generally as close as his purse, now poured forth a flood of eloquence which quite astonished me. I did not think that so much was to be said on any subject as he managed to utter on one, and that was abuse of me; he stamped, he swore, he screamed; and then, from complimenting me, he turned to Mary, and saluted her in a manner equally forcible and significant; she, who was very much frightened at the commencement of the scene, grew very angry at the coarse words he used, and the wicked motives he imputed to her.

"The child is but fourteen," she said; "he is your own nephew, and a candidate for holy orders: — father, it is a shame that you should thus speak of me, your daughter, or of one of his holy profession."

I did not particularly admire this speech myself, but it had an effect on my uncle, and was the cause of the words with which this history commences. The old gentleman persuaded his brother that I must be sent to Strasburg, and there kept until my studies for the church were concluded. I was furnished with a letter to my uncle's old college chum, Professor Schneider, who was to instruct me in theology and Greek.

I was not sorry to see Strasburg, of the wonders of which I had heard so much; but felt very loth as the time drew near when I must quit my pretty cousin, and my good old uncle. Mary and I managed, however, a parting walk, in which a number of tender things were said on both sides. I am told that you Englishmen consider it cowardly to cry; as for me, I

OLD HOUSES IN STRASBURG.

wept and roared incessantly : when Mary squeezed me, for the last time, the tears came out of me as if I had been neither more nor less than a great wet sponge. My cousin's eyes were stoically dry ; her ladyship had a part to play, and it would have been wrong for her to be in love with a young chit of fourteen — so she carried herself with perfect coolness, as if there was nothing the matter. I should not have known that she cared for me, had it not been for a letter which she wrote me a month afterwards — *then*, nobody was by, and the consequence was that the letter was half washed away with her weeping ; if she had used a watering-pot the thing could not have been better done.

Well, I arrived at Strasburg — a dismal, old-fashioned, rickety town in those days — and straightway presented myself and letter at Schneider's door ; over it was written —

COMITÉ DE SALUT PUBLIC.

Would you believe it? I was so ignorant a young fellow, that I had no idea of the meaning of the words ; however, I entered the citizen's room without fear, and sat down in his ante-chamber until I could be admitted to see him.

Here I found very few indications of his reverence's profession ; the walls were hung round with portraits of Robespierre, Marat, and the like ; a great bust of Mirabeau, mutilated, with the word *Traître* underneath ; lists and republican proclamations, tobacco-pipes and fire-arms. At a deal-table, stained with grease and wine, sat a gentleman, with a huge pigtail dangling down to that part of his person which immediately succeeds his back, and a red nightcap, containing a *tricolor* cockade as large as a pancake. He was smoking a short pipe, reading a little book, and sobbing as if his heart would break. Every now and then he would make brief remarks upon the personages or the incidents of his book, by which I could judge that he was a man of the very keenest sensibilities — " Ah, brigand ! " " O malheureuse ! " " O Charlotte, Charlotte ! " The work which this gentleman was perusing is called " The Sorrows of Werter ; " it was all the rage in those days, and my friend was only following the fashion. I asked him if I could see Father Schneider? he turned towards me a hideous, pimpled face, which I dream of now at forty years' distance.

" Father who? " said he. " Do you imagine that citizen Schneider has not thrown off the absurd mummery of priesthood? If you were a little older you would go to prison for calling him Father Schneider — many a man has died for less ; "

and he pointed to a picture of a guillotine, which was hanging in the room.

I was in amazement.

"What is he? Is he not a teacher of Greek, an abbé, a monk, until monasteries were abolished, the learned editor of the songs of ' Anacreon?'"

"He *was* all this," replied my grim friend; "he is now a Member of the Committee of Public Safety, and would think no more of ordering your head off than of drinking this tumbler of beer."

He swallowed, himself, the frothy liquid, and then proceeded to give me the history of the man to whom my uncle had sent me for instruction.

Schneider was born in 1756: was a student at Würzburg, and afterwards entered a convent, where he remained nine years. He here became distinguished for his learning and his talents as a preacher, and became chaplain to Duke Charles of Würtemberg. The doctrines of the Illuminati began about this time to spread in Germany, and Schneider speedily joined the sect. He had been a professor of Greek at Cologne; and being compelled, on account of his irregularity, to give up his chair, he came to Strasburg at the commencement of the French Revolution, and acted for some time a principal part as a revolutionary agent at Strasburg.

["Heaven knows what would have happened to me had I continued long under his tuition!" said the Captain. "I owe the preservation of my morals entirely to my entering the army. A man, sir, who is a soldier, has very little time to be wicked; except in the case of a siege and the sack of a town, when a little license can offend nobody."]

By the time that my friend had concluded Schneider's biography, we had grown tolerably intimate, and I imparted to him (with that experience so remarkable in youth) my whole history — my course of studies, my pleasant country life, the names and qualities of my dear relations, and my occupations in the vestry before religion was abolished by order of the Republic. In the course of my speech I recurred so often to the name of my cousin Mary, that the gentleman could not fail to perceive what a tender place she had in my heart.

Then we reverted to " The Sorrows of Werter," and discussed the merits of that sublime performance. Although I had before felt some misgivings about my new acquaintance, my heart now quite yearned towards him. He talked about love and sentiment in a manner which made me recollect that I was

in love myself; and you know that when a man is in that condition, his taste is not very refined, any maudlin trash of prose
or verse appearing sublime to him, provided it correspond, in
some degree, with his own situation.

"Candid youth!" cried my unknown, "I love to hear thy
innocent story and look on thy guileless face. There is, alas!
so much of the contrary in this world, so much terror and crime
and blood, that we who mingle with it are only too glad to forget it. Would that we could shake off our cares as men, and
be boys, as thou art, again!"

Here my friend began to weep once more, and fondly shook
my hand. I blessed my stars that I had, at the very outset
of my career, met with one who was so likely to aid me. What
a slanderous world it is, thought I; the people in our village
call these Republicans wicked and bloody-minded; a lamb could
not be more tender than this sentimental bottle-nosed gentleman!
The worthy man then gave me to understand that he held a
place under Government. I was busy in endeavoring to discover what his situation might be, when the door of the next
apartment opened, and Schneider made his appearance.

At first he did not notice me, but he advanced to my new
acquaintance, and gave him, to my astonishment, something
very like a blow.

"You drunken, talking fool," he said, "you are always after
your time. Fourteen people are cooling their heels yonder,
waiting until you have finished your beer and your sentiment!"

My friend slunk muttering out of the room.

"That fellow," said Schneider, turning to me, "is our public
executioner: a capital hand too if he would but keep decent
time; but the brute is always drunk, and blubbering over 'The
Sorrows of Werter!'"

.   .   .   .

I know not whether it was his old friendship for my uncle,
or my proper merits, which won the heart of this the sternest
ruffian of Robespierre's crew; but certain it is, that he became
strangely attached to me, and kept me constantly about his
person. As for the priesthood and the Greek, they were of
course very soon out of the question. The Austrians were on
our frontier; every day brought us accounts of battles won;
and the youth of Strasburg, and of all France, indeed, were
bursting with military ardor. As for me, I shared the general
mania, and speedily mounted a cockade as large as that of my
friend, the executioner.

The occupations of this worthy were unremitting. Saint

9

Just, who had come down from Paris to preside over our town, executed the laws and the aristocrats with terrible punctuality ; and Schneider used to make country excursions in search of offenders with this fellow, as a provost-marshal, at his back. In the meantime, having entered my sixteenth year, and being a proper lad of my age, I had joined a regiment of cavalry, and was scampering now after the Austrians who menaced us, and now threatening the Emigrés, who were banded at Coblentz. My love for my dear cousin increased as my whiskers grew ; and when I was scarcely seventeen, I thought myself man enough to marry her, and to cut the throat of any one who should venture to say me nay.

I need not tell you that during my absence at Strasburg, great changes had occurred in our little village, and somewhat of the revolutionary rage had penetrated even to that quiet and distant place. The hideous "Fête of the Supreme Being" had been celebrated at Paris ; the practice of our ancient religion was forbidden ; its professors were most of them in concealment, or in exile, or had expiated on the scaffold their crime of Christianity. In our poor village my uncle's church was closed, and he, himself, an inmate in my brother's house, only owing his safety to his great popularity among his former flock, and the influence of Edward Ancel.

The latter had taken in the Revolution a somewhat prominent part ; that is, he had engaged in many contracts for the army, attended the clubs regularly, corresponded with the authorities of his department, and was loud in his denunciations of the aristocrats in the neighborhood. But owing, perhaps, to the German origin of the peasantry, and their quiet and rustic lives, the revolutionary fury which prevailed in the cities had hardly reached the country people. The occasional visit of a commissary from Paris or Strasburg served to keep the flame alive, and to remind the rural swains of the existence of a Republic in France.

Now and then, when I could gain a week's leave of absence, I returned to the village, and was received with tolerable politeness by my uncle, and with a warmer feeling by his daughter.

I won't describe to you the progress of our love, or the wrath of my uncle Edward, when he discovered that it still continued. He swore and he stormed ; he locked Mary into her chamber, and vowed that he would withdraw the allowance he made me, if ever I ventured near her. His daughter, he said, should never marry a hopeless, penniless subaltern ; and Mary declared she would not marry without his consent. What had I to do ?—

to despair and to leave her.   As for my poor uncle Jacob, he
had no counsel to give me, and, indeed, no spirit left: his
little church was turned into a stable, his surplice torn off his
shoulders, and he was only too lucky in keeping *his head* on
them.   A bright thought struck him : suppose you were to ask
the advice of my old friend Schneider regarding this marriage?
he has ever been your friend, and may help you now as before.

(Here the Captain paused a little.)   You may fancy (continued he) that it was droll advice of a reverend gentleman
like uncle Jacob to counsel me in this manner; and to bid me
make friends with such a murderous cut-throat as Schneider;
but we thought nothing of it in those days ; guillotining was as
common as dancing, and a man was only thought the better
patriot the more severe he might be.   I departed forthwith to
Strasburg, and requested the vote and interest of the Citizen
President of the Committee of Public Safety.

He heard me with a great deal of attention.   I described
to him most minutely the circumstance, expatiated upon the
charms of my dear Mary, and painted her to him from head to
foot.   Her golden hair and her bright blushing cheeks, her
slim waist and her tripping tiny feet ; and furthermore, I added
that she possessed a fortune which ought, by rights, to be
mine, but for the miserly old father.   "Curse him for an
aristocrat !" concluded I, in my wrath.

As I had been discoursing about Mary's charms Schneider
listened with much complacency and attention : when I spoke
about her fortune, his interest redoubled ; and when I called
her father an aristocrat, the worthy ex-Jesuit gave a grin of
satisfaction, which was really quite terrible.   O fool that I was
to trust him so far !

.   .   .   .

The very same evening an officer waited upon me with the
following note from Saint Just : —

"STRASBURG, Fifth year of the Republic, one and
indivisible, 11 Ventose.

"The citizen Pierre Ancel is to leave Strasburg within two hours, and
to carry the enclosed despatches to the President of the Committee of
Public Safety at Paris.   The necessary leave of absence from his military
duties has been provided.   Instant punishment will follow the slightest
delay on the road.   Salut et Fraternité."

There was no choice but obedience, and off I sped on my
weary way to the capital.

As I was riding out of the Paris gate I met an equipage which I knew to be that of Schneider. The ruffian smiled at me as I passed, and wished me a *bon voyage*. Behind his chariot came a curious machine, or cart; a great basket, three stout poles, and several planks, all painted red, were lying in this vehicle, on the top of which was seated my friend with the big cockade. It was the *portable guillotine* which Schneider always carried with him on his travels. The *bourreau* was reading "The Sorrows of Werter," and looked as sentimental as usual.

I will not speak of my voyage in order to relate to you Schneider's. My story had awakened the wretch's curiosity and avarice, and he was determined that such a prize as I had shown my cousin to be should fall into no hands but his own. No sooner, in fact, had I quitted his room than he procured the order for my absence, and was on the way to Steinbach as I met him.

The journey is not a very long one; and on the next day my uncle Jacob was surprised by receiving a message that the citizen Schneider was in the village, and was coming to greet his old friend. Old Jacob was in an ecstasy, for he longed to see his college acquaintance, and he hoped also that Schneider had come into that part of the country upon the marriage-business of your humble servant. Of course Mary was summoned to give her best dinner, and wear her best frock; and her father made ready to receive the new State dignitary.

Schneider's carriage speedily rolled into the court-yard, and Schneider's *cart* followed, as a matter of course. The ex-priest only entered the house; his companion remaining with the horses to dine in private. Here was a most touching meeting between him and Jacob. They talked over their old college pranks and successes; they capped Greek verses, and quoted ancient epigrams upon their tutors, who had been dead since the Seven Years' War. Mary declared it was quite touching to listen to the merry friendly talk of these two old gentlemen.

After the conversation had continued for a time in this strain, Schneider drew up all of a sudden, and said quietly, that he had come on particular and unpleasant business — hinting about troublesome times, spies, evil reports, and so forth. Then he called uncle Edward aside, and had with him a long and earnest conversation: so Jacob went out and talked with Schneider's *friend;* they speedily became very intimate, for the ruffian detailed all the circumstances of his interview with me. When he returned into the house, some time after this pleasing colloquy, he found the tone of the society strangely altered. Edward Ancel, pale as a sheet, trembling, and crying for mercy; poor Mary weeping; and Schneider pacing energetically about the apartment, raging about the rights of man, the punishment of traitors, and the one and indivisible Republic.

"Jacob," he said, as my uncle entered the room, "I was willing, for the sake of our old friendship, to forget the crimes of your brother. He is a known and dangerous aristocrat; he holds communications with the enemy on the frontier; he is a possessor of great and ill-gotten wealth, of which he has plundered the Republic. Do you know," said he, turning to Edward Ancel, "where the least of these crimes, or the mere suspicion of them, would lead you?"

Poor Edward sat trembling in his chair, and answered not a word. He knew full well how quickly, in this dreadful time, punishment followed suspicion; and, though guiltless of all treason with the enemy, perhaps he was aware that, in certain contracts with the Government, he had taken to himself a more than patriotic share of profit.

"Do you know," resumed Schneider, in a voice of thunder, "for what purpose I came hither, and by whom I am accompanied? I am the administrator of the justice of the Republic. The life of yourself and your family is in my hands: yonder man, who follows me, is the executor of the law; he has rid the nation of hundreds of wretches like yourself. A single word from me, and your doom is sealed without hope, and your last hour is come. Ho! Gregoire!" shouted he; "is all ready?"

Gregoire replied from the court, "I can put up the machine in half an hour. Shall I go down to the village and call the troops and the law people?"

"Do you hear him?" said Schneider. "The guillotine is in the court-yard; your name is on my list, and I have witnesses to prove your crime. Have you a word in your defence?"

Not a word came; the old gentleman was dumb; but his daughter, who did not give way to her terror, spoke for him.

"You cannot, sir," said she, "although you say it, *feel* that my father is guilty; you would not have entered our house thus alone if you had thought it. You threaten him in this manner because you have something to ask and to gain from us: what is it, citizen? — tell us how much you value our lives, and what sum we are to pay for our ransom?"

" Sum ! " said uncle Jacob ; " he does not want money of us : my old friend, my college chum, does not come hither to drive bargains with anybody belonging to Jacob Ancel ? "

" Oh, no, sir, no, you can't want money of us," shrieked Edward ; " we are the poorest people of the village : ruined, Monsieur Schneider, ruined in the cause of the Republic."

" Silence, father," said my brave Mary ; " this man wants a *price :* he comes, with his worthy friend yonder, to frighten us, not to kill us. If we die, he cannot touch a sou of our money ; it is confiscated to the State. Tell us, sir, what is the price of our safety ? "

Schneider smiled, and bowed with perfect politeness.

" Mademoiselle Marie," he said, " is perfectly correct in her surmise. I do not want the life of this poor drivelling old man : my intentions are much more peaceable, be assured. It rests entirely with this accomplished young lady (whose spirit I like, and whose ready wit I admire), whether the business between us shall be a matter of love or death. I humbly offer myself, citizen Ancel, as a candidate for the hand of your charming daughter. Her goodness, her beauty, and the large fortune which I know you intend to give her, would render her a desirable match for the proudest man in the republic, and, I am sure, would make me the happiest."

" This must be a jest, Monsieur Schneider," said Mary, trembling, and turning deadly pale : " you cannot mean this ; you do not know me : you never heard of me until to-day."

" Pardon me, belle dame," replied he ; " your cousin Pierre has often talked to me of your virtues ; indeed, it was by his special suggestion that I made the visit."

" It is false ! — it is a base and cowardly lie ! " exclaimed she (for the young lady's courage was up), — " Pierre never could have forgotten himself and me so as to offer me to one like you. You come here with a lie on your lips — a lie against my father, to swear his life away, against my dear cousin's honor and love. It is useless now to deny it : father, I love Pierre Ancel ; I will marry no other but him -- no, though our last penny were paid to this man as the price of our freedom."

Schneider's only reply to this was a call to his friend Gregoire.

" Send down to the village for the maire and some gendarmes ; and tell your people to make ready."

" Shall I put *the machine* up ? " shouted he of the sentimental turn.

" You hear him," said Schneider ; " Marie Ancel, you may

decide the fate of your father. I shall return in a few hours,"
concluded he, " and will then beg to know your decision."

The advocate of the rights of man then left the apartment,
and left the family, as you may imagine, in no very pleasant
mood.

Old uncle Jacob, during the few minutes which had elapsed
in the enactment of this strange scene, sat staring wildly at
Schneider, and holding Mary on his knees : the poor little
thing had fled to him for protection, and not to her father,
who was kneeling almost senseless at the window, gazing at
the executioner and his hideous preparations. The instinct of
the poor girl had not failed her ; she knew that Jacob was her
only protector, if not of her life — heaven bless him ! — of her
honor.   "Indeed," the old man said, in a stout voice, "this
must never be, my dearest child — you must not marry this
man. If it be the will of Providence that we fall, we shall
have at least the thought to console us that we die innocent.
Any man in France at a time like this, would be a coward and
traitor if he feared to meet the fate of the thousand brave and
good who have preceded us."

"Who speaks of dying?" said Edward. "You, Brother
Jacob? — you would not lay that poor girl's head on the scaffold, or mine, your dear brother's. You will not let us die,
Mary ; you will not, for a small sacrifice, bring your poor old
father into danger?"

Mary made no answer. "Perhaps, she said, "there is
time for escape : he is to be here but in two hours ; in two
hours we may be safe, in concealment, or on the frontier."
And she rushed to the door of the chamber, as if she would
have instantly made the attempt : two *gendarmes* were at the
door. "We have orders, Mademoiselle," they said, "to allow
no one to leave this apartment until the return of the citizen
Schneider."

Alas ! all hope of escape was impossible. Mary became
quite silent for a while ; she would not speak to uncle Jacob ;
and, in reply to her father's eager questions, she only replied,
coldly, that she would answer Schneider when he arrived.

The two dreadful hours passed away only too quickly ; and,
punctual to his appointment, the ex-monk appeared. Directly
he entered, Mary advanced to him, and said, calmly, —

"Sir, I could not deceive you if I said that I freely accepted
the offer which you have made me. I will be your wife ; but I
tell you that I love another ; and that it is only to save the
lives of those two old men that I yield my person up to you."

Schneider bowed, and said, —

"It is bravely spoken. I like your candor — your beauty. As for the love, excuse me for saying that is a matter of total indifference. I have no doubt, however, that it will come as soon as your feelings in favor of the young gentleman, your cousin, have lost their present fervor. That engaging young man has, at present, another mistress — Glory. He occupies, I believe, the distinguished post of corporal in a regiment which is about to march to — Perpignan, I believe."

It was, in fact, Monsieur Schneider's polite intention to banish me as far as possible from the place of my birth; and he had, accordingly, selected the Spanish frontier as the spot where I was to display my future military talents.

Mary gave no answer to this sneer : she seemed perfectly resigned and calm : she only said, —

"I must make, however, some conditions regarding our proposed marriage, which a gentleman of Monsieur Schneider's gallantry cannot refuse."

"Pray command me," replied the husband elect. "Fair lady, you know I am your slave."

"You occupy a distinguished political rank, citizen representative," said she; "and we in our village are likewise known and beloved. I should be ashamed, I confess, to wed you here; for our people would wonder at the sudden marriage, and imply that it was only by compulsion that I gave you my hand. Let us, then, perform this ceremony at Strasburg, before the public authorities of the city, with the state and solemnity which befits the marriage of one of the chief men of the Republic."

"Be it so, madam," he answered, and gallantly proceeded to embrace his bride.

Mary did not shrink from this ruffian's kiss; nor did she reply when poor old Jacob, who sat sobbing in a corner, burst out, and said, —

"O Mary, Mary, I did not think this of thee !"

"Silence, brother !" hastily said Edward; "my good son-in-law will pardon your ill-humor."

I believe uncle Edward in his heart was pleased at the notion of the marriage; he only cared for money and rank, and was little scrupulous as to the means of obtaining them.

The matter then was finally arranged; and presently, after Schneider had transacted the affairs which brought him into that part of the country, the happy bridal party set forward for Strasburg. Uncles Jacob and Edward occupied the back seat of the old family carriage, and the young bride and bridegroom (he was nearly Jacob's age) were seated majestically in front. Mary has often since talked to me of this dreadful journey. She said she wondered at the scrupulous politeness of Schneider during the route; nay, that at another period she could have listened to and admired the singular talent of this man, his great learning, his fancy, and wit; but her mind was bent upon other things, and the poor girl firmly thought that her last day was come.

In the meantime, by a blessed chance, I had not ridden three leagues from Strasburg, when the officer of a passing troop of a cavalry regiment, looking at the beast on which I was mounted, was pleased to take a fancy to it, and ordered me, in an authoritative tone, to descend, and to give up my steed for the benefit of the Republic. I represented to him, in vain, that I was a soldier, like himself, and the bearer of despatches to Paris. "Fool!" he said; "do you think they would send despatches by a man who can ride at best but ten leagues a day?" And the honest soldier was so wroth at my supposed duplicity, that he not only confiscated my horse, but my saddle, and the little portmanteau which contained the chief part of my worldly goods and treasure. I had nothing for it but to dismount, and take my way on foot back again to Strasburg. I arrived there in the evening, determining the next morning to make my case known to the citizen St. Just; and though I made my entry without a sou, I don't know what secret exultation I felt at again being able to return.

The ante-chamber of such a great man as St. Just was, in those days, too crowded for an unprotected boy to obtain an early audience; two days passed before I could obtain a sight of the friend of Robespierre. On the third day, as I was still waiting for the interview, I heard a great bustle in the court-yard of the house, and looked out with many others at the spectacle.

A number of men and women, singing epithalamiums, and dressed in some absurd imitation of Roman costume, a troop of soldiers and gendarmerie, and an immense crowd of the *badauds* of Strasburg, were surrounding a carriage which then entered the court of the mayoralty. In this carriage, great God! I saw my dear Mary, and Schneider by her side. The truth instantly came upon me: the reason for Schneider's keen inquiries and my abrupt dismissal; but I could not believe that Mary was false to me. I had only to look in her face.

white and rigid as marble, to see that this proposed marriage was not with her consent.

I fell back in the crowd as the procession entered the great room in which I was, and hid my face in my hands : I could not look upon her as the wife of another, — upon her so long loved and truly — the saint of my childhood — the pride and hope of my youth — torn from me for ever, and delivered over to the unholy arms of the murderer who stood before me.

The door of St. Just's private apartment opened, and he took his seat at the table of mayoralty just as Schneider and his cortége arrived before it.

Schneider then said that he came in before the authorities of the Republic to espouse the citoyenne Marie Ancel.

" Is she a minor ? " asked St. Just.

" She is a minor, but her father is here to give her away."

" I am here," said uncle Edward, coming eagerly forward and bowing. " Edward Ancel, so please you, citizen representative. The worthy citizen Schneider has done me the honor of marrying into my family."

" But my father has not told you the terms of the marriage," said Mary, interrupting him, in a loud, clear voice.

Here Schneider seized her hand, and endeavored to prevent her from speaking. Her father turned pale, and cried, " Stop, Mary, stop! For heaven's sake, remember your poor old father's danger ! "

" Sir, may I speak ? "

" Let the young woman speak," said St. Just, " if she have a desire to talk." He did not suspect what would be the purport of her story.

" Sir," she said, " two days since the citizen Schneider entered for the first time our house ; and you will fancy that it must be a love of very sudden growth which has brought either him or me before you to-day. He had heard from a person who is now unhappily not present, of my name and of the wealth which my family was said to possess ; and hence arose this mad design concerning me. He came into our village with supreme power, an executioner at his heels, and the soldiery and authorities of the district entirely under his orders. He threatened my father with death if he refused to give up his daughter ; and I, who knew that there was no chance of escape, except here before you, consented to become his wife. My father I know to be innocent, for all his transactions with the State have passed through my hands. Citizen representative, I demand to be freed from this marriage ; and I charge Schneider as a

traitor to the Republic, as a man who would have murdered
an innocent citizen for the sake of private gain."

During the delivery of this little speech, uncle Jacob had
been sobbing and panting like a broken-winded horse; and
when Mary had done, he rushed up to her and kissed her, and
held her tight in his arms. "Bless thee, my child!" he cried,
"for having had the courage to speak the truth, and shame thy
old father and me, who dared not say a word."

"The girl amazes me," said Schneider, with a look of
astonishment. "I never saw her, it is true, till yesterday; but
I used no force: her father gave her to me with his free consent, and she yielded as gladly. Speak, Edward Ancel, was
it not so?"

"It was, indeed, by my free consent," said Edward, trembling.

"For shame, brother!" cried old Jacob. "Sir, it was by
Edward's free consent and my niece's; but the guillotine was
in the court-yard! Question Schneider's famulus, the man
Gregoire, him who reads 'The Sorrows of Werter.'"

Gregoire stepped forward, and looked hesitatingly at
Schneider, as he said, "I know not what took place within
doors; but I was ordered to put up the scaffold without;
and I was told to get soldiers, and let no one leave the
house."

"Citizen St. Just," cried Schneider, "you will not allow
the testimony of a ruffian like this, of a foolish girl, and a mad
ex-priest, to weigh against the word of one who has done such
service to the Republic: it is a base conspiracy to betray me;
the whole family is known to favor the interest of the *émigrés*."

"And therefore you would marry a member of the family,
and allow the others to escape; you must make a better defence,
citizen Schneider," said St. Just, sternly.

Here I came forward, and said that, three days since, I had
received an order to quit Strasburg for Paris immediately after
a conversation with Schneider, in which I had asked him his aid
in promoting my marriage with my cousin, Mary Ancel; that
he had heard from me full accounts regarding her father's
wealth; and that he had abruptly caused my dismissal, in order
to carry on his scheme against her.

"You are in the uniform of a regiment of this town; who
sent you from it?" said St. Just.

I produced the order, signed by himself, and the despatches
which Schneider had sent me.

"The signature is mine, but the despatches did not come

from my office. Can you prove in any way your conversation with Schneider?"

"Why," said my sentimental friend Gregoire, "for the matter of that, I can answer that the lad was always talking about this young woman: he told me the whole story himself, and many a good laugh I had with citizen Schneider as we talked about it."

"The charge against Edward Ancel must be examined into," said St. Just. "The marriage cannot take place. But if I had ratified it, Mary Ancel, what then would have been your course?"

Mary felt for a moment in her bosom, and said — "*He would have died to-night — I would have stabbed him with this dagger.*" *

.　　.　　.　　.　　.　　.　　.　　.

The rain was beating down the streets, and yet they were thronged; all the world was hastening to the market-place, where the worthy Gregoire was about to perform some of the pleasant duties of his office. On this occasion, it was not death that he was to inflict; he was only to expose a criminal who was to be sent on afterwards to Paris. St. Just had ordered that Schneider should stand for six hours in the public *place* of Strasburg, and then be sent on to the capital to be dealt with as the authorities might think fit.

The people followed with execrations the villain to his place of punishment; and Gregoire grinned as he fixed up to the post the man whose orders he had obeyed so often — who had delivered over to disgrace and punishment so many who merited it not.

Schneider was left for several hours exposed to the mockery and insults of the mob; he was then, according to his sentence, marched on to Paris, where it is probable that he would have escaped death, but for his own fault. He was left for some time in prison, quite unnoticed, perhaps forgotten: day by day fresh victims were carried to the scaffold, and yet the Alsacian tribune remained alive; at last, by the mediation of one of his friends, a long petition was presented to Robespierre, stating his services and his innocence, and demanding his freedom. The reply to this was an order for his instant execution: the wretch died in the last days of Robespierre's reign. His comrade, St. Just, followed him, as you know; but Edward Ancel

---

* This reply, and, indeed, the whole of the story, is historical. An account, by Charles Nodier, in the *Revue de Paris*, suggested it to the writer.

had been released before this, for the action of my brave Mary
had created a strong feeling in his favor.

"And Mary?" said I.

Here a stout and smiling old lady entered the Captain's little
room: she was leaning on the arm of a military-looking man
of some forty years, and followed by a number of noisy, rosy
children.

"This is Mary Ancel," said the Captain, "and I am Captain Pierre, and yonder is the Colonel, my son; and you see us
here assembled in force, for it is the fête of little Jacob yonder,
whose brothers and sisters have all come from their schools to
dance at his birthday."

BEATRICE MERGER.

BEATRICE MERGER, whose name might figure at the head of one of Mr. Colburn's politest romances — so smooth and aristocratic does it sound — is no heroine, except of her own simple history; she is not a fashionable French Countess, nor even a victim of the Revolution.

She is a stout, sturdy girl of two-and-twenty, with a face beaming with good nature, and marked dreadfully by small-pox; and a pair of black eyes, which might have done some execution had they been placed in a smoother face. Beatrice's station in society is not very exalted; she is a servant of all-work: she will dress your wife, your dinner, your children; she does beefsteaks and plain work; she makes beds, blacks boots, and waits at table; — such, at least, were the offices which she performed in the fashionable establishment of the writer of this book: perhaps her history may not inaptly occupy a few pages of it.

"My father died," said Beatrice, "about six years since, and left my poor mother with little else but a small cottage and a strip of land, and four children too young to work. It was hard enough in my father's time to supply so many little mouths with food; and how was a poor widowed woman to provide for them now, who had neither the strength nor the opportunity for labor?

"Besides us, to be sure, there was my old aunt; and she would have helped us, but she could not, for the old woman is bed-ridden; so she did nothing but occupy our best room, and grumble from morning till night: heaven knows, poor old soul, that she had no great reason to be very happy; for you know, sir, that it frets the temper to be sick; and that it is worse still to be sick and hungry too.

"At that time, in the country where we lived (in Picardy, not very far from Boulogne), times were so bad that the best workman could hardly find employ; and when he did, he was happy if he could earn a matter of twelve sous a day. Mother, work as she would, could not gain more than six; and it was a hard job, out of this, to put meat into six bellies, and clothing on six backs. Old Aunt Bridget would scold, as she got her portion of black bread; and my little brothers used to cry if theirs did not come in time. I, too, used to cry when I got my share; for mother kept only a little, little piece for herself, and said that she had dined in the fields, — God pardon her for the lie! and bless her, as I am sure He did; for, but for Him, no working man or woman could subsist upon such a wretched morsel as my dear mother took.

"I was a thin, ragged, barefooted girl, then, and sickly and weak for want of food; but I think I felt mother's hunger more than my own: and many and many a bitter night I lay awake, crying, and praying to God to give me means of working for myself and aiding her. And he has, indeed, been good to me," said pious Beatrice, "for He has given me all this!

"Well, time rolled on, and matters grew worse than ever; winter came, and was colder to us than any other winter, for our clothes were thinner and more torn; mother sometimes could find no work, for the fields in which she labored were hidden under the snow; so that when we wanted them most we had them least — warmth, work, or food.

"I knew that, do what I would, mother would never let me leave her, because I looked to my little brothers and my old cripple of an aunt; but still, bread was better for us than all my service; and when I left them the six would have a slice more; so I determined to bid good-by to nobody, but to go away, and look for work elsewhere. One Sunday, when mother and the little ones were at church, I went in to Aunt Bridget, and said, 'Tell mother, when she comes back, that Beatrice is gone.' I spoke quite stoutly, as if I did not care about it.

"'Gone! gone where?' said she. 'You ain't going to leave me alone, you nasty thing; you ain't going to the village to dance, you ragged, barefooted slut: you're all of a piece in this house — your mother, your brothers, and you. I know you've got meat in the kitchen, and you only give me black bread;' and here the old lady began to scream as if her heart would break; but we did not mind it, we were so used to it.

" ' Aunt,' said I, ' I'm going, and took this very opportunity because you *were* alone : tell mother I am too old now to eat her bread, and do no work for it : I am going, please God, where work and bread can be found : ' and so I kissed her : she was so astonished that she could not move or speak ; and I walked away through the old room, and the little garden, God knows whither !

" I heard the old woman screaming after me, but I did not stop nor turn round. I don't think I could, for my heart was very full ; and if I had gone back again, I should never have had the courage to go away. So I walked a long, long way, until night fell ; and I thought of poor mother coming home from mass, and not finding me ; and little Pierre shouting out, in his clear voice, for Beatrice to bring him his supper. I think I should like to have died that night, and I thought I should too ; for when I was obliged to throw myself on the cold, hard ground, my feet were too torn and weary to bear me any further.

" Just then the moon got up ; and do you know I felt a comfort in looking at it, for I knew it was shining on our little cottage, and it seemed like an old friend's face ? A little way on, as I saw by the moon, was a village : and I saw, too, that a man was coming towards me ; he must have heard me crying, I suppose.

" Was not God good to me ? This man was a farmer, who had need of a girl in his house ; he made me tell him why I was alone, and I told him the same story I have told you, and he believed me and took me home. I had walked six long leagues from our village that day, asking everywhere for work in vain ; and here, at bedtime, I found a bed and a supper !

" Here I lived very well for some months ; my master was very good and kind to me ; but, unluckily, too poor to give me any wages ; so that I could save nothing to send to my poor mother. My mistress used to scold ; but I was used to that at home, from Aunt Bridget : and she beat me sometimes, but I did not mind it ; for your hardy country girl is not like your tender town lasses, who cry if a pin pricks them, and give warning to their mistresses at the first hard word. The only drawback to my comfort was, that I had no news of my mother ; I could not write to her, nor could she have read my letter, if I had ; so there I was, at only six leagues' distance from home, as far off as if I had been to Paris or to 'Merica.

" However, in a few months I grew so listless and homesick, that my mistress said she would keep me no longer ; and though

I went away as poor as I came, I was still too glad to go back to the old village again, and see dear mother, if it were but for a day. I knew she would share her crust with me, as she had done for so long a time before; and hoped that, now, as I was taller and stronger, I might find work more easily in the neighborhood.

" You may fancy what a fête it was when I came back; though I'm sure we cried as much as if it had been a funeral. Mother got into a fit, which frightened us all; and as for Aunt Bridget, she *skreeled* away for hours together, and did not scold for two days at least. Little Pierre offered me the whole of his supper; poor little man! his slice of bread was no bigger than before I went away.

" Well, I got a little work here and a little there; but still I was a burden at home rather than a bread-winner; and, at the closing-in of the winter, was very glad to hear of a place at two leagues' distance, where work, they said, was to be had. Off I set, one morning, to find it, but missed my way, somehow, until it was night-time before I arrived. Night-time and snow again; it seemed as if all my journeys were to be made in this bitter weather.

" When I came to the farmer's door, his house was shut up, and his people all a-bed; I knocked for a long while in vain; at last he made his appearance at a window up stairs, and seemed so frightened, and looked so angry that I suppose he took me for a thief. I told him how I had come for work. ' Who comes for work at such an hour?' said he. ' Go home, you impudent baggage, and do not disturb honest people out of their sleep.' He banged the window to; and so I was left alone to shift for myself as I might. There was no shed, no cow-house, where I could find a bed; so I got under a cart, on some straw; it was no very warm berth. I could not sleep for the cold: and the hours passed so slowly, that it seemed as if I had been there a week instead of a night; but still it was not so bad as the first night when I left home, and when the good farmer found me.

" In the morning, before it was light, the farmer's people came out, and saw me crouching under the cart: they told me to get up; but I was so cold that I could not: at last the man himself came, and recognized me as the girl who had disturbed him the night before. When he heard my name, and the purpose for which I came, this good man took me into the house, and put me into one of the beds out of which his sons had just got; and, if I was cold before, you may be sure I was warm and comfortable now ! such a bed as this I had never slept in, nor ever did I have such good milk-soup as he gave me out of his own breakfast.　Well, he agreed to hire me ; and what do you think he gave me? — six sous a day ! and let me sleep in the cow-house besides : you may fancy how happy I was now, at the prospect of earning so much money.

" There was an old woman among the laborers who used to sell us soup : I got a cupful every day for a half-penny, with a bit of bread in it ; and might eat as much beet-root besides as I liked ; not a very wholesome meal, to be sure, but God took care that it should not disagree with me.

" So, every Saturday, when work was over, I had thirty sous to carry home to mother ; and tired though I was, I walked merrily the two leagues to our village, to see her again. On the road there was a great wood to pass through, and this frightened me ; for if a thief should come and rob me of my whole week's earnings, what could a poor lone girl do to help herself?　But I found a remedy for this too, and no thieves ever came near me ; I used to begin saying my prayers as I entered the forest, and never stopped until I was safe at home ; and safe I always arrived, with my thirty sous in my pocket. Ah ! you may be sure, Sunday was a merry day for us all."

.　　.　　.　　.　　.　　.　　.　　.

This is the whole of Beatrice's history which is worthy of publication ; the rest of it only relates to her arrival in Paris, and the various masters and mistresses whom she there had the honor to serve.　As soon as she enters the capital the romance disappears, and the poor girl's sufferings and privations luckily vanish with it.　Beatrice has got now warm gowns, and stout shoes, and plenty of good food.　She has had her little brother from Picardy ; clothed, fed, and educated him : that young gentleman is now a carpenter, and an honor to his profession. Madame Merger is in easy circumstances, and receives, yearly, fifty francs from her daughter.　To crown all, Mademoiselle Beatrice herself is a funded proprietor, and consulted the writer of this biography as to the best method of laying out a capital of two hundred francs, which is the present amount of her fortune.

God bless her ! she is richer than his Grace the Duke of Devonshire ; and, I dare say, has, in her humble walk, been more virtuous and more happy than all the dukes in the realm.

It is, indeed, for the benefit of dukes and such great people (who, I make no doubt, have long since ordered copies of these Sketches), that poor little Beatrice's story has been indited. Certain it is, that the young woman would never have been immortalized in this way, but for the good which her betters may derive from her example. If your ladyship will but reflect a little, after boasting of the sums which you spend in charity; the beef and blankets which you dole out at Christmas; the poonah-painting which you execute for fancy fairs; the long, long sermons which you listen to at St. George's, the whole year through; — your ladyship, I say, will allow that, although perfectly meritorious in your line, as a patroness of the Church of England, of Almack's, and of the Lying-in Asylum, yours is but a paltry sphere of virtue, a pitiful attempt at benevolence, and that this honest servant-girl puts you to shame! And you, my Lord Bishop: do you, out of your six sous a day, give away five to support your flock and family? Would you drop a single coach-horse (I do not say, *a dinner*, for such a notion is monstrous, in one of your lordship's degree), to feed any one of the starving children of your lordship's mother — the Church?

I pause for a reply. His lordship took too much turtle and cold punch for dinner yesterday, and cannot speak just now: but we have, by this ingenious question, silenced him altogether: let the world wag as it will, and poor Christians and curates starve as they may, my lord's footmen must have their new liveries, and his horses their four feeds a day.

. . . .

When we recollect his speech about the Catholics — when we remember his last charity sermon, — but I say nothing. Here is a poor benighted superstitious creature, worshipping images, without a rag to her tail, who has as much faith, and humility, and charity as all the reverend bench.

. . . .

This angel is without a place; and for this reason (besides the pleasure of composing the above slap at episcopacy) — I have indited her history. If the Bishop is going to Paris, and wants a good honest maid-of-all-work, he can have her, I have no doubt; or if he chooses to give a few pounds to her mother, they can be sent to Mr. Titmarsh, at the publisher's.

Here is Miss Merger's last letter and autograph. The note was evidently composed by an *Ecrivain public:* —

"*Madame,* — *Ayant apris par ce Monsieur, que vous vous portiez bien, ainsi que Monsieur, ayant su aussi que vous parliez de moi dans votre lettre cette nouvelle m'a fait bien plaisir Je profite de l'occasion pour vous faire passer ce petit billet où Je voudrais pouvoir*

*m'enveloper pour aller vous voir et pour vous dire que Je suis en-
core sans place Je m'ennuye tojours de ne pas vous voir ainsi que
Minette* (Minette is a cat) *qui semble m'interroger tour a tour et
demander où vous êtes. Je vous envoye aussi la note du linge a
blanchir — ah, Madame! Je vais cesser de vous ecrire mais non de
vous regretter.*"

Beatrice Merger

CARICATURES AND LITHOGRAPHY IN PARIS.

FIFTY years ago there lived at Munich a poor fellow, by name Aloys Senefelder, who was in so little repute as an author and artist, that printers and engravers refused to publish his works at their own charges, and so set him upon some plan for doing without their aid. In the first place, Aloys invented a certain kind of ink, which would resist the action of the acid that is usually employed by engravers, and with this he made his experiments upon copper-plates, as long as he could afford to purchase them. He found that to write upon the plates backwards, after the manner of engravers, required much skill and many trials ; and he thought that, were he to practise upon any other polished surface — a smooth stone, for instance, the least costly article imaginable — he might spare the expense of the copper until he had sufficient skill to use it.

One day, it is said, that Aloys was called upon to write — rather a humble composition for an author and artist — a washing-bill. He had no paper at hand, and so he wrote out the bill with some of his newly-invented ink upon one of his Kelheim stones. Some time afterwards he thought he would try and take an *impression* of his washing-bill : he did, and succeeded. Such is the story, which the reader most likely knows very well ; and having alluded to the origin of the art, we shall not follow the stream through its windings and enlargement after it issued from the little parent rock, or fill our pages with the rest of the pedigree. Senefelder invented Lithography. His invention has not made so much noise and larum in the world as some others, which have an origin quite as humble and unromantic ; but it is one to which we owe no small profit, and a great deal of pleasure : and, as such, we are bound to speak of it with all gratitude and respect. The schoolmaster, who is now abroad, has taught us, in our youth, how the cultivation of art " *emollit mores nec sinit esse* " — (it is needless to finish the quotation) ; and Lithography has been, to our thinking, the very best ally that art ever had ; the best friend of the artist, allowing him to produce rapidly multiplied and authentic copies of his own works (without trusting to the tedious and expensive assistance of the engraver) ; and the best friend to the people likewise, who have means of purchasing these cheap and beautiful productions, and thus having their ideas " mollified " and their manners " feros " no more.

With ourselves, among whom money is plenty, enterprise so great, and everything matter of commercial speculation. Lithography has not been so much practised as wood or steel engraving; which, by the aid of great original capital and spread of sale, are able more than to compete with the art of drawing on stone. The two former may be called art done by *machinery*. We confess to a prejudice in favor of the honest work of *hand*, in matters of art, and prefer the rough workmanship of the painter to the smooth copies of his performances which are produced, for the most part, on the wood-block or the steel-plate.

The theory will possibly be objected to by many of our readers : the best proof in its favor, we think, is, that the state of art amongst the people in France and Germany, where publishers are not so wealthy or enterprising as with us,* and where Lithography is more practised, is infinitely higher than in England, and the appreciation more correct. As draughtsmen, the French and German painters are incomparably superior to our own ; and with art, as with any other commodity, the demand will be found pretty equal to the supply : with us, the general demand is for neatness, prettiness, and what is called *effect* in pictures, and these can be rendered completely, nay, improved, by the engraver's conventional manner of copying the artist's performances. But to copy fine expression and fine drawing, the engraver himself must be a fine artist ; and let anybody examine the host of picture-books which appear every Christmas, and say whether, for the most part, painters or engravers possess any artistic merit? We boast, nevertheless, of some of the best engravers and painters in Europe. Here,

---

* These countries are, to be sure, inundated with the productions of our market, in the shape of Byron Beauties, reprints from the " Keepsakes," " Books of Beauty," and such trash; but these are only of late years, and their original schools of art are still flourishing.

again, the supply is accounted for by the demand ; our highest class is richer than any other aristocracy, quite as well in-structed, and can judge and pay for fine pictures and engravings. But these costly productions are for the few, and not for the many, who have not yet certainly arrived at properly appre-ciating fine art.

Take the standard " Album " for instance — that unfortunate collection of deformed Zuleikas and Medoras (from the " Byron Beauties "), the Flowers, Gems, Souvenirs, Caskets of Loveli-ness, Beauty, as they may be called ; glaring caricatures of flowers, singly, in groups, in flower-pots, or with hideous deformed little Cupids sporting among them ; of what are called " mezzotinto," pencil-drawings, " poonah-paintings," and what not. " The Album " is to be found invariably upon the round rosewood brass-inlaid drawing-room table of the middle classes, and with a couple of " Annuals " besides, which flank it on the same table, represents the art of the house ; perhaps there is a portrait of the master of the house in the dining-room, grim-glancing from above the mantel-piece ; and of the mistress over the piano up stairs ; add to these some odious miniatures of the sons and daughters, on each side of the chim-ney-glass ; and here, commonly (we appeal to the reader if this is an overcharged picture), the collection ends.   The family goes to the Exhibition once a year, to the National Gallery once in ten years : to the former place they have an inducement to go ; there are their own portraits, or the portraits of their friends, or the portraits of public characters ; and you will see them infallibly wondering over No. 2645 in the catalogue, rep-resenting " The Portrait of a Lady," or of the " First Mayor of Little Pedlington since the passing of the Reform Bill ; " or else bustling and squeezing among the miniatures, where lies the chief attraction of the Gallery.   England has produced, owing to the effects of this class of admirers of art, two admi-rable, and five hundred very clever, portrait painters.   How many *artists?*   Let the reader count upon his five fingers, and see if, living at the present moment, he can name one for each.

If, from this examination of our own worthy middle classes, we look to the same class in France, what a difference do we find !   Humble *cafés* in country towns have their walls covered with pleasing picture papers, representing " *Les Gloires de l'Armée Française*," the " Seasons," the " Four Quarters of the World," " Cupid and Psyche," or some other allegory, landscape or history, rudely painted, as papers for walls usu-ally are ; but the figures are all tolerably well drawn ; and the

common taste, which has caused a demand for such things, is
undeniable. In Paris, the manner in which the *cafés* and
houses of the *restaurateurs* are ornamented, is, of course, a
thousand times richer, and nothing can be more beautiful, or
more exquisitely finished and correct, than the designs which
adorn many of them. We are not prepared to say what sums
were expended upon the painting of " Véry's " or " Véfour's,"
of the " Salle Musard," or of numberless other places of public
resort in the capital. There is many a shop-keeper whose sign
is a very tolerable picture ; and often have we stopped to admire
(the reader will give us credit for having remained *outside*) the
excellent workmanship of the grapes and vine-leaves over the
door of some very humble, dirty, inodorous shop of a *marchand
de vin*.

These, however, serve only to educate the public taste, and
are ornaments for the most part much too costly for the people.
But the same love of ornament which is shown in their public
places of resort, appears in their houses likewise ; and every
one of our readers who has lived in Paris, in any lodging,
magnificent or humble, with any family, however poor, may
bear witness how profusely the walls of his smart *salon* in the
English quarter, or of his little room *au sixième* in the Pays
Latin, has been decorated with prints of all kinds. In the first,
probably, with bad engravings on copper from the bad and
tawdry pictures of the artists of the time of the Empire ; in the
latter, with gay caricatures of Granville or Monnier : military
pieces, such as are dashed off by Raffet, Charlet, Vernet (one
can hardly say which of the three designers has the greatest
merit, or the most vigorous hand) ; or clever pictures from the
crayon of the Deverias, the admirable Roqueplan, or Decamp.
We have named here, we believe, the principal lithographic
artists in Paris ; and those — as doubtless there are many —
of our readers who have looked over Monsieur Aubert's port-
folios, or gazed at that famous caricature-shop window in the
Rue de Coq, or are even acquainted with the exterior of Monsieur Delaporte's little emporium in the Burlington Arcade,
need not be told how excellent the productions of all these
artists are in their *genre*. We get in these engravings the
loisirs of men of genius, not the finikin performances of labored
mediocrity, as with us : all these artists are good painters, as
well as good designers ; a design from them is worth a whole
gross of Books of Beauty ; and if we might raise a humble sup-
plication to the artists in our own country of similar merit — to
such men as Leslie, Maclise, Herbert, Cattermole, and others —

ıt would be, that they should, after the example of their French brethren and of the English landscape painters, take chalk in hand, produce their own copies of their own sketches, and never more draw a single " Forsaken One," " Rejected One," " Dejected One " at the entreaty of any publisher or for the pages of any Book of Beauty, Royalty, or Loveliness whatever.

Can there be a more pleasing walk in the whole world than a stroll through the Gallery of the Louvre on a fête-day ; not to look so much at the pictures as at the lookers-on? Thousands of the poorer classes are there : mechanics in their Sunday clothes, smiling grisettes, smart dapper soldiers of the line, with bronzed wondering faces, marching together in little companies of six or seven, and stopping every now and then at Napoleon or Leonidas as they appear in proper vulgar heroics in the pictures of David or Gros. The taste of these people will hardly be approved by the connoisseur, but they have *a* taste for art. Can the same be said of our lower classes, who, if they are inclined to be sociable and amused in their holidays, have no place of resort but the tap-room or tea-garden, and no food for conversation except such as can be built upon the politics or the police reports of the last Sunday paper? So much has Church and State puritanism done for us — so well has it succeeded in materializing and binding down to the earth the imagination of men, for which God has made another world (which certain statesmen take but too little into account) — that fair and beautiful world of heart, in which there *can* be nothing selfish or sordid, of which Dulness has forgotten the existence, and which Bigotry has endeavored to shut out from sight —

> " On a banni les démons et les fées,
>   Le raisonner tristement s'accrédite :
>   On court, helas! après la vérité :
>   Ah! croyez moi, l'erreur a son mérite ! "

We are not putting in a plea here for demons and fairies, as Voltaire does in the above exquisite lines ; nor about to expatiate on the beauties of error, for it has none ; but the clank of steam-engines, and the shouts of politicians, and the struggle for gain or bread, and the loud denunciations of stupid bigots, have wellnigh smothered poor Fancy among us. We boast of our science, and vaunt our superior morality. Does the latter exist? In spite of all the forms which our policy has invented to secure it — in spite of all the preachers, all the meeting-houses, and all the legislative enactments — if any person will

take upon himself the painful labor of purchasing and perusing
some of the cheap periodical prints which form the people's
library of amusement, and contain what may be presumed to
be their standard in matters of imagination and fancy, he will
see how false the claim is that we bring forward of superior
morality. The aristocracy who are so eager to maintain, were,
of course, not the last to feel the annoyance of the legislative
restrictions on the Sabbath, and eagerly seized upon that happy
invention for dissipating the gloom and *ennui* ordered by Act
of Parliament to prevail on that day — the Sunday paper. It
might be read in a club-room, where the poor could not see
how their betters ordained one thing for the vulgar, and another
for themselves ; or in an easy-chair, in the study, whither my
lord retires every Sunday for his devotions. It dealt in private
scandal and ribaldry, only the more piquant for its pretty flimsy
veil of *double-entendre*. It was a fortune to the publisher, and
it became a necessary to the reader, which he could not do
without, any more than without his snuff-box, his opera-box,
or his *chasse* after coffee. The delightful novelty could not for
any time be kept exclusively for the *haut ton ;* and from my
lord it descended to his valet or tradesmen, and from Grosvenor Square it spread all the town through ; so that now the
lower classes have their scandal and ribaldry organs, as well as
their betters (the rogues, they *will* imitate them !) and as their
tastes are somewhat coarser than my lord's, and their numbers
a thousand to one, why of course the prints have increased,
and the profligacy has been diffused in a ratio exactly pro-
portionable to the demand, until the town is infested with such
a number of monstrous publications of the kind as would have
put Abbé Dubois to the blush, or made Louis XV. cry shame.
Talk of English morality ! — the worst licentiousness, in the
worst period of the French monarchy, scarcely equalled the
wickedness of this Sabbath-keeping country of ours.

The reader will be glad, at last, to come to the conclusion
that we would fain draw from all these descriptions — why does
this immorality exist? Because the people *must* be amused,
and have not been taught *how ;* because the upper classes,
frightened by stupid cant, or absorbed in material wants, have
not as yet learned the refinement which only the cultivation of
art can give ; and when their intellects are uneducated, and
their tastes are coarse, the tastes and amusements of classes
still more ignorant must be coarse and vicious likewise, in an
increased proportion.

Such discussions and violent attacks upon high and low,

Sabbath Bills, politicians, and what not, may appear, perhaps, out of place in a few pages which purport only to give an account of some French drawings : all we would urge is, that, in France, these prints are made because they are liked and appreciated ; with us they are not made, because they are not liked and appreciated : and the more is the pity. Nothing merely intellectual will be popular among us : we do not love beauty for beauty's sake, as Germans ; or wit, for wit's sake, as the French : for abstract art we have no appreciation. We admire H. B.'s caricatures, because they are the caricatures of well-known political characters, not because they are witty ; and Boz, because he writes us good palpable stories (if we may use such a word to a story) ; and Madame Vestris, because she has the most beautifully shaped legs ; — the *art* of the designer, the writer, the actress (each admirable in its way,) is a very minor consideration ; each might have ten times the wit, and would be quite unsuccessful without their substantial points of popularity.

In France such matters are far better managed, and the love of art is a thousand times more keen ; and (from this feeling, surely) how much superiority is there in French *society* over our own ; how much better is social happiness understood ; how much more manly equality is there between Frenchman and Frenchman, than between rich and poor in our own country, with all our superior wealth, instruction, and political freedom ! There is, amongst the humblest, a gayety, cheerfulness, politeness, and sobriety, to which, in England, no class can show a parallel : and these, be it remembered, are not only qualities for holidays, but for working-days too, and add to the enjoyment of human life as much as good clothes, good beef, or good wages. If, to our freedom, we could but add a little of their happiness ! — it is one, after all, of the cheapest commodities in the world, and in the power of every man (with means of gaining decent bread) who has the will or the skill to use it.

We are not going to trace the history of the rise and progress of art in France ; our business, at present, is only to speak of one branch of art in that country — lithographic designs, and those chiefly of a humorous character. A history of French caricature was published in Paris, two or three years back, illustrated by numerous copies of designs, from the time of Henry III. to our own day. We can only speak of this work from memory, having been unable, in London, to procure the sight of a copy ; but our impression, at the time we saw the collection, was as unfavorable as could possibly be: nothing could be more meagre than the wit, or poorer than the execution, of the whole set of drawings. Under the Empire, art, as may be imagined, was at a very low ebb; and, aping the Government of the day, and catering to the national taste and vanity, it was a kind of tawdry caricature of the sublime; of which the pictures of David and Girodet, and almost the entire collection now at the Luxembourg Palace, will give pretty fair examples. Swollen, distorted, unnatural, the painting was something like the politics of those days; with force in it, nevertheless, and something of grandeur, that will exist in spite of taste, and is born of energetic will. A man, disposed to write comparisons of characters, might, for instance, find some striking analogies between mountebank Murat, with his irresistible bravery and horsemanship, who was a kind of mixture of Duguesclin and Ducrow, and Mountebank David, a fierce, powerful painter and genius, whose idea of beauty and sublimity seemed to have been gained from the bloody melodramas on the Boulevard. Both, however, were great in their way, and were worshipped as gods, in those heathen times of false belief and hero-worship.

As for poor caricature and freedom of the press, they, like the rightful princess in a fairy tale, with the merry fantastic dwarf, her attendant, were entirely in the power of the giant who ruled the land. The Princess Press was so closely watched and guarded (with some little show, nevertheless, of respect for her rank), that she dared not utter a word of her own thoughts; and, for poor Caricature, he was gagged, and put out of the way altogether: imprisoned as completely as ever Asmodeus was in his phial.

How the Press and her attendant fared in succeeding reigns, is well known; their condition was little bettered by the downfall of Napoleon: with the accession of Charles X. they were more oppressed even than before — more than they could bear; for so hard were they pressed, that, as one has seen when sailors are working a capstan, back of a sudden the bars flew, knocking to the earth the men who were endeavoring to work them. The Revolution came, and up sprung Caricature in France; all sorts of fierce epigrams were discharged at the flying monarch, and speedily were prepared, too, for the new one.

About this time there lived at Paris (if our information be correct) a certain M. Philipon, an indifferent artist (painting was his profession), a tolerable designer, and an admirable wit

M. Philipon designed many caricatures himself, married the sister of an eminent publisher of prints (M. Aubert), and the two, gathering about them a body of wits and artists like themselves, set up journals of their own : — *La Caricature*, first published once a week ; and the *Charivari* afterwards, a daily paper, in which a design also appears daily.

At first the caricatures inserted in the *Charivari* were chiefly political ; and a most curious contest speedily commenced between the State and M. Philipon's little army in the Galérie Véro-Dodat. Half a dozen poor artists on the one side, and his Majesty Louis Philippe, his august family, and the numberless placemen and supporters of the monarchy, on the other ; it was something like Thersites girding at Ajax, and piercing through the folds of the *clypei septemplicis* with the poisonous shafts of his scorn. Our French Thersites was not always an honest opponent, it must be confessed ; and many an attack was made upon the gigantic enemy, which was cowardly, false, and malignant. But to see the monster writhing under the effects of the arrow — to see his uncouth fury in return, and the blind blows that he dealt at his diminutive opponent ! — not one of these told in a hundred ; when they *did* tell, it may be imagined that they were fierce enough in all conscience, and served almost to annihilate the adversary.

To speak more plainly, and to drop the metaphor of giant and dwarf, the King of the French suffered so much, his Ministers were so mercilessly ridiculed, his family and his own remarkable figure drawn with such odious and grotesque resemblance, in fanciful attitudes, circumstances, and disguises, so ludicrously mean, and often so appropriate, that the King was obliged to descend into the lists and battle his ridiculous enemy in form. Prosecutions, seizures, fines, regiments of furious legal officials, were first brought into play against poor M. Philipon and his little dauntless troop of malicious artists ; some few were bribed out of his ranks ; and if they did not, like Gilray in England, turn their weapons upon their old friends, at least laid down their arms, and would fight no more. The bribes, fines, indictments, and loud-tongued *avocats du Roi* made no impression ; Philipon repaired the defeat of a fine by some fresh and furious attack upon his great enemy ; if his epigrams were more covert, they were no less bitter ; if he was beaten a dozen times before a jury, he had eighty or ninety victories to show in the same field of battle, and every victory and every defeat brought him new sympathy. Every one who was at Paris a few years since must recollect the famous "*poire*" which was chalked upon all the walls of the city, and which bore so ludicrous a resemblance to Louis Philippe. The *poire* became an object of prosecution, and M. Philipon appeared before a jury to answer for the crime of inciting to contempt against the King's person, by giving such a ludicrous version of his face. Philipon, for defence, produced a sheet of paper, and drew a *poire*, a real large Burgundy pear: in the lower parts round and capacious, narrower near the stalk, and crowned with two or three careless leaves. "There was no treason in *that*," he said to the jury; "could any one object to such a harmless botanical representation?" Then he drew a second pear, exactly like the former, except that one or two lines were scrawled in the midst of it, which bore somehow a ludicrous resemblance to the eyes, nose, and mouth of a celebrated personage; and, lastly, he drew the exact portrait of Louis Philippe; the well-known toupet, the ample whiskers and jowl were there, neither extenuated nor set down in malice. "Can I help it, gentlemen of the jury, then," said he, "if his Majesty's face is like a pear? Say yourselves, respectable citizens, is it, or is it not, like a pear?" Such eloquence could not fail of its effect; the artist was acquitted, and *La poire* is immortal.

At last came the famous September laws: the freedom of the Press, which, from August, 1830, was to be "*désormais une vérité*," was calmly strangled by the Monarch who had gained his crown for his supposed championship of it; by his Ministers, some of whom had been stout Republicans on paper but a few years before; and by the Chamber, which, such is the blessed constitution of French elections, will generally vote, unvote, revote in any way the Government wishes. With a wondrous union, and happy forgetfulness of principle, monarch, ministers, and deputies issued the restriction laws; the Press was sent to prison; as for the poor dear Caricature, it was fairly murdered. No more political satires appear now, and "through the eye, correct the heart;" no more *poires* ripen on the walls of the metropolis; Philipon's political occupation is gone.

But there is always food for satire; and the French caricaturists, being no longer allowed to hold up to ridicule and reprobation the King and the deputies, have found no lack of subjects for the pencil in the ridicules and rascalities of common life. We have said that public decency is greater amongst the French than amongst us, which, to some of our readers, may appear paradoxical; but we shall not attempt to argue that, in private roguery, our neighbors are not our equals. The *procès* of Gisquet, which has appeared lately in the papers, shows how deep the demoralization must be, and how a Government, based itself on dishonesty (a tyranny, that is, under the title and fiction of a democracy,) must practise and admit corruption in its own and in its agents' dealings with the nation. Accordingly, of cheating contracts, of ministers dabbling with the funds, or extracting underhand profits for the granting of unjust privileges and monopolies, — of grasping, envious police restrictions, which destroy the freedom, and, with it, the integrity of commerce, — those who like to examine such details may find plenty in French history : the whole French finance system has been a swindle from the days of Luvois, or Law, down to the present time. The Government swindles the public, and the small traders swindle their customers, on the authority and example of the superior powers. Hence the art of roguery, under such high patronage, maintains in France a noble front of impudence, and a fine audacious openness, which it does not wear in our country.

Among the various characters of roguery which the French satirists have amused themselves by depicting, there is one of which the *greatness* (using the word in the sense which Mr. Jonathan Wild gave to it) so far exceeds that of all others, embracing, as it does, all in turn, that it has come to be considered the type of roguery in general ; and now, just as all the political squibs were made to come of old from the lips of Pasquin, all the reflections on the prevailing cant, knavery, quackery, humbug, are put into the mouth of Monsieur Robert Macaire.

A play was written, some twenty years since, called the "Auberge des Adrets," in which the characters of two robbers escaped from the galleys were introduced — Robert Macaire, the clever rogue above mentioned, and Bertrand, the stupid rogue, his friend, accomplice, butt, and scapegoat, on all occasions of danger. It is needless to describe the play — a witless performance enough, of which the joke was Macaire's exaggerated style of conversation, a farrago of all sorts of high-flown sentiments such as the French love to indulge in — contrasted with his actions, which were philosophically unscrupulous, and his appearance, which was most picturesquely sordid. The play had been acted, we believe, and forgotten, when a very clever actor, M. Frederick Lemaitre, took upon himself the performance of the character of Robert Macaire, and looked, spoke, and acted it to such admirable perfection, that the whole town

rung with applauses of the performance, and the caricaturists
delighted to copy his singular figure and costume. M. Robert
Macaire appears in a most picturesque green coat, with a
variety of rents and patches, a pair of crimson pantaloons ornamented in the same way, enormous whiskers and ringlets, an
enormous stock and shirt-frill, as dirty and ragged as stock and
shirt-frill can be, the relic of a hat very gayly cocked over one eye,
and a patch to take away somewhat from the brightness of the
other — these are the principal *pièces* of his costume — a snuff-
box like a creaking warming-pan, a handkerchief hanging together by a miracle, and a switch of about the thickness of a
man's thigh, formed the ornaments of this exquisite personage.
He is a compound of Fielding's " Blueskin " and Goldsmith's
" Beau Tibbs." He has the dirt and dandyism of the one, with
the ferocity of the other : sometimes he is made to swindle, but
where he can get a shilling more, M. Macaire will murder without scruple : he performs one and the other act (or any in the
scale between them) with a similar bland imperturbability, and
accompanies his actions with such philosophical remarks as
may be expected from a person of his talents, his energies, his
amiable life and character.

Bertrand is the simple recipient of Macaire's jokes, and
makes vicarious atonement for his crimes, acting, in fact, the
part which pantaloon performs in the pantomime, who is entirely
under the fatal influence of clown. He is quite as much a rogue
as that gentleman, but he has not his genius and courage. So,
in pantomimes, (it may, doubtless, have been remarked by the
reader,) clown always leaps first, pantaloon following after,
more clumsily and timidly than his bold and accomplished
friend and guide. Whatever blows are destined for clown, fall,
by some means of ill-luck, upon the pate of pantaloon : whenever the clown robs, the stolen articles are sure to be found in
his companion's pocket ; and thus exactly Robert Macaire and
his companion Bertrand are made to go through the world ;
both swindlers, but the one more accomplished than the other.
Both robbing all the world, and Robert robbing his friend, and,
in the event of danger, leaving him faithfully in the lurch.
There is, in the two characters, some grotesque good for the
spectator — a kind of " Beggars' Opera " moral.

Ever since Robert, with his dandified rags and airs, his cane
and snuff-box, and Bertrand with torn surtout and all-absorb-
ing pocket, have appeared on the stage, they have been popular
with the Parisians ; and with these two types of clever and
stupid knavery, M. Philipon and his companion Daumier have

created a world of pleasant satire upon all the prevailing abuses of the day.

Almost the first figure that these audacious caricaturists dared to depict was a political one : in Macaire's red breeches and tattered coat appeared no less a personage than the King himself — the old *Poire* — in a country of humbugs and swindlers the *facile princeps ;* fit to govern, as he is deeper than all the rogues in his dominions. Bertrand was opposite to him, and having listened with delight and reverence to some tale of knavery truly royal, was exclaiming with a look and voice expressive of the most intense admiration, " AH VIEUX BLA-GEUR ! va ! " — the word *blague* is untranslatable — it means *French* humbug as distinct from all other ; and only those who know the value of an epigram in France, an epigram so wonderfully just, a little word so curiously comprehensive, can fancy the kind of rage and rapture with which it was received. It was a blow that shook the whole dynasty. Thersites had there given such a wound to Ajax, as Hector in arms could scarcely have inflicted : a blow sufficient almost to create the madness to which the fabulous hero of Homer and Ovid fell a prey.

Not long, however, was French caricature allowed to attack personages so illustrious : the September laws came, and henceforth no more epigrams were launched against politics ; but the caricaturists were compelled to confine their satire to subjects and characters that had nothing to do with the State. The Duke of Orleans was no longer to figure in lithography as the fantastic Prince Rosolin ; no longer were multitudes (in chalk) to shelter under the enormous shadow of M. d'Argout's nose : Marshal Lobau's squirt was hung up in peace, and M. Thiers's pigmy figure and round spectacled face were no more to appear in print.* Robert Macaire was driven out of the Chambers and the Palace — his remarks were a great deal too appropriate and too severe for the ears of the great men who congregated in those places.

The Chambers and the Palace were shut to him ; but the rogue, driven out of his rogue's paradise, saw " that the world was all before him where to choose," and found no lack of opportunities for exercising his wit. There was the Bar, with its roguish practitioners, rascally attorneys, stupid juries, and forsworn judges ; there was the Bourse, with all its gambling, swindling, and hoaxing, its cheats and its dupes ; the Medical

---

* Almost all the principal public men had been most ludicrously caricatured in the *Charivari:* those mentioned above were usually depicted with the distinctive attributes mentioned by us.

Profession, and the quacks who ruled it, alternately ; the **Stage**, and the cant that was prevalent there ; the Fashion, and its thousand follies and extravagances. Robert Macaire had all these to *exploiter*. Of all the empire, through all the ranks, professions, the lies, crimes, and absurdities of men, he may make sport at will ; of all except of a certain class. Like Bluebeard's wife, he may see everything, but is bidden *to beware of the blue chamber*. Robert is more wise than Bluebeard's wife, and knows that it would cost him his head to enter it. Robert, therefore, keeps aloof for the moment. Would there be any use in his martyrdom? Bluebeard cannot live for ever ; perhaps, even now, those are on their way (one sees a suspicious cloud of dust or two) that are to destroy him.

In the meantime Robert and his friend have been furnishing the designs that we have before us, and of which perhaps the reader will be edified by a brief description. We are not, to be sure, to judge of the French nation by M. Macaire, any more than we are to judge of our own national morals in the last century by such a book as the "Beggars' Opera ; " but upon the morals and the national manners, works of satire afford a world of light that one would in vain look for in regular books of history. Doctor Smollett would have blushed to devote any considerable portion of his pages to a discussion of the acts and character of Mr. Jonathan Wild, such a figure being hardly admissible among the dignified personages who usually push all others out from the possession of the historical page ; but a chapter of that gentleman's memoirs, as they are recorded in that exemplary *recueil* — the "Newgate Calendar ; " nay, a canto of the great comic epic (involving many fables, and containing much exaggeration, but still having the seeds of truth) which the satirical poet of those days wrote in celebration of him — we mean Fielding's "History of Jonathan Wild the Great " — does seem to us to give a more curious picture of the manners of those times than any recognized history of them. At the close of his history of George II., Smollett condescends to give a short chapter on Literature and Manners. He speaks of Glover's "Leonidas," Cibber's "Careless Husband," the poems of Mason, Gray, the two Whiteheads, "the nervous style, extensive erudition, and superior sense of a Corke ; the delicate taste, the polished muse, and tender feeling of a Lyttelton." "King," he says, "shone unrivalled in Roman eloquence, the female sex distinguished themselves by their taste and ingenuity. Miss Carter rivalled the celebrated Dacier in learning and critical knowledge ; **Mrs. Lennox signalized** herself by many successful efforts of genius both in poetry and prose ; and Miss Reid excelled the celebrated Rosalba in portrait-painting, both in miniature and at large, in oil as well as in crayons.   The genius of Cervantes was transferred into the novels of Fielding, who painted the characters and ridiculed the follies of life with equal strength, humor, and propriety. The field of history and biography was cultivated by many writers of ability, among whom we distinguish the copious Guthrie, the circumstantial Ralph, the laborious Carte, the learned and elegant Robertson, and above all, the ingenious, penetrating, and comprehensive Hume," &c. &c.   We will quote no more of the passage.   Could a man in the best humor sit down to write a graver satire ?   Who cares for the tender muse of Lyttelton ?   Who knows the signal efforts of Mrs. Lennox's genius ?   Who has seen the admirable performances, in miniature and at large, in oil as well as in crayons, of Miss Reid? Laborious Carte, and circumstantial Ralph, and copious Guthrie, where are they, their works, and their reputation?   Mrs. Lennox's name is just as clean wiped out of the list of worthies as if she had never been born ; and Miss Reid, though she was once actual flesh and blood, " rival in miniature and at large " of the celebrated Rosalba, she is as if she had never been at all ; her little farthing rushlight of a soul and reputation having burnt out, and left neither wick nor tallow.   Death, too, has overtaken copious Guthrie and circumstantial Ralph.   Only a few know whereabouts is the grave where lies laborious Carte ; and yet, O wondrous power of genius !   Fielding's men and women are alive, though History's are not.   The progenitors of circumstantial Ralph sent forth, after much labor and pains of making, educating, feeding, clothing, a real man child, a great palpable mass of flesh, bones, and blood (we say nothing about the spirit), which was to move through the world, ponderous, writing histories, and to die, having achieved the title of circumstantial Ralph ; and lo ! without any of the trouble that the parents of Ralph had undergone, alone perhaps in a watch or spunging-house, fuddled most likely, in the blandest, easiest, and most good-humored way in the world, Henry Fielding makes a number of men and women on so many sheets of paper, not only more amusing than Ralph or Miss Reid, but more like flesh and blood, and more alive now than they.   Is not Amelia preparing her husband's little supper?   Is not Miss Snapp chastely preventing the crime of Mr. Firebrand?   Is not Parson Adams in the midst of his family, and Mr. Wild taking his last bowl of punch with the Newgate Ordinary?   Is not

every one of them a real substantial *have*-been personage now?
— more real than Reid or Ralph? For our parts, we will not
take upon ourselves to say that they do not exist somewhere
else : that the actions attributed to them have not really taken
place ; certain we are that they are more worthy of credence
than Ralph, who may or may not have been circumstantial ;
who may or may not even have existed, a point unworthy of
disputation. As for Miss Reid, we will take an affidavit that
neither in miniature nor at large did she excel the celebrated
Rosalba ; and with regard to Mrs. Lennox, we consider her
to be a mere figment, like Narcissa, Miss Tabitha Bramble, or
any hero or heroine depicted by the historian of " Peregrine
Pickle."

In like manner, after viewing nearly ninety portraits of
Robert Macaire and his friend Bertrand, all strongly resembling each other, we are inclined to believe in them as historical
personages, and to canvass gravely the circumstances of their
lives. Why should we not? Have we not their portraits? Are
not they sufficient proofs? If not, we must discredit Napoleon
(as Archbishop Whately teaches), for about his figure and himself we have no more authentic testimony.

Let the reality of M. Robert Macaire and his friend M.
Bertrand be granted, if but to gratify our own fondness for
those exquisite characters : we find the worthy pair in the
French capital, mingling with all grades of its society, *pars
magna* in the intrigues, pleasures, perplexities, rogueries, speculations, which are carried on in Paris, as in our own chief
city ; for it need not be said that roguery is of no country nor
clime, but finds ὡς πανταχοῦ γε πατρὶς ἡ βόσκουσα γῆ, is a citizen
of all countries where the quarters are good ; among our merry
neighbors it finds itself very much at its ease.

Not being endowed, then, with patrimonial wealth, but
compelled to exercise their genius to obtain distinction, or even
subsistence, we see Messrs. Bertrand and Macaire, by turns,
adopting all trades and professions, and exercising each with
their own peculiar ingenuity. As public men, we have spoken
already of their appearance in one or two important characters,
and stated that the Government grew fairly jealous of them,
excluding them from office, as the Whigs did Lord Brougham.
As private individuals, they are made to distinguish themselves
as the founders of journals, *sociétés en commandite* (companies
of which the members are irresponsible beyond the amount
of their shares), and all sorts of commercial speculations,
requiring intelligence and honesty on the part of the di-

rectors, confidence and liberal disbursements from the share-holders.

These are, among the French, so numerous, and have been of late years (in the shape of Newspaper Companies, Bitumen Companies, Galvanized-Iron Companies, Railroad Companies, &c.) pursued with such a blind *furor* and lust of gain, by that easily excited and imaginative people, that, as may be imagined, the satirist has found plenty of occasion for remark, and M. Macaire and his friend innumerable opportunities for exercising their talents.

We know nothing of M. Emile de Girardin, except that, in a duel, he shot the best man in France, Armand Carrel; and in Girardin's favor it must be said, that he had no other alternative; but was right in provoking the duel, seeing that the whole Republican party had vowed his destruction, and that he fought and killed their champion, as it were. We know nothing of M. Girardin's private character: but, as far as we can judge from the French public prints, he seems to be the most speculative of speculators, and, of course, a fair butt for the malice of the caricaturists. His one great crime, in the eyes of the French Republicans and Republican newspaper proprietors, was, that Girardin set up a journal, as he called it, "*franchement monarchique*,"— a journal in the pay of the monarchy, that is,— and a journal that cost only forty francs by the year. The *National* costs twice as much; the *Charivari* itself costs half as much again; and though all newspapers, of all parties, concurred in "snubbing" poor M. Girardin and his journal, the Republican prints, were by far the most bitter against him, thundering daily accusations and personalities; whether the abuse was well or ill founded, we know not. Hence arose the duel with Carrel; after the termination of which, Girardin put by his pistol, and vowed, very properly, to assist in the shedding of no more blood. Girardin had been the originator of numerous other speculations besides the journal: the capital of these, like that of the journal, was raised by shares, and the shareholders, by some fatality, have found themselves wofully in the lurch; while Girardin carries on the war gayly, is, or was, a member of the Chamber of Deputies, has money, goes to Court, and possesses a certain kind of reputation. He invented, we believe, the "Institution Agronome de Coetbo,"* the "Physionotype," the "Journal des Connoissances Utiles," the "Panthéon Littéraire." and the

* It is not necessary to enter into descriptions of these various inven-tions.

system of "Primes"—premiums, that is—to be given, by lottery, to certain subscribers in these institutions. Could Robert Macaire see such things going on, and have no hand in them?

Accordingly Messrs. Macaire and Bertrand are made the heroes of many speculations of the kind. In almost the first print of our collection, Robert discourses to Bertrand of his projects. "Bertrand," says the disinterested admirer of talent and enterprise, "j'adore l'industrie. Si tu veux nous créons une banque, mais là, une vraie banque : capital cent millions de millions, cent milliards de milliards d'actions. Nous enfonçons la banque de France, les banquiers, les banquistes ; nous enfonçons tout le monde." "Oui," says Bertrand, very calm and stupid, "mais les gendarmes?" "Que tu es bête, Bertrand : est-ce qu'on arrête un millionaire?" Such is the key to M. Macaire's philosophy ; and a wise creed too, as times go.

Acting on these principles, Robert appears soon after ; he has not created a bank, but a journal. He sits in a chair of state, and discourses to a shareholder. Bertrand, calm and stupid as before, stands humbly behind. "Sir," says the editor of *La Blague*, journal quotidienne, "our profits arise from a new combination. The journal costs twenty francs ; we sell it for twenty-three and a half. A million subscribers make three millions and a half of profits ; there are my figures ; contradict me by figures, or I will bring an action for libel." The reader may fancy the scene takes place in England, where many such a swindling prospectus has obtained credit ere now. At Plate 33, Robert is still a journalist ; he brings to the editor of a paper an article of his composition, a violent attack on a law. "My dear M. Macaire," says the editor, "this must be changed ; we must *praise* this law." "Bon, bon !" says our versatile Macaire. "Je vais retoucher ça, et je vous fais en faveur de la loi *un article mousseux*."

Can such things be? Is it possible that French journalists can so forget themselves? The rogues ! they should come to England and learn consistency. The honesty of the Press in England is like the air we breathe, without it we die. No, no ! in France, the satire may do very well ; but for England it is too monstrous. Call the press stupid, call it vulgar, call it violent,—but honest it *is*. Who ever heard of a journal changing its politics? *O tempora! O mores!* as Robert Macaire says, this would be carrying the joke too far.

When he has done with newspapers, Robert Macaire begins

to distinguish himself on 'Change,* as a creator of companies, a vender of shares, or a dabbler in foreign stock. "Buy my coal-mine shares," shouts Robert; "gold mines, silver mines, diamond mines, 'sont de la pot-bouille de la ratatouille en comparaison de ma houille.'" "Look," says he, on another occasion, to a very timid, open-countenanced client, "you have a property to sell! I have found the very man, a rich capitalist, a fellow whose bills are better than bank-notes." His client sells; the bills are taken in payment, and signed by that respectable capitalist, Monsieur de Saint Bertrand. At Plate 81, we find him inditing a circular letter to all the world, running thus: — "Sir, — I regret to say that your application for shares in the Consolidated European Incombustible Blacking Association cannot be complied with, as all the shares of the C. E. I. B. A. were disposed of on the day they were issued. I have, nevertheless, registered your name, and in case a second series should be put forth, I shall have the honor of immediately giving you notice. I am, sir, yours, &c., the Director, Robert Macaire." — "Print 300,000 of these," he says to Bertrand, "and poison all France with them." As usual, the stupid Bertrand remonstrates — "But we have not sold a single share; you have not a penny in your pocket, and" — "Bertrand, you are an ass; do as I bid you."

Will this satire apply anywhere in England? Have we any Consolidated European Blacking Associations amongst us? Have we penniless directors issuing El Dorado prospectuses, and jockeying their shares through the market? For information on this head, we must refer the reader to the newspapers; or if he be connected with the city, and acquainted with commercial men, he will be able to say whether *all* the persons whose names figure at the head of announcements of projected companies are as rich as Rothschild, or quite as honest as heart could desire.

When Macaire has sufficiently *exploité* the Bourse, whether as a gambler in the public funds or other companies, he sagely perceives that it is time to turn to some other profession, and, providing himself with a black gown, proposes blandly to Bertrand to set up — a new religion. "Mon ami," says the repentant sinner, "le temps de la commandite va passer, *mais les badauds ne passeront pas.*" (O rare sentence! it should be written in letters of gold!) "*Occupons nous de ce qui est éternel.* Si nous fassions une réligion?" On which M. Ber-

---

* We have given a description of a genteel Macaire in the account of M. de Bernard's novels.

trand remarks, "A religion! what the devil — a religion is not an easy thing to make." But Macaire's receipt is easy. "Get a gown, take a shop," he says, "borrow some chairs, preach about Napoleon, or the discovery of America, or Molière — and there's a religion for you."

We have quoted this sentence more for the contrast it offers with our own manners, than for its merits. After the noble paragraph, "Les badauds ne passeront pas. Occupons nous de ce qui est éternel," one would have expected better satire upon cant than the words that follow. We are not in a condition to say whether the subjects chosen are those that had been selected by Père Enfantin, or Chatel, or Lacordaire ; but the words are curious, we think, for the very reason that the satire is so poor. The fact is, there is no religion in Paris ; even clever M. Philipon, who satirizes everything, and must know, therefore, some little about the subject which he ridicules, has nothing to say but, "Preach a sermon, and that makes a religion ; anything will do." If *anything* will do, it is clear that the religious commodity is not in much demand. Tartuffe had better things to say about hypocrisy in his time ; but then Faith was alive ; now, there is no satirizing religious cant in France, for its contrary, true religion, has disappeared altogether ; and having no substance, can cast no shadow. If a satirist would lash the religious hypocrites in *England* now — the High Church hypocrites, the Low Church hypocrites, the promiscuous Dissenting hypocrites, the No Popery hypocrites — he would have ample subject enough. In France, the religious hypocrites went out with the Bourbons. Those who remain pious in that country (or, rather, we should say, in the capital, for of that we speak,) are unaffectedly so, for they have no worldly benefit to hope for from their piety ; the great majority have no religion at all, and do not scoff at the few, for scoffing is the minority's weapon, and is passed always to the weaker side, whatever that may be. Thus H. B. caricatures the Ministers : if by any accident that body of men should be dismissed from their situations, and be succeeded by H. B.'s friends, the Tories, — what must the poor artist do? He must pine away and die, if he be not converted ; he cannot always be paying compliments ; for caricature has a spice of Goethe's Devil in it, and is "der Geist der stets verneint," the Spirit that is always denying.

With one or two of the French writers and painters of caricatures, the King tried the experiment of bribery ; which succeeded occasionally in buying off the enemy, and bringing him from the republican to the royal camp ; but when there, the

deserter was never of any use.   Figaro, when so treated, grew
fat and desponding, and lost all his sprightly *verve ;* and Neme-
sis became as gentle as a Quakeress.   But these instances of
" ratting" were not many.   Some few poets were bought over ;
but, among men following the profession of the press, a change
of politics is an infringement of the point of honor, and a man
must *fight* as well as apostatize.   A very curious table might be
made, signalizing the difference of the moral standard between
us and the French.   Why is the grossness and indelicacy, publicly permitted in England, unknown in France, where private
morality is certainly at a lower ebb?   Why is the point of private honor now more rigidly maintained among the French?
Why is it, as it should be, a moral disgrace for a Frenchman to
go into debt, and no disgrace for him to cheat his customer?
Why is there more honesty and less — more propriety and less?
— and how are we to account for the particular vices or virtues
which belong to each nation in its turn?

The above is the Reverend M. Macaire's solitary exploit as
a spiritual swindler : as *Maître* Macaire in the courts of law,
as *avocat, avoué* — in a humbler capacity even, as a prisoner at
the bar, he distinguishes himself greatly, as may be imagined.
On one occasion we find the learned gentleman humanely visiting an unfortunate *détenu* — no other person, in fact, than his
friend M. Bertrand, who has fallen into some trouble, and is
awaiting the sentence of the law.   He begins —

" Mon cher Bertrand, donne moi cent écus, je te fais acquit-
ter d'emblée."

" J'ai pas d'argent."

" Hé bien, donne moi cent francs."

" Pas le sou."

" Tu n'as pas dix francs ? "

" Pas un liard."

" Alors donne moi tes bottes, je plaiderai la circonstance
atténuante."

The manner in which Maître Macaire soars from the *cent
écus* (a high point already) to the sublime of the boots, is in the
best comic style.   In another instance he pleads before a judge,
and, mistaking his client, pleads for defendant, instead of plaintiff.   " The infamy of the plaintiff's character, my *luds*, renders
his testimony on such a charge as this wholly unavailing."
" M. Macaire, M. Macaire," cries the attorney, in a fright,
" you are for the plaintiff ! "   " This, my lords, is what the
defendant *will say*.   This is the line of defence which the opposite party intend to pursue ; as if slanders like these could weigh

with an enlightened jury, or injure the spotless reputation of my client!" In this story and expedient M. Macaire has been indebted to the English bar. If there be an occupation for the English satirist in the exposing of the cant and knavery of the pretenders to religion, what room is there for him to lash the infamies of the law! On this point the French are babes in iniquity compared to us — a counsel prostituting himself for money is a matter with us so stale, that it is hardly food for satire: which, to be popular, must find some much more complicated and interesting knavery whereon to exercise its skill.

M. Macaire is more skilful in love than in law, and appears once or twice in a very amiable light while under the influence of the tender passion. We find him at the head of one of those useful establishments unknown in our country — a Bureau de Mariage: half a dozen of such places are daily advertised in the journals: and "une veuve de trente ans ayant une fortune de deux cent mille francs," or "une demoiselle de quinze ans, jolie, d'une famille très distinguée, qui possède trente mille livres de rentes," — continually, in this kind-hearted way, are offering themselves to the public: sometimes it is a gentleman, with a "physique agréable, — des talens de société" — and a place under Government, who makes a sacrifice of himself in a similar manner. In our little historical gallery we find this philanthropic anti-Malthusian at the head of an establishment of this kind, introducing a very meek, simple-looking bachelor to some distinguished ladies of his *connoissance*. "Let me present you, sir, to Madame de St. Bertrand" (it is our old friend), "veuve de la grande armée, et Mdlle Eloa de Wormspire. Ces dames brûlent de l'envie de faire votre connoissance. Je les ai invitées à dîner chez vous ce soir: vous nous menerez à l'opéra, et nous ferons une petite partie d'écarté. Tenez vous bien, M. Gobard! ces dames ont des projets sur vous!"

Happy Gobard! happy system, which can thus bring the pure and loving together, and acts as the best ally of Hymen! The announcement of the rank and titles of Madame de St. Bertrand — "veuve de la grande armée "— is very happy. "*La grande armée*" has been a father to more orphans, and a husband to more widows, than it ever made. Mistresses of *cafés*, old governesses, keepers of boarding-houses, genteel beggars, and ladies of lower rank still, have this favorite pedigree. They have all had *malheurs* (what kind it is needless to particularize), they are all connected with the *grand homme*, and their fathers were all colonels. This title exactly answers to the "clergyman's daughter" in England — as, "A young lady, the daughter of a clergyman, is desirous to teach," &c. ; "A clergyman's widow receives into her house a few select," and so forth. "Appeal to the benevolent. — By a series of unheard-of calamities, a young lady, daughter of a clergyman in the west of England, has been plunged," &c. &c. The difference is curious, as indicating the standard of respectability.

The male beggar of fashion is not so well known among us as in Paris, where street-doors are open ; six or eight families live in a house ; and the gentleman who earns his livelihood by this profession can make half a dozen visits without the trouble of knocking from house to house, and the pain of being observed by the whole street, while the footman is examining him from the area. Some few may be seen in England about the inns of court, where the locality is favorable (where, however, the owners of the chambers are not proverbially soft of heart, so that the harvest must be poor) ; but Paris is full of such adventurers, — fat, smooth-tongued, and well dressed, with gloves and gilt-headed canes, who would be insulted almost by the offer of silver, and expect your gold as their right. Among these, of course, our friend Robert plays his part ; and an excellent engraving represents him, snuff-box in hand, advancing to an old gentleman, whom, by his poodle, his powdered head, and his drivelling, stupid look, one knows to be a Carlist of the old régime. "I beg pardon," says Robert ; "is it really yourself to whom I have the honor of speaking?" — "It is." "Do you take snuff?" — "I thank you." — "Sir, I have had misfortunes — I want assistance. I am a Vendéan of illustrious birth. You know the family of *Macairbec* — we are of Brest. My grandfather served the King in his galleys ; my father and I belong, also, to the marine. Unfortunate suits at law have plunged us into difficulties, and I do not hesitate to ask you for the succor of ten francs." — "Sir, I never give to those I don't know." — "Right, sir, perfectly right. Perhaps you will have the kindness to *lend* me ten francs?"

The adventures of Doctor Macaire need not be described, because the different degrees in quackery which are taken by that learned physician are all well known in England, where we have the advantage of many higher degrees in the science, which our neighbors know nothing about. We have not Hahnemann, but we have his disciples ; we have not Broussais, but we have the College of Health ; and surely a dose of Morrison's pills is a sublimer discovery than a draught of hot water. We

had St. John Long, too — where is his science? — and we are
credibly informed that some important cures have been effected
by the inspired dignitaries of " the church" in Newman Street
— which, if it continue to practise, will sadly interfere with the
profits of the regular physicians, and where the miracles of the
Abbé of Paris are about to be acted over again.

In speaking of M. Macaire and his adventures, we have
managed so entirely to convince ourselves of the reality of the
personage, that we have quite forgotten to speak of Messrs.
Philipon and Daumier, who are, the one the inventor, the other
the designer, of the Macaire Picture Gallery. As works of
esprit, these drawings are not more remarkable than they are
as works of art, and we never recollect to have seen a series of
sketches possessing more extraordinary cleverness and variety.
The countenance and figure of Macaire and the dear stupid
Bertrand are preserved, of course, with great fidelity throughout; but the admirable way in which each fresh character is
conceived, the grotesque appropriateness of Robert's every successive attitude and gesticulation, and the variety of Bertrand's
postures of invariable repose, the exquisite fitness of all the
other characters, who act their little part and disappear from
the scene, cannot be described on paper, or too highly lauded.
The figures are very carelessly drawn; but, if the reader can
understand us, all the attitudes and limbs are perfectly *conceived*,
and wonderfully natural and various. After pondering over
these drawings for some hours, as we have been while compiling
this notice of them, we have grown to believe that the personages are real, and the scenes remain imprinted on the brain as
if we had absolutely been present at their acting. Perhaps the
clever way in which the plates are colored, and the excellent
effect which is put into each, may add to this illusion. Now,
in looking, for instance, at H. B.'s slim vapory figures, they
have struck us as excellent *likenesses* of men and women, but
no more: the bodies want spirit, action, and individuality.
George Cruikshank, as a humorist, has quite as much genius,
but he does not know the art of " effect" so well as Monsieur
Daumier; and, if we might venture to give a word of advice to
another humorous designer, whose works are extensively circu-
lated — the illustrator of " Pickwick" and " Nicholas Nickleby,"
— it would be to study well these caricatures of Monsieur
Daumier; who, though he executes very carelessly, knows very
well what he would express, indicates perfectly the attitude
and identity of his figure, and is quite aware, beforehand, of
the effect which he intends to produce. The one we should

fancy to be a practised artist, taking his ease; the other, a young one, somewhat bewildered: a very clever one, however, who, if he would think more, and exaggerate less, would add not a little to his reputation.

Having pursued, all through these remarks, the comparison between English art and French art, English and French humor, manners, and morals, perhaps we should endeavor, also, to write an analytical essay on English cant or humbug, as distinguished from French. It might be shown that the latter was more picturesque and startling, the former more substantial and positive. It has none of the poetic flights of the French genius, but advances steadily, and gains more ground in the end than its sprightlier compeer. But such a discussion would carry us through the whole range of French and English history, and the reader has probably read quite enough of the subject in this and the foregoing pages.

We shall, therefore, say no more of French and English caricatures generally, or of Mr. Macaire's particular accomplishments and adventures. They are far better understood by examining the original pictures, by which Philipon and Daumier have illustrated them, than by translations first into print and afterwards into English. They form a very curious and instructive commentary upon the present state of society in Paris, and a hundred years hence, when the whole of this struggling, noisy, busy, merry race shall have exchanged their pleasures or occupations for a quiet coffin (and a tawdry lying epitaph) at Montmartre, or Père la Chaise; when the follies here recorded shall have been superseded by new ones, and the fools now so active shall have given up the inheritance of the world to their children: the latter will, at least, have the advantage of knowing, intimately and exactly, the manners of life and being of their grandsires, and calling up, when they so choose it, our ghosts from the grave, to live, love, quarrel, swindle, suffer, and struggle on blindly as of yore. And when the amused specula tor shall have laughed sufficiently at the immensity of our follies, and the paltriness of our aims, smiled at our exploded superstitions, wondered how this man should be considered great, who is now clean forgotten (as copious Guthrie before mentioned); how this should have been thought a patriot who is but a knave spouting commonplace; or how that should have been dubbed a philosopher who is but a dull fool, blinking solemn, and pretending to see in the dark; when he shall have examined all these at his leisure, smiling in a pleasant contemp and good-humored superiority, and thanking heaven for his increased lights, he will shut the book, and be a fool as his fathers were before him.

It runs in the blood. Well hast thou said, O ragged Macaire, — " Le jour va passer, MAIS LES BADAUDS NE PASSE-RONT PAS."

LITTLE POINSINET.

ABOUT the year 1760, there lived, at Paris, a little fellow, who was the darling of all the wags of his acquaintance. Nature seemed, in the formation of this little man, to have amused herself, by giving loose to half a hundred of her most comical caprices. He had some wit and drollery of his own, which sometimes rendered his sallies very amusing; but, where his friends laughed with him once, they laughed at him a thousand times, for he had a fund of absurdity in himself that was more pleasant than all the wit in the world. He was as proud as a peacock, as wicked as an ape, and as silly as a goose. He did not possess one single grain of common sense; but, in revenge, his pretensions were enormous, his ignorance vast, and his credulity more extensive still. From his youth upwards, he had read nothing but the new novels, and the verses in the almanacs, which helped him not a little in making, what he called, poetry of his own; for, of course, our little hero was a poet. All the common usages of life, all the ways of the world, and all the customs of society, seemed to be quite unknown to him; add to these good qualities, a magnificent conceit, a cowardice inconceivable, and a face so irresistibly comic, that every one who first beheld it was compelled to burst out a-laughing, and you will have some notion of this strange little gentleman. He was very proud of his voice, and uttered all his sentences in the richest tragic tone. He was little better than a dwarf; but he elevated his eyebrows, held up his neck, walked on the tips of his toes, and gave himself the airs of a giant. He had a little pair of bandy legs, which seemed much too short to support anything like a human body; but, by the help of these crooked supporters, he thought he could dance like a Grace; and, indeed, fancied all the graces possible were to be found in his person. His goggle eyes were always rolling about wildly, as if in correspondence with the disorder of his little brain ; and his countenance thus wore an expression of perpetual wonder. With such happy natural gifts, he not only fell into all traps that were laid for him, but seemed almost to go out of his way to seek them ; although, to be sure, his friends did not give him much trouble in that search, for they prepared hoaxes for him incessantly.

One day the wags introduced him to a company of ladies, who, though not countesses and princesses exactly, took, nevertheless, those titles upon themselves for the nonce ; and were all, for the same reason, violently smitten with Master Poinsinet's person. One of them, the lady of the house, was especially tender ; and, seating him by her side at supper, so plied him with smiles, ogles, and champagne, that our little hero grew crazed with ecstasy, and wild with love. In the midst of his happiness, a cruel knock was heard below, accompanied by quick loud talking, swearing, and shuffling of feet : you would have thought a regiment was at the door. "Oh heavens!" cried the marchioness, starting up, and giving to the hand of Poinsinet one parting squeeze ; "fly — fly, my Poinsinet : 'tis the colonel — my husband!" At this, each gentleman of the party rose, and, drawing his rapier, vowed to cut his way through the colonel and all his *mousquetaires*, or die, if need be, by the side of Poinsinet.

The little fellow was obliged to lug out his sword too, and went shuddering down stairs, heartily repenting of his passion for marchionesses. When the party arrived in the street, they found, sure enough, a dreadful company of *mousquetaires*, as they seemed, ready to oppose their passage. Swords crossed, — torches blazed ; and, with the most dreadful shouts and imprecations, the contending parties rushed upon one another ; the friends of Poinsinet surrounding and supporting that little warrior, as the French knights did King Francis at Pavia, otherwise the poor fellow certainly would have fallen down in the gutter from fright.

But the combat was suddenly interrupted ; for the neighbors, who knew nothing of the trick going on, and thought the brawl was real, had been screaming with all their might for the police, who began about this time to arrive. Directly they appeared, friends and enemies of Poinsinet at once took to their heels ; and, in *this* part of the transaction, at least, our hero himself showed that he was equal to the longest-legged grenadier that ever ran away.

When, at last, those little bandy legs of his had borne him safely to his lodgings, all Poinsinet's friends crowded round him, to congratulate him on his escape and his valor.

"Egad, how he pinked that great red-haired fellow!" said one.

"No; did I?" said Poinsinet.

"Did you? Psha! don't try to play the modest, and humbug *us;* you know you did. I suppose you will say, next, that you were not for three minutes point to point with Cartentierce himself, the most dreadful swordsman of the army."

"Why, you see," says Poinsinet, quite delighted, "it was so dark that I did not know with whom I was engaged; although, *corbleu,* I *did for* one or two of the fellows." And after a little more of such conversation, during which he was fully persuaded that he had done for a dozen of the enemy at least, Poinsinet went to bed, his little person trembling with fright and pleasure; and he fell asleep, and dreamed of rescuing ladies, and destroying monsters, like a second Amadis de Gaul.

When he awoke in the morning, he found a party of his friends in his room: one was examining his coat and waistcoat; another was casting many curious glances at his inexpressibles. "Look here!" said this gentleman, holding up the garment to the light; "one — two — three gashes! I am hanged if the cowards did not aim at Poinsinet's legs! There are four holes in the sword arm of his coat, and seven have gone right through coat and waistcoat. Good heaven! Poinsinet, have you had a surgeon to your wounds?"

"Wounds!" said the little man, springing up, "I don't know — that is, I hope — that is — O Lord! O Lord! I hope I'm not wounded!" and, after a proper examination, he discovered he was not.

"Thank heaven! thank heaven!" said one of the wags (who, indeed, during the slumbers of Poinsinet had been occupied in making these very holes through the garments of that individual), "if you have escaped, it is by a miracle. Alas! alas! all your enemies have not been so lucky."

"How! is anybody wounded?" said Poinsinet.

"My dearest friend, prepare yourself; that unhappy man who came to revenge his menaced honor — that gallant officer — that injured husband, Colonel Count de Cartentierce —"

"Well?"

"Is NO MORE! he died this morning, pierced through with

12

nineteen wounds from your hand, and calling upon his country to revenge his murder."

When this awful sentence was pronounced, all the auditory gave a pathetic and simultaneous sob; and as for Poinsinet, he sank back on his bed with a howl of terror, which would have melted a Visigoth to tears, or to laughter. As soon as his terror and remorse had, in some degree, subsided, his comrades spoke to him of the necessity of making his escape; and, huddling on his clothes, and bidding them all a tender adieu, he set off, incontinently, without his breakfast, for England, America, or Russia, not knowing exactly which.

One of his companions agreed to accompany him on a part of this journey, — that is, as far as the barrier of St. Denis, which is, as everybody knows, on the high road to Dover; and there, being tolerably secure, they entered a tavern for breakfast; which meal, the last that he ever was to take, perhaps, in his native city, Poinsinet was just about to discuss, when, behold! a gentleman entered the apartment where Poinsinet and his friend were seated, and, drawing from his pocket a paper, with " Au nom du Roy" flourished on the top, read from it, or rather from Poinsinet's own figure, his exact *signalement*, laid his hand on his shoulder, and arrested him in the name of the King, and of the provost-marshal of Paris. " I arrest you, sir," said he, gravely, " with regret; you have slain, with seventeen wounds, in single combat, Colonel Count de Cartentierce, one of his Majesty's household; and, as his murderer, you fall under the immediate authority of the provost-marshal, and die without trial or benefit of clergy."

You may fancy how the poor little man's appetite fell when he heard this speech. " In the provost-marshal's hands?" said his friend : " then it is all over, indeed! When does my poor friend suffer, sir?"

" At half-past six o'clock, the day after to-morrow," said the officer, sitting down, and helping himself to wine. " But stop," said he, suddenly; " sure I can't mistake? Yes — no — yes, it is. My dear friend, my dear Durand! don't you recollect your old schoolfellow, Antoine?" And herewith the officer flung himself into the arms of Durand, Poinsinet's comrade, and they performed a most affecting scene of friendship.

" This may be of some service to you," whispered Durand to Poinsinet; and, after some further parley, he asked the officer when he was bound to deliver up his prisoner; and, hearing that he was not called upon to appear at the Marshalsea before six o'clock at night, Monsieur Durand prevailed upon Monsieur Antoine to wait until that hour, and in the meantime to allow his prisoner to walk about the town in his company. This request was, with a little difficulty, granted; and poor Poinsinet begged to be carried to the houses of his various friends, and bid them farewell. Some were aware of the trick that had been played upon him: others were not; but the poor little man's credulity was so great, that it was impossible to undeceive him; and he went from house to house bewailing his fate, and followed by the complaisant marshal's officer.

The news of his death he received with much more meekness than could have been expected; but what he could not reconcile to himself was, the idea of dissection afterwards. "What can they want with me?" cried the poor wretch, in an unusual fit of candor. "I am very small and ugly; it would be different if I were a tall fine-looking fellow." But he was given to understand that beauty made very little difference to the surgeons, who, on the contrary, would, on certain occasions, prefer a deformed man to a handsome one; for science was much advanced by the study of such monstrosities. With this reason Poinsinet was obliged to be content; and so paid his rounds of visits, and repeated his dismal adieux.

The officer of the provost-marshal, however amusing Poinsinet's woes might have been, began, by this time, to grow very weary of them, and gave him more than one opportunity to escape. He would stop at shop-windows, loiter round corners, and look up in the sky, but all in vain: Poinsinet would not escape, do what the other would. At length, luckily, about dinner-time, the officer met one of Poinsinet's friends and his own: and the three agreed to dine at a tavern, as they had breakfasted; and here the officer, who vowed that he had been up for five weeks incessantly, fell suddenly asleep, in the profoundest fatigue; and Poinsinet was persuaded, after much hesitation on his part, to take leave of him.

And now, this danger overcome, another was to be avoided. Beyond a doubt the police were after him, and how was he to avoid them? He must be disguised, of course; and one of his friends, a tall, gaunt lawyer's clerk, agreed to provide him with habits.

So little Poinsinet dressed himself out in the clerk's dingy black suit, of which the knee-breeches hung down to his heels, and the waist of the coat reached to the calves of his legs; and, furthermore, he blacked his eyebrows, and wore a huge black periwig, in which his friend vowed that no one could recognize him. But the most painful incident, with regard to the periwig, was, that Poinsinet, whose solitary beauty — if beauty it might be called — was a head of copious, curling, yellow hair, was compelled to snip off every one of his golden locks, and to rub the bristles with a black dye; "for if your wig were to come off," said the lawyer, "and your fair hair to tumble over your shoulders, every man would know, or at least suspect you." So off the locks were cut, and in his black suit and periwig little Poinsinet went abroad.

His friends had their cue; and when he appeared amongst them, not one seemed to know him. He was taken into companies where his character was discussed before him, and his wonderful escape spoken of. At last he was introduced to the very officer of the provost-marshal who had taken him into custody, and who told him that he had been dismissed the provost's service, in consequence of the escape of the prisoner. Now, for the first time, poor Poinsinet thought himself tolerably safe, and blessed his kind friends who had procured for him such a complete disguise. How this affair ended I know not, — whether some new lie was coined to account for his release, or whether he was simply told that he had been hoaxed: it mattered little; for the little man was quite as ready to be hoaxed the next day.

Poinsinet was one day invited to dine with one of the servants of the Tuileries; and, before his arrival, a person in company had been decorated with a knot of lace and a gold key, such as chamberlains wear; he was introduced to Poinsinet as the Count de Truchses, chamberlain to the King of Prussia. After dinner the conversation fell upon the Count's visit to Paris; when his Excellency, with a mysterious air, vowed that he had only come for pleasure. "It is mighty well," said a third person, "and, of course, we can't cross-question your lordship too closely;" but at the same time it was hinted to Poinsinet that a person of such consequence did not travel for *nothing*, with which opinion Poinsinet solemnly agreed; and, indeed, it was borne out by a subsequent declaration of the Count, who condescended, at last, to tell the company, in confidence, that he *had* a mission, and a most important one — to find, namely, among the literary men of France, a governor for the Prince Royal of Prussia. The company seemed astonished that the King had not made choice of Voltaire or D'Alembert, and mentioned a dozen other distinguished men who might be competent to this important duty; but the Count, as may be imagined, found objections to every one of them; and, at last, one of the guests said, that, if his Prussian Majesty was not particular as to age, he knew a person more fitted for the place than any other who could be found, — his honorable friend, M. Poinsinet, was the individual to whom he alluded.

"Good heavens!" cried the Count, "is it possible that the celebrated Poinsinet would take such a place? I would give the world to see him?" And you may fancy how Poinsinet simpered and blushed when the introduction immediately took place.

The Count protested to him that the King would be charmed to know him; and added, that one of his operas (for it must be told that our little friend was a vaudeville-maker by trade) had been acted seven-and-twenty times at the theatre at Potsdam. His Excellency then detailed to him all the honors and privileges which the governor of the Prince Royal might expect; and all the guests encouraged the little man's vanity, by asking him for his protection and favor. In a short time our hero grew so inflated with pride and vanity, that he was for patronizing the chamberlain himself, who proceeded to inform him that he was furnished with all the necessary powers by his sovereign, who had specially enjoined him to confer upon the future governor of his son the royal order of the Black Eagle.

Poinsinet, delighted, was ordered to kneel down; and the Count produced a large yellow ribbon, which he hung over his shoulder, and which was, he declared, the grand cordon of the order. You must fancy Poinsinet's face, and excessive delight at this; for as for describing them, nobody can. For four-and-twenty hours the happy chevalier paraded through Paris with this flaring yellow ribbon; and he was not undeceived until his friends had another trick in store for him.

He dined one day in the company of a man who understood a little of the noble art of conjuring, and performed some clever tricks on the cards. Poinsinet's organ of wonder was enormous; he looked on with the gravity and awe of a child, and thought the man's tricks sheer miracles. It wanted no more to set his companions to work.

"Who is this wonderful man?" said he to his neighbor.

"Why," said the other, mysteriously, "one hardly knows who he is; or, at least, one does not like to say to such an indiscreet fellow as you are." Poinsinet at once swore to be secret. "Well, then," said his friend, "you will hear that man — that wonderful man — called by a name which is not his: his real name is Acosta: he is a Portuguese Jew, a Rosicrucian, and Cabalist of the first order, and compelled to leave Lisbon for fear of the Inquisition. He performs here, as you see, some extraordinary things, occasionally; but the master of the house, who loves him excessively, would not, for the world, that his name should be made public."

" Ah, bah!" said Poinsinet, who affected the *bel esprit;* "you don't mean to say that you believe in magic, and cabalas, and such trash?"

" Do I not? You shall judge for yourself." And, accordingly, Poinsinet was presented to the magician, who pretended to take a vast liking for him, and declared that he saw in him certain marks which would infallibly lead him to great eminence in the magic art, if he chose to study it.

Dinner was served, and Poinsinet placed by the side of the miracle-worker, who became very confidential with him, and promised him — ay, before dinner was over — a remarkable instance of his power. Nobody, on this occasion, ventured to cut a single joke against poor Poinsinet; nor could he fancy that any trick was intended against him, for the demeanor of the society towards him was perfectly grave and respectful, and the conversation serious. On a sudden, however, somebody exclaimed, "Where is Poinsinet? Did any one see him leave the room?"

All the company exclaimed how singular the disappearance was; and Poinsinet himself, growing alarmed, turned round to his neighbor, and was about to explain.

" Hush!" said the magician, in a whisper; "I told you that you should see what I could do. *I have made you invisible;* be quiet, and you shall see some more tricks that I shall play with these fellows."

Poinsinet remained then silent, and listened to his neighbors, who agreed, at last, that he was a quiet, orderly personage, and had left the table early, being unwilling to drink too much. Presently they ceased to talk about him, and resumed their conversation upon other matters.

At first it was very quiet and grave, but the master of the house brought back the talk to the subject of Poinsinet, and uttered all sorts of abuse concerning him. He begged the gentleman, who had introduced such a little scamp into his house, to bring him thither no more: whereupon the other took up, warmly, Poinsinet's defence; declared that he was a man of the greatest merit, frequenting the best society, and remarkable for his talents as well as his virtues.

" Ah!" said Poinsinet to the magician, quite charmed at what he heard, "how ever shall I thank you, my dear sir, for thus showing me who my true friends are?"

The magician promised him still further favors in prospect; and told him to look out now, for he was about to throw all the company into a temporary fit of madness, which, no doubt, would be very amusing.

In consequence, all the company, who had heard every syllable of the conversation, began to perform the most extraordinary antics, much to the delight of Poinsinet. One asked a nonsensical question, and the other delivered an answer not at all to the purpose. If a man asked for a drink, they poured him out a pepper-box or a napkin : they took a pinch of snuff, and swore it was excellent wine ; and vowed that the bread was the most delicious mutton ever tasted. The little man was delighted.

" Ah ! " said he, " these fellows are prettily punished for their rascally backbiting of me ! "

" Gentlemen," said the host, " I shall now give you some celebrated champagne," and he poured out to each a glass of water.

" Good heavens ! " said one, spitting it out, with the most horrible grimace, " where did you get this detestable claret? "

" Ah, faugh ! " said a second, " I never tasted such vile corked burgundy in all my days ! " and he threw the glass of water into Poinsinet's face, as did half a dozen of the other guests, drenching the poor wretch to the skin. To complete this pleasant illusion, two of the guests fell to boxing across Poinsinet, who received a number of the blows, and received them with the patience of a fakir, feeling himself more flattered by the precious privilege of beholding this scene invisible, than hurt by the blows and buffets which the mad company bestowed upon him.

The fame of this adventure spread quickly over Paris, and all the world longed to have at their houses the representation of *Poinsinet the Invisible*. The servants and the whole company used to be put up to the trick ; and Poinsinet, who believed in his invisibility as much as he did in his existence, went about with his friend and protector the magician. People, of course, never pretended to see him, and would very often not talk of him at all for some time, but hold sober conversation about anything else in the world. When dinner was served, of course there was no cover laid for Poinsinet, who carried about a little stool, on which he sat by the side of the magician, and always ate off his plate. Everybody was astonished at the magician's appetite and at the quantity of wine he drank ; as for little Poinsinet, he never once suspected any trick, and had such a confidence in his magician, that, I do believe, if the latter had told him to fling himself out of window, he would have done so, without the slightest trepidation.

Among other mystifications in which the Portuguese enchanter plunged him, was one which used to afford always a good deal of amusement. He informed Poinsinet, with great mystery, that *he was not himself;* he was not, that is to say, that ugly, deformed little monster, called Poinsinet; but that his birth was most illustrious, and his real name *Polycarte.* He was, in fact, the son of a celebrated magician; but other magicians, enemies of his father, had changed him in his cradle, altering his features into their present hideous shape, in order that a silly old fellow, called Poinsinet, might take him to be his own son, which little monster the magician had likewise spirited away.

The poor wretch was sadly cast down at this; for he tried to fancy that his person was agreeable to the ladies, of whom he was one of the warmest little admirers possible; and to console him somewhat, the magician told him that his real shape was exquisitely beautiful, and as soon as he should appear in it, all the beauties in Paris would be at his feet. But how to regain it? " Oh, for one minute of that beauty!" cried the little man; " what would he not give to appear under that enchanting form!" The magician hereupon waved his stick over his head, pronounced some awful magical words, and twisted him round three times; at the third twist, the men in company seemed struck with astonishment and envy, the ladies clasped their hands, and some of them kissed his. Everybody declared his beauty to be supernatural.

Poinsinet, enchanted, rushed to a glass. " Fool!" said the magician; " do you suppose that *you* can see the change? My power to render you invisible, beautiful, or ten times more hideous even than you are, extends only to others, not to you. You may look a thousand times in the glass, and you will only see those deformed limbs and disgusting features with which devilish malice has disguised you." Poor little Poinsinet looked, and came back in tears. " But," resumed the magician, — " ha, ha, ha! — *I* know *a* way in which to disappoint the machinations of these fiendish magi."

" Oh, my benefactor! — my great master! — for heaven's sake tell it!" gasped Poinsinet.

" Look you — it is this. A prey to enchantment and demoniac art all your life long, you have lived until your present age perfectly satisfied; nay, absolutely vain of a person the most singularly hideous that ever walked the earth!"

"*Is* it?" whispered Poinsinet. "Indeed and indeed I didn't think it so bad!"

"He acknowledges it! he acknowledges it!" roared the magician. "Wretch, dotard, owl, mole, miserable buzzard! I have no reason to tell thee now that thy form is monstrous, that children cry, that cowards turn pale, that teeming matrons shudder to behold it. It is not thy fault that thou art thus ungainly: but wherefore so blind? wherefore so conceited of thyself! I tell thee, Poinsinet, that over every fresh instance of thy vanity the hostile enchanters rejoice and triumph. As long as thou art blindly satisfied with thyself; as long as thou pretendest, in thy present odious shape, to win the love of aught above a negress; nay, further still, until thou hast learned to regard that face, as others do, with the most intolerable horror and disgust, to abuse it when thou seest it, to despise it, in short, and treat that miserable disguise in which the enchanters have wrapped thee with the strongest hatred and scorn, so long art thou destined to wear it."

Such speeches as these, continually repeated, caused Poinsinet to be fully convinced of his ugliness; he used to go about in companies, and take every opportunity of inveighing against himself; he made verses and epigrams against himself; he talked about "that dwarf, Poinsinet;" "that buffoon, Poinsinet;" "that conceited, hump-backed Poinsinet;" and he would spend hours before the glass, abusing his own face as he saw it reflected there, and vowing that he grew handsomer at every fresh epithet that he uttered.

Of course the wags, from time to time, used to give him every possible encouragement, and declared that since this exercise, his person was amazingly improved. The ladies, too, began to be so excessively fond of him, that the little fellow was obliged to caution them at last — for the good, as he said, of society; he recommended them to draw lots, for he could not gratify them all; but promised when his metamorphosis was complete, that the one chosen should become the happy Mrs. Poinsinet; or, to speak more correctly, Mrs. Polycarte.

I am sorry to say, however, that, on the score of gallantry, Poinsinet was never quite convinced of the hideousness of his appearance. He had a number of adventures, accordingly, with the ladies, but strange to say, the husbands or fathers were always interrupting him. On one occasion he was made to pass the night in a slipper-bath full of water; where, although he had all his clothes on, he declared that he nearly caught his death of cold. Another night, in revenge, the poor fellow

——" dans le simple appareil
D'une beauté, qu'on vient d'arracher au sommeil,"

spent a number of hours contemplating the beauty of the moon on the tiles. These adventures are pretty numerous in the memoirs of M. Poinsinet ; but the fact is, that people in France were a great deal more philosophical in those days than the English are now, so that Poinsinet's loves must be passed over, as not being to our taste. His magician was a great diver, and told Poinsinet the most wonderful tales of his two minutes' absence under water. These two minutes, he said, lasted through a year, at least, which he spent in the company of a naiad, more beautiful than Venus, in a palace more splendid than even Versailles. Fired by the description, Poinsinet used to dip, and dip, but he never was known to make any mermaid acquaintances, although he fully believed that one day he should find such.

The invisible joke was brought to an end by Poinsinet's too great reliance on it ; for being, as we have said, of a very tender and sanguine disposition, he one day fell in love with a lady in whose company he dined, and whom he actually proposed to embrace ; but the fair lady, in the hurry of the moment, forgot to act up to the joke ; and instead of receiving Poinsinet's salute with calmness, grew indignant, called him an impudent little scoundrel, and lent him a sound box on the ear. With this slap the invisibility of Poinsinet disappeared, the gnomes and genii left him, and he settled down into common life again, and was hoaxed only by vulgar means.

A vast number of pages might be filled with narratives of the tricks that were played upon him ; but they resemble each other a good deal, as may be imagined, and the chief point remarkable about them is the wondrous faith of Poinsinet. After being introduced to the Prussian ambassador at the Tuileries, he was presented to the Turkish envoy at the Place Vendôme, who received him in state, surrounded by the officers of his establishment, all dressed in the smartest dresses that the wardrobe of the Opéra Comique could furnish.

As the greatest honor that could be done to him, Poinsinet was invited to eat, and a tray was produced, on which was a delicate dish prepared in the Turkish manner. This consisted of a reasonable quantity of mustard, salt, cinnamon and ginger, nutmegs and cloves, with a couple of tablespoonfuls of cayenne pepper, to give the whole a flavor; and Poinsinet's countenance may be imagined when he introduced into his mouth a quantity of this exquisite compound.

"The best of the joke was," says the author who records so many of the pitiless tricks practised upon poor Poinsinet, "that the little man used to laugh at them afterwards himself with perfect good humor; and lived in the daily hope that, from being the sufferer, he should become the agent in these hoaxes, and do to others as he had been done by." Passing, therefore, one day, on the Pont Neuf, with a friend, who had been one of the greatest performers, the latter said to him, "Poinsinet, my good fellow, thou hast suffered enough, and thy sufferings have made thee so wise and cunning, that thou art worthy of entering among the initiated, and hoaxing in thy turn." Poinsinet was charmed; he asked when he should be initiated, and how? It was told him that a moment would suffice, and that the ceremony might be performed on the spot. At this news, and according to order, Poinsinet flung himself straightway on his knees in the kennel; and the other, drawing his sword, solemnly initiated him into the sacred order of jokers. From that day the little man believed himself received into the society; and to this having brought him, let us bid him a respectful adieu.

THE DEVIL'S WAGER.

IT was the hour of the night when there be none stirring
save churchyard ghosts — when all doors are closed except the
gates of graves, and all eyes shut but the eyes of wicked men.

When there is no sound on the earth except the ticking of
the grasshopper, or the croaking of obscene frogs in the poole.

And no light except that of the blinking starres, and the
wicked and devilish wills-o'-the-wisp, as they gambol among
the marshes, and lead good men astraye.

When there is nothing moving in heaven except the owle,
as he flappeth along lazily ; or the magician, as he rides on his
infernal broomsticke, whistling through the aire like the arrowes
of a Yorkshire archere.

It was at this hour (namely, at twelve o'clock of the night,)
that two beings went winging through the black clouds, and
holding converse with each other.

Now the first was Mercurius, the messenger, not of gods
(as the heathens feigned), but of dæmons ; and the second,
with whom he held company, was the soul of Sir Roger de Rollo,
the brave knight. Sir Roger was Count of Chauchigny, in
Champagne ; Seigneur of Santerre, Villacerf and aultre lieux.
But the great die as well as the humble ; and nothing remained
of brave Rodger now, but his coffin and his deathless soul.

And Mercurius, in order to keep fast the soul, his companion,
had bound him round the neck with his tail ; which, when the
soul was stubborn, he would draw so tight as to strangle him
wellnigh, sticking into him the barbed point thereof ; whereat
the poor soul, Sir Rollo, would groan and roar lustily.

"It is hard," said the poor Sir Rollo, as they went gliding through the clouds, "that I should thus be condemned for ever, and all for want of a single ave."

"How, Sir Soul?" said the dæmon. "You were on earth so wicked, that not one, or a million of aves, could suffice to keep from hell-flame a creature like thee; but cheer up and be merry; thou wilt be but a subject of our lord the Devil, as am I; and, perhaps, thou wilt be advanced to posts of honor, as am I also:" and to show his authoritie, he lashed with his tail the ribbes of the wretched Rollo.

"Nevertheless, sinner as I am, one more ave would have saved me; for my sister, who was Abbess of St. Mary of Chauchigny, did so prevail, by her prayer and good works, for my lost and wretched soul, that every day I felt the pains of purgatory decrease; the pitchforks which, on my first entry, had never ceased to vex and torment my poor carcass, were now not applied above once a week; the roasting had ceased, the boiling had discontinued; only a certain warmth was kept up, to remind me of my situation."

"A gentle stewe," said the dæmon.

"Yea, truly, I was but in a stew, and all from the effects of the prayers of my blessed sister. But yesterday, he who watched me in purgatory told me, that yet another prayer from my sister, and my bonds should be unloosed, and I, who am now a devil, should have been a blessed angel."

"And the other ave?" said the dæmon.

"She died, sir — my sister died — death choked her in the middle of the prayer." And hereat the wretched spirit began to weepe and whine piteously; his salt tears falling over his beard, and scalding the tail of Mercurius the devil.

"It is, in truth, a hard case," said the dæmon; "but I know of no remedy save patience, and for that you will have an excellent opportunity in your lodgings below."

"But I have relations," said the Earl; "my kinsman Randal, who has inherited my lands, will he not say a prayer for his uncle?"

"Thou didst hate and oppress him when living."

"It is true; but an ave is not much; his sister, my niece, Matilda —"

"You shut her in a convent, and hanged her lover."

"Had I not reason? besides, has she not others?"

"A dozen, without doubt."

"And my brother, the prior?"

"A liege subject of my lord the Devil: he never opens

his mouth, except to utter an oath, or to swallow a cup of wine."

"And yet, if but one of these would but say an ave for me, I should be saved."

"Aves with them are raræ aves," replied Mercurius, wagging his tail right waggishly; "and, what is more, I will lay thee any wager that not one of these will say a prayer to save thee."

"I would wager willingly," responded he of Chauchigny; "but what has a poor soul like me to stake?"

"Every evening, after the day's roasting, my lord Satan giveth a cup of cold water to his servants; I will bet thee thy water for a year, that none of the three will pray for thee."

"Done!" said Rollo.

"Done!" said the dæmon; "and here, if I mistake not, is thy castle of Chauchigny."

Indeed, it was true. The soul, on looking down, perceived the tall towers, the courts, the stables, and the fair gardens of the castle. Although it was past midnight, there was a blaze of light in the banqueting-hall, and a lamp burning in the open window of the Lady Matilda.

"With whom shall we begin?" said the dæmon: "with the baron or the lady?"

"With the lady, if you will."

"Be it so; her window is open, let us enter."

So they descended, and entered silently into Matilda's chamber.

.   .   .   .

The young lady's eyes were fixed so intently on a little clock, that it was no wonder that she did not perceive the entrance of her two visitors. Her fair cheek rested on her white arm, and her white arm on the cushion of a great chair in which she sat, pleasantly supported by sweet thoughts and swan's down; a lute was at her side, and a book of prayers lay under the table (for piety is always modest). Like the amorous Alexander, she sighed and looked (at the clock) — and sighed for ten minutes or more, when she softly breathed the word "Edward!"

At this the soul of the Baron was wroth. "The jade is at her old pranks," said he to the devil; and then addressing Matilda: "I pray thee, sweet niece, turn thy thoughts for a moment from that villanous page, Edward, and give them to thine affectionate uncle."

When she heard the voice, and saw the awful apparition of

her uncle (for a year's sojourn in purgatory had not increased the comeliness of his appearance), she started, screamed, and of course fainted.

But the devil Mercurius soon restored her to herself. "What's o'clock?" said she, as soon as she had recovered from her fit: "is he come?"

"Not thy lover, Maude, but thine uncle — that is, his soul. For the love of heaven, listen to me : I have been frying in purgatory for a year past, and should have been in heaven but for the want of a single ave."

"I will say it for thee to-morrow, uncle."

"To-night, or never."

"Well, to-night be it : " and she requested the devil Mercurius to give her the prayer-book from under the table ; but he had no sooner touched the holy book than he dropped it with a shriek and a yell.   "It was hotter," he said, "than his master Sir Lucifer's own particular pitchfork." And the lady was forced to begin her ave without the aid of her missal.

At the commencement of her devotions the dæmon retired, and carried with him the anxious soul of poor Sir Roger de Rollo.

The lady knelt down — she sighed deeply ; she looked again at the clock, and began —

"Ave Maria."

When a lute was heard under the window, and a sweet voice singing —

"Hark !" said Matilda.

> "Now the toils of day are over,
>   And the sun hath sunk to rest,
>   Seeking, like a fiery lover,
>   The bosom of the blushing west—
>
> "The faithful night keeps watch and ward,
>   Raising the moon, her silver shield,
>   And summoning the stars to guard
>   The slumbers of my fair Mathilde !"

"For mercy's sake !" said Sir Rollo, "the ave first, and next the song."

So Matilda again dutifully betook her to her devotions, and began —

"Ave Maria gratiâ plena !" but the music began again, and the prayer ceased of course.

> " The faithful night !   Now all things lie
>   Hid by her mantle dark and dim,
>   In pious hope I hither hie,
>   And humbly chant mine ev'ning hymn.

> " Thou art my prayer, my saint, my shrine !
>   (For never holy pilgrim kneel'd,
>   Or wept at feet more pure than thine),
>   My virgin love, my sweet Mathilde ! "

" Virgin love ! " said the Baron.   " Upon my soul, this is
too bad ! " and he thought of the lady's lover whom he had
caused to be hanged.

But *she* only thought of him who stood singing at her window.

" Niece Matilda ! " cried Sir Roger, agonizedly, " wilt thou
listen to the lies of an impudent page, whilst thine uncle is
waiting but a dozen words to make him happy ? "

At this Matilda grew angry :   " Edward is neither impudent
nor a liar, Sir Uncle, and I will listen to the end of the song."

" Come away," said Mercurius ;   " he hath yet got wield,
field, sealed, congealed, and a dozen other rhymes beside ; and
after the song will come the supper."

So the poor soul was obliged to go ; while the lady listened,
and the page sung away till morning.

.   .   .   .

" My virtues have been my ruin," said poor Sir Rollo, as
he and Mercurius slunk silently out of the window.   " Had I
hanged that knave Edward, as I did the page his predecessor,
my niece would have sung mine ave, and I should have been
by this time an angel in heaven."

" He is reserved for wiser purposes," responded the devil :
" he will assassinate your successor, the lady Mathilde's brother ;
and, in consequence, will be hanged.   In the love of the lady
he will be succeeded by a gardener, who will be replaced by a
monk, who will give way to an ostler, who will be deposed by
a Jew pedler, who shall, finally, yield to a noble earl, the future
husband of the fair Mathilde.   So that, you see, instead of
having one poor soul a-frying, we may now look forward to a
goodly harvest for our lord the Devil."

The soul of the Baron began to think that his companion
knew too much for one who would make fair bets ; but there
was no help for it ; he would not, and he could not, cry off :
and he prayed inwardly that the brother might be found more
pious than the sister.

But there seemed little chance of this.   As they crossed the court, lackeys, with smoking dishes and full jugs, passed and repassed continually, although it was long past midnight. On entering the hall, they found Sir Randal at the head of a vast table, surrounded by a fiercer and more motley collection of individuals than had congregated there even in the time of Sir Rollo. The lord of the castle had signified that " it was his royal pleasure to be drunk," and the gentlemen of his train had obsequiously followed their master. Mercurius was delighted with the scene, and relaxed his usually rigid countenance into a bland and benevolent smile, which became him wonderfully.

The entrance of Sir Roger, who had been dead about a year, and a person with hoofs, horns, and a tail, rather disturbed the hilarity of the company. Sir Randal dropped his cup of wine; and Father Peter, the confessor, incontinently paused in the midst of a profane song, with which he was amusing the society.

" Holy Mother ! " cried he, " it is Sir Roger."

" Alive ! " screamed Sir Randal.

" No, my lord," Mercurius said ; " Sir Roger is dead, but cometh on a matter of business ; and I have the honor to act as his counsellor and attendant."

" Nephew," said Sir Roger, " the dæmon saith justly ; I am come on a trifling affair, in which thy service is essential."

" I will do anything, uncle, in my power."

" Thou canst give me life, if thou wilt ? " But Sir Randal looked very blank at this proposition. " I mean life spiritual, Randal," said Sir Roger ; and thereupon he explained to him the nature of the wager.

Whilst he was telling his story, his companion Mercurius was playing all sorts of antics in the hall ; and, by his wit and fun, became so popular with this godless crew, that they lost all the fear which his first appearance had given them. The friar was wonderfully taken with him, and used his utmost eloquence and endeavors to convert the devil ; the knights stopped drinking to listen to the argument ; the men-at-arms forbore brawling ; and the wicked little pages crowded round the two strange disputants, to hear their edifying discourse. The ghostly man, however, had little chance in the controversy, and certainly little learning to carry it on. Sir Randal interrupted him. " Father Peter," said he, " our kinsman is condemned for ever, for want of a single ave: wilt thou say it for him ? " " Willingly, my lord," said the monk, " with my book ; " and accordingly he produced his missal to read, without which aid it appeared that the holy father could not manage the desired

prayer. But the crafty Mercurius had, by his devilish **art,**
inserted a song in the place of the ave, so that Father Peter,
instead of chanting an hymn, sang the following irreverent
ditty : —

> " Some love the matin-chimes, which **tell**
>   The hour of prayer to sinner :
> But better far's the mid-day bell,
>   Which speaks the hour of **dinner ;**
> For when I see a smoking fish,
>   Or capon drown'd in gravy,
> Or noble haunch on silver **dish,**
>   Full glad I sing mine ave.

> " My pulpit is an ale-house **bench,**
>   Whereon I sit so jolly ;
> **A** smiling rosy country wench
>   My saint and patron holy.
> I kiss her cheek so red and **sleek,**
>   I press her ringlets wavy,
> And in her willing ear I speak
>   A most religious ave.

> " And if I'm blind, yet heaven is **kind,**
>   And holy saints forgiving ;
> For sure he leads a right good life
>   Who thus admires good living.
> Above, they say, our flesh is air,
>   Our blood celestial ichor :
> Oh, grant ! mid all the changes **there,**
>   They may not change our liquor ! "

And with this pious wish the holy confessor tumbled under
the table in an agony of devout drunkenness ; whilst the knights,
the men-at-arms, and the wicked little pages, rang out the last
verse with a most melodious and emphatic glee. " I am sorry,
fair uncle," hiccupped Sir Randal, " that, in the matter of the
ave, we could not oblige thee in a more orthodox manner ; but
the holy father has failed, and there is not another man in the
hall who hath an idea of a prayer."

" It is my own fault," said Sir Rollo ; " for I hanged the last
confessor." And he wished his nephew a surly good-night, as
he prepared to quit the room.

" Au revoir, gentlemen," said the devil Mercurius ; and
once more fixed his tail round the neck of his disappointed companion.

The spirit of poor Rollo was sadly cast down; the devil, on the contrary, was in high good humor. He wagged his tail with the most satisfied air in the world, and cut a hundred jokes at the expense of his poor associate. On they sped, cleaving swiftly through the cold night winds, frightening the birds that were roosting in the woods, and the owls that were watching in the towers.

In the twinkling of an eye, as it is known, devils can fly hundreds of miles: so that almost the same beat of the clock which left these two in Champagne, found them hovering over Paris. They dropped into the court of the Lazarist Convent, and winded their way, through passage and cloister, until they reached the door of the prior's cell.

Now the prior, Rollo's brother, was a wicked and malignant sorcerer; his time was spent in conjuring devils and doing wicked deeds, instead of fasting, scourging, and singing holy psalms: this Mercurius knew; and he, therefore, was fully at ease as to the final result of his wager with poor Sir Roger.

"You seem to be well acquainted with the road," said the knight.

"I have reason," answered Mercurius, "having, for a long period, had the acquaintance of his reverence, your brother; but you have little chance with him."

"And why?" said Sir Rollo.

"He is under a bond to my master, never to say a prayer, or else his soul and his body are forfeited at once."

"Why, thou false and traitorous devil!" said the enraged knight; "and thou knewest this when we made our wager?"

"Undoubtedly: do you suppose I would have done so had there been any chance of losing?"

And with this they arrived at Father Ignatius's door.

"Thy cursed presence threw a spell on my niece, and stopped the tongue of my nephew's chaplain; I do believe that had I seen either of them alone, my wager had been won."

"Certainly; therefore, I took good care to go with thee: however, thou mayest see the prior alone, if thou wilt; and lo! his door is open. I will stand without for five minutes, when it will be time to commence our journey."

It was the poor Baron's last chance: and he entered his brother's room more for the five minutes' respite than from any hope of success.

Father Ignatius, the prior, was absorbed in magic calcula- tions: he stood in the middle of a circle of skulls, with no gar- ment except his long white beard, which reached to his knees;

he was waving a silver rod, and muttering imprecations in some horrible tongue.

But Sir Rollo came forward and interrupted his incantation. " I am," said he, " the shade of thy brother Roger de Rollo; and have come, from pure brotherly love, to warn thee of thy fate."

" Whence camest thou?"

" From the abode of the blessed in Paradise," replied Sir Roger, who was inspired with a sudden thought; " it was but five minutes ago that the Patron Saint of thy church told me of thy danger, and of thy wicked compact with the fiend. ' Go,' said he, ' to thy miserable brother, and tell him there is but one way by which he may escape from paying the awful forfeit of his bond.' "

" And how may that be?" said the prior; " the false fiend hath deceived me; I have given him my soul, but have received no worldly benefit in return. Brother! dear brother! how may I escape?"

" I will tell thee. As soon as I heard the voice of blessed St. Mary Lazarus" (the worthy Earl had, at a pinch, coined the name of a saint), " I left the clouds, where, with other angels, I was seated, and sped hither to save thee. ' Thy brother,' said the Saint, ' hath but one day more to live, when he will become for all eternity the subject of Satan; if he would escape, he must boldly break his bond, by saying an ave.' "

" It is the express condition of the agreement," said the unhappy monk, " I must say no prayer, or that instant I become Satan's, body and soul."

" It is the express condition of the Saint," answered Roger, fiercely; " pray, brother, pray, or thou art lost for ever."

So the foolish monk knelt down, and devoutly sung out an ave. " Amen! " said Sir Roger, devoutly.

" Amen!" said Mercurius, as, suddenly, coming behind, he seized Ignatius by his long beard, and flew up with him to the top of the church-steeple.

The monk roared, and screamed, and swore against his brother; but it was of no avail: Sir Roger smiled kindly on him, and said, " Do not fret, brother; it must have come to this in a year or two."

And he flew alongside of Mercurius to the steeple-top: *but this time the devil had not his tail round his neck.* " I will let thee off thy bet," said he to the dæmon; for he could afford, now, to be generous.

" I believe, my lord," said the dæmon, politely, " that our

ways separate here." Sir Roger sailed gayly upwards : while Mercurius having bound the miserable monk faster than ever, he sunk downwards to earth, and perhaps lower. Ignatius was heard roaring and screaming as the devil dashed him against the iron spikes and buttresses of the church.

The moral of this story will be given in the second edition.

MADAME SAND AND THE NEW APOCALYPSE.

I DON'T know an impression more curious than that which is formed in a foreigner's mind, who has been absent from this place for two or three years, returns to it, and beholds the change which has taken place, in the meantime, in French fashions and ways of thinking. Two years ago, for instance, when I left the capital, I left the young gentlemen of France with their hair brushed *en toupet* in front, and the toes of their boots round; now the boot-toes are pointed, and the hair combed flat, and, parted in the middle, falls in ringlets on the fashionable shoulders; and, in like manner, with books as with boots, the fashion has changed considerably, and it is not a little curious to contrast the old modes with the new. Absurd as was the literary dandyism of those days, it is not a whit less absurd now: only the manner is changed, and our versatile Frenchmen have passed from one caricature to another.

The revolution may be called a caricature of freedom, as the empire was of glory; and what they borrow from foreigners undergoes the same process. They take top-boots and mackintoshes from across the water, and caricature our fashions; they read a little, very little, Shakespeare, and caricature our poetry: and while in David's time art and religion were only a caricature of Heathenism, now, on the contrary, these two commodities are imported from Germany; and distorted caricatures originally, are still farther distorted on passing the frontier.

I trust in heaven that German art and religion will take no hold in our country (where there is a fund of roast-beef that will expel any such humbug in the end); but these sprightly Frenchmen have relished the mystical doctrines mightily; and having watched the Germans, with their sanctified looks, and quaint imitations of the old times, and mysterious transcendental talk, are aping many of their fashions ; as well and solemnly as they can : not very solemnly, God wot ; for I think one should always prepare to grin when a Frenchman looks particularly grave, being sure that there is something false and ridiculous lurking under the owl-like solemnity.

When last in Paris, we were in the midst of what was called a Catholic reaction. Artists talked of faith in poems and pictures ; churches were built here and there ; old missals were copied and purchased ; and numberless portraits of saints, with as much gilding about them as ever was used in the fifteenth century, appeared in churches, ladies' boudoirs, and picture-shops. One or two fashionable preachers rose, and were eagerly followed ; the very youth of the schools gave up their pipes and billiards for some time, and flocked in crowds to Notre Dame, to sit under the feet of Lacordaire. I went to visit the Church of Notre Dame de Lorette yesterday, which was finished in the heat of this Catholic rage, and was not a little struck by the similarity of the place to the worship celebrated in it, and the admirable manner in which the architect has caused his work to express the public feeling of the moment. It is a pretty little bijou of a church : it is supported by sham marble pillars ; it has a gaudy ceiling of blue and gold, which will look very well for some time ; and is filled with gaudy pictures and carvings, in the very pink of the mode. The congregation did not offer a bad illustration of the present state of Catholic reaction. Two or three stray people were at prayers ; there was no service ; a few countrymen and idlers were staring about at the pictures ; and the Swiss, the paid guardian of the place, was comfortably and appropriately asleep on his bench at the door. I am inclined to think the famous reaction is over : the students have taken to their Sunday pipes and billiards again ; and one or two cafés have been established, within the last year, that are ten times handsomer than Notre Dame de Lorette.

However, if the immortal Görres and the German mystics have had their day, there is the immortal Göthe, and the Pantheists ; and I incline to think that the fashion has set very strongly in their favor. Voltaire and the Encyclopædians are voted, now, *barbares*, and there is no term of reprobation strong enough for heartless Humes and Helvetiuses, who lived but to destroy, and who only thought to doubt. Wretched as Voltaire's sneers and puns are, I think there is something more manly and earnest even in them, than in the present muddy

French transcendentalism. Pantheism is the word now; one and all have begun to *éprouver* the *besoin* of a religious sentiment; and we are deluged with a host of gods accordingly. Monsieur de Balzac feels himself to be inspired; Victor Hugo is a god; Madame Sand is a god; that tawdry man of genius, Jules Janin, who writes theatrical reviews for the *Débats*, has divine intimations; and there is scarce a beggarly, beardless scribbler of poems and prose, but tells you, in his preface, of the *sainteté* of the *sacerdoce littéraire;* or a dirty student, sucking tobacco and beer, and reeling home with a grisette from the chaumière, who is not convinced of the necessity of a new "Messianism," and will hiccup, to such as will listen, chapters of his own drunken Apocalypse. Surely, the negatives of the old days were far less dangerous than the assertions of the present; and you may fancy what a religion that must be, which has such high priests.

There is no reason to trouble the reader with details of the lives of many of these prophets and expounders of new revelations. Madame Sand, for instance, I do not know personally, and can only speak of her from report. True or false, the history, at any rate, is not very edifying; and so may be passed over: but, as a certain great philosopher told us, in very humble and simple words, that we are not to expect to gather grapes from thorns, or figs from thistles, we may, at least, demand, in all persons assuming the character of moralist or philosopher — order, soberness, and regularity of life; for we are apt to distrust the intellect that we fancy can be swayed by circumstance or passion; and we know how circumstance and passion *will* sway the intellect: how mortified vanity will form excuses for itself; and how temper turns angrily upon conscience, that reproves it. How often have we called our judge our enemy, because he has given sentence against us! — How often have we called the right wrong, because the right condemns us! And in the lives of many of the bitter foes of the Christian doctrine, can we find no personal reason for their hostility? The men in Athens said it was out of regard for religion that they murdered Socrates; but we have had time, since then, to reconsider the verdict; and Socrates' character is pretty pure now, in spite of the sentence and the jury of those days.

The Parisian philosophers will attempt to explain to you the changes through which Madame Sand's mind has passed, — the initiatory trials, labors, and sufferings which she has had to go through, — before she reached her present happy

state of mental illumination. She teaches her wisdom in para-
bles, that are, mostly, a couple of volumes long; and began,
first, by an eloquent attack on marriage, in the charming novel
of " Indiana." " Pity," cried she, " for the poor woman who,
united to a being whose brute force makes him her superior,
should venture to break the bondage which is imposed on her,
and allow her heart to be free."

In support of this claim of pity, she writes two volumes of
the most exquisite prose. What a tender, suffering creature
is Indiana; how little her husband appreciates that gentleness
which he is crushing by his tyranny and brutal scorn; how
natural it is that, in the absence of his sympathy, she, poor
clinging confiding creature, should seek elsewhere for shelter;
how cautious should we be, to call criminal — to visit with too
heavy a censure — an act which is one of the natural impulses
of a tender heart, that seeks but for a worthy object of love.
But why attempt to tell the tale of beautiful Indiana? Madame
Sand has written it so well, that not the hardest-hearted husband in Christendom can fail to be touched by her sorrows,
though he may refuse to listen to her argument. Let us grant,
for argument's sake, that the laws of marriage, especially the
French laws of marriage, press very cruelly upon unfortunate
women.

But if one wants to have a question of this, or any nature,
honestly argued, it is better, surely, to apply to an indifferent
person for an umpire. For instance, the stealing of pocket-
handkerchiefs or snuff-boxes may or may not be vicious; but
if we, who have not the wit, or will not take the trouble to
decide the question ourselves, want to hear the real rights
of the matter, we should not, surely, apply to a pickpocket to
know what he thought on the point. It might naturally be
presumed that he would be rather a prejudiced person — particularly as his reasoning, if successful, might get him *out of
gaol*. This is a homely illustration, no doubt; all we would
urge by it is, that Madame Sand having, according to the
French newspapers, had a stern husband, and also having,
according to the newspapers, sought " sympathy " elsewhere,
her arguments may be considered to be somewhat partial, and
received with some little caution.

And tell us who have been the social reformers? — the
haters, that is, of the present system, according to which we
live, love, marry, have children, educate them, and endow
them — *are they pure themselves?* I do believe not one; and
directly a man begins to quarrel with the world and its ways,

and to lift up, as he calls it, the voice of his despair, and preach passionately to mankind about this tyranny of faith, customs, laws; if we examine what the personal character of the preacher is, we begin pretty clearly to understand the value of the doctrine. Any one can see why Rousseau should be such a whimpering reformer, and Byron such a free and easy misanthropist, and why our accomplished Madame Sand, who has a genius and eloquence inferior to neither, should take the present condition of mankind (French-kind) so much to heart, and labor so hotly to set it right.

After " Indiana " (which, we presume, contains the lady's notions upon wives and husbands) came " Valentine," which may be said to exhibit her doctrine, in regard of young men and maidens, to whom the author would accord, as we fancy, the same tender license. " Valentine" was followed by " Lelia," a wonderful book indeed, gorgeous in eloquence, and rich in magnificent poetry: a regular topsyturvyfication of morality, a thieves' and prostitutes' apotheosis. This book has received some late enlargements and emendations by the writer; it contains her notions on morals, which, as we have said, are so peculiar, that, alas! they only can be mentioned here, not particularized: but of " Spiridion " we may write a few pages, as it is her religious manifesto.

In this work, the lady asserts her pantheistical doctrine, and openly attacks the received Christian creed. She declares it to be useless now, and unfitted to the exigencies and the degree of culture of the actual world; and, though it would be hardly worth while to combat her opinions in due form, it is, at least, worth while to notice them, not merely from the extraordinary eloquence and genius of the woman herself, but because they express the opinions of a great number of people besides: for she not only produces her own thoughts, but imitates those of others very eagerly; and one finds in her writings so much similarity with others, or, in others, so much resemblance to her, that the book before us may pass for the expression of the sentiments of a certain French party.

" Dieu est mort," says another writer of the same class, and of great genius too. — " Dieu est mort," writes Mr. Henry Heine, speaking of the Christian God; and he adds, in a daring figure of speech, — " N'entendez-vous pas sonner la Clochette? — on porte les sacremens à un Dieu qui se meurt! " Another of the pantheist poetical philosophers, Mr. Edgar Quinet, has a poem, in which Christ and the Virgin Mary are made to die similarly, and the former is classed with Prometheus. This book of "Spiridion" is a continuation of the theme, and perhaps you will listen to some of the author's expositions of it.

It must be confessed that the controversialists of the present day have an eminent advantage over their predecessors in the days of folios; it required some learning then to write a book, and some time, at least — for the very labor of writing out a thousand such vast pages would demand a considerable period. But now, in the age of duodecimos, the system is reformed altogether: a male or female controversialist draws upon his imagination, and not his learning; makes a story instead of an argument, and, in the course of 150 pages (where the preacher has it all his own way) will prove or disprove you anything. And, to our shame be it said, we Protestants have set the example of this kind of proselytism — those detestable mixtures of truth, lies, false sentiment, false reasoning, bad grammar, correct and genuine philanthropy and piety — I mean our religious tracts, which any woman or man, be he ever so silly, can take upon himself to write, and sell for a penny, as if religious instruction were the easiest thing in the world. We, I say, have set the example in this kind of composition, and all the sects of the earth will, doubtless, speedily follow it. I can point you out blasphemies in famous pious tracts that are as dreadful as those above mentioned; but this is no place for such discussions, and we had better return to Madame Sand. As Mrs Sherwood expounds, by means of many touching histories and anecdotes of little boys and girls, her notions of church history, church catechism, church doctrine; — as the author of "Father Clement, a Roman Catholic Story," demolishes the stately structure of eighteen centuries, the mighty and beautiful Roman Catholic faith, in whose bosom repose so many saints and sages, — by the means of a three-and-sixpenny duodecimo volume, which tumbles over the vast fabric, as David's pebble-stone did Goliath; — as, again, the Roman Catholic author of "Geraldine" falls foul of Luther and Calvin, and drowns the awful echoes of their tremendous protest by the sounds of her little half-crown trumpet: in like manner, by means of pretty sentimental tales, and cheap apologues, Mrs. Sand proclaims *her* truth — that we need a new Messiah, and that the Christian religion is no more! O awful, awful name of God! Light unbearable! Mystery unfathomable! Vastness immeasurable! — Who are these who come forward to explain the mystery, and gaze unblinking into the depths of the light, and measure the immeasurable vastness to a hair? O name, that God's people of old did fear to utter! O light, that God's prophet would have perished had he seen! Who are these that are now so familiar with it? — Women, truly; for the most part weak women — weak in intellect, weak mayhap in spelling and grammar, but marvellously strong in faith: — women, who step down to the people with stately step and voice of authority, and deliver their twopenny tablets, as if there were some Divine authority for the wretched nonsense recorded there!

With regard to the spelling and grammar, our Parisian Pythoness stands, in the goodly fellowship, remarkable. Her style is a noble, and, as far as a foreigner can judge, a strange tongue, beautifully rich and pure. She has a very exuberant imagination, and, with it, a very chaste style of expression. She never scarcely indulges in declamation, as other modern prophets do, and yet her sentences are exquisitely melodious and full. She seldom runs a thought to death (after the manner of some prophets, who, when they catch a little one, toy with it until they kill it), but she leaves you at the end of one of her brief, rich, melancholy sentences, with plenty of food for future cogitation. I can't express to you the charm of them; they seem to me like the sound of country bells — provoking I don't know what vein of musing and meditation, and falling sweetly and sadly on the ear.

This wonderful power of language must have been felt by most people who read Madame Sand's first books, " Valentine " and " Indiana : " in " Spiridion " it is greater, I think, than ever; and for those who are not afraid of the matter of the novel, the manner will be found most delightful. The author's intention, I presume, is to describe, in a parable, her notions of the downfall of the Catholic church; and, indeed, of the whole Christian scheme: she places her hero in a monastery in Italy, where, among the characters about him, and the events which occur, the particular tenets of Madame Dudevant's doctrine are not inaptly laid down. Innocent, faithful, tender-hearted, a young monk, by name Angel, finds himself, when he has pronounced his vows, an object of aversion and hatred to the godly men whose lives he so much respects, and whose love he would make any sacrifice to win. After enduring much, he flings himself at the feet of his confessor, and begs for his sympathy and counsel; but the confessor spurns him away, and accuses him, fiercely, of some unknown and terrible crime — bids him never return to the confessional until contrition has touched his heart, and the stains which sully his spirit are, by sincere repentance, washed away.

"Thus speaking," says Angel, "Father Hegesippus tore away his robe, which I was holding in my supplicating hands. In a sort of wildness I still grasped it tighter; he pushed me fiercely from him, and I fell with my face towards the ground. He quitted me, closing violently after him the door of the sacristy, in which this scene had passed. I was left alone in the darkness. Either from the violence of my fall, or the excess of my grief, a vein had burst in my throat, and a hæmorrhage ensued. I had not the force to rise; I felt my senses rapidly sinking, and, presently, I lay stretched on the pavement, unconscious, and bathed in my blood."

[Now the wonderful part of the story begins.]

"I know not how much time I passed in this way. As I came to myself I felt an agreeable coolness. It seemed as if some harmonious air was playing round about me, stirring gently in my hair, and drying the drops of perspiration on my brow. It seemed to approach, and then again to withdraw, breathing now softly and sweetly in the distance, and now returning, as if to give me strength and courage to rise.

"I would not, however, do so as yet; for I felt myself, as I lay, under the influence of a pleasure quite new to me; and listened, in a kind of peaceful aberration, to the gentle murmurs of the summer wind, as it breathed on me through the closed window-blinds above me. Then I fancied I heard a voice that spoke to me from the end of the sacristy: it whispered so low that I could not catch the words. I remained motionless, and gave it my whole attention. At last I heard, distinctly, the following sentence:—'*Spirit of Truth, raise up these victims of ignorance and imposture.*' 'Father Hegesippus,' said I, in a weak voice, ' is that you who are returning to me?' But no one answered. I lifted myself on my hands and knees, I listened again, but I heard nothing. I got up completely, and looked about me: I had fallen so near to the only door in this little room, that none, after the departure of the confessor, could have entered it without passing over me; besides, the door was shut, and only opened from the inside by a strong lock of the ancient shape. I touched it, and assured myself that it was closed. I was seized with terror, and, for some moments, did not dare to move. Leaning against the door, I looked round, and endeavored to see into the gloom in which the angles of the room were enveloped. A pale light, which came from an upper window, half closed, was seen to be trembling in the midst of the apartment. The wind beat the shutter to and fro, and enlarged or diminished the space through which the light issued. The objects which were in this half light — the praying-desk, surmounted by its skull — a few books lying on the benches — a surplice hanging against the wall — seemed to move with the shadow of the foliage that the air agitated behind the window. When I thought I was alone, I felt ashamed of my former timidity ; I made the sign of the cross, and was about to move forward in order to open the shutter altogether, but a deep sigh came from the praying-desk, and kept me nailed to my place. And yet I saw the desk distinctly enough to be sure that no person was near it. Then I had an idea which gave me courage. Some person, I thought, is behind the shutter, and has been saying his prayers outside without thinking of me. But who would be so bold as to express such wishes and utter such a prayer as I had just heard?

" Curiosity, the only passion and amusement permitted in a cloister, now entirely possessed me, and I advanced towards the window. But I had not made a step when a black shadow, as it seemed to me, detaching itself from the praying-desk, traversed the room, directing itself towards the window, and passed swiftly by me. The movement was so rapid that I had not time to avoid what seemed a body advancing towards me, and my fright was so great that I thought I should faint a second time. But I felt nothing, and, as if the shadow had passed through me, I saw it suddenly disappear to my left.

" I rushed to the window, I pushed back the blind with precipitation, and looked round the sacristy : I was there, entirely alone. I looked into the garden — it was deserted, and the mid-day wind was wandering among the flowers. I took courage, I examined all the corners of the room ; I looked behind the praying-desk, which was very large, and I shook all the sacerdotal vestments which were hanging on the walls, everything was in its natural condition, and could give me no explanation of what had just occurred. The sight of all the blood I had lost led me to fancy that my brain had, probably, been weakened by the hæmorrhage, and that I had been a prey to some delusion. I retired to my cell, and remained shut up there until the next day."

I don't know whether the reader has been as much struck with the above mysterious scene as the writer has ; but the fancy of it strikes me as very fine ; and the natural *supernaturalness* is kept up in the best style. The shutter swaying to and fro, the fitful *light appearing* over the furniture of the room, and giving it an air of strange motion — the awful shadow which passed through the body of the timid young novice — are surely very finely painted. "I rushed to the shutter, and flung it back: there was no one in the sacristy. I looked into the garden; it was deserted, and the mid-day wind was roaming among the flowers." The dreariness is wonderfully described: only the poor pale boy looking eagerly out from the window of the sacristy, and the hot mid-day wind walking in the solitary garden. How skilfully is each of these little strokes dashed in, and how well do all together combine to make a picture! But we must have a little more about Spiridion's wonderful visitant.

.   .   .   .

"As I entered into the garden, I stepped a little on one side, to make way for a person whom I saw before me. He was a young man of surprising beauty, and attired in a foreign costume. Although dressed in the large black robe which the superiors of our order wear, he had, underneath, a short jacket of fine cloth, fastened round the waist by a leathern belt, and a buckle of silver, after the manner of the old German students. Like them, he wore, instead of the sandals of our monks, short tight boots; and over the collar of his shirt, which fell on his shoulders, and was as white as snow, hung, in rich golden curls, the most beautiful hair I ever saw. He was tall, and his elegant posture seemed to reveal to me that he was in the habit of commanding. With much respect, and yet uncertain, I half saluted him. He did not return my salute; but he smiled on me with so benevolent an air, and at the same time, his eyes severe and blue, looked towards me with an expression of such compassionate tenderness, that his features have never since then passed away from my recollection. I stopped, hoping he would speak to me, and persuading myself, from the majesty of his aspect, that he had the power to protect me; but the monk, who was walking behind me, and who did not seem to remark him in the least, forced him brutally to step aside from the walk, and pushed me so rudely as almost to cause me to fall. Not wishing to engage in a quarrel with this coarse monk, I moved away; but, after having taken a few steps in the garden, I looked back, and saw the unknown still gazing on me with looks of the tenderest solicitude. The sun shone full upon him, and made his hair look radiant. He sighed, and lifted his fine eyes to heaven, as if to invoke its justice in my favor, and to call it to bear witness to my misery; he turned slowly towards the sanctuary, entered into the quire, and was lost, presently, in the shade. I longed to return, spite of the monk, to follow this noble stranger, and to tell him my afflictions; but who was he, that I imagined he would listen to them, and cause them to cease? I felt, even

while his softness drew me towards him, that he still inspired
me with a kind of fear ; for I saw in his physiognomy as much
austerity as sweetness."

.   .   .   .

Who was he? — we shall see that.   He was somebody very
mysterious indeed ; but our author has taken care, after the
manner of her sex, to make a very pretty fellow of him, and to
dress him in the most becoming costumes possible.

.   .   .   .

The individual in tight boots and a rolling collar, with the
copious golden locks, and the solemn blue eyes, who had just
gazed on Spiridion, and inspired him with such a feeling of tender awe, is a much more important personage than the reader
might suppose at first sight.   This beautiful, mysterious, dandy
ghost, whose costume, with a true woman's coquetry, Madame
Dudevant has so rejoiced to describe — is her religious type, a
mystical representation of Faith struggling up towards Truth,
through superstition, doubt, fear, reason, — in tight inexpressibles, with " a belt such as is worn by the old German students."
You will pardon me for treating such an awful person as this
somewhat lightly ; but there is always, I think, such a dash of
the ridiculous in the French sublime, that the critic should try
and do justice to both, or he may fail in giving a fair account of
either.   This character of Hebronius, the type of Mrs. Sand's
convictions — if convictions they may be called — or, at least,
the allegory under which her doubts are represented, is, in parts,
very finely drawn ; contains many passages of truth, very deep
and touching, by the side of others so entirely absurd and unrea-
sonable, that the reader's feelings are continually swaying between admiration and something very like contempt — always
in a kind of wonder at the strange mixture before him.   But let
us hear Madame Sand : —

"Peter Hebronius," says our author, "was not originally
so named.   His real name was Samuel.   He was a Jew, and
born in a little village in the neighborhood of Innsprück.   His
family, which possessed a considerable fortune, left him, in his
early youth, completely free to his own pursuits.   From infancy
he had shown that these were serious.   He loved to be alone ;
and passed his days, and sometimes his nights, wandering
among the mountains and valleys in the neighborhood of his
birthplace.   He would often sit by the brink of torrents, listening to the voice of their waters, and endeavoring to penetrate the meaning which Nature had hidden in those sounds.
As he advanced in years, his inquiries became more curious

and more grave. It was necessary that he should receive a solid education, and his parents sent him to study in the German universities. Luther had been dead only a century, and his words and his memory still lived in the enthusiasm of his disciples. The new faith was strengthening the conquests it had made; the Reformers were as ardent as in the first days, but their ardor was more enlightened and more measured. Proselytism was still carried on with zeal, and new converts were made every day. In listening to the morality and to the dogmas which Lutheranism had taken from Catholicism, Samuel was filled with admiration. His bold and sincere spirit instantly compared the doctrines which were now submitted to him, with those in the belief of which he had been bred; and, enlightened by the comparison, was not slow to acknowledge the inferiority of Judaism. He said to himself, that a religion made for a single people, to the exclusion of all others, — which only offered a barbarous justice for rule of conduct, — which neither rendered the present intelligible nor satisfactory, and left the future uncertain, — could not be that of noble souls and lofty intellects; and that he could not be the God of truth who had dictated, in the midst of thunder, his vacillating will, and had called to the performance of his narrow wishes the slaves of a vulgar terror. Always conversant with himself, Samuel, who had spoken what he thought, now performed what he had spoken; and, a year after his arrival in Germany, solemnly abjured Judaism, and entered into the bosom of the Reformed Church. As he did not wish to do things by halves, and desired as much as was in him to put off the old man and lead a new life, he changed his name of Samuel to that of Peter. Some time passed, during which he strengthened and instructed himself in his new religion. Very soon he arrived at the point of searching for objections to refute, and adversaries to overthrow. Bold and enterprising, he went at once to the strongest, and Bossuet was the first Catholic author that he set himself to read. He commenced with a kind of disdain; believing that the faith which he had just embraced contained the pure truth, he despised all the attacks which could be made against it, and laughed already at the irresistible arguments which he was to find in the works of the Eagle of Meaux. But his mistrust and irony soon gave place to wonder first, and then to admiration: he thought that the cause pleaded by such an advocate must, at least, be respectable; and, by a natural transition, came to think that great geniuses would only devote themselves to that which was great. He then studied Catholicism with the same ardor and impartiality which he had bestowed on Lutheranism. He went into France to gain instruction from the professors of the Mother Church, as he had from the Doctors of the reformed creed in Germany. He saw Arnauld Fénélon, that second Gregory of Nazianzen, and Bossuet himself. Guided by these masters, whose virtues made him appreciate their talents the more, he rapidly penetrated to the depth of the mysteries of the Catholic doctrine and morality. He found, in this religion, all that had for him constituted the grandeur and beauty of Protestantism, — the dogmas of the Unity and Eternity of God, which the two religions had borrowed from Judaism; and, what seemed the natural consequence of the last doctrine — a doctrine, however, to which the Jews had not arrived — the doctrine of the immortality of the soul; free will in this life; in the next, recompense for the good, and punishment for the evil. He found, more pure, perhaps, and more elevated in Catholicism than in Protestantism, that sublime morality which preaches equality to man, fraternity, love, charity, renouncement of self, devotion to your neighbor: Catholicism, in a word, seemed to possess that vast formula, and that vigorous unity, which Lutheranism wanted. The latter had, indeed, in its favor, the liberty of inquiry, which is also a want of the human mind; and had proclaimed the authority of individual reason: but it had so lost that which is the necessary basis and vital condition of all revealed religion — the principle of infallibility.; because nothing can live except in virtue of the laws that presided at its birth; and, in consequence, one revelation cannot be continued and confirmed without another. Now, infallibility is nothing but revelation continued by God, or the Word, in the person of his vicars.

.   .   .   .

"At last, after much reflection, Hebronius acknowledged himself entirely and sincerely convinced, and received baptism from the hands of Bossuet. He added the name of Spiridion to that of Peter, to signify that he had been twice enlightened by the Spirit. Resolved thenceforward to consecrate his life to the worship of the new God who had called him to Him, and to the study of His doctrines, he passed into Italy, and, with the aid of a large fortune, which one of his uncles, a Catholic like himself, had left to him, he built this convent where we now are."

.   .   .   .

A friend of mine, who has just come from Italy, says that he has there left Messrs. Sp——r, P——l, and W. Dr——d, who were the lights of the great church in Newman Street, who were themselves apostles, and declared and believed that every word of nonsense which fell from their lips was a direct spiritual intervention. These gentlemen have become Puseyites already, and are, my friend states, in the high way to Catholicism. Madame Sand herself was a Catholic some time since : having been converted to that faith along with M. N——, of the Academy of Music ; Mr. L——, the pianoforte player ; and one or two other chosen individuals, by the famous Abbé de la M——. Abbé de la M—— (so told me in the Diligence, a priest, who read his breviary and gossiped alternately very curiously and pleasantly) is himself an *âme perdue :* the man spoke of his brother clergyman with actual horror ; and it certainly appears that the Abbé's works of conversion have not prospered ; for Madame Sand, having brought her hero (and herself, as we may presume) to the point of Catholicism, proceeds directly to dispose of that as she has done of Judaism and Protestantism, and will not leave, of the whole fabric of Christianity, a single stone standing.

I think the fate of our English Newman Street apostles, and of M. de la M——, the mad priest, and his congregation of mad converts, should be a warning to such of us as are inclined to dabble in religious speculations ; for, in them, as in all others, our flighty brains soon lose themselves, and we find our reason speedily lying prostrated at the mercy of our passions ; and I think that Madame Sand's novel of Spiridion may do a vast deal of good, and bears a good moral with it ; though not such an one, perhaps, as our fair philosopher intended. For anything he learned, Samuel-Peter-Spiridion-Hebronius might have remained a Jew from the beginning to the end. Wherefore be in such a hurry to set up new faiths? Wherefore, Madame Sand, try and be so preternaturally wise? Wherefore be so eager to jump out of one religion, for the purpose of jumping into another? See what good this philosophical friskiness has done you, and on what sort of ground you are come at last. You are so wonderfully sagacious, that you flounder in mud at every step ; so amazingly clear-sighted, that your eyes cannot see an inch before you, having put out, with that extinguishing genius of yours, every one of the lights that are sufficient for the conduct of common men. And for what? Let our friend Spiridion speak for himself. After setting up his convent, and filling it with monks, who entertain an immense respect for his wealth and genius, Father Hebronius, unanimously elected prior, gives himself up to further studies, and leaves his monks to themselves. Industrious and sober as they were, originally, they grow quickly intemperate and idle; and Hebronius, who does not appear among his flock until he has freed himself of the Catholic religion, as he has of the Jewish and the Protestant, sees, with dismay, the evil condition of his disciples, and regrets, too late, the precipitancy by which he renounced, then and for ever, Christianity. "But, as he had no new religion to adopt in its place, and as, grown more prudent and calm, he did not wish to accuse himself unnecessarily, once more, of inconstancy and apostasy, he still maintained all the exterior forms of the worship which inwardly he had abjured. But it was not enough for him to have quitted error, it was necessary to discover truth. But Hebronius had well looked round to discover it; he could not find anything that resembled it. Then commenced for him a series of sufferings, unknown and terrible. Placed face to face with doubt, this sincere and religious spirit was frightened at its own solitude; and as it had no other desire nor aim on earth than truth, and nothing else here below interested it, he lived absorbed in his own sad contemplations, looked ceaselessly into the vague that surrounded him like an ocean without bounds, and seeing the horizon retreat and retreat as ever he wished to near it. Lost in this immense uncertainty, he felt as if attacked by vertigo, and his thoughts whirled within his brain. Then, fatigued with his vain toils and hopeless endeavors, he would sink down depressed, unmanned, life-wearied, only living in the sensation of that silent grief which he felt and could not comprehend."

It is a pity that this hapless Spiridion, so eager in his passage from one creed to another, and so loud in his profession of the truth, wherever he fancied that he had found it, had not waited a little, before he avowed himself either Catholic or Protestant, and implicated others in errors and follies which might, at least, have been confined to his own bosom, and there have lain comparatively harmless. In what a pretty state, for instance, will Messrs. Dr——d and P——l have left their New-man Street congregation, who are still plunged in their old superstitions, from which their spiritual pastors and masters have been set free! In what a state, too, do Mrs. Sand and her brother and sister philosophers, Templars, Saint Simonians, Fourierites, Lerouxites, or whatever the sect may be, leave the unfortunate people who have listened to their doctrines, and who have not the opportunity, or the fiery versatility of belief, which carries their teachers from one creed to another, leaving only exploded lies and useless recantations behind them! I wish the State would make a law that one individual should not

be allowed to preach more than one doctrine in his life, or, at
any rate, should be soundly corrected for every change of creed.
How many charlatans would have been silenced, — how much
conceit would have been kept within bounds, — how many fools,
who are dazzled by fine sentences, and made drunk by declamation, would have remained quiet and sober, in that quiet and
sober way of faith which their fathers held before them. However, the reader will be glad to learn that, after all his doubts
and sorrows, Spiridion does discover the truth (*the* truth, what
a wise Spiridion!) and some discretion with it; for, having
found among his monks, who are dissolute, superstitious — and
all hate him — one only being, Fulgentius, who is loving, candid, and pious, he says to him, — "If you were like myself, if
the first want of your nature were, like mine, to know, I would,
without hesitation, lay bare to you my entire thoughts. I would
make you drink the cup of truth, which I myself have filled with
so many tears, at the risk of intoxicating you with the draught.
But it is not so, alas! you are made to love rather than to know,
and your heart is stronger than your intellect. You are attached to Catholicism, — I believe so, at least, — by bonds of
sentiment which you could not break without pain, and which,
if you were to break, the truth which I could lay bare to you in
return would not repay you for what you had sacrificed. Instead of exalting, it would crush you, very likely. It is a food
too strong for ordinary men, and which, when it does not revivify, smothers. I will not, then, reveal to you this doctrine,
which is the triumph of my life, and the consolation of my last
days; because it might, perhaps, be for you only a cause of
mourning and despair. . . . . Of all the works which my long
studies have produced, there is one alone which I have not given
to the flames; for it alone is complete. In that you will find
me entire, and there LIES THE TRUTH. And, as the sage has
said you must not bury your treasures in a well, I will not confide mine to the brutal stupidity of these monks. But as this
volume should only pass into hands worthy to touch it, and be
laid open for eyes that are capable of comprehending its mysteries, I shall exact from the reader one condition, which, at
the same time, shall be a proof: I shall carry it with me to the
tomb, in order that he who one day shall read it, may have
courage enough to brave the vain terrors of the grave, in searching for it amid the dust of my sepulchre. As soon as I am
dead, therefore, place this writing on my breast. . . . . Ah!
when the time comes for reading it, I think my withered heart
will spring up again, as the frozen grass at the return of

the sun, and that, from the midst of its infinite transforma‚ tions, my spirit will enter into immediate communication with thine ! "

. . . .

Does not the reader long to be at this precious manuscript, which contains THE TRUTH ; and ought he not to be very much obliged to Mrs. Sand, for being so good as to print it for him? We leave all the story aside : how Fulgentius had not the spirit to read the manuscript, but left the secret to Alexis ; how Alexis, a stern old philosophical unbelieving monk as ever was, tried in vain to lift up the gravestone, but was taken with fever, and obliged to forego the discovery ; and how, finally, Angel, his disciple, a youth amiable and innocent as his name, was the destined person who brought the long-buried treasure to light. Trembling and delighted, the pair read this tremendous MANUSCRIPT OF SPIRIDION.

Will it be believed, that of all the dull, vague, windy documents that mortal ever set eyes on, this is the dullest? If this be absolute truth, *à quoi bon* search for it, since we have long, long had the jewel in our possession, or since, at least, it has been held up as such by every sham philosopher who has had a mind to pass off his wares on the public? Hear Spiridion : —

" How much have I wept, how much have I suffered, how much have I prayed, how much have I labored, before I understood the cause and the aim of my passage on this earth ! After many incertitudes, after much remorse, after many scruples, *I have comprehended that I was a martyr !* — But why my martyrdom? said I ; what crime did I commit before I was born, thus to be condemned to labor and groaning, from the hour when I first saw the day up to that when I am about to enter into the night of the tomb?

" At last, by dint of imploring God — by dint of inquiry into the history of man, a ray of the truth has descended on my brow, and the shadows of the past have melted from before my eyes. I have lifted a corner of the curtain : I have seen enough to know that my life, like that of the rest of the human race, has been a series of necessary errors, yet, to speak more correctly, of incomplete truths, conducting, more or less slowly and directly, to absolute truth and ideal perfection. But when will they rise on the face of the earth — when will they issue from the bosom of the Divinity — those generations who shall salute the august countenance of Truth, and proclaim the reign of the ideal on earth? I see well how humanity marches, but I neither can see its cradle nor its apotheosis. Man seems to me a transitory race, between the beast and the angel; but I know not how many centuries have been required, that he might pass from the *state of brute to the state of man*, and *I cannot tell how many ages are necessary that he may pass from the state of man to the state of angel!*

" Yet I hope, and I feel within me, at the approach of death, that which warns me that great destinies await humanity. In this life all is over for me. Much have I striven, to advance but little : I have labored without ceasing, and have done almost nothing. Yet, after pains immeasurable, I die content, for I know that I have done all I could, and am sure that the little I have done will not be lost.

" What, then, have I done? this wilt thou demand of me, man of a future age, who will seek for truth in the testaments of the past. Thou who wilt be no more Catholic — no more Christian, thou wilt ask of the poor monk, lying in the dust, an account of his life and death. Thou wouldst know wherefore were his vows, why his austerities, his labors, his retreat, his prayers?

" You who turn back to me, in order that I may guide you on your road, and that you may arrive more quickly at the goal which it has not been my lot to attain, pause, yet, for a moment, and look upon the past history of humanity. You will see that its fate has been ever to choose between the least of two evils, and ever to commit great faults in order to avoid others still greater. You will see . . . . on one side, the heathen mythology, that debased the spirit, in its efforts to deify the flesh; on the other, the austere Christian principle, that debased the flesh too much, in order to raise the worship of the spirit. You will see, afterwards, how the religion of Christ embodies itself in a church, and raises itself a generous democratic power against the tyranny of princes. Later still, you will see how that power has attained its end, and passed beyond it. You will see it, having chained and conquered princes, league itself with them, in order to oppress the people, and seize on temporal power. Schism, then, raises up against it the standard of revolt, and preaches the bold and legitimate principle of liberty of conscience : but, also, you will see how this liberty of conscience brings religious anarchy in its train ; or, worse still, religious indifference and disgust. And if your soul, shattered in the tempestuous changes which you behold humanity undergoing, would strike out for itself a passage through the rocks, amidst which, like a frail bark, lies tossing trembling truth, you will be embarrassed to choose between the new philosophers — who, in preaching tolerance, destroy religious and social unity — and the last Christians, who, to preserve society, that is, religion and philosophy, are obliged to brave the principle of toleration. Man of truth! to whom I address, at once, my instruction and my justification, at the time when you shall live, the science of truth no doubt will have advanced a step. Think, then, of all your fathers have suffered, as, bending beneath the weight of their ignorance and uncertainty, they have traversed the desert across which, with so much pain, they have conducted thee! And if the pride of thy young learning shall make thee contemplate the petty strifes in which our life has been consumed, pause and tremble, as you think of that which is still unknown to yourself, and of the judgment that your descendants will pass on you. Think of this, and learn to respect all those who, seeking their way in all sincerity, have wandered from the path, frightened by the storm, and sorely tried by the severe hand of the All-Powerful. Think of this, and prostrate yourself; for all these, even the most mistaken among them, are saints and martyrs.

" Without their conquests and their defeats, thou wert in darkness still. Yes, their failures, their errors even, have a right to your respect; for man is weak. . . . . Weep then, for us obscure travellers — unknown victims, who, by our mortal sufferings and unheard-of labors, have prepared the way before you. Pity me, who have passionately loved justice, and perseveringly sought for truth, only opened my eyes to shut them again for ever, and saw that I had been in vain endeavoring to support a ruin, to take refuge in a vault of which the foundations were worn away." . . . .

The rest of the book of Spiridion is made up of a history of the rise, progress, and (what our philosopher is pleased to call) decay of Christianity — of an assertion, that the "doctrine of Christ is incomplete;" that "Christ may, nevertheless, take his place in the Pantheon of divine men!" and of a long, disgusting, absurd, and impious vision, in which the Saviour, Moses, David, and Elijah are represented, and in which Christ is made to say — " *We are all Messiahs*, when we wish to bring the reign of truth upon earth; we are all Christs, when we suffer for it!"

And this is the ultimatum, the supreme secret, the absolute truth! and it has been published by Mrs. Sand, for so many napoleons per sheet, in the *Revue des Deux Mondes;* and the Deux Mondes are to abide by it for the future. After having attained it, are we a whit wiser? "Man is between an angel

and a beast: I don't know how long it is since he was a brute
— I can't say how long it will be before he is an angel." Think
of people living by their wits, and living by such a wit as this!
Think of the state of mental debauch and disease which must
have been passed through, ere such words could be written,
and could be popular!

When a man leaves our dismal, smoky London atmosphere,
and breathes, instead of coal-smoke and yellow fog, this bright,
clear, French air, he is quite intoxicated by it at first, and feels
a glow in his blood, and a joy in his spirits, which scarcely
thrice a year, and then only at a distance from London, he
can attain in England. Is the intoxication, I wonder, permanent among the natives? and may we not account for the ten
thousand frantic freaks of these people by the peculiar influence
of French air and sun? The philosophers are from night to
morning drunk, the politicians are drunk, the literary men reel
and stagger from one absurdity to another, and how shall we
understand their vagaries? Let us suppose, charitably, that
Madame Sand had inhaled a more than ordinary quantity of
this laughing gas when she wrote for us this precious manuscript of *Spiridion*. That great destinies are in prospect for
the human race we may fancy, without her ladyship's word for
it: but more liberal than she, and having a little retrospective
charity, as well as that easy prospective benevolence which
Mrs. Sand adopts, let us try and think there is some hope for
our fathers (who were nearer brutality than ourselves, according to the Sandean creed), or else there is a very poor chance
for us, who, great philosophers as we are, are yet, alas! far
removed from that angelic consummation which all must wish
for so devoutly. She cannot say — is it not extraordinary? —
how many centuries have been necessary before man could pass
from the brutal state to his present condition, or how many
ages will be required ere we may pass from the state of man to
the state of angels? What the deuce is the use of chronology
or philosophy? We were beasts, and we can't tell when our
tails dropped off: we shall be angels; but when our wings are
to begin to sprout, who knows? In the meantime, O man of
genius, follow our counsel: lead an easy life, don't stick at
trifles; never mind about *duty*, it is only made for slaves; if the
world reproach you, reproach the world in return, you have a
good loud tongue in your head: if your straight-laced morals
injure your mental respiration, fling off the old-fashioned stays,
and leave your free limbs to rise and fall as Nature pleases;
and when you have grown pretty sick of your liberty, and yet

unfit to return to restraint, curse the world, and scorn it, and be miserable, like my Lord Byron and other philosophers of his kidney; or else mount a step higher, and, with conceit still more monstrous, and mental vision still more wretchedly debauched and weak, begin suddenly to find yourself afflicted with a maudlin compassion for the human race, and a desire to set them right after your own fashion.   There is the quarrelsome stage of drunkenness, when a man can as yet walk and speak, when he can call names, and fling plates and wine-glasses at his neighbor's head with a pretty good aim; after this comes the pathetic stage, when the patient becomes wondrous philanthropic, and weeps wildly, as he lies in the gutter, and fancies he is at home in bed — where he ought to be; but this is an allegory.

I don't wish to carry this any farther, or to say a word in defence of the doctrine which Mrs. Dudevant has found "incomplete;" — here, at least, is not the place for discussing its merits, any more than Mrs. Sand's book was the place for exposing, forsooth, its errors: our business is only with the day and the new novels, and the clever or silly people who write them.   Oh! if they but knew their places, and would keep to them, and drop their absurd philosophical jargon!   Not all the big words in the world can make Mrs. Sand talk like a philosopher: when will she go back to her old trade, of which she was the very ablest practitioner in France?

I should have been glad to give some extracts from the dramatic and descriptive parts of the novel, that cannot, in point of style and beauty, be praised too highly.   One must suffice, — it is the descent of Alexis to seek that unlucky manuscript, *Spiridion.*

"It seemed to me," he begins, "that the descent was eternal; and that I was burying myself in the depths of Erebus: at last, I reached a level place, — and I heard a mournful voice deliver these words, as it were, to the secret centre of the earth — ' *He will mount that ascent no more !* ' — Immediately I heard arise towards me, from the depth of invisible abysses, a myriad of formidable voices united in a strange chant — ' *Let us destroy him !   Let him be destroyed !   What does he here among the dead ?   Let him be delivered back to torture !   Let him be given again to life !* '

"Then a feeble light began to pierce the darkness, and I perceived that I stood on the lowest step of a staircase, vast as the foot of a mountain.   Behind me were thousands of steps of lurid iron; before me, nothing but a void — an abyss, and ether; the blue gloom of midnight beneath my feet, as above my head. I became delirious, and quitting that staircase, which methought it was impossible for me to reascend, I sprung forth into the void with an execration. But, immediately, when I had uttered the curse, the void began to be filled with forms and colors, and I presently perceived that I was in a vast gallery, along which I advanced, trembling. There was still darkness round me; but the hollows of the vaults gleamed with a red light, and showed me the strange and hideous forms of their building. . . . . I did not distinguish the nearest objects; but those towards which I advanced assumed an appearance more and more ominous, and my terror increased with every step I took. The enormous pillars which supported the vault, and the tracery thereof itself, were figures of men, of supernatural stature, delivered to tortures without a name. Some hung by their feet, and, locked in the coils of monstrous serpents, clenched their teeth in the marble of the pavement; others, fastened by their waists, were dragged upwards, these by their feet, those by their heads, towards capitals, where other figures stooped towards them, eager to torment them. Other pillars, again, represented a struggling mass of figures devouring one another; each of which only offered a trunk severed to the knees or to the shoulders, the fierce heads whereof retained life enough to seize and devour that which was near them. There were some who, half hanging down, agonized themselves by attempting, with their upper limbs, to flay the lower moiety of their bodies, which drooped from the columns, or were attached to the pedestals; and others, who, in their fight with each other, were dragged along by morsels of flesh, — grasping which, they clung to each other with a countenance of unspeakable hate and agony. Along, or rather in place of, the frieze, there were on either side a range of unclean beings, wearing the human form, but of a loathsome ugliness, busied in tearing human corpses to pieces — in feasting upon their limbs and entrails. From the vault, instead of bosses and pendants, hung the crushed and wounded forms of children; as if to escape these eaters of man's flesh, they would throw themselves downwards, and be dashed to pieces on the pavement. . . . . The silence and motionlessness of the whole added to its awfulness. I became so faint with terror, that I stopped, and would fain have returned. But at that moment I heard, from the depths of the gloom through which I had passed, confused noises, like those of a multitude on its march. And the sounds soon became more distinct, and the

clamor fiercer, and the steps came hurrying on tumultuously —
at every new burst nearer, more violent, more threatening. I
thought that I was pursued by this disorderly crowd; and I
strove to advance, hurrying into the midst of those dismal sculp-
tures. Then it seemed as if those figures began to heave,— and
to sweat blood, — and their beady eyes to move in their sockets.
At once I beheld that they were all looking upon me, that they
were all leaning towards me, — some with frightful derision,
others with furious aversion. Every arm was raised against me,
and they made as though they would crush me with the quivering
limbs they had torn one from the other." . . . .

It is, indeed, a pity that the poor fellow gave himself the
trouble to go down into damp, unwholesome graves, for the
purpose of fetching up a few trumpery sheets of manuscript;
and if the public has been rather tired with their contents, and
is disposed to ask why Mrs. Sand's religious or irreligious
notions are to be brought forward to people who are quite satisfied with their own, we can only say that this lady is the
representative of a vast class of her countrymen, whom the
wits and philosophers of the eighteenth century have brought
to this condition. The leaves of the Diderot and Rousseau
tree have produced this goodly fruit : here it is, ripe, bursting,
and ready to fall ; — and how to fall? Heaven send that it
may drop easily, for all can see that the time is come.

THE CASE OF PEYTEL:

IN A LETTER TO EDWARD BRIEFLESS, ESQUIRE, OF PUMP COURT, TEMPLE.

PARIS, November, 1839.

MY DEAR BRIEFLESS, — Two months since, when the act of accusation first appeared, containing the sum of the charges against Sebastian Peytel, all Paris was in a fervor on the subject. The man's trial speedily followed, and kept for three days the public interest wound up to a painful point. He was found guilty of double murder at the beginning of September ; and, since that time, what with Maroto's disaffection and Turkish news, we have had leisure to forget Monsieur Peytel, and to occupy ourselves with τι νέον. Perhaps Monsieur de Balzac helped to smother what little sparks of interest might still have remained for the murderous notary. Balzac put forward a letter in his favor, so very long, so very dull, so very pompous, promising so much, and performing so little, that the Parisian public gave up Peytel and his case altogether ; nor was it until to-day that some small feeling was raised concerning him, when the newspapers brought the account how Peytel's head had been cut off at Bourg.

He had gone through the usual miserable ceremonies and delays which attend what is called, in this country, the march of justice. He had made his appeal to the Court of Cassation, which had taken time to consider the verdict of the Provincial Court, and had confirmed it. He had made his appeal for mercy ; his poor sister coming up all the way from Bourg (a sad journey, poor thing !) to have an interview with the King, who had refused to see her. Last Monday morning, at nine o'clock, an hour before Peytel's breakfast, the Greffier of Assize Court, in company with the Curé of Bourg, waited on him, and informed him that he had only three hours to live. At twelve o'clock, Peytel's head was off his body : an executioner from Lyons had come over the night before, to assist the professional throat-cutter of Bourg.

I am not going to entertain you with any sentimental lamentations for this scoundrel's fate, or to declare my belief in his innocence, as Monsieur de Balzac has done. As far as moral conviction can go, the man's guilt is pretty clearly brought home to him. But any man who has read the " Causes Célèbres," knows that men have been convicted and executed upon evidence ten times more powerful than that which was brought against Peytel. His own account of his horrible case may be true ; there is nothing adduced in the evidence which is strong enough to overthrow it. It is a serious privilege, God knows, that society takes upon itself, at any time, to deprive one of God's creatures of existence. But when the slightest doubt remains, what a tremendous risk does it incur ! In England, thank heaven, the law is more wise and more merciful : an English jury would never have taken a man's blood upon such testimony : an English judge and Crown advocate would never have acted as these Frenchmen have done ; the latter inflaming the public mind by exaggerated appeals to their passions : the former seeking, in every way, to draw confessions from the prisoner, to perplex and confound him, to do away, by fierce cross-questioning and bitter remarks from the bench, with any effect that his testimony might have on the jury. I don't·mean to say that judges and lawyers have been more violent and inquisitorial against the unhappy Peytel than against any one else ; it is the fashion of the country : a man is guilty until he proves himself to be innocent ; and to batter down his defence, if he have any, there are the lawyers, with all their horrible ingenuity, and their captivating passionate eloquence. It is hard thus to set the skilful and tried champions of the law against men unused to this kind of combat ; nay, give a man all the legal aid that he can purchase or procure, still, by this plan, you take him at a cruel, unmanly disadvantage ; he has to fight against the law, clogged with the dreadful weight of his presupposed guilt. Thank God that, in England, things are not managed so.

However, I am not about to entertain you with ignorant disquisitions about the law. Peytel's case may, nevertheless, interest you ; for the tale is a very stirring and mysterious one ; and you may see how easy a thing it is for a man's life to be talked away in France, if ever he should happen to fall under the suspicion of a crime. The French " Acte d'accusation ' begins in the following manner : —

" Of all the events which, in these latter times, have afflicted the department of the Ain, there is none which has caused a more profound and lively sensation than the tragical death of the lady, Félicité Alcazar, wife of Sebastian Benedict Peytel, notary, at Belley. At the end of October, 1838, Madame Peytel quitted that town, with her husband, and their servant Louis Rey, in order to pass a few days at Macon : at midnight, the inhabitants of Belley were suddenly awakened by the arrival of Monsieur Peytel, by his cries, and by the signs which he exhibited of the most lively agitation : he implored the succors of all the physicians in the town ; knocked violently at their doors ; rung at the bells of their houses with a sort of frenzy, and announced that his wife, stretched out, and dying, in his carriage, had just been shot, on the Lyons road, by his domestic, whose life Peytel himself had taken.

" At this recital a number of persons assembled, and what a spectacle was presented to their eyes.

" A young woman lay at the bottom of a carriage, deprived of life ; her whole body was wet, and seemed as if it had just been plunged into the water. She appeared to be severely wounded in the face ; and her garments, which were raised up, in spite of the cold and rainy weather, left the upper part of her knees almost entirely exposed. At the sight of this half-naked and inanimate body, all the spectators were affected. People said that the first duty to pay to a dying woman was, to preserve her from the cold, to cover her. A physician examined the body ; he declared that all remedies were useless ; that Madame Peytel was dead and cold.

" The entreaties of Peytel were redoubled ; he demanded fresh succors, and, giving no heed to the fatal assurance which had just been given him, required that all the physicians in the place should be sent for. A scene so strange and so melancholy ; the incoherent account given by Peytel of the murder of his wife ; his extraordinary movements ; and the avowal which he continued to make, that he had despatched the murderer, Rey, with strokes of his hammer, excited the attention of Lieutenant Wolf, commandant of gendarmes : that officer gave orders for the immediate arrest of Peytel : but the latter threw himself into the arms of a friend, who interceded for him, and begged the police not immediately to seize upon his person.

" The corpse of Madame Peytel was transported to her apartment ; the bleeding body of the domestic was likewise brought from the road, where it lay; and Peytel, asked to explain the circumstance, did so." . . . .

Now, as there is little reason to tell the reader, when an English counsel has to prosecute a prisoner on the part of the Crown for a capital offence, he produces the articles of his accusation in the most moderate terms, and especially warns the jury to give the accused person the benefit of every possible doubt that the evidence may give, or may leave. See how these things are managed in France, and how differently the French counsel for the Crown sets about his work.

He first prepares his act of accusation, the opening of which we have just read; it is published six days before the trial, so that an unimpassioned, unprejudiced jury has ample time to study it, and to form its opinions accordingly, and to go into court with a happy, just prepossession against the prisoner.

Read the first part of the Peytel act of accusation; it is as turgid and declamatory as a bad romance; and as inflated as a newspaper document, by an unlimited penny-a-liner: — " The department of the Ain is in a dreadful state of excitement; the inhabitants of Belley come trooping from their beds, — and what a sight do they behold; — a young woman at the bottom of a carriage, *toute ruisselante,* just out of a river; her garments, in spite of the cold and rain, raised, so as to leave the upper part of her knees entirely exposed, at which all the beholders were affected, and cried, that the *first duty* was to cover her from the cold." This settles the case at once; the first duty of a man is to cover the legs of the sufferer; the second to call for help. The eloquent " Substitut du Procureur du Roi" has prejudged the case, in the course of a few sentences. He is putting his readers, among whom his future jury is to be found, into a proper state of mind; he works on them with pathetic description, just as a romance-writer would: the rain pours in torrents; it is a dreary evening in November; the young creature's situation is neatly described; the distrust which entered into the breast of the keen old officer of gendarmes strongly painted, the suspicions which might, or might not, have been entertained by the inhabitants, eloquently argued. How did the advocate know that the people had such? did all the bystanders say aloud, " I suspect that this is a case of murder by Monsieur Peytel, and that his story about the domestic is all deception?" or did they go off to the mayor, and register their suspicion? or was the advocate there to hear them? Not he; but he paints you the whole scene, as though it had existed, and gives full accounts of suspicions, as if they had been facts, positive, patent, staring, that everybody could see and swear to.

Having thus primed his audience, and prepared them for the testimony of the accused party, "Now," says he, with a fine show of justice, "let us hear Monsieur Peytel;" and that worthy's narrative is given as follows : —

"He said that he had left Macon on the 31st October, at eleven o'clock in the morning, in order to return to Belley, with his wife and servant. The latter drove, or led, an open car; he himself was driving his wife in a four-wheeled carriage, drawn by one horse : they reached Bourg at five o'clock in the evening; left it at seven, to sleep at Pont d'Ain, where they did not arrive before midnight. During the journey, Peytel thought he remarked that Rey had slackened his horse's pace. When they alighted at the inn, Peytel bade him deposit in his chamber 7,500 francs, which he carried with him; but the domestic refused to do so, saying that the inn gates were secure, and there was no danger. Peytel was, therefore, obliged to carry his money up stairs himself. The next day, the 1st November, they set out on their journey again, at nine o'clock in the morning; Louis did not come, according to custom, to take his master's orders. They arrived at Tenay about three, stopped there a couple of hours to dine, and it was eight o'clock when they reached the bourg of Rossillon, where they waited half an hour to bait the horses.

"As they left Rossillon, the weather became bad, and the rain began to fall : Peytel told his domestic to get a covering for the articles in the open chariot; but Rey refused to do so, adding, in an ironical tone, that the weather was fine. For some days past, Peytel had remarked that his servant was gloomy, and scarcely spoke at all.

"After they had gone about 500 paces beyond the bridge of Andert, that crosses the river Furans, and ascended to the least steep part of the hill of Darde, Peytel cried out to his servant, who was seated in the car, to come down from it, and finish the ascent on foot.

"At this moment a violent wind was blowing from the south, and the rain was falling heavily : Peytel was seated back in the right corner of the carriage, and his wife, who was close to him, was asleep, with her head on his left shoulder. All of a sudden he heard the report of a fire-arm (he had seen the light of it at some paces' distance), and Madame Peytel cried out, 'My poor husband, take your pistols;' the horse was frightened, and began to trot. Peytel immediately

15

drew the pistol, and fired, from the interior of the carriage, upon an individual whom he saw running by the side of the road.

" Not knowing, as yet, that his wife had been hit, he jumped out on one side of the carriage, while Madame Peytel descended from the other ; and he fired a second pistol at his domestic, Louis Rey, whom he had just recognized. Redoubling his pace, he came up with Rey, and struck him, from behind, a blow with the hammer. Rey turned at this, and raised up his arm to strike his master with the pistol which he had just discharged at him ; but Peytel, more quick than he, gave the domestic a blow with the hammer, which felled him to the ground (he fell his face forwards), and then Peytel, bestriding the body, despatched him, although the brigand asked for mercy.

" He now began to think of his wife ; and ran back, calling out her name repeatedly, and seeking for her, in vain, on both sides of the road. Arrived at the bridge of Andert, he recognized his wife, stretched in a field, covered with water, which bordered the Furans. This horrible discovery had so much the more astonished him, because he had no idea, until now, that his wife had been wounded : he endeavored to draw her from the water ; and it was only after considerable exertions that he was enabled to do so, and to place her, with her face towards the ground, on the side of the road. Supposing that, here, she would be sheltered from any farther danger, and believing, as yet, that she was only wounded, he determined to ask for help at a lone house, situated on the road towards Rossillon ; and at this instant he perceived, without at all being able to explain how, that his horse had followed him back to the spot, having turned back of its own accord, from the road to Belley.

" The house at which he knocked was inhabited by two men, of the name of Thannet, father and son, who opened the door to him, and whom he entreated to come to his aid, saying that his wife had just been assassinated by his servant. The elder Thannet approached to, and examined the body, and told Peytel that it was quite dead ; he and his son took up the corpse, and placed it in the bottom of the carriage, which they all mounted themselves, and pursued their route to Belley. In order to do so, they had to pass by Rey's body, on the road, which Peytel wished to crush under the wheels of his carriage. It was to rob him of 7,500 francs, said Peytel, that the attack had been made."

Our friend, the Procureur's Substitut, has dropped, here, the eloquent and pathetic style altogether, and only gives the unlucky prisoner's narrative in the baldest and most unimaginative style. How is a jury to listen to such a fellow? they ought to condemn him, if but for making such an uninteresting statement. Why not have helped poor Peytel with some of those rhetorical graces which have been so plentifully bestowed in the opening part of the act of accusation? He might have said : —

" Monsieur Peytel is an eminent notary at Belley ; he is a man distinguished for his literary and scientific acquirements; he has lived long in the best society of the capital ; he had been but a few months married to that young and unfortunate lady, whose loss has plunged her bereaved husband into despair — almost into madness. Some early differences had marked, it is true, the commencement of their union ; but these, — which, as can be proved by evidence, were almost all the unhappy lady's fault, — had happily ceased, to give place to sentiments far more delightful and tender. Gentlemen, Madame Peytel bore in her bosom a sweet pledge of future concord between herself and her husband : in three brief months she was to become a mother.

" In the exercise of his honorable profession, — in which, to succeed, a man must not only have high talents, but undoubted probity, — and, gentlemen, Monsieur Peytel *did* succeed — *did* inspire respect and confidence, as you, his neighbors, well know ; — in the exercise, I say, of his high calling, Monsieur Peytel, towards the end of October last, had occasion to make a journey in the neighborhood, and visit some of his many clients.

" He travelled in his own carriage, his young wife beside him. Does this look like want of affection, gentlemen? or is it not a mark of love — of love and paternal care on his part towards the being with whom his lot in life was linked, — the mother of his coming child, — the young girl, who had everything to gain from the union with a man of his attainments of intellect, his kind temper, his great experience, and his high position? In this manner they travelled, side by side, lovingly together. Monsieur Peytel was not a lawyer merely, but a man of letters and varied learning; of the noble and sublime science of geology he was, especially, an ardent devotee."

(Suppose, here, a short panegyric upon geology. Allude to the creation of this mighty world, and then, naturally, to the Creator. Fancy the conversations which Peytel, a religious man,* might have with his young wife upon the subject.)

" Monsieur Peytel had lately taken into his service a man

* He always went to mass ; it is in the evidence.

named Louis Rey. Rey was a foundling, and had passed many
years in a regiment — a school, gentlemen, where much besides
bravery, alas! is taught; nay, where the spirit which familiar-
izes one with notions of battle and death, I fear, may familiarize
one with ideas, too, of murder. Rey, a dashing reckless fellow,
from the army, had lately entered Peytel's service ; was treated
by him with the most singular kindness ; accompanied him
(having charge of another vehicle) upon the journey before
alluded to ; and *knew that his master carried with him a considerable sum of money;* for a man like Rey an enormous sum, 7,500
francs. At midnight on the 1st of November, as Madame Peytel and her husband were returning home, an attack was made
upon their carriage. Remember, gentlemen, the hour at which
the attack was made ; remember the sum of money that was in
the carriage ; and remember that the Savoy frontier *is within a
league of the spot* where the desperate deed was done."

Now, my dear Briefless, ought not Monsieur Procureur, in
common justice to Peytel, after he had so eloquently proclaimed,
not the facts, but the suspicions, which weighed against that
worthy, to have given a similar florid account of the prisoner's
case? Instead of this, you will remark, that it is the advocate's
endeavor to make Peytel's statements as uninteresting in style
as possible ; and then he demolishes them in the following
way : —

" Scarcely was Peytel's statement known, when the common
sense of the public rose against it. Peytel had commenced his
story upon the bridge of Andert, over the cold body of his wife.
On the 2nd November he had developed it in detail, in the
presence of the physicians, in the presence of the assembled
neighbors — of the persons who, on the day previous only, were
his friends. Finally, he had completed it in his interrogatories,
his conversations, his writings, and letters to the magistrates ;
and everywhere these words, repeated so often, were only received with a painful incredulity. The fact was that, besides
the singular character which Peytel's appearance, attitude, and
talk had worn ever since the event, there was in his narrative
an inexplicable enigma ; its contradictions and impossibilities
were such, that calm persons were revolted at it, and that even
friendship itself refused to believe it."

Thus Mr. Attorney speaks, not for himself alone, but for the
whole French public ; whose opinions, of course, he knows.
Peytel's statement is discredited *everywhere ;* the statement
which he had made over the cold body of his wife — the monster! It is not enough simply to prove that the man committed

the murder, but to make the jury violently angry against him, and cause them to shudder in the jury-box, as he exposes the horrid details of the crime.

" Justice," goes on Mr. Substitute (who answers for the feelings of everybody), " *disturbed by the pre-occupations of public opinion*, commenced, without delay, the most active researches. The bodies of the victims were submitted to the investigations of men of art ; the wounds and projectiles were examined ; the place where the event took place explored with care.   The morality of the author of this frightful scene became the object of rigorous examination ; the *exigeances* of the prisoner, the forms affected by him, his calculating silence, and his answers, coldly insulting, were feeble obstacles ; and justice at length arrived, by its prudence, and by the discoveries it made, to the most cruel point of certainty."

You see that a man's demeanor is here made a crime against him ; and that Mr. Substitute wishes to consider him guilty, because he has actually the audacity to hold his tongue.   Now follows a touching description of the domestic, Louis Rey : —

" Louis Rey, a child of the Hospital at Lyons, was confided, at a very early age, to some honest country people, with whom he stayed until he entered the army.   At their house, and during this long period of time, his conduct, his intelligence, and the sweetness of his manners were such, that the family of his guardians became to him as an adopted family ; and his departure caused them the most sincere affliction.   When Louis quitted the army, he returned to his benefactors, and was received as a son.   They found him just as they had ever known him " (I acknowledge that this pathos beats my humble defence of Peytel entirely), " except that he had learned to read and write ; and the certificates of his commanders proved him to be a good and gallant soldier.

" The necessity of creating some resources for himself, obliged him to quit his friends, and to enter the service of Monsieur de Montrichard, a lieutenant of gendarmerie, from whom he received fresh testimonials of regard.   Louis, it is true, might have a fondness for wine and a passion for women ; but he had been a soldier, and these faults were, according to the witnesses, amply compensated for by his activity, his intelligence, and the agreeable manner in which he performed his service.   In the month of July, 1839, Rey quitted, voluntarily, the service of M. de Montrichard ; and Peytel, about this period, meeting him at Lyons, did not hesitate to attach him

to his service. Whatever may be the prisoner's present language, it is certain that up to the day of Louis's death, he
served Peytel with diligence and fidelity.

" More than once his master and mistress spoke well of him.
Everybody who has worked, or been at the house of Madame
Peytel, has spoken in praise of his character ; and, indeed, it
may be said, that these testimonials were general.

" On the very night of the 1st of November, and immediately after the catastrophe, we remark how Peytel begins to
make insinuations against his servant ; and how artfully, in
order to render them more sure, he disseminates them through
the different parts of his narrative. But, in the course of the
proceeding, these charges have met with a most complete
denial. Thus we find the disobedient servant who, at Pont
d'Ain, refused to carry the money-chest to his master's room,
under the pretext that the gates of the inn were closed securely,
occupied with tending the horses after their long journey :
meanwhile Peytel was standing by, and neither master nor
servant exchanged a word, and the witnesses who beheld
them both have borne testimony to the zeal and care of the
domestic.

" In like manner, we find that the servant, who was so
remiss in the morning as to neglect to go to his master for
orders, was ready for departure before seven o'clock, and had
eagerly informed himself whether Monsieur and Madame Peytel
were awake ; learning from the maid of the inn, that they had
ordered nothing for their breakfast. This man, who refused to
carry with him a covering for the car, was, on the contrary,
ready to take off his own cloak, and with it shelter articles of
small value ; this man, who had been for many days so silent
and gloomy, gave, on the contrary, many proofs of his gayety
— almost of his indiscretion, speaking, at all the inns, in terms
of praise of his master and mistress. The waiter at the inn at
Dauphin, says he was a tall young fellow, mild and good-
natured ; ' we talked for some time about horses, and such
things ; he seemed to be perfectly natural, and not pre-occu-
pied at all.' At Pont d'Ain, he talked of his being a foundling ; of the place where he had been brought up, and where
he had served ; and finally, at Rossillon, an hour before his
death, he conversed familiarly with the master of the port, and
spoke on indifferent subjects.

" All Peytel's insinuations against his servant had no other
end than to show, in every point of Rey's conduct, the behavior
of a man who was premeditating attack. Of what, in fact,

does he accuse him? Of wishing to rob him of 7,500 francs, and of having had recourse to assassination, in order to effect the robbery. But, for a premeditated crime, consider what singular improvidence the person showed who had determined on committing it; what folly and what weakness there is in the execution of it.

"How many insurmountable obstacles are there in the way of committing and profiting by crime! On leaving Belley, Louis Rey, according to Peytel's statement, knowing that his master would return with money, provided himself with a holster pistol, which Madame Peytel had once before perceived among his effects. In Peytel's cabinet there were some balls; four of these were found in Rey's trunk, on the 6th of November. And, in order to commit the crime, this domestic had brought away with him a pistol, and no ammunition; for Peytel has informed us that Rey, an hour before his departure from Macon, purchased six balls at a gunsmith's. To gain his point, the assassin must immolate his victims; for this, he has only one pistol, knowing, perfectly well, that Peytel, in all his travels, had two on his person; knowing that, at a late hour of the night, his shot might fail of effect; and that, in this case, he would be left to the mercy of his opponent.

"The execution of the crime is, according to Peytel's account, still more singular. Louis does not get off the carriage, until Peytel tells him to descend. He does not think of taking his master's life until he is sure that the latter has his eyes open. It is dark, and the pair are covered in one cloak; and Rey only fires at them at six paces' distance : he fires at hazard, without disquieting himself as to the choice of his victim; and the soldier, who was bold enough to undertake this double murder, has not force nor courage to consummate it. He flies, carrying in his hand a useless whip, with a heavy mantle on his shoulders, in spite of the detonation of two pistols at his ears, and the rapid steps of an angry master in pursuit, which ought to have set him upon some better means of escape. And we find this man, full of youth and vigor, lying with his face to the ground, in the midst of a public road, falling without a struggle, or resistance, under the blows of a hammer!

"And suppose the murderer had succeeded in his criminal projects, what fruit could he have drawn from them? — Leaving, on the road, the two bleeding bodies; obliged to lead two carriages at a time, for fear of discovery; not able to return himself, after all the pains he had taken to speak, at every place at which they had stopped, of the money which his master was carrying with him; too prudent to appear alone at Belley, arrested at the frontier, by the excise officers, who would present an impassable barrier to him till morning, — what could he do, or hope to do? The examination of the car has shown that Rey, at the moment of the crime, had neither linen. nor clothes, nor effects of any kind. There was found in his pockets, when the body was examined, no passport, nor certificate; one of his pockets contained a ball, of large calibre, which he had shown, in play, to a girl, at the inn at Macon, a little horn-handled knife, a snuff-box, a little packet of gunpowder, and a purse, containing only a halfpenny and some string. Here is all the baggage, with which, after the execution of his homicidal plan, Louis Rey intended to take refuge in a foreign country.* Beside these absurd contradictions, there is another remarkable fact, which must not be passed over; it is this: — the pistol found by Rey is of antique form, and the original owner of it has been found. He is a curiosity-merchant at Lyons; and, though he cannot affirm that Peytel was the person who bought this pistol of him, he perfectly recognizes Peytel as having been a frequent customer at his shop!

"No, we may fearlessly affirm that Louis Rey was not guilty of the crime which Peytel lays to his charge. If, to those who knew him, his mild and open disposition, his military career, modest and without a stain, the touching regrets of his employers, are sufficient proofs of his innocence, — the calm and candid observer, who considers how the crime was conceived, was executed, and what consequences would have resulted from it, will likewise acquit him, and free him of the odious imputation which Peytel endeavors to cast upon his memory.

"But justice has removed the veil, with which an impious hand endeavored to cover itself. Already, on the night of the 1st of November, suspicion was awakened by the extraordinary agitation of Peytel; by those excessive attentions towards his wife, which came so late; by that excessive and noisy grief, and by those calculated bursts of sorrow, which are such as Nature does not exhibit. The criminal, whom the public conscience had fixed upon; the man whose frightful combinations have been laid bare, and whose falsehoods, step by step, have been exposed, during the proceedings previous to the trial; the murderer, at whose hands a heart-stricken family, and society at large, demands an account of the blood of a wife; — that murderer is Peytel."

* This sentence is taken from another part of the "Acte d'accusation."

When, my dear Briefless, you are a judge (as I make no doubt you will be, when you have left off the club all night, cigar-smoking of mornings, and reading novels in bed), will you ever find it in your heart to order a fellow-sinner's head off upon such evidence as this? Because a romantic Substitut du Procureur de Roi chooses to compose and recite a little drama, and draw tears from juries, let us hope that severe Rhadamanthine judges are not to be melted by such trumpery. One wants but the description of the characters to render the piece complete, as thus : —

Personages.		Costumes.
SEBASTIEN PEYTEL......	Meurtrier	{ Habillement complet de notaire perfide : figure pâle, barbe noire, cheveux noirs.
LOUIS REY	{ Soldat rétiré, bon, brave, franc, jovial aimant le vin, les femmes, la gaieté, ses maîtres surtout ; vrai Français, enfin	} Costume ordinaire ; il porte sur ses épaules une couverture de cheval.
WOLF......................	Lieutenant de gendarmerie.	
FÉLICITÉ D'ALCAZAR...	Femme et victime de Peytel.	

Médecins, Villageois, Filles d'Auberge, Garçons d'Ecurie, &c. &c.
La scène se passe sur le pont d'Andert, entre Macon et Belley. Il est minuit, La pluie tombe: les tonnerres grondent. Le ciel est couvert de nuages, et sillonné d'éclairs.

All these personages are brought into play in the Procureur's drama ; the villagers come in with their chorus ; the old lieutenant of gendarmes with his suspicions ; Rey's frankness and gayety, the romantic circumstances of his birth, his gallantry and fidelity, are all introduced, in order to form a contrast with Peytel, and to call down the jury's indignation against the latter. But are these proofs? or anything like proofs? And the suspicions, that are to serve instead of proofs, what are they?

" My servant, Louis Rey, was very sombre and reserved," says Peytel ; "he refused to call me in the morning, to carry my money-chest to my room, to cover the open car when it rained." The Prosecutor disproves this by stating that Rey talked with the inn maids and servants, asked if his master was up, and stood in the inn-yard, grooming the horses, with his master by his side, neither speaking to the other. Might he not have talked to the maids, and yet been sombre when speaking to his master? Might he not have neglected to call his master, and yet have asked whether he was awake? Might he not have said that the inn-gates were safe, out of hearing of the ostler witness? Mr. Substitute's answers to Peytel's statements are no answer at all. Every word Peytel said might be true, and yet Louis Rey might not have committed the murder; or every word might have been false, and yet Louis Rey might have committed the murder.

"Then," says Mr. Substitute, "how many obstacles are there to the commission of the crime? And these are —

" 1. Rey provided himself with *one* holster pistol, to kill two people, knowing well that one of them had always a brace of pistols about him.

" 2. He does not think of firing until his master's eyes are open : fires at six paces, not caring at whom he fires, and then runs away.

" 3. He could not have intended to kill his master, because he had no passport in his pocket, and no clothes ; and because he must have been detained at the frontier until morning; and because he would have had to drive two carriages, in order to avoid suspicion.

" 4. And, a most singular circumstance, the very pistol which was found by his side had been bought at the shop of a man at Lyons, who perfectly recognized Peytel as one of his customers, though he could not say he had sold that particular weapon to Peytel."

Does it follow, from this, that Louis Rey is not the murderer, much more, that Peytel is? Look at argument No. 1. Rey had no need to kill two people : he wanted the money, and not the blood. Suppose he had killed Peytel, would he not have mastered Madame Peytel easily? — a weak woman, in an excessively delicate situation, incapable of much energy, at the best of times.

2. " He does not fire till he knows his master's eyes are open." Why, on a stormy night, does a man driving a carriage go to sleep? Was Rey to wait until his master snored? " He fires at six paces, not caring whom he hits;" — and might not this happen too? The night is not so dark but that he can see his master, in *his usual place*, driving. He fires and hits — whom? Madame Peytel, who had left her place, *and was wrapped up with Peytel in his cloak*. She screams out, " Husband, take your pistols." Rey knows that his master has a brace, thinks that he has hit the wrong person, and, as Peytel fires on him, runs away. Peytel follows, hammer in hand ; as he comes up with the fugitive, he deals him a blow on the back of the head, and Rey falls — his face to the ground. Is there anything unnatural in this story? — anything so monstrously unnatural, that is, that it might not be true?

3. These objections are absurd. Why need a man have change of linen? If he had taken none for the journey, why should he want any for the escape? Why need he drive two carriages? — He might have driven both into the river, and Mrs. Peytel in one. Why is he to go to the douane, and thrust himself into the very jaws of danger? Are there not a thousand ways for a man to pass a frontier? Do smugglers, when they have to pass from one country to another, choose exactly those spots where a police is placed?

And, finally, the gunsmith of Lyons, who knows Peytel quite well, cannot say that he sold the pistol to him; that is, he did *not* sell the pistol to him; for you have only one man's word, in this case (Peytel's), to the contrary; and the testimony, as far as it goes, is in his favor. I say, my lud, and gentlemen of the jury, that these objections of my learned friend, who is engaged for the Crown, are absurd, frivolous, monstrous; that to *suspect* away the life of a man upon such suppositions as these, is wicked, illegal, and inhuman; and, what is more, that Louis Rey, if he wanted to commit the crime — if he wanted to possess himself of a large sum of money, chose the best time and spot for so doing; and, no doubt, would have succeeded, if Fate had not, in a wonderful manner, caused Madame Peytel *to take her husband's place*, and receive the ball intended for him in her own head.

But whether these suspicions are absurd or not, hit or miss, it is the advocate's duty, as it appears, to urge them. He wants to make as unfavorable an impression as possible with regard to Peytel's character; he, therefore, must, for contrast's sake, give all sorts of praise to his victim, and awaken every sympathy in the poor fellow's favor. Having done this, as far as lies in his power, having exaggerated every circumstance that can be unfavorable to Peytel, and given his own tale in the baldest manner possible — having declared that Peytel is the murderer of his wife and servant, the Crown now proceeds to back this assertion, by showing what interested motives he had, and by relating, after its own fashion, the circumstances of his marriage.

They may be told briefly here. Peytel was of a good family, of Macon, and entitled, at his mother's death, to a considerable property. He had been educated as a notary, and had lately purchased a business, in that line, in Belley, for which he had paid a large sum of money; part of the sum, 15,000 francs, for which he had given bills, was still due.

Near Belley, Peytel first met Félicité Alcazar, who was residing with her brother-in-law, Monsieur de Montrichard; and, knowing that the young lady's fortune was considerable, he made an offer of marriage to the brother-in-law, who thought the match advantageous, and communicated on the subject with Félicité's mother, Madame Alcazar, at Paris. After a time Peytel went to Paris, to press his suit, and was accepted. There seems to have been no affectation of love on his side; and some little repugnance on the part of the lady, who yielded, however, to the wishes of her parents, and was married. The parties began to quarrel on the very day of the marriage, and continued their disputes almost to the close of the unhappy connection. Félicité was half blind, passionate, sarcastic, clumsy in her person and manners, and ill educated; Peytel, a man of considerable intellect and pretensions, who had lived for some time at Paris, where he had mingled with good literary society. The lady was, in fact, as disagreeable a person as could well be, and the evidence describes some scenes which took place between her and her husband, showing how deeply she must have mortified and enraged him.

A charge very clearly made out against Peytel, is that of dishonesty; he procured from the notary of whom he bought his place an acquittance in full, whereas there were 15,000 francs owing, as we have seen. He also, in the contract of marriage, which was to have resembled, in all respects, that between Monsieur Broussais and another Demoiselle Alcazar, caused an alteration to be made in his favor, which gave him command over his wife's funded property, without furnishing the guarantees by which the other son-in-law was bound. And, almost immediately after his marriage, Peytel sold out of the funds a sum of 50,000 francs, that belonged to his wife, and used it for his own purposes.

About two months after his marriage, *Peytel pressed his wife to make her will.* He had made his, he said, leaving everything to her, in case of his death: after some parley, the poor thing consented.* This is a cruel suspicion against him; and

---

* "Peytel," says the act of accusation, "did not fail to see the danger which would menace him, if this will (which had escaped the magistrates in their search of Peytel's papers) was discovered. He, therefore, instructed his agent to take possession of it, which he did, and the fact was not mentioned for several months afterwards. Peytel and his agent were called upon to explain the circumstance, but refused, and their silence for a long time interrupted the 'instruction'" (getting up of the evidence). "All that could be obtained from them was an avowal, that such a will existed, constituting Peytel his wife's sole legatee; and a promise, on their parts, to produce it before the court gave its sentence." But why keep the

Mr. Substitute has ·no need to enlarge upon it. As for the previous fact, the dishonest statement about the 15,000 francs, there is nothing murderous in that — nothing which a man very eager to make a good marriage might not do. The same may be said of the suppression, in Peytel's marriage contract, of the clause to be found in Broussais's, placing restrictions upon the use of the wife's money. Mademoiselle d'Alcazar's friends read the contract before they signed it, and might have refused it, had they so pleased.

After some disputes, which took place between Peytel and his wife (there were continual quarrels, and continual letters passing between them from room to room), the latter was induced to write him a couple of exaggerated letters, swearing " by the ashes of her father" that she would be an obedient wife to him, and entreating him to counsel and direct her. These letters were seen by members of the lady's family, who, in the quarrels between the couple, always took the husband's part. They were found in Peytel's cabinet, after he had been arrested for the murder, and after he had had full access to all his papers, of which he destroyed or left as many as he pleased. The accusation makes it a matter of suspicion against Peytel, that he should have left these letters of his wife's in a conspicuous situation.

" All these circumstances," says the accusation, " throw a frightful light upon Peytel's plans. The letters and will of Madame Peytel are in the hands of her husband. Three months pass away, and this poor woman is brought to her home, in the middle of the night, with two balls in her head, stretched at the bottom of her carriage, by the side of a peasant."

" What other than Sebastian Peytel could have committed this murder? — whom could it profit? — who but himself had an odious chain to break, and an inheritance to receive? Why speak of the servant's projected robbery? The pistols found by the side of Louis's body, the balls bought by him at Macon, and those discovered at Belley among his effects, were only the result of a perfidious combination. The pistol, indeed, which was found on the hill of Darde, on the night of the 1st of November, could only have belonged to Peytel, and must have been thrown by him, near the body of his domestic, with the

will secret? The anxiety about it was surely absurd and unnecessary: the whole of Madame Peytel's family knew that such a will was made. She had consulted her sister concerning it, who said — " If there is no other way of satisfying him, make the will;" and the mother, when she heard of it, cried out — " Does he intend to poison her ? "

paper which had before enveloped it. Who had seen this pistol in the hands of Louis? Among all the gendarmes, work-women, domestics, employed by Peytel and his brother-in-law, is there one single witness who had seen this weapon in Louis's possession? It is true that Madame Peytel did, on one occasion, speak to M. de Montrichard of a pistol; which had nothing to do, however, with that found near Louis Rey."

Is this justice, or good reason? Just reverse the argument, and apply it to Rey. "Who but Rey could have committed this murder? — who but Rey had a large sum of money to seize upon? — a pistol is found by his side, balls and powder in his pocket, other balls in his trunks at home. The pistol found near his body could not, indeed, have belonged to Peytel: did any man ever see it in his possession? The very gunsmith who sold it, and who knew Peytel, would he not have known that he had sold him this pistol? At his own house, Peytel has a collection of weapons of all kinds; everybody has seen them — a man who makes such collections is anxious to display them. Did any one ever see this weapon? — Not one. And Madame Peytel did, in her lifetime, remark a pistol in the valet's possession. She was short-sighted, and could not particularize what kind of pistol it was; but she spoke of it to her husband and her brother-in-law." This is not satisfactory, if you please; but, at least, it is as satisfactory as the other set of suppositions. It is the very chain of argument which would have been brought against Louis Rey by this very same compiler of the act of accusation, had Rey survived, instead of Peytel, and had he, as most undoubtedly would have been the case, been tried for the murder.

This argument was shortly put by Peytel's counsel: — "*If Peytel had been killed by Rey in the struggle, would you not have found Rey guilty of the murder of his master and mistress?*" It is such a dreadful dilemma, that I wonder how judges and lawyers could have dared to persecute Peytel in the manner which they did.

After the act of accusation, which lays down all the suppositions against Peytel as facts, which will not admit the truth of one of the prisoner's allegations in his own defence, comes the trial. The judge is quite as impartial as the preparer of the indictment, as will be seen by the following specimens of his interrogatories: —

Judge. "The act of accusation finds in your statement contradictions, improbabilities, impossibilities. Thus your domestic, who had determined to assassinate you, in order to rob you, and who *must have calculated upon the consequence of a failure*, had neither passport nor money upon him. This is very unlikely ; because he could not have gone far with only a single halfpenny, which was all he had."

Prisoner. " My servant was known, and often passed the frontier without a passport."

Judge. " *Your domestic had to assassinate two persons*, and had no weapon but a single pistol. He had no dagger ; and the only thing found on him was a knife."

Prisoner. " In the car there were several turner's implements, which he might have used."

Judge. " But he had not those arms upon him, because you pursued him immediately. He had, according to you, only this old pistol."

Prisoner. " I have nothing to say."

Judge. " Your domestic, instead of flying into woods, which skirt the road, ran straight forward on the road itself: *this, again, is very unlikely*."

Prisoner. " This is a conjecture I could answer by another conjecture ; I can only reason on the facts."

Judge. " How far did you pursue him ? "

Prisoner. " I don't know exactly."

Judge. " You said ' two hundred paces.' "

No answer from the prisoner.

Judge. " Your domestic was young, active, robust, and tall. He was ahead of you. You were in a carriage, from which you had to descend : you had to take your pistols from a cushion, and *then* your hammer ; — how are we to believe that you could have caught him, if he ran? It is *impossible*."

Prisoner. " I can't explain it : I think that Rey had some defect in one leg. I, for my part, run tolerably fast."

Judge. " At what distance from him did you fire your first shot ? "

Prisoner. " I can't tell."

Judge. " Perhaps he was not running when you fired."

Prisoner. " I saw him running."

Judge. " In what position was your wife ? "

Prisoner. " She was leaning on my left arm, and the man was on the right side of the carriage."

Judge. " The shot must have been fired *à bout portant*, because it burned the eyebrows and lashes entirely. The assassin must have passed his pistol across your breast."

Prisoner. " The shot was not fired so close ; I am convinced of it : professional gentlemen will prove it."

Judge. "*That is what you pretend, because you understand perfectly the consequences of admitting the fact.* Your wife was hit with two balls — one striking downwards, to the right, by the nose, the other going horizontally through the cheek, to the left."

Prisoner. "The contrary will be shown by the witnesses called for the purpose."

Judge. "*It is a very unlucky combination for you* that these balls, which went, you say, from the same pistol, should have taken two different directions."

Prisoner. "I can't dispute about the various combinations of fire-arms — professional persons will be heard."

Judge. "According to your statement, your wife said to you, ' My poor husband, take your pistols.'"

Prisoner. "She did."

Judge. "In a manner quite distinct."

Prisoner. "Yes."

Judge. "So distinct that you did not fancy she was hit?"

Prisoner. "Yes; that is the fact."

Judge. "*Here, again, is an impossibility;* and nothing is more precise than the declaration of the medical men. They affirm that your wife could not have spoken — their report is unanimous."

Prisoner. "I can only oppose to it quite contrary opinions from professional men, also: you must hear them."

Judge. "What did your wife do next?"

.   .   .   .

Judge. "You deny the statements of the witnesses:" (they related to Peytel's demeanor and behavior, which the judge wishes to show were very unusual; — and what if they were?) "Here, however, are some mute witnesses, whose testimony, you will not perhaps refuse. Near Louis Rey's body was found a horse-cloth, a pistol, and a whip. . . . . Your domestic must have had this cloth upon him when he went to assassinate you: it was wet and heavy. An assassin disencumbers himself of anything that is likely to impede him, especially when he is going to struggle with a man as young as himself."

Prisoner. "My servant had, I believe, this covering on his body; it might be useful to him to keep the priming of his pistol dry."

The president caused the cloth to be opened, and showed that there was no hook, or tie, by which it could be held together; and that Rey must have held it with one hand, and, in the other, his whip, and the pistol with which he intended to commit the crime ; which was impossible.

Prisoner. " These are only conjectures."

And what conjectures, my God ! upon which to take away the life of a man. Jeffreys, or Fouquier Tinville, could scarcely have dared to make such. Such prejudice, such bitter persecution, such priming of the jury, such monstrous assumptions and unreason — fancy them coming from an impartial judge! The man is worse than the public accuser.

" Rey," says the Judge, " could not have committed the murder, *because he had no money in his pocket, to fly, in case of failure.*" And what is the precise sum that his lordship thinks necessary for a gentleman to have, before he makes such an attempt? Are the men who murder for money, usually in possession of a certain independence before they begin? How much money was Rey, a servant, who loved wine and women, had been stopping at a score of inns on the road, and had, probably, an annual income of 400 francs, — how much money was Rey likely to have?

" *Your servant had to assassinate two persons.*" This I have mentioned before. Why had he to assassinate two persons,* when one was enough? If he had killed Peytel, could he not have seized and gagged his wife immediately?

" *Your domestic ran straight forward, instead of taking to the woods, by the side of the road : this is very unlikely.*" How does his worship know? Can any judge, however enlightened, tell the exact road that a man will take, who has just missed a *coup* of murder, and is pursued by a man who is firing pistols at him? And has a judge a right to instruct a jury in this way, as to what they shall, or shall not, believe?

" You have to run after an active man, who has the start of you : to jump out of a carriage ; to take your pistols ; and *then*, your hammer. *This is impossible.*" By heavens ! does it not make a man's blood boil, to read such blundering, blood-seeking sophistry? This man, when it suits him, shows that Rey would be slow in his motions ; and when it suits him, declares that Rey ought to be quick ; declares *ex cathedrâ*, what pace Rey should go, and what direction he should take ; shows, in a breath, that he must have run faster than Peytel ; and then, that he could not run fast, because the cloak clogged him ; set-

* M. Balsac's theory of the case is, that Rey had intrigued with Madame Peytel ; having known her previous to her marriage, when she was staying in the house of her brother-in-law, Monsieur de Montrichard, where Rey had been a servant.

16

tles how he is to be dressed when he commits a murder, and
what money he is to have in his pocket; gives these impossible suppositions to the jury, and tells them that the previous
statements are impossible; and, finally, informs them of the
precise manner in which Rey must have stood holding his
horse-cloth in one hand, his whip and pistol in the other, when
he made the supposed attempt at murder. Now, what is the
size of a horse-cloth? Is it as big as a pocket-handkerchief?
Is there no possibility that it might hang over one shoulder;
that the whip should be held under that very arm? Did you
never see a carter so carry it, his hands in his pockets all the
while? Is it monstrous, abhorrent to nature, that a man should
fire a pistol from under a cloak on a rainy day? — that he
should, after firing the shot, be frightened, and run; run
straight before him, with the cloak on his shoulders, and the
weapon in his hand? Peytel's story is possible, and very possible; it is almost probable. Allow that Rey had the cloth
on, and you allow that he must have been clogged in his motions; that Peytel may have come up with him — felled him
with a blow of the hammer; the doctors say that he would
have so fallen by one blow — he would have fallen on his face,
as he was found: the paper might have been thrust into his
breast, and tumbled out as he fell. Circumstances far more
impossible have occurred ere this; and men have been hanged
for them, who were as innocent of the crime laid to their
charge as the judge on the bench, who convicted them.

In like manner, Peytel may not have committed the crime
charged to him; and Mr. Judge, with his arguments as to
possibilities and impossibilities, — Mr. Public Prosecutor, with
his romantic narrative and inflammatory harangues to the jury,
— may have used all these powers to bring to death an innocent
man. From the animus with which the case had been conducted
from beginning to end, it was easy to see the result. Here it is,
in the words of the provincial paper : —

BOURG, 28 October, 1839.

" The condemned Peytel has just undergone his punishment,
which took place four days before the anniversary of his crime.
The terrible drama of the bridge of Andert, which cost the life
of two persons, has just terminated on the scaffold. Mid-day
had just sounded on the clock of the Palais: the same clock
tolled midnight when, on the 30th of August, his sentence was
pronounced.

" Since the rejection of his appeal in Cassation, on which

his principal hopes were founded, Peytel spoke little of his petition to the King. The notion of transportation was that which he seemed to cherish most. However, he made several inquiries from the gaoler of the prison, when he saw him at meal-time, with regard to the place of execution, the usual hour, and other details on the subject. From that period, the words '*Champ de Foire*' (the fair-field, where the execution was to be held), were frequently used by him in conversation.

" Yesterday, the idea that the time had arrived seemed to be more strongly than ever impressed upon him; especially after the departure of the curé, who latterly has been with him every day. The documents connected with the trial had arrived in the morning. He was ignorant of this circumstance, but sought to discover from his guardians what they tried to hide from him; and to find out whether his petition was rejected, and when he was to die.

" Yesterday, also, he had written to demand the presence of his counsel, M. Margerand, in order that he might have some conversation with him, and regulate his affairs, before he —— ; he did not write down the word, but left in its place a few points of the pen.

" In the evening, whilst he was at supper, he begged earnestly to be allowed a little wax-candle, to finish what he was writing: otherwise, he said, *Time might fail*. This was a new, indirect manner of repeating his ordinary question. As light, up to that evening, had been refused him, it was thought best to deny him in this, as in former instances; otherwise his suspicions might have been confirmed. The keeper refused his demand.

" This morning, Monday, at nine o'clock, the Greffier of the Assize Court, in fulfilment of the painful duty which the law imposes upon him, came to the prison, in company with the curé of Bourg, and announced to the convict that his petition was rejected, and that he had only three hours to live. He received this fatal news with a great deal of calmness, and showed himself to be no more affected than he had been on the trial. ' I am ready; but I wish they had given me four-and-twenty hours' notice,' — were all the words he used.

" The Greffier now retired, leaving Peytel alone with the curé, who did not thenceforth quit him. Peytel breakfasted at ten o'clock.

" At eleven, a piquet of mounted gendarmerie and infantry took their station upon the place before the prison, where a great concourse of people had already assembled. An open

car was at the door. Before he went out Peytel asked the
gaoler for a looking-glass ; and having examined his face for a
moment, said, ' At least, the inhabitants of Bourg will see that
I have not grown thin.'

" As twelve o'clock sounded, the prison gates opened, an
aide appeared, followed by Peytel, leaning on the arm of the
curé. Peytel's face was pale, he had a long black beard, a blue
cap on his head, and his great-coat flung over his shoulders,
and buttoned at the neck.

" He looked about at the place and the crowd ; he asked if
the carriage would go at a trot ; and on being told that that
would be difficult, he said he would prefer walking, and asked
what the road was. He immediately set out, walking at a firm
and rapid pace. He was not bound at all.

" An immense crowd of people encumbered the two streets
through which he had to pass to the place of execution. He
cast his eyes alternately upon them and upon the guillotine,
which was before him.

" Arrived at the foot of the scaffold, Peytel embraced the
curé, and bade him adieu. He then embraced him again ;
perhaps, for his mother and sister. He then mounted the steps
rapidly, and gave himself into the hands of the executioner,
who removed his coat and cap. He asked how he was to place
himself, and on a sign being made, he flung himself briskly on
the plank, and stretched his neck. In another moment he was
no more.

" The crowd, which had been quite silent, retired, profoundly
moved by the sight it had witnessed. As at all executions,
there was a very great number of women present.

" Under the scaffold there had been, ever since the morning,
a coffin. The family had asked for his remains, and had them
immediately buried, privately : and thus the unfortunate man's
head escaped the modellers in wax, several of whom had arrived
to take an impression of it."

Down goes the axe ; the poor wretch's head rolls gasping
into the basket ; the spectators go home, pondering ; and Mr.
Executioner and his aides have, in half an hour, removed all
traces of the august sacrifice, and of the altar on which it had
been performed. Say, Mr. Briefless, do you think that any
single person, meditating murder, would be deterred therefrom by beholding this — nay, a thousand more executions?
It is not for moral improvement, as I take it, nor for opportunity to make appropriate remarks upon the punishment of
crime, that people make a holiday of a killing-day, and leave

their homes and occupations, to flock and witness the cutting
off of a head.   Do we crowd to see Mr. Macready in the new
tragedy, or Mademoiselle Ellssler in her last new ballet and
flesh-colored stockinnet pantaloons, out of a pure love of
abstract poetry and beauty ; or from a strong notion that we
shall be excited, in different ways, by the actor and the dancer?
And so, as we go to have a meal of fictitious terror at the tragedy,
of something more questionable in the ballet, we go for a glut
of blood to the execution.   The lust is in every man's nature,
more or less.   Did you ever witness a wrestling or boxing
match?   The first clatter of the kick on the shins, or the first
drawing of blood, makes the stranger shudder a little ; but soon
the blood is his chief enjoyment, and he thirsts for it with a
fierce delight.   It is a fine grim pleasure that we have in seeing
a man killed ; and I make no doubt that the organs of destruc-
tiveness must begin to throb and swell as we witness the delightful savage spectacle.

Three or four years back, when Fieschi and Lacenaire were
executed, I made attempts to see the execution of both ; but
was disappointed in both cases.   In the first instance, the day
for Fieschi's death was, purposely, kept secret ; and he was, if
I remember rightly, executed at some remote quarter of the
town.   But it would have done a philanthropist good, to
witness the scene which we saw on the morning when his
execution did *not* take place.

It was carnival time, and the rumor had pretty generally
been carried abroad that he was to die on that morning.   A
friend, who accompanied me, came many miles, through the
mud and dark, in order to be in at the death.   We set out
before light, floundering through the muddy Champs Elysées ;
where, besides, were many other persons floundering, and all
bent upon the same errand.   We passed by the Concert of
Musard, then held in the Rue St. Honoré ; and round this, in
the wet, a number of coaches were collected.   The ball was
just up, and a crowd of people in hideous masquerade, drunk,
tired, dirty, dressed in horrible old frippery, and daubed with
filthy rouge, were trooping out of the place : tipsy women and
men, shrieking, jabbering, gesticulating, as French will do ;
parties swaggering, staggering forwards, arm in arm, reeling
to and fro across the street, and yelling songs in chorus : hundreds of these were bound for the show, and we thought ourselves lucky in finding a vehicle to the execution place, at the
Barrière d'Enfer.   As we crossed the river and entered the
Enfer Street, crowds of students, black workmen, and **more**

drunken devils from more carnival balls, were filling it; and on the grand place there were thousands of these assembled, looking out for Fieschi and his cortége. We waited and waited; but alas! no fun for us that morning: no throat-cutting; no august spectacle of satisfied justice; and the eager spectators were obliged to return, disappointed of their expected breakfast of blood. It would have been a fine scene, that execution, could it but have taken place in the midst of the mad mountebanks and tipsy strumpets who had flocked so far to witness it, wishing to wind up the delights of their carnival by a *bonne-bouche* of a murder.

The other attempt was equally unfortunate. We arrived too late on the ground to be present at the execution of Lacenaire and his co-mate in murder, Avril. But as we came to the ground (a gloomy round space, within the barrier — three roads lead to it; and, outside, you see the wine-shops and restaurateurs' of the barrier looking gay and inviting,) — as we came to the ground, we only found, in the midst of it, a little pool of ice, just partially tinged with red. Two or three idle street-boys were dancing and stamping about this pool; and when I asked one of them whether the execution had taken place, he began dancing more madly than ever, and shrieked out with a loud fantastical, theatrical voice, "Venez tous Messieurs et Dames, voyez ici le sang du monstre Lacenaire, et de son compagnon le traître Avril," or words to that effect; and straightway all the other gamins screamed out the words in chorus, and took hands and danced round the little puddle.

O august Justice, your meal was followed by a pretty appropriate grace! Was any man, who saw the show, deterred, or frightened, or moralized in any way? He had gratified his appetite for blood, and this was all. There is something singularly pleasing, both in the amusement of execution-seeing, and in the results. You are not only delightfully excited at the time, but most pleasingly relaxed afterwards; the mind, which has been wound up painfully until now, becomes quite complacent and easy. There is something agreeable in the misfortunes of others, as the philosopher has told us. Remark what a good breakfast you eat after an execution; how pleasant it is to cut jokes after it, and upon it. This merry, pleasant mood is brought on by the blood tonic.

But, for God's sake, if we are to enjoy this, let us do so in moderation; and let us, at least, be sure of a man's guilt before we murder him. To kill him, even with the full assurance that he is guilty, is hazardous enough. Who gave you the right to

do so?—you, who cry out against suicides, as impious and
contrary to Christian law? What use is there in killing him?
You deter no one else from committing the crime by so doing:
you give us, to be sure, half an hour's pleasant entertainment;
but it is a great question whether we derive much moral profit
from the sight. If you want to keep a murderer from farther
inroads upon society, are there not plenty of hulks and prisons,
God wot; treadmills, galleys, and houses of correction? Above
all, as in the case of Sebastian Peytel and his family, there have
been two deaths already; was a third death absolutely necessary?
and, taking the fallibility of judges and lawyers into his heart,
and remembering the thousand instances of unmerited punishment that have been suffered, upon similiar and stronger evidence
before, can any man declare, positively and upon his oath, that
Peytel was guilty, and that this was not *the third murder in the
family*?

FOUR IMITATIONS OF BÉRANGER.

LE ROI D'YVETOT.

Il était un roi d'Yvetot,
    Peu connu dans l'histoire ;
Se levant tard, se couchant tôt,
    Dormant fort bien sans gloire,
Et couronné par Jeanneton
D'un simple bonnet de coton,
        Dit-on.
    Oh! oh! oh! oh! ah! ah! ah! ah!
    Quel bon petit roi c'était là!
        La, la.

Il fesait ses quatre repas
    Dans son palais de chaume,
Et sur un âne, pas à pas,
    Parcourait son royaume.
Joyeux, simple et croyant le bien,
Pour toute garde il n'avait rien
        Qu'un chien.
    Oh! oh! oh! oh! ah! ah! ah! ah! &c.
        La, la.

Il n'avait de goût onéreux
    Qu'une soif un peu vive ;
Mais, en rendant son peuple heureux,
    Il faux bien qu'un roi vive.
Lui-même à table, et sans suppôt,
Sur chaque muid levait un pot
        D'impôt.
    Oh! oh! oh! oh! ah! ah! ah! ah! &c.
        La, la.

Aux filles de bonnes maisons
   Comme il avait su plaire,
Ses sujets avaient cent raisons
   De le nommer leur père :
D'ailleurs il ne levait de ban
Que pour tirer quatre fois l'an
      Au blanc.
    Oh! oh! oh! oh! ah! ah! ah! ah! &c.
     La, la.

Il n'agrandit point ses états,
   Fut un voisin commode,
Et, modèle des potentats,
   Prit le plaisir pour code.
Ce n'est que lorsqu'il expira,
Que le peuple qui l'enterra
      Pleura.
    Oh! oh! oh! oh! ah! ah! ah! ah! &c.
     La, la.

On conserve encor le portrait
   De ce digne et bon prince ;
C'est l'enseigne d'un cabaret
   Fameux dans la province.
Les jours de fête, bien souvent,
La foule s'écrie en buvant
     Devant :
    Oh! oh! oh! oh! ah! ah! ah! ah!
    Quel bon petit roi c'était là !
     La, la.

THE KING OF YVETOT.

THERE was a king of Yvetot,
   Of whom renown hath little said,
Who let all thoughts of glory go,
   And dawdled half his days a-bed ;
And every night, as night came round,
By Jenny, with a nightcap crowned,
     Slept very sound :
    Sing, ho, ho, ho! and he, he, he :
    That's the kind of king for me.

And every day it came to pass,
　That four lusty meals made he ;
And, step by step, upon an ass,
　Rode abroad, his realms to see ;
And wherever he did stir,
What think you was his escort, sir?
　　　　　Why, an old cur.
　　　Sing, ho, ho, ho ! &c.

If e'er he went into excess,
　'Twas from a somewhat lively thirst ;
But he who would his subjects bless,
　Odd's fish ! — must wet his whistle first ;
And so from every cask they got,
Our king did to himself allot,
　　　　　At least a pot,
　　　Sing, ho, ho ! &c.

To all the ladies of the land,
　A courteous king, and kind, was he ;
The reason why you'll understand,
　They named him Pater Patriæ.
Each year he called his fighting men,
And marched a league from home, and then
　　　　　Marched back again.
　　　Sing, ho, ho ! &c.

Neither by force nor false pretence,
　He sought to make his kingdom great,
And made (O princes, learn from hence) —
　" Live and let live," his rule of state.
Twas only when he came to die,
That his people who stood by,
　　　　　Were known to cry.
　　　Sing, ho, ho ! &c.

The portrait of this best of kings
　Is extant still, upon a sign
That on a village tavern swings,
　Famed in the country for good wine.
The people, in their Sunday trim,
Filling their glasses to the brim,
　　　　　Look up to him.
　　　Singing, ha, ha, ha ! and he, he he !
　　　That's the sort of king for me.

THE KING OF BRENTFORD.

ANOTHER VERSION.

THERE was a king in Brentford, — of whom no legends tell,
But who, without his glory, — could eat and sleep right well.
His Polly's cotton nightcap, — it was his crown of state,
He slept of evenings early, — and rose of mornings late.

All in a fine mud palace, — each day he took four meals,
And for a guard of honor, — a dog ran at his heels,
Sometimes, to view his kingdoms, — rode forth this monarch
          good,
And then a prancing jackass — he royally bestrode.

There were no costly habits — with which this king was curst,
Except (and where's the harm on't?) — a somewhat lively thirst;
But people must pay taxes, — and kings must have their sport,
So out of every gallon — His Grace he took a quart.

He pleased the ladies round him, — with manners soft and
          bland ;
With reason good, they named him, — the father of his land.
Each year his mighty armies — marched forth in gallant show ;
Their enemies were targets, — their bullets they were tow.

He vexed no quiet neighbor, — no useless conquest made,
But by the laws of pleasure, — his peaceful realm he swayed.
And in the years he reigned, — through all this country wide,
There was no cause for weeping, — save when the good man
          died.

The faithful men of Brentford, — do still their king deplore,
His portrait yet is swinging, — beside an ale-house door.
And topers, tender-hearted, — regard his honest phiz,
And envy times departed, — that knew a reign like his.

LE GRENIER.

Je viens revoir l'asile où ma jeunesse
De la misère a subi les leçons.
J'avais vingt ans, une folle maîtresse,
De francs amis et l'amour des chansons
Bravant le monde et les sots et les sages,
Sans avenir, riche de mon printemps,
Leste et joyeux je montais six étages.
Dans un grenier qu'on est bien à vingt ans !

C'est un grenier, point ne veux qu'on l'ignore.
Là fut mon lit, bien chétif et bien dur ;
Là fut ma table ; et je retrouve encore
Trois pieds d'un vers charbonnés sur le mur.
Apparaissez, plaisirs de mon bel âge,
Que d'un coup d'aile a fustigés le temps,
Vingt fois pour vous j'ai mis ma montre en gage.
Dans un grenier qu'on est bien à vingt ans !

Lisette ici doit surtout apparaître,
Vive, jolie, avec un frais chapeau ;
Déjà sa main à l'étroite fenêtre
Suspend son schal, en guise de rideau.
Sa robe aussi va parer ma couchette ;
Respecte, Amour, ses plis longs et flottans.
J'ai su depuis qui payait sa toilette.
Dans un grenier qu'on est bien à vingt ans !

A table un jour, jour de grande richesse,
De mes amis les voix brillaient en chœur,
Quand jusqu'ici monte un cri d'allégresse :
A Marengo Bonaparte est vainqueur.
Le canon gronde ; un autre chant commence ;
Nous célébrons tant de faits éclatans.
Les rois jamais n'envahiront la France.
Dans un grenier qu'on est bien à vingt ans !

Quittons ce toit où ma raison s'enivre.
Oh ! qu'ils sont loin ces jours si regrettés !
J'échangerais ce qu'il me reste à vivre
Contre un des mois qu'ici Dieu m'a comptés,
Pour rêver gloire, amour, plaisir, folie,
Pour dépenser sa vie en peu d'instans,
D'un long espoir pour la voir embellie,
Dans un grenier qu'on est bien à vingt ans !

THE GARRET.

WITH pensive eyes the little room I view,
　　Where, in my youth, I weathered it so long;
With a wild mistress, a stanch friend or two,
　　And a light heart still breaking into song:
Making a mock of life, and all its cares,
　　Rich in the glory of my rising sun,
Lightly I vaulted up four pair of stairs,
　　In the brave days when I was twenty-one.

Yes ; 'tis a garret — let him know't who will —
　　There was my bed — full hard it was and small.
My table there — and I decipher still
　　Half a lame couplet charcoaled on the wall.
Ye joys, that Time hath swept with him away,
　　Come to mine eyes, ye dreams of love and fun;
For you I pawned my watch how many a day,
　　In the brave days when I was twenty-one.

And see my little Jessy, first of all ;
　　She comes with pouting lips and sparkling eyes.
Behold, how roguishly she pins her shawl
　　Across the narrow casement, curtain-wise ;
Now by the bed her petticoat glides down,
　　And when did woman look the worse in none?
I have heard since who paid for many a gown,
　　In the brave days when I was twenty-one.

One jolly evening, when my friends and I
  Made happy music with our songs and cheers,
A shout of triumph mounted up thus high,
  And distant cannon opened on our ears:
We rise, — we join in the triumphant strain, —
  Napoleon conquers — Austerlitz is won —
Tyrants shall never tread us down again,
  In the brave days when I was twenty-one.

Let us begone — the place is sad and strange —
  How far, far off, these happy times appear;
All that I have to live I'd gladly change
  For one such month as I have wasted here —
To draw long dreams of beauty, love, and power,
  From founts of hope that never will outrun,
And drink all life's quintessence in an hour,
  Give me the days when I was twenty-one!

ROGER–BONTEMPS.

Aux gens atrabilaires
Pour exemple donné,
En un temps de misères
Roger-Bontemps est né.
Vivre obscur à sa guise,
Narguer les mécontens:
Eh gai! c'est la devise
Du gros Roger-Bontemps.

Du chapeau de son père
Coiffé dans le grands jours,
De roses ou de lierre
Le rajeunir toujours;
Mettre un manteau de bure
Vieil ami de vingt ans;
Eh gai! c'est la parure
Du gros Roger-Bontemps.

Posséder dans sa hutte
Une table, un vieux lit,
Des cartes, une flûte,
Un broc que Dieu remplit ;
Un portrait de maîtresse,
Un coffre et rien dedans ;
Eh gai ! c'est la richesse
Du gros Roger-Bontemps.

Aux enfans de la ville
Montrer de petits jeux ;
Etre fesseur habile
De contes graveleux ;
Ne parler que de danse
Et d'almanachs chantans
Eh gai ! c'est la science
Du gros Roger-Bontemps.

Faute de vins d'élite,
Sabler ceux du canton :
Préférer Marguerite
Aux dames du grand ton :
De joie et de tendresse
Remplir tous ses instans ;
Eh gai ! c'est la sagesse
Du gros Roger-Bontemps.

Dire au ciel : Je me fie,
Mon père, à ta bonté ;
De ma philosophie
Pardonne le gaîté :
Que ma saison dernière
Soit encore un printemps ;
Eh gai ! c'est la prière
Du gros Roger-Bontemps.

Vous, pauvres pleins d'envie
Vous, riches désireux,
Vous, dont le char dévie
Après un cours heureux ;
Vous, qui perdrez peut-être
Des titres éclatans,
Eh gai ! prenez pour maître
Le gros Roger Bontemps.

JOLLY JACK.

WHEN fierce political debate
    Throughout the isle was storming,
And Rads attacked the throne and state,
    And Tories the reforming,
To calm the furious rage of each,
    And right the land demented,
Heaven sent us Jolly Jack, to teach
    The way to be contented.

Jack's bed was straw, 'twas warm and soft,
    His chair, a three-legged stool;
His broken jug was emptied oft,
    Yet, somehow, always full.
His mistress' portrait decked the wall,
    His mirror had a crack;
Yet, gay and glad, though this was all
    His wealth, lived Jolly Jack.

To give advice to avarice,
    Teach pride its mean condition,
And preach good sense to dull pretence,
    Was honest Jack's high mission.
Our simple statesman found his rule
    Of moral in the flagon,
And held his philosophic school
    Beneath the "George and Dragon."

When village Solons cursed the Lords,
    And called the malt-tax sinful,
Jack heeded not their angry words,
    But smiled, and drunk his skinful.
And when men wasted health and life,
    In search of rank and riches,
Jack marked, aloof, the paltry strife,
    And wore his threadbare breeches.

" I enter not the church," he said,
    " But I'll not seek to rob it ; "
So worthy Jack Joe Miller read,
    While others studied Cobbett.
His talk it was of feast and fun ;
    His guide the Almanack ;
From youth to age thus gayly run
    The life of Jolly Jack.

And when Jack prayed, as oft he would,
    He humbly thanked his Maker ;
" I am," said he, " O Father good !
    Nor Catholic nor Quaker :
Give each his creed, let each proclaim
    His catalogue of curses ;
I trust in Thee, and not in them,
    In Thee, and in Thy mercies !

" Forgive me if, midst all Thy works,
    No hint I see of damning ;
And think there's faith among the Turks
    And hope for e'en the Brahmin.
Harmless my mind is, and my mirth,
    And kindly is my laughter ;
I cannot see the smiling earth,
    And think there's hell hereafter."

Jack died ; he left no legacy,
    Save that his story teaches : —
Content to peevish poverty ;
    Humility to riches.
Ye scornful great, ye envious small,
    Come, follow in his track ;
We all were happier, if we all
    Would copy JOLLY JACK.

17

FRENCH DRAMAS AND MELODRAMAS.

THERE are three kinds of drama in France, which you may subdivide as much as you please.

There is the old classical drama, wellnigh dead, and full time too: old tragedies, in which half a dozen characters appear, and spout sonorous Alexandrines for half a dozen hours. The fair Rachel has been trying to revive this *genre*, and to untomb Racine; but be not alarmed, Racine will never come to life again, and cause audiences to weep as of yore. Madame Rachel can only galvanize the corpse, not revivify it. Ancient French tragedy, red-heeled, patched, and be-periwigged, lies in the grave; and it is only the ghost of it that we see, which the fair Jewess has raised. There are classical comedies in verse, too, wherein the knavish valets, rakish heroes, stolid old guardians, and smart, free-spoken serving-women, discourse in Alexandrines, as loud as the Horaces or the Cid. An Englishman will seldom reconcile himself to the *roulement* of the verses, and the painful recurrence of the rhymes; for my part, I had rather go to Madame Saqui's or see Deburau dancing on a rope: his lines are quite as natural and poetical.

Then there is the comedy of the day, of which Monsieur Scribe is the father. Good heavens! with what a number of gay colonels, smart widows, and silly husbands has that gentleman peopled the play-books. How that unfortunate seventh commandment has been maltreated by him and his disciples. You will see four pieces, at the Gymnase, of a night; and so sure as you see them, four husbands shall be wickedly used. When is this joke to cease? Mon Dieu! Play-writers have handled it for about two thousand years, and the public, like a great baby, must have the tale repeated to it over and over again.

Finally, there is the Drama, that great monster which has sprung into life of late years; and which is said, but I don't believe a word of it, to have Shakspeare for a father. If Monsieur Scribe's plays may be said to be so many ingenious examples how to break one commandment, the *drame* is a grand and general chaos of them all; nay, several crimes are added, not prohibited in the Decalogue, which was written before dramas were. Of the drama, Victor Hugo and Dumas are the well-known and respectable guardians. Every piece Victor Hugo has written, since " Hernani," has contained a monster — a delightful monster, saved by one virtue. There is Triboulet, a foolish monster; Lucrèce Borgia, a maternal monster; Mary Tudor, a religious monster; Monsieur Quasimodo, a humpback monster; and others, that might be named, whose monstrosities we are induced to pardon — nay, admiringly to witness — because they are agreeably mingled with some exquisite display of affection. And, as the great Hugo has one monster to each play, the great Dumas has, ordinarily, half a dozen, to whom murder is nothing; common intrigue, and simple breakage of the before-mentioned commandment, nothing; but who live and move in a vast, delightful complication of crime, that cannot be easily conceived in England, much less described.

When I think over the number of crimes that I have seen Mademoiselle Georges, for instance, commit, I am filled with wonder at her greatness, and the greatness of the poets who have conceived these charming horrors for her. I have seen her make love to, and murder, her sons, in the " Tour de Nesle." I have seen her poison a company of no less than nine gentlemen, at Ferrara, with an affectionate son in the number; I have seen her, as Madame de Brinvilliers, kill off numbers of respectable relations in the first four acts; and, at the last, be actually burned at the stake, to which she comes shuddering, ghastly, barefooted, and in a white sheet. Sweet excitement of tender sympathies! Such tragedies are not so good as a real, downright execution; but, in point of interest, the next thing to it: with what a number of moral emotions do they fill the breast; with what a hatred for vice, and yet a true pity and respect for that grain of virtue that is to be found in us all: our bloody, daughter-loving Brinvilliers; our warmhearted, poisonous Lucretia Borgia; above all, what a smart appetite for a cool supper afterwards, at the Café Anglais, when the horrors of the play act as a piquant sauce to the supper!

Or, to speak more seriously, and to come, at last, to the

point. After having seen most of the grand dramas which
have been produced at Paris for the last half-dozen years, and
thinking over all that one has seen, — the fictitious murders,
rapes, adulteries, and other crimes, by which one has been
interested and excited, — a man may take leave to be heartily
ashamed of the manner in which he has spent his time ; and
of the hideous kind of mental intoxication in which he has permitted himself to indulge.

Nor are simple society outrages the only sort of crime in
which the spectator of Paris plays has permitted himself to
indulge ; he has recreated himself with a deal of blasphemy
besides, and has passed many pleasant evenings in beholding
religion defiled and ridiculed.

Allusion has been made, in a former paper, to a fashion that
lately obtained in France, and which went by the name of
Catholic reaction ; and as, in this happy country, fashion is
everything, we have had not merely Catholic pictures and
quasi religious books, but a number of Catholic plays have
been produced, very edifying to the frequenters of the theatres
or the Boulevards, who have learned more about religion from
these performances than they have acquired, no doubt, in the
whole of their lives before. In the course of a very few years
we have seen — "The Wandering Jew ; " " Belshazzar's Feast ;'
" Nebuchadnezzar :" and the " Massacre of the Innocents ;'
" Joseph and his Brethren ; " " The Passage of the Red Sea ;'
and "The Deluge."

The great Dumas, like Madame Sand before mentioned, has
brought a vast quantity of religion before the foot-lights.
There was his famous tragedy of " Caligula," which, be it
spoken to the shame of the Paris critics, was coldly received ;
nay, actually hissed, by them. And why? Because, says
Dumas, it contained a great deal too much piety for the
rogues. The public, he says, was much more religious, and
understood him at once.

" As for the critics," says he, nobly, " let those who cried
out against the immorality of Antony and Marguérite de Bour-
gogne, reproach me for *the chastity of Messalina*." (This dear
creature is the heroine of the play of " Caligula.") " It matters little to me. These people have but seen the form of my
work : they have walked round the tent, but have not seen the
arch which it covered ; they have examined the vases and candles of the altar, but have not opened the tabernacle !

" The public alone has, instinctively, comprehended that
there was, beneath this outward sign, an inward and myste-

rious grace : it followed the action of the piece in all its serpentine windings; it listened for four hours, with pious attention
(*avec recueillement et religion*), to the sound of this rolling river
of thoughts, which may have appeared to it new and bold, perhaps, but chaste and grave; and it retired, with its head on
its breast, like a man who had just perceived, in a dream, the
solution of a problem which he has long and vainly sought in
his waking hours."

You see that not only Saint Sand is an apostle, in her way;
but Saint Dumas is another. We have people in England who
write for bread, like Dumas and Sand, and are paid so much
for their line; but they don't set up for prophets. Mrs. Trollope has never declared that her novels are inspired by heaven;
Mr. Buckstone has written a great number of farces, and never
talked about the altar and the tabernacle. Even Sir Edward
Bulwer (who, on a similar occasion, when the critics found
fault with a play of his, answered them by a pretty decent
declaration of his own merits,) never ventured to say that he
had received a divine mission, and was uttering five-act revelations.

All things considered, the tragedy of "Caligula" is a decent
tragedy; as decent as the decent characters of the hero and
heroine can allow it to be; it may be almost said, provokingly
decent: but this, it must be remembered, is the characteristic
of the modern French school (nay, of the English school too);
and if the writer take the character of a remarkable scoundrel,
it is ten to one but he turns out an amiable fellow, in whom we
have all the warmest sympathy. "Caligula" is killed at the
end of the performance; Messalina is comparatively well-be-
haved; and the sacred part of the performance, the tabernacle-
characters apart from the mere "vase" and "candlestick"
personages, may be said to be depicted in the person of a
Christian convert, Stella, who has had the good fortune to be
converted by no less a person than Mary Magdalene, when she,
Stella, was staying on a visit to her aunt, near Narbonne.

     Stella (*continuant.*)   Voilà
Que je vois s'avancer, sans pilote et sans rames,
Une barque portant deux hommes et deux femmes,
Et, spectacle inouï qui me ravit encor,
Tous quatre avaient au front une auréole d'or
D'où partaient des rayons de si vive lumière
Que je fus obligée à baisser la paupière;
Et, lorsque je rouvris les yeux avec effroi,
Les voyageurs divins étaient auprès de moi.
Un jour de chacun d'eux et dans toute sa gloire

Je te raconterai la marveilleuse histoire,
Et tu l'adoreras, j'espère ; en ce moment,
Ma mère, il te suffit de savoir seulement
Que tous quatre venaient du fond de la Syrie :
Un édit les avait bannis de leur patrie,
Et, se faisant bourreaux, des hommes irrités,
Sans avirons, sans eau, sans pain et garrotés,
Sur une frêle barque échouée au rivage,
Les avaient à la mer poussés dans un orage.
Mais à peine l'esquif eut-il touché les flots
Qu'au cantique chanté par les saints matelots,
L'ouragan replia ses ailes frémissantes,
Que la mer aplanit ses vagues mugissantes,
Et qu'un soleil plus pur, reparaissant aux cieux,
Enveloppa l'esquif d'un cercle radieux ! . . .
   JUNIA. — Mais c'était un prodige.
   STELLA. —   Un miracle, ma mère !
Leurs fers tombèrent seuls, l'eau cessa d'être amère,
Et deux fois chaque jour le bateau fut couvert
D'une manne pareille à celle du désert :
C'est ainsi que, poussés par une main céleste,
Je les vis aborder.
   JUNIA. —   Oh ! dis vîte le reste !
   STELLA. — A l'aube, trois d'entre eux quittèrent la maison :
Marthe prit le chemin qui mène à Tarascon,
Lazare et Maximin celui de Massilie,
Et celle qui resta . . . . *c'etait la plus jolie*, (how truly French !)
Nous faisant appeler vers le milieu du jour,
Demanda si les monts ou les bois d'alentour
Cachaient quelque retraite inconnue et profonde,
Qui la pût séparer à tout jamais du monde. . . . .
Aquila se souvint qu'il avait pénétré
Dans un antre sauvage et de tous ignoré,
Grotte creusée aux flancs de ces Alpes sublimes,
Ou l'aigle fait son aire au-dessus des abîmes.
Il offrit cet asile, et dès le lendemain
Tous deux, pour l'y guider, nous étions en chemin.
Le soir du second jour nous touchâmes sa base :
Là, tombant à genoux dans une sainte extase,
Elle pria long-temps, puis vers l'antre inconnu,
Dénouant se chaussure, elle marcha pied nu.
Nos prières, nos cris restèrent sans réponses :
Au milieu des cailloux, des épines, des ronces,
Nous la vîmes monter, un bâton à la main,
Et ce n'est qu'arrivée au terme du chemin,
Qu'enfin elle tomba sans force et sans haleine . . . .
   JUNIA. — Comment la nommait-on, ma fille ?
   STELLA. —   Madeleine.

Walking, says Stella, by the sea-shore, " A bark drew near,
that had nor sail nor oar ; two women and two men the vessel
bore : each of that crew, 'twas wondrous to behold, wore round
his head a ring of blazing gold ; from which such radiance glittered all around, that I was fain to look towards the ground.

And when once more I raised my frightened eyne, before me stood the travellers divine; their rank, the glorious lot that each befell, at better season, mother, will I tell. Of this anon: the time will come when thou shalt learn to worship as I worship now. Suffice it, that from Syria's land they came; an edict from their country banished them. Fierce, angry men had seized upon the four, and launched them in that vessel from the shore. They launched these victims on the waters rude; nor rudder gave to steer, nor bread for food. As the doomed vessel cleaves the stormy main, that pious crew uplifts a sacred strain; the angry waves are silent as it sings; the storm, awe-stricken, folds its quivering wings. A purer sun appears the heavens to light, and wraps the little bark in radiance bright.

" JUNIA. — Sure, 'twas a prodigy.

" STELLA. — A miracle. Spontaneous from their hands the fetters fell. The salt sea-wave grew fresh, and, twice a day, manna (like that which on the desert lay) covered the bark and fed them on their way. Thus, hither led, at heaven's divine behest, I saw them land—

"JUNIA. — My daughter, tell the rest.

" STELLA. — Three of the four, our mansion left at dawn. One, Martha, took the road to Tarascon; Lazarus and Maximin to Massily; but one remained (the fairest of the three), who asked us, if i' the woods or mountains near, there chanced to be some cavern lone and drear; where she might hide, for ever, from all men. It chanced, my cousin knew of such a den; deep hidden in a mountain's hoary breast, on which the eagle builds his airy nest. And thither offered he the saint to guide. Next day upon the journey forth we hied; and came, at the second eve, with weary pace, unto the lonely mountain's rugged base. Here the worn traveller, falling on her knee, did pray awhile in sacred ecstasy; and, drawing off her sandals from her feet, marched, naked, towards that desolate retreat. No answer made she to our cries or groans; but walking midst the prickles and rude stones, a staff in hand, we saw her upwards toil; nor ever did she pause, nor rest the while, save at the entry of that savage den. Here, powerless and panting, fell she then.

" JUNIA. — What was her name, my daughter?

" STELLA.   MAGDALEN."

Here the translator must pause — having no inclination to enter " the tabernacle," in company with such a spotless high-priest as Monsieur Dumas.

Something " tabernacular " may be found in Dumas's famous piece of " Don Juan de Marana." The poet has laid the scene of his play in a vast number of places : in heaven (where we have the Virgin Mary and little angels, in blue, swinging censers before her !) — on earth, under the earth, and in a place still lower, but not mentionable to ears polite ; and the plot, as it appears from a dialogue between a good and a bad angel, with which the play commences, turns upon a contest between these two worthies for the possession of the soul of a member of the family of Marana.

" Don Juan de Marana " not only resembles his namesake, celebrated by Mozart and Molière, in his peculiar successes among the ladies, but possesses further qualities which render his character eminently fitting for stage representation : he unites the virtues of Lovelace and Lacenaire ; he blasphemes upon all occasions ; he murders, at the slightest provocation, and without the most trifling remorse ; he overcomes ladies of rigid virtue, ladies of easy virtue, and ladies of no virtue at all ; and the poet, inspired by the contemplation of such a character, has depicted his hero's adventures and conversation with wonderful feeling and truth.

The first act of the play contains a half-dozen of murders and intrigues ; which would have sufficed humbler genius than M. Dumas's, for the completion of, at least, half a dozen tragedies. In the second act our hero flogs his elder brother, and runs away with his sister-in-law ; in the third, he fights a duel with a rival, and kills him : whereupon the mistress of his victim takes poison, and dies, in great agonies, on the stage. In the fourth act, Don Juan, having entered a church for the purpose of carrying off a nun, with whom he is in love, is seized by the statue of one of the ladies whom he has previously victimized, and made to behold the ghosts of all those unfortunate persons whose deaths he has caused.

This is a most edifying spectacle. The ghosts rise solemnly, each in a white sheet, preceded by a wax-candle ; and, having declared their names and qualities, call, in chorus, for vengeance upon Don Juan, as thus : —

Don Sandoval *loquitur*.

" I am Don Sandoval d'Ojedo. I played against Don Juan my fortune, the tomb of my fathers, and the heart of my mistress ; — I lost all : I played against him my life, and I lost it. Vengeance against the murderer ! vengeance ! " — (*The candle goes out.*)

The candle goes out, and an angel descends — a flaming sword in his hand — and asks : "Is there no voice in favor of Don Juan?" when lo! Don Juan's father (like one of those ingenious toys called "Jack-in-the-box,") jumps up from his coffin, and demands grace for his son.

When Martha the nun returns, having prepared all things for her elopement, she finds Don Juan fainting upon the ground. — "I am no longer your husband," says he, upon coming to himself; "I am no longer Don Juan; I am Brother Juan the Trappist. Sister Martha, recollect that you must die!"

This was a most cruel blow upon Sister Martha, who is no less a person than an angel, an angel in disguise — the good spirit of the house of Marana, who has gone to the length of losing her wings and forfeiting her place in heaven, in order to keep company with Don Juan on earth, and, if possible, to convert him. Already, in her angelic character, she had exhorted him to repentance, but in vain; for, while she stood at one elbow, pouring not merely hints, but long sermons, into his ear, at the other elbow stood a bad spirit, grinning and sneering at all her pious counsels, and obtaining by far the greater share of the Don's attention.

In spite, however, of the utter contempt with which Don Juan treats her, — in spite of his dissolute courses, which must shock her virtue, — and his impolite neglect, which must wound her vanity, the poor creature (who, from having been accustomed to better company, might have been presumed to have had better taste), the unfortunate angel feels a certain inclination for the Don, and actually flies up to heaven to ask permission to remain with him on earth.

And when the curtain draws up, to the sound of harps, and discovers white-robed angels walking in the clouds, we find the angel of Marana upon her knees, uttering the following address : —

LE BON ANGE.

Vierge, à qui le calice à la liqueur amère
    Fut si souvent offert,
Mère, que l'on nomma la douloureuse mère,
    Tant vous avez souffert!

Vous, dont les yeux divins sur la terre des hommes
    Ont versé plus de pleurs
Que vos pieds n'ont depuis, dans le ciel où nous sommes,
    Fait éclore de fleurs.

> Vase d'élection, étoile matinale,
>   Miroir de pureté,
> Vous qui priez pour nous, d'une voix virginale,
>   La suprême bonté;
>
> A mon tour, aujourd'hui, bienheureuse Marie,
>   Je tombe à vos genoux;
> Daignez donc m'écouter, car c'est vous que je prie,
>   Vous qui priez pour nous.

Which may be thus interpreted : —

> O Virgin blest! by whom the bitter draught
>   So often has been quaffed,
> That, for thy sorrow, thou art named by us
>   The Mother Dolorous!
>
> Thou, from whose eyes have fallen more tears of woe,
>   Upon the earth below,
> Than 'neath thy footsteps, in this heaven of ours,
>   Have risen flowers!
>
> O beaming morning star! O chosen vase!
>   O mirror of all grace!
> Who, with thy virgin voice, dost ever pray
>   Man's sins away;
>
> Bend down thine ear, and list, O blessed saint!
>   Unto my sad complaint;
> Mother! to thee I kneel, on thee I call,
>   Who hearest all.

She proceeds to request that she may be allowed to return to earth, and follow the fortunes of Don Juan; and, as there is one difficulty, or, to use her own words, —

> Mais, comme vous savez qu'aux voûtes éternelles,
>   Malgré moi, tend mon vol,
> *Soufflez sur mon étoile et détachez mes ailes,*
>   *Pour m'enchaîner au sol;*

her request is granted, her star is *blown out* (O poetic allusion!) and she descends to earth to love, and to go mad, and to die for Don Juan!

The reader will require no further explanation, in order to be satisfied as to the moral of this play: but is it not a very bitter satire upon the country, which calls itself the politest nation in the world, that the incidents, the indecency, the coarse blasphemy, and the vulgar wit of this piece, should find admirers among the public, and procure reputation for the author? Could not the Government, which has re-established, in a manner, the theatrical censorship, and forbids or alters plays which touch on politics, exert the same guardianship over public morals? The honest English reader, who has a faith in his clergyman, and is a regular attendant at Sunday worship, will not be a little surprised at the march of intellect among our neighbors across the Channel, and at the kind of consideration in which they hold their religion. Here is a man who seizes upon saints and angels, merely to put sentiments in their mouths which might suit a nymph of Drury Lane. He shows heaven, in order that he may carry debauch into it; and avails himself of the most sacred and sublime parts of our creed as a vehicle for a scene-painter's skill, or an occasion for a handsome actress to wear a new dress.

M. Dumas's piece of "Kean" is not quite so sublime; it was brought out by the author as a satire upon the French critics, who, to their credit be it spoken, had generally attacked him, and was intended by him, and received by the public, as a faithful portraiture of English manners. As such, it merits special observation and praise. In the first act you find a Countess and an Ambassadress, whose conversation relates purely to the great actor. All the ladies in London are in love with him, especially the two present. As for the Ambassadress, she prefers him to her husband (a matter of course in all French plays), and to a more seducing person still — no less a person than the Prince of Wales! who presently waits on the ladies, and joins in their conversation concerning Kean. "This man," says his Royal Highness, "is the very pink of fashion. Brummell is nobody when compared to him; and I myself only an insignificant private gentleman. He has a reputation among ladies, for which I sigh in vain; and spends an income twice as great as mine." This admirable historic touch at once paints the actor and the Prince; the estimation in which the one was held, and the modest economy for which the other was so notorious.

Then we have Kean, at a place called the *Trou de Charbon*, the "Coal Hole," where, to the edification of the public, he engages in a fisty combat with a notorious boxer. This scene was received by the audience with loud exclamations of delight, and commented on, by the journals, as a faultless picture of English manners. "The Coal Hole" being on the banks of the Thames, a nobleman — *Lord Melbourn!* — has chosen the tavern as a rendezvous for a gang of pirates, who are to have their ship in waiting, in order to carry off a young lady with whom his lordship is enamored. It need not be said that Kean arrives at the nick of time, saves the innocent *Meess Anna*, and exposes the infamy of the Peer. A violent tirade against noblemen ensues, and Lord Melbourn slinks away, disappointed, to meditate revenge. Kean's triumphs continue through all the acts: the Ambassadress falls madly in love with him; the Prince becomes furious at his ill success, and the Ambassador dreadfully jealous. They pursue Kean to his dressing-room at the theatre; where, unluckily, the Ambassadress herself has taken refuge. Dreadful quarrels ensue; the tragedian grows suddenly mad upon the stage, and so cruelly insults the Prince of Wales that his Royal Highness determines to send *him to Botany Bay*. His sentence, however, is commuted to banishment to New York; whither, of course, Miss Anna accompanies him; rewarding him, previously, with her hand and twenty thousand a year!

This wonderful performance was gravely received and admired by the people of Paris: the piece was considered to be decidedly moral, because the popular candidate was made to triumph throughout, and to triumph in the most virtuous manner; for, according to the French code of morals, success among women is, at once, the proof and the reward of virtue.

The sacred personage introduced in Dumas's play behind a cloud, figures bodily in the piece of the *Massacre of the Innocents*, represented at Paris last year. She appears under a different name, but the costume is exactly that of Carlo Dolce's Madonna; and an ingenious fable is arranged, the interest of which hangs upon the grand Massacre of the Innocents, perpetrated in the fifth act. One of the chief characters is *Jean le Précurseur*, who threatens woe to Herod and his race, and is beheaded by orders of that sovereign.

In the *Festin de Balthazar*, we are similarly introduced to Daniel, and the first scene is laid by the waters of Babylon, where a certain number of captive Jews are seated in melancholy postures; a Babyloninan officer enters, exclaiming, "Chantez nous quelques chansons de Jerusalem," and the request is refused in the language of the Psalm. Belshazzar's Feast is given in a grand tableau, after Martin's picture. That painter, in like manner, furnished scenes for the *Deluge*. Vast numbers of schoolboys and children are brought to see these pieces; the lower classes delight in them. The famous *Juif Errant*, at the theatre of the Porte St. Martin, was the first of the kind, and its prodigious success, no doubt, occasioned the number of imitations which the other theatres have produced.

The taste of such exhibitions, of course, every English person will question; but we must remember the manners of the people among whom they are popular; and, if I may be allowed to hazard such an opinion, there is in every one of these Boulevard mysteries, a kind of rude moral. The Boulevard writers don't pretend to "tabernacles" and divine gifts, like Madame Sand and Dumas before mentioned. If they take a story from the sacred books, they garble it without mercy, and take sad liberties with the text; but they do not deal in descriptions of the agreeably wicked, or ask pity and admiration for tender-hearted criminals and philanthropic murderers, as their betters do. Vice is vice on the Boulevard; and it is fine to hear the audience, as a tyrant king roars out cruel sentences of death, or a bereaved mother pleads for the life of her child, making their remarks on the circumstances of the scene. "Ah, le gredin!" growls an indignant countryman. "Quel monstre!" says a grisette, in a fury. You see very fat old men crying like babies, and, like babies, sucking enormous sticks of barley-sugar. Actors and audience enter warmly into the illusion of the piece; and so especially are the former affected, that at Franconi's, where the battles of the Empire are represented, there is as regular gradation in the ranks of the mimic army as in the real imperial legions. After a man has served, with credit, for a certain number of years in the line, he is promoted to be an officer — an acting officer. If he conducts himself well, he may rise to be a Colonel or a General of Division; if ill, he is degraded to the ranks again; or, worst degradation of all, drafted into a regiment of Cossacks or Austrians. Cossacks is the lowest depth, however; nay, it is said that the men who perform these Cossack parts receive higher wages than the mimic grenadiers and old guard. They will not consent to be beaten every night, even in play; to be pursued in hundreds, by a handful of French; to fight against their beloved Emperor. Surely there is fine hearty virtue in this, and pleasant child-like simplicity.

So that while the drama of Victor Hugo, Dumas, and the enlightened classes, is profoundly immoral and absurd, the *drama* of the common people is absurd, if you will, but good and right-hearted. I have made notes of one or two of these pieces, which all have good feeling and kindness in them, and which turn, as the reader will see, upon one or two favorite points of popular morality. A drama that obtained a vast success at the Porte Saint Martin was "La Duchesse de la Vauballière." The Duchess is the daughter of a poor farmer, who was carried off in the first place, and then married by M.

le Duc de la Vauballière, a terrible roué, the farmer's landlord, and the intimate friend of Philippe d'Orléans, the Regent of France.

Now the Duke, in running away with the lady, intended to dispense altogether with ceremony, and make of Julie any-thing but his wife ; but Georges, her father, and one Morisseau, a notary, discovered him in his dastardly act, and pursued him to the very feet of the Regent, who compelled the pair to marry and make it up.

Julie complies ; but though she becomes a Duchess, her heart remains faithful to her old flame, Adrian, the doctor ; and she declares that, beyond the ceremony, no sort of intimacy shall take place between her husband and herself.

Then the Duke begins to treat her in the most ungentleman-like manner : he abuses her in every possible way ; he intro-duces improper characters into her house ; and, finally, becomes so disgusted with her, that he determines to make away with her altogether.

For this purpose, he sends forth into the highways and seizes a doctor, bidding him, on pain of death, to write a poisonous prescription for Madame la Duchesse. She swallows the potion ; and O horror ! the doctor turns out to be Dr. Adrian ; whose woe may be imagined, upon finding that he has been thus com-mitting murder on his true love !

Let not the reader, however, be alarmed as to the fate of the heroine ; no heroine of a tragedy ever yet died in the third act ; and, accordingly, the Duchess gets up perfectly well again in the fourth, through the instrumentality of Morisseau, the good lawyer.

And now it is that vice begins to be really punished. The Duke, who, after killing his wife, thinks it necessary to retreat, and take refuge in Spain, is tracked to the borders of that country by the virtuous notary, and there receives such a lesson as he will never forget to his dying day.

Morisseau, in the first instance, produces a deed (signed by his Holiness the Pope), which annuls the marriage of the Duke de la Vauballière ; then another deed, by which it is proved that he was not the eldest son of old La Vauballière, the former Duke ; then another deed, by which he shows that old La Vau-ballière (who seems to have been a disreputable old fellow) was a bigamist, and that, in consequence, the present man, styling himself Duke, is illegitimate ; and finally, Morisseau brings forward another document, which proves that the *reg'lar* Duke is no other than Adrian, the doctor !

Thus it is that love, law, and physic combined, triumph over the horrid machinations of this star-and-gartered libertine.

" Hermann l'Ivrogne " is another piece of the same order; and though not very refined, yet possesses considerable merit. As in the case of the celebrated Captain Smith of Halifax, who " took to drinking ratafia, and thought of poor Miss Bailey," — a woman and the bottle have been the cause of Hermann's ruin. Deserted by his mistress, who has been seduced from him by a base Italian Count, Hermann, a German artist, gives himself entirely up to liquor and revenge : but when he finds that force, and not infidelity, have been the cause of his mistress's ruin, the reader can fancy the indignant ferocity with which he pursues the *infame ravisseur*. A scene, which is really full of spirit, and excellently well acted, here ensues ! Hermann proposes to the Count, on the eve of their duel, that the survivor should bind himself to espouse the unhappy Marie ; but the Count declares himself to be already married, and the student, finding a duel impossible (for his object was to restore, at all events, the honor of Marie), now only thinks of his revenge, and murders the Count. Presently, two parties of men enter Hermann's apartment : one is a company of students, who bring him the news that he has obtained the prize of painting ; the other the policemen, who carry him to prison, to suffer the penalty of murder.

I could mention many more plays in which the popular morality is similiarly expressed. The seducer, or rascal of the piece, is always an aristocrat, — a wicked count, or licentious marquis, who is brought to condign punishment just before the fall of the curtain. And too good reason have the French people had to lay such crimes to the charge of the aristocracy, who are expiating now, on the stage, the wrongs which they did a hundred years since. The aristocracy is dead now ; but the theatre lives upon traditions : and don't let us be too scornful at such simple legends as are handed down by the people from race to race. Vulgar prejudice against the great it may be ; but prejudice against the great is only a rude expression of sympathy with the poor ; long, therefore, may fat *épiciers* blubber over mimic woes, and honest *prolétaires* shake their fists, shouting — " Gredin, scélérat, monstre de marquis ! " and such republican cries.

Remark, too, another development of this same popular feeling of dislike against men in power. What a number of plays and legends have we (the writer has submitted to the public, in the preceding pages, a couple of specimens ; one of French, and the other of Polish origin,) in which that great and powerful aristocrat, the Devil, is made to be miserably tricked, humiliated, and disappointed? A play of this class, which, in the midst of all its absurdities and claptraps, had much of good in it, was called " Le Maudit des Mers." Le Maudit is a Dutch captain, who, in the midst of a storm, while his crew were on their knees at prayers, blasphemed and drank punch; but what was his astonishment at beholding an archangel with a sword all covered with flaming resin, who told him that as he, in this hour of danger, was too daring, or too wicked, to utter a prayer, he never should cease roaming the seas until he could find some being who would pray to heaven for him!

Once only, in a hundred years, was the skipper allowed to land for this purpose; and this piece runs through four centuries, in as many acts, describing the agonies and unavailing attempts of the miserable Dutchman. Willing to go any lengths in order to obtain his prayer, he, in the second act, betrays a Virgin of the Sun to a follower of Pizarro : and, in the third, assassinates the heroic William of Nassau ; but ever before the dropping of the curtain, the angel and sword make their appearance : — " Treachery," says the spirit, " cannot lessen thy punishment ; — crime will not obtain thy release ! — *A la mer ! à la mer !* " and the poor devil returns to the ocean, to be lonely, and tempest-tossed, and sea-sick for a hundred years more.

But his woes are destined to end with the fourth act. Having landed in America, where the peasants on the sea-shore, all dressed in Italian costumes, are celebrating, in a quadrille, the victories of Washington, he is there lucky enough to find a young girl to pray for him. Then the curse is removed, the punishment is over, and a celestial vessel, with angels on the decks and " sweet little cherubs " fluttering about the shrouds and the poop, appear to receive him.

This piece was acted at Franconi's, where, for once, an angel-ship was introduced in place of the usual horsemanship.

One must not forget to mention here, how the English nation is satirized by our neighbors ; who have some droll traditions regarding us. In one of the little Christmas pieces produced at the Palais Royal (satires upon the follies of the past twelve months, on which all the small theatres exhaust their wit), the celebrated flight of Messrs. Green and Monck Mason was parodied, and created a good deal of laughter at the expense of John Bull. Two English noblemen, Milor Cricri and Milor Hanneton, appear as descending from a balloon, and one of them communicates to the public the philosophic observations which were made in the course of his aërial tour.

"On leaving Vauxhall," says his lordship, "we drank a bottle of Madeira, as a health to the friends from whom we parted, and crunched a few biscuits to support nature during the hours before lunch. In two hours we arrived at Canterbury, enveloped in clouds : lunch, bottled porter : at Dover, carried several miles in a tide of air, bitter cold, cherry-brandy ; crossed over the Channel safely, and thought with pity of the poor people who were sickening in the steamboats below : more bottled porter : over Calais, dinner, roast-beef of Old England ; near Dunkirk, — night falling, lunar rainbow, brandy-and-water ; night confoundedly thick ; supper, nightcap of rum-punch, and so to bed. The sun broke beautifully through the morning mist, as we boiled the kettle and took our breakfast over Cologne. In a few more hours we concluded this memorable voyage, and landed safely at Weilburg, in good time for dinner."

The joke here is smart enough ; but our honest neighbors make many better, when they are quite unconscious of the fun. Let us leave plays, for a moment, for poetry, and take an instance of French criticism, concerning England, from the works of a famous French exquisite and man of letters. The hero of the poem addresses his mistress —

> Londres, tu le sais trop, en fait de capitale,
> Est-ce que fit le ciel de plus froid et plus pâle,
> C'est la ville du gaz, des marins, du brouillard ;
> On s'y couche à minuit, et l'on s'y lève tard ;
> Ses raouts tant vantés ne sont qu'une boxade,
> Sur ses grands quais jamais échelle ou sérénade,
> Mais de volumineux bourgeois pris de porter
> Qui passent sans lever le front à Westminster ;
> Et n'était sa forêt de mâts perçant la brume,
> Sa tour dont à minuit le vieil œil s'allume,
> Et tes deux yeux, Zerline, illuminés bien plus,
> Je dirais que, ma foi, des romans que j'ai lus,
> Il n'en est pas un seul, plus lourd, plus léthargique
> Que cette nation qu'on nomme Britannique!

The writer of the above lines (which let any man who can translate) is Monsieur Roger de Beauvoir, a gentleman who actually lived many months in England, as an attaché to the embassy of M. de Polignac. He places the heroine of his tale in a *petit réduit près le Strand*, "with a green and fresh jalousie, and a large blind, let down all day ; you fancied you were entering a bath of Asia, as soon as you had passed the per-

18

fumed threshold of this charming retreat!" He next places
her —

> Dans un square écarté, morne et couverte de givre,
> Où se cache un hôtel, aux vieux lions de cuivre ;

and the hero of the tale, a young French poet, who is in London,
is truly unhappy in that village.

> Arthur dessèche et meurt. Dans la ville de Sterne,
> Rien qu'en voyant le peuple il a le mal de mer ·
> Il n'aime ni le Parc, gai comme une citerne,
> Ni le tir au pigeon, ni le *soda-water*.*

> *Liston* ne le fait plus sourciller ! Il rumine
> Sur les trottoirs du Strand, droit comme un échiquier,
> Contre le peuple anglais, les nègres, la vermine,
> Et les mille *cokneys* du peuple boutiquier,

> Contre tous les bas-bleus, contre les pâtissières,
> Les parieurs d'Epsom, le gin, le parlement,
> La *quaterly*, le roi, la pluie et les libraires,
> Dont il ne touche plus, hélas ! un sou d'argent !

> Et chaque gentleman lui dit : L'heureux poète !

" L'heureux poète " indeed ! I question if a poet in this
wide world is so happy as M. de Beauvoir, or has made such
wonderful discoveries. " The bath of Asia, with green jalou-
sies," in which the lady dwells ; " the old hotel, with copper
lions, in a lonely square ; " — were ever such things heard of,
or imagined, but by a Frenchman? The sailors, the negroes,
the vermin, whom he meets in the street, — how great and
happy are all these discoveries ! Liston no longer makes the
happy poet frown ; and " gin," " cokneys," and the " quaterly "
have not the least effect upon him ! And this gentleman has
lived many months amongst us ; admires *Williams Shakspear*,
the " grave et vieux prophète," as he calls him, and never,
for an instant, doubts that his description contains anything
absurd !

I don't know whether the great Dumas has passed any time
in England ; but his plays show a similar intimate knowledge
of our habits. Thus in *Kean*, the stage-manager is made to
come forward and address the pit, with a speech beginning,
" *My Lords and Gentlemen ;* " and a company of Englishwomen
are introduced (at the memorable " Coal Hole "), and they all
wear *pinafores ;* as if the British female were in the invariable

* The italics are the author's own.

habit of wearing this outer garment, or slobbering her gown without it.   There was another celebrated piece, enacted some years since, upon the subject of Queen Caroline, where our late adored sovereign, George, was made to play a most despicable part ; and where Signor Bergami fought a duel with Lord Londonderry.   In the last act of this play, the House of Lords was represented, and Sir Brougham made an eloquent speech in the Queen's favor.   Presently the shouts of the mob were heard without ; from shouting they proceeded to pelting ; and pasteboard-brickbats and cabbages came flying among the representatives of our hereditary legislature.   At this unpleasant juncture, *Sir Hardinge*, the Secretary-at-War, rises and calls in the military ; the act ends in a general row, and the ignominious fall of Lord Liverpool, laid low by a brickbat from the mob !

The description of these scenes is, of course, quite incapable of conveying any notion of their general effect.   You must have the solemnity of the actors, as they Meess and Milor one another, and the perfect gravity and good faith with which the audience listen to them.   Our stage Frenchman is the old Marquis, with sword, and pigtail, and spangled court coat. The Englishman of the French theatre has, invariably, a red wig, and almost always leather gaiters, and a long white upper Benjamin : he remains as he was represented in the old caricatures after the peace, when Vernet designed him.

And to conclude this catalogue of blunders : in the famous piece of the " Naufrage de la Meduse," the first act is laid on board an English ship-of-war, all the officers of which appeared in light blue or green coats (the lamp-light prevented our distinguishing the color accurately), and TOP-BOOTS !

.   .   .   .   .   .

Let us not attempt to deaden the force of this tremendous blow by any more remarks.   The force of blundering can go no further.   Would a Chinese playwright or painter have stranger notions about the barbarians than our neighbors, who are separated from us but by two hours of salt water?

MEDITATIONS AT VERSAILLES.

THE palace of Versailles has been turned into a bricabrac shop of late years, and its time-honored walls have been covered with many thousand yards of the worst pictures that eye ever looked on. I don't know how many leagues of battles and sieges the unhappy visitor is now obliged to march through, amidst a crowd of chattering Paris cockneys, who are never tired of looking at the glories of the Grenadier Français; to the chronicling of whose deeds this old palace of the old kings is now altogether devoted. A whizzing, screaming steam-engine rushes hither from Paris, bringing shoals of *badauds* in its wake. The old *coucous* are all gone, and their place knows them no longer. Smooth asphaltum terraces, tawdry lamps, and great hideous Egyptian obelisks, have frightened them away from the pleasant station they used to occupy under the trees of the Champs Elysées; and though the old *coucous* were just the most uncomfortable vehicles that human ingenuity ever constructed, one can't help looking back to the days of their existence with a tender regret; for there was pleasure then in the little trip of three leagues: and who ever had pleasure in a railway journey? Does any reader of this venture to say that, on such a voyage, he ever dared to be pleasant? Do the most hardened stokers joke with one another? I don't believe it. Look into every single car of the train, and you will see that every single face is solemn. They take their seats gravely, and are silent, for the most part, during the journey; they dare not look out of window, for fear of being blinded by the smoke that comes whizzing by, or of losing their heads in one of the windows of the down train; they ride for miles in utter damp and darkness: through awful pipes of brick, that have been run pitilessly through the bowels of gentle mother earth, the cast-iron Frankenstein of an engine gallops on, puffing and screaming. Does any man pretend to say that he *enjoys* the journey? — he might as well say that he enjoyed having his hair cut; he bears it, but that is all: he will not allow the world to laugh at him, for any exhibition of slavish fear; and pretends, therefore, to be at his ease; but he *is* afraid: nay, ought to be, under the circumstances. I am sure Hannibal or Napoleon would, were they locked suddenly into a car; there kept close prisoners for a certain number of hours, and whirled along at this dizzy pace. You can't stop, if you would: — you may die, but you can't stop; the engine may explode upon the road, and up you go along with it; or, may be a bolter and take a fancy to go down a hill, or into a river: all this you must bear, for the privilege of travelling twenty miles an hour.

This little journey, then, from Paris to Versailles, that used to be so merry of old, has lost its pleasures since the disappearance of the *coucous;* and I would as lief have for companions the statues that lately took a coach from the bridge opposite the Chamber of Deputies, and stepped out in the court of Versailles, as the most part of the people who now travel on the railroad. The stone figures are not a whit more cold and silent than these persons, who used to be, in the old *coucous*, so talkative and merry. The prattling grisette and her swain from the Ecole de Droit; the huge Alsacian carabineer, grimly smiling under his sandy moustaches and glittering brass helmet; the jolly nurse, in red calico, who had been to Paris to show mamma her darling Lolo, or Auguste; — what merry companions used one to find squeezed into the crazy old vehicles that formerly performed the journey! But the age of horse-flesh is gone — that of engineers, economists, and calculators has succeeded; and the pleasure of *coucoudom* is extinguished for ever. Why not mourn over it, as Mr. Burke did over his cheap defence of nations and unbought grace of life; that age of chivalry, which he lamented, àpropos of a trip to Versailles, some half a century back?

Without stopping to discuss (as might be done, in rather a neat and successful manner) whether the age of chivalry was cheap or dear, and whether, in the time of the unbought grace of life, there was not more bribery, robbery, villainy, tyranny, and corruption, than exists even in our own happy days, — let us make a few moral and historical remarks upon the town of Versailles; where, between railroad and *coucou*, we are surely arrived by this time.

The town is, certainly, the most moral of towns. You pass from the railroad station through a long, lonely suburb, with dusty rows of stunted trees on either side, and some few miserable beggars, idle boys, and ragged old women under them. Behind the trees are gaunt, mouldy houses; palaces once, where (in the days of the unbought grace of life) the cheap defence of nations gambled, ogled, swindled, intrigued; whence high-born duchesses used to issue, in old times, to act as chambermaids to lovely Du Barri; and mighty princes rolled away, in gilt caroches, hot for the honor of lighting his Majesty to bed, or of presenting his stockings when he rose, or of holding his napkin when he dined. Tailors, chandlers, tinmen, wretched hucksters, and greengrocers, are now established in the mansions of the old peers; small children are yelling at the doors, with mouths besmeared with bread and treacle; damp rags are hanging out of every one of the windows, steam· ing in the sun; oyster-shells, cabbage-stalks, broken crockery, old papers, lie basking in the same cheerful light. A solitary water-cart goes jingling down the wide pavement, and spirts a feeble refreshment over the dusty, thirsty stones.

After pacing for some time through such dismal streets, we *deboucher* on the *grande place;* and before us lies the palace dedicated to all the glories of France. In the midst of the great lonely plain this famous residence of King Louis looks low and mean. — Honored pile! Time was when tall musketeers and gilded body-guards allowed none to pass the gate. Fifty years ago, ten thousand drunken women from Paris broke through the charm; and now a tattered commissioner will conduct you through it for a penny, and lead you up to the sacred entrance of the palace.

We will not examine all the glories of France, as here they are portrayed in pictures and marble: catalogues are written about these miles of canvas, representing all the revolutionary battles, from Valmy to Waterloo, — all the triumphs of Louis XIV. — all the mistresses of his successor — and all the great men who have flourished since the French empire began. Military heroes are most of these — fierce constables in shining steel, marshals in voluminous wigs, and brave grenadiers in bearskin caps; some dozens of whom gained crowns, principalities, dukedoms; some hundreds, plunder and epaulets; some millions, death in African sands, or in icy Russian plains, under the guidance, and for the good, of that arch-hero, Napoleon. By far the greater part of "all the glories" of France (as of most other countries) is made up of these military men: and a fine satire it is on the cowardice of mankind, that they pay such an extraordinary homage to the virtue called courage; filling their history-books with tales about it, and nothing but it.

Let them disguise the place, however, as they will, and plaster the walls with bad pictures as they please, it will be hard to think of any family but one, as one traverses this vast gloomy edifice. It has not been humbled to the ground, as a certain palace of Babel was of yore; but it is a monument of fallen pride, not less awful, and would afford matter for a whole library of sermons. The cheap defence of nations expended a thousand millions in the erection of this magnificent dwelling-place. Armies were employed, in the intervals of their warlike labors, to level hills, or pile them up; to turn rivers, and to build aqueducts, and transplant woods, and construct smooth terraces, and long canals. A vast garden grew up in a wilderness, and a stupendous palace in the garden, and a stately city round the palace: the city was peopled with parasites, who daily came to do worship before the creator of these wonders — the Great King. "Dieu seul est grand," said courtly Massillon; but next to him, as the prelate thought, was certainly Louis, his vicegerent here upon earth — God's lieutenant-governor of the world, — before whom courtiers used to fall on their knees, and shade their eyes, as if the light of his countenance, like the sun, which shone supreme in heaven, the type of him, was too dazzling to bear.

Did ever the sun shine upon such a king before, in such a palace? — or, rather, did such a king ever shine upon the sun? When Majesty came out of his chamber, in the midst of his superhuman splendors, viz. in his cinnamon-colored coat, embroidered with diamonds; his pyramid of a wig;* his red-heeled shoes, that lifted him four inches from the ground, "that he scarcely seemed to touch;" when he came out, blazing upon the dukes and duchesses that waited his rising, — what could the latter do, but cover their eyes, and wink, and tremble? And did he not himself believe, as he stood there, on his high heels, under his ambrosial periwig, that there was something in him more than man — something above Fate?

This, doubtless, was he fain to believe; and if, on very fine days, from his terrace before his gloomy palace of Saint Germains, he could catch a glimpse, in the distance, of a certain white spire of St. Denis, where his race lay buried, he would say to his courtiers, with a sublime condescension, "Gentlemen,

---

* It is fine to think that, in the days of his youth, his **Majesty Louis XIV.** used to *powder his wig with gold-dust.*

you must remember that I, too, am mortal. " Surely the lords in waiting could hardly think him serious, and vowed that his Majesty always loved a joke. However, mortal or not, the sight of that sharp spire wounded his Majesty's eyes ; and is said, by the legend, to have caused the building of the palace of Babel-Versailles.

In the year 1681, then, the great king, with bag and bag-gage, — with guards, cooks, chamberlains, mistresses, Jesuits, gentlemen, lackeys, Fénélons, Molières, Lauzuns, Bossuets, Villars, Villeroys, Louvois, Colberts, — transported himself to his new palace : the old one being left for James of England and Jaquette his wife, when their time should come. And when the time did come, and James sought his brother's kingdom, it is on record that Louis hastened to receive and console him, and prom-ised to restore, incontinently, those islands from which the *ca-naille* had turned him. Between brothers such a gift was a trifle ; and the courtiers said to one another reverently : * "The Lord said unto my Lord, Sit thou on my right hand, until I make thine enemies thy footstool." There was no blasphemy in the speech : on the contrary, it was gravely said, by a faithful be-lieving man, who thought it no shame to the latter, to compare his Majesty with God Almighty. Indeed, the books of the time will give one a strong idea how general was this Louis-worship. I have just been looking at one, which was written by an hon-est Jesuit and Protégé of Père la Chaise, who dedicates a book of medals to the august Infants of France, which does, indeed, go almost as far in print. He calls our famous monarch " Louis le Grand : — 1, l'invincible ; 2, le sage ; 3, le conquérant ; 4, la merveille de son siècle ; 5, la terreur de ses ennemis ; 6, l'amour de ses peuples ; 7, l'arbitre de la paix et de la guerre ; 8, l'ad-miration de l'univers ; 9, et digne d'en être le maître : 10, le modèle d'un héros achevé ; 11, digne de l'immortalité, et de la vénération de tous les siècles ! "

A pretty Jesuit declaration, truly, and a good honest judg-ment upon the great king ! In thirty years more — 1.   The invincible had been beaten a vast number of times. 2. The sage was the puppet of an artful old woman, who was the puppet of more artful priests. 3. The conqueror had quite forgotten his early knack of conquering. 5. The terror of his enemies (for 4, the marvel of his age, we pretermit, it being a loose term, that may apply to any person or thing) was now terrified by his

---

* I think it is in the amusing "Memoirs of Madame de Crequi" (a for-gery, but a work remarkable for its learning and accuracy) that the above anecdote is related.

enemies in turn. 6. The love of his people was as heartily detested by them as scarcely any other monarch, not even his great-grandson, has been, before or since. 7. The arbiter of peace and war was fain to send superb ambassadors to kick their heels in Dutch shopkeepers' ante-chambers. 8, is again a general term. 9. The man fit to be master of the universe, was scarcely master of his own kingdom. 10. The finished hero was all but finished, in a very commonplace and vulgar way. And 11. The man worthy of immortality was just at the point of death, without a friend to soothe or deplore him ; only withered old Maintenon to utter prayers at his bedside, and croaking Jesuits to prepare him,* with heaven knows what wretched tricks and mummeries, for his appearance in that Great Republic that lies on the other side of the grave. In the course of his fourscore splendid miserable years, he never had but one friend, and he ruined and left her. Poor La Vallière, what a sad tale is yours ! " Look at this Galerie des Glaces," cries Monsieur Vatout, staggering with surprise at the appearance of the room, two hundred and forty-two feet long, and forty high. " Here it was that Louis displayed all the grandeur of royalty ; and such was the splendor of his court, and the luxury of the times, that this immense room could hardly contain the crowd of courtiers that pressed around the monarch." Wonderful ! wonderful ! Eight thousand four hundred and sixty square feet of courtiers ! Give a square yard to each, and you have a matter of three thousand of them. Think of three thousand courtiers per day, and all the chopping and changing of them for near forty years : some of them dying, some getting their wishes, and retiring to their provinces to enjoy their plunder ; some disgraced, and going home to pine away out of the light of the sun ; † new ones perpetually arriving, — pushing, squeezing, for their place, in the crowded Galerie des Glaces. A quarter of a million of noble countenances, at the very least, must those glasses have reflected. Rouge, diamonds, ribbons, patches, upon the faces of smiling ladies : towering periwigs, sleek shaven crowns, tufted moustaches, scars, and grizzled whiskers, worn by ministers, priests, dandies, and grim old commanders. — So many faces, O ye gods ! and every one of them lies ! So many tongues, vowing devotion and respectful love to the great king in his six-inch wig ; and only poor La Vallière's amongst them all

* They made a Jesuit of him on his death-bed.
† Saint Simon's account of Lauzun, in disgrace, is admirably facetious and pathetic ; Lauzun's regrets are as monstrous as those of Raleigh when deprived of the sight of his adorable Queen and Mistress, Elizabeth.

which had a word of truth for the dull ears of Louis of Bourbon.

" Quand j'aurai de la peine aux Carmélites," says unhappy Louise, about to retire from these magnificent courtiers and their grand Galerie des Glaces, " je me souviendrai de ce que ces gens là m'ont fait souffrir ! " — A troop of Bossuets inveighing against the vanities of courts could not preach such an affecting sermon. What years of anguish and wrong had the poor thing suffered, before these sad words came from her gentle lips ! How these courtiers have bowed and flattered, kissed the ground on which she trod, fought to have the honor of riding by her carriage, written sonnets, and called her goddess ; who, in the days of her prosperity, was kind and beneficent, gentle and compassionate to all ; then (on a certain day, when it is whispered that his Majesty hath cast the eyes of his gracious affection upon another) behold three thousand courtiers are at the feet of the new divinity. — " O divine Athenais ! what blockheads have we been to worship any but you. — *That* a goddess ? — a pretty goddess forsooth ; — a witch, rather, who, for a while, kept our gracious monarch blind ! Look at her : the woman limps as she walks ; and, by sacred Venus, her mouth stretches almost to her diamond ear-rings ? " * The same tale may be told of many more deserted mistresses ; and fair Athenais de Montespan was to hear it of herself one day. Meantime, while La Vallière's heart is breaking, the model of a finished hero is yawning ; as, on such paltry occasions, a finished hero should. *Let* her heart break : a plague upon her tears and repentance ; what right has she to repent? Away with her to her convent. She goes, and the finished hero never sheds a tear. What a noble pitch of stoicism to have reached ! Our Louis was so great, that the little woes of mean people were beyond him : his friends died, his mistresses left him ; his children, one by one, were cut off before his eyes, and great Louis is not moved in the slightest degree ! As how, indeed, should a god be moved?

I have often liked to think about this strange character in the world, who moved in it, bearing about a full belief in his own infallibility ; teaching his generals the art of war, his ministers the science of government, his wits taste, his courtiers dress ; ordering deserts to become gardens, turning villages into palaces at a breath ; and indeed the august figure of the man,

* A pair of diamond ear-rings, given by the King to La Vallière, caused much scandal ; and some lampoons are extant, which impugn the taste of Louis XIV. for loving a lady with such an enormous mouth.

as he towers upon his throne, cannot fail to inspire one with respect and awe : — how grand those flowing locks appear ; how awful that sceptre ; how magnificent those flowing robes ! In Louis, surely, if in any one, the majesty of kinghood is represented.

But a king is not every inch a king, for all the poet may say ; and it is curious to see how much precise majesty there is in that majestic figure of Ludovicus Rex. In the Frontispiece, we have endeavored to make the exact calculation. The idea of kingly dignity is equally strong in the two outer figures ; and you see, at once, that majesty is made out of the wig, the high-heeled shoes, and cloak, all fleurs-de-lis bespangled. As for the little lean, shrivelled, paunchy old man, of five feet two, in a jacket and breeches, there is no majesty in *him* at any rate ; and yet he has just stepped out of that very suit of clothes. Put the wig and shoes on him, and he is six feet high ; — the other fripperies, and he stands before you majestic, imperial, and heroic ! Thus do barbers and cobblers make the gods that we worship : for do we not all worship him ? Yes; though we all know him to be stupid, heartless, short, of doubtful personal courage, worship and admire him we must ; and have set up, in our hearts, a grand image of him, endowed with wit, magnanimity, valor, and enormous heroical stature.

And what magnanimous acts are attributed to him ! or, rather, how differently do we view the actions of heroes and common men, and find that the same thing shall be a wonderful virtue in the former, which, in the latter, is only an ordinary act of duty. Look at yonder window of the king's chamber ; — one morning a royal cane was seen whirling out of it, and plumped among the courtiers and guard of honor below. King Louis had absolutely, and with his own hand, flung his own cane out of the window, " because," said he, " I won't demean myself by striking a gentleman ! " O miracle of magnanimity ! Lauzun was not caned, because he besought majesty to keep his promise, — only imprisoned for ten years in Pignerol, along with banished Fouquet ; — and a pretty story is Fouquet's too.

Out of the window the king's august head was one day thrust, when old Condé was painfully toiling up the steps of the court below. " Don't hurry yourself, my cousin," cries Magnanimity ; " one who has to carry so many laurels cannot walk fast." At which all the courtiers, lackeys, mistresses, chamberlains, Jesuits, and scullions, clasp their hands and burst into tears. Men are affected by the tale to this very day. For a century and three-quarters, have not all the books that

speak of Versailles, or Louis Quatorze, told the story?—
"Don't hurry yourself, my cousin!" O admirable king and
Christian! what a pitch of condescension is here, that the
greatest king of all the world should go for to say anything so
kind, and really tell a tottering old gentleman, worn out with
gout, age, and wounds, not to walk too fast!

What a proper fund of slavishness is there in the composition of mankind, that histories like these should be found to
interest and awe them. Till the world's end, most likely, this
story will have its place in the history-books; and unborn generations will read it, and tenderly be moved by it. I am sure
that Magnanimity went to bed that night, pleased and happy,
intimately convinced that he had done an action of sublime
virtue, and had easy slumbers and sweet dreams,—especially
if he had taken a light supper, and not too vehemently attacked
his *en cas de nuit*.

That famous adventure, in which the *en cas de nuit* was
brought into use, for the sake of one Poquelin *alias* Molière;—how often has it been described and admired? This
Poquelin, though king's valet-de-chambre, was by profession
a vagrant; and as such, looked coldly on by the great lords
of the palace, who refused to eat with him. Majesty hearing
of this, ordered his *en cas de nuit* to be placed on the table,
and positively cut off a wing with his own knife and fork for
Poquelin's use. O thrice happy Jean Baptiste! The king has
actually sat down with him cheek by jowl, had the liver-wing
of a fowl, and given Molière the gizzard; put his imperial legs
under the same mahogany (*sub iisdem trabibus*). A man, after
such an honor, can look for little else in this world: he has
tasted the utmost conceivable earthly happiness, and has nothing to do now but to fold his arms, look up to heaven, and
sing "Nunc dimittis" and die.

Do not let us abuse poor old Louis on account of this monstrous pride; but only lay it to the charge of the fools who
believed and worshipped it. If, honest man, he believed himself to be almost a god, it was only because thousands of
people had told him so — people only half liars, too; who did,
in the depths of their slavish respect, admire the man almost
as much as they said they did. If, when he appeared in his
five-hundred-million coat, as he is said to have done, before
the Siamese ambassadors, the courtiers began to shade their
eyes and long for parasols, as if this Bourbonic sun was too
hot for them; indeed, it is no wonder that he should believe
that there was something dazzling about his person: he had

half a million of eager testimonies to this idea. Who was to tell him the truth? — Only in the last years of his life did trembling courtiers dare whisper to him, after much circumlocution, that a certain battle had been fought at a place called Blenheim, and that Eugene and Marlborough had stopped his long career of triumphs.

"On n'est plus heureux à notre âge," says the old man, to one of his old generals, welcoming Tallard after his defeat; and he rewards him with honors, as if he had come from a victory. There is, if you will, something magnanimous in this welcome to his conquered general, this stout protest against Fate. Disaster succeeds disaster; armies after armies march out to meet fiery Eugene and that dogged, fatal Englishman, and disappear in the smoke of the enemies' cannon. Even at Versailles you may almost hear it roaring at last; but when courtiers, who have forgotten their god, now talk of quitting this grand temple of his, old Louis plucks up heart and will never hear of surrender. All the gold and silver at Versailles he melts, to find bread for his armies : all the jewels on his five-hundred-million coat he pawns resolutely ; and, bidding Villars go and make the last struggle but one, promises, if his general is defeated, to place himself at the head of his nobles, and die King of France. Indeed, after a man, for sixty years, has been performing the part of a hero, some of the real heroic stuff must have entered into his composition, whether he would or not. When the great Elliston was enacting the part of King George the Fourth, in the play of "The Coronation," at Drury Lane, the galleries applauded very loudly his suavity and majestic demeanor, at which Elliston, inflamed by the popular loyalty (and by some fermented liquor in which, it is said, he was in the habit of indulging), burst into tears, and spreading out his arms, exclaimed : "Bless ye, bless ye, my people !" Don't let us laugh at his Ellistonian majesty, nor at the people who clapped hands and yelled "bravo!" in praise of him. The tipsy old manager did really feel that he was a hero at that moment ; and the people, wild with delight and attachment for a magnificent coat and breeches, surely were uttering the true sentiments of loyalty : which consists in reverencing these and other articles of costume. In this fifth act, then, of his long royal drama, old Louis performed his part excellently ; and when the curtain drops upon him, he lies, dressed majestically, in a becoming kingly attitude, as a king should.

The king his successor has not left, at Versailles, half so much occasion for moralizing; perhaps the neighboring Parc aux Cerfs would afford better illustrations of his reign. The life of his great grandsire, the Grand Llama of France, seems to have frightened Louis the well-beloved; who understood that loneliness is one of the necessary conditions of divinity, and being of a jovial, companionable turn, aspired not beyond manhood. Only in the matter of ladies did he surpass his predecessor, as Solomon did David. War he eschewed, as his grandfather bade him; and his simple taste found little in this world to enjoy beyond the mulling of chocolate and the frying of pancakes. Look, here is the room called Laboratoire du Roi, where, with his own hands, he made his mistress's breakfast: — here is the little door through which, from her apartments in the upper story, the chaste Du Barri came stealing down to the arms of the weary, feeble, gloomy old man. But of women he was tired long since, and even pancake-frying had palled upon him. What had he to do, after forty years of reign; — after having exhausted everything? Every pleasure that Dubois could invent for his hot youth, or cunning Lebel could minister to his old age, was flat and stale; used up to the very dregs: every shilling in the national purse had been squeezed out, by Pompadour and Du Barri and such brilliant ministers of state. He had found out the vanity of pleasure, as his ancestor had discovered the vanity of glory: indeed it was high time that he should die. And die he did; and round his tomb, as round that of his grandfather before him, the starving people sang a dreadful chorus of curses, which were the only epitaphs for good or for evil that were raised to his memory.

As for the courtiers — the knights and nobles, the unbought grace of life — they, of course, forgot him in one minute after his death, as the way is. When the king dies, the officer appointed opens his chamber window, and calling out into the court below, *Le Roi est mort*, breaks his cane, takes another and waves it, exclaiming, *Vive le Roi!* Straightway all the loyal nobles begin yelling *Vive le Roi!* and the officer goes round solemnly and sets yonder great clock in the Cour de Marbre to the hour of the king's death. This old Louis had solemnly ordained; but the Versailles clock was only set twice: there was no shouting of *Vive le Roi* when the successor of Louis XV. mounted to heaven to join his sainted family.

Strange stories of the deaths of kings have always been very recreating and profitable to us: what a fine one is that of the death of Louis XV., as Madame Campan tells it. One night the gracious monarch came back ill from Trianon ; the disease turned out to be the small-pox ; so violent that ten people of those who had to enter his chamber caught the infection and died. The whole court flies from him ; only poor old fat Mesdames the King's daughters persist in remaining at his bedside, and praying for his soul's welfare.

On the 10th May, 1774, the whole court had assembled at the château ; the Œil de Bœuf was full. The Dauphin had determined to depart as soon as the king had breathed his last. And it was agreed by the people of the stables, with those who watched in the king's room, that a lighted candle should be placed in a window, and should be extinguished as soon as he had ceased to live. The candle was put out. At that signal, guards, pages, and squires mounted on horseback, and everything was made ready for departure. The Dauphin was with the Dauphiness, waiting together for the news of the king's demise. *An immense noise, as if of thunder, was heard in the next room ;* it was the crowd of courtiers, who were deserting the dead king's apartment, in order to pay their court to the new power of Louis XVI. Madame de Noailles entered, and was the first to salute the queen by her title of Queen of France, and begged their Majesties to quit their apartments, to receive the princes and great lords of the court desirous to pay their homage to the new sovereigns. Leaning on her husband's arm, a handkerchief to her eyes, in the most touching attitude, Marie Antoinette received these first visits. On quitting the chamber where the dead king lay, the Duc de Villequier bade M. Anderville, first surgeon of the king, to open and embalm the body : it would have been certain death to the surgeon. " I am ready, sir," said he ; " but whilst I am operating, you must hold the head of the corpse : your charge demands it." The Duke went away without a word, and the body was neither opened nor embalmed. A few humble domestics and poor workmen watched by the remains, and performed the last offices to their master. The surgeons ordered spirits of wine to be poured into the coffin.

They huddled the king's body into a post-chaise ; and in this deplorable equipage, with an escort of about forty men, Louis the well-beloved was carried, in the dead of night, from Versailles to St. Denis, and then thrown into the tomb of the kings of France !

If any man is curious, and can get permission, he may mount to the roof of the palace, and see where Louis XVI. used royally to amuse himself, by gazing upon the doings of all the townspeople below with a telescope. Behold that balcony, where, one morning, he, his queen, and the little Dauphin stood, with Cromwell Grandison Lafayette by their side, who kissed her Majesty's hand, and protected her; and then, lovingly surrounded by his people, the king got into a coach and came to Paris : nor did his Majesty ride much in coaches after that.

There is a portrait of the king, in the upper galleries, clothed in red and gold, riding a fat horse, brandishing a sword, on which the word "Justice" is inscribed, and looking remarkably stupid and uncomfortable. You see that the horse will throw him at the very first fling; and as for the sword, it never was made for such hands as his, which were good at holding a corkscrew or a carving-knife, but not clever at the management of weapons of war. Let those pity him who will : call him saint and martyr if you please ; but a martyr to what principle was he? Did he frankly support either party in his kingdom, or cheat and tamper with both? He might have escaped ; but he must have his supper : and so his family was butchered and his kingdom lost, and he had his bottle of Burgundy in comfort at Varennes. A single charge upon the fatal 10th of August, and the monarchy might have been his once more ; but he is so tender-hearted, that he lets his friends be murdered before his eyes almost : or, at least, when he has turned his back upon his duty and his kingdom, and has skulked for safety into the reporters' box, at the National Assembly. There were hundreds of brave men who died that day, and were martyrs, if you will ; poor neglected tenth-rate courtiers, for the most part, who had forgotten old slights and disappointments, and left their places of safety to come and die, if need were, sharing in the supreme hour of the monarchy. Monarchy was a great deal too humane to fight along with these, and so left them to the pikes of Santerre and the mercy of the men of the Sections. But we are wandering a good ten miles from Versailles, and from the deeds which Louis XVI. performed there.

He is said to have been such a smart journeyman blacksmith, that he might, if Fate had not perversely placed a crown on his head, have earned a couple of louis every week by the making of locks and keys. Those who will may see the workshop where he employed many useful hours : Madame Elizabeth was at prayers meanwhile ; the queen was making pleasant parties with her ladies. Monsieur the Count d'Artois was learning to dance on the tight-rope ; and Monsieur de Provence was cultivating *l'eloquence du billet* and studying his favorite Horace. It is said that each member of the august family succeeded remarkably well in his or her pursuits; big Monsieur's little notes are still cited. At a minuet or syllabub, poor Antoinette was unrivalled; and Charles, on the tight-rope, was so graceful and so *gentil*, that Madame Saqui might envy him. The time only was out of joint. O cursed spite, that ever such harmless creatures as these were bidden to right it!

A walk to the little Trianon is both pleasing and moral: no doubt the reader has seen the pretty fantastical gardens which environ it; the groves and temples; the streams and caverns (whither, as the guide tells you, during the heat of summer, it was the custom of Marie Antoinette to retire, with her favorite, Madame de Lamballe): the lake and Swiss village are pretty little toys, moreover; and the cicerone of the place does not fail to point out the different cottages which surround the piece of water, and tell the names of the royal masqueraders who inhabited each. In the long cottage, close upon the lake, dwelt the Seigneur du Village, no less a personage than Louis XV.; Louis XVI., the Dauphin, was the Bailli; near his cottage is that of Monseigneur the Count d'Artois, who was the Miller; opposite lived the Prince de Condé, who enacted the part of Gamekeeper (or, indeed, any other rôle, for it does not signify much); near him was the Prince de Rohan, who was the Aumônier; and yonder is the pretty little dairy, which was under the charge of the fair Marie Antoinette herself.

I forget whether Monsieur the fat Count of Provence took any share of this royal masquerading; but look at the names of the other six actors of the comedy, and it will be hard to find any person for whom Fate had such dreadful visitations in store. Fancy the party, in the days of their prosperity, here gathered at Trianon, and seated under the tall poplars by the lake, discoursing familiarly together: suppose of a sudden some conjuring Cagliostro of the time is introduced among them, and foretells to them the woes that are about to come. "You, Monsieur l'Aumônier, the descendant of a long line of princes, the passionate admirer of that fair queen who sits by your side, shall be the cause of her ruin and your own,* and shall die in disgrace and exile. You, son of the Condés, shall live long enough to see your royal race overthrown, and shall die by the hands of a hangman.† You, oldest son of Saint Louis, shall perish by the executioner's axe; that beautiful head, O Antoinette, the same ruthless blade shall sever." "They shall kill

---

* In the diamond-necklace affair.
† He was found hanging in his own bedroom.

me first," says Lamballe, at the queen's side. "Yes, truly,"
replies the soothsayer, "for Fate prescribes ruin for your mistress and all who love her." *   "And," cries Monsieur d'Artois,
"do I not love my sister, too? I pray you not to omit me in
your prophecies."

To whom Monsieur Cagliostro says, scornfully, "You may
look forward to fifty years of life, after most of these are laid
in the grave. You shall be a king, but not die one; and shall
leave the crown only; not the worthless head that shall wear
it. Thrice shall you go into exile: you shall fly from the people, first, who would have no more of you and your race; and
you shall return home over half a million of human corpses,
that have been made for the sake of you, and of a tyrant as
great as the greatest of your family. Again driven away, your
bitterest enemy shall bring you back. But the strong limbs of
France are not to be chained by such a paltry yoke as you can
put on her: you shall be a tyrant, but in will only; and shall
have a sceptre, but to see it robbed from your hand."

"And pray, Sir Conjurer, who shall be the robber?" asked
Monsieur the Count d'Artois.

.   .   .   .   .   .

This I cannot say, for here my dream ended. The fact is,
I had fallen asleep on one of the stone benches in the Avenue
de Paris, and at this instant was awakened by a whirling of
carriages and a great clattering of national guards, lancers and
outriders, in red. HIS MAJESTY LOUIS PHILIPPE was going to
pay a visit to the palace; which contains several pictures of his
own glorious actions, and which has been dedicated, by him, to
all the glories of France.

---

* Among the many lovers that rumor gave to the queen, poor Ferscu
is the most remarkable. He seems to have entertained for her a high and
perfectly pure devotion. He was the chief agent in the luckless escape to
Varennes; was lurking in Paris during the time of her captivity; and was
concerned in the many fruitless plots that were made for her rescue.
Ferscu lived to be an old man, but died a dreadful and violent death. He
was dragged from his carriage by the mob, in Stockholm, and murdered
by them.

THE LITTLE TRIANON OF MARIE ANTOINETTE.

EASTERN SKETCHES

TO

CAPTAIN SAMUEL LEWIS,

OF THE PENINSULAR AND ORIENTAL STEAM NAVIGATION COMPANY'S
SERVICE.

MY DEAR LEWIS, — After a voyage, during which the captain of the ship has displayed uncommon courage, seamanship, affability, or other good qualities, grateful passengers often present him with a token of their esteem, in the shape of teapots, tankards, trays, &c. of precious metal. Among authors, however, bullion is a much rarer commodity than paper, whereof I beg you to accept a little in the shape of this small volume. It contains a few notes of a voyage which your skill and kindness rendered doubly pleasant; and of which I don't think there is any recollection more agreeable than that it was the occasion of making your friendship.

If the noble company in whose service you command (and whose fleet alone makes them a third-rate maritime power in Europe) should appoint a few admirals in their navy, I hope to hear that your flag is hoisted on board one of the grandest of their steamers. But, I trust, even there you will not forget the " Iberia," and the delightful Mediterranean cruise we had in her in the Autumn of 1844.

Most faithfully yours,

My dear LEWIS,

W. M. THACKERAY.

LONDON, December 24, 1845.

PREFACE.

On the 20th of August, 1844, the writer of this little book went to dine at the "———— Club," quite unconscious of the wonderful events which Fate had in store for him.

Mr. William was there, giving a farewell dinner to his friend, Mr. James (now Sir James). These two asked Mr. Titmarsh to join company with them, and the conversation naturally fell upon the tour Mr. James was about to take. The Peninsular and Oriental Company had arranged an excursion in the Mediterranean, by which, in the space of a couple of months, as many men and cities were to be seen as Ulysses surveyed and noted in ten years. Malta, Athens, Smyrna, Constantinople, Jerusalem, Cairo, were to be visited, and everybody was to be back in London by Lord Mayor's Day.

The idea of beholding these famous places inflamed Mr. Titmarsh's mind; and the charms of such a journey were eloquently impressed upon him by Mr. James. "Come," said that kind and hospitable gentleman, "and make one of my family party; in all your life you will never probably have a chance again to see so much in so short a time. Consider — it is as easy as a journey to Paris or to Baden." Mr. Titmarsh considered all these things; but also the difficulties of the situation: he had but six-and-thirty hours to get ready for so portentous a journey — he had engagements at home — finally, could he afford it? In spite of these objections, however, with every glass of claret the enthusiasm somehow rose, and the difficulties vanished.

But when Mr. James, to crown all, said he had no doubt that his friends, the Directors of the Peninsular and Oriental Company, would make Mr. Titmarsh the present of a berth for the voyage, all objections ceased on his part : to break his outstanding engagements — to write letters to his amazed family, stating that they were not to expect him at dinner on Saturday fortnight, as he would be at Jerusalem on that day — to purchase eighteen shirts and lay in a sea stock of Russia ducks, — was the work of four-and-twenty hours ; and on the 22nd of August, the "Lady Mary Wood" was sailing from Southampton with the "subject of the present memoir," quite astonished to find himself one of the passengers on board.

These important statements are made partly to convince some incredulous friends — who insist still that the writer never went abroad at all, and wrote the following pages, out of pure fancy, in retirement at Putney ; but mainly, to give him an opportunity of thanking the Directors of the Company in question for a delightful excursion.

It was one so easy, so charming, and I think profitable — it leaves such a store of pleasant recollections for after days — and creates so many new sources of interest (a newspaper letter from Beyrout, or Malta, or Algiers, has twice the interest now that it had formerly), — that I can't but recommend all persons who have time and means to make a similar journey — vacation idlers to extend their travels and pursue it : above all, young well-educated men entering life, to take this course, we will say, after that at college ; and, having their book-learning fresh in their minds, see the living people and their cities, and the actual aspect of Nature, along the famous shores of the Mediterranean.

A JOURNEY FROM CORNHILL TO CAIRO.

CHAPTER I.

VIGO.

THE sun brought all the sick people out of their berths this morning, and the indescribable moans and noises which had been issuing from behind the fine painted doors on each side of the cabin happily ceased. Long before sunrise, I had the good fortune to discover that it was no longer necessary to maintain the horizontal posture, and, the very instant this truth was apparent, came on deck, at two o'clock in the morning, to see a noble full moon sinking westward, and millions of the most brilliant stars shining overhead. The night was so serenely pure, that you saw them in magnificent airy perspective ; the blue sky around and over them, and other more distant orbs sparkling above, till they glittered away faintly into the immeasurable distance. The ship went rolling over a heavy, sweltering, calm sea. The breeze was a warm and soft one ; quite different to the rigid air we had left behind us, two days since, off the Isle of Wight. The bell kept tolling its half-hours, and the mate explained the mystery of watch and dog-watch.

The sight of that noble scene cured all the woes and discomfitures of sea-sickness at once, and if there were any need to communicate such secrets to the public, one might tell of much more good that the pleasant morning-watch effected ; but there are a set of emotions about which a man had best be shy of talking lightly, — and the feelings excited by contemplating this vast, magnificent, harmonious Nature are among these. The view of it inspires a delight and ecstasy which is not only hard to describe, but which has something secret in it that a man should not utter loudly. Hope, memory, humility, tender yearnings towards dear friends, and inexpressible love and reverence towards the Power which created the infinite universe blazing above eternally, and the vast ocean shining and rolling around — fill the heart with a solemn, humble happiness, that a person dwelling in a city has rarely occasion to enjoy. They are coming away from London parties at this time : the dear little eyes are closed in sleep under mother's wing. How far off city cares and pleasures appear to be! how small and mean they seem, dwindling out of sight before this magnificent brightness of Nature! But the best thoughts only grow and strengthen under it. Heaven shines above, and the humbled spirit looks up reverently towards that boundless aspect of wisdom and beauty. You are at home, and with all at rest there, however far away they may be ; and through the distance the heart broods over them, bright and wakeful like yonder peaceful stars overhead.

The day was as fine and calm as the night ; at seven bells, suddenly a bell began to toll very much like that of a country church, and on going on deck we found an awning raised, a desk with a flag flung over it close to the compass, and the ship's company and passengers assembled there to hear the captain read the Service in a manly respectful voice. This, too, was a novel and touching sight to me. Peaked ridges of purple mountains rose to the left of the ship, — Finisterre and the coast of Galicia. The sky above was cloudless and shining ; the vast dark ocean smiled peacefully round about, and the ship went rolling over it, as the people within were praising the Maker of all.

In honor of the day, it was announced that the passengers would be regaled with champagne at dinner ; and accordingly that exhilarating liquor was served out in decent profusion, the company drinking the captain's health with the customary orations of compliment and acknowledgment. This feast was scarcely ended, when we found ourselves rounding the headland into Vigo Bay, passing a grim and tall island of rocky mountains which lies in the centre of the bay.

Whether it is that the sight of land is always welcome to weary mariners, after the perils and annoyances of a voyage of three days, or whether the place is in itself extraordinarily beautiful, need not be argued ; but I have seldom seen anything more charming than the amphitheatre of noble hills into which the ship now came — all the features of the landscape being lighted up with a wonderful clearness of air, which rarely adorns a view in our country. The sun had not yet set, but over the town and lofty rocky castle of Vigo a great ghost of a moon was faintly visible, which blazed out brighter and brighter as the superior luminary retired behind the purple mountains of the headland to rest. Before the general background of waving heights which encompassed the bay, rose a second semicircle of undulating hills, as cheerful and green as the mountains behind them were gray and solemn. Farms and gardens, convent towers, white villages and churches, and buildings that no doubt were hermitages once, upon the sharp peaks of the hills, shone brightly in the sun. The sight was delightfully cheerful, animated, and pleasing.

Presently the captain roared out the magic words, "Stop her!" and the obedient vessel came to a stand-still, at some three hundred yards from the little town, with its white houses clambering up a rock, defended by the superior mountain whereon the castle stands. Numbers of people, arrayed in various brilliant colors of red, were standing on the sand close by the tumbling, shining, purple waves : and there we beheld, for the first time, the royal red and yellow standard of Spain floating on its own ground, under the guardianship of a light blue sentinel, whose musket glittered in the sun. Numerous boats were seen, incontinently, to put off from the little shore.

And now our attention was withdrawn from the land to a sight of great splendor on board. This was Lieutenant Bundy, the guardian of her Majesty's mails, who issued from his cabin in his long swallow-tailed coat with anchor buttons ; his sabre clattering between his legs ; a magnificent shirt-collar, of several inches in height, rising round his good-humored sallow face ; and above it a cocked hat, that shone so, I thought it was made of polished tin (it may have been that or oilskin), handsomely laced with black worsted, and ornamented with a shining gold cord. A little squat boat, rowed by three ragged gallegos, came bouncing up to the ship. Into this Mr. Bundy and her Majesty's royal mail embarked with much majesty ; and in the twinkling of an eye, the royal standard of England, about the size of a pocket-handkerchief, — and at the bows of the boat, the man-of-war's pennant, being a strip of bunting considerably under the value of a farthing, — streamed out.

"They know that flag, sir," said the good-natured old tar, quite solemnly, in the evening afterwards : "they respect it, sir." The authority of her Majesty's lieutenant on board the steamer is stated to be so tremendous, that he may order it to stop, to move, to go larboard, starboard, or what you will; and the captain dare only disobey him *suo periculo.*

It was agreed that a party of us should land for half an hour, and taste real Spanish chocolate on Spanish ground. We followed Lieutenant Bundy, but humbly in the provider's boat; that officer going on shore to purchase fresh eggs, milk for tea (in place of the slimy substitute of whipped yolk of egg which we had been using for our morning and evening meals), and, if possible, oysters, for which it is said the rocks of Vigo are famous.

It was low tide, and the boat could not get up to the dry shore. Hence it was necessary to take advantage of the offers of sundry gallegos, who rushed barelegged into the water, to land on their shoulders. The approved method seems to be, to sit upon one shoulder only, holding on by the porter's whiskers; and though some of our party were of the tallest and fattest men whereof our race is composed, and their living sedans exceedingly meagre and small, yet all were landed without accident upon the juicy sand, and forthwith surrounded by a host of mendicants, screaming, " I say, sir! penny, sir! I say, English! tam your ays! penny!" in all voices, from extreme youth to the most lousy and venerable old age. When it is said that these beggars were as ragged as those of Ireland, and still more voluble, the Irish traveller will be able to form an opinion of their capabilities.

Through this crowd we passed up some steep rocky steps, through a little low gate, where, in a little guard-house and barrack, a few dirty little sentinels were keeping a dirty little guard; and by low-roofed, whitewashed houses, with balconies, and women in them, — the very same women, with the very same head-clothes, and yellow fans and eyes, at once sly and solemn, which Murillo painted, — by a neat church into which we took a peep, and, finally, into the Plaza del Constitucion, or *grand place* of the town, which may be about as big as that pleasing square, Pump Court, Temple. We were taken to an inn, of which I forget the name, and were shown from one chamber and story to another, till we arrived at that apartment where the real Spanish chocolate was finally to be served out. All these rooms were as clean as scrubbing and whitewash could make them; with simple French prints (with Spanish titles) on the walls; a few rickety half-finished articles of furniture; and, finally, an air of extremely respectable poverty. A jolly, black-eyed, yellow-shawled Dulcinea conducted us througn the apartment, and provided us with the desired refreshment.

Sounds of clarions drew our eyes to the Place of the Constitution; and, indeed, I had forgotten to say, that that majestic square was filled with military, with exceedingly small firelocks, the men ludicrously young and diminutive for the most part, in a uniform at once cheap and tawdry, — like those supplied to the warriors at Astley's, or from still humbler theatrical wardrobes: indeed, the whole scene was just like that of a little theatre; the houses curiously small, with arcades and balconies, out of which looked women apparently a great deal too big for the chambers they inhabited; the warriors were in ginghams, cottons, and tinsel; the officers had huge epaulets of sham silver lace drooping over their bosoms, and looked as as if they were attired at a very small expense. Only the general — the captain-general (Pooch, they told us, was his name: I know not how 'tis written in Spanish) — was well got up, with a smart hat, a real feather, huge stars glittering on his portly chest, and tights and boots of the first order. Presently, after a good deal of trumpeting, the little men marched off the place, Pooch and his staff coming into the very inn in which we were awaiting our chocolate.

Then we had an opportunity of seeing some of the civilians of the town. Three or four ladies passed, with fan and mantle; to them came three or four dandies, dressed smartly in the French fashion, with strong Jewish physiognomies. There was one, a solemn lean fellow in black, with his collars extremely turned over, and holding before him a long ivory-tipped ebony cane, who tripped along the little place with a solemn smirk, which gave one an indescribable feeling of the truth of Gil Blas, and of those delightful bachelors and licentiates who have appeared to us all in our dreams.

In fact we were but half an hour in this little queer Spanish town; and it appeared like a dream, too, or a little show got up to amuse us. Boom! the gun fired at the end of the funny little entertainment. The women and the balconies, the beggars and the walking Murillos, Pooch and the little soldiers in tinsel, disappeared, and were shut up in their box again. Once more we were carried on the beggars' shoulders out off the shore, and we found ourselves again in the great stalwart roast-beef world; the stout British steamer bearing out of the bay whose purple waters had grown more purple. The sun had set by this time, and the moon above was twice as big and bright as our degenerate moons are.

The provider had already returned with his fresh stores, and Bundy's tin hat was popped into its case, and he walking the deck of the packet denuded of tails. As we went out of the bay, occurred a little incident with which the great incidents of the day may be said to wind up. We saw before us a little vessel, tumbling and plunging about in the dark waters of the bay, with a bright light beaming from the mast. It made for us at about a couple of miles from the town, and came close up, flouncing and bobbing in the very jaws of the paddle, which looked as if it would have seized and twirled round that little boat and its light, and destroyed them for ever and ever. All the passengers, of course, came crowding to the ship's side to look at the bold little boat.

"I say!" howled a man; "I say!—a word!—I say! Pasagero! Pasagero! Pasage-e-ero!" We were two hundred yards ahead by this time.

"Go on," says the captain.

"You may stop if you like," says Lieutenant Bundy, exerting his tremendous responsibility. It is evident that the lieutenant has a soft heart, and felt for the poor devil in the boat who was howling so piteously "Pasagero!"

But the captain was resolute. His duty was *not* to take the man up. He was evidently an irregular customer — some one trying to escape, possibly.

The lieutenant turned away, but did not make any further hints. The captain was right; but we all felt somehow disappointed, and looked back wistfully at the little boat, jumping up and down far astern now; the poor little light shining in vain, and the poor wretch within screaming out in the most heart-rending accents a last faint desperate "I say! Pasagero-o!"

We all went down to tea rather melancholy; but the new milk, in the place of that abominable whipped egg, revived us again; and so ended the great events on board the "Lady Mary Wood" steamer, on the 25th August, 1844.

CHAPTER II.

LISBON—CADIZ.

A GREAT misfortune which befalls a man who has but a single day to stay in a town, is that fatal duty which superstition entails upon him of visiting the chief lions of the city in which he may happen to be. You must go through the ceremony, however much you may sigh to avoid it; and however much you know that the lions in one capital roar very much like the lions in another; that the churches are more or less large and splendid, the palaces pretty spacious, all the world over; and that there is scarcely a capital city in this Europe but has its pompous bronze statue or two of some periwigged, hook-nosed emperor, in a Roman habit, waving his bronze bâton on his broad-flanked brazen charger. We only saw these state old lions in Lisbon, whose roar has long since ceased to frighten one. First we went to the church of St. Roch, to see a famous piece of mosaic-work there. It is a famous work of art, and was bought by I don't know what king for I don't know how much money. All this information may be perfectly relied on, though the fact is, we did not see the mosaic-work: the sacristan, who guards it, was yet in bed; and it was veiled from our eyes in a side-chapel by great dirty damask curtains, which could not be removed, except when the sacristan's toilette was done; and at the price of a dollar. So we were spared this mosaic exhibition; and I think I always feel relieved when such an event occurs. I feel I have done my duty in coming to see the enormous animal; if he is not at home, *virtute meâ me, &c.* — we have done our best, and mortal can do no more.

In order to reach that church of the forbidden mosaic, we had sweated up several most steep and dusty streets — hot and dusty, although it was but nine o'clock in the morning. Thence the guide conducted us into some little dust-powdered gardens, in which the people make believe to enjoy the verdure, and whence you look over a great part of the arid, dreary, stony city. There was no smoke, as in honest London, only dust — dust over the gaunt houses and the dismal yellow strips of gardens. Many churches were there, and tall, half-baked-looking public edifices, that had a dry, uncomfortable, earth-quaky look, to my idea. The ground-floors of the spacious houses by which we passed seemed the coolest and pleasantest portions of the mansion. They were cellars or warehouses, for the most part, in which white-jacketed clerks sat smoking easy cigars. The streets were plastered with placards of a bull-fight, to take place the next evening (there was no opera at that season) ; but it was not a real Spanish tauromachy — only a theatrical combat, as you could see by the picture, in which the horseman was cantering off at three miles an hour, the bull tripping after him with tips to his gentle horns. Mules interminable, and almost all excellently sleek and handsome, were pacing down every street : here and there, but later in the day, came clattering along a smart rider on a prancing Spanish horse ; and in the afternoon a few families might be seen in the queerest old-fashioned little carriages, drawn by their jolly mules, and swinging between, or rather before, enormous wheels.

The churches I saw were of the florid periwig architecture — I mean of that pompous, cauliflower kind of ornament which was the fashion in Louis the Fifteenth's time, at which unlucky period a building mania seems to have seized upon many of the monarchs of Europe, and innumerable public edifices were erected. It seems to me to have been the period in all history when society was the least natural, and perhaps the most dissolute ; and I have always fancied that the bloated artificial forms of the architecture partake of the social disorganization of the time. Who can respect a simpering ninny, grinning in a Roman dress and a full-bottomed wig, who is made to pass off for a hero ; or a fat woman in a hoop, and of a most doubtful virtue, who leers at you as a goddess? In the palaces which we saw, several court allegories were represented, which, atrocious as they were in point of art, might yet serve to attract the regard of the moralizer. There were Faith, Hope, and Charity restoring Don John to the arms of his happy Portugal : there were Virtue, Valor, and Victory saluting Don Emanuel : Reading, Writing, and Arithmetic (for what I know, or some mythologic nymphs) dancing before Don Miguel — the picture is there still, at the Ajuda ; and ah me ! where is poor Mig? Well, it is these state lies and ceremonies that we persist in going to see ; whereas a man would have a much better insight into Portuguese manners, by planting himself at a corner, like yonder beggar, and watching the real transactions of the day.

A drive to Belem is the regular route practised by the traveller who has to make only a short stay, and accordingly a couple of carriages were provided for our party, and we were

driven through the long merry street of Belem, peopled by endless strings of mules — by thousands of gallegos, with water-
barrels on their shoulders, or lounging by the fountains to hire,
— by the Lisbon and Belem omnibuses, with four mules, jingling along at a good pace ; and it seemed to me to present a
far more lively and cheerful, though not so regular, an appearance as the stately quarters of the city we had left behind us.
The little shops were at full work — the men brown, well-
dressed, manly, and handsome : so much cannot, I am sorry
to say, be said for the ladies, of whom, with every anxiety to
do so, our party could not perceive a single good-looking specimen all day.   The noble blue Tagus accompanies you all along
these three miles of busy, pleasant street, whereof the chief
charm, as I thought, was its look of genuine business — that
appearance of comfort which the cleverest court-architect never
knows how to give.

The carriages (the canvas one with four seats and the chaise
in which I drove) were brought suddenly up to a gate with the
royal arms over it ; and here we were introduced to as queer
an exhibition as the eye has often looked on.   This was the
state carriage-house, where there is a museum of huge old
tumble-down gilded coaches of the last century, lying here,
mouldy and dark, in a sort of limbo.   The gold has vanished
from the great lumbering old wheels and panels ; the velvets
are wofully tarnished.   When one thinks of the patches and
powder that have simpered out of those plate-glass windows —
the mitred bishops, the big-wigged marshals, the shovel-hatted
abbés which they have borne in their time — the human mind
becomes affected in no ordinary degree.   Some human minds
heave a sigh for the glories of bygone days ; while others, considering rather the lies and humbug, the vice and servility,
which went framed and glazed and enshrined, creaking along
in those old Juggernaut cars, with fools worshipping under the
wheels, console themselves for the decay of institutions that
may have been splendid and costly, but were ponderous,
clumsy, slow, and unfit for daily wear.   The guardian of these
defunct old carriages tells some prodigious fibs concerning them :
he pointed out one carriage that was six hundred years old in
his calendar ; but any connoisseur in bricabrac can see it was
built at Paris in the Regent Orleans' time.

Hence it is but a step to an institution in full life and vigor,
— a noble orphan-school for one thousand boys and girls,
founded by Don Pedro, who gave up to its use the superb convent of Belem, with its splendid cloisters, vast airy dormitories,

and magnificent church. Some Oxford gentlemen would have
wept to see the desecrated edifice, — to think that the shaven
polls and white gowns were banished from it to give place to
a thousand children, who have not even the clergy to instruct
them. " Every lad here may choose his trade," our little informant said, who addressed us in better French than any of
our party spoke, whose manners were perfectly gentlemanlike
and respectful, and whose clothes, though of a common cotton
stuff, were cut and worn with a military neatness and precision.
All the children whom we remarked were dressed with similar
neatness, and it was a pleasure to go through their various
rooms for study, where some were busy at mathematics, some
at drawing, some attending a lecture on tailoring, while others
were sitting at the feet of a professor of the science of shoemaking. All the garments of the establishment were made
by the pupils ; even the deaf and dumb were drawing and reading, and the blind were, for the most part, set to perform on
musical instruments, and got up a concert for the visitors. It
was then we wished ourselves of the numbers of the deaf and
dumb, for the poor fellows made noises so horrible, that even
as blind beggars they could hardly get a livelihood in the musical way.

Hence we were driven to the huge palace of Necessidades,
which is but a wing of a building that no King of Portugal
ought ever to be rich enough to complete, and which, if perfect,
might outvie the Tower of Babel. The mines of Brazil must
have been productive of gold and silver indeed when the founder
imagined this enormous edifice. From the elevation on which
it stands it commands the noblest views, — the city is spread
before it, with its many churches and towers, and for many
miles you see the magnificent Tagus, rolling by banks crowned
with trees and towers. But to arrive at this enormous building
you have to climb a steep suburb of wretched huts, many of
them with dismal gardens of dry, cracked earth, where a few
reedy sprouts of Indian corn seemed to be the chief cultivation,
and which were guarded by huge plants of spiky aloes, on
which the rags of the proprietors of the huts were sunning
themselves. The terrace before the palace was similarly en-
croached upon by these wretched habitations. A few millions
judiciously expended might make of this arid hill one of the
most magnificent gardens in the world ; and the palace seems
to me to excel for situation any royal edifice I have ever seen.
But the huts of these swarming poor have crawled up close to
its gates, — the superb walls of hewn stone stop all of a sudden

TOWER OF BELEM.

with a lath-and-plaster *hitch ;* and capitals, and hewn stones for
columns, still lying about on the deserted terrace, may lie there
for ages to come, probably, and never take their places by the
side of their brethren in yonder tall bankrupt galleries. The
air of this pure sky has little effect upon the edifices, — the
edges of the stone look as sharp as if the builders had just left
their work ; and close to the grand entrance stands an out-
building, part of which may have been burnt fifty years ago,
but is in such cheerful preservation that you might fancy the
fire had occurred yesterday. It must have been an awful sight
from this hill to have looked at the city spread before it, and
seen it reeling and swaying in the time of the earthquake. I
thought it looked so hot and shaky, that one might fancy a return of the fit. In several places still remain gaps and chasms,
and ruins lie here and there as they cracked and fell.

Although the palace has not attained anything like its full
growth, yet what exists is quite big enough for the monarch of
such a little country ; and Versailles or Windsor has not apartments more nobly proportioned. The Queen resides in the
Ajuda, a building of much less pretensions, of which the yellow
walls and beautiful gardens are seen between Belem and the
city. The Necessidades are only used for grand galas, recep-
tions of ambassadors, and ceremonies of state. In the throne-
room is a huge throne, surmounted by an enormous gilt crown,
than which I have never seen anything larger in the finest pantomime at Drury Lane ; but the effect of this splendid piece is
lessened by a shabby old Brussels carpet, almost the only other
article of furniture in the apartment, and not quite large enough
to cover its spacious floor. The looms of Kidderminster have
supplied the web which ornaments the " Ambassadors' Waiting-
Room," and the ceilings are painted with huge allegories in
distemper, which pretty well correspond with the other furniture. Of all the undignified objects in the world, a palace out
at elbows is surely the meanest. Such places ought not to be
seen in adversity, — splendor is their decency, — and when no
longer able to maintain it, they should sink to the level of their
means, calmly subside into manufactories, or go shabby in
seclusion.

There is a picture-gallery belonging to the palace that is
quite of a piece with the furniture, where are the mythological
pieces relative to the kings before alluded to, and where the
English visitor will see some astonishing pictures of the Duke
of Wellington, done in a very characteristic style of Portuguese
art. There is also a chapel, which has been decorated with

much care and sumptuousness of ornament, — the altar surmounted by a ghastly and horrible carved figure in the taste of
the time when faith was strengthened by the shrieks of Jews
on the rack, and enlivened by the roasting of heretics. Other
such frightful images may be seen in the churches of the city;
those which we saw were still rich, tawdry, and splendid to
outward show, although the French, as usual, had robbed their
shrines of their gold and silver, and the statues of their jewels
and crowns. But brass and tinsel look to the visitor full as
well at a little distance, — as doubtless Soult and Junot thought,
when they despoiled these places of worship, like French philosophers as they were.

A friend, with a classical turn of mind, was bent upon seeing the aqueduct, whither we went on a dismal excursion of
three hours, in the worst carriages, over the most diabolical
clattering roads, up and down dreary parched hills, on which
grew a few gray olive-trees and many aloes. When we arrived,
the gate leading to the aqueduct was closed, and we were entertained with a legend of some respectable character who had
made a good livelihood there for some time past lately, having
a private key to this very aqueduct, and lying in wait there for
unwary travellers like ourselves, whom he pitched down the
arches into the ravines below, and there robbed them at leisure.
So that all we saw was the door and the tall arches of the aqueduct, and by the time we returned to town it was time to go on
board the ship again. If the inn at which we had sojourned
was not of the best quality, the bill, at least, would have done
honor to the first establishment in London. We all left the
house of entertainment joyfully, glad to get out of the sunburnt
city and go *home*. Yonder in the steamer was home, with its
black funnel and gilt portraiture of " Lady Mary Wood" at
the bows; and every soul on board felt glad to return to the
friendly little vessel. But the authorities of Lisbon, however,
are very suspicious of the departing stranger, and we were
made to lie an hour in the river before the Sanita boat, where
a passport is necessary to be procured before the traveller can
quit the country. Boat after boat, laden with priests and peasantry, with handsome red-sashed gallegos clad in brown, and
ill-favored women, came and got their permits, and were off, as
we lay bumping up against the old hull of the Sanita boat: but
the officers seemed to take a delight in keeping us there bumping, looked at us quite calmly over the ship's sides, and smoked
their cigars without the least attention to the prayers which we
shrieked out for release.

If we were glad to get away from Lisbon, we were quite as sorry to be obliged to quit Cadiz, which we reached the next night, and where we were allowed a couple of hours' leave to land and look about. It seemed as handsome within as it is stately without; the long narrow streets of an admirable cleanliness, many of the tall houses of rich and noble decorations, and all looking as if the city were in full prosperity. I have seen no more cheerful and animated sight than the long street leading from the quay where we were landed, and the market blazing in sunshine, piled with fruit, fish, and poultry, under many-colored awnings; the tall white houses with their balconies and galleries shining round about, and the sky above so blue that the best cobalt in all the paint-box looks muddy and dim in comparison to it. There were pictures for a year in that market-place — from the copper-colored old hags and beggars who roared to you for the love of heaven to give money, to the swaggering dandies of the market, with red sashes and tight clothes, looking on superbly, with a hand on the hip and a cigar in the mouth. These must be the chief critics at the great bull-fight house yonder by the Alameda, with its scanty trees and cool breezes, facing the water. Nor are there any corks to the bulls' horns here as at Lisbon. A small old English guide, who seized upon me the moment my foot was on shore, had a store of agreeable legends regarding the bulls, men, and horses that had been killed with unbounded profusion in the late entertainments which have taken place.

It was so early an hour in the morning that the shops were scarcely opened as yet; the churches, however, stood open for the faithful, and we met scores of women tripping towards them with pretty feet, and smart black mantillas, from which looked out fine dark eyes and handsome pale faces, very different from the coarse brown countenances we had seen at Lisbon. A very handsome modern cathedral, built by the present bishop at his own charges, was the finest of the public edifices we saw; it was not, however, nearly so much frequented as another little church, crowded with altars and fantastic ornaments, and lights and gilding, where we were told to look behind a huge iron grille, and beheld a bevy of black nuns kneeling. Most of the good ladies in the front ranks stopped their devotions, and looked at the strangers with as much curiosity as we directed at them through the gloomy bars of their chapel. The men's convents are closed; that which contains the famous Murillos has been turned into an academy of the fine arts; but the English guide did not think the pictures were of sufficient interest to detain strangers, and so hurried us back to the shore, and grumbled at only getting three shillings at parting for his trouble and his information. And so our residence in Andalusia began and ended before breakfast, and we went on board and steamed for Gibraltar, looking, as we passed, at Joinville's black squadron, and the white houses of St. Mary's across the bay, with the hills of Medina Sidonia and Granada lying purple beyond them. There's something even in those names which is pleasant to write down; to have passed only two hours in Cadiz is something — to have seen real donnas with comb and mantle — real caballeros with cloak and cigar — real Spanish barbers lathering out of brass basins, — and to have heard guitars under the balconies: there was one that an old beggar was jangling in the market, whilst a huge leering fellow in bushy whiskers and a faded velvet dress came singing and jumping after our party, — not singing to a guitar, it is true, but imitating one capitally with his voice, and cracking his fingers by way of castanets, and performing a dance such as Figaro or Lablache might envy. How clear that fellow's voice thrums on the ear even now; and how bright and pleasant remains the recollection of the fine city and the blue sea, and the Spanish flags floating on the boats that danced over it, and Joinville's band beginning to play stirring marches as we puffed out of the bay.

The next stage was Gibraltar, where we were to change horses. Before sunset we skirted along the dark savage mountains of the African coast, and came to the Rock just before gun-fire. It is the very image of an enormous lion, crouched between the Atlantic and the Mediterranean, and set there to guard the passage for its British mistress. The next British lion is Malta, four days further on in the Midland Sea, and ready to spring upon Egypt or pounce upon Syria, or roar so as to be heard at Marseilles in case of need.

To the eyes of the civilian the first-named of these famous fortifications is by far the most imposing. The Rock looks so tremendous, that to ascend it, even without the compliment of shells or shot, seems a dreadful task — what would it be when all those mysterious lines of batteries were vomiting fire and brimstone; when all those dark guns that you see poking their grim heads out of every imaginable cleft and zigzag should salute you with shot, both hot and cold; and when, after tugging up the hideous perpendicular place, you were to find regiments of British grenadiers ready to plunge bayonets into your poor panting stomach, and let out artificially the little breath left there? It is a marvel to think that soldiers will mount such places for a shilling — ensigns for five and ninepence — a day: a cabman would ask double the money to go half way! One meekly reflects upon the above strange truths, leaning over the ship's side, and looking up the huge mountain, from the tower nestled at the foot of it to the thin flagstaff at the summit, up to which have been piled the most ingenious edifices for murder Christian science ever adopted. My hobby-horse is a quiet beast, suited for Park riding, or a gentle trot to Putney and back to a snug stable, and plenty of feeds of corn: — it can't abide climbing hills, and is not at all used to gunpowder. Some men's animals are so spirited that the very appearance of a stone-wall sets them jumping at it; regular chargers of hobbies, which snort and say — "Ha, ha!" at the mere notion of a battle.

CHAPTER III.

THE "LADY MARY WOOD."

OUR week's voyage is now drawing to a close. We have just been to look at Cape Trafalgar, shining white over the finest blue sea. (We, who were looking at Trafalgar Square only the other day!) The sight of that cape must have disgusted Joinville and his fleet of steamers, as they passed yesterday into Cadiz bay, and to-morrow will give them a sight of St. Vincent.

One of their steam-vessels has been lost off the coast of Africa; they were obliged to burn her, lest the Moors should take possession of her. She was a virgin vessel, just out of Brest. Poor innocent! to die in the very first month of her union with the noble whiskered god of war!

We Britons on board the English boat received the news of the "Groenenland's" abrupt demise with grins of satisfaction. It was a sort of national compliment, and cause of agreeable congratulation. "The lubbers!" we said; "the clumsy humbugs! there's none but Britons to rule the waves!" and we gave ourselves piratical airs, and went down presently and were sick in our little buggy berths. It was pleasant certainly, to laugh at Joinville's admiral's flag floating at his foremast, in yonder black ship, with its two thundering great guns at the bows and stern, its busy crew swarming on the deck, and a crowd of obsequious shore-boats bustling round the vessel — and to sneer at the Mogador warrior, and vow that we English, had we been inclined to do the business, would have performed it a great deal better.

Now yesterday at Lisbon we saw H. M. S. " Caledonia." *This*, on the contrary, inspired us with feelings of respect and awful pleasure. There she lay — the huge sea-castle — bearing the unconquerable flag of our country. She had but to open her jaws, as it were, and she might bring a second earthquake on the city — batter it into kingdom-come — with the Ajuda palace and the Necessidades, the churches, and the lean, dry, empty streets, and Don John, tremendous on horseback, in the midst of Black Horse Square. Wherever we looked we could see that enormous " Caledonia," with her flashing three lines of guns. We looked at the little boats which ever and anon came out of this monster, with humble wonder. There was the lieutenant who boarded us at midnight before we dropped anchor in the river: ten white-jacketed men pulling as one, swept along with the barge, gig, boat, curricle, or coach-and-six, with which he came up to us. We examined him — his red whiskers — his collars turned down — his duck trousers, his bullion epaulets — with awe. With the same reverential feeling we examined the seamen — the young gentleman in the bows of the boat — the handsome young officers of marines we met sauntering in the town next day — the Scotch surgeon who boarded us as we weighed anchor — every man, down to the broken-nosed mariner who was drunk in a wine-house, and had " Caledonia" written on his hat. Whereas at the Frenchmen we looked with undisguised contempt. We were ready to burst with laughter as we passed the Prince's vessel — there was a little French boy in a French boat alongside cleaning it, and twirling about a little French mop — we thought it the most comical, contemptible French boy, mop, boat, steamer, prince — Psha! it is of this wretched vaporing stuff that false patriotism is made. I write this as a sort of homily àpropos of the day, and Cape Trafalgar, off which we lie. What business have I to strut the deck, and clap my wings, and cry " Cock-a-doodle-doo " over it? Some compatriots are at that work even now.

We have lost one by one all our jovial company. There were the five Oporto wine-merchants — all hearty English gen

tlemen — gone to their wine-butts, and their red-legged part-
ridges, and their duels at Oporto. It appears that these gallant
Britons fight every morning among themselves, and give the
benighted people among whom they live an opportunity to
admire the spirit national. There is the brave, honest major,
with his wooden leg — the kindest and simplest of Irishmen :
he has embraced his children, and reviewed his little invalid
garrison of fifteen men, in the fort which he commands at
Belem, by this time, and, I have no doubt, played to every
soul of them the twelve tunes of his musical-box. It was
pleasant to see him with that musical-box — how pleased he
wound it up after dinner — how happily he listened to the little
clinking tunes as they galloped, ding-dong, after each other.
A man who carries a musical-box is always a good-natured
man.

Then there was his Grace, or his Grandeur, the Archbishop
of Beyrouth (in the parts of the infidels), his Holiness's Nuncio
to the court of her Most Faithful Majesty, and who mingled
among us like any simple mortal, — except that he had an extra
smiling courtesy, which simple mortals do not always possess ;
and when you passed him as such, and puffed your cigar in his
face, took off his hat with a grin of such prodigious rapture,
as to lead you to suppose that the most delicious privilege of
his whole life was that permission to look at the tip of your
nose or of your cigar. With this most reverend prelate was his
Grace's brother and chaplain — a very greasy and good-natured
ecclesiastic, who, from his physiognomy, I would have imagined
to be a dignitary of the Israelitish rather than the Romish church
— as profuse in smiling courtesy as his Lordship of Beyrouth.
These two had a meek little secretary between them, and a tall
French cook and valet, who, at meal times, might be seen busy
about the cabin where their reverences lay. They were on
their backs for the greater part of the voyage ; their yellow
countenances were not only unshaven, but, to judge from ap-
pearances, unwashed. They ate in private ; and it was only
of evenings, as the sun was setting over the western wave, and,
comforted by the dinner, the cabin passengers assembled on
the quarter-deck, that we saw the dark faces of the reverend
gentlemen among us for a while. They sank darkly into their
berths when the steward's bell tolled for tea.

At Lisbon, where we came to anchor at midnight, a special
boat came off, whereof the crew exhibited every token of reverence for the ambassador of the ambassador of heaven, and
carried him off from our company. This abrupt departure in

the darkness disappointed some of us, who had promised ourselves the pleasure of seeing his Grandeur depart in state in the
morning, shaved, clean, and in full pontificals, the tripping little
secretary swinging an incense-pot before him, and the greasy
chaplain bearing his crosier.

Next day we had another bishop, who occupied the very
same berth his Grace of Beyrouth had quitted — was sick in
the very same way — so much so that this cabin of the " Lady
Mary Wood " is to be christened " the bishop's berth " henceforth ; and a handsome mitre is to be painted on the basin.

Bishop No. 2 was a very stout, soft, kind-looking old gentleman in a square cap, with a handsome tassel of green and gold
round his portly breast and back. He was dressed in black
robes and tight purple stockings : and we carried him from Lisbon to the little flat coast of Faro, of which the meek old gentleman was the chief pastor.

We had not been half an hour from our anchorage in the
Tagus, when his lordship dived down into the episcopal berth.
All that night there was a good smart breeze ; it blew fresh all
the next day, as we went jumping over the blue bright sea ; and
there was no sign of his lordship the bishop until we were opposite the purple hills of Algarve, which lay some ten miles distant, — a yellow sunny shore stretching flat before them, whose
long sandy flats and villages we could see with our telescope
from the steamer.

Presently a little vessel, with a huge shining lateen sail,
and bearing the blue and white Portuguese flag, was seen playing a sort of leap-frog on the jolly waves, jumping over them,
and ducking down as merry as could be. This little boat came
towards the steamer as quick as ever she could jump ; and
Captain Cooper roaring out, " Stop her ! " to " Lady Mary
Wood," her ladyship's paddles suddenly ceased twirling, and
news was carried to the good bishop that his boat was almost
alongside, and that his hour was come.

It was rather an affecting sight to see the poor old fat gentleman, looking wistfully over the water as the boat now came
up, and her eight seamen, with great noise, energy, and gesticulation laid her by the steamer. The steamer steps were let
down ; his lordship's servant, in blue and yellow livery, (like
the " Edinburgh Review,") cast over the episcopal luggage into
the boat, along with his own bundle and the jack-boots with
which he rides postilion on one of the bishop's fat mules at Faro.
The blue and yellow domestic went down the steps into the
boat. Then came the bishop's turn ; but he couldn't do it for

a long while. He went from one passenger to another, sadly
shaking them by the hand, often taking leave and seeming loth
to depart, until Captain Cooper, in a stern but respectful tone,
touched him on the shoulder, and said, I know not with what
correctness, being ignorant of the Spanish language, " Señor
'Bispo, Señor 'Bispo!" on which summons the poor old man,
looking ruefully round him once more, put his square cap under.
his arm, tucked up his long black petticoats, so as to show his
purple stockings and jolly fat calves, and went trembling down
the steps towards the boat. The good old man! I wish I had
had a shake of that trembling podgy hand somehow before he
went upon his sea martyrdom. I felt a love for that soft-hearted
old Christian. Ah! let us hope his governante tucked him comfortably in bed when he got to Faro that night, and made him
a warm gruel and put his feet in warm water. The men clung
around him, and almost kissed him as they popped him into the
boat, but he did not heed their caresses. Away went the boat
scudding madly before the wind. Bang! another lateen-sailed
boat in the distance fired a gun in his honor ; but the wind was
blowing away from the shore, and who knows when that meek
bishop got home to his gruel!

I think these were the notables of our party. I will not
mention the laughing, ogling lady of Cadiz, whose manners, I
very much regret to say, were a great deal too lively for my
sense of propriety ; nor those fair sufferers, her companions, who
lay on the deck with sickly, smiling, female resignation : nor
the heroic children, who no sooner ate biscuit than they were
ill, and no sooner were ill than they began eating biscuit
again ; but just allude to one other martyr, the kind lieutenant
in charge of the mails, and who bore his cross with what I can't
but think a very touching and noble resignation.

There's a certain sort of man whose doom in the world is
disappointment, — who excels in it, — and whose luckless triumphs in his meek career of life, I have often thought, must
be regarded by the kind eyes above with as much favor as
the splendid successes and achievements of coarser and more
prosperous men. As I sat with the lieutenant upon deck, his
telescope laid over his lean legs, and he looking at the sunset
with a pleased, withered old face, he gave me a little account
of his history. I take it he is in nowise disinclined to talk
about it, simple as it is : he has been seven-and-thirty years in
the navy, being somewhat more mature in the service than
Lieutenant Peel, Rear-Admiral Prince de Joinville, and other
commanders who need not be mentioned. He is a very well-

educated man, and reads prodigiously,— travels, histories, lives of eminent worthies and heroes, in his simple way. He is not in the least angry at his want of luck in the profession. " Were I a boy to-morrow," he said, " I would begin it again ; and when I see my schoolfellows, and how they have got on in life, if some are better off than I am, I find many are worse, and have no call to be discontented." So he carries her Majesty's mails meekly through this world, waits upon port-admirals and captains in his old glazed hat, and is as proud of the pennon at the bow of his little boat, as if it were flying from the mainmast of a thundering man-of-war. He gets two hundred a year for his services, and has an old mother and a sister living in England somewhere, who I will wager (though he never, I swear, said a word about it) have a good portion of this princely income.

Is it breaking a confidence to tell Lieutenant Bundy's history? Let the motive excuse the deed. It is a good, kind, wholesome, and noble character. Why should we keep all our admiration for those who win in this world, as we do, sycophants as we are? When we write a novel, our great, stupid imaginations can go no further than to marry the hero to a fortune at the end, and to find out that he is a lord by right. O blundering, lickspittle morality ! And yet I would like to fancy some happy retributive Utopia in the peaceful cloudland, where my friend the meek lieutenant should find the yards of his ship manned as he went on board, all the guns firing an enormous salute (only without the least noise or vile smell of powder), and he be saluted on the deck as Admiral Sir James, or Sir Joseph — ay, or Lord Viscount Bundy, knight of all the orders above the sun.

I think this is a sufficient, if not a complete catalogue of the worthies on board the " Lady Mary Wood." In the week we were on board — it seemed a year by the way — we came to regard the ship quite as a home. We felt for the captain — the most good-humored, active, careful, ready of captains — a filial, a fraternal regard ; for the provider, who provided for us with admirable comfort and generosity, a genial gratitude ; and for the brisk steward's lads — brisk in serving the banquet, sympathizing in handing the basin — every possible sentiment of regard and good-will. What winds blew, and how many knots we ran, are all noted down, no doubt, in the ship's log : and as for what ships we saw — every one of them with their gunnage, tonnage, their nation, their direction whither they were bound — were not these all noted down with surprising ingenuity and precision by the lieutenant, at a family desk at which he sat every night, before a great paper elegantly and mysteriously ruled off with his large ruler? I have a regard for every man on board that ship, from the captain down to the crew — down even to the cook, with tattooed arms, sweating among the saucepans in the galley, who used (with a touching affection) to send us locks of his hair in the soup. And so, while our feelings and recollections are warm, let us shake hands with this knot of good fellows, comfortably floating about in their little box of wood and iron, across Channel, Biscay Bay, and the Atlantic, from Southampton Water to Gibraltar Straits.

CHAPTER IV.

GIBRALTAR.

SUPPOSE all the nations of the earth to send fitting ambassadors to represent them at Wapping or Portsmouth Point, with each, under its own national signboard and language, its appropriate house of call, and your imagination may figure the Main Street of Gibraltar: almost the only part of the town, I believe, which boasts of the name of street at all, the remaining houserows being modestly called lanes, such as Bomb Lane, Battery Lane, Fusee Lane, and so on. In Main Street the Jews predominate, the Moors abound; and from the " Jolly Sailor," or the brave " Horse Marine," where the people of our nation are drinking British beer and gin, you hear choruses of " Garryowen " or " The Lass I left behind me ; " while through the flaring lattices of the Spanish ventas come the clatter of castanets and the jingle and moan of Spanish guitars and ditties. It is a curious sight at evening this thronged street, with the people, in a hundred different costumes, bustling to and fro under the coarse flare of the lamps ; swarthy Moors, in white or crimson robes ; dark Spanish smugglers in tufted hats, with gay silk handkerchiefs round their heads ; fuddled seamen from men-of-war, or merchantmen ; porters, Galician or Genoese ; and at every few minutes' interval, little squads of soldiers tramping to relieve guard at some one of the innumerable posts in the town.

Some of our party went to a Spanish venta, as a more convenient or romantic place of residence than an English house ;

others made choice of the club-house in Commercial Square, of which I formed an agreeable picture in my imagination; rather, perhaps, resembling the Junior United Service Club in Charles Street, by which every Londoner has passed ere this with respectful pleasure, catching glimpses of magnificent blazing candelabras, under which sit neat half-pay officers, drinking half-pints of port. The club-house of Gibraltar is not, however, of the Charles Street sort; it may have been cheerful once, and there are yet relics of splendor about it. When officers wore pigtails, and in the time of Governor O'Hara, it may have been a handsome place; but it is mouldy and decrepit now; and though his Excellency, Mr. Bulwer, was living there, and made no complaints that I heard of, other less distinguished persons thought they had reason to grumble. Indeed, what is travelling made of? At least half its pleasures and incidents come out of inns; and of them the tourist can speak with much more truth and vivacity than of historical recollections compiled out of histories, or filched out of handbooks. But to speak of the best inn in a place needs no apology; that, at least, is useful information; as every person intending to visit Gibraltar cannot have seen the flea-bitten countenances of our companions, who fled from their Spanish venta to take refuge at the club the morning after our arrival, they may surely be thankful for being directed to the best house of accommodation in one of the most unromantic, uncomfortable, and prosaic of towns.

If one had a right to break the sacred confidence of the mahogany, I could entertain you with many queer stories of Gibraltar life, gathered from the lips of the gentlemen who enjoyed themselves round the dingy tablecloth of the club-house coffee-room, richly decorated with cold gravy and spilt beer. I heard there the very names of the gentlemen who wrote the famous letters from the "Warspite" regarding the French proceedings at Mogador; and met several refugee Jews from that place, who said that they were much more afraid of the Kabyles without the city than of the guns of the French squadron, of which they seemed to make rather light. I heard the last odds on the ensuing match between Captain Smith's b. g. Bolter, and Captain Brown's ch. c. Roarer: how the gun-room of her Majesty's ship "Purgatory" had "cobbed" a tradesman of the town, and of the row in consequence. I heard capital stories of the way in which Wilkins had escaped the guard, and Thompson had been locked up among the mosquitoes for being out after ten without the lantern. I heard how the governor was an old ——, but to say what, would be breaking a confidence; only this may be divulged, that the epithet was exceedingly complimentary to Sir Robert Wilson. All the while these conversations were going on, a strange scene of noise and bustle was passing in the market-place, in front of the window, where Moors, Jews, Spaniards, soldiers were thronging in the sun ; and a ragged fat fellow, mounted on a tobacco-barrel, with his hat cocked on his ear, was holding an auction, and roaring with an energy and impudence that would have done credit to Covent Garden.

The Moorish castle is the only building about the Rock which has an air at all picturesque or romantic ; there is a plain Roman Catholic cathedral, a hideous new Protestant church of the cigar-divan architecture, and a Court-house with a portico which is said to be an imitation of the Parthenon : the ancient religious houses of the Spanish town are gone, or turned into military residences, and marked so that you would never know their former pious destination. You walk through narrow white-washed lanes, bearing such martial names as are before mentioned, and by-streets with barracks on either side : small Newgate-like looking buildings, at the doors of which you may see the sergeants' ladies conversing ; or at the open windows of the officers' quarters, Ensign Fipps lying on his sofa and smoking his cigar, or Lieutenant Simson practising the flute to while away the weary hours of garrison dulness. I was surprised not to find more persons in the garrison library, where is a magnificent reading-room, and an admirable collection of books.

In spite of the scanty herbage and the dust on the trees, the Alameda is a beautiful walk ; of which the vegetation has been as laboriously cared for as the tremendous fortifications which flank it on either side. The vast Rock rises on one side with its interminable works of defence, and Gibraltar Bay is shining on the other, out on which from the terraces immense cannon are perpetually looking, surrounded by plantations of cannon-balls and beds of bomb-shells, sufficient, one would think, to blow away the whole Peninsula. The horticultural and military mixture is indeed very queer : here and there temples, rustic summer-seats, &c. have been erected in the garden, but you are sure to see a great squat mortar look up from among the flower-pots : and amidst the aloes and geraniums sprouts the green petticoat and scarlet coat of a Highlander. Fatigue-parties are seen winding up the hill, and busy about the endless cannon-ball plantations ; awkward squads are drilling in the open spaces : sentries marching everywhere, and (this is a caution to artists) I am told have orders to run any man through, who is discovered making a sketch of the place. It is always beautiful.

especially at evening, when the people are sauntering along the walks, and the moon is shining on the waters of the bay and the hills and twinkling white houses of the opposite shore. Then the place becomes quite romantic : it is too dark to see the dust on the dried leaves ; the cannon-balls do not intrude too much, but have subsided into the shade ; the awkward squads are in bed ; even the loungers are gone, the fan-flirting Spanish ladies, the sallow black-eyed children, and the trim white-jacketed dandies. A fife is heard from some craft at roost on the quiet waters somewhere ; or a faint cheer from yonder black steamer at the Mole, which is about to set out on some night expedition. You forget that the town is at all like Wapping, and deliver yourself up entirely to romance ; the sentries look noble pacing there, silent in the moonlight, and Sandy's voice is quite musical as he challenges with a " Who goes there?"

" All's well " is very pleasant when sung decently in tune, and inspires noble and poetic ideas of duty, courage, and danger : but when you hear it shouted all the night through, accompanied by a clapping of muskets in a time of profound peace, the sentinel's cry becomes no more romantic to the hearer than it is to the sandy Connaught-man or the barelegged Highlander who delivers it. It is best to read about wars comfortably in Harry Lorrequer or Scott's novels, in which knights shout their war-cries, and jovial Irish bayoneteers hurrah, without depriving you of any blessed rest. Men of a different way of thinking, however, can suit themselves perfectly at Gibraltar ; where there is marching and counter-marching, challenging and relieving guard all the night through. And not here in Commercial Square alone, but all over the huge Rock in the darkness — all through the mysterious zig-zags, and round the dark cannon-ball pyramids, and along the vast rock-galleries, and up to the topmost flagstaff, where the sentry can look out over two seas, poor fellows are marching and clapping muskets, and crying " All's Well," dressed in cap and feather, in place of honest nightcaps best befitting the decent hours of sleep.

All these martial noises three of us heard to the utmost advantage, lying on iron bedsteads at the time in a cracked old room on the ground floor, the open windows of which looked into the square. No spot could be more favorably selected for watching the humors of a garrison-town by night. About midnight, the door hard by us was visited by a party of young officers, who having had quite as much drink as was good for them, were naturally inclined for more ; and when we remonstrated through the windows, one of them in a young

tipsy voice asked after our mothers, and finally reeled away.
How charming is the conversation of high-spirited youth! I
don't know whether the guard got hold of them: but certainly
if a civilian had been hiccupping through the streets at that hour
he would have been carried off to the guard-house, and left to
the mercy of the mosquitoes there, and had up before the Governor in the morning. The young man in the coffee-room tells
me he goes to sleep every night with the keys of Gibraltar under
his pillow. It is an awful image, and somehow completes the
notion of the slumbering fortress. Fancy Sir Robert Wilson,
his nose just visible over the sheets, his nightcap and the huge
key (you see the very identical one in Reynolds's portrait of
Lord Heathfield) peeping out from under the bolster!

If I entertain you with accounts of inns and nightcaps it is
because I am more familiar with these subjects than with history
and fortifications: as far as I can understand the former, Gibraltar is the great British depot for smuggling goods into the
Peninsula. You see vessels lying in the harbor, and are told
in so many words they are smugglers; all those smart Spaniards with cigar and mantles are smugglers, and run tobaccos
and cotton into Catalonia; all the respected merchants of the
place are smugglers. The other day a Spanish revenue vessel
was shot to death under the thundering great guns of the fort,
for neglecting to bring to, but it so happened that it was in
chase of a smuggler; in this little corner of her dominions
Britain proclaims war to custom-houses, and protection to free
trade. Perhaps ere a very long day, England may be acting
that part towards the world, which Gibraltar performs towards
Spain now; and the last war in which we shall ever engage may
be a custom-house war. For once establish railroads and
abolish preventive duties through Europe, and what is there
left to fight for? It will matter very little then under what flag
people live, and foreign ministers and ambassadors may enjoy
a dignified sinecure; the army will rise to the rank of peaceful
constables, not having any more use for their bayonets than
those worthy people have for their weapons now who accompany the law at assizes under the name of javelin-men. The
apparatus of bombs and eighty-four-pounders may disappear
from the Alameda, and the crops of cannon-balls which now
grow there may give place to other plants more pleasant to the
eye; and the great key of Gibraltar may be left in the gate for
anybody to turn at will, and Sir Robert Wilson may sleep at
quiet.

I am afraid I thought it was rather a release, when, having made up our minds to examine the Rock in detail and view the magnificent excavations and galleries, the admiration of all military men, and the terror of any enemies who may attack the fortress, we received orders to embark forthwith in the " Tagus," which was to carry us to Malta and Constantinople. So we took leave of this famous Rock — this great blunderbuss — which we seized out of the hands of the natural owners a hundred and forty years ago, and which we have kept ever since tremendously loaded and cleaned and ready for use.   To seize and have it is doubtless a gallant thing ; it is like one of those tests of courage which one reads of in the chivalrous romances, when, for instance, Sir Huon of Bordeaux is called upon to prove his knighthood by going to Babylon and pulling out the Sultan's beard and front teeth in the midst of his court there.   But, after all, justice must confess it was rather hard on the poor Sultan.   If we had the Spaniards established at Land's End, with impregnable Spanish fortifications on St. Michael's Mount, we should perhaps come to the same conclusion.   Meanwhile let us hope, during this long period of deprivation, the Sultan of Spain is reconciled to the loss of his front teeth and bristling whiskers — let us even try to think that he is better without them.   At all events, right or wrong, whatever may be our title to the property, there is no Englishman but must think with pride of the manner in which his countrymen have kept it, and of the courage, endurance, and sense of duty with which stout old Eliot and his companions resisted Crillion and the Spanish battering-ships and his fifty thousand men.   There seems to be something more noble in the success of a gallant resistance than of an attack, however brave.   After failing in his attack on the fort, the French General visited the English Commander who had foiled him, and parted from him and his garrison in perfect politeness and good humor.   The English troops, Drinkwater says, gave him thundering cheers as he went away, and the French in return complimented us on our gallantry, and lauded the humanity of our people.   If we are to go on murdering each other in the old-fashioned way, what a pity it is that our battles cannot end in the old-fashioned way too.

One of our fellow-travellers, who had written a book, and had suffered considerably from sea-sickness during our passage along the coasts of France and Spain, consoled us all by saying that the very minute we got into the Mediterranean we might consider ourselves entirely free from illness ; and, in fact, that

It was unheard of in the Inland Sea.   Even in the Bay of Gibraltar the water looked bluer than anything I have ever seen —
except Miss Smith's eyes.   I thought, somehow, the delicious
faultless azure never could look angry — just like the eyes before alluded to — and under this assurance we passed the Strait,
and began coasting the African shore calmly and without the
least apprehension, as if we were as much used to the tempest
as Mr. T. P. Cooke.

But when, in spite of the promise of the man who had written
the book, we found ourselves worse than in the worst part of
the Bay of Biscay, or off the storm-lashed rocks of Finisterre,
we set down the author in question as a gross impostor, and
had a mind to quarrel with him for leading us into this cruel
error.   The most provoking part of the matter, too, was, that
the sky was deliciously clear and cloudless, the air balmy, the
sea so insultingly blue that it seemed as if we had no right to be
ill at all, and that the innumerable little waves that frisked
round about our keel were enjoying an *anerithmon gelasma* (this
is one of my four Greek quotations : depend on it I will manage
to introduce the other three before the tour is done) — seemed
to be enjoying, I say, the above named Greek quotation at our
expense.   Here is the dismal log of Wednesday, 4th of September : — " All attempts at dining very fruitless.   Basins in
requisition.   Wind hard ahead.   *Que diable allais-je faire dans
cette galère ?*   Writing or thinking impossible : so read letters
from the Ægean."   These brief words give, I think, a complete
idea of wretchedness, despair, remorse, and prostration of soul
and body.   Two days previously we passed the forts and moles
and yellow buildings of Algiers, rising very stately from the
sea, and skirted by gloomy purple lines of African shore, with
fires smoking in the mountains, and lonely settlements here and
there.

On the 5th, to the inexpressible joy of all, we reached
Valetta, the entrance to the harbor of which is one of the most
stately and agreeable scenes ever admired by sea-sick traveller.   The small basin was busy with a hundred ships, from the
huge guard-ship, which lies there a city in itself ; — merchantmen loading and crews cheering, under all the flags of the world
flaunting in the sunshine ; a half-score of busy black steamers
perpetually coming and going, coaling and painting, and puffing
and hissing in and out of harbor ; slim men-of-war's barges shooting to and fro, with long shining oars flashing like wings over the
water ; hundreds of painted town-boats, with high heads and
white awnings, — down to the little tubs in which some naked,

tawny young beggars came paddling up to the steamer, entreating us to let them dive for halfpence. Round this busy blue water rise rocks, blazing in sunshine, and covered with every imaginable device of fortification; to the right, St. Elmo, with flag and light-house; and opposite, the Military Hospital, looking like a palace; and all round, the houses of the city, for its size the handsomest and most stately in the world.

Nor does it disappoint you on a closer inspection, as many a foreign town does. The streets are thronged with a lively, comfortable-looking population; the poor seem to inhabit handsome stone palaces, with balconies and projecting windows of heavy carved stone. The lights and shadows, the cries and stenches, the fruit-shops and fish-stalls, the dresses and chatter of all nations; the soldiers in scarlet, and women in black mantillas; the beggars, boatmen, barrels of pickled herrings and maccaroni; the shovel-hatted priests and bearded capuchins; the tobacco, grapes, onions, and sunshine; the signboards, bottled-porter stores, the statues of saints and little chapels which jostle the stranger's eyes as he goes up the famous stairs from the Water-gate, make a scene of such pleasant confusion and liveliness as I have never witnessed before. And the effects of the groups of multitudinous actors in this busy, cheerful drama is heightened, as it were, by the decorations of the stage. The sky is delightfully brilliant; all the houses and ornaments are stately; castles and palaces are rising all around; and the flag, towers, and walls of Fort St. Elmo look as fresh and magnificent as if they had been erected only yesterday.

The Strada Reale has a much more courtly appearance than that one described. Here are palaces, churches, court-houses and libraries, the genteel London shops, and the latest articles of perfumery. Gay young officers are strolling about in shell-jackets much too small for them: midshipmen are clattering by on hired horses; squads of priests, habited after the fashion of Don Basilio in the opera, are demurely pacing to and fro; professional beggars run shrieking after the stranger; and agents for horses, for inns, and for worse places still, follow him and insinuate the excellence of their goods. The houses where they are selling carpet-bags and pomatum were the palaces of the successors of the goodliest company of gallant knights the world ever heard tell of. It seems unromantic; but *these* were not the romantic Knights of St. John. The heroic days of the Order ended as the last Turkish galley lifted anchor after the memorable siege. The present stately houses were built in times of peace and splendor and decay. I doubt whether the Auberge de Provence, where the " Union Club " flourishes now, has ever seen anything more romantic than the pleasant balls held in the great room there.

The Church of Saint John, not a handsome structure without, is magnificent within : a noble hall covered with a rich embroidery of gilded carving, the chapels of the different nations on either side, but not interfering with the main structure, of which the whole is simple, and the details only splendid ; it seemed to me a fitting place for this wealthy body of aristocratic soldiers, who made their devotions as it were on parade, and, though on their knees, never forgot their epaulets or their quarters of nobility. This mixture of religion and worldly pride seems incongruous at first ; but have we not at church at home similar relics of feudal ceremony? — the verger with the silver mace who precedes the vicar to the desk ; the two chaplains of my lord archbishop, who bow over his grace as he enters the communion-table gate ; even poor John, who follows my lady with a coroneted prayer-book, and makes his *congé* as he hands it into the pew. What a chivalrous absurdity is the banner of some high and mighty prince, hanging over his stall in Windsor Chapel, when you think of the purpose for which men are supposed to assemble there ! The Church of the Knights of St. John is paved over with sprawling heraldic devices of the dead gentlemen of the dead Order ; as if, in the next world, they expected to take rank in conformity with their pedigrees, and would be marshalled into heaven according to the orders of precedence. Cumbrous handsome paintings adorn the walls and chapels, decorated with pompous monuments of Grand Masters. Beneath is a crypt, where more of these honorable and reverend warriors lie, in a state that a Simpson would admire. In the altar are said to lie three of the most gallant relics in the world : the keys of Acre, Rhodes, and Jerusalem. What blood was shed in defending these emblems ! What faith, endurance, genius, and generosity ; what pride, hatred, ambition, and savage lust of blood were roused together for their guardianship !

In the lofty halls and corridors of the Governor's house, some portraits of the late Grand Masters still remain : a very fine one, by Caravaggio, of a knight in gilt armor, hangs in the dining-room, near a full-length of poor Louis XVI., in royal robes, the very picture of uneasy impotency. But the portrait of De Vignacourt is the only one which has a respectable air ; the other chiefs of the famous society are pompous old gentlemen in black, with huge periwigs, and crowns round their hats, and a couple of melancholy pages in yellow and red. But pages and wigs and Grand Masters have almost faded out of the canvas, and are vanishing into Hades with a most melancholy indistinctness. The names of most of these gentlemen, however, live as yet in the forts of the place, which all seem to have been eager to build and christen : so that it seems as if, in the Malta mythology, they had been turned into freestone.

In the armory is the very suit painted by Caravaggio, by the side of the armor of the noble old La Valette, whose heroism saved his island from the efforts of Mustapha and Dragut, and an army quite as fierce and numerous as that which was baffled before Gibraltar, by similar courage and resolution. The sword of the last-named famous corsair (a most truculent little scimitar), thousands of pipes and halberts, little old cannons and wall-pieces, helmets and cuirasses, which the knights or their people wore, are trimly arranged against the wall, and, instead of spiking Turks or arming warriors, now serve to point morals and adorn tales. And here likewise are kept many thousand muskets, swords, and boarding-pikes for daily use, and a couple of ragged old standards of one of the English regiments, who pursued and conquered in Egypt the remains of the haughty and famous French Republican army, at whose appearance the last knights of Malta flung open the gates of all their fortresses, and consented to be extinguished without so much as a remonstrance, or a kick, or a struggle.

We took a drive into what may be called the country ; where the fields are rocks, and the hedges are stones — passing by the stone gardens of the Florian, and wondering at the number and handsomeness of the stone villages and churches rising everywhere among the stony hills. Handsome villas were passed everywhere, and we drove for a long distance along the sides of an aqueduct, quite a royal work of the Caravaggio in gold armor, the Grand Master De Vignacourt. A most agreeable contrast to the arid rocks of the general scenery was the garden at the Governor's country-house ; with the orange-trees and water, its beautiful golden grapes, luxuriant flowers, and thick cool shrubberies. The eye longs for this sort of refreshment, after being seared with the hot glare of the general country ; and St. Antonio was as pleasant after Malta as Malta was after the sea.

We paid the island a subsequent visit in November, passing seventeen days at an establishment called Fort Manuel there, and by punsters the Manuel des Voyageurs ; where Government accommodates you with quarters ; where the authorities are so attentive as to scent your letters with aromatic vinegar

before you receive them, and so careful of your health as to
lock you up in your room every night lest you should walk in
your sleep, and so over the battlements into the sea: if you
escaped drowning in the sea, the sentries on the opposite shore
would fire at you, hence the nature of the precaution. To drop,
however, this satirical strain: those who know what quarantine
is, may fancy that the place somehow becomes unbearable in
which it has been endured. And though the November climate
of Malta is like the most delicious May in England, and though
there is every gayety and amusement in the town, a comfortable
little opera, a good old library filled full of good old books
(none of your works of modern science, travel, and history, but
good old *useless* books of the last two centuries), and nobody
to trouble you in reading them, and though the society of
Valetta is most hospitable, varied, and agreeable, yet somehow
one did not feel *safe* in the island, with perpetual glimpses of
Fort Manuel from the opposite shore; and, lest the quarantine
authorities should have a fancy to fetch one back again, on a
pretext of posthumous plague, we made our way to Naples by
the very first opportunity — those who remained, that is, of the
little Eastern expedition. They were not all there. The Giver
of life and death had removed two of our company: one was
left behind to die in Egypt, with a mother to bewail his loss;
another we buried in the dismal lazaretto cemetery.

.   .   .   .

One is bound to look at this, too, as a part of our journey.
Disease and death are knocking perhaps at your next cabin
door. Your kind and cheery companion has ridden his last
ride and emptied his last glass beside you. And while fond
hearts are yearning for him far away, and his own mind, if conscious, is turning eagerly towards the spot of the world whither
affection or interest calls it — the Great Father summons the
anxious spirit from earth to himself, and ordains that the
nearest and dearest shall meet here no more.

Such an occurrence as a death in a lazaretto, mere selfishness renders striking. We were walking with him but two days
ago on deck. One has a sketch of him, another his card, with
the address written yesterday, and given with an invitation to
come and see him at home in the country, where his children
are looking for him. He is dead in a day, and buried in the
walls of the prison. A doctor felt his pulse by deputy — a
clergyman comes from the town to read the last service over
him — and the friends, who attend his funeral, are marshalled
by lazaretto-guardians, so as not to touch each other. Every

man goes back to his room and applies the lesson to himself.
One would not so depart without seeing again the dear, dear
faces. We reckon up those we love: they are but very few,
but I think one loves them better than ever now. Should it be
your turn next? — and why not? Is it pity or comfort to think
of that affection which watches and survives you?

The Maker has linked together the whole race of man with
this chain of love. I like to think that there is no man but has
had kindly feelings for some other, and he for his neighbor,
until we bind together the whole family of Adam. Nor does it
end here. It joins heaven and earth together. For my friend
or my child of past days is still my friend or my child to me
here, or in the home prepared for us by the Father of all.
If identity survives the grave, as our faith tells us, is it not a
consolation to think that there may be one or two souls among
the purified and just, whose affection watches us invisible, and
follows the poor sinner on earth?

CHAPTER V.

ATHENS.

Not feeling any enthusiasm myself about Athens, my
bounden duty of course is clear, to sneer and laugh heartily at
all who have. In fact, what business has a lawyer, who was
in Pump Court this day three weeks, and whose common reading is law reports or the newspaper, to pretend to fall in love
for the long vacation with mere poetry, of which I swear a great
deal is very doubtful, and to get up an enthusiasm quite foreign
to his nature and usual calling in life? What call have ladies
to consider Greece "romantic," they who get their notions of
mythology from the well-known pages of "Tooke's Pantheon?"
What is the reason that blundering Yorkshire squires, young
dandies from Corfu regiments, jolly sailors from ships in the
harbor, and yellow old Indians returning from Bundelcund,
should think proper to be enthusiastic about a country of which
they know nothing; the mere physical beauty of which they
cannot, for the most part, comprehend; and because certain
characters lived in it two thousand four hundred years ago?
What have these people in common with Pericles, what have

these ladies in common with Aspasia (O fie)? Of the race of Englishmen who come wondering about the tomb of Socrates, do you think the majority would not have voted to hemlock him? Yes: for the very same superstition which leads men by the nose now, drove them onward in the days when the lowly husband of Xantippe died for daring to think simply and to speak the truth. I know of no quality more magnificent in fools than their faith: that perfect consciousness they have, that they are doing virtuous and meritorious actions, when they are performing acts of folly, murdering Socrates, or pelting Aristides with holy oyster-shells, all for Virtue's sake; and a "History of Dulness in all Ages of the World," is a book which a philosopher would surely be hanged, but as certainly blessed, for writing.

If papa and mamma (honor be to them!) had not followed the faith of their fathers, and thought proper to send away their only beloved son (afterwards to be celebrated under the name of Titmarsh) into ten years' banishment of infernal misery, tyranny, annoyance; to give over the fresh feelings of the heart of the little Michael Angelo to the discipline of vulgar bullies, who, in order to lead tender young children to the Temple of Learning (as they do in the spelling-books), drive them on with clenched fists and low abuse; if they fainted, revived them with a thump, or assailed them with a curse; — if, I say, my dear parents, instead of giving me the inestimable benefit of a ten years' classical education, had kept me at home with my dear thirteen sisters, it is probable I should have liked this country of Attica, in sight of the blue shores of which the present pathetic letter is written; but I was made so miserable in youth by a classical education, that all connected with it is disagreeable in my eyes; and I have the same recollection of Greek in youth that I have of castor-oil.

So in coming in sight of the promontory of Sunium, where the Greek muse, in an awful vision, came to me, and said in a patronizing way, "Why, my dear," (she always, the old spinster, adopts this high and mighty tone,)—"Why, my dear, are you not charmed to be in this famous neighborhood, in this land of poets and heroes, of whose history your classical education ought to have made you a master; if it did not, you have wofully neglected your opportunities, and your dear parents have wasted their money in sending you to school. I replied: "Madam, your company in youth was made so laboriously disagreeable to me, that I can't at present reconcile myself to you in age. I read your poets, but it was in fear and trembling; and a cold sweat is but an ill accompaniment to poetry. I blundered through your histories; but history is so dull (saving your presence) of herself, that when the brutal dulness of a schoolmaster is superadded to her own slow conversation, the union becomes intolerable: hence I have not the slightest pleasure in renewing my acquaintance with a lady who has been the source of so much bodily and mental discomfort to me." To make a long story short, I am anxious to apologize for a want of enthusiasm in the classical line, and to excuse an ignorance which is of the most undeniable sort.

This is an improper frame of mind for a person visiting the land of Æschylus and Euripides; add to which, we have been abominably overcharged at the inn: and what are the blue hills of Attica, the silver calm basin of Piræus, the heathery heights of Pentelicus, and yonder rocks crowned by the Doric columns of the Parthenon, and the thin Ionic shafts of the Erechtheum, to a man who has had little rest, and is bitten all over by bugs? Was Alcibiades bitten by bugs, I wonder; and did the brutes crawl over him as he lay in the rosy arms of Phryne? I wished all night for Socrates' hammock or basket, as it is described in the "Clouds;" in which resting-place, no doubt, the abominable animals kept perforce clear of him.

A French man-of-war, lying in the silvery little harbor, sternly eying out of its stern port-holes a saucy little English corvette beside, began playing sounding marches as a crowd of boats came paddling up to the steamer's side to convey us travellers to shore. There were Russian schooners and Greek brigs lying in this little bay; dumpy little windmills whirling round on the sunburnt heights round about it; an improvised town of quays and marine taverns has sprung up on the shore; a host of jingling barouches, more miserable than any to be seen even in Germany, were collected at the landing-place; and the Greek drivers (how queer they looked in skull-caps, shabby jackets with profuse embroidery of worsted, and endless petticoats of dirty calico!) began, in a generous ardor for securing passengers, to abuse each other's horses and carriages in the regular London fashion. Satire could certainly hardly caricature the vehicle in which we were made to journey to Athens; and it was only by thinking that, bad as they were, these coaches were much more comfortable contrivances than any Alcibiades or Cimon ever had, that we consoled ourselves along the road. It was flat for six miles along the plain to the city: and you see for the greater part of the way the purple mount on which the Acropolis rises, and the gleaming houses of the town spread beneath. Round this wide, yellow, barren plain, — a stunt district of olive-trees is almost the only vegetation visible — there rises, as it were, a sort of chorus of the most beautiful mountains; the most elegant, gracious, and noble the eye ever looked on. These hills did not appear at all lofty or terrible, but superbly rich and aristocratic. The clouds were dancing round about them; you could see their rosy, purple shadows sweeping round the clear, serene summits of the hill. To call a hill aristocratic seems affected or absurd; but the difference between these hills and the others, is the difference between Newgate Prison and the "Travellers' Club," for instance: both are buildings; but the one stern, dark, and coarse; the other rich, elegant, and festive. At least, so I thought. With such a stately palace as munificent Nature had built for these people, what could they be themselves but lordly, beautiful, brilliant, brave, and wise? We saw four Greeks on donkeys on the road (which is a dust-whirlwind where it is not a puddle); and other four were playing with a dirty pack of cards, at a barrack that English poets have christened the "Half-way House." Does external nature and beauty influence the soul to good? You go about Warwickshire, and fancy that from merely being born and wandering in those sweet sunny plains and fresh woodlands Shakspeare must have drunk in a portion of that frank, artless sense of beauty, which lies about his works like a bloom or dew; but a Coventry ribbon-maker, or a slang Leamington squire, are looking on those very same landscapes too, and what do they profit? You theorize about the influence which the climate and appearance of Attica must have had in ennobling those who were born there; yonder dirty, swindling, ragged blackguards, lolling over greasy cards three hours before noon, quarrelling and shrieking, armed to the teeth and afraid to fight, are bred out of the same land which begot the philosophers and heroes. But the "Half-way House" is past by this time, and behold! we are in the capital of King Otho.

I swear solemnly that I would rather have two hundred a year in Fleet Street, than be King of the Greeks, with Basileus written before my name round their beggarly coin; with the bother of perpetual revolutions in my huge plaster-of-Paris palace, with no amusement but a drive in the afternoon over a wretched arid country, where roads are not made, with ambassadors (the deuce knows why, for what good can the English, or the French, or the Russian party get out of such a bankrupt alliance as this?) perpetually pulling and tugging at me, away from honest Germany, where there is beer and æsthetic conversation, and operas at a small cost. The shabbiness of this place actually beats Ireland, and that is a strong word. The palace of the Basileus is an enormous edifice of plaster, in a square containing six houses, three donkeys, no roads, no fountains (except in the picture of the inn) ; backwards it seems to look straight to the mountain — on one side is a beggarly garden — the King goes out to drive (revolutions permitting) at five — some four-and-twenty blackguards saunter up to the huge sandhill of a terrace, as his Majesty passes by in a gilt barouche and an absurd fancy dress ; the gilt barouche goes plunging down the sandhills : the two dozen soldiers, who have been presenting arms, slouch off to their quarters : the vast barrack of a palace remains entirely white, ghastly, and lonely : and, save the braying of a donkey now and then, (which long-eared minstrels are more active and sonorous ·in Athens than in any place I know,) all is entirely silent round Basileus's palace. How could people who knew Leopold fancy he would be so "jolly green" as to take such a berth? It was only a gobemouche of a Bavarian that could ever have been induced to accept it.

I beseech you to believe that it was not the bill and the bugs at the inn which induced the writer hereof to speak so slightingly of the residence of Basileus. These evils are now cured and forgotten. This is written off the leaden flats and mounds which they call the Troad. It is stern justice alone which pronounces this excruciating sentence. It was a farce to make this place into a kingly capital ; and I make no manner of doubt that King Otho, the very day he can get away unperceived, and get together the passage-money, will be off for dear old Deutschland, Fatherland, Beerland !

I have never seen a town in England which may be compared to this ; for though Herne Bay is a ruin now, money was once spent upon it and houses built ; here, beyond a few score of mansions comfortably laid out, the town is little better than a rickety agglomeration of larger and smaller huts, tricked out here and there with the most absurd cracked ornaments and cheap attempts at elegance. But neatness is the elegance of poverty, and these people despise such a homely ornament. I have got a map with squares, fountains, theatres, public gardens, and Places d'Othon marked out ; but they only exist in the paper capital — the wretched tumble-down wooden one boasts of none.

One is obliged to come back to the old disagreeable comparison of Ireland. Athens may be about as wealthy a place as Carlow or Killarney, — the streets swarm with idle crowds, the innumerable little lanes flow over with dirty little children, they are playing and puddling about in the dirt everywhere, with great big eyes, yellow faces, and the queerest little gowns and skull-caps. But in the outer man, the Greek has far the advantage of the Irishman : most of them are well and decently dressed (if five-and-twenty yards of petticoat may not be called decent, what may?) they swagger to and fro with huge knives in their girdles. Almost all the men are handsome, but live hard, it is said, in order to decorate their backs with those fine clothes of theirs. I have seen but two or three handsome women, and these had the great drawback which is common to the race — I mean, a sallow, greasy, coarse complexion, at which it was not advisable to look too closely.

And on this score I think we English may pride ourselves on possessing an advantage (by *we*, I mean the lovely ladies to whom this is addressed with the most respectful compliments) over the most classical country in the world. I don't care for beauty which will only bear to be looked at from a distance, like a scene in a theatre. What is the most beautiful nose in the world, if it be covered with a skin of the texture and color of coarse whity-brown paper ; and if Nature has made it as slippery and shining as though it had been anointed with pomatum? They may talk about beauty, but would you wear a flower that had been dipped in a grease-pot? No ; give me a fresh, dewy, healthy rose out of Somersetshire ; not one of those superb, tawdry, unwholesome exotics, which are only good to make poems about. Lord Byron wrote more cant of this sort than any poet I know of. Think of "the peasant girls with dark blue eyes" of the Rhine — the brown-faced, flat-nosed, thick-lipped, dirty wenches ! Think of "filling high a cup of Samian wine ; " small beer is nectar compared to it, and Byron himself always drank gin. That man *never* wrote from his heart. He got up rapture and enthusiasm with an eye to the public ; but this is dangerous ground, even more dangerous than to look Athens full in the face, and say that your eyes are not dazzled by its beauty. The Great Public admires Greece and Byron ; the public knows best. Murray's " Guide-book " calls the latter " our native bard." Our native bard ! *Mon Dieu !* *He* Shakspeare's, Milton's, Keats's, Scott's native bard ! Well, woe be to the man who denies the public gods !

The truth is, then, that Athens is a disappointment; and I am angry that it should be so. To a skilled antiquarian, or an enthusiastic Greek scholar, the feelings created by a sight of the place of course will be different; but you who would be inspired by it must undergo a long preparation of reading, and possess, too, a particular feeling; both of which, I suspect, are uncommon in our busy commercial newspaper-reading country. Men only say they are enthusiastic about the Greek and Roman authors and history, because it is considered proper and respectable. And we know how gentlemen in Baker Street have editions of the classics handsomely bound in the library, and how they use them. Of course they don't retire to read the newspaper; it is to look over a favorite ode of Pindar, or to discuss an obscure passage in Athenæus! Of course country magistrates and Members of Parliament are always studying Demosthenes and Cicero; we know it from their continual habit of quoting the Latin grammar in Parliament. But it is agreed that the classics are respectable; therefore we are to be enthusiastic about them. Also let us admit that Byron is to be held up as " our native bard."

I am not so entire a heathen as to be insensible to the beauty of those relics of Greek art, of which men much more learned and enthusiastic have written such piles of descriptions. I thought I could recognize the towering beauty of the prodigious columns of the Temple of Jupiter; and admire the astonishing grace, severity, elegance, completeness of the Parthenon. The little Temple of Victory, with its fluted Corinthian shafts, blazed under the sun almost as fresh as it must have appeared to the eyes of its founders; I saw nothing more charming and brilliant, more graceful, festive, and aristocratic than this sumptuous little building. The Roman remains which lie in the town below look like the works of barbarians beside these perfect structures. They jar strangely on the eye, after it has been accustoming itself to perfect harmony and proportions. If, as the schoolmaster tells us, the Greek writing is as complete as the Greek art; if an ode of Pindar is as glittering and pure as the Temple of Victory; or a discourse of Plato as polished and calm as yonder mystical portico of the Erechtheum; what treasures of the senses and delights of the imagination have those lost to whom the Greek books are as good as sealed!

And yet one meets with very dull first-class men. Genius won't transplant from one brain to another, or is ruined in the carriage, like fine Burgundy. Sir Robert Peel and Sir John Hobhouse are both good scholars; but their poetry in Parliament does not strike one as fine. Muzzle, the schoolmaster, who is bullying poor trembling little boys, was a fine scholar when he was a sizar, and a ruffian then and ever since. Where is the great poet, since the days of Milton, who has improved the natural offshoots of his brain by grafting it from the Athenian tree?

I had a volume of Tennyson in my pocket, which somehow settled that question, and ended the querulous dispute between me and Conscience, under the shape of the neglected and irritated Greek muse, which had been going on ever since I had commenced my walk about Athens. The old spinster saw me wince at the idea of the author of Dora and Ulysses, and tried to follow up her advantage by further hints of time lost, and precious opportunities thrown away. " You might have written poems like them," said she ; " or, no, not like them perhaps, but you might have done a neat prize-poem, and pleased your papa and mamma. You might have translated Jack and Gill into Greek iambics, and been a credit to your college." I turned testily away from her. " Madam," says I, " because an eagle houses on a mountain, or soars to the sun, don't you be angry with a sparrow that perches on a garret-window, or twitters on a twig. Leave me to myself; look, my beak is not aquiline by any means."

And so, my dear friend, you who have been reading this last page in wonder, and who, instead of a description of Athens, have been accommodated with a lament on the part of the writer, that he was idle at school, and does not know Greek, excuse this momentary outbreak of egotistic despondency. To say truth, dear Jones, when one walks among the nests of the eagles, and sees the prodigious eggs they laid, a certain feeling of discomfiture must come over us smaller birds. You and I could not invent — it even stretches our minds painfully to try and comprehend part of the beauty of the Parthenon — ever so little of it, — the beauty of a single column, — a fragment of a broken shaft lying under the astonishing blue sky there, in the midst of that unrivalled landscape. There may be grander aspects of nature, but none more deliciously beautiful. The hills rise in perfect harmony, and fall in the most exquisite cadences, — the sea seems brighter, the islands more purple, the clouds more light and rosy than elsewhere. As you look up through the open roof, you are almost oppressed by the serene depth of the blue overhead. Look even at the fragments of the marble, how soft and pure it is, glittering, and white like fresh snow ! " I was all beautiful," it seems to say : " even the hidden parts of me were spotless, precious, and fair" — and so, musing over this wonderful scene, perhaps I get some feeble glimpse or idea of that ancient Greek spirit which peopled it with sublime races of heroes and gods ; * and which I never could get out of a Greek book, — no, not though Muzzle flung it at my head.

CHAPTER VI.

SMYRNA — FIRST GLIMPSES OF THE EAST.

I AM glad that the Turkish part of Athens was extinct, so that I should not be balked of the pleasure of entering an Eastern town by an introduction to any garbled or incomplete specimen of one. Smyrna seems to me the most Eastern of all I have seen ; as Calais will probably remain to the Englishman the most French town in the world. The jack-boots of the postilions don't seem so huge elsewhere, or the tight stockings of the maid-servants so Gallic. The churches and the ramparts, and the little soldiers on them, remain for ever impressed upon your memory ; from which larger temples and buildings, and whole armies have subsequently disappeared : and the first words of actual French heard spoken, and the first dinner at " Quillacq's," remain after twenty years as clear as on the first day. Dear Jones, can't you remember the exact smack of the white hermitage, and the toothless old fellow singing " Largo al factotum" ?

The first day in the East is like that. After that there is nothing. The wonder is gone, and the thrill of that delightful shock, which so seldom touches the nerves of plain men of the world, though they seek for it everywhere. One such looked out at Smyrna from our steamer, and yawned without the least excitement, and did not betray the slightest emotion, as boats with real Turks on board came up to the ship. There lay the town with minarets and cypresses, domes and

---

* Saint Paul, speaking from the Areopagus and rebuking these superstitions away, yet speaks tenderly to the people before him, whose devotions he had marked ; quotes their poets, to bring them to think of the God unknown, whom they had ignorantly worshipped ; and says, that the times of this ignorance *God winked at,* but that now it was time to repent. No rebuke can surely be more gentle than this delivered by the upright Apostle.

castles; great guns were firing off, and the blood-red flag of the Sultan flaring over the fort ever since sunrise; woods and mountains came down to the gulf's edge, and as you looked at them with the telescope, there peeped out of the general mass a score of pleasant episodes of Eastern life — there were cottages with quaint roofs; silent cool kiosks, where the chief of the eunuchs brings down the ladies of the harem. I saw Hassan, the fisherman, getting his nets; and Ali Baba going off with his donkey to the great forest for wood. Smith looked at these wonders quite unmoved; and I was surprised at his apathy: but he had been at Smyrna before. A man only sees the miracle once; though you yearn after it ever so, it won't come again. I saw nothing of Ali Baba and Hassan the next time we came to Smyrna, and had some doubts (recollecting the badness of the inn) about landing at all. A person who wishes to understand France and the East should come in a yacht to Calais or Smyrna, land for two hours, and never afterwards go back again.

But those two hours are beyond measure delightful. Some of us were querulous up to that time, and doubted of the wisdom of making the voyage. Lisbon, we owned, was a failure; Athens a dead failure; Malta very well, but not worth the trouble and sea-sickness: in fact, Baden-Baden or Devonshire would be a better move than this; when Smyrna came, and rebuked all mutinous Cockneys into silence. Some men may read this who are in want of a sensation. If they love the odd and picturesque, if they loved the "Arabian Nights" in their youth, let them book themselves on board one of the Peninsular and Oriental vessels, and try one *dip* into Constantinople or Smyrna. Walk into the bazaar, and the East is unveiled to you; how often and often have you tried to fancy this, lying out on a summer holiday at school! It is wonderful, too, how *like* it is; you may imagine that you have been in the place before, you seem to know it so well!

The beauty of that poetry is, to me, that it was never too handsome; there is no fatigue of sublimity about it. Shacabac and the little Barber play as great a part in it as the heroes; there are no uncomfortable sensations of terror; you may be familiar with the great Afreet, who was going to execute the travellers for killing his son with a date-stone. Morgiana, when she kills the forty robbers with boiling oil, does not seem to hurt them in the least; and though King Schahriar makes a practice of cutting off his wives' heads, yet you fancy they have got them on again in some of the back rooms of the palace, where they are dancing and playing on dulcimers. How fresh, easy, good-natured, is all this! How delightful is that notion of the pleasant Eastern people about knowledge, where the height of science is made to consist in the answering of riddles! and all the mathematicians and magicians bring their great beards to bear on a conundrum!

When I got into the bazaar, among this race, somehow I felt as if they were all friends. There sat the merchants in their little shops, quiet and solemn, but with friendly looks. There was no smoking, it was the Ramazan; no eating, the fish and meats fizzing in the enormous pots of the cook-shops are only for the Christians. The children abounded; the law is not so stringent upon them, and many wandering merchants were there selling figs (in the name of the Prophet, doubtless), for their benefit, and elbowing onwards with baskets of grapes and cucumbers. Countrymen passed bristling over with arms, each with a huge bellyful of pistols and daggers in his girdle; fierce, but not the least dangerous. Wild swarthy Arabs, who had come in with the caravans, walked solemnly about, very different in look and demeanor from the sleek inhabitants of the town. Greeks and Jews squatted and smoked, their shops tended by sallow-faced boys, with large eyes, who smiled and welcomed you in; negroes bustled about in gaudy colors; and women, with black nose-bags and shuffling yellow slippers, chattered and bargained at the doors of the little shops. There was the rope quarter and the sweetmeat quarter, and the pipe bazaar, and the arm bazaar, and the little turned-up shoe quarter, and the shops where ready-made jackets and pelisses were swinging, and the region where, under the ragged awnings, regiments of tailors were at work. The sun peeps through these awnings of mat or canvas, which are hung over the narrow lanes of the bazaar, and ornaments them with a thousand freaks of light and shadow. Cogia Hassan Alhabbal's shop is in a blaze of light; while his neighbor, the barber and coffee-house keeper, has his premises, his low seats and narghilés, his queer pots and basins, in the shade. The cobblers are always good-natured; there was one, who, I am sure, has been revealed to me in my dreams, in a dirty old green turban, with a pleasant wrinkled face like an apple, twinkling his little gray eyes as he held them up to talk to the gossips, and smiling under a delightful old gray beard, which did the heart good to see. You divine the conversation between him and the cucumber-man, as the Sultan used to understand the language of birds. Are any of those cucumbers stuffed with pearls, and is that

Armenian with the black square turban Haroun Alraschid in disguise, standing yonder by the fountain where the children are drinking — the gleaming marble fountain, chequered all over with light and shadow, and engraved with delicate Arabesques and sentences from the Koran?

But the greatest sensation of all is when the camels come. Whole strings of real camels, better even than in the procession of Blue Beard, with soft rolling eyes and bended necks, swaying from one side of the bazaar to the other to and fro, and treading gingerly with their great feet. O you fairy dreams of boyhood! O you sweet meditations of half-holidays, here you are realized for half an hour! The genius which presides over youth led us to do a good action that day. There was a man sitting in an open room, ornamented with fine long-tailed sentences of the Koran : some in red, some in blue ; some written diagonally over the paper ; some so shaped as to represent ships, dragons, or mysterious animals. The man squatted on a carpet in the middle of this room, with folded arms, waggling his head to and fro, swaying about, and singing through his nose choice phrases from the sacred work. But from the room above came a clear noise of many little shouting voices, much more musical than that of Naso in the matted parlor, and the guide told us it was a school, so we went up stairs to look.

I declare, on my conscience, the master was in the act of bastinadoing a little mulatto boy ; his feet were in a bar, and the brute was laying on with a cane ; so we witnessed the howling of the poor boy, and the confusion of the brute who was administering the correction. The other children were made to shout, I believe, to drown the noise of their little comrade's howling ; but the punishment was instantly discontinued as our hats came up over the stairtrap, and the boy cast loose, and the bamboo huddled into a corner, and the schoolmaster stood before us abashed. All the small scholars in red caps, and the little girls in gaudy handkerchiefs, turned their big wondering dark eyes towards us ; and the caning was over for *that* time, let us trust. I don't envy some schoolmasters in a future state. I pity that poor little blubbering Mahometan ; he will never be able to relish the " Arabian Nights " in the original all his life long.

From this scene we rushed off somewhat discomposed to make a breakfast off red mullets and grapes, melons, pomegranates, and Smyrna wine, at a dirty little comfortable inn, to which we were recommended : and from the windows of which we had a fine cheerful view of the gulf and its busy craft, and the loungers and merchants along the shore. There were camels unloading at one wharf, and piles of melons much bigger than the Gibraltar cannon-balls at another. It was the fig-season, and we passed through several alleys encumbered with long rows of fig-dressers, children and women for the most part, who were packing the fruit diligently into drums, dipping them in salt-water first, and spreading them neatly over with leaves; while the figs and leaves are drying, large white worms crawl out of them, and swarm over the decks of the ships which carry them to Europe and to England, where small children eat them with pleasure — I mean the figs, not the worms — and where they are still served at wine-parties at the Universities. When fresh they are not better than elsewhere; but the melons are of admirable flavor, and so large, that Cinderella might almost be accommodated with a coach made of a big one, without any very great distention of its original proportions.

Our guide, an accomplished swindler, demanded two dollars as the fee for entering the mosque, which others of our party subsequently saw for sixpence, so we did not care to examine that place of worship. But there were other cheaper sights, which were to the full as picturesque, for which there was no call to pay money, or, indeed, for a day, scarcely to move at all. I doubt whether a man who would smoke his pipe on a bazaar counter all day, and let the city flow by him, would not be almost as well employed as the most active curiosity-hunter.

To be sure he would not see the women. Those in the bazaar were shabby people for the most part, whose black masks nobody would feel a curiosity to remove. You could see no more of their figures than if they had been stuffed in bolsters; and even their feet were brought to a general splay uniformity by the double yellow slippers which the wives of true believers wear. But it is in the Greek and Armenian quarters and among those poor Christians who were pulling figs, that you see the beauties; and a man of a generous disposition may lose his heart half a dozen times a day in Smyrna. There was the pretty maid at work at a tambour-frame in an open porch, with an old duenna spinning by her side, and a goat tied up to the railings of the little court-garden; there was the nymph who came down the stair with the pitcher on her head, and gazed with great calm eyes, as large and stately as Juno's; there was the gentle mother, bending over a queer cradle, in which lay a small crying bundle of infancy. All these three charmers were seen in a single street in the Armenian quarter, where the

house-doors are all open, and the women of the families sit
under the arches in the court. There was the fig-girl, beautiful
beyond all others, with an immense coil of deep black hair
twisted round a head of which Raphael was worthy to draw the
outline, and Titian to paint the color. I wonder the Sultan has
not swept her off, or that the Persian merchants, who come
with silks and sweetmeats, have not kidnapped her for the
Shah of Tehran.

We went to see the Persian merchants at their khan, and
purchased some silks there from a swarthy, black-bearded man,
with a conical cap of lambswool. Is it not hard to think that
silks bought of a man in a lambswool cap, in a caravanserai,
brought hither on the backs of camels, should have been manufactured after all at Lyons? Others of our party bought carpets,
for which the town is famous ; and there was one who absolutely
laid in a stock of real Smyrna figs ; and purchased three or four
real Smyrna sponges for his carriage ; so strong was his passion
for the genuine article.

I wonder that no painter has given us familiar views of the
East : not processions, grand sultans, or magnificent landscapes ;
but faithful transcripts of every-day Oriental life, such as each
street will supply to him. The camels afford endless motives,
couched in the market-places, lying by thousands in the camel
square, snorting and bubbling after their manner, the sun blazing down on their backs, their slaves and keepers lying behind
them in the shade : and the Caravan Bridge, above all, would
afford a painter subjects for a dozen of pictures. Over this
Roman arch, which crosses the Meles river, all the caravans
pass on their entrance to the town. On one side, as we sat and
looked at it, was a great row of plane-trees ; on the opposite
bank, a deep wood of tall cypresses — in the midst of which
rose up innumerable gray tombs, surmounted with the turbans
of the defunct believers. Beside the stream, the view was less
gloomy. There was under the plane-trees a little coffee-house,
shaded by a trellis-work, covered over with a vine, and ornamented with many rows of shining pots and water-pipes, for
which there was no use at noonday now, in the time of Ramazan. Hard by the coffee-house was a garden and a bubbling
marble fountain, and over the stream was a broken summer-
house, to which amateurs may ascend, for the purpose of examining the river ; and all round the plane-trees plenty of stools
for those who were inclined to sit and drink sweet thick coffee,
or cool lemonade made of fresh green citrons. The master of
the house, dressed in a white turban and light blue pelisse,

lolled under the coffee-house awning; the slave in white with a
crimson striped jacket, his face as black as ebony, brought us
pipes and lemonade again, and returned to his station at the
coffee-house, where he curled his black legs together, and began
singing out of his flat nose to the thrumming of a long guitar
with wire strings. The instrument was not bigger than a soup-
ladle, with a long straight handle, but its music pleased the
performer; for his eyes rolled shining about, and his head
wagged, and he grinned with an innocent intensity of enjoyment that did one good to look at. And there was a friend to
share his pleasure: a Turk dressed in scarlet, and covered all
over with daggers and pistols, sat leaning forward on his little
stool, rocking about, and grinning quite as eagerly as the black
minstrel. As he sang and we listened, figures of women bearing pitchers went passing over the Roman bridge, which we saw
between the large trunks of the planes; or gray forms of camels
were seen stalking across it, the string preceded by the little
donkey, who is always here their long-eared conductor.

These are very humble incidents of travel. Wherever the
steamboat touches the shore adventure retreats into the interior,
and what is called romance vanishes. It won't bear the vulgar
gaze; or rather the light of common day puts it out, and it is
only in the dark that it shines at all. There is no cursing and
insulting of Giaours now. If a Cockney looks or behaves in a
particularly ridiculous way, the little Turks come out and laugh
at him. A Londoner is no longer a spittoon for true believers:
and now that dark Hassan sits in his divan and drinks champagne, and Selim has a French watch, and Zuleika perhaps
takes Morrison's pills, Byronism becomes absurd instead of
sublime, and is only a foolish expression of Cockney wonder.
They still occasionally beat a man for going into a mosque,
but this is almost the only sign of ferocious vitality left in the
Turk of the Mediterranean coast, and strangers may enter
scores of mosques without molestation. The paddle-wheel is
the great conqueror. Wherever the captain cries "Stop her!"
Civilization stops, and lands in the ship's boat, and makes a
permanent acquaintance with the savages on shore. Whole
hosts of crusaders have passed and died, and butchered here in
vain. But to manufacture European iron into pikes and helmets
was a waste of metal: in the shape of piston-rods and furnace-
pokers it is irresistible; and I think an allegory might be made
showing how much stronger commerce is than chivalry, and
finishing with a grand image of Mahomet's crescent being extinguished in Fulton's boiler.

This I thought was the moral of the day's sights and adventures. We pulled off to the steamer in the afternoon — the Inbat blowing fresh, and setting all the craft in the gulf dancing over its blue waters. We were presently under weigh again, the captain ordering his engines to work only at half power, so that a French steamer which was quitting Smyrna at the same time might come up with us, and fancy she could beat the irresistible "Tagus." Vain hope! Just as the Frenchman neared us, the "Tagus" shot out like an arrow, and the discomfited Frenchman went behind. Though we all relished the joke exceedingly, there was a French gentleman on board who did not seem to be by any means tickled with it; but he had received papers at Smyrna, containing news of Marshal Bugeaud's victory at Isley, and had this land victory to set against our harmless little triumph at sea.

That night we rounded the Island of Mitylene : and the next day the coast of Troy was in sight, and the tomb of Achilles — a dismal-looking mound that rises in a low, dreary, barren shore — less lively and not more picturesque than the Scheldt or the mouth of the Thames. Then we passed Tenedos and the forts and town at the mouth of the Dardanelles. The weather was not too hot, the water as smooth as at Putney, and everybody happy and excited at the thought of seeing Constantinople to-morrow. We had music on board all the way from Smyrna. A German commis-voyageur, with a guitar, who had passed unnoticed until that time, produced his instrument about mid-day, and began to whistle waltzes. He whistled so divinely that the ladies left their cabins, and men laid down their books. He whistled a polka so bewitchingly that two young Oxford men began whirling round the deck, and performed that popular dance with much agility until they sank down tired. He still continued an unabated whistling, and as nobody would dance, pulled off his coat, produced a pair of castanets, and whistling a mazurka, performed it with tremendous agility. His whistling made everybody gay and happy — made those acquainted who had not spoken before, and inspired such a feeling of hilarity in the ship, that that night, as we floated over the sea of Marmora, a general vote was expressed for broiled bones and a regular supper-party. Punch was brewed, and speeches were made, and after a lapse of fifteen years, I heard the "Old English Gentleman" and "Bright Chanticleer Proclaims the Morn," sung in such style that you would almost fancy the proctors must hear, and send us all home.

CHAPTER VII.

CONSTANTINOPLE.

WHEN we rose at sunrise to see the famous entry to Constantinople, we found, in the place of the city and the sun, a
bright white fog, which hid both from sight, and which only
disappeared as the vessel advanced towards the Golden Horn.
There the fog cleared off as it were by flakes, as you see gauze
curtains lifted away, one by one, before a great fairy scene at
the theatre. This will give idea enough of the fog; the difficulty is to describe the scene afterwards, which was in truth the
great fairy scene, than which it is impossible to conceive anything more brilliant and magnificent. I can't go to any more
romantic place than Drury Lane to draw my similes from —
Drury Lane, such as we used to see it in our youth, when to
our sight the grand last pictures of the melodrama or pantomime
were as magnificent as any objects of nature we have seen with
maturer eyes. Well, the view of Constantinople is as fine as
any of Stanfield's best theatrical pictures, seen at the best
period of youth, when fancy had all the bloom on her — when
all the heroines who danced before the scene appeared as
ravishing beauties, when there shone an unearthly splendor
about Baker and Diddear — and the sound of the bugles
and fiddles, and the cheerful clang of the cymbals, as the
scene unrolled, and the gorgeous procession meandered tri-
umphantly through it — caused a thrill of pleasure, and awakened an innocent fulness of sensual enjoyment that is only
given to boys.

The above sentence contains the following propositions : —
The enjoyments of boyish fancy are the most intense and delicious in the world. Stanfield's panorama used to be the
realization of the most intense youthful fancy. I puzzle my
brains and find no better likeness for the place. The view of
Constantinople resembles the *ne plus ultra* of a Stanfield dio-
rama, with a glorious accompaniment of music, spangled
houris, warriors, and winding processions, feasting the eyes
and the soul with light, splendor, and harmony. If you were
never in this way during your youth ravished at the play-house,
of course the whole comparison is useless : and you have no
idea, from this description, of the effect which Constantinople

produces on the mind. But if you were never affected by a theatre, no words can work upon your fancy, and typographical attempts to move it are of no use. For, suppose we combine mosque, minaret, gold, cypress, water, blue, caïques, seventy-four, Galata, Tophana, Ramazan, Backallum, and so forth, together, in ever so many ways, your imagination will never be able to depict a city out of them. Or, suppose I say the Mosque of St. Sophia is four hundred and seventy-three feet in height, measuring from the middle nail of the gilt crescent surmounting the dome to the ring in the centre stone; the circle of the dome is one hundred and twenty-three feet in diameter, the windows ninety-seven in number — and all this may be true, for anything I know to the contrary: yet who is to get an idea of St. Sophia from dates, proper names, and calculations with a measuring-line? It can't be done by giving the age and measurement of all the buildings along the river, the names of all the boatmen who ply on it. Has your fancy, which pooh-poohs a simile, faith enough to build a city with a foot-rule? Enough said about descriptions and similes (though whenever I am uncertain of one I am naturally most anxious to fight for it): it is a scene not perhaps sublime, but charming, magnificent, and cheerful beyond any I have ever seen — the most superb combination of city and gardens, domes and shipping, hills and water, with the healthiest breeze blowing over it, and above it the brightest and most cheerful sky.

It is proper, they say, to be disappointed on entering the town, or any of the various quarters of it, because the houses are not so magnificent on inspection, and seen singly as they are when beheld *en masse* from the waters. But why form expectations so lofty? If you see a group of peasants picturesquely disposed at a fair, you don't suppose that they are all faultless beauties, or that the men's coats have no rags, and the women's gowns are made of silk and velvet: the wild ugliness of the interior of Constantinople or Pera has a charm of its own, greatly more amusing than rows of red bricks or drab stones, however symmetrical. With brick or stone they could never form those fantastic ornaments, railings, balconies, roofs, galleries, which jut in and out of the rugged houses of the city. As we went from Galata to Pera up a steep hill, which new-comers ascend with some difficulty, but which a porter, with a couple of hundredweight on his back, paces up without turning a hair, I thought the wooden houses far from being disagreeable objects, sights quite as surprising and striking as the grand one we had just left.

I do not know how the custom-house of his Highness is made to be a profitable speculation. As I left the ship, a man pulled after my boat, and asked for backsheesh, which was given him to the amount of about twopence. He was a custom-house officer, but I doubt whether this sum which he levied ever went to the revenue.

I can fancy the scene about the quays somewhat to resemble the river of London in olden times, before coal-smoke had darkened the whole city with soot, and when, according to the old writers, there really was bright weather. The fleets of caïques bustling along the shore, or scudding over the blue water, are beautiful to look at: in Hollar's print London river is so studded over with wherry-boats, which bridges and steamers have since destroyed. Here the caïque is still in full perfection: there are thirty thousand boats of the kind plying between the cities; every boat is neat, and trimly carved and painted; and I scarcely saw a man pulling in one of them that was not a fine specimen of his race, brawny and brown, with an open chest and a handsome face. They wear a thin shirt of exceedingly light cotton, which leaves their fine brown limbs full play; and with a purple sea for a background, every one of these dashing boats forms a brilliant and glittering picture. Passengers squat in the inside of the boat; so that as it passes you see little more than the heads of the true believers, with their red fez and blue tassel, and that placid gravity of expression which the sucking of a tobacco-pipe is sure to give to a man.

The Bosphorus is enlivened by a multiplicity of other kinds of craft. There are the dirty men-of-war's boats of the Russians, with unwashed, mangy crews; the great ferry-boats carrying hundreds of passengers to the villages; the melon-boats piled up with enormous golden fruit; his Excellency the Pasha's boat, with twelve men bending to their oars; and his Highness's own caïque, with a head like a serpent, and eight-and-twenty tugging oarsmen, that goes shooting by amidst the thundering of the cannon. Ships and steamers, with black sides and flaunting colors, are moored everywhere, showing their flags, Russian and English, Austrian, American, and Greek; and along the quays country ships from the Black Sea or the islands, with high carved poops and bows, such as you see in the pictures of the shipping of the seventeenth century. The vast groves and towers, domes and quays, tall minarets

and spired spreading mosques of the three cities, rise all
around in endless magnificence and variety, and render this
water-street a scene of such delightful liveliness and beauty,
that one never tires of looking at it.   I lost a great number of
the sights in and round Constantinople through the beauty of
this admirable scene : but what are sights after all? and isn't
that the best sight which makes you most happy?

We were lodged at Pera at "Misseri's Hotel," the host of
which has been made famous ere this time by the excellent
book "Eothen," — a work for which all the passengers on
board our ship had been battling, and which had charmed all
— from our great statesman, our polished lawyer, our young
Oxonian, who sighed over certain passages that he feared were
wicked, down to the writer of this, who, after perusing it with
delight, laid it down with wonder, exclaiming, "Aut Diabolus
aut" — a book which has since (greatest miracle of all) excited
a feeling of warmth and admiration in the bosom of the godlike,
impartial, stony *Athenæum*.   Misseri, the faithful and chivalrous Tartar, is transformed into the most quiet and gentlemanlike of landlords, a great deal more gentlemanlike in manner
and appearance than most of us who sat at his table, and
smoked cool pipes on his house-top, as we looked over the hill
and the Russian palace to the water, and the Seraglio gardens
shining in the blue.   We confronted Misseri, "Eothen" in
hand, and found, on examining him, that it *was* "aut Diabolus aut amicus" — but the name is a secret; I will never
breathe it, though I am dying to tell it.

The last good description of a Turkish bath, I think, was
Lady Mary Wortley Montagu's — which voluptuous picture
must have been painted at least a hundred and thirty years
ago : so that another sketch may be attempted by a humbler
artist in a different manner.   The Turkish bath is certainly a
novel sensation to an Englishman, and may be set down as a
most queer and surprising event of his life.   I made the valet-
de-place or dragoman (it is rather a fine thing to have a dragoman in one's service) conduct me forthwith to the best appointed
hummums in the neighborhood ; and we walked to a house at
Tophana, and into a spacious hall lighted from above, which is
the cooling-room of the bath.

The spacious hall has a large fountain in the midst, a
painted gallery running round it ; and many ropes stretched
from one gallery to another, ornamented with profuse draperies
of towels and blue cloths, for the use of the frequenters of the
place.   All round the room and the galleries were matted in-

closures, fitted with numerous neat beds and cushions for reposing on, where lay a dozen of true believers smoking, or
sleeping, or in the happy half-dozing state. I was led up to
one of these beds, to rather a retired corner, in consideration
of my modesty; and to the next bed presently came a dancing
dervish, who forthwith began to prepare for the bath.

When the dancing dervish had taken off his yellow sugar-
loaf cap, his gown, shawl, &c., he was arrayed in two large
blue cloths; a white one being thrown over his shoulders, and
another in the shape of a turban plaited neatly round his head;
the garments of which he divested himself were folded up in
another linen, and neatly put by. I beg leave to state I was
treated in precisely the same manner as the dancing dervish.

The reverend gentleman then put on a pair of wooden
pattens, which elevated him about six inches from the ground;
and walked down the stairs, and paddled across the moist
marble floor of the hall, and in at a little door, by the which
also Titmarsh entered. But I had none of the professional
agility of the dancing dervish; I staggered about very ludicrously upon the high wooden pattens; and should have been
down on my nose several times, had not the dragoman and the
master of the bath supported me down stairs and across the
hall. Dressed in three large cotton napkins, with a white
turban round my head, I thought of Pall Mall with a sort of
despair. I passed the little door, it was closed behind me — I
was in the dark — I couldn't speak the language — in a white
turban. Mon Dieu! what was going to happen!

The dark room was the tepidarium, a moist oozing arched
den, with a light faintly streaming from an orifice in the domed
ceiling. Yells of frantic laughter and song came booming and
clanging through the echoing arches, the doors clapped to with
loud reverberations. It was the laughter of the followers of
Mahound, rollicking and taking their pleasure in the public
bath. I could not go into that place: I swore I would not;
they promised me a private room, and the dragoman left me.
My agony at parting from that Christian cannot be described.

When you get into the sudarium, or hot room, your first
sensations only occur about half a minute after entrance, when
you feel that you are choking. I found myself in that state,
seated on a marble slab; the bath man was gone; he had taken
away the cotton turban and shoulder shawl: I saw I was in a
narrow room of marble, with a vaulted roof, and a fountain of
warm and cold water; the atmosphere was in a steam, the choking sensation went off, and I felt a sort of pleasure presently in

a soft boiling simmer, which, no doubt, potatoes feel when they are steaming. You are left in this state for about ten minutes; it is warm certainly, but odd and pleasant, and disposes the mind to reverie.

But let any delicate mind in Baker Street fancy my horror, when, on looking up out of this reverie, I saw a great brown wretch extended before me, only half dressed, standing on pattens, and exaggerated by them and the steam until he looked like an ogre, grinning in the most horrible way, and waving his arm, on which was a horsehair glove. He spoke, in his unknown nasal jargon, words which echoed through the arched room; his eyes seemed astonishingly large and bright, his ears stuck out, and his head was all shaved, except a bristling top-knot, which gave it a demoniac fierceness.

This description, I feel, is growing too frightful; ladies who read it will be going into hysterics, or saying, "Well, upon my word, this is the most singular, the most extraordinary kind of language. Jane, my love, you will not read that odious book" — and so I will be brief. This grinning man belabors the patient violently with the horse brush. When he has completed the horse-hair part, and you lie expiring under a squirting fountain of warm water, and fancying all is done, he reappears with a large brass basin containing a quantity of lather, in the midst of which is something like old Miss Mac-Whirter's flaxen wig that she is so proud of, and that we have all laughed at. Just as you are going to remonstrate, the thing like the wig is dashed into your face and eyes, covered over with soap, and for five minutes you are drowned in lather: you can't see, the suds are frothing over your eyeballs; you can't hear, the soap is whizzing into your ears; can't gasp for breath, Miss MacWhirter's wig is down your throat with half a pailful of suds in an instant — you are all soap. Wicked children in former days have jeered you, exclaiming, "How are you off for soap?" You little knew what saponacity was till you entered a Turkish bath.

When the whole operation is concluded, you are led — with what heartfelt joy I need not say — softly back to the cooling-room, having been robed in shawls and turbans as before. You are laid gently on the reposing bed; somebody brings a narghilé, which tastes as tobacco must taste in Mahomet's Paradise; a cool sweet dreamy languor takes possession of the purified frame, and half an hour of such delicious laziness is spent over the pipe as is unknown in Europe, where vulgar prejudice has most shamefully maligned indolence, calls it foul names, such as the father of all evil, and the like ; in fact, does not know how to educate idleness as those honest Turks do, and the fruit, which, when properly cultivated, it bears.

The after-bath state is the most delightful condition of laziness I ever knew, and I tried it wherever we went afterwards on our little tour. At Smyrna the whole business was much inferior to the method employed in the capital. At Cairo, after the soap, you are plunged into a sort of stone coffin, full of water, which is all but boiling. This has its charms ; but I could not relish the Egyptian shampooing. A hideous old blind man (but very dexterous in his art) tried to break my back and dislocate my shoulders, but I could not see the pleasure of the practice ; and another fellow began tickling the soles of my feet, but I rewarded him with a kick that sent him off the bench. The pure idleness is the best, and I shall never enjoy such in Europe again.

Victor Hugo, in his famous travels on the Rhine, visiting Cologne, gives a learned account of what he *didn't* see there. I have a remarkable catalogue of similar objects at Constantinople. I didn't see the dancing dervishes, it was Ramazan ; nor the howling dervishes at Scutari, it was Ramazan ; nor the interior of St. Sophia, nor the women's apartment of the Seraglio, nor the fashionable promenade at the Sweet Waters, always because it was Ramazan ; during which period the dervishes dance and howl but rarely, their legs and lungs being unequal to much exertion during a fast of fourteen hours. On account of the same holy season, the royal palaces and mosques are shut ; and though the valley of the Sweet Waters is there, no one goes to walk ; the people remaining asleep all day, and passing the night in feasting and carousing. The minarets are illuminated at this season ; even the humblest mosque at Jerusalem, or Jaffa, mounted a few circles of dingy lamps ; those of the capital were handsomely lighted with many festoons of lamps, which had a fine effect from the water. I need not mention other and constant illuminations of the city which innumerable travellers have described — I mean the fires. There were three in Pera during our eight days' stay there ; but they did not last long enough to bring the Sultan out of bed to come and lend his aid. Mr. Hobhouse (quoted in the " Guide-book ") says, if a fire lasts an hour, the Sultan is bound to attend it in person ; and that people having petitions to present, have often set houses on fire for the purpose of forcing out this royal trump. The Sultan can't lead a very " jolly life," if this rule be universal. Fancy his Highness, in the midst of his moon-faced beauties, handkerchief in hand, and obliged to tie it round his face, and go out of his warm harem at midnight at the cursed cry of " Yang en Var ! "

We saw his Highness in the midst of his people and their petitions, when he came to the mosque at Tophana ; not the largest, but one of the most picturesque of the public buildings of the city. The streets were crowded with people [watching for the august arrival, and lined with the squat military in their bastard European costume ; the sturdy police, with bandeliers and brown surtouts, keeping order, driving off the faithful from the railings of the Esplanade through which their Emperor was to pass, and only admitting (with a very unjust partiality, I thought) us Europeans into that reserved space. Before the august arrival, numerous officers collected, colonels and pashas went by with their attendant running footmen ; the most active, insolent, and hideous of these great men, as I thought, being his Highness's black eunuchs, who went prancing through the crowd, which separated before them with every sign of respect.

The common women were assembled by many hundreds : the yakmac, a muslin chin-cloth which they wear, makes almost every face look the same ; but the eyes and noses of these beauties are generally visible, and, for the most part, both these features are good. The jolly negresses wear the same white veil, but they are by no means so particular about hiding the charms of their good-natured black faces, and they let the cloth blow about as it lists, and grin unconfined. Wherever we went the negroes seemed happy. They have the organ of child-loving ; little creatures were always prattling on their shoulders, queer little things in night-gowns of yellow dimity, with great flowers, and pink, or red, or yellow shawls, with great eyes glistening underneath. Of such the black women seemed always the happy guardians. I saw one at a fountain, holding one child in her arms, and giving another a drink — a ragged little beggar — a sweet and touching picture of a black charity.

I am almost forgetting his Highness the Sultan. About a hundred guns were fired off at clumsy intervals from the Esplanade facing the Bosphorus, warning us that the monarch had set off from his Summer Palace, and was on the way to his grand canoe. At last that vessel made its appearance ; the band struck up his favorite air ; his caparisoned horse was led down to the shore to receive him ; the eunuchs, fat pashas, colonels, and officers of state gathering round as the Commander of the Faithful mounted. I had the indescribable happiness of seeing him at a very short distance. The Padishah, or Father of all

the Sovereigns on earth, has not that majestic air which some
sovereigns possess, and which makes the beholder's eyes wink,
and his knees tremble under him: he has a black beard, and
a handsome well-bred face, of a French cast; he looks like a
young French *roué* worn out by debauch; his eyes bright, with
black rings round them; his cheeks pale and hollow. He was
lolling on his horse as if he could hardly hold himself on the
saddle: or as if his cloak, fastened with a blazing diamond clasp
on his breast, and falling over his horse's tail, pulled him back.
But the handsome sallow face of the Refuge of the World looked
decidedly interesting and intellectual. I have seen many a
young Don Juan at Paris, behind a counter, with such a beard
and countenance; the flame of passion still burning in his hollow eyes, while on his damp brow was stamped the fatal mark
of premature decay. The man we saw cannot live many sum-
mers. Women and wine are said to have brought the Zilullah
to this state; and it is whispered by the dragomans, or laquais-
de-place, (from whom travellers at Constantinople generally
get their political information,) that the Sultan's mother and
his ministers conspire to keep him plunged in sensuality, that
they may govern the kingdom according to their own fancies.
Mr. Urquhart, I am sure, thinks that Lord Palmerston has something to do with the business, and drugs the Sultan's champagne
for the benefit of Russia.

As the Pontiff of Mussulmans passed into the mosque, a
shower of petitions was flung from the steps where the crowd
was collected, and over the heads of the gendarmes in brown.
A general cry, as for justice, rose up; and one old ragged woman came forward and burst through the throng, howling, and
flinging about her lean arms, and baring her old shrunken
breast. I never saw a finer action of tragic woe, or heard
sounds more pitiful than those old passionate groans of hers.
What was your prayer, poor old wretched soul? The gendarmes
hemmed her round, and hustled her away, but rather kindly.
The Padishah went on quite impassible — the picture of debauch
and ennui.

I like pointing morals, and inventing for myself cheap con-
solations, to reconcile me to that state of life into which it has
pleased heaven to call me; and as the Light of the World disappeared round the corner, I reasoned pleasantly with myself
about his Highness, and enjoyed that secret selfish satisfaction
a man has, who sees he is better off than his neighbor. "Michael Angelo," I said, "you are still (by courtesy) young: if
you had five hundred thousand a year, and were a great prince,

MINNE

SUMMER PALACE, CONSTANTINOPLE.

I would lay a wager that men would discover in you a magnificent courtesy of demeanor, and a majestic presence that only belongs to the sovereigns of the world. If you had such an income, you think you could spend it with splendor! distributing genial hospitalities, kindly alms, soothing misery, bidding humility be of good heart, rewarding desert. If you had such means of purchasing pleasure, you think, you rogue, you could relish it with gusto. But fancy being brought to the condition of the poor Light of the Universe yonder; and reconcile yourself with the idea that you are only a farthing rushlight. The cries of the poor widow fall as dead upon him as the smiles of the brightest eyes out of Georgia. He can't stir abroad but those abominable cannon begin roaring and deafening his ears. He can't see the world but over the shoulders of a row of fat pashas, and eunuchs, with their infernal ugliness. His ears can never be regaled with a word of truth, or blessed with an honest laugh. The only privilege of manhood left to him, he enjoys but for a month in the year, at this time of Ramazan, when he is forced to fast for fifteen hours; and, by consequence, has the blessing of feeling hungry." Sunset during Lent appears to be his single moment of pleasure; they say the poor fellow is ravenous by that time, and as the gun fires the dish-covers are taken off, so that for five minutes a day he lives and is happy over pillau, like another mortal.

And yet, when floating by the Summer Palace, a barbaric edifice of wood and marble, with gilded suns blazing over the porticos, and all sorts of strange ornaments and trophies figuring on the gates and railings — when we passed a long row of barred and filigreed windows, looking on the water — when we were told that those were the apartments of his Highness's ladies, and actually heard them whispering and laughing behind the bars — a strange feeling of curiosity came over some ill-regulated minds — just to have *one* peep, one look at all those wondrous beauties, singing to the dulcimers, paddling in the fountains, dancing in the marble halls, or lolling on the golden cushions, as the gaudy black slaves brought pipes and coffee. This tumultuous movement was calmed by thinking of that dreadful statement of travellers, that in one of the most elegant halls there is a trap-door, on peeping below which you may see the Bosphorus running underneath, into which some luckless beauty is plunged occasionally, and the trap-door is shut, and the dancing and the singing, and the smoking and the laughing go on as before. They say it is death to pick up any of the sacks thereabouts, if a stray one should float by you. There were

23

none any day when I passed, *at least, on the surface of the water*.

It has been rather a fashion of our travellers to apologize for Turkish life, of late, and paint glowing, agreeable pictures of many of its institutions. The celebrated author of " Palm-Leaves" (his name is famous under the date-trees of the Nile, and uttered with respect beneath the tents of the Bedaween,) has touchingly described Ibrahim Pasha's paternal fondness, who cut off a black slave's head for having dropped and maimed one of his children ; and has penned a melodious panegyric of "The Harem," and of the fond and beautiful duties of the inmates of that place of love, obedience, and seclusion. I saw, at the mausoleum of the late Sultan Mahmoud's family, a good subject for a Gnazul, in the true new Oriental manner.

These royal burial-places are the resort of the pious Moslems. Lamps are kept burning there ; and in the ante-chambers, copies of the Koran are provided for the use of believers ; and you never pass these cemeteries but you see Turks washing at the cisterns, previous to entering for prayer, or squatted on the benches, chanting passages from the sacred volume. Christians, I believe, are not admitted, but may look through the bars, and see the coffins of the defunct monarchs and children of the royal race. Each lies in his narrow sarcophagus, which is commonly flanked by huge candles, and covered with a rich embroidered pall. At the head of each coffin rises a slab, with a gilded inscription ; for the princesses, the slab is simple, not unlike our own monumental stones. The head-stones of the tombs of the defunct princes are decorated with a turban, or, since the introduction of the latter article of dress, with the red fez. That of Mahmoud is decorated with the imperial aigrette.

In this dismal but splendid museum, I remarked two little tombs with little red fezzes, very small, and for very young heads evidently, which were lying under the little embroidered palls of state. I forget whether they had candles too ; but their little flame of life was soon extinguished, and there was no need of many pounds of wax to typify it. These were the tombs of Mahmoud's grandsons, nephews of the present Light of the Universe, and children of his sister, the wife of Halil Pacha. Little children die in all ways ; these of the much-maligned Mahometan royal race perished by the bowstring. Sultan Mahmoud (may he rest in glory !) strangled the one ; but, having some spark of human feeling, was so moved by the wretchedness and agony of the poor bereaved mother, his daughter, that his royal heart relented towards her, and he promised that, should she ever have another child, it should be allowed to live. He died; and Abdul Medjid (may his name be blessed!) the debauched young man whom we just saw riding to the mosque, succeeded. His sister, whom he is said to have loved, became again a mother, and had a son. But she relied upon her father's word and her august brother's love, and hoped that this little one should be spared. The same accursed hand tore this infant out of its mother's bosom, and killed it. The poor woman's heart broke outright at this second calamity, and she died. But on her death-bed she sent for her brother, rebuked him as a perjurer and an assassin, and expired calling down the divine justice on his head. She lies now by the side of the two little fezzes.

Now I say this would be a fine subject for an Oriental poem. The details are dramatic and noble, and could be grandly touched by a fine artist. If the mother had borne a daughter, the child would have been safe; that perplexity might be pathetically depicted as agitating the bosom of the young wife, about to become a mother. A son is born: you can see her despair and the pitiful looks she casts on the child, and the way in which she hugs it every time the curtains of her door are removed. The Sultan hesitated probably; he allowed the infant to live for six weeks. He could not bring his royal soul to inflict pain. He yields at last; he is a martyr — to be pitied, not to be blamed. If he melts at his daughter's agony, he is a man and a father. There are men and fathers too in the much-maligned Orient.

Then comes the second act of the tragedy. The new hopes, the fond yearnings, the terrified misgivings, the timid belief, and weak confidence; the child that is born — and dies smiling prettily — and the mother's heart is rent so, that it can love, or hope, or suffer no more. Allah is God! She sleeps by the little fezzes. Hark! the guns are booming over the water, and his Highness is coming from his prayers.

After the murder of that little child, it seems to me one can never look with anything but horror upon the butcherly Herod who ordered it. The death of the seventy thousand Janissaries ascends to historic dignity, and takes rank as war. But a great Prince and Light of the Universe, who procures abortions and throttles little babies, dwindles away into such a frightful insignificance of crime, that those may respect him who will. I pity their Excellencies the Ambassadors, who are obliged to smirk and cringe to such a rascal. To do the Turks justice — and two days' walk in Constantinople will settle this fact as well as a year's residence in the city — the people do not seem in the least animated by this Herodian spirit. I never saw more kindness to children than among all classes, more fathers walking about with little solemn Mahometans in red caps and big trousers, more business going on than in the toy quarter, and in the Atmeidan. Although you may see there the Thebaic stone set up by the Emperor Theodosius, and the bronze column of serpents which Murray says was brought from Delphi, but which my guide informed me was the very one exhibited by Moses in the wilderness, yet I found the examination of these antiquities much less pleasant than to look at the many troops of children assembled on the plain to play; and to watch them as they were dragged about in little queer arobas, or painted carriages, which are there kept for hire. I have a picture of one of them now in my eyes: a little green oval machine, with flowers rudely painted round the window, out of which two smiling heads are peeping, the pictures of happiness. An old, good-humored, gray-bearded Turk is tugging the cart; and behind it walks a lady in a yakmac and yellow slippers, and a black female slave, grinning as usual, towards whom the little coach-riders are looking. A small, sturdy, barefooted Mussulman is examining the cart with some feelings of envy: he is too poor to purchase a ride for himself and the round-faced puppy-dog, which he is hugging in his arms as young ladies in our country do dolls.

All the neighborhood of the Atmeidan is exceedingly picturesque — the mosque court and cloister, where the Persians have their stalls of sweetmeats and tobacco; a superb sycamore-tree grows in the middle of this, overshadowing an aromatic fountain; great flocks of pigeons are settling in corners of the cloister, and barley is sold at the gates, with which the good-natured people feed them. From the Atmeidan you have a fine view of St. Sophia: and here stands a mosque which struck me as being much more picturesque and sumptuous — the Mosque of Sultan Achmed, with its six gleaming white minarets and its beautiful courts and trees. Any infidels may enter the court without molestation, and, looking through the barred windows of the mosque, have a view of its airy and spacious interior. A small audience of women was collected there when I looked in, squatted on the mats, and listening to a preacher, who was walking among them, and speaking with great energy. My dragoman interpreted to me the sense of a few words of his sermon: he was warning them of the danger of gadding about to public places, and of the immorality of too much talking; and, I dare say, we might have had more valuable information from him regarding the follies of womankind, had not a tall Turk clapped my interpreter on the shoulder, and pointed him to be off.

Although the ladies are veiled, and muffled with the ugliest dresses in the world, yet it appears their modesty is alarmed in spite of all the coverings which they wear. One day, in the bazaar, a fat old body, with diamond rings on her fingers, that were tinged with henné of a logwood color, came to the shop where I was purchasing slippers, with her son, a young Aga of six years of age, dressed in a braided frock-coat, with a huge tassel to his fez, exceeding fat, and of a most solemn demeanor. The young Aga came for a pair of shoes, and his contortions were so delightful as he tried them, that I remained looking on with great pleasure, wishing for Leech to be at hand to sketch his lordship and his fat mamma, who sat on the counter. That lady fancied I was looking at her, though, as far as I could see, she had the figure and complexion of a roly-poly pudding; and so, with quite a premature bashfulness, she sent me a message by the shoemaker, ordering me to walk away if I had made my purchases, for that ladies of her rank did not choose to be stared at by strangers; and I was obliged to take my leave, though with sincere regret, for the little lord had just squeezed himself into an attitude than which I never saw anything more ludicrous in General Tom Thumb. When the ladies of the Seraglio come to that bazaar with their *cortége* of infernal black eunuchs, strangers are told to move on briskly. I saw a bevy of about eight of these, with their aides-de-camp; but they were wrapped up, and looked just as vulgar and ugly as the other women, and were not, I suppose, of the most beautiful sort. The poor devils are allowed to come out, half a dozen times in the year, to spend their little wretched allowance of pocket-money in purchasing trinkets and tobacco; all the rest of the time they pursue the beautiful duties of their existence in the walls of the sacred harem.

Though strangers are not allowed to see the interior of the cage in which these birds of Paradise are confined, yet many parts of the Seraglio are free to the curiosity of visitors, who choose to drop a backsheesh here and there. I landed one morning at the Seraglio point from Galata, close by an ancient pleasure-house of the defunct Sultan; a vast broad-brimmed pavilion, that looks agreeable enough to be a dancing-room for ghosts now: there is another summer-house, the Guide-book cheerfully says, whither the Sultan goes to sport with his women and *mutes*. A regiment of infantry, with their music at their head, were marching to exercise in the outer grounds of the Seraglio; and we followed them, and had an opportunity of seeing their evolutions, and hearing their bands, upon a fine green plain under the Seraglio walls, where stands one solitary column, erected in memory of some triumph of some Byzantian emperor.

There were three battalions of the Turkish infantry exercising here; and they seemed to perform their evolutions in a very satisfactory manner: that is, they fired all together, and charged and halted in very straight lines, and bit off imaginary cartridge-tops with great fierceness and regularity, and made all their ramrods ring to measure, just like so many Christians. The men looked small, young, clumsy, and ill-built; uncomfortable in their shabby European clothes; and about the legs, especially, seemed exceedingly weak and ill-formed. Some score of military invalids were lolling in the sunshine, about a fountain and a marble summer-house that stand on the ground, watching their comrades' manœuvres (as if they could never have enough of that delightful pastime); and these sick were much better cared for than their healthy companions. Each man had two dressing-gowns, one of white cotton, and an outer wrapper of warm brown woollen. Their heads were accommodated with wadded cotton nightcaps; and it seemed to me, from their condition and from the excellent character of the military hospitals, that it would be much more wholesome to be ill than to be well in the Turkish service.

Facing this green esplanade, and the Bosphorus shining beyond it, rise the great walls of the outer Seraglio Gardens: huge masses of ancient masonry, over which peep the roofs of numerous kiosks and outhouses, amongst thick evergreens, planted so as to hide the beautiful frequenters of the place from the prying eyes and telescopes. We could not catch a glance of a single figure moving in these great pleasure-grounds. The road winds round the walls; and the outer park, which is likewise planted with trees, and diversified by garden-plots and cottages, had more the air of the outbuildings of a homely English park, than of a palace which we must all have imagined to be the most stately in the world. The most commonplace water-carts were passing here and there; roads were being repaired in the Macadamite manner; and carpenters were mending the park-palings, just as they do in Hampshire. The next thing you might fancy would be the Sultan walking out with a spud and a couple of dogs, on the way to meet the post-bag and the *Saint James's Chronicle.*

The palace is no palace at all. It is a great town of pavilions, built without order, here and there, according to the fancy of succeeding Lights of the Universe, or their favorites. The only row of domes which looked particularly regular or stately, were the kitchens. As you examined the buildings they had a ruinous, dilapidated look: they are not furnished, it is said, with particular splendor, — not a bit more elegantly than Miss Jones's seminary for young ladies, which we may be sure is much more comfortable than the extensive establishment of his Highness Abdul Medjid.

In the little stable I thought to see some marks of royal magnificence, and some horses worthy of the king of all kings. But the Sultan is said to be a very timid horseman: the animal that is always kept saddled for him did not look to be worth twenty pounds; and the rest of the horses in the shabby, dirty stalls, were small, ill-kept, common-looking brutes. You might see better, it seemed to me, at a country inn stable on any market-day.

The kitchens are the most sublime part of the Seraglio. There are nine of these great halls, for all ranks, from his Highness downwards, where many hecatombs are roasted daily, according to the accounts, and where cooking goes on with a savage Homeric grandeur. Chimneys are despised in these primitive halls; so that the roofs are black with the smoke of hundreds of furnaces, which escapes through apertures in the domes above. These, too, give the chief light in the rooms, which streams downwards, and thickens and mingles with the smoke, and so murkily lights up hundreds of swarthy figures busy about the spits and the caldrons. Close to the door by which we entered they were making pastry for the sultanas; and the chief pastry-cook, who knew my guide, invited us courteously to see the process, and partake of the delicacies prepared for those charming lips. How those sweet lips must shine after eating these puffs! First, huge sheets of dough are rolled out till the paste is about as thin as silver paper: then an artist forms the dough-muslin into a sort of drapery, curling it round and round in many fanciful and pretty shapes, until it is all got into the circumference of a round metal tray in which it is baked. Then the cake is drenched in grease most profusely; and, finally, a quantity of syrup is poured over it, when the delectable mixture is complete. The moon-faced ones are said to devour immense quantities of this wholesome food; and, in fact, are eating grease and sweetmeats from morning till night. I don't like to think what the consequences may be, or allude to the agonies which the delicate creatures must inevitably suffer.

The good-natured chief pastry-cook filled a copper basin with greasy puffs; and, dipping a dubious ladle into a large caldron, containing several gallons of syrup, poured a liberal portion over the cakes, and invited us to eat. One of the tarts was quite enough for me: and I excused myself on the plea of ill-health from imbibing any more grease and sugar. But my companion, the dragoman, finished some forty puffs in a twinkling. They slipped down his opened jaws as the sausages do down clowns' throats in a pantomime. His moustaches shone with grease, and it dripped down his beard and fingers. We thanked the smiling chief pastry-cook, and rewarded him handsomely for the tarts. It is something to have eaten of the dainties prepared for the ladies of the harem; but I think Mr. Cockle ought to get the names of the chief sultanas among the exalted patrons of his antibilious pills.

From the kitchens we passed into the second court of the Seraglio, beyond which is death. The Guide-book only hints at the dangers which would befall a stranger caught prying in the mysterious *first* court of the palace. I have read "Blue-beard," and don't care for peeping into forbidden doors; so that the second court was quite enough for me; the pleasure of beholding it being heightened, as it were, by the notion of the invisible danger sitting next door, with uplifted scimitar ready to fall on you — present though not seen.

A cloister runs along one side of this court; opposite is the hall of the divan, "large but low, covered with lead, and gilt, after the Moorish manner, plain enough." The Grand Vizier sits in this place, and the ambassadors used to wait here, and be conducted hence on horseback, attired with robes of honor. But the ceremony is now, I believe, discontinued; the English envoy, at any rate, is not allowed to receive any backsheesh, and goes away as he came, in the habit of his own nation. On the right is a door leading into the interior of the Seraglio; *none pass through it but such as are sent for*, the Guide-book says: it is impossible to top the terror of that description.

About this door lads and servants were lolling, ichoglans and pages, with lazy looks and shabby dresses; and among them, sunning himself sulkily on a bench, a poor old fat, wrinkled, dismal white eunuch, with little fat white hands, and a great head sunk into his chest, and two sprawling little legs that seemed incapable to hold up his bloated old body. He squeaked out some surly reply to my friend the dragoman, who, softened and sweetened by the tarts he had just been devouring, was, no doubt, anxious to be polite: and the poor worthy fellow walked away rather crestfallen at this return of his salutation, and hastened me out of the place.

The palace of the Seraglio, the cloister with marble pillars, the hall of the ambassadors, the impenetrable gate guarded by eunuchs and ichoglans, have a romantic look in print; but not so in reality. Most of the marble is wood, almost all the gilding is faded, the guards are shabby, the foolish perspectives painted on the walls are half cracked off. The place looks like Vauxhall in the daytime.

We passed out of the second court under THE SUBLIME PORTE — which is like a fortified gate of a German town of the middle ages — into the outer court, round which are public offices, hospitals, and dwellings of the multifarious servants of the palace. This place is very wide and picturesque: there is a pretty church of Byzantine architecture at the further end; and in the midst of the court a magnificent plane-tree, of prodigious dimensions and fabulous age according to the guides; St. Sophia towers in the further distance: and from here, perhaps, is the best view of its light swelling domes and beautiful proportions. The Porte itself, too, forms an excellent subject for the sketcher, if the officers of the court will permit him to design it. I made the attempt, and a couple of Turkish beadles looked on very good-naturedly for some time at the progress of the drawing; but a good number of other spectators speedily joined them, and made a crowd, which is not permitted, it would seem, in the Seraglio; so I was told to pack up my portfolio, and remove the cause of the disturbance, and lost my drawing of the Ottoman Porte.

I don't think I have anything more to say about the city which has not been much better told by graver travellers. I, with them, could see (perhaps it was the preaching of the politicians that warned me of the fact) that we are looking on at the last days of an empire; and heard many stories of weakness, disorder, and oppression. I even saw a Turkish lady drive up to Sultan Achmet's mosque *in a brougham*. Is not that a subject to moralize upon? And might one not draw endless conclusions from it, that the knell of the Turkish dominion is rung; that the European spirit and institutions once admitted can never be rooted out again; and that the scepticism prevalent amongst the higher orders must descend ere very long to the lower; and the cry of the muezzin from the mosque become a mere ceremony?

But as I only stayed eight days in this place, and knew not a syllable of the language, perhaps it is as well to pretermit any disquisitions about the spirit of the people. I can only say that they looked to be very good-natured, handsome and lazy; that the women's yellow slippers are very ugly; that the kabobs at the shop hard by the Rope Bazaar are very hot and good; and that at the Armenian cook-shops they serve you delicious fish, and a stout raisin wine of no small merit. There came in, as we sat and dined there at sunset, a good old Turk, who called for a penny fish, and sat down under a tree very humbly, and ate it with his own bread. We made that jolly old Mussulman happy with a quart of the raisin wine; and his eyes twinkled with every fresh glass, and he wiped his old beard delighted, and talked and chirped a good deal, and, I dare say, told us the whole state of the empire. He was the only Mussulman with whom I attained any degree of intimacy during my stay in Constantinople; and you will see that, for obvious reasons, I cannot divulge the particulars of our conversation.

"You have nothing to say, and you own it," says somebody: "then why write?" That question perhaps (between ourselves) I have put likewise; and yet, my dear sir, there are *some* things worth remembering even in this brief letter: that woman in the brougham is an idea of significance: that comparison of the Seraglio to Vauxhall in the daytime is a true and real one; from both of which your own great soul and ingenious philosophic spirit may draw conclusions, that I myself have modestly forborne to press. You are too clever to require a moral to be tacked to all the fables you read, as is done for children in the spelling-books; else I would tell you that the government of the Ottoman Porte seems to be as rotten, as wrinkled, and as feeble as the old eunuch I saw crawling about it in the sun; that when the lady drove up in a brougham to Sultan Achmet, I felt that the schoolmaster was really abroad; and that the crescent will go out before that luminary, as meekly as the moon does before the sun.

CHAPTER VIII.

RHODES.

THE sailing of a vessel direct for Jaffa brought a great number of passengers together, and our decks were covered with Christian, Jew, and Heathen. In the cabin we were Poles and Russians, Frenchmen, Germans, Spaniards, and Greeks; on the deck were squatted several little colonies of people of different race and persuasion. There was a Greek Papa, a noble figure with a flowing and venerable white beard, who had been living on bread-and-water for I don't know how many years, in order to save a little money to make the pilgrimage to Jerusalem. There were several families of Jewish Rabbis, who celebrated their " feast of tabernacles " on board; their chief men performing worship twice or thrice a day, dressed in their pontifical habits, and bound with phylacteries; and there were Turks, who had their own ceremonies and usages, and wisely kept aloof from their neighbors of Israel.

The dirt of these children of captivity exceeds all possibility of description; the profusion of stinks which they raised, the grease of their venerable garments and faces, the horrible messes cooked in the filthy pots, and devoured with the nasty fingers, the squalor of mats, pots, old bedding, and foul carpets of our Hebrew friends, could hardly be painted by Swift, in his dirtiest mood, and cannot be, of course, attempted by my timid and genteel pen. What would they say in Baker Street to some sights with which our new friends favored us? What would your ladyship have said if you had seen the interesting Greek nun combing her hair over the cabin — combing it with the natural fingers, and, averse to slaughter, flinging the delicate little intruders, which she found in the course of her investigation, gently into the great cabin? Our attention was a good deal occupied in watching the strange ways and customs of the various comrades of ours.

The Jews were refugees from Poland, going to lay their bones to rest in the valley of Jehoshaphat, and performing with exceeding rigor the offices of their religion. At morning and evening you were sure to see the chiefs of the families, arrayed in white robes, bowing over their books, at prayer. Once a week, on the eve before the Sabbath, there was a general

washing in Jewry, which sufficed until the ensuing **Friday.**
The men wore long gowns, and caps of fur, or else broad-
brimmed hats, or, in service-time, bound on their heads little
iron boxes, with the sacred name engraved on them. Among
the lads there were some beautiful faces; and among the women your humble servant discovered one who was a perfect rose-
bud of beauty when first emerging from her Friday's toilette,
and for a day or two afterwards, until each succeeding day's
smut darkened those fresh and delicate cheeks of hers. We
had some very rough weather in the course of the passage
from Constantinople to Jaffa, and the sea washed over and
over our Israelitish friends and their baggages and bundles;
but though they were said to be rich, they would not afford to
pay for cabin shelter. One father of a family, finding his progeny half drowned in a squall, vowed he *would* pay for a cabin;
but the weather was somewhat finer the next day, and he could
not squeeze out his dollars, and the ship's authorities would not
admit him except upon payment.

This unwillingness to part with money is not only found
amongst the followers of Moses, but in those of Mahomet, and
Christians too. When we went to purchase in the bazaars,
after offering money for change, the honest fellows would frequently keep back several piastres, and when urged to refund,
would give most dismally: and begin doling out penny by
penny, and utter pathetic prayers to their customer not to take
any more. I bought five or six pounds' worth of Broussa silks
for the womenkind, in the bazaar at Constantinople, and the
rich Armenian who sold them begged for three-halfpence to
pay his boat to Galata. There is something naïf and amusing in this exhibition of cheatery — this simple cringing, and
wheedling, and passion for twopence-halfpenny. It was pleasant to give a millionnaire beggar an alms, and laugh in his face
and say, "There, Dives, there's a penny for you: be happy,
you poor old swindling scoundrel, as far as a penny goes." I
used to watch these Jews on shore, and making bargains with
one another as soon as they came on board; the battle between
vender and purchaser was an agony — they shrieked, clasped
hands, appealed to one another passionately; their handsome,
noble faces assumed a look of woe — quite an heroic eagerness
and sadness about a farthing.

Ambassadors from our Hebrews descended at Rhodes to
buy provisions, and it was curious to see their dealings: there
was our venerable Rabbi, who, robed in white and silver, and
bending over his book at the morning service, looked like a

patriarch, and whom I saw chaffering about a fowl with a brother Rhodian Israelite. How they fought over the body of that lean animal! The street swarmed with Jews : goggling eyes looked out from the old carved casements — hooked noses issued from the low antique doors — Jew boys driving donkeys, Hebrew mothers nursing children, dusky, tawdry, ragged young beauties and most venerable gray-bearded fathers were all gathered round about the affair of the hen! And at the same time that our Rabbi was arranging the price of it, his children were instructed to procure bundles of green branches to decorate the ship during their feast. Think of the centuries during which these wonderful people have remained unchanged ; and how, from the days of Jacob downwards, they have believed and swindled!

The Rhodian Jews, with their genius for filth, have made their quarter of the noble, desolate old town, the most ruinous and wretched of all. The escutcheons of the proud old knights are still carved over the doors, whence issue these miserable greasy hucksters and pedlars. The Turks respected these emblems of the brave enemies whom they had overcome, and left them untouched. When the French seized Malta they were by no means so delicate : they effaced armorial bearings with their usual hot-headed eagerness ; and a few years after they had torn down the coats-of-arms of the gentry, the heroes of Malta and Egypt were busy devising heraldry for themselves, and were wild to be barons and counts of the empire.

The chivalrous relics at Rhodes are very superb. I know of no buildings whose stately and picturesque aspect seems to correspond better with one's notions of their proud founders. The towers and gates are warlike and strong, but beautiful and aristocratic : you see that they must have been high-bred gentlemen who built them. The edifices appear in almost as perfect a condition as when they were in the occupation of the noble Knights of St. John ; and they have this advantage over modern fortifications, that they are a thousand times more picturesque. Ancient war condescended to ornament itself, and built fine carved castles and vaulted gates : whereas, to judge from Gibraltar and Malta, nothing can be less romantic than the modern military architecture ; which sternly regards the fighting, without in the least heeding the war-paint. Some of the huge artillery with which the place was defended still lies in the bastions ; and the touch-holes of the guns are preserved by being covered with rusty old corselets, worn by defenders of the fort three hundred years ago. The Turks, who battered down chivalry, seem to be waiting their turn of destruction now. In walking through Rhodes one is strangely affected by witnessing the signs of this double decay. For instance, in the streets of the knights, you see noble houses, surmounted by noble escutcheons of superb knights, who lived there, and prayed, and quarrelled, and murdered the Turks; and were the most gallant pirates of the inland seas; and made vows of chastity, and robbed and ravished; and, professing humility, would admit none but nobility into their order; and died recommending themselves to sweet St. John, and calmly hoping for heaven in consideration of all the heathen they had slain. When this superb fraternity was obliged to yield to courage as great as theirs, faith as sincere, and to robbers even more dexterous and audacious than the noblest knight who ever sang a canticle to the Virgin, these halls were filled by magnificent Pashas and Agas, who lived here in the intervals of war, and having conquered its best champions, despised Christendom and chivalry pretty much as an Englishman despises a Frenchman. Now the famous house is let to a shabby merchant, who has his little beggarly shop in the bazaar; to a small officer, who ekes out his wretched pension by swindling, and who gets his pay in bad coin. Mahometanism pays in pewter now, in place of silver and gold. The lords of the world have run to seed. The powerless old sword frightens nobody now — the steel is turned to pewter too, somehow, and will no longer shear a Christian head off any shoulders. In the Crusades my wicked sympathies have always been with the Turks. They seem to me the best Christians of the two; more humane, less brutally presumptuous about their own merits, and more generous in esteeming their neighbors. As far as I can get at the authentic story, Saladin is a pearl of refinement compared to the brutal beef-eating Richard — about whom Sir Walter Scott has led all the world astray.

When shall we have a real account of those times and heroes — no good-humored pageant, like those of the Scott romances — but a real authentic story to instruct and frighten honest people of the present day, and make them thankful that the grocer governs the world now in place of the baron? Meanwhile a man of tender feelings may be pardoned for twaddling a little over this sad spectacle of the decay of two of the great institutions of the world. Knighthood is gone — amen; it expired with dignity, its face to the foe: and old Mahometanism is lingering about just ready to drop. But it is unseemly to see such a Grand Potentate in such a state of decay: the son of

Bajazet Ilderim insolvent; the descendants of the Prophet bullied by Calmucs and English and whippersnapper Frenchmen; the Fountain of Magnificence done up, and obliged to coin pewter! Think of the poor dear houris in Paradise, how sad they must look as the arrivals of the Faithful become less and less frequent every day. I can fancy the place beginning to wear the fatal Vauxhall look of the Seraglio, and which has pursued me ever since I saw it: the fountains of eternal wine are beginning to run rather dry, and of a questionable liquor; the ready-roasted-meat trees may cry, "Come eat me," every now and then, in a faint voice, without any gravy in it — but the Faithful begin to doubt about the quality of the victuals. Of nights you may see the houris sitting sadly under them, darning their faded muslins: Ali, Omar, and the Imaums are reconciled and have gloomy consultations: and the Chief of the Faithful himself, the awful camel-driver, the supernatural husband of Khadijah, sits alone in a tumble-down kiosk, thinking moodily of the destiny that is impending over him; and of the day when his gardens of bliss shall be as vacant as the bankrupt Olympus.

All the town of Rhodes has this appearance of decay and ruin, except a few consuls' houses planted on the sea-side, here and there, with bright flags flaunting in the sun; fresh paint; English crockery; shining mahogany, &c., — so many emblems of the new prosperity of *their* trade, while the old inhabitants were going to rack — the fine Church of St. John, converted into a mosque, is a ruined church, with a ruined mosque inside; the fortifications are mouldering away, as much as time will let them. There was considerable bustle and stir about the little port; but it was a bustle of people who looked for the most part to be beggars; and I saw no shop in the bazaar that seemed to have the value of a pedlar's pack.

I took, by way of guide, a young fellow from Berlin, a journeyman shoemaker, who had just been making a tour in Syria, and who professed to speak both Arabic and Turkish quite fluently — which I thought he might have learned when he was a student at college, before he began his profession of shoemaking; but I found he only knew about three words of Turkish, which were produced on every occasion, as I walked under his guidance through the desolate streets of the noble old town. We went out upon the lines of fortification, through an ancient gate and guard-house, where once a chapel probably stood, and of which the roofs were richly carved and gilded.

A ragged squad of Turkish soldiers lolled about the gate now ; a couple of boys on a donkey ; a grinning slave on a mule ; a pair of women flapping along in yellow papooshes ; a basket-maker sitting under an antique carved portal, and chanting or howling as he plaited his osiers : a peaceful well of water, at which knights' chargers had drunk, and at which the double-boyed donkey was now refreshing himself — would have made a pretty picture for a sentimental artist.   As he sits, and endeavors to make a sketch of this plaintive little comedy, a shabby dignitary of the island comes clattering by on a thirty-shilling horse, and two or three of the ragged soldiers leave their pipes to salute him as he passes under the Gothic arch-way.

The astonishing brightness and clearness of the sky under which the island seemed to bask, struck .me as surpassing anything I had seen — not even at Cadiz, or the Piræus, had I seen sands so yellow, or water so magnificently blue.   The houses of the people along the shore were but poor tenements, with humble court-yards and gardens ; but every fig-tree was gilded and bright, as if it were in an Hesperian orchard ; the palms, planted here and there, rose with a sort of halo of light round about them ; the creepers on the walls quite dazzled with the brilliancy of their flowers and leaves ; the people lay in the cool shadows, happy and idle, with handsome solemn faces ; nobody seemed to be at work ; they only talked a very little, as if idleness and silence were a condition of the delight-ful shining atmosphere in which they lived.

We went down to an old mosque by the sea-shore, with a cluster of ancient domes hard by it, blazing in the sunshine, and carved all over with names of Allah, and titles of old pirates and generals who reposed there.   The guardian of the mosque sat in the garden-court, upon a high wooden pulpit, lazily wag-ging his body to and fro, and singing the praises of the Prophet gently through his nose, as the breeze stirred through the trees overhead, and cast chequered and changing shadows over the paved court, and the little fountains, and the nasal psalmist on his perch.   On one side was the mosque, into which you could see, with its white walls and cool matted floor, and quaint carved pulpit and ornaments, and nobody at prayers.   In the middle distance rose up the noble towers and battlements of the knightly town, with the deep sea-line behind them.

It really seemed as if everybody was to have a sort of sober cheerfulness, and must yield to indolence under this charming atmosphere.   I went into the court-yard by the sea-shore (where

GATE OF THE GRAND MASTER'S PALACE.

a few lazy ships were lying, with no one on board), and found it was the prison of the place. The door was as wide open as Westminster Hall. Some prisoners, one or two soldiers and functionaries, and some prisoners' wives, were lolling under an arcade by a fountain ; other criminals were strolling about here and there, their chains clinking quite cheerfully : and they and the guards and officials came up chatting quite friendly together, and gazed languidly over the portfolio, as I was endeavoring to get the likeness of one or two of these comfortable malefactors. One old and wrinkled she-criminal, whom I had selected on account of the peculiar hideousness of her countenance, covered it up with a dirty cloth, at which there was a general roar of laughter among this good-humored auditory of cut-throats, pickpockets, and policemen. The only symptom of a prison about the place was a door, across which a couple of sentinels were stretched, yawning ; while within lay three freshly-caught pirates, chained by the leg. They had committed some murders of a very late date, and were awaiting sentence ; but their wives were allowed to communicate freely with them : and it seemed to me, that if half a dozen friends would set them free, and they themselves had energy enough to move, the sentinels would be a great deal too lazy to walk after them.

The combined influence of Rhodes and Ramazan, I suppose, had taken possession of my friend the Schuster-gesell from Berlin. As soon as he received his fee, he cut me at once, and went and lay down by a fountain near the port, and ate grapes out of a dirty pocket-handkerchief. Other Christian idlers lay near him, dozing, or sprawling in the boats, or listlessly munching watermelons. Along the coffee-houses of the quay sat hundreds more, with no better employment ; and the captain of the " Iberia " and his officers, and several of the passengers in that famous steamship, were in this company, being idle with all their might. Two or three adventurous young men went off to see the valley where the dragon was killed ; but others, more susceptible of the real influence of the island, I am sure would not have moved though we had been told that the Colossus himself was taking a walk half a mile off.

CHAPTER IX.

THE WHITE SQUALL.

On deck, beneath the awning,
I dozing lay and yawning;
It was the gray of dawning,
    Ere yet the sun arose;
And above the funnel's roaring,
And the fitful wind's deploring,
I heard the cabin snoring
    With universal nose.
I could hear the passengers snorting,
I envied their disporting,
Vainly I was courting
    The pleasure of a doze.

So I lay, and wondered why light
Came not, and watched the twilight
And the glimmer of the skylight,
    That shot across the deck;
And the binnacle pale and steady,
And the dull glimpse of the dead-eye,
And the sparks in fiery eddy,
    That whirled from the chimney neck:
In our jovial floating prison
There was sleep from fore to mizzen,
And never a star had risen
    The hazy sky to speck.

Strange company we harbored;
We'd a hundred Jews to larboard,
Unwashed, uncombed, unbarbered,
    Jews black, and brown, and gray;
With terror it would seize ye,
And make your souls uneasy,
To see those Rabbis greasy,
    Who did nought but scratch and pray:
Their dirty children pucking,
Their dirty saucepans cooking,
Their dirty fingers hooking
    Their swarming fleas away.

To starboard Turks and Greeks were,
Whiskered, and brown their cheeks were,
Enormous wide their breeks were,
    Their pipes did puff alway ;
Each on his mat allotted,
In silence smoked and squatted,
Whilst round their children trotted,
    In pretty, pleasant play.
He can't but smile who traces
The smiles on those brown faces,
And the pretty prattling graces
    Of those small heathens gay.

And so the hours kept tolling,
And through the ocean rolling,
Went the brave " Iberia " bowling
Before the break of day ——
When a SQUALL upon a sudden
Came o'er the waters scudding ;
And the clouds began to gather,
And the sea was lashed to lather,
And the lowering thunder grumbled,
And the lightning jumped and tumbled.
And the ship, and all the ocean,
Woke up in wild commotion.
Then the wind set up a howling,
And the poodle-dog a yowling,
And the cocks began a crowing,
And the old cow raised a lowing,
As she heard the tempest blowing ;
And fowls and geese did cackle,
And the cordage and the tackle
Began to shriek and crackle ;
And the spray dashed o'er the funnels,
And down the deck in runnels ;
And the rushing water soaks all,
From the seamen in the fo'ksal
To the stokers, whose black faces
Peer out of their bed-places ;
And the captain he was bawling,
And the sailors pulling, hauling ;
And the quarter-deck tarpauling
Was shivered in the squalling ;

And the passengers awaken,
Most pitifully shaken ;
And the steward jumps up, and hastens
For the necessary basins.

Then the Greeks they groaned and quivered,
And they knelt, and moaned, and shivered,
As the plunging waters met them,
And splashed and overset them ;
And they call in their emergence
Upon countless saints and virgins ;
And their marrowbones are bended,
And they think the world is ended.

And the Turkish women for'ard
Were frightened and behorror'd ;
And, shrieking and bewildering,
The mothers clutched their children ;
The men sung " Allah Illah !
Mashallah Bismillah ! "
As the warring waters doused them,
And splashed them and soused them ;
And they called upon the Prophet,
And thought but little of it.

Then all the fleas in Jewry
Jumped up and bit like fury ;
And the progeny of Jacob
Did on the main-deck wake up
(I wot those greasy Rabbins
Would never pay for cabins) ;
And each man moaned and jabbered in
His filthy Jewish gaberdine,
In woe and lamentation,
And howling consternation.
And the splashing water drenches
Their dirty brats and wenches ;
And they crawl from bales and benches,
In a hundred thousand stenches.

This was the White Squall famous
Which latterly o'ercame us,
And which all will well remember
On the 28th September ;

When a Prussian Captain of Lancers
(Those tight-laced, whiskered prancers)
Came on the deck astonished,
By that wild squall admonished,
And wondering cried, "Potztausend!
Wie ist der Sturm jetzt brausend!"
And looked at Captain Lewis,
Who calmly stood and blew his
Cigar in all the bustle,
And scorned the tempest's tussle.
And oft we've thought thereafter
How he beat the storm to laughter;
For well he knew his vessel
With that vain wind could wrestle;
And when a wreck we thought her
And doomed ourselves to slaughter,
How gayly he fought her,
And through the hubbub brought her,
And, as the tempest caught her,
Cried, "GEORGE! SOME BRANDY AND WATER!"

And when, its force expended,
The harmless storm was ended,
And, as the sunrise splendid
Came blushing o'er the sea;
I thought, as day was breaking,
My little girls were waking,
And smiling, and making
A prayer at home for me.

CHAPTER X.

TELMESSUS. — BEYROUT.

THERE should have been a poet in our company to describe
that charming little bay of Glaucus, into which we entered on the
26th of September, in the first steamboat that ever disturbed its
beautiful waters. You can't put down in prose that delicious
episode of natural poetry; it ought to be done in a symphony,
full of sweet melodies and swelling harmonies; or sung in a

strain of clear crystal iambics, such as Milnes knows how to write. A mere map, drawn in words, gives the mind no notion of that exquisite nature. What do mountains become in type, or rivers in Mr. Vizetelly's best brevier? Here lies the sweet bay, gleaming peaceful in the rosy sunshine : green islands dip here and there in its waters ; purple mountains swell circling round it; and towards them, rising from the bay, stretches a rich green plain, fruitful with herbs and various foliage, in the midst of which the white houses twinkle. I can see a little minaret, and some spreading palm-trees ; but, beyond these, the description would answer as well for Bantry Bay as for Makri. You could write so far, nay, much more particularly and grandly, without seeing the place at all, and after reading Beaufort's "Caramania," which gives you not the least notion of it.

Suppose the great hydrographer of the Admiralty himself can't describe it, who surveyed the place ; suppose Mr. Fellowes, who discovered it afterwards — suppose, I say, Sir John Fellowes, Knt., can't do it (and I defy any man of imagination to get an impression of Telmessus from his book) — can you, vain man, hope to try? The effect of the artist, as I take it, ought to be, to produce upon his hearer's mind, by his art, an effect something similar to that produced on his own by the sight of the natural object. Only music, or the best poetry, can do this. Keats's " Ode to the Grecian Urn " is the best description I know of that sweet, old, silent ruin of Telmessus. After you have once seen it, the remembrance remains with you, like a tune from Mozart, which he seems to have caught out of heaven, and which rings sweet harmony in your ears for ever after ! It's a benefit for all after life ! You have but to shut your eyes, and think, and recall it, and the delightful vision comes smiling back, to your order ! — the divine air — the delicious little pageant, which nature set before you on this lucky day.

Here is the entry made in the note-book on the eventful day : — " In the morning steamed into the Bay of Glaucus — landed at Makri — cheerful old desolate village — theatre by the beautiful sea-shore — great fertility, oleanders — a palm-tree in the midst of the village, spreading out like a Sultan's aigrette — sculptured caverns, or tombs, up the mountain — camels over the bridge.

Perhaps it is best for a man of fancy to make his own landscape out of these materials : to group the couched camels under the plane-trees ; the little crowd of wandering, ragged heathens come down to the calm water, to behold the nearing steamer ;

to fancy a mountain, in the sides of which some scores of tombs are rudely carved; pillars and porticos, and Doric entablatures.   But it is of the little theatre that he must make the most beautiful picture — a charming little place of festival, lying out on the shore, and looking over the sweet bay and the swelling purple islands.   No theatre-goer ever looked out on a fairer scene.   It encourages poetry, idleness, delicious sensual reverie.   O Jones! friend of my heart! would you not like to be a white-robed Greek, lolling languidly on the cool benches here, and pouring compliments (in the Ionic dialect) into the rosy ears of Neæra?   Instead of Jones, your name should be Ionides; instead of a silk hat, you should wear a chaplet of roses in your hair: you would not listen to the choruses they were singing on the stage, for the voice of the fair one would be whispering a rendezvous for the *mesonuktiais horais*, and my Ionides would have no ear for aught beside.   Yonder, in the mountain, they would carve a Doric cave temple, to receive your urn when all was done; and you would be accompanied thither by a dirge of the surviving Ionidæ.   The caves of the dead are empty now, however, and their place knows them not any more among the festal haunts of the living.   But, by way of supplying the choric melodies sung here in old time, one of our companions mounted on the scene and spouted,

"My name is Norval."

On the same day we lay to for a while at another ruined theatre, that of Antiphilos.   The Oxford men, fresh with recollections of the little-go, bounded away up the hill on which it lies to the ruin, measured the steps of the theatre, and calculated the width of the scene; while others, less active, watched them with telescopes from the ship's sides, as they plunged in and out of the stones and hollows.

Two days after the scene was quite changed.   We were out of sight of the classical country, and lay in St. George's Bay, behind a huge mountain, upon which St. George fought the dragon, and rescued the lovely Lady Sabra, the King of Babylon's daughter.   The Turkish fleet was lying about us, commanded by that Halil Pacha whose two children the two last Sultans murdered.   The crimson flag, with the star and crescent, floated at the stern of his ship.   Our diplomatist put on his uniform and cordons, and paid his Excellency a visit.   He spoke in rapture, when he returned, of the beauty and order of the ship, and the urbanity of the infidel admiral.   He sent us bottles of ancient Cyprus wine to drink: and the captain of her

Majesty's ship, "Trump," alongside which we were lying, confirmed that good opinion of the Capitan Pasha which the reception of the above present led us to entertain, by relating many instances of his friendliness and hospitalities. Captain G—— said the Turkish ships were as well manned, as well kept, and as well manœuvred, as any vessels in any service; and intimated a desire to command a Turkish seventy-four, and a perfect willingness to fight her against a French ship of the same size. But I heartily trust he will neither embrace the Mahometan opinions, nor be called upon to engage any seventy-four whatever. If he do, let us hope he will have his own men to fight with. If the crew of the "Trump" were all like the crew of the captain's boat, they need fear no two hundred and fifty men out of any country, with any Joinville at their head. We were carried on shore by this boat. For two years, during which the "Trump" had been lying off Beyrout, none of the men but these eight had ever set foot on shore. Mustn't it be a happy life? We were landed at the busy quay of Beyrout, flanked by the castle that the fighting old commodore half battered down.

Along the Beyrout quays, civilization flourishes under the flags of the consul, which are streaming out over the yellow buildings in the clear air. Hither she brings from England her produce of marine stores and woollens, her crockeries, her portable soups, and her bitter ale. Hither she has brought politeness, and the last modes from Paris. They were exhibited in the person of a pretty lady, superintending the great French store, and who, seeing a stranger sketching on the quay, sent forward a man with a chair to accommodate that artist, and greeted him with a bow and a smile, such as only can be found in France. Then she fell to talking to a young French officer with a beard, who was greatly smitten with her. They were making love just as they do on the Boulevard. An Arab porter left his bales, and the camel he was unloading, to come and look at the sketch. Two stumpy, flat-faced Turkish soldiers, in red caps and white undresses, peered over the paper. A noble little Lebanonian girl, with a deep yellow face, and curly dun-colored hair, and a blue tattooed chin, and for all clothing a little ragged shift of blue cloth, stood by like a little statue, holding her urn, and stared with wondering brown eyes. How magnificently blue the water was! — how bright the flags and buildings as they shone above it, and the lines of the rigging tossing in the bay! The white crests of the blue waves jumped and sparkled like quicksilver; the shadows were as broad and cool as the lights were brilliant and rosy; the battered old towers of the commodore looked quite cheerful in the delicious atmosphere; and the mountains beyond were of an amethyst color. The French officer and the lady went on chattering quite happily about love, the last new bonnet, or the battle of Isley, or the "Juif Errant." How neatly her gown and sleeves fitted her pretty little person! We had not seen a woman for a month except honest Mrs. Flanigan, the stewardess, and the ladies of our party, and the tips of the noses of the Constantinople beauties as they passed by leering from their yakmacs, waddling and plapping in their odious yellow papooshes.

And this day is to be marked with a second white stone, for having given the lucky writer of the present, occasion to behold a second beauty. This was a native Syrian damsel, who bore the sweet name of Mariam. So it was she stood as two of us (I mention the number for fear of scandal) took her picture.

So it was that the good-natured black cook looked behind her young mistress, with a benevolent grin, that only the admirable Leslie could paint.

Mariam was the sister of the young guide whom we hired to show us through the town, and to let us be cheated in the purchase of gilt scarfs, and handkerchiefs, which strangers think proper to buy. And before the above authentic drawing could be made, many were the stratagems the wily artists were obliged to employ, to subdue the shyness of the little Mariam. In the first place, she would stand behind the door (from which in the darkness her beautiful black eyes gleamed out like penny tapers); nor could the entreaties of her brother and mamma bring her from that hiding-place. In order to conciliate the latter, we began by making a picture of her too — that is, not of her, who was an enormous old fat woman in yellow, quivering all over with strings of pearls, and necklaces of sequins, and other ornaments, the which descended from her neck, and down her ample stomacher: we did not depict that big old woman, who would have been frightened at an accurate representation of her own enormity; but an ideal being, all grace and beauty, dressed in her costume, and still simpering before me in my sketch-book like a lady in a book of fashions.

This portrait was shown to the old woman, who handed it over to the black cook, who, grinning, carried it to little Mariam — and the result was, that the young creature stepped forward, and submitted; and has come over to Europe as you see.

A very snug and happy family did this of Mariam's appear to be. If you could judge by all the laughter and giggling, by the splendor of the women's attire, by the neatness of the little house, prettily decorated with arabesque paintings, neat mats, and gay carpets, they were a family well to do in the Beyrout world, and lived with as much comfort as any Europeans. They had one book; and, on the wall of the principal apart-ment, a black picture of the Virgin, whose name is borne by pretty Mariam.

The camels and the soldiers, the bazaars and khans, the fountains and awnings, which chequer, with such delightful variety of light and shade, the alleys and markets of an Oriental town, are to be seen in Beyrout in perfection; and an artist might here employ himself for months with advantage and pleasure. A new costume was here added to the motley and picturesque assembly of dresses. This was the dress of the blue-veiled women from the Lebanon, stalking solemnly through the markets, with huge horns, near a yard high, on their foreheads. For thousands of years, since the time the Hebrew prophets wrote, these horns have so been exalted in the Lebanon.

At night Captain Lewis gave a splendid ball and supper to the "Trump." We had the "Trump's" band to perform the music; and a grand sight it was to see the captain himself enthusiastically leading on the drum. Blue lights and rockets were burned from the yards of our ship; which festive signals were answered presently from the " Trump," and from another English vessel in the harbor.

They must have struck the Capitan Pasha with wonder, for he sent his secretary on board of us to inquire what the fire-works meant. And the worthy Turk had scarcely put his foot on the deck, when he found himself seized round the waist by one of the " Trump's " officers, and whirling round the deck in a waltz, to his own amazement, and the huge delight of the company. His face of wonder and gravity, as he went on twirling, could not have been exceeded by that of a dancing dervish at Scutari ; and the manner in which he managed to *enjamber* the waltz excited universal applause.

I forget whether he accommodated himself to European ways so much further as to drink champagne at supper-time ; to say that he did would be telling tales out of school, and might inter-fere with the future advancement of that jolly dancing Turk.

We made acquaintance with another of the Sultan's sub-jects, who, I fear, will have occasion to doubt of the honor of the English nation, after the foul treachery with which he was treated.

Among the occupiers of the little bazaar watchboxes, ven-ders of embroidered handkerchiefs and other articles of showy Eastern haberdashery, was a good-looking, neat young fellow, who spoke English very fluently, and was particularly atten-tive to all the passengers on board our ship. This gentleman was not only a pocket-handkerchief merchant in the bazaar, but earned a further livelihood by letting out mules and donkeys ; and he kept a small lodging-house, or inn, for travellers, as we were informed.

No wonder he spoke good English, and was exceedingly polite and well-bred ; for the worthy man had passed some time in England, and in the best society too. That humble haberdasher at Beyrout had been a lion here, at the very best houses of the great people, and had actually made his appear-ance at Windsor, where he was received as a Syrian Prince, and treated with great hospitality by royalty itself.

I don't know what waggish propensity moved one of the officers of the " Trump " to say that there was an equerry of his Royal Highness the Prince on board, and to point me out as the dignified personage in question. So the Syrian Prince was introduced to the royal equerry, and a great many compli-ments passed between us. I even had the audacity to state that on my very last interview with my royal master, his Royal Highness had said, " Colonel Titmarsh, when you go to Beyrout, you will make special inquiries regarding my interesting friend Cogia Hassan."

Poor Cogia Hassan (I forget whether that was his name, but it is as good as another) was overpowered with this royal message; and we had an intimate conversation together, at which the waggish officer of the "Trump" assisted with the greatest glee.

But see the consequences of deceit! The next day, as we were getting under way, who should come on board but my friend the Syrian Prince, most eager for a last interview with the Windsor equerry; and he begged me to carry his protestations of unalterable fidelity to the gracious consort of her Majesty. Nor was this all. Cogia Hassan actually produced a great box of sweetmeats, of which he begged my excellency to accept, and a little figure of a doll dressed in the costume of Lebanon. Then the punishment of imposture began to be felt severely by me. How to accept the poor devil's sweetmeats? How to refuse them? And as we know that one fib leads to another, so I was obliged to support the first falsehood by another; and putting on a dignified air — "Cogia Hassan," says I, "I am surprised you don't know the habits of the British Court better, and are not aware that our gracious master solemnly forbids his servants to accept any sort of backsheesh upon our travels."

So Prince Cogia Hassan went over the side with his chest of sweetmeats, but insisted on leaving the doll, which may be worth twopence-halfpenny; of which, and of the costume of the women of Lebanon, the following is an accurate likeness.*

CHAPTER XI.

A DAY AND NIGHT IN SYRIA.

WHEN, after being for five whole weeks at sea, with a general belief that at the end of a few days the marine malady leaves you for good, you find that a brisk wind and a heavy rolling swell create exactly the same inward effects which they occasioned at the very commencement of the voyage — you begin to fancy that you are unfairly dealt with: and I, for my part, had thought of complaining to the company of this atrocious

* This refers to an illustrated edition of the work.

violation of the rules of their prospectus; but we were perpetually coming to anchor in various ports, at which intervals of peace and good humor were restored to us.

On the 3rd of October our cable rushed with a huge rattle into the blue sea before Jaffa, at a distance of considerably more than a mile off the town, which lay before us very clear, with the flags of the consuls flaring in the bright sky, and making a cheerful and hospitable show. The houses a great heap of sun-baked stones, surmounted here and there by minarets and countless little whitewashed domes; a few date-trees spread out their fan-like heads over these dull-looking buildings; long sands stretched away on either side, with low purple hills behind them; we could see specks of camels crawling over these yellow plains; and those persons who were about to land, had the leisure to behold the sea-spray flashing over the sands, and over a heap of black rocks which lie before the entry to the town. The swell is very great, the passage between the rocks narrow, and the danger sometimes considerable. So the guide began to entertain the ladies and other passengers in the huge country boat which brought us from the steamer, with an agreeable story of a lieutenant and eight seamen of one of her Majesty's ships, who were upset, dashed to pieces, and drowned upon these rocks, through which two men and two boys, with a very moderate portion of clothing, each standing and pulling half an oar — there were but two oars between them, and another by way of rudder — were endeavoring to guide us.

When the danger of the rocks and surf was passed, came another danger of the hideous brutes in brown skins and the briefest shirts, who came towards the boat, straddling through the water with outstretched arms, grinning and yelling their Arab invitations to mount their shoulders. I think these fellows frightened the ladies still more than the rocks and the surf; but the poor creatures were obliged to submit; and, trembling, were accommodated somehow upon the mahogany backs of these ruffians, carried through the shallows, and flung up to a ledge before the city gate, where crowds more of dark people were swarming, howling after their fashion. The gentlemen, meanwhile, were having arguments about the eternal backsheesh with the roaring Arab boatmen; and I recall with wonder and delight especially, the curses and screams of one small and extremely loud-lunged fellow, who expressed discontent at receiving a five, instead of a six piastre piece. But how is one to know, without possessing the language? Both coins are made of a greasy pewtery sort of tin; and I thought the biggest was the most valuable: but the fellow showed a sense of their value, and a disposition seemingly to cut any man's throat who did not understand it. Men's throats have been cut for a less difference before now.

Being cast upon the ledge, the first care of our gallantry was to look after the ladies, who were scared and astonished by the naked savage brutes, who were shouldering the poor things to and fro; and bearing them through these and a dark archway, we came into a street crammed with donkeys and their packs and drivers, and towering camels with leering eyes looking into the second-floor rooms, and huge splay feet, through which *mesdames et mesdemoiselles* were to be conducted. We made a rush at the first open door, and passed comfortably under the heels of some horses gathered under the arched court, and up a stone staircase, which turned out to be that of the Russian consul's house. His people welcomed us most cordially to his abode, and the ladies and the luggage (objects of our solicitude) were led up many stairs and across several terraces to a most comfortable little room, under a dome of its own, where the representative of Russia sat. Women with brown faces and draggle-tailed coats and turbans, and wondering eyes, and no stays, and blue beads and gold chains hanging round their necks, came to gaze, as they passed, upon the fair neat English women. Blowsy black cooks puffing over fires and the strangest pots and pans on the terraces, children paddling about in long striped robes, interrupted their sports or labors to come and stare; and the consul, in his cool domed chamber, with a lattice overlooking the sea, with clean mats, and pictures of the Emperor, the Virgin, and St. George, received the strangers with smiling courtesies, regaling the ladies with pomegranates and sugar, the gentlemen with pipes of tobacco, whereof the fragrant tubes were three yards long.

The Russian amenities concluded, we left the ladies still under the comfortable, cool dome of the Russian consulate, and went to see our own representative. The streets of the little town are neither agreeable to horse nor foot travellers. Many of the streets are mere flights of rough steps, leading abruptly into private houses: you pass under archways and passages numberless; a steep, dirty labyrinth of stone-vaulted stables and sheds occupies the ground-floor of the habitations; and you pass from flat to flat of the terraces; at various irregular corners of which, little chambers, with little private domes, are erected, and the people live seemingly as much upon the terrace as in the room.

We found the English consul in a queer little arched chamber, with a strange old picture of the King's arms to decorate one side of it : and here the consul, a demure old man, dressed in red flowing robes, with a feeble janissary bearing a shabby tin-mounted staff, or mace, to denote his office, received such of our nation as came to him for hospitality. He distributed pipes and coffee to all and every one ; he made us a present of his house and all his beds for the night, and went himself to lie quietly on the terrace ; and for all this hospitality he declined to receive any reward from us, and said he was but doing his duty in taking us in. This worthy man, I thought, must doubtless be very well paid by our Government for making such sacrifices ; but it appears that he does not get one single farthing, and that the greater number of our Levant consuls are paid at a similar rate of easy remuneration. If we have bad consular agents, have we a right to complain? If the worthy gentlemen cheat occasionally, can we reasonably be angry? But in travelling through these countries, English people, who don't take into consideration the miserable poverty and scanty resources of their country, and are apt to brag and be proud of it, have their vanity hurt by seeing the representatives of every nation but their own well and decently maintained, and feel ashamed at sitting down under the shabby protection of our mean consular flag.

The active young men of our party had been on shore long before us, and seized upon all the available horses in the town ; but we relied upon a letter from Halil Pacha, enjoining all governors and pashas to help us in all ways : and hearing we were the bearers of this document, the cadi and vice-governor of Jaffa came to wait upon the head of our party ; declared that it was his delight and honor to set eyes upon us ; that he would do everything in the world to serve us ; that there were no horses, unluckily, but he would send and get some in three hours ; and so left us with a world of grinning bows and many choice compliments from one side to the other, which came to each filtered through an obsequious interpreter. But hours passed, and the clatter of horses' hoofs was not heard. We had our dinner of eggs and flaps of bread, and the sunset gun fired : we had our pipes and coffee again, and the night fell. Is this man throwing dirt upon us? we began to think. Is he laughing at our beards, and are our mothers' graves ill-treated by this smiling, swindling cadi? We determined to go and seek in his own den this shuffling dispenser of infidel justice. This time we would be no more bamboozled by compliments ;

but we would use the language of stern expostulation, and, being roused, would let the rascal hear the roar of the indignant British lion; so we rose up in our wrath. The poor consul got a lamp for us with a bit of wax-candle, such as I wonder his means could afford; the shabby janissary marched ahead with his tin mace; the two laquais-de-place, that two of our company had hired, stepped forward, each with an old sabre, and we went clattering and stumbling down the streets of the town, in order to seize upon this cadi in his own divan. I was glad, for my part (though outwardly majestic and indignant in demeanor), that the horses had not come, and that we had a chance of seeing this little queer glimpse of Oriental life, which the magistrate's faithlessness procured for us.

As piety forbids the Turks to eat during the weary daylight hours of the Ramazan, they spend their time profitably in sleeping until the welcome sunset, when the town wakens: all the lanterns are lighted up; all the pipes begin to puff, and the narghilés to bubble; all the sour-milk-and-sherbet-men begin to yell out the excellence of their wares; all the frying-pans in the little dirty cookshops begin to friz, and the pots to send forth a steam: and through this dingy, ragged, bustling, beggarly, cheerful scene, we began now to march towards the Bow Street of Jaffa. We bustled through a crowded narrow archway which led to the cadi's police-office, entered the little room, atrociously perfumed with musk, and passing by the rail-board, where the common sort stood, mounted the stage upon which his worship and friends sat, and squatted down on the divans in stern and silent dignity. His honor ordered us coffee, his countenance evidently showing considerable alarm. A black slave, whose duty seemed to be to prepare this beverage in a side-room with a furnace, prepared for each of us about a teaspoonful of the liquor: his worship's clerk, I presume, a tall Turk of a noble aspect, presented it to us; and having lapped up the little modicum of drink, the British lion began to speak.

All the other travellers (said the lion with perfect reason) have good horses and are gone; the Russians have got horses, the Spaniards have horses, the English have horses, but we, we vizirs in our country, coming with letters of Halil Pacha, are laughed at, spit upon! Are Halil Pacha's letters dirt, that you attend to them in this way? Are British lions dogs that you treat them so? — and so on. This speech with many variations was made on our side for a quarter of an hour; and we finally swore that unless the horses were forthcoming we would write to Halil Pacha the next morning, and to his Excellency the

English Minister at the Sublime Porte. Then you should have heard the chorus of Turks in reply: a dozen voices rose up from the divan, shouting, screaming, ejaculating, expectorating, (the Arabic spoken language seems to require a great employment of the two latter oratorical methods), and uttering what the meek interpreter did not translate to us, but what I dare say were by no means complimentary phrases towards us and our nation. Finally, the palaver concluded by the cadi declaring that by the will of heaven horses should be forthcoming at three o'clock in the morning; and that if not, why, then, we might write to Halil Pacha.

This posed us, and we rose up and haughtily took leave. I should like to know that fellow's real opinion of us lions very much: and especially to have had the translation of the speeches of a huge-breeched turbaned roaring infidel, who looked and spoke as if he would have liked to fling us all into the sea, which was hoarsely murmuring under our windows an accompaniment to the concert within.

We then marched through the bazaars, that were lofty and grim, and pretty full of people. In a desolate broken building, some hundreds of children were playing and singing; in many corners sat parties over their water-pipes, one of whom every now and then would begin twanging out a most queer chant; others there were playing at casino — a crowd squatted around the squalling gamblers, and talking and looking on with eager interest. In one place of the bazaar we found a hundred people at least listening to a story-teller, who delivered his tale with excellent action, voice, and volubility: in another they were playing a sort of thimblerig with coffee-cups, all intent upon the game, and the player himself very wild lest one of our party, who had discovered where the pea lay, should tell the company. The devotion and energy with which all these pastimes were pursued, struck me as much as anything. These people have been playing thimblerig and casino; that story-teller has been shouting his tale of Antar for forty years; and they are just as happy with this amusement now as when first they tried it. Is there no ennui in the Eastern countries, and are blue-devils not allowed to go abroad there?

From the bazaars we went to see the house of Mustapha, said to be the best house and the greatest man of Jaffa. But the great man had absconded suddenly, and had fled into Egypt. The Sultan had made a demand upon him for sixteen thousand purses, 80,000*l*. — Mustapha retired — the Sultan pounced down upon his house, and his goods, his horses and

his mules. His harem was desolate. Mr. Milnes could have
written six affecting poems, had he been with us, on the dark
loneliness of that violated sanctuary. We passed from hall to
hall, terrace to terrace — a few fellows were slumbering on the
naked floors, and scarce turned as we went by them. We
entered Mustapha's particular divan — there was the raised
floor, but no bearded friends squatting away the night of Ramazan ; there was the little coffee furnace, but where was the
slave and the coffee and the glowing embers of the pipes?
Mustapha's favorite passages from the Koran were still painted
up on the walls, but nobody was the wiser for them. We
walked over a sleeping negro, and opened the windows which
looked into his gardens. The horses and donkeys, the camels
and mules were picketed there below, but where is the said
Mustapha? From the frying-pan of the Porte, has he not
fallen into the fire of Mehemet Ali? And which is best, to broil
or to fry? If it be but to read the " Arabian Nights " again on
getting home, it is good to have made this little voyage and
seen these strange places and faces.

Then we went out through the arched lowering gateway of
the town into the plain beyond, and that was another famous
and brilliant scene of the " Arabian Nights." The heaven shone
with a marvellous brilliancy — the plain disappeared far in the
haze — the towers and battlements of the town rose black
against the sky — old outlandish trees rose up here and there —
clumps of camels were couched in the rare herbage — dogs were
baying about — groups of men lay sleeping under their haicks
round about — round about the tall gates many lights were
twinkling — and they brought us water-pipes and sherbet — and
we wondered to think that London was only three weeks off.

Then came the night at the consul's. The poor demure old
gentleman brought out his mattresses ; and the ladies sleeping
round on the divans, we lay down quite happy ; and I for my
part intended to make as delightful dreams as Alnaschar ; but
— lo, the delicate mosquito sounded his horn : the active flea
jumped up, and came to feast on Christian flesh (the Eastern
flea bites more bitterly than the most savage bug in Christendom), and the bug — oh, the accursed ! Why was he made?
What duty has that infamous ruffian to perform in the world,
save to make people wretched? Only Bulwer in his most pathetic style could describe the miseries of that night — the
moaning, the groaning, the cursing, the tumbling, the blistering,
the infamous despair and degradation ! I heard all the cocks
in Jaffa crow ; the children crying, and the mothers hushing

them; the donkeys braying fitfully in the moonlight; at last, I heard the clatter of hoofs below, and the hailing of men. It was three o'clock, the horses were actually come; nay, there were camels likewise; asses and mules, pack-saddles and drivers,' all bustling together under the moonlight in the cheerful street — and the first night in Syria was over.

CHAPTER XII.

FROM JAFFA TO JERUSALEM.

It took an hour or more to get our little caravan into marching order, to accommodate all the packs to the horses, the horses to the riders; to see the ladies comfortably placed in their litter, with a sleek and large black mule fore and aft, a groom to each mule, and a tall and exceedingly good-natured and mahogany-colored infidel to walk by the side of the carriage, to balance it as it swayed to and fro, and to offer his back as a step to the inmates whenever they were minded to ascend or alight. These three fellows, fasting through the Ramazan, and over as rough a road, for the greater part, as ever shook mortal bones, performed their fourteen hours' walk of near forty miles, with the most admirable courage, alacrity, and good humor. They once or twice drank water on the march, and so far infringed the rule; but they refused all bread or edible refreshment offered to them, and tugged on with an energy that the best camel, and I am sure the best Christian, might envy. What a lesson of good-humored endurance it was to certain Pall Mall Sardanapaluses, who grumble if club sofa-cushions are not soft enough!

If I could write sonnets at leisure, I would like to chronicle in fourteen lines my sensations on finding myself on a high Turkish saddle, with a pair of fire-shovel stirrups and worsted reins, red padded saddle-cloth, and innumerable tags, fringes, glass-beads, ends of rope, to decorate the harness of the horse, the gallant steed on which I was about to gallop into Syrian life. What a figure we cut in the moonlight, and how they would have stared in the Strand! Ay, or in Leicestershire, where I warrant such a horse and rider are not often visible! The shovel stirrups are deucedly short; the clumsy leathers cut the shins of some equestrians abominably; you sit over your horse as it were on a tower, from which the descent would be very easy, but for the big peak of the saddle. A good way for the inexperienced is to put a stick or umbrella across the saddle peak again, so that it is next to impossible to go over your horse's neck. I found this a vast comfort in going down the hills, and recommend it conscientiously to other dear simple brethren of the city.

Peaceful men, we did not ornament our girdles with pistols, yataghans, &c., such as some pilgrims appeared to bristle all over with; and as a lesson to such rash people, a story may be told which was narrated to us at Jerusalem, and carries a wholesome moral. The Honorable Hoggin Armer, who was lately travelling in the East, wore about his stomach two brace of pistols, of such exquisite finish and make, that a Sheikh, in the Jericho country, robbed him merely for the sake of the pistols. I don't know whether he has told the story to his friends at home.

Another story about Sheikhs may here be told àpropos. That celebrated Irish Peer, Lord Oldgent (who was distinguished in the Buckinghamshire Dragoons), having paid a sort of black mail to the Sheikh of Jericho country, was suddenly set upon by another Sheikh, who claimed to be the real Jerichonian governor; and these twins quarrelled over the body of Lord Oldgent, as the widows for the innocent baby before Solomon. There was enough for both — but these digressions are interminable.

The party got under way at near four o'clock: the ladies in the litter, the French *femme-de-chambre* manfully caracoling on a gray horse; the cavaliers, like your humble servant, on their high saddles; the domestics, flunkies, guides, and grooms, on all sorts of animals, — some fourteen in all. Add to these, two most grave and stately Arabs in white beards, white turbans, white haicks and raiments; sabres curling round their military thighs, and immense long guns at their backs. More venerable warriors I never saw; they went by the side of the litter soberly prancing. When we emerged from the steep clattering streets of the city into the gray plains, lighted by the moon and starlight, these militaries rode onward, leading the way through the huge avenues of strange diabolical-looking prickly pears (plants that look as if they had grown in Tartarus), by which the first mile or two of route from the city is bounded; and as the dawn arose before us, exhibiting first a streak of gray, then of green, then of red in the sky, it was fine to see these martial

figures defined against the rising light.   The sight of that little
cavalcade, and of the nature around it, will always remain with
me, I think, as one of the freshest and most delightful sensations I have enjoyed since the day I first saw Calais pier.   It
was full day when they gave their horses a drink at a large
pretty Oriental fountain, and then presently we entered the open
plain — the famous plain of Sharon — so fruitful in roses once,
now hardly cultivated, but always beautiful and noble.

Here presently, in the distance, we saw another cavalcade
pricking over the plain.   Our two white warriors spread to the
right and left, and galloped to reconnoitre.   We, too, put our
steeds to the canter, and handling our umbrellas as Richard did
his lance against Saladin, went undaunted to challenge this
caravan.   The fact is, we could distinguish that it was formed
of the party of our pious friends the Poles, and we hailed them
with cheerful shouting, and presently the two caravans joined
company, and scoured the plain at the rate of near four miles
per hour.   The horse-master, a courier of this company, rode
three miles for our one.   He was a broken-nosed Arab, with
pistols, a sabre, a fusee, a yellow Damascus cloth flapping over
his head, and his nose ornamented with diachylon.   He rode
a hog-necked gray Arab, bristling over with harness, and
jumped, and whirled, and reared, and halted, to the admiration
of all.

Scarce had the diachylonian Arab finished his evolutions,
when lo ! yet another cloud of dust was seen, and another party
of armed and glittering horsemen appeared.   They, too, were
led by an Arab, who was followed by two janissaries, with
silver maces shining in the sun.   'Twas the party of the new
American Consul-General of Syria and Jerusalem, hastening to
that city, with the inferior consuls of Ramleh and Jaffa to escort
him.   He expects to see the Millennium in three years, and has
accepted the office of consul at Jerusalem, so as to be on the
spot in readiness.

When the diachylon Arab saw the American Arab, he
straightway galloped his steed towards him, took his pipe,
which he delivered at his adversary in guise of a jereed, and
galloped round and round, and in and out, and there and back
again, as in a play of war.   The American replied in a similar
playful ferocity — the two warriors made a little tournament
for us there on the plains before Jaffa, in the which diachylon
being a little worsted, challenged his adversary to a race, and
fled away on his gray, the American following on his bay.   Here

poor sticking-plaster was again worsted, the Yankee contemptuously riding round him, and then declining further exercise.

What more could mortal man want? A troop of knights
and paladins could have done no more. In no page of Walter
Scott have I read a scene more fair and sparkling. The sober
warriors of our escort did not join in the gambols of the young
men. There they rode soberly, in their white turbans, by their
ladies' litter, their long guns rising up behind them.

There was no lack of company along the road : donkeys
numberless, camels by twos and threes ; now a mule-driver,
trudging along the road, chanting a most queer melody ; now a
lady, in white veil, black mask, and yellow papooshes, bestriding her ass, and followed by her husband, — met us on the way ;
and most people gave a salutation. Presently we saw Ramleh,
in a smoking mist, on the plain before us, flanked to the right
by a tall lonely tower, that might have held the bells of some
moutier of Caen or Evreux. As we entered, about three hours
and a half after starting, among the white domes and stone
houses of the little town, we passed the place of tombs. Two
women were sitting on one of them, — the one bending her
head towards the stone, and rocking to and fro, and moaning
out a very sweet, pitiful lamentation. The American consul
invited us to breakfast at the house of his subaltern, the hospitable one-eyed Armenian, who represents the United States at
Jaffa. The stars and stripes were flaunting over his terraces,
to which we ascended, leaving our horses to the care of a multitude of roaring, ragged Arabs beneath, who took charge of
and fed the animals, though I can't say in the least why ; but,
in the same way as getting off my horse on entering Jerusalem,
I gave the rein into the hand of the first person near me, and
have never heard of the worthy brute since. At the American
consul's we were served first with rice soup in pishpash, flavored
with cinnamon and spice ; then with boiled mutton, then with
stewed ditto and tomatoes ; then with fowls swimming in grease ;
then with brown ragoûts belabored with onions ; then with a
smoking pilaff of rice : several of which dishes I can pronounce
to be of excellent material and flavo' When the gentry had
concluded this repast, it was handed to a side-table, where the
commonalty speedily discussed it. We left them licking their
fingers as we hastened away upon the second part of the
ride.

And as we quitted Ramleh, the scenery lost that sweet and
peaceful look which characterizes the pretty plain we had traversed ; and the sun, too, rising in the heaven, dissipated all

those fresh, beautiful tints in which God's world is clothed of early morning, and which city people have so seldom the chance of beholding. The plain over which we rode looked yellow and gloomy; the cultivation little or none; the land across the road-side fringed, for the most part, with straggling wild carrot plants; a patch of green only here and there. We passed several herds of lean, small, well-conditioned cattle: many flocks of black goats, tended now and then by a ragged negro shepherd, his long gun slung over his back, his hand over his eyes to shade them as he stared at our little cavalcade. Most of the half-naked countryfolks we met, had this dismal appendage to Eastern rustic life; and the weapon could hardly be one of mere defence, for, beyond the faded skull-cup, or tattered coat of blue or dirty white, the brawny, brown-chested, solemn-looking fellows had nothing seemingly to guard. As before, there was no lack of travellers on the road: more donkeys trotted by, looking sleek and strong; camels singly and by pairs, laden with a little humble ragged merchandise, on their way between the two towns. About noon we halted eagerly at a short distance from an Arab village and well, where all were glad of a drink of fresh water. A village of beavers, or a colony of ants, make habitations not unlike these dismal huts piled together on the plain here. There were no single huts along the whole line of road; poor and wretched as they are, the Fellahs huddle all together for protection from the other thieves their neighbors. The government (which we restored to them) has no power to protect them, and is only strong enough to rob them. The women, with their long blue gowns and ragged veils, came to and fro with pitchers on their heads. Rebecca had such an one when she brought drink to the lieutenant of Abraham. The boys came staring round, bawling after us with their fathers for the inevitable backsheesh. The village dogs barked round the flocks, as they were driven to water or pasture.

We saw a gloomy, not very lofty-looking ridge of hills in front of us; the highest of which the guide pointing out to us, told us that from it we should see Jerusalem. It looked very near, and we all set up a trot of enthusiasm to get into this hill country.

But that burst of enthusiasm (it may have carried us nearly a quarter of a mile in three minutes) was soon destined to be checked by the disagreeable nature of the country we had to traverse. Before we got to the real mountain district, we were in a manner prepared for it, by the mounting and descent of several lonely outlying hills, up and down which our rough stony track wound. Then we entered the hill district, and our path lay through the clattering bed of an ancient stream, whose brawling waters have rolled away into the past, along with the fierce and turbulent race who once inhabited these savage hills. There may have been cultivation here two thousand years ago. The mountains, or huge stony mounds environing this rough path, have level ridges all the way up to their summits; on these parallel ledges there is still some verdure and soil: when water flowed here, and the country was thronged with that extraordinary population, which, according to the Sacred Histories, was crowded into the region, these mountain steps may have been gardens and vineyards, such as we see now thriving along the hills of the Rhine. Now the district is quite deserted, and you ride among what seem to be so many petrified waterfalls. We saw no animals moving among the stony brakes; scarcely even a dozen little birds in the whole course of the ride. The sparrows are all at Jerusalem, among the housetops, where their ceaseless chirping and twittering forms the most cheerful sound of the place.

The company of Poles, the company of Oxford men, and the little American army, travelled too quick for our caravan, which was made to follow the slow progress of the ladies' litter, and we had to make the journey through the mountains in a very small number. Not one of our party had a single weapon more dreadful than an umbrella: and a couple of Arabs, wickedly inclined, might have brought us all to the halt, and rifled every carpet-bag and pocket belonging to us. Nor can I say that we journeyed without certain qualms of fear. When swarthy fellows, with girdles full of pistols and yataghans, passed us without unslinging their long guns: — when scowling camel-riders, with awful long bending lances, decorated with tufts of rags, or savage plumes of scarlet feathers, went by without molestation, I think we were rather glad that they did not stop and parley: for, after all, a British lion with an umbrella is no match for an Arab with his infernal long gun. What, too, would have become of our women? So we tried to think that it was entirely out of anxiety for them that we were inclined to push on.

There is a shady resting-place and village in the midst of the mountain district, where the travellers are accustomed to halt for an hour's repose and refreshment; and the other caravans were just quitting this spot, having enjoyed its cool shades and waters, when we came up. Should we stop? Regard for the ladies (of course no other earthly consideration) made us say, "No!" What admirable self-denial and chivalrous devotion! So our poor devils of mules and horses got no rest and no water, our panting litter-men no breathing time, and we staggered desperately after the procession ahead of us. It wound up the mountain in front of us: the Poles with their guns and attendants, the American with his janissaries; fifty or sixty all riding slowly like the procession in "Bluebeard."

But alas, they headed us very soon; when we got up the weary hill they were all out of sight. Perhaps thoughts of Fleet Street did cross the minds of some of us then, and a vague desire to see a few policemen. The district now seemed peopled, and with an ugly race. Savage personages peered at us out of huts, and grim holes in the rocks. The mules began to loiter most abominably — water the muleteers must have — and, behold, we came to a pleasant-looking village of trees standing on a hill; children were shaking figs from the trees — women were going about — before us was the mosque of a holy man — the village, looking like a collection of little forts, rose up on the hill to our right, with a long view of the fields and gardens stretching from it, and camels arriving with their burdens. Here we must stop; Paolo, the chief servant, knew the Sheikh of the village — he very good man — give him water and supper — water very good here — in fact we began to think of the propriety of halting here for the night, and making our entry into Jerusalem on the next day.

A man on a handsome horse dressed in red came prancing up to us, looking hard at the ladies in the litter, and passed away. Then two others sauntered up, one handsome, and dressed in red too, and he stared into the litter without ceremony, began to play with a little dog that lay there, asked if we were Inglees, and was answered by me in the affirmative. Paolo had brought the water, the most delicious draught in the world. The gentlefolks had had some, the poor muleteers were longing for it. The French maid, the courageous Victoire (never since the days of Joan of Arc has there surely been a more gallant and virtuous female of France) refused the drink; when suddenly a servant of the party scampers up to his master and says; "Abou Gosh says the ladies must get out and show themselves to the women of the village!"

It was Abou Gosh himself, the redoubted robber Sheikh about whom we had been laughing and crying "Wolf!" all day. Never was seen such a skurry! "March!" was the instant order given. When Victoire heard who it was and the message, you should have seen how she changed countenance; trembling for her virtue in the ferocious clutches of a Gosh. "Un verre d'eau pour l'amour de Dieu!" gasped she, and was ready to faint on her saddle. "Ne buvez plus, Victoire!" screamed a little fellow of our party. "Push on, push on!" cried one and all. "What's the matter!" exclaimed the ladies in the litter, as they saw themselves suddenly jogging on again. But we took care not to tell them what had been the designs of the redoubtable Abou Gosh. Away then we went — Victoire was saved — and her mistresses rescued from dangers they knew not of, until they were a long way out of the village.

Did he intend insult or good-will? Did Victoire escape the odious chance of becoming Madame Abou Gosh? Or did the mountain chief simply propose to be hospitable after his fashion? I think the latter was his desire; if the former had been his wish, a half-dozen of his long guns could have been up with us in a minute, and had all our party at their mercy. But now, for the sake of the mere excitement, the incident was, I am sorry to say, rather a pleasant one than otherwise: especially for a traveller who is in the happy condition of being able to sing before robbers, as is the case with the writer of the present.

A little way out of the land of Goshen we came upon a long stretch of gardens and vineyards, slanting towards the setting sun, which illuminated numberless golden clusters of the most delicious grapes, of which we stopped and partook. Such grapes were never before tasted; water so fresh as that which a countryman fetched for us from a well never sluiced parched throats before. It was the ride, the sun, and above all Abou Gosh, who made that refreshment so sweet, and hereby I offer him my best thanks. Presently, in the midst of a most diabolical ravine, down which our horses went sliding, we heard the evening gun; it was fired from Jerusalem. The twilight is brief in this country, and in a few minutes the landscape was gray round about us, and the sky lighted up by a hundred thousand stars, which made the night beautiful.

Under this superb canopy we rode for a couple of hours to our journey's end. The mountains round about us dark, lonely, and sad; the landscape as we saw it at night (it is not more cheerful in the daytime), the most solemn and forlorn I have ever seen. The feelings of almost terror with which, riding through the night, we approached this awful place, the centre of the world's past and future history, have no need to be noted down here. The recollection of those sensations must remain with a man as long as his memory lasts ; and he should think of them as often, perhaps, as he should talk of them little.

CHAPTER XIII.

JERUSALEM.

The ladies of our party found excellent quarters in readiness for them at the Greek convent in the city ; where airy rooms, and plentiful meals, and wines and sweetmeats delicate and abundant, were provided to cheer them after the fatigues of their journey. I don't know whether the worthy fathers of the convent share in the good things which they lavish on their guests ; but they look as if they do. Those whom we saw bore every sign of easy conscience and good living ; there were a pair of strong, rosy, greasy, lazy lay-brothers, dawdling in the sun on the convent terrace, or peering over the parapet into the street below, whose looks gave one a notion of anything but asceticism.

In the principal room of the strangers' house (the lay traveller is not admitted to dwell in the sacred interior of the convent), and over the building, the Russian double-headed eagle is displayed. The place is under the patronage of the Emperor Nicholas : an Imperial Prince has stayed in these rooms : the Russian consul performs a great part in the city ; and a considerable annual stipend is given by the Emperor towards the maintenance of the great establishment in Jerusalem. The Great Chapel of the Church of the Holy Sepulchre is by far the richest, in point of furniture, of all the places of worship under that roof. We were in Russia, when we came to visit our friends here ; under the protection of the Father of the Church and the Imperial Eagle ! This butcher and tyrant, who sits on his throne only through the crime of those who held it before him — every step in whose pedigree is stained by some horrible mark of murder, parricide, adultery — this padded and whiskered pontiff — who rules in his jack-boots over a system of spies and soldiers, of deceit, ignorance, dissoluteness, and brute force, such as surely the history of the world never told of before — has a tender interest in the welfare of his spiritual children : in the Eastern Church ranks after divinity, and is worshipped by millions of men. A pious ex-emplar of Christianity truly! and of the condition to which its union with politics has brought it! Think of the rank to which he pretends, and gravely believes that he possesses, no doubt! — think of those who assumed the same ultra-sacred character before him! — and then of the Bible and the Founder of the Religion, of which the Emperor assumes to be the chief priest and defender!

We had some Poles of our party; but these poor fellows went to the Latin convent, declining to worship after the Em-peror's fashion. The next night after our arrival, two of them passed in the Sepulchre. There we saw them, more than once on subsequent visits, kneeling in the Latin Church before the pictures, or marching solemnly with candles in processions, or lying flat on the stones, or passionately kissing the spots which their traditions have consecrated as the authentic places of the Saviour's sufferings. More honest or more civilized, or from opposition, the Latin fathers have long given up and disowned the disgusting mummery of the Eastern Fire — which lie the Greeks continue annually to tell.

Their travellers' house and convent, though large and com-modious, are of a much poorer and shabbier condition than those of the Greeks. Both make believe not to take money; but the traveller is expected to pay in each. The Latin fathers enlarge their means by a little harmless trade in beads and crosses, and mother-of-pearl shells, on which figures of saints are engraved; and which they purchase from the manufac-turers, and vend at a small profit. The English, until of late, used to be quartered in these sham inns; but last year two or three Maltese took houses for the reception of tourists, who can now be accommodated with cleanly and comfortable board, at a rate not too heavy for most pockets.

To one of these we went very gladly; giving our horses the bridle at the door, which went off of their own will to their stables, through the dark inextricable labyrinths of streets, archways, and alleys, which we had threaded after leaving the main street from the Jaffa Gate. There, there was still some life. Numbers of persons were collected at their doors, or smoking before the dingy coffee-houses, where singing and story-telling were going on; but out of this great street every-thing was silent, and no sign of a light from the windows of the low houses which we passed.

We ascended from a lower floor up to a terrace, on which were several little domed chambers, or pavilions. From this terrace, whence we looked in the morning, a great part of the city spread before us : — white domes upon domes, and terraces of the same character as our own. Here and there, from among these whitewashed mounds round about, a minaret rose, or a rare date-tree ; but the chief part of the vegetation near was that odious tree the prickly pear, — one huge green wart growing out of another, armed with spikes, as inhospitable as the aloe, without shelter or beauty. To the right the Mosque of Omar rose ; the rising sun behind it. Yonder steep tortuous lane before us, flanked by ruined walls on either side, has borne, time out of mind, the title of Via Dolorosa ; and tradition has fixed the spots where the Saviour rested, bearing his cross to Calvary. But of the mountain, rising immediately in front of us, a few gray olive-trees speckling the yellow side here and there, there can be no question. That is the Mount of Olives. Bethany lies beyond it. The most sacred eyes that ever looked on this world have gazed on those ridges : it was there He used to walk and teach. With shame and humility one looks towards the spot where that inexpressible Love and Benevolence lived and breathed ; where the great yearning heart of the Saviour interceded for all our race ; and whence the bigots and traitors of his day led him away to kill him !

That company of Jews whom we had brought with us from Constantinople, and who had cursed every delay on the route, not from impatience to view the Holy City, but from rage at being obliged to purchase dear provisions for their maintenance on ship-board, made what bargains they best could at Jaffa, and journeyed to the Valley of Jehoshaphat at the cheapest rate. We saw the tall form of the old Polish Patriarch, venerable in filth, stalking among the stinking ruins of the Jewish quarter. The sly old Rabbi, in the greasy folding hat, who would not pay to shelter his children from the storm off Beyrout, greeted us in the bazaars ; the younger Rabbis were furbished up with some smartness. We met them on Sunday at the kind of promenade by the walls of the Bethlehem Gate ; they were in company of some red-bearded co-religionists, smartly attired in Eastern raiment ; but their voice was the voice of the Jews of Berlin, and of course as we passed they were talking about so many hundert thaler. You may track one of the people, and be sure to hear mention of that silver calf that they worship.

The English mission has been very unsuccessful with these religionists. I don't believe the Episcopal apparatus — the chaplains, and the colleges, and the beadles — have succeeded in converting a dozen of them; and a sort of martyrdom is in store for the luckless Hebrew at Jerusalem who shall secede from his faith. Their old community spurn them with horror; and I heard of the case of one unfortunate man, whose wife, in spite of her husband's change of creed, being resolved, like a true woman, to cleave to him, was spirited away from him in his absence; was kept in privacy in the city, in spite of all exertions of the mission, of the consul and the bishop, and the chaplains and the beadles; was passed away from Jerusalem to Beyrout, and thence to Constantinople; and from Constantinople was whisked off into the Russian territories, where she still pines after her husband. May that unhappy convert find consolation away from her. I could not help thinking, as my informant, an excellent and accomplished gentleman of the mission, told me the story, that the Jews had done only what the Christians do under the same circumstances. The woman was the daughter of a most learned Rabbi, as I gathered. Suppose a daughter of the Rabbi of Exeter, or Canterbury, were to marry a man who turned Jew, would not her Right Reverend Father be justified in taking her out of the power of a person likely to hurl her soul to perdition? These poor converts should surely be sent away to England out of the way of persecution. We could not but feel a pity for them, as they sat there on their benches in the church conspicuous; and thought of the scorn and contumely which attended them without, as they passed, in their European dresses and shaven beards, among their grisly, scowling, long-robed countrymen.

As elsewhere in the towns I have seen, the Ghetto of Jerusalem is pre-eminent in filth. The people are gathered round about the dung-gate of the city. Of a Friday you may hear their wailings and lamentations for the lost glories of their city. I think the Valley of Jehoshaphat is the most ghastly sight I have seen in the world. From all quarters they come hither to bury their dead. When his time is come yonder hoary old miser, with whom we made our voyage, will lay his carcass to rest here. To do that, and to claw together money, has been the purpose of that strange, long life.

We brought with us one of the gentlemen of the mission, a Hebrew convert, the Rev. Mr. E——; and lest I should be supposed to speak with disrespect above of any of the converts of the Hebrew faith, let me mention this gentleman as the only one whom I had the fortune to meet on terms of intimacy. I never saw a man whose outward conduct was more touching, whose sincerity was more evident, and whose religious feeling seemed more deep, real, and reasonable.

Only a few feet off, the walls of the Anglican Church of Jerusalem rise up from their foundations, on a picturesque open spot, in front of the Bethlehem Gate. The English bishop has his church hard by: and near it is the house where the Christians of our denomination assemble and worship.

There seem to be polyglot services here. I saw books of prayer, or Scripture, in Hebrew, Greek, and German: in which latter language Dr. Alexander preaches every Sunday. A gentleman who sat near me at church used all these books indifferently: reading the first lesson from the Hebrew book, and the second from the Greek. Here we all assembled on the Sunday after our arrival: it was affecting to hear the music and language of our country sounding in this distant place; to have the decent and manly ceremonial of our service; the prayers delivered in that noble language. Even that stout anti-prelatist, the American consul, who has left his house and fortune in America in order to witness the coming of the Millennium, who believes it to be so near that he has brought a dove with him from his native land (which bird he solemnly informed us was to survive the expected Advent), was affected by the good old words and service. He swayed about and moaned in his place at various passages; during the sermon he gave especial marks of sympathy and approbation. I never heard the service more excellently and impressively read than by the Bishop's chaplain, Mr. Veitch. But it was the music that was most touching I thought, — the sweet old songs of home.

There was a considerable company assembled: near a hundred people I should think. Our party made a large addition to the usual congregation. The Bishop's family is proverbially numerous: the consul, and the gentlemen of the mission, have wives, and children, and English establishments. These, and the strangers, occupied places down the room, to the right and left of the desk and communion-table. The converts, and the members of the college, in rather a scanty number, faced the officiating clergyman; before whom the silver maces of the janissaries were set up, as they set up the beadles' maces in England.

I made many walks round the city to Olivet and Bethany,

to the tombs of the kings, and the fountains sacred in story. These are green and fresh, but all the rest of the landscape seemed to me to be *frightful.* Parched mountains, with a gray bleak olive-tree trembling here and there; savage ravines and valleys, paved with tombstones — a landscape unspeakably ghastly and desolate, meet the eye wherever you wander round about the city. The place seems quite adapted to the events which are recorded in the Hebrew histories. It and they, as it seems to me, can never be regarded without terror. Fear and blood, crime and punishment, follow from page to page in frightful succession. There is not a spot at which you look, but some violent deed has been done there: some massacre has been committed, some victim has been murdered, some idol has been worshipped with bloody and dreadful rites. Not far from hence is the place where the Jewish conqueror fought for the possession of Jerusalem. "The sun stood still, and hasted not to go down about a whole day;" so that the Jews might have daylight to destroy the Amorites, whose iniquities were full, and whose land they were about to occupy. The fugitive heathen king, and his allies, were discovered in their hiding-place, and hanged: "and the children of Judah smote Jerusalem with the edge of the sword, and set the city on fire; and they left none remaining, but utterly destroyed all that breathed."

I went out at the Zion Gate, and looked at the so-called tomb of David. I had been reading all the morning in the Psalms, and his history in Samuel and Kings. "*Bring thou down Shimei's hoar head to the grave with blood,*" are the last words of the dying monarch as recorded by the history. What they call the tomb is now a crumbling old mosque; from which Jew and Christian are excluded alike. As I saw it, blazing in the sunshine, with the purple sky behind it, the glare only served to mark the surrounding desolation more clearly. The lonely walls and towers of the city rose hard by. Dreary mountains, and declivities of naked stones, were round about: they are burrowed with holes in which Christian hermits lived and died. You see one green place far down in the valley: it is called En Rogel. Adonijah feasted there, who was killed by his brother Solomon, for asking for Abishag for wife. The Valley of Hinnom skirts the hill: the dismal ravine was a fruitful garden once. Ahaz, and the idolatrous kings, sacrificed to idols under the green trees there, and "caused their children to pass through the fire." On the mountain opposite, Solomon, with the thousand women of his harem, worshipped the gods of all their nations, "Ashtoreth," and "Milcom, and Molech, the abomination of the Ammonites." An enormous charnel-house stands on the hill where the bodies of dead pilgrims used to be thrown; and common belief has fixed upon this spot as the Aceldama, which Judas purchased with the price of his treason. Thus you go on from one gloomy place to another, each seared with its bloody tradition. Yonder is the Temple, and you think of Titus's soldiery storming its flaming porches, and entering the city, in the savage defence of which two million human souls perished. It was on Mount Zion that Godfrey and Tancred had their camp: when the Crusaders entered the mosque, they rode knee-deep in the blood of its defenders, and of the women and children who had fled thither for refuge: it was the victory of Joshua over again. Then, after three days of butchery, they purified the desecrated mosque and went to prayer. In the centre of this history of crime rises up the Great Murder of all. . . . .

I need say no more about this gloomy landscape. After a man has seen it once, he never forgets it — the recollection of it seems to me to follow him like a remorse, as it were to implicate him in the awful deed which was done there. Oh! with what unspeakable shame and terror should one think of that crime, and prostrate himself before the image of that Divine Blessed Sufferer.

Of course the first visit of the traveller is to the famous Church of the Sepulchre.

In the archway, leading from the street to the court and church, there is a little bazaar of Bethlehemites, who must interfere considerably with the commerce of the Latin fathers. These men bawl to you from their stalls, and hold up for your purchase their devotional baubles, — bushels of rosaries and scented beads, and carved mother-of-pearl shells, and rude stone salt-cellars and figures. Now that inns are established, — envoys of these pedlars attend them on the arrival of strangers, squat all day on the terraces before your door, and patiently entreat you to buy of their goods. Some worthies there are who drive a good trade by tattooing pilgrims with the five crosses, the arms of Jerusalem; under which the name of the city is punctured in Hebrew, with the auspicious year of the Hadji's visit. Several of our fellow-travellers submitted to this queer operation, and will carry to their grave this relic of their journey. Some of them had engaged a servant, a man at Beyrout, who had served as a lad on board an English ship in the

26

Mediterranean. Above his tattooage of the five crosses, the fellow had a picture of two hearts united, and the pathetic motto, "Betsy my dear." He had parted with Betsy my dear five years before at Malta. He had known a little English there, but had forgotten it. Betsy my dear was forgotten too. Only her name remained engraved with a vain simulacrum of constancy on the faithless rogue's skin: on which was now printed another token of equally effectual devotion. The beads and the tattooing, however, seem essential ceremonies attendant on the Christian pilgrim's visit; for many hundreds of years, doubtless, the palmers have carried off with them these simple reminiscences of the sacred city. That symbol has been engraven upon the arms of how many Princes, Knights, and Crusaders! Don't you see a moral as applicable to them as to the swindling Beyrout horseboy? I have brought you back that cheap and wholesome apologue, in lieu of any of the Bethlehemite shells and beads.

After passing through the porch of the pedlars, you come to the court-yard in front of the noble old towers of the Church of the Sepulchre, with pointed arches and Gothic traceries, rude, but rich and picturesque in design. Here crowds are waiting in the sun, until it shall please the Turkish guardians of the church-door to open. A swarm of beggars sit here permanently: old tattered hags with long veils, ragged children, blind old bearded beggars, who raise up a chorus of prayers for money, holding out their wooden bowls, or clattering with their sticks on the stones, or pulling your coat-skirts and moaning and whining; yonder sit a group of coal-black Coptish pilgrims, with robes and turbans of dark blue, fumbling their perpetual beads. A party of Arab Christians have come up from their tents or villages: the men half-naked, looking as if they were beggars, or banditti, upon occasion; the women have flung their head-cloths back, and are looking at the strangers under their tattooed eyebrows. As for the strangers, there is no need to describe *them;* that figure of the Englishman, with his hands in his pockets, has been seen all the world over: staring down the crater of Vesuvius, or into a Hottentot kraal — or at a pyramid, or a Parisian coffee-house, or an Esquimaux hut — with the same insolent calmness of demeanor. When the gates of the church are open, he elbows in among the first, and flings a few scornful piastres to the Turkish door-keeper; and gazes round easily at the place, in which people of every other nation in the world are in tears, or in rapture, or wonder. He has never seen the place until now, and looks as indifferent

ARAB FOUNTAIN IN JERUSALEM.

as the Turkish guardian who sits in the doorway, and swears at the people as they pour in.

Indeed, I believe it is impossible for us to comprehend the source and nature of the Roman Catholic devotion. I once went into a church at Rome at the request of a Catholic friend, who described the interior to be so beautiful and glorious, that he thought (he said) it must be like heaven itself. I found walls hung with cheap stripes of pink and white calico, altars covered with artificial flowers, a number of wax-candles, and plenty of gilt-paper ornaments. The place seemed to me like a shabby theatre ; and here was my friend on his knees at my side, plunged in a rapture of wonder and devotion.

I could get no better impression out of this the most famous church in the world. The deceits are too open and flagrant ; the inconsistencies and contrivances too monstrous. It is hard even to sympathize with persons who receive them as genuine ; and though (as I know and saw in the case of my friend at Rome) the believer's life may be passed in the purest exercise of faith and charity, it is difficult even to give him credit for honesty, so barefaced seem the impostures which he professes to believe and reverence. It costs one no small effort even to admit the possibility of a Catholic's credulity : to share in his rapture and devotion is still further out of your power ; and I could get from this church no other emotions but those of shame and pain.

The legends with which the Greeks and Latins have garnished the spot have no more sacredness for you than the hideous, unreal, barbaric pictures and ornaments which they have lavished on it. Look at the fervor with which pilgrims kiss and weep over a tawdry Gothic painting, scarcely better fashioned than an idol in a South Sea Morai. The histories which they are called upon to reverence are of the same period and order, — savage Gothic caricatures. In either a saint appears in the costume of the middle ages, and is made to accommodate himself to the fashion of the tenth century.

The different churches battle for the possession of the various relics. The Greeks show you the Tomb of Melchisedec, while the Armenians possess the Chapel of the Penitent Thief ; the poor Copts (with their little cabin of a chapel) can yet boast of possessing the thicket in which Abraham caught the Ram, which was to serve as the vicar of Isaac ; the Latins point out the Pillar to which the Lord was bound. The place of the Invention of the Sacred Cross, the Fissure in the Rock of Golgotha, the Tomb of Adam himself — are all here within a few yards' space. You mount a few steps, and are told it is Calvary upon which you stand. All this in the midst of flaring candles, reeking incense, savage pictures of Scripture story, or portraits of kings who have been benefactors to the various chapels ; a din and clatter of strange people, — these weeping, bowing, kissing, — those utterly indifferent ; and the priests clad in outlandish robes, snuffling and chanting incomprehensible litanies, robing, disrobing, lighting up candles or extinguishing them, advancing, retreating, bowing with all sorts of unfamiliar genuflexions. Had it pleased the inventors of the Sepulchre topography to have fixed on fifty more spots of ground as the places of the events of the sacred story, the pilgrim would have believed just as now. The priest's authority has so mastered his faith, that it accommodates itself to any demand upon it ; and the English stranger looks on the scene, for the first time, with a feeling of scorn, bewilderment, and shame at that grovelling credulity, those strange rites and ceremonies, that almost confessed imposture.

Jarred and distracted by these, the Church of the Holy Sepulchre, for some time, seems to an Englishman the least sacred spot about Jerusalem. It is the lies, and the legends, and the priests, and their quarrels, and their ceremonies, which keep the Holy Place out of sight. A man has not leisure to view it, for the brawling of the guardians of the spot. The Roman conquerors, they say, raised up a statue of Venus in this sacred place, intending to destroy all memory of it. I don't think the heathen was as criminal as the Christian is now. To deny and disbelieve, is not so bad as to make belief a ground to cheat upon. The liar Ananias perished for that ; and yet out of these gates, where angels may have kept watch — out of the tomb of Christ — Christian priests issue with a lie in their hands. What a place to choose for imposture, good God ! to sully, with brutal struggles for self-aggrandizement, or shameful schemes of gain !

The situation of the Tomb (into which, be it authentic or not, no man can enter without a shock of breathless fear, and deep and awful self-humiliation,) must have struck all travellers. It stands in the centre of the arched rotunda, which is common to all denominations, and from which branch off the various chapels belonging to each particular sect. In the Coptic Chapel I saw one coal-black Copt, in blue robes, cowering in the little Cabin, surrounded by dingy lamps, barbarous pictures, and cheap, faded trumpery. In the Latin Church there was no service going on, only two fathers dusting the mouldy gewgaws along the brown walls, and laughing to one another. The gorgeous church of the Fire impostors, hard by, was always more fully attended; as was that of their wealthy neighbors, the Armenians. These three main sects hate each other; their quarrels are interminable; each bribes and intrigues with the heathen lords of the soil, to the prejudice of his neighbor. Now it is the Latins who interfere, and allow the common church to go to ruin, because the Greeks purpose to roof it; now the Greeks demolish a monastery on Mount Olivet, and leave the ground to the Turks, rather than allow the Armenians to possess it. On another occasion, the Greeks having mended the Armenian steps, which led to the (so-called) Cave of the Nativity at Bethlehem, the latter asked for permission to destroy the work of the Greeks, and did so. And so round this sacred spot, the centre of Christendom, the representatives of the three great sects worship under one roof, and hate each other!

Above the Tomb of the Saviour, the cupola *is open*, and you see the blue sky overhead. Which of the builders was it that had the grace to leave that under the high protection of heaven, and not confine it under the mouldering old domes and roofs, which cover so much selfishness, and uncharitableness, and imposture!

We went to Bethlehem, too; and saw the apocryphal wonders there.

Five miles' ride brings you from Jerusalem to it, over naked wavy hills; the aspect of which, however, grows more cheerful as you approach the famous village. We passed the Convent of Mar Elyas on the road, walled and barred like a fort. In spite of its strength, however, it has more than once been stormed by the Arabs, and the luckless fathers within put to death. Hard by was Rebecca's Well: a dead body was lying there, and crowds of male and female mourners dancing and howling round it. Now and then a little troop of savage scowling horsemen — a shepherd driving his black sheep, his gun over his shoulder — a troop of camels — or of women, with long blue robes and white veils, bearing pitchers, and staring at the strangers with their great solemn eyes — or a company of laborers, with their donkeys, bearing grain or grapes to the city, — met us and enlivened the little ride. It was a busy and cheerful scene. The Church of the Nativity, with the adjoining Convents, forms a vast and noble Christian structure. A party of travellers were going to the Jordan that day, and scores of their followers — of the robbing Arabs, who profess to protect

them, (magnificent figures some of them, with flowing haicks
and turbans, with long guns and scimitars, and wretched horses,
covered with gaudy trappings,) were standing on the broad
pavement before the little Convent gate. It was such a scene
as Cattermole might paint. Knights and Crusaders may have
witnessed a similar one. You could fancy them issuing out of
the narrow little portal, and so greeted by the swarms of swarthy
clamorous women and merchants and children.

The scene within the building was of the same Gothic character. We were entertained by the Superior of the Greek Convent, in a fine refectory, with ceremonies and hospitalities that
pilgrims of the middle ages might have witnessed. We were
shown over the magnificent Barbaric Church, visited of course
the Grotto where the Blessed Nativity is said to have taken
place, and the rest of the idols set up for worship by the clumsy
legend. When the visit was concluded, the party going to the
Dead Sea filed off with their armed attendants ; each individual
traveller making as brave a show as he could, and personally
accoutred with warlike swords and pistols. The picturesque
crowds, and the Arabs and the horsemen, in the sunshine ; the
noble old convent, and the gray-bearded priests, with their
feast ; and the church, and its pictures and columns, and incense ; the wide brown hills spreading round the village ; with
the accidents of the road, — flocks and shepherds, wells and
funerals, and camel-trains, — have left on my mind a brilliant,
romantic, and cheerful picture. But you, Dear M——, without visiting the place, have imagined one far finer ; and Bethlehem, where the Holy Child was born, and the angels sang,
" Glory to God in the highest, and on earth peace and good-
will towards men," is the most sacred and beautiful spot in the
earth to you.

By far the most comfortable quarters in Jerusalem are those
of the Armenians, in their convent of St. James. Wherever
we have been, these Eastern quakers look grave, and jolly, and
sleek. Their convent at Mount Zion is big enough to contain
two or three thousand of their faithful ; and their church is
ornamented by the most rich and hideous gifts ever devised by
uncouth piety. Instead of a bell, the fat monks of the convent
beat huge noises on a board, and drub the faithful in to prayers.
I never saw men more lazy and rosy, than these reverend
fathers, kneeling in their comfortable matted church, or sitting
in easy devotion. Pictures, images, gilding, tinsel, wax-candles,
twinkle all over the place ; and ten thousand ostrichs' eggs (or

any lesser number you may allot) dangle from the vaulted ceiling. There were great numbers of people at worship in this gorgeous church; they went on their knees, kissing the walls with much fervor, and paying reverence to the most precious relic of the convent, — the chair of St. James, their patron, the first Bishop of Jerusalem.

The chair pointed out with greatest pride in the church of the Latin Convent, is that shabby red damask one appropriated to the French Consul, — the representative of the king of that nation, — and the protection which it has from time immemorial accorded to the Christians of the Latin rite in Syria. All French writers and travellers speak of this protection with delightful complacency. Consult the French books of travel on the subject, and any Frenchman whom you may meet: he says, " La France, Monsieur, de tous les temps protège les Chrétiens d'Orient ;" and the little fellow looks round the church with a sweep of the arm, and protects it accordingly. It is *bon ton* for them to go in processions ; and you see them on such errands, marching with long candles, as gravely as may be. But I have never been able to edify myself with their devotion ; and the religious outpourings of Lamartine and Chateaubriand, which we have all been reading àpropos of the journey we are to make, have inspired me with an emotion anything but respectful. " Voyez comme M. de Chateaubriand prie Dieu," the Viscount's eloquence seems always to say. There is a sanctified grimace about the little French pilgrim which it is very difficult to contemplate gravely.

The pictures, images, and ornaments of the principal Latin convent are quite mean and poor, compared to the wealth of the Armenians. The convent is spacious, but squalid. Many hopping and crawling plagues are said to attack the skins of pilgrims who sleep there. It is laid out in courts and galleries, the mouldy doors of which are decorated with twopennny pictures of favorite saints and martyrs : and so great is the shabbiness and laziness, that you might fancy yourself in a convent in Italy. Brown-clad fathers, dirty, bearded, and sallow, go gliding about the corridors. The relic manufactory before mentioned carries on a considerable business, and despatches bales of shells, crosses, and beads to believers in Europe. These constitute the chief revenue of the convent now. *La France* is no longer the most Christian kingdom, and her protection of the Latins is not good for much since Charles X. was expelled : and Spain, which used likewise to be generous on occasions, (the gifts, arms, candlesticks, baldaquins of the Spanish sovereigns figure pretty frequently in the various Latin chapels,) has been stingy since the late disturbances, the spoliation of the clergy, &c. After we had been taken to see the humble curiosities of the place, the Prior treated us in his wooden parlor with little glasses of pink Rosolio, brought with many bows and genuflexions by his reverence the convent butler.

After this community of holy men, the most important perhaps is the American Convent, a Protestant congregation of Independents chiefly, who deliver tracts, propose to make converts, have meetings of their own, and also swell the little congregation that attends the Anglican service. I have mentioned our fellow-traveller, the Consul-General for Syria of the United States. He was a tradesman, who had made a considerable fortune, and lived at a country-house in comfortable retirement. But his opinion is, that the prophecies of Scripture are about to be accomplished ; that the day of the return of the Jews is at hand, and the glorification of the restored Jerusalem. He is to witness this — he and a favorite dove with which he travels ; and he forsook home and comfortable country-house, in order to make this journey. He has no other knowledge of Syria but what he derives from the prophecy ; and this (as he takes the office gratis) has been considered a sufficient reason for his appointment by the United States Government. As soon as he arrived, he sent and demanded an interview with the Pasha ; explained to him his interpretation of the Apocalypse, in which he has discovered that the Five Powers and America are about to intervene in Syrian affairs, and the infallible return of the Jews to Palestine. The news must have astonished the Lieutenant of the Sublime Porte ; and since the days of the Kingdom of Munster, under his Anabaptist Majesty, John of Leyden, I doubt whether any Government has received or appointed so queer an ambassador. The kind, worthy, simple man took me to his temporary consulate-house at the American Missionary Establishment ; and, under pretence of treating me to white wine, expounded his ideas ; talked of futurity as he would about an article in *The Times ;* and had no more doubt of seeing a divine kingdom established in Jerusalem than you that there will be a levée next spring at St. James's. The little room in which we sat was padded with missionary tracts, but I heard of scarce any converts — not more than are made by our own Episcopal establishment.

But if the latter's religious victories are small, and very few people are induced by the American tracts, and the English preaching and catechising, to forsake their own manner of worshipping the Divine Being in order to follow ours; yet surely our religious colony of men and women can't fail to do good, by the sheer force of good example, pure life, and kind offices. The ladies of the mission have numbers of clients, of all persuasions, in the town, to whom they extend their charities. Each of their houses is a model of neatness, and a dispensary of gentle kindnesses; and the ecclesiastics have formed a modest centre of civilization in the place. A dreary joke was made in the House of Commons about Bishop Alexander and the Bishopess his lady, and the Bishoplings, his numerous children, who were said to have scandalized the people of Jerusalem. That sneer evidently came from the Latins and Greeks; for what could the Jews and Turks care because an English clergyman had a wife and children as their own priests have? There was no sort of ill-will exhibited towards them, as far as I could learn; and I saw the Bishop's children riding about the town as safely as they could about Hyde Park. All Europeans, indeed, seemed to me to be received with forbearance, and almost courtesy, within the walls. As I was going about making sketches, the people would look on very good-humoredly, without offering the least interruption; nay, two or three were quite ready to stand still for such a humble portrait as my pencil could make of them; and the sketch done, it was passed from one person to another, each making his comments, and signifying a very polite approval. Here are a pair of

them, Fath Allah and Ameenut Daoodee his father, horse-dealers by trade, who came and sat with us at the inn, and smoked pipes (the sun being down), while the original of this masterpiece was made. With the Arabs outside the walls, however, and the freshly arriving country-people, this politeness was not so much exhibited. There was a certain tattooed girl, with

black eyes and huge silver ear rings, and a chin delicately picked out with blue, who formed one of a group of women outside the great convent, whose likeness I longed to carry off; — there was a woman with a little child, with wondering eyes, drawing water at the pool of Siloam, in such an attitude and dress as Rebecca may have had when Isaac's lieutenant asked her for drink : — both of these parties standing still for half a minute, at the next cried out for backsheesh ; and not content with the five piastres which I gave them individually, screamed out for more, and summoned their friends, who screamed out backsheesh too. I was pursued into the convent by a dozen howling women calling for pay, barring the door against them, to the astonishment of the worthy papa who kept it; and at Miriam's Well the women were joined by a man with a large stick, who backed their petition. But him we could afford to laugh at, for we were two, and had sticks likewise.

In the village of Siloam I would not recommend the artist to loiter. A colony of ruffians inhabit the dismal place, who have guns as well as sticks at need. Their dogs howl after the strangers as they pass through ; and over the parapets of their walls you are saluted by the scowls of a villanous set of countenances, that it is not good to see with one pair of eyes. They shot a man at mid-day at a few hundred yards from the gates while we were at Jerusalem, and no notice was taken of the murder. Hordes of Arab robbers infest the neighborhood of the city, with the Sheikhs of whom travellers make terms when minded to pursue their journey. I never could understand why the walls stopped these warriors if they had a mind to plunder the city, for there are but a hundred and fifty men in the garrison to man the long lonely lines of defence.

I have seen only in Titian's pictures those magnificent purple shadows in which the hills round about lay, as the dawn rose faintly behind them ; and we looked at Olivet for the last time from our terrace, where we were awaiting the arrival of the horses that were to carry us to Jaffa. A yellow moon was still blazing in the midst of countless brilliant stars overhead ; the nakedness and misery of the surrounding city were hidden in that beautiful rosy atmosphere of mingling night and dawn. The city never looked so noble ; the mosques, domes, and minarets rising up into the calm starlit sky.

By the gate of Bethlehem there stands one palm-tree, and a house with three domes. Put these and the huge old Gothic gate as a background dark against the yellowing eastern sky :

the foreground is a deep gray : as you look into it dark forms
of horsemen come out of the twilight : now there come lanterns, more horsemen, a litter with mules, a crowd of Arab
horseboys and dealers accompanying their beasts to the gate ;
all the members of our party come up by twos and threes ;
and, at last, the great gate opens just before sunrise, and we
get into the gray plains.

Oh! the luxury of an English saddle ! An English servant
of one of the gentlemen of the mission procured it for me, on
the back of a little mare, which (as I am a light weight) did
not turn a hair in the course of the day's march — and after
we got quit of the ugly, stony, clattering, mountainous Abou
Gosh district, into the fair undulating plain, which stretches to
Ramleh, carried me into the town at a pleasant hand-gallop.
A negro, of preternatural ugliness, in a yellow gown, with a
crimson handkerchief streaming over his head, digging his
shovel spurs into the lean animal he rode, and driving three
others before — swaying backwards and forwards on his horse,
now embracing his ears, and now almost under his belly,
screaming " yallah " with the most frightful shrieks, and singing country songs — galloped along ahead of me. I acquired
one of his poems pretty well, and could imitate his shriek accurately ; but I shall not have the pleasure of singing it to you
in England. I had forgotten the delightful dissonance two
days after, both the negro's and that of a real Arab minstrel,
a donkey-driver accompanying our baggage, who sang and
grinned with the most amusing good-humor.

We halted, in the middle of the day, in a little wood of
olive-trees, which forms almost the only shelter between Jaffa
and Jerusalem, except that afforded by the orchards in the
odious village of Abou Gosh, through which we went at a
double-quick pace. Under the olives, or up in the branches,
some of our friends took a siesta. I have a sketch of four of
them so employed. Two of them were dead within a month of
the fatal Syrian fever. But we did not know how near fate was
to us then. Fires were lighted, and fowls and eggs divided, and
tea and coffee served round in tin panikins, and here we lighted
pipes, and smoked and laughed at our ease. I believe everybody was happy to be out of Jerusalem. The impression I
have of it now is of ten days passed in a fever.

We all found quarters in the Greek convent at Ramleh,
where the monks served us a supper on a terrace, in a pleasant
sunset ; a beautiful and cheerful landscape stretching around ;
the land in graceful undulations, the towers and mosques rosy

in the sunset, with no lack of verdure, especially of graceful palms. Jaffa was nine miles off. As we rode all the morning we had been accompanied by the smoke of our steamer, twenty miles off at sea.

The convent is a huge caravanserai; only three or four monks dwell in it, the ghostly hotel-keepers of the place. The horses were tied up and fed in the court-yard, into which we rode; above were the living-rooms, where there is accommodation, not only for an unlimited number of pilgrims, but for a vast and innumerable host of hopping and crawling things, who usually persist in partaking of the traveller's bed. Let all thin-skinned travellers in the East be warned on no account to travel without the admirable invention described in Mr. Fellowes' book; nay, possibly invented by that enterprising and learned traveller. You make a sack, of calico or linen, big enough for the body, appended to which is a closed chimney of muslin, stretched out by cane-hoops, and fastened up to a beam, or against the wall. You keep a sharp eye to see that no flea or bug is on the look-out, and when assured of this, you pop into the bag, tightly closing the orifice after you. This admirable bug-disappointer I tried at Ramleh, and had the only undisturbed night's rest I enjoyed in the east. To be sure it was a short night, for our party were stirring at one o'clock, and those who got up insisted on talking and keeping awake those who inclined to sleep. But I shall never forget the terror inspired in my mind, being shut up in the bug-disappointer, when a facetious lay-brother of the convent fell upon me and began *tickling* me. I never had the courage again to try the anti-flea contrivance, preferring the friskiness of those animals to the sports of such a greasy grinning wag as my friend at Ramleh.

In the morning, and long before sunrise, our little caravan was in marching order again. We went out with lanterns and shouts of "yallah" through the narrow streets, and issued into the plain, where, though there was no moon, there were blazing stars shining steadily overhead. They become friends to a man who travels, especially under the clear Eastern sky; whence they look down as if protecting you, solemn, yellow, and refulgent. They seem *nearer* to you than in Europe; larger and more awful. So we rode on till the dawn rose, and Jaffa came in view. The friendly ship was lying out in waiting for us; the horses were given up to their owners: and in the midst of a crowd of naked beggars, and a perfect storm of curses and yells for backsheesh, our party got into their boats.

and to the ship, where we were welcomed by the very best captain that ever sailed upon this maritime globe, namely, Captain Samuel Lewis of the Peninsular and Oriental Company's Service.

CHAPTER XIV.

FROM JAFFA TO ALEXANDRIA.

[From the Provider's Log-Book.]

BILL OF FARE, OCTOBER 12TH.

Mulligatawny Soup.	Cabbage.
Salt Fish and Egg Sauce.	French Beans.
Roast Haunch of Mutton.	Boiled Potatoes.
Boiled Shoulder and Onion Sauce.	Baked ditto.
Boiled Beef.	
Roast Fowls.	Damson Tart.
Pillau ditto.	Currant ditto.
Ham.	Rice Puddings.
Haricot Mutton.	Currant Fritters.
Curry and Rice.	

WE were just at the port's mouth — and could see the towers and buildings of Alexandria rising purple against the sunset, when the report of a gun came booming over the calm golden water; and we heard, with much mortification, that we had no chance of getting pratique that night. Already the ungrateful passengers had begun to tire of the ship, — though in our absence in Syria it had been carefully cleansed and purified; though it was cleared of the swarming Jews who had infested the decks all the way from Constantinople; and though we had been feasting and carousing in the manner described above.

But very early next morning we bore into the harbor, busy with a great quantity of craft. We passed huge black hulks of mouldering men-of-war, from the sterns of which trailed the dirty red flag, with the star and crescent; boats, manned with red-capped seamen, and captains and steersmen in beards and tarbooshes, passed continually among these old hulks, the rowers bending to their oars, so that at each stroke they disappeared bodily in the boat. Besides these, there was a large fleet of country ships, and stars and stripes, and tricolors, and Union Jacks; and many active steamers, of the

French and English companies, shooting in and out of the harbor, or moored in the briny waters. The ship of *our* company, the "Oriental," lay there — a palace upon the brine, and some of the Pasha's steam-vessels likewise, looking very like Christian boats; but it was queer to look at some unintelligible Turkish flourish painted on the stern, and the long-tailed Arabian hieroglyphics gilt on the paddle-boxes. Our dear friend and comrade of Beyrout (if we may be permitted to call her so), H.M.S. "Trump," was in the harbor; and the captain of that gallant ship, coming to greet us, drove some of us on shore in his gig.

I had been preparing myself overnight, by the help of a cigar and a moonlight contemplation on deck, for sensations on landing in Egypt. I was ready to yield myself up with solemnity to the mystic grandeur of the scene of initiation. Pompey's Pillar must stand like a mountain, in a yellow plain, surrounded by a grove of obelisks as tall as palm-trees. Placid sphinxes brooding o'er the Nile — mighty Memnonian countenances calm — had revealed Egypt to me in a sonnet of Tennyson's, and I was ready to gaze on it with pyramidal wonder and hieroglyphic awe.

The landing quay at Alexandria is like the dockyard quay at Portsmouth: with a few score of brown faces scattered among the population. There are slop-sellers, dealers in marine-stores, bottled-porter shops, seamen lolling about; flies and cabs are plying for hire: and a yelling chorus of donkey-boys, shrieking, "Ride, sir! — donkey, sir! — I say, sir!" in excellent English, dispel all romantic notions. The placid sphinxes brooding o'er the Nile disappeared with that shriek of the donkey-boys. You might be as well impressed with Wapping as with your first step on Egyptian soil.

The riding of a donkey is, after all, not a dignified occupation. A man resists the offer at first, somehow, as an indignity. How is that poor little, red-saddled, long-eared creature to carry you? Is there to be one for you and another for your legs? Natives and Europeans, of all sizes, pass by, it is true, mounted upon the same contrivance. I waited until I got into a very private spot, where nobody could see me, and then ascended — why not say descended, at once? — on the poor little animal. Instead of being crushed at once, as perhaps the rider expected, it darted forward, quite briskly and cheerfully, at six or seven miles an hour; requiring no spur or admonitive to haste, except the shrieking of the little Egyptian gamin, who ran along by ʼsinus's side.

The character of the houses by which you pass is scarcely Eastern at all. The streets are busy with a motley population of Jews and Armenians, slave-driving-looking Europeans, large-breeched Greeks, and well-shaven buxom merchants, looking as trim and fat as those on the Bourse or on 'Change; only, among the natives, the stranger can't fail to remark (as the Caliph did of the Calendars, in the "Arabian Nights") that so many of them *have only one eye*. It is the horrid ophthalmia which has played such frightful ravages with them. You see children sitting in the doorways, their eyes completely closed up with the green sickening sore, and the flies feeding on them. Five or six minutes of the donkey-ride brings you to the Frank quarter, and the handsome broad street (like a street of Marseilles) where the principal hotels and merchants' houses are to be found, and where the consuls have their houses, and hoist their flags. The palace of the French Consul-General makes the grandest show in the street, and presents a great contrast to the humble abode of the English representative, who protects his fellow-countrymen from a second floor.

But that Alexandrian two-pair-front of a Consulate was more welcome and cheering than a palace to most of us. For there lay certain letters, with post-marks of *Home* upon them; and kindly tidings, the first heard for two months : — though we had seen so many men and cities since, that Cornhill seemed to be a year off, at least, with certain persons dwelling (more or less) in that vicinity. I saw a young Oxford man seize his despatches, and slink off with several letters, written in a tight, neat hand, and sedulously crossed; which any man could see, without looking farther, were the handiwork of Mary Ann, to whom he is attached. The lawyer received a bundle from his chambers, in which his clerk eased his soul regarding the state of Snooks *v.* Rodgers, Smith *ats* Tomkins, &c. The statesman had a packet of thick envelopes, decorated with that profusion of sealing-wax in which official recklessness lavishes the resources of the country : and your humble servant got just one little, modest letter containing another, written in pencil characters, varying in size between one and two inches; but how much pleasanter to read than my lord's despatch, or the clerk's account of Smith *ats* Tomkins, — yes, even than the Mary Ann correspondence! . . . . Yes, my dear madam, you will understand me, when I say that it was from little Polly at home, with some confidential news about a cat, and the last report of her new doll.

It is worth while to have made the journey for this pleasure : to have walked the deck on long nights, and have thought of home. You have no leisure to do so in the city. You don't see the heavens shine above you so purely there, or the stars so clearly. How, after the perusal of the above documents, we enjoyed a file of the admirable *Galignani ;* and what O'Connell was doing ; and the twelve last new victories of the French in Algeria ; and, above all, six or seven numbers of *Punch !* There might have been an avenue of Pompey's Pillars within reach, and a live sphinx sporting on the banks of the Mahmoodieh Canal, and we would not have stirred to see them, until *Punch-* had had his interview and *Galignani* was dismissed.

The curiosities of Alexandria are few, and easily seen. We went into the bazaars, which have a much more Eastern look than the European quarter, with its Anglo-Gallic-Italian inhabitants, and Babel-like civilization. Here and there a large hotel, clumsy and whitewashed, with Oriental trellised windows, and a couple of slouching sentinels at the doors, in the ugliest composite uniform that ever was seen, was pointed out as the residence of some great officer of the Pasha's Court, or of one of the numerous children of the Egyptian Solomon. His Highness was in his own palace, and was consequently not visible. He was in deep grief, and strict retirement. It was at this time that the European newspapers announced that he was about to resign his empire ; but the quidnuncs of Alexandria hinted that a love-affair, in which the old potentate had engaged with senile extravagance, and the effects of a potion of hachich, or some deleterious drug, with which he was in the habit of intoxicating himself, had brought on that languor and desperate weariness of life and governing, into which the venerable Prince was plunged. Before three days were over, however, the fit had left him, and he determined to live and reign a little longer. A very few days afterwards several of our party were presented to him at Cairo, and found the great Egyptian ruler perfectly convalescent.

This and the Opera, and the quarrels of the two *prime donne*, and the beauty of one of them, formed the chief subjects of conversation ; and I had this important news in the shop of a certain barber in the town, who conveyed it in a language composed of French, Spanish, and Italian, and with a volubility quite worthy of a barber of Gil Blas.

Then we went to see the famous obelisk presented by Mehemet Ali to the British Government, who have not shown a particular alacrity to accept this ponderous present. The huge shaft lies on the ground prostrate, and desecrated by all sorts of abominations. Children were sprawling about, attracted by the dirt there. Arabs, negroes, and donkey-boys were passing, quite indifferent, by the fallen monster of a stone, — as indifferent as the British Government, who don't care for recording the glorious termination of their Egyptian campaign of 1801. If our country takes the compliment so coolly, surely it would be disloyal upon our parts to be more enthusiastic. I wish they would offer the Trafalgar Square Pillar to the Egyptians; and that both of the huge, ugly monsters were lying in the dirt there, side by side.

Pompey's Pillar is by no means so big as the Charing Cross trophy. This venerable column has not escaped ill-treatment either. Numberless ships' companies, travelling Cockneys, &c., have affixed their rude marks upon it. Some daring ruffian even painted the name of "Warren's blacking" upon it, effacing other inscriptions, — one, Wilkinson says, "of the second Psammetichus." I regret deeply, my dear friend, that I cannot give you this document respecting a lamented monarch, in whose history I know you take such an interest.

The best sight I saw in Alexandria was a negro holiday; which was celebrated outside of the town by a sort of negro village of huts, swarming with old, lean, fat, ugly, infantine, happy faces, that nature has smeared with a preparation even more black and durable than that with which Psammetichus's base has been polished. Every one of these jolly faces was on the broad grin, from the dusky mother to the India-rubber child sprawling upon her back, and the venerable jetty senior whose wool was as white as that of a sheep in Florian's pastorals.

To these dancers a couple of fellows were playing on a drum and a little banjo. They were singing a chorus, which was not only singular, and perfectly marked in the rhythm, but exceeding sweet in the tune. They danced in a circle; and performers came trooping from all quarters, who fell into the round, and began waggling their heads, and waving their left hands, and tossing up and down the little thin rods which they each carried, and all singing to the very best of their power.

I saw the chief eunuch of the Grand Turk at Constantinople pass by — but with what a different expression! Though he is one of the greatest of the great in the Turkish Empire (ranking with a Cabinet Minister or Lord Chamberlain here), his fine countenance was clouded with care, and savage with ennui.

27

Here his black brethren were ragged, starving, and happy; and I need not tell such a fine moralist as you are, how it is the case, in the white as well as the black world, that happiness (republican leveller, who does not care a fig for the fashion) often disdains the turrets of kings, to pay a visit to the "tabernas pauperum."

We went the round of the coffee-houses in the evening, both the polite European places of resort, where you get ices and the French papers, and those in the town, where Greeks, Turks, and general company resort, to sit upon uncomfortable chairs, and drink wretched muddy coffee, and to listen to two or three miserable musicians, who keep up a variation of howling for hours together. But the pretty song of the niggers had spoiled me for that abominable music.

CHAPTER XV.

TO CAIRO.

WE had no need of hiring the country boats which ply on the Mahmoodieh Canal to Atfeh, where it joins the Nile, but were accommodated in one of the Peninsular and Oriental Company's fly-boats; pretty similar to those narrow Irish canal-boats in which the enterprising traveller has been carried from Dublin to Ballinasloe. The present boat was, to be sure, tugged by a little steamer, so that the Egyptian canal is ahead of the Irish in so far: in natural scenery, the one prospect is fully equal to the other; it must be confessed that there is nothing to see. In truth, there was nothing but this: you saw a muddy bank on each side of you, and a blue sky overhead. A few round mud-huts and palm-trees were planted along the line here and there. Sometimes we would see, on the water-side, a woman in a blue robe, with her son by her, in that tight brown costume with which Nature had supplied him. Now, it was a hat dropped by one of the party into the water; a brown Arab plunged and disappeared incontinently after the hat, re-issued from the muddy water, prize in hand, and ran naked after the little steamer (which was by this time far ahead of him), his brawny limbs shining in the sun: then we had half-cold fowls and bitter ale: then we had dinner — bitter ale and cold fowls;

with which incidents the day on the canal passed away, as harmlessly as if we had been in a Dutch trackschuyt.

Towards evening we arrived at the town of Atfeh — half land, half houses, half palm-trees, with swarms of half-naked people crowding the rustic shady bazaars, and bartering their produce of fruit or many-colored grain. Here the canal came to a check, ending abruptly with a large lock. A little fleet of masts and country ships were beyond the lock, and it led into THE NILE.

After all, it is something to have seen these red waters. It is only low green banks, mud-huts, and palm-clumps, with the sun setting red behind them, and the great, dull, sinuous river flashing here and there in the light. But it is the Nile, the old Saturn of a stream — a divinity yet, though younger river-gods have deposed him. Hail! O venerable father of crocodiles! We were all lost in sentiments of the profoundest awe and respect; which we proved by tumbling down into the cabin of the Nile steamer that was waiting to receive us, and fighting and cheating for sleeping berths.

At dawn in the morning we were on deck; the character had not altered of the scenery about the river. Vast flat stretches of land were on either side, recovering from the subsiding inundations: near the mud villages, a country ship or two was roosting under the date-trees; the landscape everywhere stretching away level and lonely. In the sky in the east was a long streak of greenish light, which widened and rose until it grew to be of an opal color, then orange; then, behold, the round red disc of the sun rose flaming up above the horizon. All the water blushed as he got up; the deck was all red; the steersman gave his helm to another, and prostrated himself on the deck, and bowed his head eastward, and praised the Maker of the sun: it shone on his white turban as he was kneeling, and gilt up his bronzed face, and sent his blue shadow over the glowing deck. The distances, which had been gray, were now clothed in purple; and the broad stream was illuminated. As the sun rose higher, the morning blush faded away; the sky was cloudless and pale, and the river and the surrounding landscape were dazzlingly clear.

Looking ahead in an hour or two, we saw the Pyramids. Fancy my sensations, dear M——; — two big ones and a little one:

!   !   !

There they lay, rosy and solemn in the distance — those old, majestical, mystical, familiar edifices. Several of us tried to be impressed; but breakfast supervening, a rush was made at the coffee and cold pies, and the sentiment of awe was lost in the scramble for victuals.

Are we so blasés of the world that the greatest marvels in it do not succeed in moving us? Have society, Pall Mall clubs, and a habit of sneering, so withered up our organs of veneration that we can admire no more? My sensation with regard to the Pyramids was, that I had seen them before: then came a feeling of shame that the view of them should awaken no respect. Then I wanted (naturally) to see whether my neighbors were any more enthusiastic than myself — Trinity College, Oxford, was busy with the cold ham: Downing Street was particularly attentive to a bunch of grapes: Fig-tree Court behaved with decent propriety; he is in good practice, and of a Conservative turn of mind, which leads him to respect from principle *les faits accomplis;* perhaps he remembered that one of them was as big as Lincoln's Inn Fields. But, the truth is, nobody was seriously moved. . . . . And why should they, because of an exaggeration of bricks ever so enormous? I confess, for my part, that the Pyramids are very big.

After a voyage of about thirty hours, the steamer brought up at the quay of Boulak, amidst a small fleet of dirty comfortless Cangias, in which cottons and merchandise were loading and unloading, and a huge noise and bustle on the shore. Numerous villas, parks, and country-houses, had begun to decorate the Cairo bank of the stream ere this: residences of the Pasha's nobles, who have had orders to take their pleasure here and beautify the precincts of the capital; tall factory chimneys also rise here; there are foundries and steam-engine manufactories. These, and the pleasure-houses, stand as trim as soldiers on parade; contrasting with the swarming, slovenly, close, tumble-down, eastern old town, that forms the outport of Cairo, and was built before the importation of European taste and discipline.

Here we alighted upon donkeys, to the full as brisk as those of Alexandria, invaluable to timid riders, and equal to any weight. We had a Jerusalem pony race into Cairo; my animal beating all the rest by many lengths. The entrance to the capital, from Boulak, is very pleasant and picturesque — over a fair road, and the wide-planted plain of the Ezbekieh; where are gardens, canals, fields, and avenues of trees, and where the great ones of the town come and take their pleasure. We saw

EGYPTIAN VILLA.

many barouches driving about with fat Pashas lolling on the cushions; stately-looking colonels and doctors taking their ride, followed by their orderlies or footmen; lines of people taking pipes and sherbet in the coffee-houses; and one of the pleasantest sights of all, — a fine new white building with Hôtel d'Orient written up in huge French characters, and which, indeed, is an establishment as large and comfortable as most of the best inns of the South of France. As a hundred Christian people, or more, come from England and from India every fortnight, this inn has been built to accommodate a large proportion of them; and twice a month, at least, its sixty rooms are full.

The gardens from the windows give a very pleasant and animated view: the hotel-gate is besieged by crews of donkey-drivers; the noble stately Arab women, with tawny skins (of which a simple robe of floating blue cotton enables you liberally to see the color) and large black eyes, come to the well hard by for water: camels are perpetually arriving and setting down their loads: the court is full of bustling dragomans, ayahs, and children from India; and poor old venerable he-nurses, with gray beards and crimson turbans, tending little white-faced babies that have seen the light at Dumdum or Futtyghur: a copper-colored barber, seated on his hams, is shaving a camel-driver at the great inn-gate. The bells are ringing prodigiously; and Lieutenant Waghorn is bouncing in and out of the court-yard full of business. He only left Bombay yesterday morning, was seen in the Red Sea on Tuesday, is engaged to dinner this afternoon in the Regent's Park, and (as it is about two minutes since I saw him in the court-yard) I make no doubt he is by this time at Alexandria or at Malta, say, perhaps at both. *Il en est capable*. If any man can be at two places at once (which I don't believe or deny) Waghorn is he.

Six-o'clock bell rings. Sixty people sit down to a quasi French banquet: thirty Indian officers in moustaches and jackets; ten civilians in ditto and spectacles; ten pale-faced ladies with ringlets, to whom all pay prodigious attention. All the pale ladies drink pale ale, which, perhaps, accounts for it; in fact the Bombay and Suez passengers have just arrived, and hence this crowding and bustling, and display of military jackets and moustaches, and ringlets and beauty. The windows are open, and a rush of mosquitoes from the Ezbekieh waters, attracted by the wax-candles, adds greatly to the excitement of the scene. There was a little tough old Major, who persisted in flinging open the windows, to admit these volatile creatures, with a noble disregard to their sting — and the pale ringlets did not seem to heed them either, though the delicate shoulders of some of them were bare.

All the meat, ragoûts, fricandeaux, and roasts, which are served round at dinner, seem to me to be of the same meat : a black uncertain sort of viand do these " flesh-pots of Egypt" contain. But what the meat is no one knew ; is it the donkey? The animal is more plentiful than any other in Cairo.

After dinner, the ladies retiring, some of us take a mixture of hot water, sugar, and pale French brandy, which is said to be deleterious, but is by no means unpalatable. One of the Indians offers a bundle of Bengal cheroots ; and we make acquaintance with those honest bearded white-jacketed Majors and military Commanders, finding England here in a French hotel kept by an Italian, at the city of Grand Cairo, in Africa.

On retiring to bed you take a towel with you into the sacred interior, behind the mosquito curtains. Then your duty is, having tucked the curtains closely around, to flap and bang violently with this towel, right and left, and backwards and forwards, until every mosquito shall have been massacred that may have taken refuge within your muslin canopy.

Do what you will, however, one of them always escapes the murder ; and as soon as the candle is out the miscreant begins his infernal droning and trumpeting ; descends playfully upon your nose and face, and so lightly that you don't know that he touches you. But that for a week afterwards you bear about marks of his ferocity, you might take the invisible little being to be a creature of fancy — a mere singing in your ears.

This, as an account of Cairo, dear M——, you will probably be disposed to consider as incomplete : the fact is, I have seen nothing else as yet. I have peered into no harems. The magicians, proved to be humbugs, have been bastinadoed out of town. The dancing-girls, those lovely Alme, of whom I had hoped to be able to give a glowing and elegant, though strictly moral, description, have been whipped into Upper Egypt, and as you are saying in your mind . . . . Well, it *isn't* a good description of Cairo ; you are perfectly right. It is England in Egypt. I like to see her there with her pluck, enterprise, manliness, bitter ale, and Harvey sauce. Wherever they come they stay and prosper. From the summit of yonder Pyramids forty centuries may look down on them if they are minded ; and I say, those venerable daughters of time ought to be better pleased by the examination, than by regarding the

French bayonets and General Bonaparte, Member of the Institute, fifty years ago, running about with sabre and pigtail. Wonders he did, to be sure, and then ran away, leaving Kleber, to be murdered, in the lurch — a few hundred yards from the spot where these disquisitions are written. But what are his wonders compared to Waghorn? Nap massacred the Mamelukes at the Pyramids: Wag has conquered the Pyramids themselves; dragged the unwieldy structures a month nearer England than they were, and brought the country along with them. All the trophies and captives that ever were brought to Roman triumph were not so enormous and wonderful as this. All the heads that Napoleon ever caused to be struck off (as George Cruikshank says) would not elevate him a monument as big. Be ours the trophies of peace! O my country! O Waghorn! *Hæ tibi erunt artes.* When I go to the Pyramids I will sacrifice in your name, and pour out libations of bitter ale and Harvey sauce in your honor.

One of the noblest views in the world is to be seen from the citadel, which we ascended to-day. You see the city stretching beneath it, with a thousand minarets and mosques, — the great river curling through the green plains, studded with innumerable villages. The Pyramids are beyond, brilliantly distinct; and the lines and fortifications of the height, and the arsenal lying below. Gazing down, the guide does not fail to point out the famous Mameluke leap, by which one of the corps escaped death, at the time that his Highness the Pasha arranged the general massacre of the body.

The venerable Patriarch's harem is close by, where he received, with much distinction, some of the members of our party. We were allowed to pass very close to the sacred precincts, and saw a comfortable white European building, approached by flights of steps, and flanked by pretty gardens. Police and law-courts were here also, as I understood; but it was not the time of the Egyptian assizes. It would have been pleasant, otherwise, to see the chief cadi in his hall of justice; and painful, though instructive, to behold the immediate application of the bastinado.

The great lion of the place is a new mosque which Mehemet Ali is constructing very leisurely. It is built of alabaster of a fair white, with a delicate blushing tinge; but the ornaments are European — the noble, fantastic, beautiful Oriental art is forgotten. The old mosques of the city, of which I entered two, and looked at many, are a thousand times more beautiful. Their variety of ornament is astonishing, — the difference in the shapes of the domes, the beautiful fancies and caprices in the forms of the minarets, which violate the rules of proportion with the most happy, daring grace, must have struck every architect who has seen them. As you go through the streets, these architectural beauties keep the eye continually charmed : now it is a marble fountain, with its arabesque and carved over-hanging roof, which you can look at with as much pleasure as an antique gem, so neat and brilliant is the execution of it ; then, you come to the arched entrance to a mosque, which shoots up like — like what? — like the most beautiful pirouette by Taglioni, let us say. This architecture is not sublimely beautiful, perfect loveliness and calm, like that which was revealed to us at the Parthenon (and in comparison of which the Pantheon and Colosseum are vulgar and coarse, mere broad-shouldered Titans before ambrosial Jove) ; but these fantastic spires, and cupolas, and galleries, excite, amuse, *tickle* the imagination, so to speak, and perpetually fascinate the eye. There were very few believers in the famous mosque of Sultan Hassan when we visited it, except the Moslemitish beadle, who was on the look-out for backsheesh, just like his brother officer in an English cathedral ; and who, making us put on straw slippers, so as not to pollute the sacred pavement of the place, conducted us through it.

It is stupendously light and airy ; the best specimens of Norman art that I have seen (and surely the Crusaders must have carried home the models of these heathenish temples in their eyes) do not exceed its noble grace and simplicity. The mystics make discoveries at home, that the Gothic architecture is Catholicism carved in stone — (in which case, and if archi-tectural beauty is a criterion or expression of religion, what a dismal barbarous creed must that expressed by the Bethesda meeting-house and Independent chapels be?) — if, as they would gravely hint, because Gothic architecture is beautiful, Catholicism is therefore lovely and right, — why, Mahometan-ism must have been right and lovely too once. Never did a creed possess temples more elegant ; as elegant as the Cathedral at Rouen, or the Baptistery at Pisa.

But it is changed now. There was nobody at prayers ; only the official beadles, and the supernumerary guides, who came for backsheesh. Faith hath degenerated. Accordingly they can't build these mosques, or invent these perfect forms, any more. Witness the tawdry incompleteness and vulgarity of the Pasha's new temple, and the woful failures among the very late edifices in Constantinople !

However, they still make pilgrimages to Mecca in great force. The Mosque of Hassan is hard by the green plain on which the *Hag* encamps before it sets forth annually on its pious peregrination. It was not yet its time, but I saw in the bazaars that redoubted Dervish, who is the Master of the Hag — the leader of every procession, accompanying the sacred camel; and a personage almost as much respected as Mr. O'Connell in Ireland.

This fellow lives by alms (I mean the head of the Hag). Winter and summer he wears no clothes but a thin and scanty white shirt. He wields a staff, and stalks along scowling and barefoot. His immense shock of black hair streams behind him, and his brown, brawny body is curled over with black hair, like a savage man. This saint has the largest harem in the town; he is said to be enormously rich by the contributions he has levied; and is so adored for his holiness by the infatuated folk, that when he returns from the Hag (which he does on horseback, the chief Mollahs going out to meet him and escort him home in state along the Ezbekieh road,) the people fling themselves down under the horse's feet, eager to be trampled upon and killed, and confident of heaven if the great Hadji's horse will but kick them into it. Was it my fault if I thought of Hadji Daniel, and the believers in him?

There was no Dervish of repute on the plain when I passed; only one poor, wild fellow, who was dancing, with glaring eyes and grizzled beard, rather to the contempt of the bystanders, as I thought, who by no means put coppers into his extended bowl. On this poor devil's head there was a poorer devil still — a live cock, entirely plucked, but ornamented with some bits of ragged tape and scarlet and tinsel, the most horribly grotesque and miserable object I ever saw.

A little way from him, there was a sort of play going on — a clown and a knowing one, like Widdicombe and the clown with us, — the buffoon answering with blundering responses, which made all the audience shout with laughter; but the only joke which was translated to me would make you do anything but laugh, and shall therefore never be revealed by these lips. All their humor, my dragoman tells me, is of this questionable sort; and a young Egyptian gentleman, son of a Pasha, whom I subsequently met at Malta, confirmed the statement, and gave a detail of the practices of private life which was anything but edifying. The great aim of woman, he said, in the much-maligned Orient, is to administer to the brutality of her lord; her merit is in knowing how to vary the beast's pleasures.

He could give us no idea, he said, of the *wit* of the Egyptian women, and their skill in *double entendre ;* nor, I presume, did we lose much by our ignorance. What I would urge, humbly, however, is this — Do not let us be led away by German writers and æsthetics, Semilassoisms, Hahnhahnisms, and the like. The life of the East is a life of brutes. The much-maligned Orient, I am confident, has not been maligned near enough ; for the good reason that none of us can tell the amount of horrible sensuality practised there.

Beyond the jack-pudding rascal and his audience, there was on the green a spot, on which was pointed out to me a mark, as of blood. That morning the blood had spouted from the neck of an Arnaoot soldier, who had been executed for murder. These Arnaoots are the curse and terror of the citizens. Their camps are without the city ; but they are always brawling, or drunken, or murdering within, in spite of the rigid law which is applied to them, and which brings one or more of the scoundrels to death almost every week.

Some of our party had seen this fellow borne by the hotel the day before, in the midst of a crowd of soldiers who had apprehended him. The man was still formidable to his score of captors ; his clothes had been torn off ; his limbs were bound with cords ; but he was struggling frantically to get free ; and my informant described the figure and appearance of the naked, bound, writhing savage, as quite a model of beauty.

Walking in the street, this fellow had just before been struck by the looks of a woman who was passing, and laid hands on her. She ran away, and he pursued her. She ran into the police-barrack, which was luckily hard by ; but the Arnaoot was nothing daunted, and followed into the midst of the police. One of them tried to stop him. The Arnaoot pulled out a pistol, and shot the policeman dead. He cut down three or four more before he was secured. He knew his inevitable end must be death : that he could not seize upon the woman : that he could not hope to resist half a regiment of armed soldiers : yet his instinct of lust and murder was too strong ; and so he had his head taken off quite calmly this morning, many of his comrades attending their brother's last moments. He cared not the least about dying ; and knelt down and had his head off as coolly as if he were looking on at the same ceremony performed on another.

When the head was off, and the blood was spouting on the ground, a married woman, who had no children, came forward very eagerly out of the crowd, to smear herself with it, — the application of criminals' blood being considered a very favorable medicine for women afflicted with barrenness, — so she indulged in this remedy.

But one of the Arnaoots standing near said, " What, you like blood, do you?" (or words to that effect). " Let's see how yours mixes with my comrade's." And thereupon, taking out a pistol, he shot the woman in the midst of the crowd and the guards who were attending the execution; was seized of course by the latter; and no doubt to-morrow morning will have *his* head off too. It would be a good chapter to write — the Death of the Arnaoot — but I shan't go. Seeing one man hanged is quite enough in the course of a life. *J'y ai été*, as the Frenchman said of hunting.

These Arnaoots are the terror of the town. They seized hold of an Englishman the other day, and were very nearly pistolling him. Last week one of them murdered a shopkeeper at Boulak, who refused to sell him a watermelon at a price which he, the soldier, fixed upon it. So, for the matter of three-halfpence, he killed the shopkeeper; and had his own rascally head chopped off, universally regretted by his friends. Why, I wonder, does not his Highness the Pasha invite the Arnaoots to a *déjeûné* at the Citadel, as he did the Mamelukes, and serve them up the same sort of breakfast? The walls are considerably heightened since Emin Bey and his horse leapt them, and it is probable that not one of them would escape.

This sort of pistol practice is common enough here, it would appear; and not among the Arnaoots merely, but the higher orders. Thus, a short time since, one of his Highness's grandsons, whom I shall call Bluebeard Pasha (lest a revelation of the name of the said Pasha might interrupt our good relations with his country) — one of the young Pashas being backward rather in his education, and anxious to learn mathematics, and the elegant deportment of civilized life, sent to England for a tutor. I have heard he was a Cambridge man, and had learned both algebra and politeness under the Reverend Doctor Whizzle, of —— College.

One day when Mr. MacWhirter, B.A., was walking in Shoubra gardens, with his Highness the young Bluebeard Pasha, inducting him into the usages of polished society, and favoring him with reminiscences of Trumpington, there came up a poor fellah, who flung himself at the feet of young Bluebeard, and calling for justice in a loud and pathetic voice, and holding out a petition, besought his Highness to cast a gracious

eye upon the same, and see that his slave had justice done
him.

Bluebeard Pasha was so deeply engaged and interested by
his respected tutor's conversation, that he told the poor fellah
to go to the deuce, and resumed the discourse which his ill-
timed outcry for justice had interrupted. But the unlucky
wight of a fellah was pushed by his evil destiny, and thought
he would make yet another application. So he took a short
cut down one of the garden lanes, and as the Prince and the
Reverend Mr. MacWhirter, his tutor, came along once more
engaged in pleasant disquisition, behold the fellah was once
more in their way, kneeling at the august Bluebeard's feet,
yelling out for justice as before, and thrusting his petition into
the royal face.

When the Prince's conversation was thus interrupted a
second time, his royal patience and clemency were at an end.
" Man," said he, " once before I bade thee not to pester me
with thy clamor, and lo ! you have disobeyed me, — take the
consequences of disobedience to a Prince, and thy blood be
upon thine own head." So saying, he drew out a pistol and
blew out the brains of that fellah, so that he never bawled out
for justice any more.

The Reverend Mr. MacWhirter was astonished at this sudden mode of proceeding : " Gracious Prince," said he, " we do
not shoot an undergraduate at Cambridge even for walking over
a college grass-plot. — Let me suggest to your Royal Highness
that this method of ridding yourself of a poor devil's importuni-
ties is such as we should consider abrupt and almost cruel in
Europe. Let me beg you to moderate your royal impetuosity
for the future ; and, as your Highness's tutor, entreat you to be
a little less prodigal of your powder and shot."

" O Mollah ! " said his Highness, here interrupting his governor's affectionate appeal, — " you are good to talk about
Trumpington and the Pons Asinorum, but if you interfere with
the course of justice in any way, or prevent me from shooting
any dog of an Arab who snarls at my heels, I have another pistol ; and, by the beard of the Prophet ! a bullet for you too."
So saying he pulled out the weapon, with such a terrific and
significant glance at the Reverend Mr. MacWhirter, that that
gentleman wished himself back in his Combination Room again ;
and is by this time, let us hope, safely housed there.

Another facetious anecdote, the last of those I had from
a well-informed gentleman residing at Cairo, whose name (as
many copies of this book that is to be will be in the circulating

libraries there) I cannot, for obvious reasons, mention. The revenues of the country come into the august treasury through the means of farmers, to whom the districts are let out, and who are personally answerable for their quota of the taxation. This practice involves an intolerable deal of tyranny and extortion on the part of those engaged to levy the taxes, and creates a corresponding duplicity among the fellahs, who are not only wretchedly poor among themselves, but whose object is to appear still more poor, and guard their money from their rapacious overseers. Thus the Orient is much maligned; but everybody cheats there : that is a melancholy fact. The Pasha robs and cheats the merchants ; knows that the overseer robs him, and bides his time, until he makes him disgorge by the application of the tremendous bastinado ; the overseer robs and squeezes the laborer ; and the poverty-stricken devil cheats and robs in return ; and so the government moves in a happy cycle of roguery.

Deputations from the fellahs and peasants come perpetually before the august presence, to complain of the cruelty and exactions of the chiefs set over them : but, as it is known that the Arab never will pay without the bastinado, their complaints, for the most part, meet with but little attention. His Highness's treasury must be filled, and his officers supported in their authority.

However, there was one village, of which the complaints were so pathetic, and the inhabitants so supremely wretched, that the royal indignation was moved at their story, and the chief of the village, Skinflint Beg, was called to give an account of himself at Cairo.

When he came before the presence, Mehemet Ali reproached him with his horrible cruelty and exactions ; asked him how he dared to treat his faithful and beloved subjects in this way, and threatened him with disgrace, and the utter confiscation of his property, for thus having reduced a district to ruin.

" Your Highness says I have reduced these fellahs to ruin," said Skinflint Beg ; " what is the best way to confound my enemies, and to show you the falsehood of their accusations that I have ruined them? — To bring more money from them. If I bring you five hundred purses from my village, will you acknowledge that my people are not ruined yet?"

The heart of the Pasha was touched : " I will have no more bastinadoing, O Skinflint Beg ; you have tortured these poor people so much, and have got so little from them, that my royal heart relents for the present, and I will have them suffer no farther."

"Give me free leave — give me your Highness's gracious pardon, and I will bring the five hundred purses as surely as my name is Skinflint Beg. I demand only the time to go home, the time to return, and a few days to stay, and I will come back as honestly as Regulus Pasha did to the Carthaginians, — I will come back and make my face white before your Highness."

Skinflint Beg's prayer for a reprieve was granted, and he returned to his village, where he forthwith called the elders together. "O friends," he said, "complaints of our poverty and misery have reached the royal throne, and the benevolent heart of the sovereign has been melted by the words that have been poured into his ears. 'My heart yearns towards my people of El Muddee,' he says; 'I have thought how to relieve their miseries. Near them lies the fruitful land of El Guanee. It is rich in maize and cotton, in sesame and barley; it is worth a thousand purses; but I will let it to my children for seven hundred, and I will give over the rest of the profit to them, as an alleviation for their affliction.'"

The elders of El Muddee knew the great value and fertility of the lands of Guanee, but they doubted the sincerity of their governor, who, however, dispelled their fears, and adroitly quickened their eagerness to close with the proffered bargain. "I will myself advance two hundred and fifty purses," he said, "do you take counsel among yourselves, and subscribe the other five hundred; and when the sum is ready, a deputation of you shall carry it to Cairo, and I will come with my share; and we will lay the whole at the feet of his Highness." So the gray-bearded ones of the village advised with one another; and those who had been inaccessible to bastinadoes, somehow found money at the calling of interest; and the Sheikh, and they, and the five hundred purses, set off on the road to the capital.

When they arrived, Skinflint Beg and the elders of El Muddee sought admission to the royal throne, and there laid down their purses. "Here is your humble servant's contribution," said Skinflint, producing his share; "and here is the offering of your loyal village of El Muddee. Did I not before say that enemies and deceivers had maligned me before the august presence, pretending that not a piastre was left in my village, and that my extortion had entirely denuded the peasantry? See! here is proof that there is plenty of money still in El Muddee;

in twelve hours the elders have subscribed five hundred purses, and lay them at the feet of their lord."

Instead of the bastinado, Skinflint Beg was instantly rewarded with the royal favor, and the former mark of attention was bestowed upon the fellahs who had maligned him; Skinflint Beg was promoted to the rank of Skinflint Bey; and his manner of extracting money from his people may be studied with admiration in a part of the United Kingdom.*

At the time of the Syrian quarrel, and when, apprehending some general rupture with England, the Pasha wished to raise the spirit of the fellahs, and *relever la morale nationale*, he actually made one of the astonished Arabs a colonel. He degraded him three days after peace was concluded. The young Egyptian colonel, who told me this, laughed and enjoyed the joke with the utmost gusto. " Is it not a shame," he said, " to make me a colonel at three-and-twenty; I, who have no particular merit, and have never seen any service?" Death has since stopped the modest and good-natured young fellow's further promotion. The death of —— Bey was announced in the French papers a few weeks back.

My above kind-hearted and agreeable young informant used to discourse, in our evenings in the Lazaretto at Malta, very eloquently about the beauty of his wife, whom he had left behind him at Cairo — her brown hair, her brilliant complexion, and her blue eyes. It is this Circassian blood, I suppose, to which the Turkish aristocracy that governs Egypt must be indebted for the fairness of their skin. Ibrahim Pasha, riding by in his barouche, looked like a bluff, jolly-faced English dragoon officer, with a gray moustache and red cheeks, such as you might see on a field-day at Maidstone. All the numerous officials riding through the town were quite as fair as Europeans. We made acquaintance with one dignitary, a very jovial and fat Pasha, the proprietor of the inn, I believe, who was continually lounging about the Ezbekieh garden, and who, but for a slight Jewish cast of countenance, might have passed any day for a Frenchman. The ladies whom we saw were equally fair; that is, the very slight particles of the persons of ladies which our lucky eyes were permitted to gaze on. These lovely creatures go through the town by parties of three or four, mounted on donkeys, and attended by slaves holding on at the crupper, to receive the lovely riders lest they should fall, and shouting out shrill cries of " Schmaalek," " Ameenek " (or how-

* At Derrynane Beg, for instance.

ever else these words may be pronounced), and flogging off the people right and left with the buffalo-thong. But the dear creatures are even more closely disguised than at Constantinople : their bodies are enveloped with a large black silk hood, like a cab-head ; the fashion seemed to be to spread their arms out, and give this covering all the amplitude of which it was capable, as they leered and ogled you from under their black masks with their big rolling eyes.

Everybody has big rolling eyes here (unless, to be sure, they lose one of ophthalmia). The Arab women are some of the noblest figures I have ever seen. The habit of carrying jars on the head always gives the figure grace and motion ; and the dress the women wear certainly displays it to full advantage. I have brought a complete one home with me, at the service of any lady for a masqued ball. It consists of a coarse blue dress of calico, opened in front, and fastened with a horn button. Three yards of blue stuff for a veil ; on the top of the veil a jar to be balanced on the head ; and a little black strip of silk to fall over the nose, and leave the beautiful eyes full liberty to roll and roam. But such a costume, not aided by any stays or any other article of dress whatever, can be worn only by a very good figure. I suspect it won't be borrowed for many balls next season.

The men, a tall, handsome, noble race, are treated like dogs. I shall never forget riding through the crowded bazaars, my interpreter, or laquais-de-place, ahead of me to clear the way — when he took his whip and struck it over the shoulders of a man who could not or would not make way !

The man turned round — an old, venerable, handsome face, with awfully sad eyes, and a beard long and quite gray. He did not make the least complaint, but slunk out of the way, piteously shaking his shoulder. The sight of that indignity gave me a sickening feeling of disgust. I shouted out to the cursed lackey to hold his hand, and forbade him ever in my presence to strike old or young more ; but everybody is doing it. The whip is in everybody's hands : the Pasha's running footman, as he goes bustling through the bazaar ; the doctor's attendant, as he soberly threads the crowd on his mare ; the negro slave, who is riding by himself, the most insolent of all, strikes and slashes about without mercy, and you never hear a single complaint.

How to describe the beauty of the streets to you ! — the fantastic splendor ; the variety of the houses, and archways, and hanging roofs, and balconies, and porches ; the delightful accidents of light and shade which chequer them; the noise, the bustle, the brilliancy of the crowd; the interminable vast bazaars with their barbaric splendor! There is a fortune to be made for painters in Cairo, and materials for a whole Academy of them. I never saw such a variety of architecture, of life, of picturesqueness, of brilliant color, and light and shade. There is a picture in every street, and at every bazaar stall. Some of these our celebrated water-color painter, Mr. Lewis, has produced with admirable truth and exceeding minuteness and beauty; but there is room for a hundred to follow him; and should any artist (by some rare occurrence) read this, who has leisure, and wants to break new ground, let him take heart, and try a winter in Cairo, where there is the finest climate and the best subjects for his pencil.

A series of studies of negroes alone would form a picture-book, delightfully grotesque. Mounting my donkey to-day, I took a ride to the desolate, noble old buildings outside the city, known as the Tombs of the Caliphs. Every one of these edifices, with their domes, and courts, and minarets, is strange and beautiful. In one of them there was an encampment of negro slaves newly arrived: some scores of them were huddled against the sunny wall; two or three of their masters lounged about the court, or lay smoking upon carpets. There was one of these fellows, a straight-nosed, ebony-faced Abyssinian, with an expression of such sinister good-humor in his handsome face as would form a perfect type of villany. He sat leering at me, over his carpet, as I endeavored to get a sketch of that incarnate rascality. "Give me some money," said the fellow. "I know what you are about. You will sell my picture for money when you get back to Europe; let me have some of it now!" But the very rude and humble designer was quite unequal to depict such a consummation and perfection of roguery; so flung him a cigar, which he began to smoke, grinning at the giver. I requested the interpreter to inform him, by way of assurance of my disinterestedness, that his face was a great deal too ugly to be popular in Europe, and that was the particular reason why I had selected it.

Then one of his companions got up and showed us his black cattle. The male slaves were chiefly lads, and the women young, well formed, and abominably hideous. The dealer pulled her blanket off one of them and bade her stand up, which she did with a great deal of shuddering modesty. She was coal black, her lips were the size of sausages, her eyes large and good-humored; the hair or wool on this young person's head

28

was curled and greased into a thousand filthy little ringlets. She was evidently the beauty of the flock.

They are not unhappy; they look to being bought, as many a spinster looks to an establishment in England; once in a family they are kindly treated and well clothed, and fatted, and are the merriest people of the whole community. These were of a much more savage sort than the slaves I had seen in the horrible market at Constantinople, where I recollect a young creature — whilst I was looking at her and forming pathetic conjectures regarding her fate — smiling very good-humoredly, and bidding the interpreter ask me to buy her for twenty pounds.

From these Tombs of the Caliphs the Desert is before you. It comes up to the walls of the city, and stops at some gardens which spring up all of a sudden at its edge. You can see the first Station-house on the Suez Road; and so from distance point to point, could ride thither alone without a guide.

Asinus trotted gallantly into this desert for the space of a quarter of an hour. There we were (taking care to keep our backs to the city walls), in the real actual desert: mounds upon mounds of sand, stretching away as far as the eye can see, until the dreary prospect fades away in the yellow horizon! I had formed a finer idea of it out of "Eothen." Perhaps in a simoom it may look more awful. The only adventure that befell in this romantic place was that asinus's legs went deep into a hole: whereupon his rider went over his head, and bit the sand, and measured his length there; and upon this hint rose up, and rode home again. No doubt one should have gone out for a couple of days' march — as it was, the desert did not seem to me sublime, only *uncomfortable*.

Very soon after this perilous adventure the sun likewise dipped into the sand (but not to rise therefrom so quickly as I had done); and I saw this daily phenomenon of sunset with pleasure, for I was engaged at that hour to dine with our old friend J——, who has established himself here in the most complete Oriental fashion.

You remember J——, and what a dandy he was, the faultlessness of his boots and cravats, the brilliancy of his waistcoats and kid-gloves; we have seen his splendor in Regent Street, in the Tuileries, or on the Toledo. My first object on arriving here was to find out his house, which he has taken far away from the haunts of European civilization, in the Arab quarter. It is situated in a cool, shady, narrow alley; so narrow, that it was with great difficulty — his Highness Ibrahim Pasha happening to pass at the same moment — that my little procession of two donkeys, mounted by self and valet-de-place, with the two donkey-boys our attendants, could range ourselves along the wall, and leave room for the august cavalcade. His Highness having rushed on (with an affable and good-humored salute to our imposing party), we made J.'s quarters; and in the first place, entered a broad covered court or porch, where a swarthy, tawny attendant, dressed in blue, with white turban, keeps a perpetual watch. Servants in the East lie about all the doors, it appears; and you clap your hands, as they do in the dear old " Arabian Nights," to summon them.

This servant disappeared through a narrow wicket, which he closed after him; and went into the inner chambers to ask if his lord would receive us. He came back presently, and rising up from my donkey, I confided him to his attendant, (lads more sharp, arch, and wicked than these donkey-boys don't walk the pavé of Paris or London,) and passed the mysterious outer door.

First we came into a broad open court, with a covered gallery running along one side of it. A camel was reclining on the grass there; near him was a gazelle, to glad J. with his dark blue eye; and a numerous brood of hens and chickens, who furnish his liberal table. On the opposite side of the covered gallery rose up the walls of his long, queer, many-windowed, many-galleried house. There were wooden lattices to those arched windows, through the diamonds of one of which I saw two of the most beautiful, enormous, ogling, black eyes in the world, looking down upon the interesting stranger. Pigeons were flapping, and hopping, and fluttering, and cooing about. Happy pigeons, you are, no doubt, fed with crumbs from the henné-tipped fingers of Zuleika! All this court, cheerful in the sunshine, cheerful with the astonishing brilliancy of the eyes peering out from the lattice bars, was as mouldy, ancient, and ruinous — as any gentleman's house in Ireland, let us say. The paint was peeling off the rickety old carved galleries; the arabesques over the windows were chipped and worn; — the ancientness of the place rendered it doubly picturesque. I have detained you a long time in the outer court. Why the deuce was Zuleika there, with the beautiful black eyes!

Hence we passed into a large apartment, where there was a fountain; and another domestic made his appearance, taking me in charge, and relieving the tawny porter of the gate. This fellow was clad in blue too, with a red sash and a gray beard. He conducted me into a great hall, where there was a great, large Saracenic oriel window. He seated me on a divan: and stalking off, for a moment, returned with a long pipe and a brass chafing-dish : he blew the coal for the pipe, which he motioned me to smoke, and left me there with a respectful bow. This delay, this mystery of servants, that outer court with the camels, gazelles, and other beautiful-eyed things, affected me prodigiously all the time he was staying away ; and while I was examining the strange apartment and its contents, my respect and awe for the owner increased vastly.

As you will be glad to know how an Oriental nobleman (such as J. undoubtedly is) is lodged and garnished, let me describe the contents of this hall of audience. It is about forty feet long, and eighteen or twenty high. All the ceiling is carved, gilt, painted and embroidered with arabesques, and choice sentences of Eastern writing. Some Mameluke Aga, or Bey, whom Mehemet Ali invited to breakfast and massacred, was the proprietor of this mansion once : it has grown dingier, but, perhaps, handsomer, since his time. Opposite the divan is a great bay-window, with a divan likewise round the niche. It looks out upon a garden about the size of Fountain Court, Temple ; surrounded by the tall houses of the quarter. The garden is full of green. A great palm-tree springs up in the midst, with plentiful shrubberies, and a talking fountain. The room beside the divan is furnished with one deal table, value five shillings ; four wooden chairs, value six shillings ; and a couple of mats and carpets. The tables and chairs are luxuries imported from Europe. The regular Oriental dinner is put upon copper trays, which are laid upon low stools. Hence J—— Effendi's house may be said to be much more sumptuously furnished than those of the Beys and Agas his neighbors.

When these things had been examined at leisure, J—— appeared. Could it be the exquisite of the " Europa" and the " Trois Frères?" A man — in a long yellow gown, with a long beard somewhat tinged with gray, with his head shaved, and wearing on it first a white wadded cotton nightcap, second, a red tarboosh — made his appearance and welcomed me cordially. It was some time, as the Americans say, before I could " realize " the *semillant* J. of old times.

He shuffled off his outer slippers before he curled up on the divan beside me. He clapped his hands, and languidly called " Mustapha." Mustapha came with more lights, pipes, and coffee ; and then we fell to talking about London, and I gave him the last news of the comrades in that dear city. As we talked, his Oriental coolness and languor gave way to British cordiality ; he was the most amusing companion of the —— Club once more.

He has adapted himself outwardly, however, to the Oriental life. When he goes abroad he rides a gray horse with red housings, and has two servants to walk beside him. He wears a very handsome, grave costume of dark blue, consisting of an embroidered jacket and gaiters, and a pair of trousers, which would make a set of dresses for an English family. His beard curls nobly over his chest, his Damascus scimitar on his thigh. His red cap gives him a venerable and Bey-like appearance. There is no gewgaw or parade about him, as in some of your dandified young Agas. I should say that he is a Major-General of Engineers, or a grave officer of State. We and the Turkified European, who found us at dinner, sat smoking in solemn divan.

His dinners were excellent ; they were cooked by a regular Egyptian female cook. We had delicate cucumbers stuffed with forced-meats ; yellow smoking pilaffs, the pride of the Oriental cuisine ; kid and fowls à l'Aboukir and à la Pyramide : a number of little savory plates of legumes of the vegetable marrow sort : kibobs with an excellent sauce of plums and piquant herbs. We ended the repast with ruby pomegranates, pulled to pieces, deliciously cool and pleasant. For the meats, we certainly ate them with the Infidel knife and fork ; but for the fruit, we put our hands into the dish and flicked them into our mouths in what cannot but be the true Oriental manner. I asked for lamb and pistachio-nuts, and cream-tarts *au poivre;* but J.'s cook did not furnish us with either of those historic dishes. And for drink, we had water freshened in the porous little pots of gray clay, at whose spout every traveller in the East has sucked delighted. Also, it must be confessed, we drank certain sherbets, prepared by the two great rivals, Hadji Hodson and Bass Bey — the bitterest and most delicious of draughts ! O divine Hodson ! a camel's load of thy beer came from Beyrout to Jerusalem while we were there. How shall I ever forget the joy inspired by one of those foaming cool flasks?

We don't know the luxury of thirst in English climes. Sedentary men in cities at least have seldom ascertained it ; but when they travel, our countrymen guard against it well. The road between Cairo and Suez is *jonché* with soda-water corks. Tom Thumb and his brothers might track their way across the desert by those landmarks.

Cairo is magnificently picturesque ; it is fine to have palm-trees in your gardens, and ride about on a camel; but, after all, I was anxious to know what were the particular excitements of Eastern life, which detained J., who is a town-bred man, from his natural pleasures and occupations in London; where his family don't hear from him, where his room is still kept ready at home, and his name is on the list of his club; and where his neglected sisters tremble to think that their Frederick is going about with a great beard and a crooked sword, dressed up like an odious Turk. In a "lark" such a costume may be very well; but home, London, a razor, your sister to make tea, a pair of moderate Christian breeches in lieu of those enormous Turkish shulwars, are vastly more convenient in the long run. What was it that kept him away from these decent and accustomed delights?

It couldn't be the black eyes in the balcony — upon his honor she was only the black cook, who has done the pilaff, and stuffed the cucumbers. No, it was an indulgence of laziness such as Europeans, Englishmen at least, don't know how to enjoy. Here he lives like a languid Lotus-eater — a dreamy, hazy, lazy, tobaccofied life. He was away from evening-parties, he said; he needn't wear white kid-gloves, or starched neck-cloths, or read a newspaper. And even this life at Cairo was too civilized for him; Englishmen passed through; old acquaintances would call: the great pleasure of pleasures was life in the desert, — under the tents, with still *more* nothing to do than in Cairo; now smoking, now cantering on Arabs, and no crowd to jostle you; solemn contemplations of the stars at night, as the camels were picketed, and the fires and the pipes were lighted.

The night-scene in the city is very striking for its vastness and loneliness. Everybody has gone to rest long before ten o'clock. There are no lights in the enormous buildings; only the stars blazing above, with their astonishing brilliancy, in the blue, peaceful sky. Your guides carry a couple of little lanterns, which redouble the darkness in the solitary, echoing street. Mysterious people are curled up and sleeping in the porches. A patrol of soldiers passes, and hails you. There is a light yet in one mosque, where some devotees are at prayers all night; and you hear the queerest nasal music proceeding from those pious believers. As you pass the mad-house, there is one poor fellow still talking to the moon — no sleep for him. He howls and sings there all the night — quite cheerfully, however. He has not lost his vanity with his reason; he is a Prince in spite of the bars and the straw.

What to say about those famous edifices, which has not been better said elsewhere?—but you will not believe that we visited them, unless I bring some token from them. Here is one.*

That white-capped lad skipped up the stones with a jug of water in his hand, to refresh weary climbers; and, squatting himself down on the summit, was designed as you see. The vast, flat landscape stretches behind him; the great winding river; the purple city, with forts, and domes, and spires; the green fields, and palm-groves, and speckled villages; the plains still covered with shining inundations — the landscape stretches far, far away, until it is lost and mingled in the golden horizon. It is poor work, this landscape-painting in print. Shelley's two sonnets are the best views that I know of the Pyramids — better than the reality; for a man may lay down the book, and in quiet fancy conjure up a picture out of these magnificent words, which shan't be disturbed by any pettinesses or mean realities, — such as the swarms of howling beggars, who jostle you about the actual place, and scream in your ears incessantly, and hang on your skirts and bawl for money.

The ride to the Pyramids is one of the pleasantest possible. In the fall of the year, though the sky is almost cloudless above you, the sun is not too hot to bear; and the landscape, refreshed by the subsiding inundations, delightfully green and cheerful. We made up a party of some half-dozen from the hotel, a lady (the kind soda-water provider, for whose hospitality the most grateful compliments are hereby offered) being of the company, bent like the rest upon going to the summit of Cheops. Those who were cautious and wise, took a brace of donkeys. At least five times during the route did my animals fall with me, causing me to repeat the Desert experiment over again, but with more success. The pace between a moderate pair of legs and the ground is not many inches. By eschewing stirrups, the donkey could fall, and the rider alight on the ground, with the greatest ease and grace. Almost everybody was down and up again in the course of the day.

We passed through the Ezbekieh and by the suburbs of the town, where the garden-houses of the Egyptian noblesse are situated, to Old Cairo, where a ferry-boat took the whole party across the Nile, with that noise and bawling volubility in which the Arab people seem to be so unlike the grave and silent Turks; and so took our course for some eight or ten miles over the devious track which the still outlying waters obliged us to pursue. The Pyramids were in sight the whole way. One or

* This refers to an illustrated edition of the work.

two thin, silvery clouds were hovering over them, and casting delicate, rosy shadows, upon the grand, simple, old piles. Along the track we saw a score of pleasant pictures of Eastern life : — The Pasha's horses and slaves stood caparisoned at his door ; at the gate of one country-house, I am sorry to say, the Bey's *gig* was in waiting, — a most unromantic chariot : the husbandmen were coming into the city, with their strings of donkeys and their loads ; as they arrived, they stopped and sucked at the fountain : a column of red-capped troops passed to drill, with slouched gait, white uniforms, and glittering bayonets. Then we had the pictures at the quay : the ferry-boat, and the red-sailed river-boat, getting under weigh, and bound up the stream. There was the grain market, and the huts on the opposide side ; and that beautiful woman, with silver armlets, and a face the color of gold, which (the nose-bag having been luckily removed) beamed solemnly on us Europeans, like a great yellow harvest-moon. The bunches of purpling dates were pending from the branches ; gray cranes or herons were flying over the cool, shining lakes, that the river's overflow had left behind ; water was gurgling through the courses by the rude locks and barriers formed there, and overflowing this patch of ground ; whilst the neighboring field was fast budding into the more brilliant fresh green. Single dromedaries were stepping along, their riders lolling on their hunches ; low sail-boats were lying in the canals ; now, we crossed an old marble bridge ; now, we went, one by one, over a ridge of slippery earth ; now, we floundered through a small lake of mud. At last, at about half a mile off the Pyramid, we came to a piece of water some two score yards broad, where a regiment of half-naked Arabs, seizing upon each individual of the party, bore us off on their shoulders, to the laughter of all, and the great perplexity of several, who every moment expected to be pitched into one of the many holes with which the treacherous lake abounded.

It was nothing but joking and laughter, bullying of guides, shouting for interpreters, quarrelling about sixpences. We were acting a farce, with the Pyramids for the scene. There they rose up enormous under our eyes, and the most absurd, trivial things were going on under their shadow. The sublime had disappeared, vast as they were. Do you remember how Gulliver lost his awe of the tremendous Brobdingnag ladies? Every traveller must go through all sorts of chaffering, and bargaining, and paltry experiences, at this spot. You look up the tremendous steps, with a score of savage ruffians bellowing round you ; you hear faint cheers and cries high up, and catch sight of little reptiles crawling upwards; or, having achieved the summit, they come hopping and bouncing down again from degree to degree, — the cheers and cries swell louder and more disagreeable; presently the little jumping thing, no bigger than an insect a moment ago, bounces down upon you expanded into a panting Major of Bengal cavalry. He drives off the Arabs with an oath, — wipes his red shining face with his yellow handkerchief, drops puffing on the sand in a shady corner, where cold fowl and hard eggs are awaiting him, and the next minute you see his nose plunged in a foaming beaker of brandy and soda-water. He can say now, and for ever, he has been up the Pyramid. There is nothing sublime in it. You cast your eye once more up that staggering perspective of a zigzag line, which ends at the summit, and wish you were up there — and down again. Forwards! — Up with you! It must be done. Six Arabs are behind you, who won't let you escape if you would.

The importunity of these ruffians is a ludicrous annoyance to which a traveller must submit. For two miles before you reach the Pyramids they seize on you and never cease howling. Five or six of them pounce upon one victim, and never leave him until they have carried him up and down. Sometimes they conspire to run a man up the huge stair, and bring him, half-killed and fainting, to the top. Always a couple of brutes insist upon impelling you sternwards; from whom the only means to release yourself is to kick out vigorously and unmercifully, when the Arabs will possibly retreat. The ascent is not the least romantic, or difficult, or sublime: you walk up a great broken staircase, of which some of the steps are four feet high. It's not hard, only a little high. You see no better view from the top than you beheld from the bottom; only a little more river, and sand, and rice-field. You jump down the big steps at your leisure; but your meditations you must keep for after-times, — the cursed shrieking of the Arabs prevents all thought or leisure.

— And this is all you have to tell about the Pyramids? Oh! for shame! Not a compliment to their age and size? Not a big phrase, — not a rapture? Do you mean to say that you had no feeling of respect and awe? Try, man, and build up a monument of words as lofty as they are — they, whom " imber edax" and " aquilo impotens" and the flight of ages have not been able to destroy!

— No: be that work for great geniuses, great painters, great poets! This quill was never made to take such flights;

it comes of the wing of a humble domestic bird, who walks a common; who talks a great deal (and hisses sometimes); who can't fly far or high, and drops always very quickly; and whose unromantic end is, to be laid on a Michaelmas or Christmas table, and there to be discussed for half an hour — let us hope, with some relish.

Another week saw us in the Quarantine Harbor at Malta, where seventeen days of prison and quiet were almost agreeable, after the incessant sight-seeing of the last two months. In the interval, between the 23rd of August and the 27th of October, we may boast of having seen more men and cities than most travellers have seen in such a time : — Lisbon, Cadiz, Gibraltar, Malta, Athens, Smyrna, Constantinople, Jerusalem, Cairo. I shall have the carpet-bag which has visited these places in company with its owner, embroidered with their names; as military flags are emblazoned, and laid up in ordinary, to be looked at in old age. With what a number of sights and pictures, — of novel sensations, and lasting and delightful remembrances, does a man furnish his mind after such a tour! You forget all the annoyances of travel; but the pleasure remains with you, through that kind provision of nature by which a man forgets being ill, but thinks with joy of getting well, and can remember all the minute circumstances of his convalescence. I forget what sea-sickness is now · though it occupies a woful portion of my Journal. There was a time on board when the bitter ale was decidedly muddy; and the cook of the ship deserting at Constantinople, it must be confessed his successor was for some time before he got his hand in. These sorrows have passed away with the soothing influence of time : the pleasures of the voyage remain, let us hope, as long as life will endure. It was but for a couple of days that those shining columns of the Parthenon glowed under the blue sky there; but the experience of a life could scarcely impress them more vividly. We saw Cadiz only for an hour; but the white buildings, and the glorious blue sea, how clear they are to the memory! — with the tang of that gipsy's guitar dancing in the market-place, in the midst of the fruit, and the beggars, and the sunshine. Who can forget the Bosphorus, the brightest and fairest scene in all the world; or the towering lines of Gibraltar; or the great piles of Mafra, as we rode into the Tagus? As I write this, and think, back comes Rhodes, with its old towers and artillery, and that wonderful atmosphere, and that astonishing blue sea which environs the island. The Arab riders go pacing over the plains of Sharon, in the rosy twilight, just before sunrise; and I can see the ghastly Moab mountains, with the Dead Sea gleaming before them, from the mosque on the way towards Bethany. The black, gnarled trees of Gethsemane lie at the foot of Olivet, and the yellow ramparts of the city rise up on the stony hills beyond.

But the happiest and best of all the recollections, perhaps, are those of the hours passed at night on the deck, when the stars were shining overhead, and the hours were tolled at their time, and your thoughts were fixed upon home far away. As the sun rose I once heard the priest, from the minaret of Constantinople, crying out, "Come to prayer," with his shrill voice ringing through the clear air; and saw, at the same hour, the Arab prostrate himself and pray, and the Jew Rabbi, bending over his book, and worshipping the Maker of Turk and Jew. Sitting at home in London, and writing this last line of farewell, those figures come back the clearest of all to the memory, with the picture, too, of our ship sailing over the peaceful Sabbath sea, and our own prayers and services celebrated there. So each, in his fashion, and after his kind, is bowing down, and adoring the Father, who is equally above all. Cavil not, you brother or sister, if your neighbor's voice is not like yours; only hope that his words are honest (as far as they may be), and his heart humble and thankful.

THE END.

THE IRISH SKETCH BOOK

OF 1842.

TO

CHARLES LEVER, ESQ.,

OF TEMPLEOGUE HOUSE, NEAR DUBLIN.

MY DEAR LEVER, — Harry Lorrequer needs no complimenting in a dedication ; and I would not venture to inscribe this volume to the Editor of the "Dublin University Magazine," who, I fear, must disapprove of a great deal which it contain?

But allow me to dedicate my little book to a good Irishman (the hearty charity of whose visionary red-coats, some substantial personages in black might imitate to advantage), and to a friend from whom I have received a hundred acts of kindness and cordial hospitality.

Laying aside for a moment the travelling-title of Mr. Titmarsh, let me acknowledge these favors in my own name, and subscribe myself, my dear Lever,

Most sincerely and gratefully yours,

W. M. THACKERAY.

LONDON, April 27, 1843.

THE IRISH SKETCH BOOK.

CHAPTER I.

A SUMMER DAY IN DUBLIN, OR THERE AND THEREABOUTS.

THE coach that brings the passenger by wood and mountain, by brawling waterfall and gloomy plain, by the lonely lake of Festiniog and across the swinging world's wonder of a Menai Bridge, through dismal Anglesea to dismal Holyhead — the Birmingham mail, — manages matters so cleverly, that after ten hours' ride the traveller is thrust incontinently on board the packet, and the steward says there's no use in providing dinner on board because the passage is so short.

That is true : but why not give us half an hour on shore ? Ten hours spent on a coach-box render the dinner question one of extreme importance ; and as the packet reaches Kingstown at midnight, when all the world is asleep, the inn-larders locked up, and the cook in bed ; and as the mail is not landed until five in the morning (at which hour the passengers are considerately awakened by a great stamping and shouting overhead), might not "Lord Lowther" give us one little half-hour ? Even the steward agreed that it was a useless and atrocious tyranny ; and, indeed, after a little demur, produced a half-dozen of fried eggs, a feeble makeshift for a dinner.

Our passage across from the Head was made in a rain so pouring and steady, that sea and coast were entirely hidden from us, and one could see very little beyond the glowing tip of the cigar which remained alight nobly in spite of the weather. When the gallant exertions of that fiery spirit were over for ever, and burning bravely to the end it had breathed its last in doing its master service, all became black and cheerless around ; the passengers had dropped off one by one, preferring to be dry and ill below rather than wet and squeamish

above: even the mate with his gold-laced cap (who is so astonishingly like Mr. Charles Dickens that he might pass for that
gentleman) — even the mate said he would go to his cabin and
turn in. So there remained nothing for it but to do as all the
world had done.

Hence it was impossible to institute the comparison between
the Bay of Naples and that of Dublin (the Bee of Neeples the
former is sometimes called in this country), where I have heard
the likeness asserted in a great number of societies and conversations. But how could one see the Bay of Dublin in the
dark? and how, supposing one could see it, should a person
behave who has never seen the Bay of Naples? It is but to
take the similarity for granted, and remain in bed till morning.

When everybody was awakened at five o'clock by the noise
made upon the removal of the mail-bags, there was heard a
cheerless dribbling and pattering overhead, which led one to
wait still further until the rain should cease. At length the
steward said the last boat was going ashore, and receiving
half a crown for his own services (the regular tariff) intimated
likewise that it was the custom for gentlemen to compliment
the stewardess with a shilling, which ceremony was also complied with. No doubt she is an amiable woman, and deserves
any sum of money. As for inquiring whether she merited it
or not in this instance, that surely is quite unfair. A traveller who stops to inquire the deserts of every individual claim-
ant of a shilling on his road, had best stay quiet at home. If
we only got what we *deserved*, — heaven save us! — many of
us might whistle for a dinner.

A long pier, with a steamer or two at hand, and a few
small vessels lying on either side of the jetty; a town irreg-
ularly built, with many handsome terraces, some churches, and
showy-looking hotels; a few people straggling on the beach;
two or three cars at the railroad station, which runs along the
shore as far as Dublin; the sea stretching interminably eastward; to the north the Hill of Howth, lying gray behind the
mist; and, directly under his feet upon the wet, black, shining, slippery deck, an agreeable reflection of his own legs, disappearing seemingly in the direction of the cabin from which
he issues; are the sights which a traveller may remark on coming on deck at Kingstown pier on a wet morning — let us say
on an *average* morning; for, according to the statement of well-
informed natives, the Irish day is more often rainy than otherwise. A hideous obelisk, stuck upon four fat balls, and surmounted with a crown on a cushion (the latter were no bad

emblems perhaps of the monarch in whose honor they were raised), commemorates the sacred spot at which George IV. *quitted* Ireland. You are landed here from the steamer; and a carman, who is dawdling in the neighborhood, with a straw in his mouth, comes leisurely up to ask whether you will go to Dublin? Is it natural indolence, or the effect of despair because of the neighboring railroad, which renders him so indifferent? — He does not even take the straw out of his mouth as he proposes the question — he seems quite careless as to the answer.

He said he would take me to Dublin " in three quarthers," as soon as we began a parley. As to the fare, he would not hear of it — he said he would leave it to my honor; he would take me for nothing. Was it possible to refuse such a genteel offer? The times are very much changed since those described by the facetious Jack Hinton, when the carmen tossed up for the passenger, and those who won him took him: for the remaining cars on the stand did not seem to take the least interest in the bargain, or to offer to overdrive or underbid their comrade in any way.

Before that day, so memorable for joy and sorrow, for rapture at receiving its monarch and tearful grief at losing him, when George IV. came and left the maritime resort of the citizens of Dublin, it bore a less genteel name than that which it owns at present, and was called Dunleary. After that glorious event Dunleary disdained to be Dunleary any longer, and became Kingstown henceforward and for ever. Numerous terraces and pleasure-houses have been built in the place — they stretch row after row along the banks of the sea, and rise one above another on the hill. The rents of these houses are said to be very high; the Dublin citizens crowd into them in summer; and a great source of pleasure and comfort must it be to them to have the fresh sea-breezes and prospects so near to the metropolis.

The better sort of houses are handsome and spacious; but the fashionable quarter is yet in an unfinished state, for enterprising architects are always beginning new roads, rows and terraces: nor are those already built by any means complete. Beside the aristocratic part of the town is a commercial one, and nearer to Dublin stretch lines of low cottages which have not a Kingstown look at all, but are evidently of the Dunleary period. It is quite curious to see in the streets where the shops are, how often the painter of the signboards begins with big letters, and ends, for want of space, with small; and the Eng-

lishman accustomed to the thriving neatness and regularity
which characterize towns great and small in his own country,
can't fail to notice the difference here. The houses have a
battered, rakish look, and seem going to ruin before their time.
As seamen of all nations come hither who have made no vow
of temperance, there are plenty of liquor-shops still, and shabby
cigar-shops, and shabby milliners' and tailors' with fly-blown
prints of old fashions. The bakers and apothecaries make a
great brag of their calling, and you see MEDICAL HALL, or PUB-
LIC BAKERY, BALLYRAGGET FLOUR-STORE, (or whatever the name
may be,) pompously inscribed over very humble tenements.
Some comfortable grocers' and butchers' shops, and numbers
of shabby sauntering people, the younger part of whom are
barelegged and bareheaded, make up the rest of the picture
which the stranger sees as his car goes jingling through the
street.

After the town come the suburbs of pleasure-houses; low
one-storied cottages for the most part: some neat and fresh,
some that have passed away from the genteel state altogether,
and exhibit downright poverty; some in a state of transition,
with broken windows and pretty romantic names upon tumble-
down gates. Who lives in them? One fancies that the chairs
and tables inside are broken, that the teapot on the breakfast-
table has no spout, and the tablecloth is ragged and sloppy;
that the lady of the house is in dubious curl-papers, and the
gentleman, with an imperial to his chin, wears a flaring dressing-gown all ragged at the elbows.

To be sure, a traveller who in ten minutes can see not only
the outsides of houses, but the interiors of the same, must
have remarkably keen sight; and it is early yet to speculate.
It is clear, however, that these are pleasure-houses for a certain
class; and looking at the houses, one can't but fancy the inhabitants resemble them somewhat. The car, on its road to Dublin, passes by numbers of these — by more shabbiness than a
Londoner will see in the course of his home peregrinations for
a year.

The capabilities of the country, however, are very great,
and in many instances have been taken advantage of: for you
see, besides the misery, numerous handsome houses and parks
along the road, having fine lawns and woods; and the sea is
in our view at a quarter of an hour's ride from Dublin. It is
the continual appearance of this sort of wealth which makes
the poverty more striking: and thus between the two (for there
is no vacant space of fields between Kingstown and Dublin)

the car reaches the city. There is but little commerce on this road, which was also in extremely bad repair. It is neglected for the sake of its thriving neighbor the railroad; on which a dozen pretty little stations accommodate the inhabitants of the various villages through which we pass.

The entrance to the capital is very handsome. There is no bustle and throng of carriages, as in London; but you pass by numerous rows of neat houses, fronted with gardens and adorned with all sorts of gay-looking creepers. Pretty market-gardens, with trim beds of plants and shining glass-houses, give the suburbs a *riante* and cheerful look; and, passing under the arch of the railway, we are in the city itself. Hence you come upon several old-fashioned, well-built, airy, stately streets, and through Fitzwilliam Square, a noble place, the garden of which is full of flowers and foliage. The leaves are green, and not black as in similar places in London; the red brick houses tall and handsome. Presently the car stops before an extremely big red house, in that extremely large square, Stephen's Green, where Mr. O'Connell says there is one day or other to be a Parliament. There is room enough for that, or for any other edifice which fancy or patriotism may have a mind to erect, for part of one of the sides of the square is not yet built, and you see the fields and the country beyond.

This then is the chief city of the aliens. — The hotel to which I had been directed is a respectable old edifice, much frequented by families from the country, and where the solitary traveller may likewise find society: for he may either use the " Shelburne " as an hotel or a boarding-house, in which latter case he is comfortably accommodated at the very moderate daily charge of six-and-eight-pence. For this charge a copious breakfast is provided for him in the coffee-room, a perpetual luncheon is likewise there spread, a plentiful dinner is ready at six o'clock: after which there is a drawing-room and a rubber of whist, with *tay* and coffee and cakes in plenty to satisfy the largest appetite. The hotel is majestically conducted by clerks and other officers; the landlord himself does not appear, after the honest, comfortable English fashion, but lives in a private mansion hard by, where his name may be read inscribed on a brass-plate, like that of any other private gentleman.

A woman melodiously crying " Dublin Bay herrings " passed just as we came up to the door, and as that fish is famous throughout Europe, I seized the earliest opportunity and ordered a broiled one for breakfast   It merits all its reputation : and in this respect I should think the Bay of Dublin is far superior to its rival of Naples.   Are there any herrings in Naples Bay? Dolphins there may be ; and Mount Vesuvius, to be sure, is bigger than even the Hill of Howth ; but a dolphin is better in a sonnet than at a breakfast, and what poet is there that, at certain periods of the day, would hesitate in his choice between the two ?

With this famous broiled herring the morning papers are served up ; and a great part of these, too, gives opportunity of reflection to the new-comer, and shows him how different this country is from his own.   Some hundred years hence, when students want to inform themselves of the history of the present day, and refer to files of *Times* and *Chronicle* for the purpose, I think it is possible that they will consult, not so much those luminous and philosophical leading-articles which call our attention at present both by the majesty of their eloquence and the largeness of their type, but that they will turn to those parts of the journals into which information is squeezed in the smallest possible print : to the advertisements, namely, the law and police reports, and to the instructive narratives supplied by that ill-used body of men who transcribe knowledge at the rate of a penny a line.

The papers before me (*The Morning Register*, Liberal and Roman Catholic, *Saunders's News-Letter*, neutral and Conservative,) give a lively picture of the movement of city and country on this present fourth day of July, 1842, and the Englishman can scarcely fail, as he reads them, to note many small points of difference existing between his own country and this.   How do the Irish amuse themselves in the capital?   The love for theatrical exhibitions is evidently not very great.   Theatre Royal — Miss Kemble and the Sonnambula, an Anglo-Italian importation.   Theatre Royal, Abbey Street — The Temple of Magic and the Wizard, last week.   Adelphi Theatre, Great Brunswick Street — The Original Seven Lancashire Bell-ringers : a delicious excitement indeed !   Portobello Gardens — " THE LAST ERUPTION BUT SIX," says the advertisement in capitals.   And, finally, " Miss Hayes will give her first and farewell concert at the Rotunda, previous to leaving her native country."   Only one instance of Irish talent do we read of, and that, in a desponding tone, announces its intention of quitting its native country.   All the rest of the pleasures of the evening are importations from cockney-land.   The Sonnambula from

Covent Garden, the Wizard from the Strand, the Seven Lancashire Bell-ringers from Islington, or the City Road, no doubt; and as for "The last Eruption but Six," it has *erumped* near the "Elephant and Castle" any time these two years, until the cockneys would wonder at it no longer.

The commercial advertisements are but few — a few horses and cars for sale; some flaming announcements of insurance companies; some "emporiums" of Scotch tweeds and English broadcloths; an auction for damaged sugar; and an estate or two for sale. They lie in the columns languidly, and at their ease as it were: how different from the throng, and squeeze, and bustle of the commercial part of a London paper, where every man (except Mr. George Robins) states his case as briefly as possible, because thousands more are to be heard besides himself, and as if he had no time for talking!

The most active advertisers are the schoolmasters. It is now the happy time of the Midsummer holidays; and the pedagogues make wonderful attempts to encourage parents, and to attract fresh pupils for the ensuing half-year. Of all these announcements that of Madame SHANAHAN (a delightful name) is perhaps the most brilliant. "To Parents and Guardians. — Paris. — Such parents and guardians as may wish to entrust their children for education *in its fullest extent* to Madame SHANAHAN, *can have the advantage of being conducted to Paris* by her brother, the Rev. J. P. O'Reilly, of Church Street Chapel:" which admirable arrangement carries the parents to Paris and leaves the children in Dublin. Ah, Madame, you may take a French title; but your heart is still in your country, and you are to the *fullest extent* an Irishwoman still!

Fond legends are to be found in Irish books regarding places where you may now see a round tower and a little old chapel, twelve feet square, where famous universities are once said to have stood, and which have accommodated myriads of students. Mrs. Hall mentions Glendalough, in Wicklow, as one of these places of learning; nor can the fact be questioned, as the universities existed hundreds of years since, and no sort of records are left regarding them. A century hence some antiquary may light upon a Dublin paper, and form marvellous calculations regarding the state of education in the country. For instance, at Bective House Seminary, conducted by Dr. J. L. Burke, ex-Scholar T.C.D., no less than *two hundred and three* young gentlemen took prizes at the Midsummer examination: nay, some of the most meritorious carried off a dozen premiums apiece. A Dr. Delamere, ex-Scholar T.C.D., dis-

tributed three hundred and twenty rewards to his young friends:
and if we allow that one lad in twenty is a prizeman, it is clear
that there must be six thousand four hundred and forty youths
under the Doctor's care.

Other schools are advertised in the same journals, each with
its hundred of prize-bearers; and if other schools are advertised,
how many more must there be in the country which are not advertised! There must be hundreds of thousands of prizemen,
millions of scholars; besides national-schools, hedge-schools,
infant-schools, and the like. The English reader will see the
accuracy of the calculation.

In the *Morning Register*, the Englishman will find something
to the full as curious and startling to him; you read gravely in
the English language how the Bishop of Aureliopolis has just
been consecrated; and that the distinction has been conferred
upon him by — the Holy Pontiff! — the Pope of Rome, by all
that is holy! Such an announcement sounds quite strange *in
English*, and in your own country, as it were: or isn't it your own
country? Suppose the Archbishop of Canterbury were to send
over a clergyman to Rome, and consecrate him Bishop of the Pal-
atine or the Suburra, I wonder how his Holiness would like *that?*

There is a report of Dr. Miley's sermon upon the occasion
of the new bishop's consecration; and the *Register* happily
lauds the discourse for its " refined and fervent eloquence."
The Doctor salutes the Lord Bishop of Aureliopolis on his admission among the " Princes of the Sanctuary," gives a blow
en passant at the Established Church, whereof the revenues, he
elegantly says, " might excite the zeal of Dives or Epicurus to
become a bishop," and having vented his sly wrath upon the
" courtly artifice and intrigue " of the Bench, proceeds to make
the most outrageous comparisons with regard to my Lord of
Aureliopolis; his virtues, his sincerity, and the severe privations and persecutions which acceptance of the episcopal office
entails upon him.

" That very evening," says the *Register*, " the new bishop
entertained at dinner, in the chapel-house, a select number of
friends; amongst whom were the officiating prelates and clergymen who assisted in the ceremonies of the day. The repast
was provided by Mr. Jude, of Grafton Street, and was served
up in a style of elegance and comfort that did great honor to
that gentleman's character as a *restaurateur*. *The wines were
of the richest and rarest quality*. It may be truly said to have
been an entertainment where the feast of reason and the flow
of soul predominated. The company broke up at nine."

And so my lord is scarcely out of chapel but his privations begin! Well. Let us hope that, in the course of his episcopacy, he may incur no greater hardships, and that Dr. Miley may come to be a bishop too in his time ; when perhaps he will have a better opinion of the Bench.

The ceremony and feelings described are curious, I think ; and more so perhaps to a person who was in England only yesterday, and quitted it just as their Graces, Lordships, and Reverences were sitting down to dinner. Among what new sights, ideas, customs, does the English traveller find himself after that brief six-hours' journey from Holyhead!

There is but one part more of the papers to be looked at ; and that is the most painful of all. In the law-reports of the Tipperary special commission sitting at Clonmel, you read that Patrick Byrne is brought up for sentence, for the murder of Robert Hall, Esq.: and Chief Justice Doherty says, " Patrick Byrne, I will not now recapitulate the circumstances of your enormous crime, but guilty as you are of the barbarity of having perpetrated with your hand the foul murder of an unoffending old man — barbarous, cowardly, and cruel as that act was — there lives one more guilty man, and that is he whose diabolical mind hatched the foul conspiracy of which you were but the instrument and the perpetrator. Whoever that may be, I do not envy him his protracted existence. He has sent that aged gentleman, without one moment's warning, to face his God ; but he has done more : he has brought you, unhappy man, with more deliberation and more cruelty, to face your God, *with the weight of that man's blood upon you.* I have now only to pronounce the sentence of the law : " — it is the usual sentence, with the usual prayer of the judge, that the Lord may have mercy upon the convict's soul.

Timothy Woods, a young man of twenty years of age, is then tried for the murder of Michael Laffan. The Attorney-General states the case : — On the 19th of May last, two assassins dragged Laffan from the house of Patrick Cummins, fired a pistol-shot at him, and left him dead as they thought. Laffan, though mortally wounded, crawled away after the fall ; when the assassins, still seeing him give signs of life, rushed after him, fractured his skull by blows of a pistol, and left him on a dunghill dead. There Laffan's body lay for several hours, and *nobody dared to touch it.* Laffan's widow found the body there two hours after the murder, and *an inquest was held on the body as it lay on the dunghill.* Laffan was driver on the lands of Kilnertin, which were formerly held by **Pat** Cummins, *the man who* *had the charge of the lands before Laffan was murdered;* the latter was dragged out of Cummins's house in the presence of a witness who refused to swear to the murderers, and was shot in sight of another witness, James Meara, who with other men was on the road : when asked whether he cried out, or whether he went to assist the deceased, Meara answers, *" Indeed I did not ; we would not interfere — it was no business of ours ! "*

Six more instances are given of attempts to murder ; on which the judge, in passing sentence, comments in the following way : —

" The Lord Chief Justice addressed the several persons, and said — It was now his painful duty to pronounce upon them severally and respectively the punishment which the law and the court awarded against them for the crimes of which they had been convicted. Those crimes were one and all of them of no ordinary enormity — they were crimes which, in point of morals, involved the atrocious guilt of murder ; and if it had pleased God to spare their souls from the pollution of that offence, the court could not still shut its eyes to the fact, that although death had not ensued in consequence of the crimes of which they had been found guilty, yet it was not owing to their forbearance that such a dreadful crime had not been perpetrated. The prisoner, Michael Hughes, had been convicted of firing a gun at a person of the name of John Ryan (Luke) ; his horse had been killed, and no one could say that the balls were not intended for the prosecutor himself. The prisoner had fired one shot himself, and then called on his companion in guilt to discharge another. One of these shots killed Ryan's mare, and it was by the mercy of God that the life of the prisoner had not become forfeited by his own act. The next culprit was John Pound, who was equally guilty of the intended outrage perpetrated on the life of an unoffending individual — that individual a female, surrounded by her little children, five or six in number — with a complete carelessness to the probable consequences, while she and her family were going, or had gone, to bed. The contents of a gun were discharged through the door, which entered the panel in three different places. The deaths resulting from this act might have been extensive, but it was not a matter of any moment how many were deprived of life. The woman had just risen from her prayers, preparing herself to sleep under the protection of that arm which would shield the child and protect the innocent, when she was wounded. As to Cornelius Flynn and Patrick Dwyer, they likewise were the subjects of similar imputations and similar observations. There was a very slight difference between them, but not such as to amount to any real distinction. They had gone upon a common, illegal purpose, to the house of a respectable individual, for the purpose of interfering with the domestic arrangements he thought fit to make. They had no sort of right to interfere with the disposition of a man's affairs ; and what would be the consequences if the reverse were to be held? No imputation had ever been made upon the gentleman whose house was visited, but he was desired to dismiss another, under the pains and penalties of death, although that other was not a retained servant, but a friend who had come to Mr. Hogan on a visit. Because this visitor used sometimes to inspect the men at work, the lawless edict issued that he should be put away. Good God! to what extent did the prisoners and such misguided men intend to carry out their objects? Where was their dictation to cease? are they, and those in a similar rank, to take upon themselves to regulate how many and what men a farmer should take into his employment? Were they to be the judges whether a servant had discharged his duty to his principal? or was it because a visitor happened to come, that the host should turn him away, under the pains and penalties of death? His lordship, after adverting to the guilt of the prisoners in this case — the last two persons convicted, Thos. Stapleton and Thos. Gleeson — said their case was so recently before the public, that it was sufficient to say they were morally guilty of what might be considered wilful and deliberate murder. Murder was most awful, because it could only be suggested by deliberate malice, and the act of the prisoners was the result of that base, malicious, and diabolical disposition. What was the cause of resentment against the unfortunate man who had been shot at, and so desperately wounded? Why, he had dared to comply with the wishes of a just landlord ; and because the landlord, for the benefit of his tenantry, proposed that the farms should be squared, those who acquiesced in his wishes were to be equally the victims of the assassin. What were the facts in this case? The two prisoners at the bar, Stapleton and Gleeson, sprung out at the man as he was leaving work, placed him on his knees, and without giving him a moment of preparation, commenced the work of blood, intending deliberately to despatch that unprepared and unoffending individual to eternity. What country was it that they lived in, in which such crimes could be perpetrated in the open light of day? It was not necessary that deeds of darkness should be shrouded in the clouds of night, for the darkness of the deeds themselves was considered a sufficient protection. He (the Chief Justice) was not aware of any solitary instance at the present commission, to show that the crimes committed were the consequences of poverty. Poverty should be no justification, however; it might be some little palliation, but on no trial at this commission did it appear that the crime could be attributed to distress. His lordship concluded a most impressive address, by sentencing the six prisoners called up, to transportation for life.

"The clock was near midnight as the court was cleared, and the whole of the proceedings were solemn and impressive in the extreme. The commission is likely to prove extremely beneficial in its results on the future tranquillity of the country."

I confess, for my part, to that common cant and sickly sentimentality, which, thank God! is felt by a great number of people now-a-days, and which leads them to revolt against murder, whether performed by a ruffian's knife or a hangman's rope: whether accompanied with a curse from the thief as he blows his victim's brains out, or a prayer from my lord on the bench in his wig and black cap. Nay, is all the cant and sickly sentimentality on our side, and might not some such charge be applied to the admirers of the good old fashion? Long ere this is printed, for instance, Byrne and Woods have been hanged: * sent "to face their God," as the Chief Justice says, "with the weight of their victim's blood upon them," — a just observation; and remember that it is *we who send them*. It is true that the judge hopes Heaven will have mercy upon their souls; but are such recommendations of particular weight because they come from the bench? Psha! If we go on killing people without giving them time to repent, let us at least give up the cant of praying for their souls' salvation. We find a man drowning in a well, shut the lid upon him, and heartily pray that he may get out. Sin has hold of him, as the two ruffians of Laffan yonder, and we stand aloof, and hope that he may escape. Let us give up this ceremony of condolence, and be honest, like the witness, and say, "Let him save himself or not, it's no business of ours." . . . . Here a waiter, with a very broad, though insinuating accent says, "Have you done with the *Sandthers*, sir! there's a gentleman waiting for't these two hours." And so

---

* The two men were executed pursuant to sentence, and both persisted solemnly in denying their guilt. There can be no doubt of it: but it appears to be a point of honor with these unhappy men to make no statement which may incriminate the witnesses who appeared on their behalf, and on their part perjured themselves equally

he carries off that strange picture of pleasure and pain, trade, theatres, schools, courts, churches, life and death, in Ireland, which a man may buy for a fourpenny-piece.

The papers being read, it became my duty to discover the town; and a handsomer town, with fewer people in it, it is impossible to see on a summer's day. In the whole wide square of Stephen's Green, I think there were not more than two nursery-maids to keep company with the statue of George I., who rides on horseback in the middle of the garden, the horse having his foot up to trot, as if he wanted to go out of town too. Small troops of dirty children (too poor and dirty to have lodgings at Kingstown) were squatting here and there upon the sunshiny steps, the only clients at the thresholds of the professional gentlemen whose names figure on brass-plates on the doors. A stand of lazy carmen, a policeman or two with clinking boot-heels, a couple of moaning beggars leaning against the rails and calling upon the Lord, and a fellow with a toy and book stall, where the lives of St. Patrick, Robert Emmett, and Lord Edward Fitzgerald may be bought for double their value, were all the population of the Green.

At the door of the Kildare Street Club, I saw eight gentlemen looking at two boys playing at leapfrog: at the door of the University six lazy porters, in jockey-caps, were sunning themselves on a bench — a sort of blue-bottle race; and the Bank on the opposite side did not look as if sixpence-worth of change had been negotiated there during the day. There was a lad pretending to sell umbrellas under the colonnade, almost the only instance of trade going on; and I began to think of Juan Fernandez, or Cambridge in the long vacation. In the courts of the College, scarce the ghost of a gyp or the shadow of a bed-maker.

In spite of the solitude, the square of the College is a fine sight: a large ground, surrounded by buildings of various ages and styles, but comfortable, handsome, and in good repair; a modern row of rooms; a row that has been Elizabethan once; a hall and senate-house, facing each other, of the style of George I.; and a noble library, with a range of many windows, and a fine manly, simple façade of cut stone. The library was shut. The librarian, I suppose, is at the seaside; and the only part of the establishment which I could see was the museum, to which one of the jockey-capped porters conducted me, up a

2

wide, dismal staircase, (adorned with an old pair of jack-boots, a dusty canoe or two, a few helmets, and a South Sea Islander's armor,) which passes through a hall hung round with cobwebs (with which the blue-bottles are too wise to meddle), into an old mouldy room, filled with dingy glass-cases, under which the articles of curiosity or science were partially visible. In the middle was a very *seedy* camelopard (the word has grown to be English by this time), the straw splitting through his tight old skin and the black cobbler's-wax stuffing the dim orifices of his eyes. Other beasts formed a pleasing group around him, not so tall, but equally mouldy and old. The porter took me round to the cases, and told me a great number of fibs concerning their contents : there was the harp of Brian Borou, and the sword of some one else, and other cheap old gimcracks with their corollary of lies. The place would have been a disgrace to Don Saltero. I was quite glad to walk out of it, and down the dirty staircase again : about the ornaments of which the jockey-capped gyp had more figments to tell ; an atrocious one (I forget what) relative to the pair of boots ; near which — a fine specimen of collegiate taste — were the shoes of Mr. O'Brien, the Irish giant. If the collection is worth preserving, — and indeed the mineralogical specimens look quite as awful as those in the British Museum, — one thing is clear, that the rooms are worth sweeping. A pail of water costs nothing, a scrubbing-brush not much, and a charwoman might be hired for a trifle, to keep the room in a decent state of cleanliness.

Among the curiosities is a mask of the Dean — not the scoffer and giber, not the fiery politician, nor the courtier of St. John and Harley, equally ready with servility and scorn ; but the poor old man, whose great intellect had deserted him, and who died old, wild, and sad. The tall forehead is fallen away in a ruin, the mouth has settled in a hideous, vacant smile. Well, it was a mercy for Stella that she died first : it was better that she should be killed by his unkindness than by the sight of his misery ; which, to such a gentle heart as that, would have been harder still to bear.

The Bank, and other public buildings of Dublin, are justly famous. In the former may still be seen the room which was the House of Lords formerly, and where the Bank directors now sit, under a clean marble image of George III. The House of Commons has disappeared, for the accommodation of clerks and cashiers. The interior is light, splendid, airy, well-furnished, and the outside of the building not less so. The Exchange, hard by, is an equally magnificent structure ; but the genius of commerce has deserted it, for all its architectural beauty. There was nobody inside when I entered but a pert statue of George III. in a Roman toga, simpering and turning out his toes ; and two dirty children playing, whose hoop-sticks caused great clattering echoes under the vacant sounding dome. The neighborhood is not cheerful, and has a dingy, poverty-stricken look.

Walking towards the river, you have on either side of you, at Carlisle Bridge, a very brilliant and beautiful prospect : the Four Courts and their dome to the left, the Custom House and its dome to the right ; and in this direction seaward, a considerable number of vessels are moored, and the quays are black and busy with the cargoes discharged from ships. Seamen cheering, herring-women bawling, coal-carts loading — the scene is animated and lively. Yonder is the famous Corn Exchange ; but the Lord Mayor is attending to his duties in Parliament, and little of note is going on. I had just passed his lordship's mansion in Dawson Street, — a queer old dirty brick house, with dumpy urns at each extremity, and looking as if a story of it had been cut off — a rasée-house. Close at hand, and peering over a paling, is a statue of our blessed sovereign George II. How absurd these pompous images look, of defunct majesties, for whom no breathing soul cares a half-penny ! It is not so with the effigy of William III., who has done something to merit a statue. At this minute the Lord Mayor has William's effigy under a canvas, and is painting him of a bright green, picked out with yellow — his lordship's own livery.

The view along the quays to the Four Courts has no small resemblance to a view along the quays at Paris, though not so lively as are even those quiet walks. The vessels do not come above-bridge, and the marine population remains constant about them, and about numerous dirty liquor-shops, eating-houses, and marine-store establishments, which are kept for their accommodation along the quay. As far as you can see, the shining Liffey flows away eastward, hastening (like the rest of the inhabitants of Dublin) to the sea.

In front of Carlisle Bridge, and not in the least crowded, though in the midst of Sackville Street, stands Nelson upon a stone pillar. The Post Office is on his right hand (only it is cut off) ; and on his left, " Gresham's " and the " Imperial Hotel." Of the latter let me say (from subsequent experience) that it is ornamented by a cook who could dress a dinner by the side of M. Borel or M. Soyer. Would there were more such artists in this ill-fated country ! The street is exceedingly

broad and handsome ; the shops at the commencement, rich
and spacious ; but in Upper Sackville Street, which closes with
the pretty building and gardens of the Rotunda, the appearance
of wealth begins to fade somewhat, and the houses look as if
they had seen better days.   Even in this, the great street of
the town, there is scarcely any one, and it is as vacant and
listless as Pall Mall in October.   In one of the streets off Sackville Street, is the house and exhibition of the Irish Academy,
which I went to see, as it was positively to close at the end of
the week.   While I was there, two *other* people came in ; and
we had, besides, the money-taker and a porter, to whom the
former was reading, out of a newspaper, those Tipperary murders which were mentioned in a former page.   The echo took
up the theme, and hummed it gloomily through the vacant
place.

The drawings and reputation of Mr. Burton are well known
in England : his pieces were the most admired in the collection.
The best draughtsman is an imitator of Maclise, Mr. Bridgeman,
whose pictures are full of vigorous drawing, and remarkable
too for their grace.   I gave my catalogue to the two young ladies
before mentioned, and have forgotten the names of other artists
of merit, whose works decked the walls of the little gallery.
Here, as in London, the Art Union is making a stir ; and
several of the pieces were marked as the property of members
of that body.   The possession of some of these one would not be
inclined to covet ; but it is pleasant to see that people begin to
buy pictures at all, and there will be no lack of artists presently,
in a country where nature is so beautiful, and genius so plenty.
In speaking of the fine arts and of views of Dublin, it may be
said that Mr. Petrie's designs for Curry's Guide-book of the
City are exceedingly beautiful, and, above all, *trustworthy :* no
common quality in a descriptive artist at present.

Having a couple of letters of introduction to leave, I had the
pleasure to find the blinds down at one house, and the window
in papers at another ; and at each place the knock was answered
in that leisurely way, by one of those dingy female lieutenants
who have no need to tell you that families are out of town.   So
the solitude became very painful, and I thought I would go
back and talk to the waiter at the " Shelburne," the only man
in the whole kingdom that I knew.   I had been accommodated
with a queer little room, and dressing-room on the ground-floor,
looking towards the Green : a black-faced, good-humored chamber-maid had promised to perform a deal of scouring which was
evidently necessary, (a fact she might have observed for six

months back, only she is no doubt of an absent turn,) and when I came back from the walk, I saw the little room was evidently enjoying itself in the sunshine, for it had opened its window, and was taking a breath of fresh air, as it looked out upon the Green.

As I came up to it in the street, its appearance made me burst out laughing, very much to the surprise of a ragged cluster of idlers lolling upon the steps next door; and I have drawn it here, not because it is a particularly picturesque or rare kind of window, but because, as I fancy, there is a sort of *moral* in it.* You don't see such windows commonly in respectable English inns — windows leaning gracefully upon hearthbrooms for support. Look out of that window without the hearth-broom and it would cut your head off: how the beggars would start that are always sitting on the steps next door! Is it prejudice that makes one prefer the English window, that relies on its own ropes and ballast (or lead if you like), and does not need to be propped by any foreign aid? or is this only a solitary instance of the kind, and are there no other specimens in Ireland of the careless, dangerous, extravagant hearth-broom system?

In the midst of these reflections (which might have been carried much farther, for a person with an allegorical turn might examine the entire country through this window), a most wonderful cab, with an immense prancing cab-horse, was seen to stop at the door of the hotel, and Pat the waiter tumbling into the room swiftly with a card in his hand, says, " Sir, the gentleman of this card is waiting for you at the door." *Mon Dieu!* it was an invitation to dinner! and I almost leapt into the arms of the man in the cab — so delightful was it to find a friend in a place where, a moment before, I had been as lonely as Robinson Crusoe.

The only drawback, perhaps, to pure happiness, when riding in such a gorgeous equipage as this, was that we could not drive up Regent Street, and meet a few creditors, or acquaintances at least. However, Pat, I thought, was exceedingly awestricken by my disappearance in this vehicle; which had evidently, too, a considerable effect upon some other waiters at the "Shelburne," with whom I was not as yet so familiar. The mouldy camelopard at the Trinity College " Musayum" was scarcely taller than the bay-horse in the cab; the groom behind was of a corresponding smallness. The cab was of a lovely olive-green, picked out with white, high on high springs and

* This refers to an illustrated edition of the work.

enormous wheels, which, big as they were, scarcely seemed to touch the earth. The little tiger swung gracefully up and down, holding on by the hood, which was of the material of which the most precious and polished boots are made. As for the *lining* — but here we come too near the sanctity of private life ; suffice that there was a kind friend inside, who (though by no means of the fairy sort) was as welcome as any fairy in the finest chariot. W—— had seen me landing from the packet that morning, and was the very man who in London, a month previous, had recommended me to the " Shelburne." These facts are not of much consequence to the public, to be sure, except that an explanation was necessary of the miraculous appearance of the cab and horse.

Our course, as may be imagined, was towards the seaside ; for whither else should an Irishman at this season go? Not far from Kingstown is a house devoted to the purpose of festivity : it is called Salt Hill, stands upon a rising ground, commanding a fine view of the bay and the railroad, and is kept by persons bearing the celebrated name of Lovegrove. It is in fact a sea-Greenwich, and though there are no marine whitebait, other fishes are to be had in plenty, and especially the famous Bray trout, which does not ill deserve its reputation.

Here we met three young men, who may be called by the names of their several counties — Mr. Galway, Mr. Roscommon, and Mr. Clare ; and it seemed that I was to complain of solitude no longer : for one straightway invited me to his county, where was the finest salmon-fishing in the world ; another said he would drive me through the county Kerry in his four-in-hand drag ; and the third had some propositions of sport equally hospitable. As for going down to some races, on the Curragh of Kildare I think, which were to be held on the next and the three following days, there seemed to be no question about *that*. That a man should miss a race within forty miles, seemed to be a point never contemplated by these jovial sporting fellows.

Strolling about in the neighborhood before dinner, we went down to the sea-shore, and to some caves which had lately been discovered there : and two Irish ladies, who were standing at the entrance of one of them, permitted me to take the following portraits, which were pronounced to be pretty accurate.

They said they had not acquiesced in the general Temperance movement that had taken place throughout the country ; and, indeed, if the truth must be known, it was only under promise of a glass of whiskey apiece that their modesty could be so far overcome as to permit them to sit for their portraits.

By the time they were done, a crowd of both sexes had gathered round, and expressed themselves quite ready to sit upon the same terms. But though there was great variety in their coun-tenances, there was not much beauty ; and besides, dinner was by this time ready, which has at certain periods a charm even greater than art.

The bay, which had been veiled in mist and gray in the morning, was now shining under the most beautiful clear sky, which presently became rich with a thousand gorgeous hues of sunset. The view was as smiling and delightful a one as can be conceived, — just such a one as should be seen *à travers* a good dinner ; with no fatiguing sublimity or awful beauty in it, but brisk, brilliant, sunny, enlivening. In fact, in placing his banqueting-house here, Mr. Lovegrove had, as usual, a brilliant idea. You must not have too much view, or a severe one, to give a relish to a good dinner ; nor too much music, nor too quick, nor too slow, nor too loud. Any reader who has dined at a *table-d'hôte* in Germany will know the annoyance of this : a set of musicians immediately at your back will sometimes play you a melancholy polonaise ; and a man with a good ear must perforce eat in time, and your soup is quite cold before it is swallowed. Then, all of a sudden, crash goes a brisk gallop ! and you are obliged to gulp your victuals at the rate of ten miles an hour. And in respect of conversation during a good dinner, the same rules of propriety should be consulted. Deep and sublime talk is as improper as sublime prospects. Dante and champagne (I was going to say Milton and oysters, but that is a pun) are quite unfit themes of dinner-talk. Let it be light, brisk, not oppressive to the brain. Our conversation was, I recollect, just the thing. We talked about the last Derby the whole time, and the state of the odds for the St. Leger ; nor was the Ascot Cup forgotten ; and a bet or two was gayly booked.

Meanwhile the sky, which had been blue and then red, as-sumed, towards the horizon, as the red was sinking under it, a gentle, delicate cast of green. Howth Hill became of a darker purple, and the sails of the boats rather dim. The sea grew deeper and deeper in color. The lamps at the railroad dotted the line with fire ; and the light-houses of the bay began to flame. The trains to and from the city rushed flashing and hissing by. In a word, everybody said it was time to light a cigar ; which was done, the conversation about the Derby still continuing.

" Put out that candle," said Roscommon to Clare. This the

latter instantly did by flinging the taper out of the window upon the lawn, which is a thoroughfare ; and where a great laugh arose among half a score of beggar-boys, who had been under the window for some time past, repeatedly requesting the company to throw out sixpence between them.

Two other sporting young fellows had now joined the company ; and as by this time claret began to have rather a mawkish taste, whiskey-and-water was ordered, which was drunk upon the *perron* before the house, whither the whole party adjourned, and where for many hours we delightfully tossed for sixpences — a noble and fascinating sport. Nor would these remarkable events have been narrated, had I not received express permission from the gentlemen of the party to record all that was said and done. Who knows but, a thousand years hence, some antiquary or historian may find a moral in this description of the amusement of the British youth at the present enlightened time?

HOT LOBSTER.

P.S. — You take a lobster, about three feet long if possible, remove the shell, cut or break the flesh of the fish in pieces not too small. Some one else meanwhile makes a mixture of mustard, vinegar, catsup, and lots of cayenne pepper. You produce a machine called a *despatcher*, which has a spirit-lamp under it that is usually illuminated with whiskey. The lobster, the sauce, and near half a pound of butter are placed in the despatcher, which is immediately closed. When boiling, the mixture is stirred up, the lobster being sure to heave about in the pan in a convulsive manner, while it emits a remarkably rich and agreeable odor through the apartment. A glass and a half of sherry is now thrown into the pan, and the contents served out hot, and eaten by the company. Porter is commonly drunk, and whiskey-punch afterwards, and the dish is fit for an emperor.

N.B. — You are recommended not to hurry yourself in getting up the next morning, and may take soda-water with advantage — *Probatum est.*

CHAPTER II.

A COUNTRY-HOUSE IN KILDARE — SKETCHES OF AN IRISH FAMILY AND FARM.

It had been settled among my friends, I don't know for what particular reason, that the Agricultural Show at Cork was an exhibition I was specially bound to see. When, therefore, a gentleman to whom I had brought a letter of introduction kindly offered me a seat in his carriage, which was to travel by short days' journeys to that city, I took an abrupt farewell of Pat the waiter, and some other friends in Dublin : proposing to renew our acquaintance, however, upon some future day.

We started then one fine afternoon on the road from Dublin to Naas, which is the main southern road from the capital to Munster, and met, in the course of the ride of a score of miles, a dozen of coaches very heavily loaded, and bringing passengers to the city. The exit from Dublin this way is not much more elegant than the outlet by way of Kingstown : for though the great branches of the city appear flourishing enough as yet, the small outer ones are in a sad state of decay. Houses drop off here and there, and dwindle wofully in size ; we are got into the back-premises of the seemingly prosperous place, and it looks miserable, careless, and deserted. We passed through a street which was thriving once, but has fallen since into a sort of decay, to judge outwardly, — St. Thomas Street. Emmett was hanged in the midst of it. And on pursuing the line of street, and crossing the Great Canal, you come presently to a fine tall square building in the outskirts of the town, which is no more nor less than Kilmainham Gaol, or Castle. Poor Emmett is the Irish darling still — his history is on every bookstall in the city, and yonder trim-looking brick gaol a spot where Irishmen may go and pray. Many a martyr of theirs has appeared and died in front of it, — found guilty of " wearing of the green."

There must be a fine view from the gaol windows, for we presently come to a great stretch of brilliant green country, leaving the Dublin hills lying to the left, picturesque in their outline, and of wonderful color. It seems to me to be quite a different color to that in England — different-shaped clouds — different shadows and lights. The country is well tilled, well peopled ; the hay-harvest on the ground, and the people taking advantage of the sunshine to gather it in ; but in spite of everything, — green meadows, white villages and sunshine, — the place has a sort of sadness in the look of it.

The first town we passed, as appears by reference to the Guidebook, is the little town of Rathcoole ; but in the space of three days Rathcoole has disappeared from my memory, with the exception of a little low building which the village contains, and where are the quarters of the Irish constabulary. Nothing can be finer than the trim, orderly, and soldier-like appearance of this splendid corps of men.

One has glimpses all along the road of numerous gentlemen's places, looking extensive and prosperous, of a few mills by streams here and there ; but though the streams run still, the mill-wheels are idle for the chief part ; and the road passes more than one long low village, looking bare and poor, but neat and whitewashed : it seems as if the inhabitants were determined to put a decent look upon their poverty. One or two villages there were evidently appertaining to gentlemen's seats ; these are smart enough, especially that of Johnstown, near Lord Mayo's fine domain, where the houses are of the Gothic sort, with pretty porches, creepers, and railings. Noble purple hills to the left and right keep up, as it were, an accompaniment to the road.

As for the town of Naas, the first after Dublin that I have seen, what can be said of it but that it looks poor, mean, and yet somehow cheerful? There was a little bustle in the small shops, a few cars were jingling along the broadest street of the town — some sort of dandies and military individuals were lolling about right and left ; and I saw a fine court-house, where the assizes of Kildare county are held.

But by far the finest, and I think the most extensive edifice in Naas, was a haystack in the inn-yard, the proprietor of which did not fail to make me remark its size and splendor. It was of such dimensions as to strike a cockney with respect and pleasure ; and here standing just as the new crops were coming in, told a tale of opulent thrift and good husbandry. Are there many more such haystacks, I wonder, in Ireland? The crops along the road seemed healthy, though rather light : wheat and oats plenty, and especially flourishing ; hay and clover not so good ; and turnips (let the important remark be taken at its full value) almost entirely wanting.

The little town as they call it of Kilcullen tumbles down a hill and struggles up another ; the two being here picturesquely divided by the Liffey, over which goes an antique bridge. It boasts, moreover, of a portion of an abbey wall, and a piece of round tower, both on the hill summit, and to be seen (says the Guide-book) for many miles round. Here we saw the first public evidences of the distress of the country. There was no trade in the little place, and but few people to be seen, except a crowd round a meal-shop, where meal is distributed once a week by the neighboring gentry. There must have been some hundreds of persons waiting about the doors; women for the most part: some of their children were to be found loitering about the bridge much farther up the street: but it was curious to note, amongst these undeniably starving people, how healthy their looks were. Going a little farther we saw women pulling weeds and nettles in the hedges, on which dismal sustenance the poor creatures live, having no bread, no potatoes, no work. Well! these women did not look thinner or more unhealthy than many a well-fed person. A company of English lawyers, now, look more cadaverous than these starving creatures.

Stretching away from Kilcullen bridge, for a couple of miles or more, near the fine house and plantations of the Latouche family, is to be seen a much prettier sight, I think, than the finest park and mansion in the world. This is a tract of excessively green land, dotted over with brilliant white cottages, each with its couple of trim acres of garden, where you see thick potato-ridges covered with blossom, great blue plots of comfortable cabbages and such pleasant plants of the poor man's garden. Two or three years since, the land was a marshy common, which had never since the days of the Deluge fed any being bigger than a snipe, and into which the poor people descended, draining and cultivating and rescuing the marsh from the water, and raising their cabins and setting up their little inclosures of two or three acres upon the land which they had thus created. "Many of 'em has passed months in jail for that," said my informant (a groom on the back seat of my host's phaeton): for it appears that certain gentlemen in the neighborhood looked upon the titles of these new colonists with some jealousy, and would have been glad to depose them; but there were some better philosophers among the surrounding gentry, who advised that instead of discouraging the settlers it would be best to help them; and the consequence has been, that there are now two hundred flourishing little homesteads upon this rescued land, and as many families in comfort and plenty.

Just at the confines of this pretty rustic republic, our pleas-

ant afternoon's drive ended; and I must begin this tour with
a monstrous breach of confidence, by first describing what I
saw.

Well, then, we drove through a neat lodge-gate, with no
stone lions or supporters, but riding well on its hinges, and
looking fresh and white; and passed by a lodge, not Gothic,
but decorated with flowers and evergreens, with clean windows,
and a sound slate roof; and then went over a trim road, through
a few acres of grass, adorned with plenty of young firs and other
healthy trees, under which were feeding a dozen of fine cows or
more. The road led up to a house, or rather a congregation
of rooms, built seemingly to suit the owner's convenience, and
increasing with his increasing wealth, or whim, or family.
This latter is as plentiful as everything else about the place;
and as the arrows increased, the good-natured, lucky father
has been forced to multiply the quivers.

First came out a young gentleman, the heir of the house,
who, after greeting his papa, began examining the horses with
much interest; whilst three or four servants, quite neat and
well dressed, and, wonderful to say, without any talking, began
to occupy themselves with the carriage, the passengers, and the
trunks. Meanwhile, the owner of the house had gone into
the hall, which is snugly furnished as a morning-room, and
where one, two, three young ladies came in to greet him. The
young ladies having concluded their embraces performed (as I
am bound to say from experience, both in London and Paris)
some very appropriate and well-finished curtsies to the strangers
arriving. And these three young persons were presently succeeded by some still younger, who came without any curtsies
at all; but, bounding and jumping, and shouting out "Papa"
at the top of their voices, they fell forthwith upon that worthy
gentleman's person, taking possession this of his knees, that
of his arms, that of his whiskers, as fancy or taste might
dictate.

"Are there any more of you?" says he, with perfect good-
humor; and, in fact, it appeared that there were some more in
the nursery, as we subsequently had occasion to see.

Well, this large happy family are lodged in a house than
which a prettier or more comfortable is not to be seen even in
England; of the furniture of which it may be in confidence
said, that each article is only made to answer one purpose: —
thus, that chairs are never called upon to exercise the versatility of their genius by propping up windows; that chests of
drawers are not obliged to move their unwieldy persons in order

to act as locks to doors; that the windows are not variegated by paper, or adorned with wafers, as in other places which I have seen: in fact, that the place is just as comfortable as a place can be.

And if these comforts and reminiscences of three days' date are enlarged upon at some length, the reason is simply this: — this is written at what is supposed to be the best inn at one of the best towns of Ireland, Waterford. Dinner is just over; it is assize-week, and the *table-d'hôte* was surrounded for the chief part by English attorneys — the cyouncillors (as the bar are pertinaciously called) dining up stairs in private. Well, on going to the public room and being about to lay down my hat on the sideboard, I was obliged to pause — out of regard to a fine thick coat of dust which had been kindly left to gather for some days past I should think, and which it seemed a shame to displace. Yonder is a chair basking quietly in the sunshine; some round object has evidently reposed upon it (a hat or plate probably), for you see a clear circle of black horsehair in the middle of the chair, and dust all round it. Not one of those dirty napkins that the four waiters carry, would wipe away the grime from the chair, and take to itself a little dust more! The people in the room are shouting out for the waiters, who cry, " Yes, sir," peevishly, and don't come; but stand bawling and jangling, and calling each other names, at the sideboard. The dinner is plentiful and nasty — raw ducks, raw pease, on a crumpled tablecloth, over which a waiter has just spirted a pint of obstreperous cider. The windows are open, to give free view of a crowd of old beggar-women, and of a fellow playing a cursed Irish pipe. Presently this delectable apartment fills with choking peat-smoke; and on asking what is the cause of this agreeable addition to the pleasures of the place, you are told that they are lighting a fire in a back-room.

Why should lighting a fire in a back-room fill a whole enormous house with smoke? Why should four waiters stand and *jaw* and gesticulate among themselves, instead of waiting on the guests? Why should ducks be raw, and dust lie quiet in places where a hundred people pass daily? All these points make one think very regretfully of neat, pleasant, comfortable, prosperous H—— town, where the meat was cooked, and the rooms were clean, and the servants didn't talk. Nor need it be said here, that it is as cheap to have a house clean as dirty, and that a raw leg of mutton costs exactly the same sum as one *cuit à point*. And by this moral earnestly hoping that all Ireland may profit, let us go back to H——, and the sights to be seen there.

There is no need to particularize the chairs and tables any farther, nor to say what sort of conversation and claret we had; nor to set down the dishes served at dinner. If an Irish gentleman does not give you a more hearty welcome than an Englishman, at least he has a more hearty manner of welcoming you; and while the latter reserves his fun and humor (if he possess those qualities) for his particular friends, the former is ready to laugh and talk his best with all the world, and give way entirely to his mood. And it would be a good opportunity here for a man who is clever at philosophizing to expound various theories upon the modes of hospitality practised in various parts of Europe. In a couple of hours' talk, an Englishman will give you his notions on trade, politics, the crops; the last run with the hounds, or the weather: it requires a long sitting, and a bottle of wine at the least, to induce him to laugh cordially, or to speak unreservedly; and if you joke with him before you know him, he will assuredly set you down as a low impertinent fellow. In two hours, and over a pipe, a German will be quite ready to let loose the easy floodgates of his sentiment, and confide to you many of the secrets of his soft heart. In two hours a Frenchman will say a hundred and twenty smart, witty, brilliant, false things, and will care for you as much then as he would if you saw him every day for twenty years — that is, not one single straw; and in two hours an Irishman will have allowed his jovial humor to unbutton, and gambolled and frolicked to his heart's content. Which of these, putting *Monsieur* out of the question, will stand by his friend with the most constancy, and maintain his steady wish to serve him? That is a question which the Englishman (and I think with a little of his ordinary cool assumption) is disposed to decide in his own favor; but it is clear that for a stranger the Irish ways are the pleasantest, for here he is at once made happy and at home; or at ease rather: for home is a strong word, and implies much more than any stranger can expect, or even desire to claim.

Nothing could be more delightful to witness than the evident affection which the children and parents bore to one another, and the cheerfulness and happiness of their family-parties. The father of one lad went with a party of his friends and family on a pleasure-party, in a handsome coach-and-four. The little fellow sat on the coach-box and played with the whip very wistfully for some time: the sun was shining, the horses came out in bright harness, with glistening coats; one of the girls brought a geranium to stick in papa's button-hole, who was to drive. But although there was room in the coach, and though papa said he should go if he liked, and though the lad longed to go — as who wouldn't? — he jumped off the box, and said he would not go: mamma would like him to stop at home and keep his sister company; and so down he went like a hero. Does this story appear trivial to any one who reads it? If so, he is a pompous fellow, whose opinion is not worth the having; or he has no children of his own; or he has forgotten the day when he was a child himself; or he has never repented of the surly selfishness with which he treated brothers and sisters, after the habit of young English gentlemen.

"That's a list that uncle keeps of his children," said the same young fellow, seeing his uncle reading a paper; and to understand this joke, it must be remembered that the children of the gentleman called uncle came into the breakfast-room by half-dozens. "That's a *rum* fellow," said the eldest of these latter to me, as his father went out of the room, evidently thinking his papa was the greatest wit and wonder in the whole world. And a great merit, as it appeared to me, on the part of these worthy parents was, that they consented not only to make, but to take jokes from their young ones: nor was the parental authority in the least weakened by this kind familiar intercourse.

A word with regard to the ladies so far. Those I have seen appear to the full as well educated and refined, and far more frank and cordial, than the generality of the fair creatures on the other side of the Channel. I have not heard anything about poetry, to be sure, and in only one house have seen an album; but I have heard some capital music, of an excellent family sort — that sort which is used, namely, to set young people dancing, which they have done merrily for some nights. In respect of drinking, among the gentry teetotalism does not, thank heaven! as yet appear to prevail; but although the claret has been invariably good, there has been no improper use of it.* Let all English be recommended to be very careful of whiskey, which experience teaches to be a very deleterious drink. Natives say that it is wholesome, and may be sometimes seen to use it with impunity; but the whiskey-fever is naturally more fatal to strangers than inhabitants of the coun-

---

* The only instances of intoxication that I have heard of as yet, have been on the part of two "cyouncillors," undeniably drunk and noisy yesterday after the bar dinner at Waterford.

try; and whereas an Irishman will sometimes imbibe a half-
dozen tumblers of the poison, two glasses will be often found
to cause headaches, heartburns, and fevers to a person newly
arrived in the country. The said whiskey is always to be had for
the asking, but is not produced at the bettermost sort of tables.

Before setting out on our second day's journey, we had time
to accompany the well-pleased owner of H—— town over some
of his fields and out-premises. Nor can there be a pleasanter
sight to owner or stranger. Mr. P—— farms four hundred
acres of land about his house; and employs on this estate no
less than a hundred and ten persons. He says there is full
work for every one of them; and to see the elaborate state of
cultivation in which the land was, it is easy to understand how
such an agricultural regiment were employed. The estate is
like a well-ordered garden: we walked into a huge field of potatoes, and the landlord made us remark that there was not a
single weed between the furrows; and the whole formed a vast
flower-bed of a score of acres. Every bit of land up to the
hedge-side was fertilized and full of produce: the space left for
the plough having afterwards been gone over, and yielding its
fullest proportion of "fruit." In a turnip-field were a score
or more of women and children, who were marching through
the ridges, removing the young plants where two or three had
grown together, and leaving only the most healthy. Every
individual root in the field was thus the object of culture; and
the owner said that this extreme cultivation answered his purpose, and that the employment of all these hands, (the women
and children earn 6d. and 8d. a day all the year round,) which
gained him some reputation as a philanthropist, brought him
profit as a farmer too; for his crops were the best that land
could produce. He has further the advantage of a large stock
for manure, and does everything for the land which art can do.

Here we saw several experiments in manuring: an acre
of turnips prepared with bone-dust; another with " Murray's
Composition," whereof I do not pretend to know the ingre-
dients; another with a new manure called guano. As far as
turnips and a first year's crop went, the guano carried the
day. The plants on the guano acre looked to be three weeks
in advance of their neighbors, and were extremely plentiful
and healthy. I went to see this field two months after the
above passage was written: the guano acre still kept the lead;
the bone-dust ran guano very hard; and composition was
clearly distanced.

Behind the house is a fine village of corn and hayricks, and a street of out-buildings, where all the work of the farm is prepared. Here were numerous people coming with pails for buttermilk, which the good-natured landlord made over to them. A score of men or more were busied about the place ; some at a grindstone, others at a forge — other fellows busied in the cart-houses and stables, all of which were as neatly kept as in the best farm in England. A little further on was a flower-garden, a kitchen-garden, a hot-house just building, a kennel of fine pointers and setters ; — indeed a noble feature of country neatness, thrift, and plenty.

We went into the cottages and gardens of several of Mr. P——'s laborers, which were all so neat that I could not help fancying they were pet cottages, erected under the landlord's own superintendence, and ornamented to his order. But he declared that it was not so ; that the only benefit his laborers got from him was constant work, and a house rent-free ; and that the neatness of the gardens and dwellings was of their own doing. By making them a present of the house, he said, he made them a present of the pig and live stock, with which almost every Irish cotter pays his rent, so that each workman could have a bit of meat for his support ; — would that all laborers in the empire had as much! With regard to the neatness of the houses, the best way to ensure this, he said, was for the master constantly to visit them — to awaken as much emulation as he could amongst the cottagers, so that each should make his place as good as his neighbor's — and to take them good-humoredly to task if they failed in the requisite care.

And so this pleasant day's visit ended. A more practical person would have seen, no doubt, and understood much more than a mere citizen could, whose pursuits have been very different from those noble and useful ones here spoken of. But a man has no call to be a judge of turnips or live stock, in order to admire such an establishment as this, and heartily to appreciate the excellence of it. There are some happy organizations in the world which possess the great virtue of *prosperity.* It implies cheerfulness, simplicity, shrewdness, perseverance, honesty, good health. See how, before the good-humored resolution of such characters, ill-luck gives way, and fortune assumes their own smiling complexion ! Such men grow rich without driving a single hard bargain ; their condition being to make others prosper along with themselves. Thus, his very charity, another informant tells me, is one of the causes of my host's good fortune. He might have three pounds a year from each of forty cottages, but instead prefers a hundred healthy workmen; or he might have a fourth of the number of workmen, and a farm yielding a produce proportionately less; but instead of saving the money of their wages, prefers a farm the produce of which, as I have heard from a gentleman whom I take to be good authority, is unequalled elsewhere.

Besides the cottages, we visited a pretty school where children of an exceeding smallness were at their work, — the children of the Catholic peasantry. The few Protestants of the district do not attend the national-school, nor learn their alphabet or their multiplication-table in company with their little Roman Catholic brethren. The clergyman who lives hard by the gate of H—— town, in his communication with his parishioners cannot fail to see how much misery is relieved and how much good is done by his neighbor; but though the two gentlemen are on good terms, the clergyman will not break bread with his Catholic fellow-Christian. There can be no harm, I hope, in mentioning this fact, as it is rather a public than a private matter; and, unfortunately, it is only a stranger that is surprised by such a circumstance, which is quite familiar to residents of the country. There are Catholic inns and Protestant inns in the towns; Catholic coaches and Protestant coaches on the roads; nay, in the North, I have since heard of a High Church coach and a Low Church coach adopted by travelling Christians of either party.

CHAPTER III.

FROM CARLOW TO WATERFORD.

THE next morning being fixed for the commencement of our journey towards Waterford, a carriage made its appearance in due time before the hall-door: an amateur stage-coach, with four fine horses, that were to carry us to Cork. The crew of the "drag," for the present, consisted of two young ladies, and two who will not be old, please heaven! for these thirty years; three gentlemen whose collected weights might amount to fifty-four stone; and one of smaller proportions, being as yet only twelve years old: to these were added a couple of grooms and a lady's-maid. Subsequently we took in a dozen or so more pas·

sengers, who did not seem in the slightest degree to inconvenience the coach or the horses ; and thus was formed a tolerably numerous and merry party. The governor took the reins, with his geranium in his button-hole, and the place on the box was quarrelled for without ceasing, and taken by turns.

Our day's journey lay through a country more picturesque, though by no means so prosperous and well cultivated as the district through which we had passed on our drive from Dublin. This trip carried us through the County of Carlow and the town of that name : a wretched place enough, with a fine court-house, and a couple of fine churches : the Protestant church a noble structure, and the Catholic cathedral said to be built after some continental model. The Catholics point to the structure with considerable pride : it was the first, I believe, of the many handsome cathedrals for their worship which have been built of late years in this country by the noble contributions of the poor man's penny, and by the untiring energies and sacrifices of the clergy. Bishop Doyle, the founder of the church, has the place of honor within it ; nor, perhaps, did any Christian pastor ever merit the affection of his flock more than that great and high-minded man. He was the best champion the Catholic Church and cause ever had in Ireland : in learning, and admirable kindness and virtue, the best example to the clergy of his religion : and if the country is now filled with schools, where the humblest peasant in it can have the benefit of a liberal and wholesome education, it owes this great boon mainly to his noble exertions, and to the spirit which they awakened.

As for the architecture of the cathedral, I do not fancy a professional man would find much to praise in it ; it seems to me overloaded with ornaments, nor were its innumerable spires and pinnacles the more pleasing to the eye because some of them were out of the perpendicular. The interior is quite plain, not to say bare and unfinished. Many of the chapels in the country that I have since seen are in a similar condition : for when the walls are once raised, the enthusiasm of the subscribers to the building seems somewhat characteristically to grow cool, and you enter at a porch that would suit a palace, with an interior scarcely more decorated than a barn. A wide large floor, some confession-boxes against the blank walls here and there, with some humble pictures at the " stations," and the statue, under a mean canopy of red woollen stuff, were the chief furniture of the cathedral.

The severe homely features of the good bishop were not very favorable subjects for Mr. Hogan's chisel ; but a figure of pros-

trate, weeping Ireland, kneeling by the prelate's side, and for
whom he is imploring protection, has much beauty. In the
chapels of Dublin and Cork some of this artist's work may be
seen, and his countrymen are exceedingly proud of him.

Connected with the Catholic cathedral is a large tumble-
down-looking divinity college : there are upwards of a hundred
students here, and the college is licensed to give degrees in arts
as well as divinity ; at least so the officer of the church said,
as he showed us the place through the bars of the sacristy-
windows, in which apartment may be seen sundry crosses, a
pastoral letter of Dr. Doyle, and a number of ecclesiastical
vestments formed of laces, poplins, and velvets handsomely
laced with gold. There is a convent by the side of the cathedral, and, of course, a parcel of beggars all about, and indeed
all over the town, profuse in their prayers and invocations of
the Lord, and whining flatteries of the persons whom they
address. One wretched old tottering hag began whining the
Lord's Prayer as a proof of her sincerity, and blundered in
the very midst of it, and left us thoroughly disgusted after
the very first sentence.

It was market-day in the town, which is tolerably full of
poor-looking shops, the streets being thronged with donkey-
carts, and people eager to barter their small wares. Here
and there were picture-stalls, with huge hideous-colored engravings of the Saints : and indeed the objects of barter upon
the banks of the clear bright river Barrow seemed scarcely to
be of more value than the articles which change hands, as one
reads of, in a town of African huts and traders on the banks of
the Quorra. Perhaps the very bustle and cheerfulness of the
people served only, to a Londoner's eye, to make it look the
more miserable. It seems as if they had no *right* to be eager
about such a parcel of wretched rags and trifles as were exposed
to sale.

There are some old towers of a castle here, looking finely
from the river ; and near the town is a grand modern residence
belonging to Colonel Bruen, with an oak-park on one side of
the road, and a deer-park on the other. These retainers of the
Colonel's lay in their rushy green inclosures, in great numbers,
and seemingly in flourishing condition.

The road from Carlow to Leighlin Bridge is exceedingly
beautiful : noble pure hills rising on either side, and the broad
silver Barrow flowing through rich meadows of that astonishing verdure which is only to be seen in this country. Here and
there was a country-house, or a tall mill by a stream-side : but

the latter buildings were for the most part empty, the gaunt windows gaping without glass, and their great wheels idle. Leighlin Bridge, lying up and down a hill by the river contains a considerable number of pompous-looking warehouses, that looked for the most part to be doing no more business than the mills on the Carlow road, but stood by the roadside staring at the coach as it were, and basking in the sun, swaggering, idle, insolvent, and out-at-elbows. There are one or two very pretty, modest, comfortable-looking country places about Leighlin Bridge, and on the road thence to a miserable village called the Royal Oak, a beggarly sort of bustling place.

Here stands a dilapidated hotel and posting-house: and indeed on every road, as yet, I have been astonished at the great movement and stir; — the old coaches being invariably crammed, cars jingling about equally full, and no want of gentlemen's carriages to exercise the horses of the " Royal Oak" and similar establishments. In the time of the rebellion, the landlord of this " Royal Oak," a great character in those parts, was a fierce United Irishman. One day it happened that Sir John Anderson came to the inn, and was eager for horses on. The landlord, who knew Sir John to be a Tory, vowed and swore he had no horses; that the judges had the last going to Kilkenny; that the yeomanry had carried off the best of them; that he could not give a horse for love or money. " Poor Lord Edward!" said Sir John, sinking down in a chair, and clasping his hands, " my poor dear misguided friend, and must you die for the loss of a few hours and the want of a pair of horses?"

" Lord *What?*" says the landlord.

" Lord Edward Fitzgerald," replied Sir John. " The Government has seized his papers, and got scent of his hiding-place. If I can't get to him before two hours, Sirr will have him."

" My dear Sir John," cried the landlord, " it's not two horses but it's eight I'll give you, and may the judges go hang for me! Here, Larry! Tim! First and second pair for Sir John Anderson; and long life to you, Sir John, and the Lord reward you for your good deed this day!"

Sir John, my informant told me, had invented this predicament of Lord Edward's in order to get the horses; and by way of corroborating the whole story, pointed out an old chaise which stood at the inn-door with its window broken, a great crevice in the panel, some little wretches crawling underneath the wheels, and two huge blackguards lolling against the pole.

" And that," says he, " is no doubt the very post-chaise Sir John Anderson had." It certainly looked ancient enough.

Of course, as we stopped for a moment in the place, troops of slatternly, ruffianly-looking fellows assembled round the carriage, dirty heads peeped out of all the dirty windows, beggars came forward with a joke and a prayer, and troops of children raised their shouts and halloos. I confess, with regard to the beggars, that I have never yet had the slightest sentiment of compassion for the very oldest or dirtiest of them, or been inclined to give them a penny : they come crawling round you with lying prayers and loathsome compliments, that make the stomach turn ; they do not even disguise that they are lies ; for, refuse them and the wretches turn off with a laugh and a joke, a miserable grinning cynicism that creates distrust and indifference, and must be, one would think, the very best way to close the purse, not to open it, for objects so unworthy.

How do all these people live ? one can't help wondering ; — these multifarious vagabonds, without work or workhouse, or means of subsistence ? The Irish Poor Law Report says that there are twelve hundred thousand people in Ireland — a sixth of the population — who have no means of livelihood but charity, and whom the State, or individual members of it, must maintain. How *can* the State support such an enormous burden ; or the twelve hundred thousand be supported ? What a strange history it would be, could one but get it true, — that of the manner in which a score of these beggars have maintained themselves for a fortnight past !

Soon after quitting the " Royal Oak," our road branches off to the hospitable house where our party, consisting of a dozen persons, was to be housed and fed for the night. Fancy the look which an English gentleman of moderate means would assume, at being called on to receive such a company ! A pretty road of a couple of miles, thickly grown with ash and oak trees, under which the hats of coach-passengers suffered some danger, leads to the house of D——. A young son of the house, on a white pony, was on the look-out, and great cheering and shouting took place among the young people as we came in sight.

Trotting away by the carriage-side he brought us through a gate with a pretty avenue of trees leading to the pleasure-grounds of the house — a handsome building commanding noble views of river, mountains, and plantations. Our entertainer only rents the place ; so I may say, without any imputation against him, that the house was by no means so handsome within as without, — not that the want of finish in the interior made our party the less merry, or the host's entertainment less hearty and cordial.

The gentleman who built and owns the house, like many other proprietors in Ireland, found his mansion too expensive for his means, and has relinquished it. I asked what his income might be, and no wonder that he was compelled to resign his house; which a man with four times the income in England would scarcely venture to inhabit. There were numerous sitting-rooms below; a large suite of rooms above, in which our large party, with their servants, disappeared without any seeming inconvenience, and which already accommodated a family of at least a dozen persons, and a numerous train of domestics. There was a great court-yard surrounded by capital offices, with stabling and coach-houses sufficient for a half-dozen of country gentlemen. An English squire of ten thousand a year might live in such a place — the original owner, I am told, had not many more hundreds.

Our host has wisely turned the chief part of the pleasure-ground round the house into a farm; nor did the land look a bit the worse, as I thought, for having rich crops of potatoes growing in place of grass, and fine plots of waving wheat and barley. The care, skill, and neatness everywhere exhibited, and the immense luxuriance of the crops, could not fail to strike even a cockney: and one of our party, a very well-known, practical farmer, told me that there was at least five hundred pounds' worth of produce upon the little estate of some sixty acres, of which only five-and-twenty were under the plough.

As at H—— town, on the previous day, several men and women appeared sauntering in the grounds, and as the master came up, asked for work, or sixpence, or told a story of want. There are lodge-gates at both ends of the demesne; but it appears the good-natured practice of the country admits a beggar as well as any other visitor. To a couple our landlord gave money, to another a little job of work; another he sent roughly out of the premises: and I could judge thus what a continual tax upon the Irish gentleman these travelling paupers must be, of whom his ground is never free.

There, loitering about the stables and out-houses, were several people who seemed to have acquired a sort of right to be there: women and children who had a claim upon the butter-milk; men who did an odd job now and then; loose hangers-on of the family: and in the lodging-houses and inns I have entered, the same sort of ragged vassals are to be found; in a house however poor, you are sure to see some poorer dependant who is a stranger, taking a meal of potatoes in the kitchen; a Tim or Mike loitering hard by, ready to run on a message, or carry a bag. This is written, for instance, at a lodging over a shop at Cork. There sits in the shop a poor old fellow quite past work, but who totters up and down stairs to the lodgers, and does what little he can for his easily-won bread. There is another fellow outside who is sure to make his bow to anybody issuing from the lodging, and ask if his honor wants an errand done? Neither class of such dependants exists with us. What housekeeper in London is there will feed an old man of seventy that's good for nothing, or encourage such a disreputable hanger-on as yonder shuffling, smiling cad?

Nor did Mr. M——'s " irregulars " disappear with the day; for when, after a great deal of merriment, and kind, happy dancing and romping of young people, the fineness of the night suggested the propriety of smoking a certain cigar (it is never more acceptable than at that season), the young squire voted that we should adjourn to the stables for the purpose, where accordingly the cigars were discussed. There were still the inevitable half-dozen hangers-on : one came grinning with a lantern, all nature being in universal blackness except his grinning face ; another ran obsequiously to the stables to show a favorite mare — I think it was a mare — though it may have been a mule, and your humble servant not much the wiser. The cloths were taken off ; the fellows with the candles crowded about ; and the young squire bade me admire the beauty of her fore-leg, which I did with the greatest possible gravity. " Did you ever see such a fore-leg as that in your life?" says the young squire, and further discoursed upon the horse's points, the amateur grooms joining in chorus.

There was another young squire of our party, a pleasant gentlemanlike young fellow, who danced as prettily as any Frenchman, and who had ridden over from a neighboring house : as I went to bed, the two lads were arguing whether young Squire B—— should go home or stay at D—— that night. There was a bed for him — there was a bed for everybody it seemed, and a kind welcome too. How different was all this to the ways of a severe English house !

Next morning the whole of our merry party assembled round a long, jovial breakfast-table, stored with all sorts of good things ; and the biggest and jovialest man of all, who had just come in fresh from a walk in the fields, and vowed that he was as hungry as a hunter, and was cutting some slices out of an inviting ham on the side-table, suddenly let fall his knife and fork with dismay. " Sure, John, don't you know it's Friday?" cried a lady from the table ; and back John came with a most lugubrious queer look on his jolly face, and fell to work upon bread-and-butter, as resigned as possible, amidst no small laughter, as may be well imagined. On this I was bound, as a Protestant, to eat a large slice of pork, and discharged that duty nobly, and with much self-sacrifice.

The famous " drag " which had brought us so far, seemed to be as hospitable and elastic as the house which we now left, for the coach accommodated, inside and out, a considerable party from the house ; and we took our road leisurely, in a cloudless scorching day, towards Waterford. The first place we passed through was the little town of Gowran, near which is a grand, well-ordered park, belonging to Lord Clifden, and where his mother resides, with whose beautiful face, in Lawrence's pictures, every reader must be familiar. The kind English lady has done the greatest good in the neighborhood, it is said, and the little town bears marks of her beneficence, in its neatness, prettiness, and order. Close by the church there are the ruins of a fine old abbey here, and a still finer one a few miles on, at Thomastown, most picturesquely situated amidst trees and meadow, on the river Nore. The place within, however, is dirty and ruinous — the same wretched suburbs, the same squalid congregation of beggarly loungers, that are to be seen elsewhere. The monastic ruin is very fine, and the road hence to Thomastown rich with varied cultivation and beautiful verdure, pretty gentlemen's mansions shining among the trees on either side of the way. There was one place along this rich tract that looked very strange and ghastly — a huge old pair of gate pillars, flanked by a ruinous lodge, and a wide road winding for a mile up a hill. There had been a park once, but all the trees were gone ; thistles were growing in the yellow sickly land, and rank thin grass on the road. Far away you saw in this desolate tract a ruin of a house : many a butt of claret has been emptied there, no doubt, and many a merry party come out with hound and horn. But what strikes the Englishman with wonder is not so much, perhaps, that an owner of the place should have been ruined and a spendthrift, as that the land should lie there useless ever since. If one is not successful with us another man will be, or another will try, at least. Here lies useless a great capital of hundreds of acres of land ; barren, where the commonest effort might make it productive, and looking as if for a quarter of a century past no soul ever looked or cared for it. You might travel five hundred miles through England and not see such a spectacle.

A short distance from Thomastown is another abbey; and presently, after passing through the village of Knocktopher, we came to a posting-place called Ballyhale, of the *moral* aspect of which the following scrap taken in the place will give a notion.*

A dirty, old, contented, decrepit idler was lolling in the sun at a shop-door, and hundreds of the population of the dirty, old, decrepit, contented place were employed in the like way. A dozen of boys were playing at pitch-and-toss; other male and female beggars were sitting on a wall looking into a stream; scores of ragamuffins, of course, round the carriage; and beggars galore at the door of the little ale-house or hotel. A gentleman's carriage changed horses as we were baiting here. It was a rich sight to see the cattle, and the way of starting them: "Halloo! Yoop — hoop!" a dozen ragged ostlers and amateurs running by the side of the miserable old horses, the postilion shrieking, yelling, and belaboring them with his whip. Down goes one horse among the new-laid stones; the postilion has him up with a cut of the whip and a curse, and takes advantage of the start caused by the stumble to get the brute into a gallop, and to go down the hill. "I know it for a fact," a gentleman of our party says, "that no horses *ever* got out of Ballyhale without an accident of some kind."

"Will your honor like to come and see a big pig?" here asked a man of the above gentleman, well known as a great farmer and breeder. We all went to see the big pig, not very fat as yet, but, upon my word, it is as big as a pony. The country round is, it appears, famous for the breeding of such, especially a district called the Welsh mountains, through which we had to pass on our road to Waterford.

This is a curious country to see, and has curious inhabitants: for twenty miles there is no gentleman's house: gentlemen dare not live there. The place was originally tenanted by a clan of Welshes; hence its name; and they maintain themselves in their occupancy of the farms in Tipperary fashion, by simply putting a ball into the body of any man who would come to take a farm over any one of them. Some of the crops in the fields of the Welsh country seemed very good, and the fields well tilled; but it is common to see, by the side of one

* This refers to an illustrated edition of the work.

field that is well cultivated, another that is absolutely barren; and the whole tract is extremely wretched. Appropriate histories and reminiscences accompany the traveller : at a chapel near Mullinavat is the spot where sixteen policemen were murdered in the tithe-campaign ; farther on you come to a lime-kiln, where the guard of a mail-coach was seized and *roasted alive*. I saw here the first hedge-school I have seen : a crowd of half-savage-looking lads and girls looked up from their studies in the ditch, their college or lecture-room being in a mud cabin hard by.

And likewise, in the midst of this wild tract, a fellow met us who was trudging the road with a fish-basket over his shoulder, and who stopped the coach, hailing two of the gentlemen in it by name, both of whom seemed to be much amused by his humor. He was a handsome rogue, a poacher, or salmon-taker, by profession, and presently poured out such a flood of oaths, and made such a monstrous display of grinning wit and blackguardism, as I have never heard equalled by the best Billingsgate practitioner, and as it would be more than useless to attempt to describe. Blessings, jokes, and curses trolled off the rascal's lips with a volubility which caused his Irish audience to shout with laughter, but which were quite beyond a cockney. It was a humor so purely national as to be understood by none but natives, I should think. I recollect the same feeling of perplexity while sitting, the only Englishman, in a company of jocular Scotchmen. They bandied about puns, jokes, imitations, and applauded with shrieks of laughter what, I confess, appeared to me the most abominable dulness ; nor was the salmon-taker's jocularity any better. I think it rather served to frighten than to amuse ; and I am not sure but that I looked out for a band of jocular cut-throats of this sort to come up at a given guffaw, and playfully rob us all round. However, he went away quite peaceably, calling down for the party the benediction of a great number of saints, who must have been somewhat ashamed to be addressed by such a rascal.

Presently we caught sight of the valley through which the Suir flows, and descended the hill towards it, and went over the thundering old wooden bridge to Waterford.

CHAPTER IV.

FROM WATERFORD TO CORK.

THE view of the town from the bridge and the heights above it is very imposing; as is the river both ways. Very large vessels sail up almost to the doors of the houses, and the quays are flanked by tall red warehouses, that look at a little distance as if a world of business might be doing within them. But as you get into the place, not a soul is there to greet you, except the usual society of beggars, and a sailor or two, or a green-coated policeman sauntering down the broad pavement. We drove up to the " Coach Inn," a huge, handsome, dirty build-ing, of which the discomforts have been pathetically described elsewhere. The landlord is a gentleman and considerable horse-proprietor, and though a perfectly well-bred, active, and intelligent man, far too much of a gentleman to play the host well: at least as an Englishman understands that character.

Opposite the town is a tower of questionable antiquity and undeniable ugliness; for though the inscription says it was built in the year one thousand and something, the same docu-ment adds that it was rebuilt in 1819 — to either of which dates the traveller is thus welcomed. The quays stretch for a con-siderable distance along the river, poor, patched-windowed, mouldy-looking shops forming the basement-story of most of the houses. We went into one, a jeweller's, to make a pur-chase — it might have been of a gold watch for anything the owner knew; but he was talking with a friend in his back-parlor, gave us a look as we entered, allowed us to stand some minutes in the empty shop, and at length to walk out without being served. In another shop a boy was lolling behind a counter, but could not say whether the articles we wanted were to be had; turned out a heap of drawers, and could not find them; and finally went for the master, who could not come. True commercial independence, and an easy way enough of life.

In one of the streets leading from the quay is a large, dingy Catholic chapel, of some pretensions within; but, as usual, there had been a failure for want of money, and the front of the chapel was unfinished, presenting the butt-end of a portico, and walls on which the stone coating was to be laid. But a much

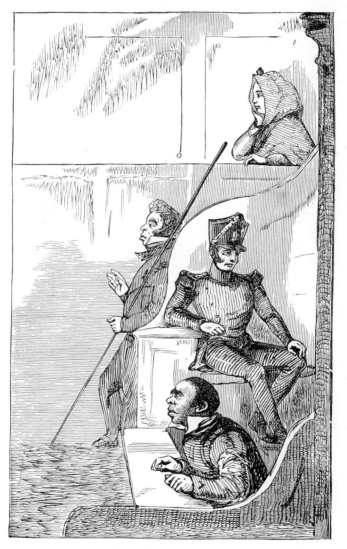

THE COURT-HOUSE AT WATERFORD.

finer ornament to the church than any of the questionable gew-gaws which adorned the ceiling was the piety, stern, simple, and unaffected, of the people within. Their whole soul seemed to be in their prayers, as rich and poor knelt indifferently on the flags. There is of course an episcopal cathedral, well and neatly kept, and a handsome Bishop's palace: near it was a convent of nuns, and a little chapel-bell clinking melodiously. I was prepared to fancy something romantic of the place; but as we passed the convent gate, a shoeless slattern of a maid opened the door — the most dirty and unpoetical of house-maids.

Assizes were held in the town, and we ascended to the court-house through a steep street, a sort of rag-fair, but more villa-nous, and miserable than any rag-fair in St. Giles's: the houses and stock of the Seven Dials look as if they belonged to capi-talists when compared with the scarecrow wretchedness of the goods here hung out for sale. Who wanted to buy such things? I wondered. One would have thought that the most part of the articles had passed the possibility of barter for money, even out of the reach of the half-farthings coined of late. All the street was lined with wretched hucksters and their merchandise of gooseberries, green apples, children's dirty cakes, cheap crockeries, brushes, and tinware; among which objects the peo-ple were swarming about busily.

Before the court is a wide street, where a similar market was held, with a vast number of donkey-carts urged hither and thither, and great shrieking, chattering, and bustle. It is five hundred years ago since a poet who accompanied Richard II. in his voyage hither spoke of " *Watreforde ou moult vilaine et orde y sont la gente.*" They don't seem to be much changed now, but remain faithful to their ancient habits.

About the court-house swarms of beggars of course were collected, varied by personages of a better sort: gray-coated farmers, and women with their picturesque blue cloaks, who had trudged in from the country probably. The court-house is as beggarly and ruinous as the rest of the neighborhood; smart-looking policemen kept order about it, and looked very hard at me as I ventured to take a sketch.

The figures as I saw them were accurately disposed as follows: the man in the dock, the policeman seated easily above him, the woman looking down from a gallery. The man was accused of stealing a sack of wool, and, having no counsel, made for himself as adroit a defence as any one of the counsellors (they are without robes or wigs here, by the way,) could have made for him. He had been seen examining a certain sack of wool in a coffee-shop at Dungarvan, and next day was caught sight of in Waterford Market, standing under an archway from the rain, with the sack by his side.

" Wasn't there twenty other people under the arch?" said he to a witness, a noble-looking beautiful girl — the girl was obliged to own there were. " Did you see me touch the wool, or stand nearer to it than a dozen of the dacent people there?" and the girl confessed she had not. " And this it is, my lord," says he to the bench, " they attack me because I am poor and ragged, but they never think of charging the crime on a rich farmer."

But alas for the defence! another witness saw the prisoner with his legs round the sack, and being about to charge him with the theft, the prisoner fled into the arms of a policeman, to whom his first words were, " I know nothing about the sack." So, as the sack had been stolen, as he had been seen handling it four minutes before it was stolen, and holding it for sale the day after, it was concluded that Patrick Malony had stolen the sack, and he was accommodated with eighteen months accordingly.

In another case we had a woman and her child on the table; and others followed, in the judgment of which it was impossible not to admire the extreme leniency, acuteness, and sensibility of the judge presiding, Chief Justice Pennefather: — the man against whom all the Liberals in Ireland, and every one else who has read his charge too, must be angry, for the ferocity of his charge against a Belfast newspaper editor. It seems as if no parties here will be dispassionate when they get to a party question, and that natural kindness has no claim when Whig and Tory come into collision.

The witness is here placed on a table instead of a witness-box; nor was there much farther peculiarity to remark, except in the dirt of the court, the absence of the barristerial wig and gown, and the great coolness with which a fellow who seemed a sort of clerk, usher, and Irish interpreter to the court, recommended a prisoner, who was making rather a long defence, to be quiet. I asked him why the man might not have his say. " Sure," says he, " he's said all he has to say, and there's no use in any more." But there was no use in attempting to convince Mr. Usher that the prisoner was best judge on this point: in fact the poor devil shut his mouth at the admonition, and was found guilty with perfect justice.

A considerable poor-house has been erected at Waterford,

but the beggars of the place as yet prefer their liberty, and less certain means of gaining support. We asked one who was calling down all the blessings of all the saints and angels upon us, and telling a most piteous tale of poverty, why she did not go to the poor-house. The woman's look at once changed from a sentimental whine to a grin. "Dey owe two hundred pounds at dat house," said she, "and faith, an honest woman can't go dere." With which wonderful reason ought not the most squeamish to be content?

After describing, as accurately as words may, the features of a landscape, and stating that such a mountain was to the left, and such a river or town to the right, and putting down the situations and names of the villages, and the bearings of the roads, it has no doubt struck the reader of books of travels that the writer has not given him the slightest idea of the country, and that he would have been just as wise without perusing the letter-press landscape through which he has toiled. It will be as well then, under such circumstances, to spare the public any lengthened description of the road from Waterford to Dungarvan; which was the road we took, followed by benedictions delivered gratis from the beggarhood of the former city. Not very far from it you see the dark plantations of the magnificent domain of Curraghmore, and pass through a country, blue, hilly, and bare, except where gentlemen's seats appear with their ornaments of wood. Presently, after leaving Waterford, we came to a certain town called Kilmacthomas, of which all the information I have to give is, that it is situated upon a hill and river, and that you may change horses there. The road was covered with carts of seaweed, which the people were bringing for manure from the shore some four miles distant; and beyond Kilmacthomas we beheld the Cummeragh Mountains, "often named in maps the Nennavoulagh," either of which names the reader may select at pleasure.

Thence we came to "Cushcam," at which village be it known that the turnpike-man kept the drag a very long time waiting. "I think the fellow must be writing a book," said the coachman, with a most severe look of drollery at a cockney tourist, who tried, under the circumstances, to blush, and not to laugh. I wish I could relate or remember half the mad jokes that flew about among the jolly Irish crew on the top of the coach, and which would have made a journey through the Desert jovial.

When the 'pike-man had finished his composition (that of a turn-pike-ticket, which he had to fill,) we drove on to Dungarvan ; the two parts of which town, separated by the river Colligan, have been joined by a causeway three hundred yards along, and a bridge erected at an enormous outlay by the Duke of Devon-shire. In former times, before his Grace spent his eighty thousand pounds upon the causeway, this wide estuary was called "Dungarvan Prospect," because the ladies of the coun-try, walking over the river at low water, took off their shoes and stockings (such as had them), and tucking up their clothes, exhibited — what I have never seen, and cannot therefore be expected to describe. A large and handsome Catholic chapel, a square with some pretensions to regularity of building, a very neat and comfortable inn, and beggars and idlers still more numerous than at Waterford, were what we had leisure to re-mark in half an hour's stroll through the town.

Near the prettily situated village of Cappoquin is the Trap-pist House of Mount Meilleraie, of which we could only see the pinnacles. The brethren were presented some years since with a barren mountain, which they have cultivated most success-fully. They have among themselves workmen to supply all their frugal wants : ghostly tailors and shoemakers, spiritual gardeners and bakers, working in silence, and serving heaven after their way. If this reverend community, for fear of the opportunity of sinful talk, choose to hold their tongues, the next thing will be to cut them out altogether, and so render the danger impossible : if, being men of education and intel-ligence, they incline to turn butchers and cobblers, and smother their intellects by base and hard menial labor, who knows but one day a sect may be more pious still, and rejecting even butchery and bakery as savoring too much of worldly con-venience and pride, take to a wild-beast life at once? Let us concede that suffering, and mental and bodily debasement, are the things most agreeable to heaven, and there is no knowing where such piety may stop. I was very glad we had not time to see the grovelling place ; and as for seeing shoes made or fields tilled by reverend amateurs, we can find cobblers and ploughboys to do the work better.

By the way, the Quakers have set up in Ireland a sort of monkery of their own. Not far from Carlow we met a couple of cars drawn by white horses, and holding white Quakers and Quakeresses, in white hats, clothes, shoes, with wild maniacal-looking faces, bumping along the road. Let us hope that we may soon get a community of Fakeers and howling Dervishes into the country. It would be a refreshing thing to see such ghostly men in one's travels, standing at the corners of roads and praising the Lord by standing on one leg, or cutting and hacking themselves with knives like the prophets of Baal. Is it not as pious for a man to deprive himself of his leg as of his tongue, and to disfigure his body with the gashes of a knife, as with the hideous white raiment of the illuminated Quakers?

While these reflections were going on, the beautiful Blackwater river suddenly opened before us, and driving along it for three miles through some of the most beautiful, rich country ever seen, we came to Lismore. Nothing can be certainly more magnificent than this drive. Parks and rocks covered with the grandest foliage; rich, handsome seats of gentlemen in the midst of fair lawns and beautiful bright plantations and shrubberies; and at the end, the graceful spire of Lismore church, the prettiest I have seen in, or, I think, out of Ireland. Nor in any country that I have visited have I seen a view more noble — it is too rich and peaceful to be what is called romantic, but lofty, large, and *generous*, if the term may be used; the river and banks as fine as the Rhine; the castle not as large, but as noble and picturesque as Warwick. As you pass the bridge, the banks stretch away on either side in amazing verdure, and the castle-walks remind one somewhat of the dear old terrace of St. Germains, with its groves, and long grave avenues of trees.

The salmon-fishery of the Blackwater is let, as I hear, for a thousand a year. In the evening, however, we saw some gentlemen who are likely to curtail the profits of the farmer of the fishery — a company of ragged boys, to wit — whose occupation, it appears, is to poach. These young fellows were all lolling over the bridge, as the moon rose rather mistily, and pretended to be deeply enamored of the view of the river. They answered the questions of one of our party with the utmost innocence and openness, and one would have supposed the lads were so many Arcadians, but for the arrival of an old woman, who, suddenly coming up among them, poured out, upon one and all, a volley of curses, both deep and loud, saying that perdition would be their portion, and calling them "shchamers" at least a hundred times. Much to my wonder, the young men did not reply to the voluble old lady for some time, who then told us the cause of her anger. She had a son, — "Look at him there, the villain." The lad was standing, looking very unhappy. "His father, that's now dead, paid a fistful of money to bind him 'prentice at Dungarvan: but these shchamers followed him there; made him break his indentures, and go poaching and thieving and shchaming with them." The poor old woman shook her hands in the air, and shouted at the top of her deep voice: there was something very touching in her grotesque sorrow; nor did the lads make light of it at all, contenting themselves with a surly growl, or an oath, if directly appealed to by the poor creature.

So, cursing and raging, the woman went away. The son, a lad of fourteen, evidently the fag of the big bullies round about him, stood dismally away from them, his head sunk down. I went up and asked him, "Was that his mother?" He said, "Yes." "Was she good and kind to him when he was at home?" He said, "Oh yes." "Why not come back to her?" I asked him; but he said "he couldn't." Whereupon I took his arm, and tried to lead him away by main force; but he said, "Thank you, sir, but I can't go back," and released his arm. We stood on the bridge some minutes longer, looking at the view; but the boy, though he kept away from his comrades, would not come. I wonder what they have done together, that the poor boy is past going home? The place seemed to be so quiet and beautiful, and far away from London, that I thought crime couldn't have reached it; and yet here it lurks somewhere among six boys of sixteen, each with a stain in his heart, and some black history to tell. The poor widow's yonder was the only family about which I had a chance of knowing anything in this remote place; nay, in all Ireland: and God help us, hers was a sad lot! — a husband gone dead, — an only child gone to ruin. It is awful to think that there are eight millions of stories to be told in this island. Seven million nine hundred and ninety-nine thousand nine hundred and ninety-eight more lives that I, and all brother cockneys, know nothing about. Well, please God, they are not all like this.

That day I heard *another* history. A little old disreputable man in tatters, with a huge steeple of a hat, came shambling down the street, one among the five hundred blackguards there. A fellow standing under the "Sun" portico (a sort of swaggering, chattering, cringing *touter*, and master of ceremonies to the gutter,) told us something with regard to the old disreputable man. His son had been hanged the day before at Clonmel, for one of the Tipperary murders. That blackguard in our eyes instantly looked quite different from all other blackguards: I saw him gesticulating at the corner of a street, and watched him with wonderful interest.

The church with the handsome spire that looks so graceful

among the trees, is a cathedral church, and one of the neatest-kept and prettiest edifices I have seen in Ireland. In the old graveyard Protestants and Catholics lie together — that is, not together ; for each has a side of the ground where they sleep, and, so occupied, do not quarrel. The sun was shining down upon the brilliant grass — and I don't think the shadows of the Protestant graves were any longer or shorter than those of the Catholics ! Is it the right or the left side of the graveyard which is nearest heaven I wonder? Look, the sun shines upon both alike, "and the blue sky bends over all."

Raleigh's house is approached by a grave old avenue, and well-kept wall, such as is rare in this country ; and the court of the castle within has the solid, comfortable, quiet look, equally rare. It is like one of our colleges at Oxford : there is a side of the quadrangle with pretty ivy-covered gables ; another part of the square is more modern ; and by the main body of the castle is a small chapel exceedingly picturesque. The interior is neat and in excellent order ; but it was unluckily done up some thirty years ago (as I imagine from the style), before our architects had learned Gothic, and all the ornamental work is consequently quite ugly and out of keeping. The church has probably been arranged by the same hand. In the castle are some plainly-furnished chambers, one or two good pictures, and a couple of oriel windows, the views from which up and down the river are exceedingly lovely. You hear praises of the Duke of Devonshire as a landlord wherever you go among his vast estates : it is a pity that, with such a noble residence as this, and with such a wonderful country round about it, his Grace should not inhabit it more.

Of the road from Lismore to Fermoy it does not behove me to say much, for a pelting rain came on very soon after we quitted the former place, and accompanied us almost without ceasing to Fermoy. Here we had a glimpse of a bridge across the Blackwater, which we had skirted in our journey from Lismore. Now enveloped in mist and cloud, now spanned by a rainbow, at another time, basking in sunshine, Nature attired the charming prospect for us in a score of different ways ; and it appeared before us like a coquettish beauty who was trying what dress in her wardrobe might most become her. At Fermoy we saw a vast barrack, and an overgrown inn, where, however, good fare was provided ; and thence hastening came by Rathcormack, and Watergrass Hill, famous for the residence of Father Prout, whom my friend the Rev. Francis Sylvester has made immortal ; from which descending we arrived at the beautiful wooded village of Glanmire, with its mills, and steeples, and streams, and neat school-houses, and pleasant country residences. This brings us down upon the superb stream which leads from the sea to Cork.

The view for three miles on both sides is magnificently beautiful. Fine gardens, and parks, and villas cover the shore on each bank; the river is full of brisk craft moving to the city or out to sea; and the city finely ends the view, rising upon two hills on either side of the stream. I do not know a town to which there is an entrance more beautiful, commodious, and stately.

Passing by numberless handsome lodges, and nearer the city, many terraces in neat order, the road conducts us near a large tract of some hundred acres which have been reclaimed from the sea, and are destined to form a park and pleasure-ground for the citizens of Cork. In the river, and up to the bridge, some hundreds of ships were lying; and a fleet of steamboats opposite the handsome house of the St. George's Steam-Packet Company. A church stands prettily on the hill above it, surrounded by a number of new habitations very neat and white. On the road is a handsome Roman Catholic chapel, or a chapel which will be handsome so soon as the necessary funds are raised to complete it. But, as at Waterford, the chapel has been commenced, and the money has failed, and the fine portico which is to decorate it one day, as yet only exists on the architect's paper. Saint Patrick's Bridge, over which we pass, is a pretty building; and Patrick Street, the main street of the town, has an air of business and cheerfulness, and looks densely thronged.

As the carriage drove up to those neat, comfortable, and extensive lodgings which Mrs. MacO'Boy has to let, a magnificent mob was formed round the vehicle, and we had an opportunity of at once making acquaintance with some of the dirtiest rascally faces that all Ireland presents. Besides these professional rogues and beggars, who make a point to attend on all vehicles, everybody else seemed to stop too, to see that wonder, a coach and four horses. People issued from their shops, heads appeared at windows. I have seen the Queen pass in state in London, and not bring together a crowd near so great as that which assembled in the busiest street of the second city of the kingdom, just to look at a green coach and four bay horses. Have they nothing else to do?—or is it that they *will* do nothing but stare, swagger, and be idle in the streets?

CHAPTER V.

CORK — THE AGRICULTURAL SHOW — FATHER MATHEW.

A MAN has no need to be an agriculturist in order to take a warm interest in the success of the Irish Agricultural Society, and to see what vast good may result from it to the country. The National Education scheme — a noble and liberal one, at least as far as a stranger can see, which might have united the Irish people, and brought peace into this most distracted of all countries — failed unhappily of one of its greatest ends. The Protestant clergy have always treated the plan with bitter hostility : and I do believe, in withdrawing from it, have struck the greatest blow to themselves as a body, and to their own influence in the country, which has been dealt to them for many a year. Rich, charitable, pious, well-educated, to be found in every parish in Ireland, had they chosen to fraternize with the people and the plan, they might have directed the educational movement ; they might have attained the influence which is now given over entirely to the priest ; and when the present generation, educated in the national schools, were grown up to manhood, they might have had an interest in almost every man in Ireland. Are they as pious, and more polished, and better educated than their neighbors the priests? There is no doubt of it ; and by constant communion with the people, they would have gained all the benefits of the comparison, and advanced the interests of their religion far more than now they can hope to do. Look at the national school : throughout the country it is commonly by the chapel side — it is a Catholic school, directed and fostered by the priest ; and as no people are more eager for learning, more apt to receive it, or more grateful for kindness than the Irish, he gets all the gratitude of the scholars who flock to the school, and all the future influence over them, which naturally and justly comes to him. The Protestant wants to better the condition of these people : he says that the woes of the country are owing to its prevalent religion ; and in order to carry his plans of amelioration into effect, he obstinately refuses to hold communion with those whom he is desirous to convert to what he believes are sounder principles and purer doctrines. The clergyman will reply, that points of principle prevented him : with this fatal doctrinal objection, it is not, of course, the province of a layman to meddle ; but this is clear, that the parson might have had an influence over the country, and he would not ; that he might have rendered the Catholic population friendly to him, and he would not ; but, instead, has added one cause of estrangement and hostility more to the many which already existed against him. This is one of the attempts at union in Ireland, and one can't but think with the deepest regret and sorrow of its failure.

Mr. O'Connell and his friends set going another scheme for advancing the prosperity of the country, — the notable project of home manufactures, and of a coalition against foreign importation. This was a union certainly, but a union of a different sort to that noble and peaceful one which the National Education Board proposed. It was to punish England, while it pretended to secure the independence of Ireland, by shutting out our manufactures from the Irish markets ; which were one day or other, it was presumed, to be filled by native produce. Large bodies of tradesmen and private persons in Dublin and other towns in Ireland associated together, vowing to purchase no articles of ordinary consumption or usage but what were manufactured in the country. This bigoted, old-world scheme of restriction — not much more liberal than Swing's crusade against the threshing-machines, or the coalitions in England against machinery — failed, as it deserved to do. For the benefit of a few tradesmen, who might find their account in selling at dear rates their clumsy and imperfect manufactures, it was found impossible to tax a people that are already poor enough ; nor did the party take into account the cleverness of the merchants across sea, who were by no means disposed to let go their Irish customers. The famous Irish frieze uniform which was to distinguish these patriots, and which Mr. O'Connell lauded so loudly and so simply, came over made at half-price from Leeds and Glasgow, and was retailed as real Irish by many worthies who had been first to join the union. You may still see shops here and there with their pompous announcement of " Irish Manufactures ; " but the scheme is long gone to ruin : it could not stand against the vast force of English and Scotch capital and machinery, any more than the Ulster spinning-wheel against the huge factories and steam-engines which one may see about Belfast.

The scheme of the Agricultural Society is a much more feasible one ; and if, please God, it can be carried out, likely to give not only prosperity to the country, but union likewise in a great degree. As yet Protestants and Catholics concerned in it have worked well together; and it is a blessing to see them meet upon *any* ground without heartburning and quarrelling. Last year, Mr. Purcell, who is well known in Ireland as the principal mail-coach contractor for the country, — who himself employs more workmen in Dublin than perhaps any other person there, and has also more land under cultivation than most of the great landed proprietors in the country, — wrote a letter to the news-papers, giving his notions of the fallacy of the exclusive-dealing system, and pointing out at the same time how he considered the country might be benefited — by agricultural improvement, namely. He spoke of the neglected state of the country, and its amazing natural fertility; and, for the benefit of all, called upon the landlords and landholders to use their interest and develop its vast agricultural resources. Manufactures are at best but of slow growth, and demand not only time, but capi-tal; meanwhile, until the habits of the people should grow to be such as to render manufactures feasible, there was a great neglected treasure, lying under their feet, which might be the source of prosperity to all. He pointed out the superior meth-ods of husbandry employed in Scotland and England, and the great results obtained upon soils naturally much poorer; and, taking the Highland Society for an example, the establishment of which had done so much for the prosperity of Scotland, he proposed the formation in Ireland of a similar association.

The letter made an extraordinary sensation throughout the country. Noblemen and gentry of all sides took it up; and numbers of these wrote to Mr. Purcell, and gave him their cordial adhesion to the plan. A meeting was held, and the Society formed: subscriptions were set on foot, headed by the Lord Lieutenant (Fortescue) and the Duke of Leinster, each with a donation of 200*l.*; and the trustees had soon 5,000*l.* at their disposal: with, besides, an annual revenue of 1,000*l.* The subscribed capital is funded; and political subjects strictly excluded. The Society has a show yearly in one of the prin-cipal towns of Ireland: it corresponds with the various local agricultural associations throughout the country; encourages the formation of new ones; and distributes prizes and rewards. It has further in contemplation, to establish a large Agricultural school for farmers' sons; and has formed in Dublin an Agricul-tural Bazaar and Museum.

It was the first meeting of the Society which we were come to see at Cork. Will it be able to carry its excellent intentions into effect? Will the present enthusiasm of its founders and members continue? Will one political party or another get the upper hand in it? One can't help thinking of these points with some anxiety — of the latter especially : as yet, happily, the clergy of either side have kept aloof, and the union seems pretty cordial and sincere.

There are in Cork, as no doubt in every town of Ireland sufficiently considerable to support a plurality of hotels, some especially devoted to the Conservative and Liberal parties. Two dinners were to be given àpropos of the Agricultural meeting; and in order to conciliate all parties, it was determined that the Tory landlord should find the cheap ten-shilling dinner for one thousand, the Whig landlord the genteel guinea dinner for a few select hundreds.

I wish Mr. Cuff, of the " Freemasons' Tavern," could have been at Cork to take a lesson from the latter gentleman : for he would have seen that there are means of having not merely enough to eat, but enough of the very best, for the sum of a guinea ; that persons can have not only wine, but good wine, and if inclined (as some topers are on great occasions) to pass to another bottle, — a second, a third, or a fifteenth bottle, for what I know is very much at their service. It was a fine sight to see Mr. MacDowall presiding over an ice-well and extracting the bottles of champagne. With what calmness he did it! How the corks popped, and the liquor fizzed, and the agriculturalists drank the bumpers off! And how good the wine was too — the greatest merit of all! Mr. MacDowall did credit to his liberal politics by his liberal dinner.

" Sir," says a waiter whom I asked for currant-jelly for the haunch — (there were a dozen such smoking on various parts of the table — think of that, Mr. Cuff!) — " Sir," says the waiter, " there's no jelly, but I've brought you *some very fine lobster-sauce.*" I think this was the most remarkable speech of the evening ; not excepting that of my Lord Bernard, who, to three hundred gentlemen more or less connected with farming, had actually the audacity to quote the words of the great agricultural poet of Rome —

" *O fortunatos nimium sua si,*" &c.

How long are our statesmen in England to continue to back their opinions by the Latin grammar? Are the Irish agriculturalists so *very* happy, if they did but know it — at least those out of doors? Well, those within were jolly enough. Champagne and claret. turbot and haunch, are gifts of the *justissima tellus*, with which few husbandmen will be disposed to quarrel: — no more let us quarrel either with eloquence after dinner.

If the Liberal landlord had shown his principles in his dinner, the Conservative certainly showed his ; by conserving as much profit as possible for himself. We sat down one thousand to some two hundred and fifty cold joints of meat. Every man was treated with a pint of wine, and very bad too, so that there was the less cause to grumble because more was not served. Those agriculturalists who had a mind to drink whiskey-and-water had to pay extra for their punch. Nay, after shouting in vain for half an hour to a waiter for some cold water, the unhappy writer could only get it by promising a shilling. The sum was paid on delivery of the article ; but as everybody round was thirsty too, I got but a glassful from the decanter, which only served to make me long for more. The waiter (the rascal !) promised more, but never came near us afterwards : he had got his shilling, and so he left us in a hot room, surrounded by a thousand hot fellow-creatures, one of them making a dry speech. The agriculturalists were not on this occasion *nimium fortunati*.

To have heard a nobleman, however, who discoursed to the meeting, you would have fancied that we were the luckiest mortals under the broiling July sun. He said he could conceive nothing more delightful than to see, " on proper occasions," — (mind, *on proper occasions!*) — " the landlord mixing with his tenantry ; and to look around him at a scene like this, and see *the condescension* with which the gentry mingled with the farmers !" Prodigious condescension truly ! This neat speech seemed to me an oratoric slap on the face to about nine hundred and seventy persons present ; and being one of the latter, I began to hiss by way of acknowledgment of the compliment, and hoped that a strong party would have destroyed the harmony of the evening, and done likewise. But not one hereditary bondsman would join in the compliment — and they were quite right too. The old lord who talked about condescension is one of the greatest and kindest landlords in Ireland. If he thinks he condescends by doing his duty and mixing with men as good as himself, the fault lies with the latter. Why are they so ready to go down on their knees to my lord? A man can't help " condescending " to another who will persist in kissing his shoestrings. They respect rank in England — the people seem almost to adore it here.

As an instance of the intense veneration for lords which distinguishes this county of Cork, I may mention what occurred afterwards. The members of the Cork Society gave a dinner to their guests of the Irish Agricultural Association. The founder of the latter, as Lord Downshire stated, was Mr. Purcell: and as it was agreed on all hands that the Society so founded was likely to prove of the greatest benefit to the country, one might have supposed that any compliment paid to it might have been paid to it through its founder. Not so. The Society asked the lords to dine, and Mr. Purcell to meet the lords.

After the grand dinner came a grand ball, which was indeed one of the gayest and prettiest sights ever seen; nor was it the less agreeable, because the ladies of the city mixed with the ladies from the country, and vied with them in grace and beauty. The charming gayety and frankness of the Irish ladies have been noted and admired by every foreigner who has had the good fortune to mingle in their society; and I hope it is not detracting from the merit of the upper classes to say that the lower are not a whit less pleasing. I never saw in any country such a general grace of manner and *ladyhood*. In the midst of their gayety, too, it must be remembered that they are the chastest of women, and that no country in Europe can boast of such a general purity.

In regard of the Munster ladies, I had the pleasure to be present at two or three evening-parties at Cork, and must say that they seem to excel the English ladies not only in wit and vivacity, but in the still more important article of the toilette. They are as well dressed as Frenchwomen, and incomparably handsomer; and if ever this book reaches a thirtieth edition, and I can find out better words to express admiration, they shall be inserted here. Among the ladies' accomplishments, I may mention that I have heard in two or three private families such fine music as is rarely to be met with out of a capital. In one house we had a supper and songs afterwards, in the old honest fashion. Time was in Ireland when the custom was a common one; but the world grows languid as it grows genteel; and I fancy it requires more than ordinary spirit and courage now for a good old gentleman, at the head of his kind family table, to strike up a good old family song.

The delightful old gentleman who sung the song here mentioned could not help talking of the Temperance movement with a sort of regret, and said that all the fun had gone out of Ireland since Father Mathew banished the whiskey from it. Indeed, any stranger going amongst the people can perceive that they are now anything but gay. I have seen a great number of crowds and meetings of people in all parts of Ireland, and found them all gloomy. There is nothing like the merry-making one reads of in the Irish novels. Lever and Maxwell must be taken as chroniclers of the old times — the pleasant but wrong old times — for which one can't help having an antiquarian fondness.

On the day we arrived at Cork, and as the passengers descended from "the drag," a stout, handsome, honest-looking man, of some two-and-forty years, was passing by, and received a number of bows from the crowd around. It was THEOBALD MATHEW, with whose face a thousand little print-shop windows had already rendered me familiar. He shook hands with the master of the carriage very cordially, and just as cordially with the master's coachman, a disciple of temperance, as at least half Ireland is at present. The day after the famous dinner at MacDowall's, some of us came down rather late, perhaps in consequence of the events of the night before — (I think it was Lord Bernard's quotation from Virgil, or else the absence of the currant-jelly for the venison, that occasioned a slight headache among some of us, and an extreme longing for sodawater,) — and there was the Apostle of Temperance seated at the table drinking tea. Some of us felt a little ashamed of ourselves, and did not like to ask somehow for the soda-water in such an awful presence as that. Besides, it would have been a confession to a Catholic priest, and, as a Protestant, I am above it.

The world likes to know how a great man appears even to a valet-de-chambre, and I suppose it is one's vanity that is flattered in such rare company to find the great man quite as unassuming as the very smallest personage present; and so like to other mortals, that we would not know him to be a great man at all, did we not know his name, and what he had done. There is nothing remarkable in Mr. Mathew's manner, except that it is exceedingly simple, hearty, and manly, and that he does not wear the downcast, demure look which, I know not why, certainly characterizes the chief part of the gentlemen of his profession. Whence comes that general scowl which darkens the faces of the Irish priesthood? I have met a score of these reverend gentlemen in the country, and not one of them seemed to look or speak frankly, except Mr. Mathew, and a couple more. He is almost the only man, too, that I have met in Ireland, who, in speaking of public matters, did not talk as a partisan. With the state of the country, of landlord, tenant, and peasantry, he seemed to be most curiously and intimately acquainted ; speaking of their wants, differences, and the means of bettering them, with the minutest practical knowledge. And it was impossible in hearing him to know, but from previous acquaintance with his character, whether he was Whig or Tory, Catholic or Protestant. Why does not Government make a Privy Councillor of him? — that is, if he would honor the Right Honorable body by taking a seat amongst them. His knowledge of the people is prodigious, and their confidence in him as great ; and what a touching attachment that is which these poor fellows show to any one who has their cause at heart — even to any one who says he has !

Avoiding all political questions, no man seems more eager than he for the practical improvement of this country. Leases and rents, farming improvements, reading-societies, music-societies — he was full of these, and of his schemes of temperance above all. He never misses a chance of making a convert, and has his hand ready and a pledge in his pocket for sick or poor. One of his disciples in a livery-coat came into the room with a tray — Mr. Mathew recognized him, and shook him by the hand directly ; so he did with the strangers who were presented to him ; and not with a courtly popularity-hunting air, but, as it seemed, from sheer hearty kindness, and a desire to do every one good.

When breakfast was done — (he took but one cup of tea, and says that, from having been a great consumer of tea and refreshing liquids before, a small cup of tea, and one glass of water at dinner, now serve him for his day's beverage) — he took the ladies of our party to see his burying-ground — a new and handsome cemetery, lying a little way out of the town, and where, thank God ! Protestants and Catholics may lie together, without clergymen quarrelling over their coffins.

It is a handsome piece of ground, and was formerly a botanic garden ; but the funds failed for that undertaking, as they have for a thousand other public enterprises in this poor disunited country ; and so it has been converted into a *hortus siccus* for us mortals. There is already a pretty large collection. In the midst is a place for Mathew himself — honor to him living or dead ! Meanwhile, numerous stately monuments have been built, flowers planted here and there over dear remains, and the garden in which they lie is rich, green, and beautiful. Here is a fine statue, by Hogan, of a weeping genius that broods over the tomb of an honest merchant and clothier of the city. He took a liking to the artist, his fellow-townsman, and ordered his own monument, and had the gratification to see it arrive from Rome a few weeks before his death. A prettier thing even than the statue is the tomb of a little boy, which has been shut in by a large and curious *grille* of iron-work. The father worked it, a blacksmith, whose darling the child was, and he spent three years in hammering out this mausoleum. It is the beautiful story of the pot of ointment told again at the poor blacksmith's anvil; and who can but like him for placing this fine gilded cage over the body of his poor little one? Presently you come to a Frenchwoman's tomb, with a French epitaph by a French husband, and a pot of artificial flowers in a niche — a wig, and a pot of rouge, as it were, just to make the dead look passably well. It is *his* manner of showing his sympathy for an immortal soul that has passed away. The poor may be buried here for nothing; and here, too, once more THANK GOD! each may rest without priests or parsons scowling hell-fire at his neighbor unconscious under the grass.

CHAPTER VI.

CORK — THE URSULINE CONVENT.

THERE is a large Ursuline convent at Blackrock, near Cork, and a lady who had been educated there was kind enough to invite me to join a party to visit the place. Was not this a great privilege for a heretic? I have peeped into convent chapels abroad, and occasionally caught glimpses of a white veil or black gown; but to see the pious ladies in their own retreat was quite a novelty — much more exciting than the exhibition of Long Horns and Short Horns by which we had to pass on our road to Blackrock.

The three miles' ride is very pretty. As far as Nature goes, she has done her best for the neighborhood; and the noble hills on the opposite coast of the river, studded with innumerable pretty villas and garnished with fine trees and meadows, the river itself dark blue under a brilliant cloudless heaven, and lively with its multiplicity of gay craft, accompany the traveller along the road; except here and there where the view is shut out by fine avenues of trees, a beggarly row of cottages, or a villa wall. Rows of dirty cabins, and smart bankers' country-houses, meet one at every turn; nor do the latter want for fine names, you may be sure. The Irish grandiloquence displays itself finely in the invention of such ; and, to the great inconvenience, I should think, of the postman, the names of the houses appear to change with the tenants : for I saw many old houses with new placards in front, setting forth the *last* title of the house.

I had the box of the carriage (a smart vehicle that would have done credit to the ring), and found the gentleman by my side very communicative. He named the owners of the pretty mansions and lawns visible on the other side of the river : they appear almost all to be merchants, who have made their fortunes in the city. In the like manner, though the air of the town is extremely fresh and pure to a pair of London lungs, the Cork shopkeeper is not satisfied with it, but contrives for himself a place (with an euphonious name, no doubt) in the suburbs of the city. These stretch to a great extent along the beautiful, liberal-looking banks of the stream.

I asked the man about the Temperance, and whether he was a temperance man? He replied by pulling a medal out of his waistcoat pocket, saying that he always carried it about with him for fear of temptation. He said that he took the pledge two years ago, before which time, as he confessed, he had been a sad sinner in the way of drink. "I used to take," said he, "from eighteen to twenty glasses of whiskey a day ; I was always at the drink ; I'd be often up all night at the public : I was turned away by my present master on account of it ;"— and all of a sudden he resolved to break it off. I asked him whether he had not at first experienced ill-health from the suddenness of the change in his habits ; but he said — and let all persons meditating a conversion from liquor remember the fact — that the abstinence never affected him in the least, but that he went on growing better and better in health every day, stronger and more able of mind and body.

The man was a Catholic, and in speaking of the numerous places of worship along the road as we passed, I'm sorry to confess, dealt some rude cuts with his whip regarding the Protestants. Coachman as he was, the fellow's remarks seemed to be correct : for it appears that the religious world of Cork is of so excessively enlightened a kind, that one church will not content one pious person ; but that, on the contrary, they will be at Church of a morning, at Independent church of an after-noon, at a Darbyite congregation of an evening, and so on, gathering excitement or information from all sources which they could come at. Is not this the case? are not some of the ultra

serious as eager after a new preacher, as the ultra-worldly for a
new dancer? don't they talk and gossip about him as much?
Though theology from the coach-box is rather questionable,
(after all the man was just as much authorized to propound his
notions as many a fellow from an amateur pulpit,) yet he certainly had the right here as far as his charge against certain
Protestants went.

The reasoning from it was quite obvious, and I'm sure was
in the man's mind, though he did not utter it, as we drove by
this time into the convent gate. "Here," says coachman, " is
our church. *I* don't drive my master and mistress from church
to chapel, from chapel to conventicle, hunting after new
preachers every Sabbath. I bring them every Sunday and set
them down at the same place, where they know that everything
they hear *must* be right. Their fathers have done the same
thing before them; and the young ladies and gentlemen will
come here too ; and all the new-fangled doctors and teachers
may go roaring through the land, and still here we come regularly, not caring a whit for the vagaries of others, knowing that
we ourselves are in the real old right original way."

I am sure this is what the fellow meant by his sneer at the
Protestants, and their gadding from one doctrine to another ;
but there was no call and no time to have a battle with him, as
by this time we had entered a large lawn covered with haycocks,
and prettily, as I think, ornamented with a border of blossoming
potatoes, and drove up to the front door of the convent. It is
a huge old square house, with many windows, having probably
been some flaunting squire's residence ; but the nuns have taken
off somewhat from its rakish look, by flinging out a couple of
wings with chapels, or buildings like chapels, at either end.

A large, lofty, clean, trim hall was open to a flight of steps,
and we found a young lady in the hall, playing, instead of a
pious sonata — which I vainly thought was the practice in such
godly seminaries of learning — that abominable rattling piece
of music called *la Violette*, which it has been my lot to hear
executed by other young ladies ; and which (with its like) has
always appeared to me to be constructed upon this simple
fashion — to take a tune, and then, as it were, to fling it down
and up stairs. As soon as the young lady playing "the
Violet" saw us, she quitted the hall and retired to an inner
apartment, where she resumed that delectable piece at her leisure.
Indeed there were pianos all over the educational part of the
house.

We were shown into a gay parlor (where hangs a pretty

drawing representing the melancholy old convent which the Sisters previously inhabited in Cork), and presently Sister No. Two-Eight made her appearance — a pretty and graceful lady, attired as on the next page.*

"'Tis the prettiest nun of the whole house," whispered the lady who had been educated at the convent; and I must own that slim gentle, and pretty as this young lady was, and calculated with her kind smiling face and little figure to frighten no one in the world, a great six-foot Protestant could not help looking at her with a little tremble. I had never been in a nun's company before; I'm afraid of such — I don't care to own — in their black mysterious robes and awful veils. As priests in gorgeous vestments, and little rosy incense-boys in red, bob their heads and knees up and down before altars, or clatter silver pots full of smoking odors, I feel I don't know what sort of thrill and secret creeping terror. Here I was, in a room with a real live nun, pretty and pale — I wonder has she any of her sisterhood immured in *oubliettes* down below; is her poor little weak, delicate body scarred all over with scourgings, iron collars, hair shirts? What has she had for dinner to-day? — as we passed the refectory there was a faint sort of vapid nun-like vegetable smell, speaking of fasts and wooden platters; and I could picture to myself silent sisters eating their meal — a grim old yellow one in the reading-desk, croaking out an extract from a sermon for their edification.

But is it policy, or hypocrisy, or reality? These nuns affect extreme happiness and content with their condition: a smiling beatitude, which they insist belongs peculiarly to them, and about which the only doubtful point is the manner in which it is produced before strangers. Young ladies educated in convents have often mentioned this fact — how the nuns persist in declaring and proving to them their own extreme enjoyment of life.

Were all the smiles of that kind-looking Sister Two-Eight perfectly sincere? Whenever she spoke her face was lighted up with one. She seemed perfectly radiant with happiness, tripping lightly before us, and distributing kind compliments to each, which made me in a very few minutes forget the introductory fright which her poor little presence had occasioned.

She took us through the hall (where was the vegetable savor before mentioned), and showed us the contrivance by which the name of Two-Eight was ascertained. Each nun has a number, or a combination of numbers, prefixed to her name; and a bell is pulled a corresponding number of times, by which

* This refers to an illustrated edition of the work.

eacu sister knows when she is wanted. Poor souls! are they always on the look-out for that bell, that the ringing of it should be supposed infallibly to awaken their attention.

From the hall the sister conducted us through ranges of apartments, and I had almost said avenues of pianofortes, whence here and there a startled pensioner would rise *hinnuleo similis*, at our approach, seeking a *pavidam matrem* in the person of a demure old stout mother hard by. We were taken through a hall decorated with a series of pictures of Pope Pius VI.,— wonderful adventures, truly, in the life of the gentle old man. In one you see him gracefully receiving a Prince and Princess of Russia (tremendous incident!). The Prince has a pigtail, the Princess powder and a train, the Pope a — but never mind, we shall never get through the house at this rate.

Passing through Pope Pius's gallery, we came into a long, clean, lofty passage, with many little doors on each side; and here I confess my heart began to thump again. These were the doors of the cells of the Sisters. Bon Dieu! and is it possible that I shall see a nun's cell? Do I not recollect the nun's cell in "The Monk," or in "The Romance of the Forest?" or, if not there, at any rate, in a thousand noble romances, read in early days of half-holiday perhaps — romances at twopence a volume.

Come in, in the name of the saints! Here is the cell. I took off my hat and examined the little room with much curious wonder and reverence. There was an iron bed, with comfortable curtains of green serge. There was a little clothes-chest of yellow wood, neatly cleaned, and a wooden chair beside it, and a desk on the chest, and about six pictures on the wall — little religious pictures: a saint with gilt paper round him; the Virgin showing on her breast a bleeding heart, with a sword run through it; and other sad little subjects, calculated to make the inmate of the cell think of the sufferings of the saints and martyrs of the Church. Then there was a little crucifix, and a wax-candle on the ledge; and here was the place where the poor black-veiled things were to pass their lives for ever!

After having seen a couple of these little cells, we left the corridors in which they were, and were conducted, with a sort of pride on the nun's part, I thought, into the grand room of the convent — a parlor with pictures of saints, and a gay paper, and a series of small fineries, such only as women very idle know how to make. There were some portraits in the room, one an atrocious daub of an ugly old woman, surrounded by children still more hideous. Somebody had told the poor nun that this was a fine thing, and she believed it — heaven bless her! — quite implicitly : nor is the picture of the ugly old Canadian woman the first reputation that has been made this way.

Then from the fine parlor we went to the museum. I don't know how we should be curious of such trifles ; but the chronicling of small-beer is the main business of life — people only differing, as Tom Moore wisely says in one of his best poems, about their own peculiar tap. The poor nun's little collection of gimcracks was displayed in great state : there were spars in one drawer; and, I think, a Chinese shoe and some Indian wares in another ; and some medals of the Popes, and a couple of score of coins ; and a clean glass case, full of antique works of French theology of the distant period of Louis XV., to judge by the bindings — and this formed the main part of the museum. "The chief objects were gathered together by a single nun," said the sister with a look of wonder, as she went prattling on, and leading us hither and thither, like a child showing her toys.

What strange mixture of pity and pleasure is it which comes over you sometimes when a child takes you by the hand, and leads you up solemnly to some little treasure of its own — a feather or a string of glass beads? I declare I have often looked at such with more delight than at diamonds ; and felt the same sort of soft wonder examining the nun's little treasure-chamber. There was something touching in the very poverty of it : — had it been finer, it would not have been half so good.

And now we had seen all the wonders of the house but the chapel, and thither we were conducted ; all the ladies of our party kneeling down as they entered the building, and saying a short prayer.

This, as I am on sentimental confessions, I must own affected me too. It was a very pretty and tender sight. I should have liked to kneel down too, but was ashamed ; our northern usages not encouraging — among men at least — that sort of abandonment of dignity. Do any of us dare to sing psalms at church? and don't we look with rather a sneer at a man who does?

The chapel had nothing remarkable in it except a very good organ, as I was told ; for we were allowed only to see the exterior of that instrument, our pious guide with much pleasure removing an oil-cloth which covered the mahogany. At one side of the altar is a long high *grille*, through which you see a hall, where the nuns have their stalls, and sit in chapel time ;

and beyond this hall is another small chapel, with a couple of altars, and one beautiful print in one of them — a German Holy Family — a prim, mystical, tender piece, just befitting the place.

In the *grille* is a little wicket and a ledge before it. It is to this wicket that women are brought to kneel; and a bishop is in the chapel on the other side, and takes their hands in his, and receives their vows. I had never seen the like before, and own that I felt a sort of shudder at looking at the place. There rest the girl's knees as she offers herself up, and for-swears the sacred affections which God gave her; there she kneels and denies for ever the beautiful duties of her being : — no tender maternal yearnings, no gentle attachments are to be had for her or from her, — there she kneels and commits sui-cide upon her heart. O honest Martin Luther ! thank God, you came to pull that infernal, wicked, unnatural altar down — that cursed Paganism ! Let people, solitary, worn out by sorrow or oppressed with extreme remorse, retire to such places ; fly and beat your breasts in caverns and wildernesses, O women, if you will, but be Magdalens first. It is shameful that any young girl, with any vocation however seemingly strong, should be allowed to bury herself in this small tomb of a few acres. Look at yonder nun, — pretty, smiling, graceful, and young, — what has God's world done to *her*, that she should run from it, or she done to the world, that she should avoid it? What call has she to give up all her duties and affections? and would she not be best serving God with a husband at her side, and a child on her knee?

The sights in the house having been seen, the nun led us through the grounds and gardens. There was the hay in front, a fine yellow cornfield at the back of the house, and a large melancholy-looking kitchen-garden ; in all of which places the nuns, for certain hours in the day, are allowed to take recrea-tion. " The nuns here are allowed to amuse themselves more than ours at New Hall," said a little girl who is educated at that English convent : " do you know that here the nuns may make hay?" What a privilege is this ! We saw none of the black sisterhood availing themselves of it, however : the hay was neatly piled into cocks and ready for housing ; so the poor souls must wait until next year before they can enjoy this blessed sport once more.

Turning into a narrow gate with the nun at our head, we found ourselves in a little green, quiet inclosure — it was the burial-ground of the convent. The poor things know the places

where they are to lie : she who was with us talked smilingly of
being stretched there one day, and pointed out the resting-place
of a favorite old sister who had died three months back, and
been buried in the very midst of the little ground.   And here
they come to live and die.   The gates are open, but they never
go out.   All their world lies in a dozen acres of ground ; and
they sacrifice their lives in early youth, many of them passing from the grave up stairs in the house to the one scarcely
narrower in the churchyard here ; and are seemingly not unhappy.

I came out of the place quite sick ; and looking before me,
— there, thank God ! was the blue spire of Monkstown church
soaring up into the free sky — a river in front rolling away to
the sea — liberty, sunshine, all sorts of glad life and motion
round about : and I couldn't but thank heaven for it, and the
Being whose service is freedom, and who has given us affections
that we may use them — not smother and kill them ; and a noble
world to live in, that we may admire it and Him who made it
— not shrink from it, as though we dared not live there, but
must turn our backs upon it and its bountiful Provider.

And in conclusion, if that most cold-blooded and precise of
all personages, the respectable and respected English reader,
may feel disposed to sneer at the above sentimental homily, or
to fancy that it has been written for effect — let him go and see
a convent for himself.   I declare I think for my part that we
have as much right to permit Sutteeism in India as to allow
women in the United Kingdom to take these wicked vows, or
Catholic bishops to receive them ; and that Government has
as good a right to interpose in such cases, as the police have to
prevent a man from hanging himself, or the doctor to refuse a
glass of prussic-acid to any one who may have a wish to go
out of the world.

CHAPTER VII.

CORK.

AMIDST the bustle and gayeties of the Agricultural meeting,
the working-day aspect of the city was not to be judged of : but
I passed a fortnight in the place afterwards, during which time
it settled down to its calm and usual condition.   The flashy

French and plated goods' shops, which made a show for the occasion of the meeting, disappeared; you were no longer crowded and jostled by smart male and female dandies in walking down Patrick Street or the Mall; the poor little theatre had scarcely a soul on its bare benches: I went once, but the dreadful brass-band of a dragoon regiment blew me. out of doors. This music could be heard much more pleasantly at some distance off in the street.

One sees in this country many a grand and tall iron gate leading into a very shabby field covered with thistles; and the simile to the gate will in some degree apply to this famous city of Cork, — which is certainly not a city of palaces, but of which the outlets are magnificent. That towards Killarney leads by the Lee, the old avenue of Mardyke, and the rich green pastures stretching down to the river; and as you pass by the portico of the county gaol, as fine and as glancing as a palace, you see the wooded heights on the other side of the fair stream, crowded with a thousand pretty villas and terraces, presenting every image of comfort and prosperity. The entrance from Cove has been mentioned before; nor is it easy to find anywhere a nobler, grander, and more cheerful scene.

Along the quays up to St. Patrick's Bridge there is a certain bustle. Some forty ships may be lying at anchor along the walls of the quay, and its pavements are covered with goods of various merchandise: here a cargo of hides; yonder a company of soldiers, their kits, and their Dollies, who are taking leave of the red-coats at the steamer's side. Then you shall see a fine, squeaking, shrieking drove of pigs embarking by the same conveyance, and insinuated into the steamer by all sorts of coaxing, threatening, and wheedling. Seamen are singing and yeehoing on board; grimy colliers smoking at the liquor-shops along the quay; and as for the bridge — there is a crowd of idlers on *that*, you may be sure, sprawling over the balustrade for ever and ever, with long ragged coats, steeple-hats, and stumpy doodeens.

Then along the Coal Quay you may see a clump of jingle-drivers, who have all a word for your honor; and in Patrick Street, at three o'clock, when "The Rakes of Mallow" gets under weigh (a cracked old coach with the paint rubbed off, some smart horses, and an exceedingly dingy harness) — at three o'clock, you will be sure to see at least forty persons waiting to witness the departure of the said coach: so that the neighborhood of the inn has an air of some bustle.

At the other extremity of the town, if it be assize time, you will see some five hundred persons squatting by the court-house, or buzzing and talking within. The rest of the respectable quarter of the city is pretty free from anything like bustle : there is no more life in Patrick Street than in Russell Square of a sunshiny day ; and as for the Mall, it is as lonely as the chief street of a German Residenz.

I have mentioned the respectable quarter of the city — for there are quarters in it swarming with life, but of such a frightful kind as no pen need care to describe : alleys where the odors and rags and darkness are so hideous, that one runs frightened away from them. In some of them, they say, not the policeman, only the priest, can penetrate. I asked a Roman Catholic clergyman of the city to take me into some of these haunts, but he refused very justly ; and indeed a man may be quite satisfied with what he can see in the mere outskirts of the districts, without caring to penetrate further. Not far from the quays is an open space where the poor hold a market or bazaar. Here is liveliness and business enough : ragged women chattering and crying their beggarly wares ; ragged boys gloating over dirty apple- and pie-stalls ; fish frying, and raw and stinking ; clothes-booths, where you might buy a wardrobe for scarecrows ; old nails, hoops, bottles, and marine-wares ; old battered furniture, that has been sold against starvation. In the streets round about this place, on a sunshiny day, all the black gaping windows and mouldy steps are covered with squatting lazy figures — women, with bare breasts, nursing babies, and leering a joke as you pass by — ragged children paddling everywhere. It is but two minutes' walk out of Patrick Street, where you come upon a fine flashy shop of plated-goods, or a grand French emporium of dolls, walking-sticks, carpet-bags, and perfumery. The markets hard by have a rough, old-fashioned, cheerful look ; it's a comfort after the misery to hear a red butcher's wife crying after you to buy an honest piece of meat.

The poor-house, newly established, cannot hold a fifth part of the poverty of this great town : the richer inhabitants are untiring in their charities, and the Catholic clergyman before mentioned took me to see a delivery of rice, at which he presides every day until the potatoes shall come in. This market, over which he presides so kindly, is held in an old bankrupt warehouse, and the rice is sold considerably under the prime cost to hundreds of struggling applicants who come when lucky enough to have wherewithal to pay.

That the city contains much wealth is evidenced by the number of handsome villas round about it, where the rich merchants dwell; but the warehouses of the wealthy provision-merchants make no show to the stranger walking the streets; and of the retail-shops, if some are spacious and handsome, most look as if too big for the business carried on within. The want of ready money was quite curious. In three of the principal shops I purchased articles, and tendered a pound in exchange — not one of them had silver enough; and as for a five-pound note, which I presented at one of the topping bookseller's, his boy went round to various places in vain, and finally set forth to the Bank, where change was got. In another small shop I offered half a crown to pay for a sixpenny article — it was all the same. "Tim," says the good woman, "run out in a hurry and fetch the gentleman change." Two of the shopmen, seeing an Englishman, were very particular to tell me in what years they themselves had been in London. It seemed a merit in these gentlemen's eyes to have once dwelt in that city; and I see in the papers continually ladies advertising as governesses, and specifying particularly that they are "English ladies."

I received six 5l. post-office orders; I called four times on as many different days at the Post Office before the capital could be forthcoming, getting on the third application 20l. (after making a great clamor, and vowing that such things were unheard-of in England), and on the fourth call the remaining 10l. I saw poor people, who may have come from the country with their orders, refused payment of an order of some 40s.; and a gentleman who tendered a pound-note in payment of a foreign letter, was told to "leave his letter and pay some other time." Such things could not take place in the hundred-and-second city in England; and as I do not pretend to doctrinize at all, I leave the reader to draw his own deductions with regard to the commercial condition and prosperity of the second city in Ireland.

Half a dozen of the public buildings I saw were spacious and shabby beyond all cockney belief. Adjoining the "Imperial Hotel" is a great, large, handsome, desolate reading-room, which was founded by a body of Cork merchants and tradesmen, and is the very picture of decay. Not Palmyra — not the Russell Institution in Great Coram Street — presents a more melancholy appearance of faded greatness. Opposite this is another institution called the Cork Library, where there are plenty of books and plenty of kindness to the stranger; but the shabbiness and faded splendor of the place are quite painful. There are three handsome Catholic churches commenced of late years ; not one of them is complete : two want their porticos ; the other is not more than thirty feet from the ground, and according to the architectural plan was to rise as high as a cathedral. There is an Institution, with a fair library of scientific works, a museum, and a drawing-school with a supply of casts. The place is in yet more dismal condition than the Library : the plasters are spoiled incurably for want of a sixpenny feather-brush ; the dust lies on the walls, and nobody seems to heed it. Two shillings a year would have repaired much of the evil which has happened to this institution ; and it is folly to talk of inward dissensions and political differences as causing the ruin of such institutions : kings or law don't cause or cure dust and cobwebs, but indolence leaves them to accumulate, and imprudence will not calculate its income, and vanity exaggerates its own powers, and the fault is laid upon that tyrant of a sister kingdom. The whole country is filled with such failures ; swaggering beginnings that could not be carried through ; grand enterprises begun dashingly, and ending in shabby compromises or downright ruin.

I have said something in praise of the manners of the Cork ladies : in regard of the gentlemen, a stranger too must remark the extraordinary degree of literary taste and talent amongst them, and the wit and vivacity of their conversation. The love for literature seems to an Englishman doubly curious. What, generally speaking, do a company of grave gentlemen and ladies in Baker Street know about it? Who ever reads books in the City, or how often does one hear them talked about at a Club? The Cork citizens are the most book-loving men I ever met. The town has sent to England a number of literary men, of reputation too, and is not a little proud of their fame. Everybody seemed to know what Maginn was doing, and that Father Prout had a third volume ready, and what was Mr. Croker's last article in the *Quarterly*. The young clerks and shopmen seemed as much *au fait* as their employers, and many is the conversation I heard about the merits of this writer or that — Dickens, Ainsworth, Lover, Lever.

I think, in walking the streets, and looking at the ragged urchins crowding there, every Englishman must remark that the superiority of intelligence is here, and not with us. I never saw such a collection of bright-eyed, wild, clever, eager faces. Mr. Maclise has carried away a number of them in his memory ; and the lovers of his admirable pictures will find more than one Munster countenance under a helmet in company of Macbeth, or in a slashed doublet alongside of Prince Hamlet, or in the very midst of Spain in company with Señor Gil Blas. Gil Blas himself came from Cork, and not from Oviedo.

I listened to two boys almost in rags : they were lolling over the quay balustrade, and talking about *one of the Ptolemys !* and talking very well too. One of them had been reading in " Rollin," and was detailing his information with a great deal of eloquence and fire. Another day, walking in the Mardyke, I followed three boys, not half so well dressed as London errand-boys : one was telling the other about Captain Ross's voyages, and spoke with as much brightness and intelligence as the best-read gentleman's son in England could do. He was as much of a gentleman too, the ragged young student ; his manner as good, though perhaps more eager and emphatic ; his language was extremely rich, too, and eloquent. Does the reader remember his school-days, when half a dozen lads in the bedrooms took it by turns to tell stories ? how poor the language generally was, and how exceedingly poor the imagination ! Both of those ragged Irish lads had the making of gentlemen, scholars, orators, in them. Apropos of love of reading, let me mention here a Dublin story. Dr. Lever, the celebrated author of " Harry Lorrequer," went into Dycer's stables to buy a horse. The groom who brought the animal out, directly he heard who the gentleman was, came out and touched his cap, and pointed to a little book in his pocket in a pink cover. " *I can't do without it, sir*," says the man. It was " Harry Lorrequer." I wonder does any one of Mr. Rymell's grooms take in " Pickwick," or would they have any curiosity to see Mr. Dickens, should he pass that way?

The Corkagians are eager for a Munster University ; asking for, and having a very good right to, the same privilege which has been granted to the chief city of the North of Ireland. It would not fail of being a great benefit to the city and to the country too, which would have no need to go so far as Dublin for a school of letters and medicine ; nor, Whig and Catholic for the most part, to attend a Tory and Protestant University. The establishing of an open college in Munster would bring much popularity to any Ministry that should accord such a boon. People would cry out, " Popery and Infidelity," doubtless, as they did when the London University was established ; as the same party in Spain would cry out, " Atheism and Heresy." But the time, thank God! is gone by in England when it was necessary to legislate for *them ;* and Sir Robert Peel, in giving his adherence to the National Education scheme, has sanctioned the principle of which this so much longed-for college would only be a consequence.

The medical charities and hospitals are said to be very well arranged, and the medical men of far more than ordinary skill. Other public institutions are no less excellent. I was taken over the Lunatic Asylum, where everything was conducted with admirable comfort, cleanliness, and kindness; and as for the county gaol, it is so neat, spacious, and comfortable, that we can only pray to see every cottager in the country as cleanly, well lodged, and well fed as the convicts are. They get a pound of bread and a pint of milk twice a day : there must be millions of people in this wretched country, to whom such food would be a luxury that their utmost labors can never by possibility procure for them ; and in going over this admirable institution, where everybody is cleanly, healthy, and well-clad, I could not but think of the rags and filth of the horrid starvation market before mentioned ; so that the prison seemed almost a sort of premium for vice. But the people like their freedom, such as it is, and prefer to starve and be ragged as they list. They will not go to the poor-houses, except at the greatest extremity, and leave them on the slightest chance of existence elsewhere.

Walking away from this palace of a prison, you pass amidst all sorts of delightful verdure, cheerful gardens, and broad green luscious pastures, down to the beautiful River Lee. On one side, the river shines away towards the city with its towers and purple steeples ; on the other it is broken by little water-falls and bound in by blue hills, an old castle towering in the distance, and innumerable parks and villas lying along the pleasant wooded banks. How beautiful the scene is, how rich and how happy ! Yonder, in the old Mardyke Avenue, you hear the voices of a score of children, and along the bright green meadows, where the cows are feeding, the gentle shadows of the clouds go playing over the grass. Who can look at such a charming scene but with a thankful swelling heart?

In the midst of your pleasure, three beggars have hobbled up, and are howling supplications to the Lord. One is old and blind, and so diseased and hideous, that straightway all the pleasure of the sight round about vanishes from you — that livid ghastly face interposing between you and it. And so it is throughout the south and west of Ireland ; the traveller is haunted by the face of the popular starvation. It is not the exception, it is the condition of the people. In this fairest and richest of countries, men are suffering and starving by millions. There are thousands of them at this minute stretched

In the sunshine at their cabin doors with no work, scarcely any food, no hope seemingly. Strong countrymen are lying in bed "*for the hunger*" — because a man lying on his back does not need so much food as a person afoot. Many of them have torn up the unripe potatoes from their little gardens, to exist now, and must look to winter, when they shall have to suffer starvation and cold too. The epicurean, and traveller for pleasure, had better travel anywhere than here : where there are miseries that one does not dare to think of ; where one is always feeling how helpless pity is, and how hopeless relief, and is perpetually made ashamed of being happy.

I have just been strolling up a pretty little height called Grattan's Hill, that overlooks the town and the river, and where the artist that comes Cork-wards may find many subjects for his pencil. There is a kind of pleasure-ground at the top of this eminence — a broad walk that draggles up to a ruined wall, with a ruined niche in it, and a battered stone bench. On the side that shelves down to the water are some beeches, and opposite them a row of houses from which you see one of the prettiest prospects possible — the shining river with the craft along the quays, and the busy city in the distance, the active little steamers puffing away towards Cove, the farther bank crowned with rich woods, and pleasant-looking country-houses : perhaps they are tumbling, rickety and ruinous, as those houses close by us, but you can't see the ruin from here.

What a strange air of forlorn gayety there is about the place ! — the sky itself seems as if it did not know whether to laugh or cry, so full is it of clouds and sunshine. Little fat, ragged, smiling children are clambering about the rocks, and sitting on mossy door-steps, tending other children yet smaller, fatter, and more dirty. "Stop till I get you a posy" (pronounced *pawawawsee*), cries one urchin to another. "Tell me who is it ye love, Jooly?" exclaims another, cuddling a redfaced infant with a very dirty nose. More of the same race are perched about the summer-house, and two wenches with large purple feet are flapping some carpets in the air. It is a wonder the carpets will bear this kind of treatment at all, and do not be off at once to mingle with the elements : I never saw things that hung to life by such a frail thread.

This dismal pleasant place is a suburb of the second city in Ireland, and one of the most beautiful spots about the town. What a prim, bustling, active, green-railinged, tea-gardened, gravelwalked place would it have been in the five-hundredth town in

England! — but you see the people can be quite as happy in the rags and without the paint, and I hear a great deal more heartiness and affection from these children than from their fat little brethren across the Channel.

If a man wanted to study ruins, here is a house close at hand, not forty years old no doubt, but yet as completely gone to wreck as Netley Abbey. It is quite curious to study that house; and a pretty ruinous fabric of improvidence, extravagance, happiness, and disaster may the imagination build out of it! In the first place, the owners did not wait to finish it before they went to inhabit it! This is written in just such another place; — a handsome drawing-room with a good carpet, a lofty marble mantel-piece, and no paper to the walls. The door is prettily painted white and blue, and though not six weeks old, a great piece of the wood-work is off already (Peggy uses it to prevent the door from banging to); and there are some fine chinks in every one of the panels, by which my neighbor may see all my doings.

A couple of score of years, and this house will be just like yonder place on Grattan's Hill.

Like a young prodigal, the house begins to use its constitution too early; and when it should yet (in the shape of carpenters and painters) have all its masters and guardians to watch and educate it, my house on Grattan's Hill must be a man at once, and enjoy all the privileges of strong health! I would lay a guinea they were making punch in that house before they could keep the rain out of it! that they had a dinner-party and ball before the floors were firm or the wainscots painted, and a fine tester-bed in the best room, where my lady might catch cold in state, in the midst of yawning chimneys, creaking window-sashes, and smoking plaster.

Now look at the door of the coach-house, with its first coat of paint seen yet, and a variety of patches to keep the feeble barrier together. The loft was arched once, but a great corner has tumbled at one end, leaving a gash that unites the windows with the coach-house door. Several of the arch-stones are removed, and the whole edifice is about as rambling and disorderly as — as the arrangement of this book, say. Very tall tufts of mouldy moss are on the drawing-room windows, with long white heads of grass. As I am sketching this — *honk!* — a great lean sow comes trampling through the slush within the court-yard, breaks down the flimsy apparatus of rattling boards and stones which had passed for the gate, and walks with her seven squeaking little ones to disport on the grass on the hill.

The drawing-room of the tenement mentioned just now, with its pictures, and pulleyless windows and lockless doors, was tenanted by a friend who lodged there with a sick wife and a couple of little children; one of whom was an infant in arms. It is not, however, the lodger — who is an Englishman — but the kind landlady and her family who may well be described here — for their like are hardly to be found on the other side of the Channel. Mrs. Fagan is a young widow who has seen better days, and that portrait over the grand mantel-piece is the picture of her husband that is gone, a handsome young man, and well to do at one time as a merchant. But the widow (she is as pretty, as lady-like, as kind, and as neat as ever widow could be,) has little left to live upon but the rent of her lodgings and her furniture; of which we have seen the best in the drawing-room.

She has three fine children of her own : there is Minny, and Katey, and Patsey, and they occupy indifferently the dining-room on the ground-floor or the kitchen opposite; where in the midst of a great smoke sits an old nurse, by a copper of potatoes which is always bubbling and full. Patsey swallows quantities of them, that's clear : his cheeks are as red and shining as apples, and when he roars, you are sure that his lungs are in the finest condition. Next door to the kitchen is the pantry, and there is a bucketful of the before-mentioned fruit and a grand service of china for dinner and dessert. The kind young widow shows them with no little pride, and says with reason that there are few lodging-houses in Cork that can match such china as that. They are relics of the happy old times when Fagan kept his gig and horse, doubtless, and had his friends to dine — the happy prosperous days which she has exchanged for poverty and the sad black gown.

Patsey, Minny, and Katey have made friends with the little English people up stairs; the elder of whom, in the course of a month, has as fine a Munster brogue as ever trolled over the lips of any born Corkagian. The old nurse carries out the whole united party to walk, with the exception of the English baby, that jumps about in the arms of a countrywoman of her own. That is, unless one of the four Miss Fagans takes her; for four of them there are, four *other* Miss Fagans, from eighteen downwards to fourteen : —handsome, fresh, lively, dancing, bouncing girls. You may always see two or three of them smiling at the parlor-window, and they laugh and turn away their heads when any young fellow looks and admires them.

Now it stands to reason that a young widow of five-and-twenty can't be the mother of four young ladies of eighteen downwards; and, if anybody wants to know how they come to be living with the poor widow their cousin, the answer is, they are on a visit. Peggy the maid says their papa is a gentleman of property, and can " spend his eight hundred a year."

Why don't they remain with the old gentleman then, instead of quartering on the poor young widow, who has her own little mouths to feed? The reason is, the old gentleman has gone and *married his cook;* and the daughters have quitted him in a body, refusing to sit down to dinner with a person who ought by rights to be in the kitchen. The whole family (the Fagans are of good family) take the quarrel up, and here are the young people under shelter of the widow.

Four merrier tender-hearted girls are not to be found in all Ireland; and the only subject of contention amongst them is, which shall have the English baby: they are nursing it, and singing to it, and dandling it by turns all day long. When they are not singing to the baby, they are singing to an old piano: such an old wiry, jingling, wheezy piano! It has plenty of work, playing jigs and song accompaniments between meals, and acting as a sideboard at dinner. I am not sure that it is at rest at night either; but have a shrewd suspicion that it is turned into a four-post bed. And for the following reason : —

Every afternoon, at four o'clock, you see a tall old gentleman walking leisurely to the house. He is dressed in a long great-coat with huge pockets, and in the huge pockets are sure to be some big apples for all the children — the English child amongst the rest, and she generally has the biggest one. At seven o'clock, you are sure to hear a deep voice shouting " PAGGY ! " in an awful tone — it is the old gentleman calling for his " materials ; " which Peggy brings without any farther ado ; and a glass of punch is made, no doubt, for everybody. Then the party separates : the children and the old nurse have long since trampled up stairs ; Peggy has the kitchen for her sleeping apartment, and the four young ladies make it out somehow in the back drawing-room. As for the old gentleman, he reposes in the parlor ; and it must be somewhere about the piano, for there is no furniture in the room except that, a table, a few old chairs, a work-box, and a couple of albums.

The English girl's father met her in the street one day, talking confidentially with a tall old gentleman in a great-coat. " Who's your friend? " says the Englishman afterwards to the little girl. " Don't you know him, papa? " said the child in the purest brogue. "Don't you know him? — THAT's UNCLE JAMES!" And so it was: in this kind, poor, generous, bare-backed house, the English child found a set of new relations; little rosy brothers and sisters to play with, kind women to take the place of the almost dying mother, a good old Uncle James to bring her home apples and care for her — one and all ready to share their little pittance with her, and to give her a place in their simple friendly hearts. God Almighty bless the widow and her mite, and all the kind souls under her roof!

How much goodness and generosity — how much purity, fine feeling — nay, happiness — may dwell amongst the poor whom we have been just looking at! Here, thank God, is an instance of this happy and cheerful poverty: and it is good to look, when one can, at the heart that beats under the thread-bare coat, as well as the tattered old garment itself. Well, please heaven, some of those people whom we have been look-ing at, are as good, and not much less happy: but though they are accustomed to their want, the stranger does not reconcile himself to it quickly; and I hope no Irish reader will be of-fended at my speaking of this poverty, not with scorn or ill-feeling, but with hearty sympathy and good-will.

One word more regarding the Widow Fagan's house. When Peggy brought in coals for the drawing-room fire, she carried them — in what do you think? "In a coal-scuttle, to be sure," says the English reader, down on you as sharp as a needle.

No, you clever Englishman, it wasn't a coal-scuttle.

"Well, then, it was in a fire-shovel," says that brightest of wits, guessing again.

No, it *wasn't* a fire-shovel, you heaven-born genius; and you might guess from this until Mrs. Snooks called you up to coffee, and you would never find out. It was in something which I have already described in Mrs. Fagan's pantry.

"Oh, I have you now, it was the bucket where the potatoes were; the thlatternly wetch!" says Snooks.

Wrong again! Peggy brought up the coals — in a CHINA PLATE!

Snooks turns quite white with surprise and almost chokes himself with his port. "Well," says he, "of all the *wum countwith* that I ever wead of, hang me if Ireland ithn't the *wummetht*. Coalth in a plate! Mawyann, do you hear that? In Ireland they alwayth thend up their coalth in a plate!"

CHAPTER VIII.

FROM CORK TO BANTRY; WITH AN ACCOUNT OF THE CITY OF
SKIBBEREEN.

THAT light four-inside, four-horse coach, the "Skibbereen Perseverance," brought me fifty-two miles to-day, for the sum of three-and-sixpence, through a country which is, as usual, somewhat difficult to describe. We issued out of Cork by the western road, in which, as the Guide-book says, there is something very imposing. "The magnificence of the county court-house, the extent, solidity, and characteristic sternness of the county gaol," were visible to us for a few minutes; when, turning away southward from the pleasant banks of the stream, the road took us towards Bandon, through a country that is bare and ragged-looking, but yet green and pretty; and it always seems to me, like the people, to look cheerful in spite of its wretchedness, or, more correctly, to look tearful and cheerful at the same time.

The coach, like almost every other public vehicle I have seen in Ireland, was full to the brim and over it. What can send these restless people travelling and hurrying about from place to place as they do? I have heard one or two gentlemen hint that they had "business" at this place or that; and found afterwards that one was going a couple of score of miles to look at a mare, another to examine a setter-dog, and so on. I did not make it my business to ask on what errand the gentlemen on the coach were bound; though two of them, seeing an Englishman, very good-naturedly began chalking out a route for him to take, and showing a sort of interest in his affairs which is not with us generally exhibited. The coach, too, seemed to have the elastic hospitality of some Irish houses; it accommodated an almost impossible number. For the greater part of the journey the little guard sat on the roof among the carpet-bags, holding in one hand a huge tambour-frame, in the other a band-box marked "Foggarty, Hatter." (What is there more ridiculous in the name of Foggarty than in that of Smith? and yet, had Smith been the name, I never should have laughed at or remarked it). Presently by his side clambered a green-coated policeman with his carbine, and we had a talk about the vitriol-throwers at Cork, and the sentence just passed upon them. The populace has decidedly taken part with the vitriol-throwers : parties of dragoons were obliged to surround the avenues of the court ; and the judge who sentenced them was abused as he entered his carriage, and called an old villain, and many other opprobious names.

This case the reader very likely remembers. A saw-mill was established at Cork, by which some four hundred sawyers were thrown out of employ. In order to deter the proprietors of this and all other mills from using such instruments further, the sawyers determined to execute a terrible vengeance, and cast lots among themselves which of their body should fling vitriol into the faces of the mill-owners. The men who were chosen by the lot were to execute this horrible office on pain of death, and did so, — frightfully burning and blinding one of the gentlemen owning the mill. Great rewards were offered for the apprehension of the criminals, and at last one of their own body came forward as an approver, and the four principal actors in this dreadful outrage were sentenced to be transported for life. Crowds of the ragged admirers of these men were standing round " the magnificent county court-house " as we passed the building. Ours is a strange life indeed. What a history of poverty and barbarity, and crime and even kindness, was that by which we passed before the magnificent county court-house at eight miles an hour ! What a chapter might a philosopher write on them ! Look yonder at those two hundred ragged fellow-subjects of yours : they are kind, good, pious, brutal, starving. If the priest tells them, there is scarce any penance they will not perform ; there is scarcely any pitch of misery which they have not been known to endure, nor any degree of generosity of which they are not capable : but if a man comes among these people, and can afford to take land over their heads, or if he invents a machine which can work more economically than their labor, they will shoot the man down without mercy, murder him, or put him to horrible tortures, and glory almost in what they do. There stand the men ; they are only separated from us by a few paces : they are as fond of their mothers and children as we are ; their gratitude for small kindnesses shown to them is extraordinary ; they are Christians as we are ; but interfere with their interests, and they will murder you without pity.

It is not revenge so much which these poor fellows take, as a brutal justice of their own. Now, will it seem a paradox to say, in regard to them and their murderous system, that the way to put an end to the latter is to *kill them no more !* **Let the** priest be able to go amongst them and say, The law holds a man's life so sacred that it will on *no account* take it away. No man, nor body of men, has a right to meddle with human life: not the Commons of England any more than the Commons of Tipperary. This may cost two or three lives, probably, until such time as the system may come to be known and understood; but which will be the greatest economy of blood in the end?

By this time the vitriol-men were long passed away, and we began next to talk about the Cork and London steamboats; which are made to pay, on account of the number of paupers whom the boats bring over from London at the charge of that city. The passengers found here, as in everything else almost which I have seen as yet, another instance of the injury which England inflicts on them. "As long as these men are strong and can work," says one, "you keep them; when they are in bad health, you fling them upon us." Nor could I convince him that the agricultural gentlemen were perfectly free to stay at home if they liked: that we did for them what was done for English paupers — sent them, namely, as far as possible on the way to their parishes; nay, that some of them (as I have seen with my own eyes) actually saved a bit of money during the harvest, and took this cheap way of conveying it and themselves to their homes again. But nothing would convince the gentleman that there was not some wicked scheming on the part of the English in the business; and, indeed, I find upon almost every other subject a peevish and puerile suspiciousness which is worthy of France itself.

By this time we came to a pretty village called Innishannon, upon the noble banks of the Bandon river; leading for three miles by a great number of pleasant gentlemen's seats to Bandon town. A good number of large mills were on the banks of the stream; and the chief part of them, as in Carlow, useless. One mill we saw was too small for the owner's great speculations; and so he built another and larger one: the big mill cost him 10,000*l.*, for which his brothers went security; and, a lawsuit being given against the mill-owner, the two mills stopped, the two brothers went off, and yon fine old house, in the style of Anne, with terraces and tall chimneys — one of the oldest country-houses I have seen in Ireland — is now inhabited by the natural son of the mill-owner, who has more such interesting progeny. Then we came to a tall, comfortable house, in a plantation; opposite to which was a stone castle, in its shrubberies on the other side of the road. The tall house

in the plantation shot the opposite side of the road in a duel,
and nearly killed him; on which the opposite side of the road
built this castle, *in order to plague* the tall house. They are
good friends now; but the opposite side of the road ruined
himself in building his house. I asked, "Is the house finished?" — "*A good deal of it is*," was the answer. — And then
we came to a brewery, about which was a similar story of
extravagance and ruin; but, whether before or after entering
Bandon, does not matter.

We did not, it appears, pass through the best part of Bandon: I looked along one side of the houses in the long street
through which we went, to see if there was a window without
a broken pane of glass, and can declare on my conscience that
every single window had three broken panes. There we changed
horses, in a market-place, surrounded, as usual, by beggars;
then we passed through a suburb still more wretched and ruinous than the first street, and which, in very large letters, is
called DOYLE STREET: and the next stage was at a place called
Dunmanway.

Here it was market-day, too, and, as usual, no lack of attendants: swarms of peasants in their blue cloaks, squatting
by their stalls here and there. There is a little miserable old
market-house, where a few women were selling buttermilk; another, bullocks' hearts, liver, and such like scraps of meat;
another had dried mackerel on a board; and plenty of people
huckstering of course. Round the coach came crowds of rag-
gery, and blackguards fawning for money. I wonder who gives
them any! I have never seen any one give yet; and were
they not even so numerous that it would be impossible to gratify
them all, there is something in their cant and supplications
to the Lord so disgusting to me, that I could not give a halfpenny.

In regard of pretty faces, male or female, this road is very
unfavorable. I have not seen one for fifty miles; though, as
it was market-day all along the road, we have had the opportunity to examine vast numbers of countenances. The women
are, for the most part, stunted, short, with flat Tartar faces;
and the men no handsomer. Every woman has bare legs, of
course; and as the weather is fine, they are sitting outside their
cabins, with the pig, and the geese, and the children sporting
around.

Before many doors we saw a little flock of these useful animals, and the family pig almost everywhere: you might see
him browsing and poking along the hedges, his fore and hind

leg attached with a wisp of hay to check his propensity to roaming. Here and there were a small brood of turkeys ; now and then a couple of sheep or a single one grazing upon a scanty field, of which the chief crop seemed to be thistles and stone ; and, by the side of the cottage, the potato-field always.

The character of the landscape for the most part is bare and sad ; except here and there in the neighborhood of the towns, where people have taken a fancy to plant, and where nature has helped them, as it almost always will in this country. If we saw a field with a good hedge to it, we were sure to see a good crop inside. Many a field was there that had neither crop nor hedge. We passed by and over many pretty streams, running bright through brilliant emerald meadows : and I saw a thousand charming pictures, which want as yet an Irish Berghem. A bright road winding up a hill ; on it a country cart, with its load, stretching a huge shadow ; the before-mentioned emerald pastures and silver rivers in the foreground ; a noble sweep of hills rising up from them, and contrasting their magnificent purple with the green ; in the extreme distance the clear cold outline of some far-off mountains, and the white clouds tumbled about in the blue sky overhead. It has no doubt struck all persons who love to look at nature, how different the skies are in different countries. I fancy Irish or French clouds are as characteristic as Irish or French landscapes. It would be well to have a daguerreotype and get a series of each. Some way beyond Dunmanway the road takes us through a noble savage country of rocks and heath. Nor must the painter forget long black tracts of bog here and there, and the water glistening brightly at the places where the turf has been cut away. Add to this, and chiefly by the banks of rivers, a ruined old castle or two : some were built by the Danes, it is said. The O'Connors, the O'Mahonys, the O'Driscolls were lords of many others, and their ruined towers may be seen here and along the sea.

Near Dunmanway that great coach, "The Skibbereen Industry," dashed by us at seven miles an hour ; a wondrous vehicle : there were gaps between every one of the panels ; you could see daylight through-and-through it. Like our machine, it was full, with three complementary sailors on the roof, as little harness as possible to the horses, and as long stages as horses can well endure : ours were each eighteen-mile stages. About eight miles from Skibbereen a one-horse car met us, and carried away an offshoot of passengers to Bantry. Five passengers and their luggage, and a very wild, steep road : all this had one poor little pony to overcome ! About the towns there were some show of gentlemen's cars, smart and well appointed, and on the road great numbers of country carts : an army of them met us coming from Skibbereen, and laden with gray sand for manure.

Before you enter the city of Skibbereen, the tall new poorhouse presents itself to the eye of the traveller ; of the common model, being a bastard-Gothic edifice, with a profusion of cottage-ornée (is cottage masculine or feminine in French?) — of cottage-ornée roofs, and pinnacles, and insolent-looking stacks of chimneys. It is built for 900 people, but as yet not more than 400 have been induced to live in it ; the beggars preferring the freedom of their precarious trade to the dismal certainty within its walls. Next we come to the chapel. a very large, respectable-looking building of dark-gray stone ; and presently, behold, by the crowd of blackguards in waiting, " The Skibbereen Perseverance " has found its goal, and you are inducted to the " hotel " opposite.

Some gentlemen were at the coach, besides those of lower degree. Here was a fat fellow with large whiskers, a geranium, and a cigar ; yonder a tall handsome old man that I would swear was a dragoon on half-pay. He had a little cap, a Taglioni coat, a pair of beautiful spaniels, and a pair of knee-breeches which showed a very handsome old leg ; and his object seemed to be to invite everybody to dinner as they got off the coach. No doubt he has seen the " Skibbereen Perseverance " come in ever since it was a " Perseverance." It is wonderful to think what will interest men in prisons or country towns !

There is a dirty coffee-room, with a strong smell of whiskey : indeed three young " materialists " are employed at the moment : and I hereby beg to offer an apology to three other gentlemen — the captain, another, and the gentleman of the geranium, who had caught hold of a sketching-stool which is my property, and were stretching it, and sitting upon it, and wondering, and talking of it, when the owner came in, and they bounced off to their seats like so many school-boys. Dirty as the place was, this was no reason why it should not produce an exuberant dinner of trout and Kerry mutton ; after which Dan the waiter, holding up a dingy decanter, asks how much whiskey I'd have.

That calculation need not be made here ; and if a man sleeps well, has he any need to quarrel with the appointments of his bedroom, and spy out the deficiencies of the land? As it was Sunday, it was impossible for me to say what sort of shops " the active and flourishing town " of Skibbereen contains.

There were some of the architectural sort, viz. with gilt letters and cracked mouldings, and others into which I thought I saw the cows walking; but it was only into their little cribs and paddocks at the back of the shops. There is a trim Wesleyan chapel, without any broken windows; a neat church standing modestly on one side. The Lower Street crawls along the river to a considerable extent, having by-streets and boulevards of cabins here and there.

The people came flocking into the place by hundreds, and you saw their blue cloaks dotting the road and the bare open plains beyond. The men came with shoes and stockings to-day, the women all barelegged, and many of them might be seen washing their feet in the stream before they went up to the chapel. The street seemed to be lined on either side with blue cloaks, squatting along the doorways as is their wont. Among these, numberless cows were walking to and fro, and pails of milk passing, and here and there a hound or two went stalking about. Dan the waiter says they are hunted by the handsome old captain who was yesterday inviting everybody to dinner.

Anybody at eight o'clock of a Sunday morning in summer may behold the above scene from a bridge just outside the town. He may add to it the river, with one or two barges lying idle upon it; a flag flying at what looks like a custom-house; bare country all around; and the chapel before him, with a swarm of the dark figures round about it.

I went into it, not without awe (for, as I confessed before, I always feel a sort of tremor on going into a Catholic place of worship: the candles, and altars, and mysteries, the priest and his robes, and nasal chanting, and wonderful genuflexions, will frighten me as long as I live). The chapel-yard was filled with men and women; a couple of shabby old beadles were at the gate with copper shovels to collect money; and inside the chapel four or five hundred people were on their knees, and scores more of the blue-mantles came in, dropping their curtsies as they entered, and then taking their places on the flags.

And now the pangs of hunger beginning to make themselves felt, it became necessary for your humble servant (after making several useless applications to a bell, which properly declined to work on Sundays) to make a personal descent to the inn-kitchen, where was not a bad study for a painter. It was a huge room, with a peat fire burning, and a staircase walking up one side of it, on which stair was a damsel in a partial though by no means picturesque dishabille. The cook had just come in with a great frothing pail of milk, and sat with her arms folded; the ostler's boy sat dangling his legs from the table; the ostler was dandling a noble little boy of a year old, at whom Mrs. Cook likewise grinned delighted. Here, too, sat Mr. Dan the waiter; and no wonder the breakfast was delayed, for all three of these worthy domestics seemed delighted with the infant.

He was handed over to the gentleman's arms for the space of thirty seconds; the gentleman being the father of a family, and of course an amateur.

" Say Dan for the gentleman," says the delighted cook.

" Dada," says the baby; at which the assembly grinned with joy: and Dan promised I should have my breakfast " in a hurry."

But of all the wonderful things to be seen in Skibbereen, Dan's pantry is the most wonderful: every article within is a makeshift, and has been ingeniously perverted from its original destination. Here lie bread, blacking, fresh butter, tallow-candles, dirty knives — all in the same cigar-box with snuff, milk, cold bacon, brown sugar, broken teacups, and bits of soap. No pen can describe that establishment, as no English imagination could have conceived it. But lo! the sky has cleared after a furious fall of rain — (in compliance with Dan's statement to that effect, " that the weather would be fine ") — and a car is waiting to carry us to Loughine.

Although the description of Loughine can make but a poor figure in a book, the ride thither is well worth the traveller's short labor. You pass by one of the cabin-streets out of the town into a country which for a mile is rich with grain, though bare of trees; then through a boggy bleak district, from which you enter into a sort of sea of rocks, with patches of herbage here and there. Before the traveller, almost all the way, is a huge pile of purple mountain, on which, as one comes nearer, one perceives numberless waves and breaks, as you see small waves on a billow in the sea; then clambering up a hill, we look down upon a bright green flat of land, with the lake beyond it, girt round by gray melancholy hills. The water may be a mile in extent; a cabin tops the mountain here and there; gentlemen have erected one or two anchorite pleasure-houses on the banks, as cheerful as a summer-house would be on Salisbury Plain. I felt not sorry to have seen this lonely lake, and still happier to leave it. There it lies with crags all round it, in the midst of desolate plains: it escapes somewhere to the sea; its waters are salt: half a dozen boats lie here and there upon its banks, and we saw a small crew of boys plashing about and swimming in it, laughing and yelling. It seemed a shame to disturb the silence so.

The crowd of swaggering "gents" (I don't know the corresponding phrase in the Anglo-Irish vocabulary to express a shabby dandy) awaiting the Cork mail, which kindly goes twenty miles out of its way to accommodate the town of Skibbereen, was quite extraordinary. The little street was quite blocked up with shabby gentlemen, and shabby beggars, awaiting this daily phenomenon. The man who had driven us to Loughine did not fail to ask for his fee as driver; and then, having received it, came forward in his capacity of boots and received another remuneration. The ride is desolate, bare, and yet beautiful. There are a set of hills that keep one company the whole way; they were partially hidden in a gray sky, which flung a general hue of melancholy too over the green country through which we passed. There was only one wretched village along the road, but no lack of population : ragged people who issued from their cabins as the coach passed, or were sitting by the wayside. Everybody seems sitting by the wayside here : one never sees this general repose in England — a sort of ragged lazy contentment. All the children seem to be on the watch for the coach; waited very knowingly and carefully their opportunity, and then hung on by scores behind. What a pleasure to run over flinty roads with bare feet, to be whipped off, and to walk back to the cabin again! These were very different cottages to those neat ones I had seen in Kildare. The wretchedness of them is quite painful to look at; many of the potato-gardens were half dug up, and it is only the first week in August, near three months before the potato is ripe and at full growth ; and the winter still six months away. There were chapels occasionally, and smart new-built churches — one of them has a congregation of ten souls, the coachman told me. Would it not be better that the clergyman should receive them in his room, and that the church-building money should be bestowed otherwise? —

At length, after winding up all sorts of dismal hills speckled with wretched hovels, a ruinous mill every now and then, black bog-lands, and small winding streams, breaking here and there into little falls, we come upon some ground well tilled and planted, and descending (at no small risk from stumbling horses) a bleak long hill, we see the water before us, and turning to the right by the handsome little park of Lord Bearhaven, enter Bantry. The harbor is beautiful. Small mountains in green undulations rising on the opposite side ; great gray ones farther back ; a pretty island in the midst of the water, which is wonderfully bright and calm. A handsome yacht, and two or three vessels with their Sunday colors out, were lying in the bay. It looked like a seaport scene at a theatre, gay, cheerful, neat, and picturesque. At a little distance the town, too, is very pretty. There·are some smart houses on the quays, a handsome court-house as usual, a fine large hotel, and plenty of people flocking round the wonderful coach.

The town is most picturesquely situated, climbing up a wooded hill, with numbers of neat cottages here and there, an ugly church with an air of pretension, and a large grave Roman Catholic chapel the highest point of the place. The Main Street was as usual thronged with the squatting blue cloaks, carrying on their eager trade of buttermilk and green apples, and such cheap wares. With the exception of this street and the quay, with their whitewashed and slated houses, it is a town of cabins. The wretchedness of some of them is quite curious : I tried to make a sketch of a row which lean against an old wall, and are built upon a rock that tumbles about in the oddest and most fantastic shapes, with a brawling waterfall dashing down a channel in the midst. These are, it appears, the beggars' houses : any one may build a lodge against that wall, rent-free ; and such places were never seen ! As for drawing them, it was in vain to try ; one might as well make a sketch of a bundle of rags. An ordinary pigsty in England is really more comfortable. Most of them were not six feet long or five feet high, built of stones huddled together, a hole being left for the people to creep in at, a ruined thatch to keep out some little portion of the rain. The occupiers of these places sat at their doors in tolerable contentment, or the children came down and washed their feet in the water. I declare I believe a Hottentot kraal has more comforts in it : even to write of the place makes one unhappy, and the words move slow. But in the midst of all this misery there is an air of actual cheerfulness ; and go but a few score yards off, and these wretched hovels lying together look really picturesque and pleasing.

CHAPTER IX.

A SMART two-horse car takes the traveller thrice a week from Bantry to Killarney, by way of Glengariff and Kenmare. Unluckily, the rain was pouring down furiously as we passed to the first-named places, and we had only opportunity to see a part of the astonishing beauty of the country. What sends picturesque tourists to the Rhine and Saxon Switzerland? within five miles round the pretty inn of Glengariff there is a country of the magnificence of which no pen can give an idea. I would like to be a great prince, and bring a train of painters over to make, if they could, and according to their several capabilities, a set of pictures of the place. Mr. Creswick would find such rivulets and waterfalls, surrounded by a luxuriance of foliage and verdure that only his pencil can imitate. As for Mr. Cattermole, a red-shanked Irishman should carry his sketching-books to all sorts of wild noble heights, and vast rocky valleys, where he might please himself by piling crag upon crag, and by introducing, if he had a mind, some of the wild figures which peopled this country in old days. There is the Eagle's Nest, for instance, regarding which the Guide-book gives a pretty legend. The Prince of Bantry being conquered by the English soldiers, fled away, leaving his Princess and children to the care of a certain faithful follower of his, who was to provide them with refuge and food. But the whole country was overrun by the conquerors; all the flocks driven away by them, all the houses ransacked, and the crops burnt off the ground, and the faithful servitor did not know where he should find a meal or a resting-place for the unhappy Princess O'Donovan.

He made, however, a sort of shed by the side of a mountain, composing it of sods and stones so artfully that no one could tell but that it was a part of the hill itself; and here, having speared or otherwise obtained a salmon, he fed their Highnesses for the first day; trusting to heaven for a meal when the salmon should be ended.

The Princess O'Donovan and her princely family soon came to an end of the fish; and cried out for something more.

So the faithful servitor, taking with him a rope and his little son Shamus, mounted up to the peak where the eagles rested; and, from the spot to which he climbed, saw their nest, and the young eaglets in it, in a cleft below the precipice.

"Now," said he, "Shamus my son, you must take these thongs with you, and I will let you down by the rope" (it was a straw-rope, which he had made himself, and though it might be considered a dangerous thread to hang by in other countries, you'll see plenty of such contrivances in Ireland to the present day).

"I will let you down by the rope, and you must tie the thongs round the necks of the eaglets, not so as to choke them, but to prevent them from swallowing much." So Shamus went down and did as his father bade him, and came up again when the eaglets were doctored.

Presently the eagles came home: one bringing a rabbit and the other a grouse. These they dropped into the nest for the young ones; and soon after went away in quest of other adventures.

Then Shamus went down into the eagle's nest again, gutted the grouse and rabbit, and left the garbage to the eaglets (as was their right), and brought away the rest. And so the Princess and Princes had game that night for their supper. How long they lived in this way, the Guide-book does not say: but let us trust that the Prince, if he did not come to his own again, was at least restored to his family and decently mediatized: and, for my part, I have very little doubt but that Shamus, the gallant young eagle-robber, created a favorable impression upon one of the young Princesses, and (after many adventures in which he distinguished himself,) was accepted by her Highness for a husband, and her princely parents for a gallant son-in-law.

And here, while we are travelling to Glengariff, and ordering painters about with such princely liberality (by the way, Mr. Stanfield should have a boat in the bay, and paint both rock and sea at his ease), let me mention a wonderful, awful incident of real life which occurred on the road. About four miles from Bantry, at a beautiful wooded place, hard by a mill and waterfall, up rides a gentleman to the car with his luggage, going to Killarney races. The luggage consisted of a small carpet-bag and a pistol-case. About two miles farther on, a fellow stops the car: "Joe," says he, "my master is going to ride to Killarney, so you please to take his luggage." The luggage consisted of a small carpet-bag, and — a pistol-case as before. Is this a gentleman's usual travelling baggage in Ireland?

As there is more rain in this country than in any other, and as, therefore, naturally the inhabitants should be inured to the weather, and made to despise an inconvenience which they cannot avoid, the travelling-conveyances are arranged so that you may get as much practice in being wet as possible. The traveller's baggage is stowed in a place between the two rows of seats, and which is not inaptly called the well, as in a rainy season you might possibly get a bucketful of water out of that orifice. And I confess I saw, with a horrid satisfaction, the pair of pistol-cases lying in this moist aperture, with water pouring above them and lying below them; nay, prayed that all such weapons might one day be consigned to the same fate. But as the waiter at Bantry, in his excessive zeal to serve me, had sent my portmanteau back to Cork by the coach, instead of allowing me to carry it with me to Killarney, and as the rain had long since begun to insinuate itself under the seat-cushion and through the waterproof apron of the car, I dropped off at Glengariff, and dried the only suit of clothes I had by the kitchen-fire. The inn is very pretty: some thorn-trees stand before it, where many barelegged people were lolling, in spite of the weather. A beautiful bay stretches out before the house, the full tide washing the thorn-trees; mountains rise on either side of the little bay, and there is an island, with a castle in it, in the midst, near which a yacht was moored. But the mountains were hardly visible for the mist, and the yacht, island, and castle looked as if they had been washed against the flat gray sky in Indian-ink.

The day did not clear up sufficiently to allow me to make any long excursion about the place, or indeed to see a very wide prospect round about it: at a few hundred yards, most of the objects were enveloped in mist; but even this, for a lover of the picturesque, had its beautiful effect, for you saw the hills in the foreground pretty clear, and covered with their wonderful green, while immediately behind them rose an immense blue mass of mist and mountain that served to *relieve* (to use the painter's phrase) the nearer objects. Annexed to the hotel is a flourishing garden, where the vegetation is so great that the landlord told me it was all he could do to check the trees from growing: round about the bay, in several places, they come clustering down to the water's edge, nor does the salt-water interfere with them.

Winding up a hill to the right, as you quit the inn, is the

beautiful road to the cottage and park of Lord Bantry. One or two parties on pleasure bent went so far as the house, and were partially consoled for the dreadful rain which presently poured down upon them, by wine, whiskey, and refreshments which the liberal owner of the house sent out to them. I myself had only got a few hundred yards when the rain overtook me, and sent me for refuge into a shed, where a blacksmith had arranged a rude furnace and bellows, and where he was at work, with a rough gilly to help him, and of course a lounger or two to look on.

The scene was exceedingly wild and picturesque, and I took out a sketch-book and began to draw. The blacksmith was at first very suspicious of the operation which I had commenced, nor did the poor fellow's sternness at all yield until I made him a present of a shilling to buy tobacco — when he, his friend, and his son became good-humored, and said their little say. This was the first shilling he had earned these three years : he was a small farmer, but was starved out, and had set up a forge here, and was trying to get a few pence. What struck me was the great number of people about the place. We had at least twenty visits while the sketch was being made ; cars, and single and double horsemen, were continually passing ; between the intervals of the shower a couple of ragged old women would creep out from some hole and display baskets of green apples for sale : wet or not, men and women were lounging up and down the road. You would have thought it was a fair, and yet there was not even a village at this place, only the inn and post-house, by which the cars to Tralee pass thrice a week.

The weather, instead of mending, on the second day was worse than ever. All the view had disappeared now under a rushing rain, of which I never saw anything like the violence. We were visited by five maritime — nay, buccaneering-looking gentlemen in moustaches, with fierce caps and jackets, just landed from a yacht : and then the car brought us three Englishmen wet to the skin and thirsting for whiskey-and-water.

And with these three Englishmen a great scene occurred, such as we read of in Smollett's and Fielding's inns. One was a fat old gentleman from Cambridge — who, I was informed, was a Fellow of a college in that university, but whom I shrewdly suspect * to be butler or steward of the same. The

---

* The suspicion turned out to be very correct. The gentleman is the respected cook of C——, as I learned afterwards from a casual Cambridge man.

younger men, burly, manly, good-humored fellows of seventeen stone, were the nephews of the elder — who, says one, " could draw a cheque for his thousand pounds."

Two-and-twenty years before, on landing at the Pigeon-House at Dublin, the old gentleman had been cheated by a carman, and his firm opinion seemed to be that all carmen — nay, all Irishmen — were cheats.

And a sad proof of this depravity speedily showed itself: for having hired a three-horse car at Killarney, which was to carry them to Bantry, the Englishmen saw, with immense indignation, after they had drunk a series of glasses of whiskey, that the three-horse car had been removed, a one-horse vehicle standing in its stead.

Their wrath no pen can describe. "I tell you they are all so!" shouted the elder. "When I landed at the Pigeon-House . . . ." "Bring me a post-chaise!" roars the second. "Waiter, get some more whiskey!" exclaims the third. "If they don't send us on with three horses, I'll stop here for a week." Then issuing, with his two young friends, into the passage, to harangue the populace assembled there, the elder Englishman began a speech about dishonesty, "d—d rogues and thieves, Pigeon-House: he was a gentleman, and wouldn't be done, d—n his eyes and everybody's eyes." Upon the affrighted landlord, who came to interpose, they all fell with great ferocity: the elder man swearing, especially, that he " would write to Lord Lansdowne regarding his conduct, likewise to Lord Bandon, also to Lord Bantry: he was a gentleman; he'd been cheated in the year 1815, on his first landing at the Pigeon-House: and, d—n the Irish, they were all alike." After roaring and cursing for half an hour, a gentleman at the door, seeing the meek bearing of the landlord — who stood quite lost and powerless in the whirlwind of rage that had been excited about his luckless ears — said, "If men cursed and swore in that way in his house, he would know how to put them out."

"Put *me* out!" says one of the young men, placing himself before the fat old blasphemer his relative. "Put *me* out, my fine fellow!" But it was evident the Irishman did not like his customer. "Put *me* out!" roars the old gentleman, from behind his young protector. " —— my eyes, who are *you*, sir? who *are* you, sir? I insist on knowing who you are."

"And who are you?" asks the Irishman.

"Sir, I'm a gentleman, and *pay my way!* and as soon as I get into Bantry, I swear I'll write a letter to Lord Bandon Bantry. and complain of the treatment I have received here."

Now, as the unhappy landlord had not said one single word, and as, on the contrary, to the annoyance of the whole house, the stout old gentleman from Cambridge had been shouting, raging, and cursing for two hours, I could not help, like a great ass as I was, coming forward and (thinking the landlord might be a tenant of Lord Bantry's) saying, " Well, sir, if you write and say the landlord has behaved ill, I will write to say that he has acted with extraordinary forbearance and civility."

O fool! to interfere in disputes where one set of the disputants have drunk half a dozen glasses of whiskey in the middle of the day! No sooner had I said this than the other young man came and fell upon me, and in the course of a few minutes found leisure to tell me " that I was no gentleman ; that I was ashamed to give my name, or say where I lived ; that I was a liar, and didn't live in London, and couldn't mention the name of a single respectable person there ; that he was a merchant and tradesman, and hid his quality from no one : " and, finally, " that though bigger than himself, there was nothing he would like better than that I should come out on the green and stand to him like a man."

This invitation, although repeated several times, I refused with as much dignity as I could assume ; partly because I was sober and cool, while the other was furious and drunk ; also because I felt a strong suspicion that in about ten minutes the man would manage to give me a tremendous beating, which I did not merit in the least ; thirdly, because a victory over him would not have been productive of the least pleasure to me ; and lastly, because there was something really honest and gallant in the fellow coming out to defend his old relative. Both of the younger men would have fought like tigers for this disreputable old gentleman, and desired no better sport. The last I heard of the three was that they and the driver made their appearance before a magistrate in Bantry ; and a pretty story will the old man have to tell to his club at the " Hoop," or the " Red Lion," of those swindling Irish, and the ill-treatment he met with in their country.

As for the landlord, the incident will be a blessed theme of conversation to him for a long time to come. I heard him discoursing of it in the passage during the rest of the day ; and next morning when I opened my window and saw with much delight the bay clear and bright as silver — except where the green hills were reflected in it, the blue sky above, and the purple mountains round about with only a few clouds veiling their peaks — the first thing I heard was the voice of Mr. Eccles repeating the story to a new customer.

" I thought thim couldn't be gintlemin," was the appropriate remark of Mr. Tom the waiter, " from the way in which they took their whiskey — raw with cold wather, widout *mixing or iny thing.*" Could an Irish waiter give a more excellent definition of the ungenteel?

At nine o'clock in the morning of the next day, the unlucky car which had carried the Englishmen to Bantry came back to Glengariff, and as the morning was very fine, I was glad to take advantage of it, and travel some five-and-thirty English miles to Killarney.

CHAPTER X.

FROM GLENGARIFF TO KILLARNEY.

The Irish car seems accommodated for any number of persons : it appeared to be full when we left Glengariff, for a traveller from Bearhaven, and the five gentlemen from the yacht, took seats upon it with myself, and we fancied it was impossible more than seven should travel by such a conveyance ; but the driver showed the capabilities of his vehicle presently. The journey from Glengariff to Kenmare is one of astonishing beauty ; and I have seen Killarney since, and am sure that Glengariff loses nothing by comparison with this most famous of lakes. Rock, wood, and sea stretch around the traveller — a thousand delightful pictures : the landscape is at first wild without being fierce, immense woods and plantations enriching the valleys — beautiful streams to be seen everywhere.

Here again I was surprised at the great population along the road ; for one saw but few cabins, and there is no village between Glengariff and Kenmare. But men and women were on banks and in fields ; children, as usual, came trooping up to the car ; and the jovial men of the yacht had great conversations with most of the persons whom we met on the road. A merrier set of fellows it were hard to meet. " Should you like anything to drink, sir ? " says one, commencing the acquaintance. " We have the best whiskey in the world, and plenty of porter in the basket." Therewith the jolly seamen produced a long bottle of grog, which was passed round from one to another; and then began singing, shouting, laughing, roaring for the whole journey. "British sailors have a knack, pull away — ho, boys!" "Hurroo, my fine fellow! does your mother know you're out?" "Hurroo, Tim Herlihy! you're a *fluke*, Tim Herlihy." One man sang on the roof, one *hurroo'd* to the echo, another apostrophized the aforesaid Herlihy as he passed grinning on a car; a third had a pocket-handkerchief flaunting from a pole, with which he performed exercises in the face of any horseman whom we met; and great were their yells as the ponies shied off at the salutation and the riders swerved in their saddles. In the midst of this rattling chorus we went along: gradually the country grew wilder and more desolate, and we passed through a grim mountain region, bleak and bare, the road winding round some of the innumerable hills, and once or twice by means of a tunnel rushing boldly through them. One of these tunnels, they say, is a couple of hundred yards long; and a pretty howling, I need not say, was made through that pipe of rock by the jolly yacht's crew. "We saw you sketching in the blacksmith's shed at Glengariff," says one, "and we wished we had you on board. Such a jolly life we led of it!" — They roved about the coast, they said, in their vessel; they feasted off the best of fish, mutton, and whiskey; they had Gamble's turtle-soup on board, and fun from morning till night, and *vice versâ*. Gradually it came out that there was not, owing to the tremendous rains, a dry corner in their ship: that they slung two in a huge hammock in the cabin, and that one of their crew had been ill, and shirked off. What a wonderful thing pleasure is! To be wet all day and night; to be scorched and blistered by the sun and rain; to beat in and out of little harbors, and to exceed diurnally upon whiskey-punch — 'faith, London, and an arm-chair at the club, are more to the tastes of some men.

After much mountain-work of ascending and descending, (in which latter operation, and by the side of precipices that make passing cockneys rather squeamish, the carman drove like mad to the whooping and screeching of the red-rovers,) we at length came to Kenmare, of which all that I know is that it lies prettily in a bay or arm of the sea; that it is approached by a little hanging-bridge, which seems to be a wonder in these parts; that it is a miserable little place when you enter it; and that, finally, a splendid luncheon of all sorts of meat and excellent cold salmon may sometimes be had for a shilling at the hotel of the place. It is a great vacant house, like the rest of them, and would frighten people in England; but after a few days one grows used to the Castle Rackrent style. I am not sure that there is not a certain sort of comfort to be had in these rambling rooms, and among these bustling, blundering waiters, which one does not always meet with in an orderly English house of entertainment.

After discussing the luncheon, we found the car with fresh horses, beggars, idlers, policemen, &c., standing round of course; and now the miraculous vehicle, which had held hitherto seven with some difficulty, was called upon to accommodate thirteen.

A pretty noise would our three Englishmen of yesterday — nay, any other Englishmen for the matter of that — have made, if coolly called upon to admit an extra party of four into a mail-coach! The yacht's crew did not make a single objection; a couple clambered up on the roof, where they managed to locate themselves with wonderful ingenuity, perched upon hard wooden chests, or agreeably reposing upon the knotted ropes which held them together; one of the new passengers scrambled between the driver's legs, where he held on somehow, and the rest were pushed and squeezed astonishingly in the car.

Now the fact must be told, that five of the new passengers (I don't count a little boy besides) were women, and very pretty, gay, frolicksome, lively, kind-hearted, innocent women too; and for the rest of the journey there was no end of laughing and shouting, and singing, and hugging, so that the caravan presented the appearance which is depicted in the frontispiece of this work.

Now it may be a wonder to some persons, that with such a cargo the carriage did not upset, or some of us did not fall off; to which the answer is that we *did* fall off. A very pretty woman fell off, and showed a pair of never-mind-what-colored garters, and an interesting English traveller fell off too: but heaven bless you! these cars are made to fall off from; and considering the circumstances of the case, and in the same company, I would rather fall off than not. A great number of polite allusions and genteel inquiries were, as may be imagined, made by the jolly boat's crew. But though the lady affected to be a little angry at first, she was far too good-natured to be angry long, and at last fairly burst out laughing with the passengers. We did not fall off again, but held on very tight, and just as we were reaching Killarney, saw somebody else fall off from another car. But in this instance the gentleman had no lady to tumble with.

For almost half the way from Kenmare, this wild, beautiful

road commands views of the famous lake and vast blue mountains about Killarney. Turk, Tomies, and Mangerton were clothed in purple, like kings in mourning; great heavy clouds were gathered round their heads, parting away every now and then, and leaving their noble features bare. The lake lay for some time underneath us, dark and blue, with dark misty islands in the midst. On the right-hand side of the road would be a precipice covered with a thousand trees, or a green rocky flat, with a reedy mere in the midst, and other mountains rising as far as we could see. I think of that diabolical tune in "Der Freischutz" while passing through this sort of country. Every now and then, in the midst of some fresh country or inclosed trees, or at a turn of the road, you lose the sight of the great big awful mountain: but, like the aforesaid tune in "Der Freischutz," it is always there close at hand. You feel that it keeps you company. And so it was that we rode by dark old Mangerton, then presently past Muckross, and then through two miles of avenues of lime-trees, by numerous lodges and gentlemen's seats, across an old bridge, where you see the mountains again and the lake, until, by Lord Kenmare's house, a hideous row of houses informed us that we were at Killarney.

Here my companion suddenly let go my hand, and by a certain uneasy motion of the waist, gave me notice to withdraw the other too; and so we rattled up to the "Kenmare Arms:" and so ended, not without a sigh on my part, one of the merriest six-hour rides that five yachtmen, one cockney, five women and a child, the carman, and a countryman with an alpeen, ever took in their lives.

As for my fellow-companion, she would hardly speak the next day; but all the five maritime men made me vow and promise that I would go and see them at Cork, where I should have horses to ride, the fastest yacht out of the harbor to sail in, and the best of whiskey, claret, and welcome. Amen, and may every single person who buys a copy of this book meet with the same deserved fate.

The town of Killarney was in a violent state of excitement with a series of horse-races, hurdle-races, boat-races, and stag-hunts by land and water, which were taking place, and attracted a vast crowd from all parts of the kingdom. All the inns were full, and lodgings cost five shillings a day — nay, more in some places; for though my landlady, Mrs. Macgillicuddy, charges that sum, a leisurely old gentleman, whom I never saw in my life before, made my acquaintance by stopping me in the

street yesterday, and said he paid a pound a day for his two
bedrooms.   The old gentleman is eager for company; and
indeed, when a man travels alone, it is wonderful how little he
cares to select his society; how indifferent company pleases
him; how a good fellow delights him: how sorry he is when
the time for parting comes, and he has to walk off alone, and
begin the friendship-hunt over again.

The first sight I witnessed at Killarney was a race-ordinary,
where, for a sum of twelve shillings, any man could take his
share of turbot, salmon, venison, and beef, with port, and sherry,
and whiskey-punch at discretion. Here were the squires of Cork
and Kerry, one or two Englishmen, whose voices amidst the
rich humming brogue round about sounded quite affected (not
that they were so, but there seems a sort of impertinence in the
shrill, high-pitched tone of the English voice here). At the
head of the table, near the chairman, sat some brilliant young
dragoons, neat, solemn, dull, with huge moustaches, and boots
polished to a nicety.

And here of course the conversation was of the horse,
horsey: how Mr. This had refused fifteen hundred guineas for
a horse which he bought for a hundred; how Bacchus was the
best horse in Ireland; which horses were to run at Something
races; and how the Marquis of Waterford gave a plate or a
purse. We drank "the Queen," with hip! hip! hurrah! the
"winner of the Kenmare stakes" — hurrah! Presently the
gentleman next me rose and made a speech: he had brought
a mare down and won the stakes — a hundred and seventy
guineas — and I looked at him with a great deal of respect.
Other toasts ensued, and more talk about horses. Nor am I in
the least disposed to sneer at gentlemen who like sporting and
talk about it: for I do believe that the conversation of a dozen
fox-hunters is just as clever as that of a similar number of merchants, barristers, or literary men.   But to this trade, as to all
others, a man must be bred; if he has not learnt it thoroughly
or in early life, he will not readily become a proficient afterwards,
and when therefore the subject is broached, had best maintain
a profound silence.

A young Edinburgh cockney, with an easy self-confidence
that the reader may have perhaps remarked in others of his
calling and nation, and who evidently knew as much of sporting
matters as the individual who writes this, proceeded nevertheless to give the company his opinions, and greatly astonished
them all; for these simple people are at first willing to believe
that a stranger is sure to be a knowing fellow, and did not seem

inclined to be undeceived even by this little pert, grinning Scotchman. It was good to hear him talk of Haddington, Musselburgh — and heaven knows what strange outlandish places, as if they were known to all the world. And here would be a good opportunity to enter into a dissertation upon natural characteristics : to show that the bold, swaggering Irishman is really a modest fellow, while the canny Scot is a most brazen one ; to wonder why the inhabitant of one country is ashamed of it — which is in itself so fertile and beautiful, and has produced more than its fair proportion of men of genius, valor, and wit ; whereas it never enters into the head of a Scotchman to question his own equality (and something more) at all : but that such discussions are quite unprofitable ; nay, that exactly the contrary propositions may be argued to just as much length. Has the reader ever tried with a dozen of De Tocqueville's short crisp philosophic apophthegms and taken the converse of them ? The one or other set of propositions will answer equally well ; and it is the best way to avoid all such. Let the above passage, then, simply be understood to say, that on a certain day the writer met a vulgar little Scotchman — not that all Scotchmen are vulgar ; — that this little pert creature prattled about his country as if he and it were ornaments to the world — which the latter is, no doubt ; and that one could not but contrast his behavior with that of great big stalwart simple Irishmen, who asked your opinion of their country with as much modesty as if you — because an Englishman — must be somebody, and they the dust of the earth.

Indeed, this want of self-confidence at times becomes quite painful to the stranger. If in reply to their queries, you say you like the country, people seem really quite delighted. Why should they ? Why should a stranger's opinion who doesn't know the country be more valued than a native's who does?— Suppose an Irishman in England were to speak in praise or abuse of the country, would one be particularly pleased or annoyed ? One would be glad that the man liked his trip ; but as for his good or bad opinion of the country, the country stands on its own bottom, superior to any opinion of any man or men.

I must beg pardon of the little Scotchman for reverting to him (let it be remembered that there were *two* Scotchmen at Killarney, and that I speak of the other one) ; but I have seen no specimen of that sort of manners in any Irishman since I have been in the country. I have met more gentlemen here than in any place I ever saw : gentlemen of high and low ranks.

that is to say : men shrewd and delicate of perception, observant of society, entering into the feelings of others, and anxious
to set them at ease or to gratify them ; of course exaggerating
their professions of kindness and in so far insincere ; but the
very exaggeration seems to be a proof of a kindly nature, and
I wish in England we were a little more complimentary. In
Dublin, a lawyer left his chambers, and a literary man his books,
to walk the town with me — the town, which they must know
a great deal too well : for, pretty as it is, it is but a small place
after all, not like that great bustling, changing, struggling world,
the Englishman's capital. Would a London man leave his business to trudge to the Tower or the Park with a stranger ?   We
would ask him to dine at the club, or to eat whitebait at Lovegrove's, and think our duty done, neither caring for him, nor
professing to care for him ; and we pride ourselves on our
honesty accordingly. Never was honesty more selfish. And
so a vulgar man in England disdains to flatter his equals, and
chiefly displays his character of snob by assuming as much as
he can for himself, swaggering and showing off in his coarse,
dull, stupid way.

" I am a gentleman, and pay my way," as the old fellow
said at Glengariff. I have not heard a sentence near so vulgar
from any man in Ireland. Yes, by the way, there was another
Englishman at Cork : a man in a middling, not to say humble,
situation of life. When introduced to an Irish gentleman, his
formula seemed to be, " I think, sir, I have met you somewhere
before." " I am sure, sir, I have met you before," he said for
the second time in my hearing, to a gentleman of great note in
Ireland. " Yes, I have met you at Lord X——'s." " I don't
know my Lord X——," replied the Irishman. " Sir," says the
other, " *I shall have great pleasure in introducing you to him.*"
Well, the good-natured simple Irishman thought this gentleman
a very fine fellow. There was only one, of some dozen who
spoke about him, that found out snob. I suppose the Spaniards
lorded it over the Mexicans in this way : their drummers passing for generals among the simple red men, their glass beads
for jewels, and their insolent bearing for heroic superiority.

Leaving, then, the race-ordinary (that little Scotchman with
his airs has carried us the deuce knows how far out of the way),
I came home just as the gentlemen of the race were beginning
to " mix," that is, to forsake the wine for the punch. At the
lodgings I found my five companions of the morning with a
bottle of that wonderful whiskey of which they spoke ; and
which they had agreed to exchange against a bundle of Liver-

pool cigars : so we discussed them, the whiskey, and other topics in common. Now there is no need to violate the sanctity
of private life, and report the conversation which took place, the
songs which were sung, the speeches which were made, and
the other remarkable events of the evening. Suffice it to say,
that the English traveller gradually becomes accustomed to
whiskey-punch (in moderation of course), and finds the beverage very agreeable at Killarney ; against which I recollect a
protest was entered at Dublin.

But after we had talked of hunting, racing, regatting, and
all other sports, I came to a discovery which astonished me,
and for which these honest, kind fellows are mentioned publicly
here. The portraits, or a sort of resemblance of four of them,
may be seen in the foregoing drawing of the car. The man
with the straw-hat and handkerchief tied over it is the captain
of an Indiaman ; three others, with each a pair of moustaches,
sported yacht-costumes, jackets, club anchor-buttons, and so
forth ; and, finally, one on the other side of the car (who cannot
be seen on account of the portmanteaus, otherwise the likeness
would be perfect,) was dressed with a coat and a hat in the
ordinary way. One with the gold band and moustaches is a
gentleman of property ; the other three are attorneys every man
of them ; two in large practice in Cork and Dublin, the other,
and owner of the yacht, under articles to the attorney of Cork.
Now did any Englishman ever live with three attorneys for a
whole day without hearing a single syllable of law spoken? Did
we ever see in our country attorneys with moustaches ; or, above
all, an attorney's clerk the owner of a yacht of thirty tons?
He is a gentleman of property too — the heir, that is, to a good
estate ; and has had a yacht of his own, he says, ever since he
was fourteen years old. Is there any English boy of fourteen
who commands a ship with a crew of five men under him? We
all agreed to have a boat for the stag-hunt on the lake next
day ; and I went to bed wondering at this strange country more
than ever. An attorney with moustaches ! What would they
say of him in Chancery Lane?

CHAPTER XI.

KILLARNEY — STAG-HUNTING ON THE LAKE.

MRS. MACGILLICUDDY's house is at the corner of the two principal streets of Killarney town, and the drawing-room windows command each a street. Before one window is a dismal, rickety building, with a slated face, that looks like an ex-town-hall. There is a row of arches to the ground-floor, the angles at the base of which seem to have mouldered or to have been kicked away. Over the centre arch is a picture with a flourishing yellow inscription above, importing that it is the meeting-place of the Total Abstinence Society. Total abstinence is represented by the figures of a gentleman in a blue coat and drab tights, with gilt garters, who is giving his hand to a lady; between them is an escutcheon surmounted with a cross and charged with religious emblems. Cupids float above the heads and between the legs of this happy pair, while an exceedingly small tea-table with the requisite crockery reposes against the lady's knee; a still, with death's-head and bloody bones, filling up the naked corner near the gentleman. A sort of market is held here, and the place is swarming with blue cloaks and groups of men talking; here and there is a stall with coarse linens, crockery, a cheese; and crowds of egg- and milk-women are squatted on the pavement, with their ragged customers or gossips; and the yellow-haired girl, on the next page, with a barrel containing nothing at all, has been sitting, as if for her portrait, this hour past.

Carts, cars, jingles, barouches, horses and vehicles of all descriptions rattle presently through the streets: for the town is crowded with company for the races and other sports, and all the world is bent to see the stag-hunt on the lake. Where the ladies of the Macgillicuddy family have slept, heaven knows, for their house is full of lodgers. What voices you hear! "Bring me some hot wa*tah*," says a genteel, high-piped English voice. "Hwhere's me hot wather?" roars a deep-toned Hibernian. See, over the way, three ladies in ringlets and green tabbinet taking their "tay" preparatory to setting out. I wonder whether they heard the sentimental songs of the law-marines last night? They must have been edified if they did.

My companions came, true to their appointment, and we walked down to the boats, lying at a couple of miles from the town, near the "Victoria Inn," a handsome mansion, in pretty grounds, close to the lake, and owned by the patriotic Mr. Finn. A nobleman offered Finn eight hundred pounds for the use of his house during the races, and, to Finn's eternal honor be it said, he refused the money, and said he would keep his house for his friends and patrons, the public. Let the Cork Steam-Packet Company think of this generosity on the part of Mr. Finn, and blush for shame : at the Cork Agricultural Show they raised their fares, and were disappointed in their speculation, as they deserved to be, by indignant Englishmen refusing to go at all.

The morning had been bright enough ; but for fear of accidents we took our mackintoshes, and at about a mile from the town found it necessary to assume those garments and wear them for the greater part of the day. Passing by the "Victoria," with its beautiful walks, park, and lodge, we came to a little creek where the boats were moored ; and there was the wonderful lake before us, with its mountains, and islands, and trees. Unluckily, however, the mountains happened to be invisible ; the islands looked like gray masses in the fog, and all that we could see for some time was the gray silhouette of the boat ahead of us, in which a passenger was engaged in a witty conversation with some boat still further in the mist.

Drumming and trumpeting was heard at a little distance, and presently we found ourselves in the midst of a fleet of boats upon the rocky shores of the beautiful little Innisfallen.

Here we landed for a while, and the weather clearing up allowed us to see this charming spot : rocks, shrubs, and little abrupt rises and falls of ground, covered with the brightest emerald grass ; a beautiful little ruin of a Saxon chapel, lying gentle, delicate, and plaintive on the shore ; some noble trees round about it, and beyond, presently, the tower of Ross Castle : island after island appearing in the clearing sunshine, and the huge hills throwing their misty veils off, and wearing their noble robes of purple. The boats' crews were grouped about the place, and one large barge especially had landed some sixty people, being the Temperance band, with its drums, trumpets, and wives. They were marshalled by a grave old gentleman with a white waistcoat and queue, a silver medal decorating one side of his coat, and a brass heart reposing on the other flap. The horns performed some Irish airs prettily ; and at length, at the instigation of a fellow who went swaggering about with a pair

of whirling drumsticks, all formed together and played Garryowen — the active drum of course most dreadfully out of time.

Having strolled about the island for a quarter of an hour, it
became time to take to the boats again, and we were rowed
over to the wood opposite Sullivan's cascade, where the hounds
had been laid in in the morning, and the stag was expected to
take water. Fifty or sixty men are employed on the mountain
to drive the stag lakewards, should he be inclined to break
away : and the sport generally ends by the stag — a wild one —
making for the water with the pack swimming afterwards ; and
here he is taken and disposed of : how I know not. It is rather
a parade than a stag-hunt ; but, with all the boats around and
the noble view, must be a fine thing to see.

Presently, steering his barge, the " Erin," with twelve oars
and a green flag sweeping the water, came by the president of
the sports, Mr. John O'Connell, a gentleman who appears to
be liked by rich and poor here, and by the latter especially is
adored. " Sure we'd dhrown ourselves for him," one man told
me ; and proceeded to speak eagerly in his praise, and to tell
numberless acts of his generosity and justice. The justice is
rather rude in this wild country sometimes, and occasionally
the judges not only deliver the sentence but execute it ; nor
does any one think of appealing to any more regular jurisdiction. The likeness of Mr. O'Connell to his brother is very
striking : one might have declared it was the Liberator sitting
at the stern of the boat.

Some scores more boats were there, darting up and down in
the pretty, busy waters. Here came a Cambridge boat ; and
where, indeed, will not the gentlemen of that renowned university be found ? Yonder were the dandy dragoons, stiff,
silent, slim, faultlessly appointed, solemnly puffing cigars.
Every now and then a hound would be heard in the wood,
whereon numbers of voices, right and left, would begin to yell
in chorus — " Hurroo ! Hoop ! Yow — yow — yow !" in accents
the most shrill or the most melancholious. Meanwhile the
sun had had enough of the sport, the mountains put on their
veils again, the islands retreated into the mist, the word went
through the fleet to spread all umbrellas, and ladies took shares
of mackintoshes and disappeared under the flaps of silk cloaks.

The wood comes down to the very edge of the water, and
many of the crews thought fit to land and seek this green
shelter. There you might see how the *dandium summâ genus
hæsit ulmo,* clambering up thither to hide from the rain, and
many " membra " in dabbled russia-ducks cowering *viridi sub*

arbuto ad aquæ lene caput. To behold these moist dandies the natives of the country came eagerly. Strange, savage faces might be seen peering from out of the trees : long-haired, bare-legged girls came down the hill, some with green apples and very sickly-looking plums ; some with whiskey and goat's-milk : a ragged boy had a pair of stag's-horns to sell : the place swarmed with people. We went up the hill to see the noble cascade, and when you say that it comes rushing down over rock and through tangled woods, alas ! one has said all the dictionary can help you to, and not enough to distinguish this particular cataract from any other. This seen and admired, we came back to the harbor where the boats lay, and from which spot the reader might have seen the foregoing view of the lake — that is, you *would* see the lake, if the mist would only clear away.*

But this for hours it did not seem inclined to do. We rowed up and down industriously for a period of time which seemed to me atrociously long. The bugles of the " Erin " had long since sounded " Home, sweet home ! " and the greater part of the fleet had dispersed. As for the stag-hunt, all I saw of it was four dogs that appeared on the shore at different intervals, and a huntsman in a scarlet coat, who similarly came and went : once or twice we were gratified by hearing the hounds : but at last it was agreed that there was no chance for the day, and we rowed off to Kenmare Cottage — where, on the lovely lawn, or in a cottage adjoining, the gentry picnic, and where, with a handkerchiefful of potatoes, we made as pleasant a meal as ever I recollect. Here a good number of the boats were assembled ; here you might see cloths spread and dinner going on ; here were those wonderful officers, looking as if they had just stepped from band-boxes, with — by heavens ! — not a shirt-collar disarranged nor a boot dimmed by the wet. An old piper was making a very feeble music, with a handkerchief spread over his face ; and, farther on, a little smiling German boy was playing an accordion and singing a ballad of Hauff's. I had a silver medal in my pocket, with Victoria on one side and Britannia on the other, and gave it him, for the sake of old times and his round friendly face. Oh, little German boy, many a night as you trudge lonely through this wild land, must you yearn after *Bruderlein* and *Schwesterlein* at home — yonder in stately Frankfürt city that lies by silver Mayn. I thought of vineyards and sunshine, and the greasy clock in the theatre, and the railroad all the way to Wiesbaden, and the handsome

* This refers to an illustrated edition of the work.

Jew country-houses by the Bockenheimer-Thor . . . . "Come along," says the boatman. "All the gintlemin are waiting for your honor." And I found them finishing the potatoes, and we all had a draught of water from the lake, and so pulled to the Middle or Turk Lake through the picturesque green rapid that floats under Brickeen Bridge.

What is to be said about Turk Lake? When there, we agreed that it was more beautiful than the large lake, of which it is not one fourth the size; then, when we came back, we said, " No, the large lake is the most beautiful." And so, at every point we stopped at, we determined that that particular spot was the prettiest in the whole lake. The fact is — and I don't care to own it — they are too handsome. As for a man coming from his desk in London or Dublin and seeing " the whole lakes in a day," he is an ass for his pains; a child doing sums in addition might as well read the whole multiplication-table, and fancy he had it by heart. We should look at these wonderful things leisurely and thoughtfully; and even then, blessed is he who understands them. I wonder what impression the sight made upon the three tipsy Englishmen at Glengariff? What idea of natural beauty belongs to an old fellow who says he is " a gentleman, and pays his way?" What to a jolly fox-hunter, who had rather see a good " screeching" run with the hounds than the best landscape ever painted? And yet they all come hither, and go through the business regularly, and would not miss seeing every one of the lakes and going up every one of the hills. By which circumlocution the writer wishes ingenuously to announce that he will not see any more lakes, ascend any mountains or towers, visit any gaps of Dunloe, or any prospects whatever, except such as nature shall fling in his way in the course of a quiet reasonable walk.

In the Middle Lake we were carried to an island where a ceremony of goat's-milk and whiskey is performed by some travellers, and where you are carefully conducted to a spot that " Sir Walter Scott admired more than all." Whether he did or not, we can only say on the authority of the boatman; but the place itself was a quiet nook, where three waters meet, and indeed of no great picturesqueness when compared with the beauties around. But it is of a gentle, homely beauty — not like the lake, which is as a princess dressed out in diamonds and velvet for a drawing-room, and knowing herself to be faultless too. As for Innisfallen, it was just as if she gave one smiling peep into the nursery before she went away, so quiet, innocent, and tender is that lovely spot; but, depend on it, if there is a lake fairy or princess, as Crofton Croker and other historians assert, she is of her nature a vain creature, proud of her person, and fond of the finest dresses to adorn it. May I confess that I would rather, for a continuance, have a house facing a paddock, with a cow in it, than be always looking at this immense, overpowering splendor. You would not, my dear brother cockney from Tooley Street? No, those brilliant eyes of thine were never meant to gaze at anything less bright than the sun. Your mighty spirit finds nothing too vast for its comprehension, spurns what is humble as unworthy, and only, like Foote's bear, dances to " the genteelest of tunes."

The long and short of the matter is, that on getting off the lake, after seven hours' rowing, I felt as much relieved as if I had been dining for the same length of time with her Majesty the Queen, and went jumping home as gayly as possible ; but those marine lawyers insisted so piteously upon seeing Ross Castle, close to which we were at length landed, that I was obliged (in spite of repeated oaths to the contrary) to ascend that tower, and take a bird's-eye view of the scene. Thank heaven, I have neither tail nor wings, and have not the slightest wish to be a bird : that continual immensity of prospect which stretches beneath those little wings of theirs must deaden their intellects, depend on it. Tomkins and I are not made for the immense : we can enjoy a little at a time, and enjoy that little very much ; or if like birds, we are like the ostrich — not that we have fine feathers to our backs, but because we cannot fly. Press us too much, and we become flurried, and run off and bury our heads in the quiet bosom of dear mother earth, and so get rid of the din, and the dazzle, and the shouting.

Because we dined upon potatoes, that was no reason we should sup on buttermilk. Well, well ! salmon is good, and whiskey is good too.

CHAPTER XII.

KILLARNEY — THE RACES — MUCKROSS.

THE races were as gay as races could be, in spite of one or two untoward accidents that arrived at the close of the day's sport. Where all the people came from that thronged out of the town was a wonder ; where all the vehicles, the cars,

barouches and shandrydans, the carts, the horse- and donkey-
men could have found stable and shelter, who can tell? Of all
these equipages and donkeypages I had a fine view from Mrs.
Macgillicuddy's window, and it was pleasant to see the happy
faces shining under the blue cloaks as the carts rattled by.

A very handsome young lady — I presume Miss MacG. —
who gives a hand to the drawing-room and comes smiling in
with the teapot — Miss MacG., I say, appeared to-day in a
silk bonnet and stiff silk dress, with a brooch and a black
mantle, as smart as any lady in the land, and looking as if she
was accustomed to her dress too, which the housemaid on
banks of Thames does not. Indeed, I have not met a more
ladylike young person in Ireland than Miss MacG.; and when
I saw her in a handsome car on the course, I was quite proud
of a bow.

Tramping thither, too, as hard as they could walk, and as
happy and smiling as possible, were Mary the coachman's wife
of the day before, and Johanna with the child, and presently
the other young lady: the man with the stick, you may be
sure: he would toil a year for that day's pleasure. They are
all mad for it: people walk for miles and miles round to the
race; they come without a penny in their pockets often, trusting to chance and charity, and that some worthy gentleman
may fling them a sixpence. A gentleman told me that he saw
on the course persons from his part of the country, who must
have walked eighty miles for the sport.

For a mile and a half to the racecourse there could be no
pleasanter occupation than looking at the happy multitudes
who were thronging thither; and I am bound to say that on
rich or poor shoulders I never saw so many handsome faces in
my life. In the carriages, among the ladies of Kerry, every
second woman was handsome; and there is something peculiarly tender and pleasing in the looks of the young female
peasantry that is perhaps even better than beauty. Beggars
had taken their stations along the road in no great numbers,
for I suspect they were most of them on the ground, and those
who remained were consequently of the oldest and ugliest. It
is a shame that such horrible figures are allowed to appear in
public as some of the loathsome ones which belong to these
unhappy people. On went the crowd, however, laughing and
as gay as possible; all sorts of fun passing from car- to foot-
passengers as the pretty girls came clattering by, and the
" boys " had a word for each. One lady, with long flowing
auburn hair, who was turning away her head from some " boys "

very demurely, I actually saw, at a pause of the cart, kissed by one of them. She gave the fellow a huge box on the ear and he roared out, "O murther!" and she frowned for some time as hard as she could, whilst the ladies in the blue cloaks at the back of the car uttered a shrill rebuke in Irish. But in a minute the whole party was grinning, and the young fellow who had administered the salute may, for what I know, have taken another without the slap on the face by way of exchange.

And here, lest the fair public may have a bad opinion of the personage who talks of kissing with such awful levity, let it be said that with all this laughing, romping, kissing, and the like, there are no more innocent girls in the world than the Irish girls; and that the women of our squeamish country are far more liable to err. One has but to walk through an English and Irish town, and see how much superior is the morality of the latter. That great terror-striker, the Confessional, is before the Irish girl, and sooner or later her sins must be told there.

By this time we are got upon the course, which is really one of the most beautiful spots that ever was seen: the lake and mountains lying along two sides of it, and of course visible from all. They were busy putting up the hurdles when we arrived: stiff bars and poles, four feet from the ground, with furze-bushes over them. The grand stand was already full; along the hedges sat thousands of the people, sitting at their ease doing nothing, and happy as kings. A daguerreotype would have been of great service to have taken their portraits, and I never saw a vast multitude of heads and attitudes so picturesque and lively. The sun lighted up the whole course and the lakes with amazing brightness, though behind the former lay a huge rack of the darkest clouds, against which the cornfields and meadows shone in the brightest green and gold, and a row of white tents was quite dazzling.

There was a brightness and intelligence about this immense Irish crowd, which I don't remember to have seen in an English one. The women in their blue cloaks, with red smiling faces peering from one end, and bare feet from the other, had seated themselves in all sorts of pretty attitudes of cheerful contemplation; and the men, who are accustomed to lie about, were doing so now with all their might — sprawling on the banks, with as much ease and variety as club-room loungers on their soft cushions, — or squatted leisurely among the green potatoes. The sight of so much happy laziness did one good to look on. Nor did the honest fellows seem to weary of this amusement. Hours passed on, and the gentlefolks (judging from our party) began to grow somewhat weary; but the finest peasantry in Europe never budged from their posts, and continued to indulge in greetings, indolence, and conversation.

When we came to the row of white tents, as usual it did not look so brilliant or imposing as it appeared from a little distance, though the scene around them was animating enough. The tents were long humble booths stretched on hoops, each with its humble streamer or ensign without, and containing, of course, articles of refreshment within. But Father Mathew has been busy among the publicans, and the consequence is that the poor fellows are now condemned for the most part to sell "tay" in place of whiskey; for the concoction of which beverage huge caldrons were smoking, in front of each hut-door, in round graves dug for the purpose and piled up with black smoking sod.

Behind this camp were the carts of the poor people, which were not allowed to penetrate into the quarter where the quality cars stood. And a little way from the huts, again, you might see (for you could scarcely hear) certain pipers executing their melodies and inviting people to dance.

Anything more lugubrious than the drone of the pipe, or the jig danced to it, or the countenances of the dancers and musicians, I never saw. Round each set of dancers the people formed a ring, in the which the figurantes and coryphées went through their operations. The toes went in and the toes went out; then there came certain mystic figures of hands across, and so forth. I never saw less grace or seemingly less enjoyment — no, not even in a quadrille. The people, however, took a great interest, and it was "Well done, Tim!" "Step out, Miss Brady!" and so forth during the dance.

Thimble-rig too obtained somewhat, though in a humble way. A ragged scoundrel — the image of Hogarth's Bad Apprentice — went bustling and shouting through the crowd with his dirty tray and thimble, and as soon as he had taken his post, stated that this was the "royal game of thimble" and called upon "gintlemin" to come forward. And then a ragged fellow would be seen to approach, with as innocent an air as he could assume, and the bystanders might remark that the second ragged fellow almost always won. Nay, he was so benevolent in many instances, as to point out to various people who had a mind to bet, under which thimble the pea actually was. Meanwhile, the first fellow was sure to be looking away and talking to some one in the crowd; but somehow it generally happened — and how

of course I can't tell — that any man who listened to the advice
of rascal No. 2, lost his money.   I believe it is so even in England.

Then you would see gentlemen with halfpenny roulette-
tables, and, again, here were a pair who came forward disinter-
estedly with a table and a pack of cards, and began playing
against each other for ten shillings a game, betting crowns as
freely as possible.

Gambling, however, must have been fatal to both of these
gentlemen, else might not one have supposed that, if they were
in the habit of winning much, they would have treated themselves to better clothes?   This, however, is the way with all
gamblers, as the reader has no doubt remarked : for, look at a
game of loo or *vingt-et-un* played in a friendly way, and where
you, and three or four others, have certainly lost three or four
pounds, — well, ask at the end of the game who has won, and
you invariably find that nobody has.   Hopkins has only covered himself ; Snooks has neither lost nor won ; Smith has won
four shillings ; and so on.   Who gets the money?   The devil
gets it, I dare say ; and so, no doubt, he has laid hold of the
money of yonder gentleman in the handsome great-coat.

But, to the shame of the stewards, be it spoken, they are extremely averse to this kind of sport ; and presently comes up
one, a stout old gentleman on a bay horse, wielding a huge
hunting-whip, at the sight of which all fly, amateurs, idlers, professional men, and all.   He is a rude customer to deal with,
that gentleman with the whip : just now he was clearing the
course, and cleared it with such a vengeance, that a whole
troop on a hedge retreated backwards into a ditch opposite,
where was rare kicking, and sprawling, and disarrangement
of petticoats, and cries of " O murther ! "   " Mother of God ! "
" I'm kilt ! " and so on.   But as soon as the horsewhip was
gone, the people clambered out of their ditch again, and were
as thick as ever on the bank.

The last instance of the exercise of the whip shall be this.
A groom rode insolently after a gentleman, calling him names,
and inviting him to fight.   This the great flagellator hearing,
rode up to the groom, lifted him gracefully off his horse into
the air, and on to the ground, and when there administered
to him a severe and merited fustigation ; after which he told
the course-keepers to drive the fellow off the course, and enjoined the latter not to appear again at his peril.

As for the races themselves, I won't pretend to say that they
were better or worse than other such amusements ; or to quarrel

with gentlemen who choose to risk their lives in manly exercise.
In the first race there was a fall : one of the gentlemen was
carried off the ground, and it was said *he was dead*. In the
second race, a horse and man went over and over each other,
and the fine young man (we had seen him five minutes before,
full of life and triumph, clearing the hurdles on his gray horse,
at the head of the race) : — in the second heat of the second
race the poor fellow missed his leap, was carried away stunned
and dying, and the bay horse won.

I was standing, during the first heat of this race, (this is the
second man the gray has killed — they ought to call him the
Pale Horse,) by half a dozen young girls from the gentleman's
village, and hundreds more of them were there, anxious for the
honor of their village, the young squire, and the gray horse.
Oh, how they hurrah'd as he rode ahead ! I saw these girls —
they might be fourteen years old — after the catastrophe.
" Well," says I, " this is a sad end to the race." " *And is it
the pink jacket or the blue has won this time?* " says one of the
girls. It was poor Mr. C——'s only epitaph : and wasn't it a
sporting answer? That girl ought to be a hurdle-racer's wife ;
and I would like, for my part, to bestow her upon the groom
who won the race.

I don't care to confess that the accident to the poor young
gentleman so thoroughly disgusted my feeling as a man and a
cockney, that I turned off the racecourse short, and hired a
horse for sixpence to carry me back to Miss Macgillicuddy. In
the evening at the inn, (let no man who values comfort go to an
Irish inn in race-time,) a blind old piper, with silvery hair and
of a most respectable, bard-like appearance, played a great deal
too much for us after dinner. He played very well, and with
very much feeling, ornamenting the airs with flourishes and variations that were very pretty indeed, and his pipe was by far the
most melodious I have heard ; but honest truth compels me to
say, that the bad pipes are execrable, and the good inferior to
a clarionet.

Next day, instead of going back to the racecourse, a car
drove me out to Muckross, where, in Mr. Herbert's beautiful
grounds, lies the prettiest little *bijou* of a ruined abbey ever seen
— a little chapel with a little chancel, a little cloister, a little
dormitory, and in the midst of the cloister a wonderful huge
yew-tree which darkens the whole place. The abbey is famous
in book and legend ; nor could two young lovers, or artists in
search of the picturesque, or picnic-parties with the cold chicken
and champagne in the distance, find a more charming place to

while away a summer's day than in the park of Mr. Herbert. But depend on it, for show-places, and the due enjoyment of scenery, that distance of cold chickens and champagne is the most pleasing perspective one can have. I would have sacrificed a mountain or two for the above, and would have pitched Mangerton into the lake for the sake of a friend with whom to enjoy the rest of the landscape.

The walk through Mr. Herbert's demesne carries you, through all sorts of beautiful avenues, by a fine house which he is building in the Elizabethan style, and from which, as from the whole road, you command the most wonderful rich views of the lake. The shore breaks into little bays, which the water washes; here and there are picturesque gray rocks to meet it, the bright grass as often, or the shrubs of every kind which bathe their roots in the lake. It was August, and the men before Turk Cottage were cutting a second crop of clover, as fine, seemingly, as a first crop elsewhere: a short walk from it brought us to a neat lodge whence issued a keeper with a key, quite willing, for the consideration of sixpence, to conduct us to Turk Waterfall.

Evergreens and other trees in their brightest livery; blue sky; roaring water, here black, and yonder foaming of a dazzling white; rocks shining in the dark places, or frowning black against the light, all the leaves and branches keeping up a perpetual waving and dancing round about the cascade: what is the use of putting down all this? A man might describe the cataract of the Serpentine in exactly the same terms, and the reader be no wiser. Suffice it to say, that the Turk cascade is even handsomer than the before-mentioned waterfall of O'Sullivan, and that a man may pass half an hour there, and look, and listen, and muse, and not even feel the want of a companion, or so much as think of the iced champagne. There is just enough of savageness in the Turk cascade to make the view *piquante*. It is not, at this season at least, by any means fierce, only wild; nor was the scene peopled by any of the rude, red-shanked figures that clustered about the trees of O'Sullivan's waterfall, — savages won't pay sixpence for the prettiest waterfall ever seen — so that this only was for the best of company.

The road hence to Killarney carries one through Muckross village, a pretty cluster of houses, where the sketcher will find abundant materials for exercising his art and puzzling his hand. There are not only noble trees, but a green common and an old water-gate to a river, lined on either side by beds of rushes and discharging itself beneath an old mill-wheel. But the old mill-wheel was perfectly idle, like most men and mill-wheels in this country; by it is a ruinous house, and a fine garden of stinging nettles; opposite it, on the common, is another ruinous house, with another garden containing the same plant; and far away are sharp ridges of purple hills, which make as pretty a landscape as the eye can see. I don't know how it is, but throughout the country the men and the landscapes seem to be the same, and one and the other seem ragged, ruined, and cheerful.

Having been employed all day (making some abominable attempts at landscape-drawing, which shall not be exhibited here), it became requisite, as the evening approached, to re-cruit an exhausted cockney stomach — which, after a very moderate portion of exercise, begins to sigh for beefsteaks in the most peremptory manner. Hard by is a fine hotel with a fine sign stretching along the road for the space of a dozen windows at least, and looking inviting enough. All the doors were open, and I walked into a great number of rooms, but the only person I saw was a woman with trinkets of arbutus, who offered me, by way of refreshment, a walking-stick or a card-rack. I suppose everybody was at the races; and an evilly-disposed person might have laid *main-basse* upon the great-coats which were there, and the silver spoons, if by any miracle such things were kept — but Britannia-metal is the favorite compo-sition in Ireland; or else iron by itself; or else iron that has been silvered over, but that takes good care to peep out at all the corners of the forks: and blessed is the traveller who has not other observations to make regarding his fork, besides the mere abrasion of the silver.

This was the last day's race, and on the next morning (Sunday), all the thousands who had crowded to the race seemed trooping to the chapels, and the streets were blue with cloaks. Walking in to prayers, and without his board, came my young friend of the thimble-rig, and presently after saun-tered in the fellow with the long coat, who had played at cards for sovereigns. I should like to hear the confession of himself and friend the next time they communicate with his reverence.

The extent of this town is very curious, and I should imagine its population to be much greater than five thousand, which was the number, according to Miss Macgillicuddy. Along the three main streets are numerous arches, down every one of which runs an alley, intersected by other alleys, and swarming with people. A stream or gutter runs commonly down these alleys, in which the pigs and children are seen paddling about. The men and women loll at their doors or windows, to enjoy the detestable prospect. I saw two pigs under a fresh-made deal staircase in one of the main streets near the Bridewell: two very well-dressed girls, with their hair in ringlets, were looking out of the parlor-window: almost all the glass in the upper rooms was of course smashed, the windows patched here and there (if the people were careful), the wood-work of the door loose, the whitewash peeling off, — and the house evidently not two years old.

By the Bridewell is a busy potato-market, picturesque to the sketcher, if not very respectable to the merchant: here were the country carts and the country cloaks, and the shrill beggarly bargains going on — a world of shrieking and gesticulating, and talk, about a pennyworth of potatoes.

All round the town miserable streets of cabins are stretched. You see people lolling at each door, women staring and combing their hair, men with their little pipes, children whose rags hang on by a miracle, idling in a gutter. Are we to set all this down to absenteeism, and pity poor injured Ireland? Is the landlord's absence the reason why the house is filthy, and Biddy lolls in the porch all day? Upon my word, I have heard people talk as if, when Pat's thatch was blown off, the landlord ought to go fetch the straw and the ladder, and mend it himself. People need not be dirty if they are ever so idle; if they are ever so poor, pigs and men need not live together. Half an hour's work, and digging a trench, might remove that filthy dunghill from that filthy window. The smoke might as well come out of the chimney as out of the door. Why should not Tim do that, instead of walking a hundred and sixty miles to a race? The priests might do much more to effect these reforms than even the landlords themselves: and I hope now that the excellent Father Mathew has succeeded in arraying his clergy to work with him in the abolition of drunkenness, they will attack the monster Dirt, with the same good-will, and surely with the same success.

CHAPTER XIII.

TRALEE — LISTOWEL — TARBERT.

I MADE the journey to Tralee next day, upon one of the famous Bianconi cars — very comfortable conveyances too, if the booking-officers would only receive as many persons as the car would hold, and not have too many on the seats. For half an hour before the car left Killarney, I observed people had taken their seats : and, let all travellers be cautious to do likewise, lest, although they have booked their places, they be requested to mount on the roof, and accommodate themselves on a band-box, or a pleasant deal trunk with a knotted rope, to prevent it from being slippery, while the corner of another box jolts against your ribs for the journey. I had put my coat on a place, and was stepping to it, when a lovely lady with great activity jumped up and pushed the coat on the roof, and not only occupied my seat, but insisted that her husband should have the next one to her. So there was nothing for it but to make a huge shouting with the book-keeper and call instantly for the taking down of my luggage, and vow my great gods that I would take a post-chaise and make the office pay : on which, I am ashamed to say, some other person was made to give up a decently comfortable seat on the roof, which I occupied, the former occupant hanging on — heaven knows where or how.

A company of young squires were on the coach, and they talked of horse-racing and hunting punctually for three hours, during which time I do believe they did not utter one single word upon any other subject. What a wonderful faculty it is ! The writers of Natural Histories, in describing the noble horse, should say he is made not only to run, to carry burdens, &c., but to be talked about. What would hundreds of thousands of dashing young fellows do with their tongues, if they had not this blessed subject to discourse on ?

As far as the country went, there was here, to be sure, not much to be said. You pass through a sad-looking, bare, undulating country, with few trees, and poor stone-hedges, and poorer crops ; nor have I yet taken in Ireland so dull a ride. About half-way between Tralee and Killarney is a wretched town, where horses are changed, and where I saw more hideous beggary than anywhere else, I think. And I was glad to get over this gloomy tract of country, and enter the capital of Kerry.

It has a handsome description in the guide-books; but, if I mistake not, the English traveller will find a stay of a couple of hours in the town quite sufficient to gratify his curiosity with respect to the place. There seems to be a great deal of poor business going on; the town thronged wtth people as usual; the shops large and not too splendid. There are two or three rows of respectable houses, and a mall, and the townspeople have the further privilege of walking in the neighboring grounds of a handsome park, which the proprietor has liberally given to their use. Tralee has a newspaper, and boasts of a couple of clubs: the one I saw was a big white house, no windows broken, and looking comfortable. But the most curious sight of the town was the chapel, with the festival held there. It was the feast of the Assumption of the Virgin, (let those who are acquainted with the calendar and the facts it commemorates say what the feast was, and when it falls,) and all the country seemed to be present on the occasion: the chapel and the large court leading to it were thronged with worshippers, such as one never sees in our country, where devotion is by no means so crowded as here. Here, in the court-yard, there were thousands of them on their knees, rosary in hand, for the most part praying, and mumbling, and casting a wistful look round as the strangers passed. In a corner was an old man groaning in the agonies of death or colic, and a woman got off her knees to ask us for charity for the unhappy old fellow. In the chapel the crowd was enormous: the priest and his people were kneeling, and bowing, and humming, and chanting, and censer-rattling; the ghostly crew being attended by a fellow that I don't remember to have seen in Continental churches, a sort of Catholic clerk, a black shadow to the parson, bowing his head when his reverence bowed, kneeling when he knelt, only three steps lower.

But we who wonder at copes and candlesticks, see nothing strange in surplices and beadles. A Turk, doubtless, would sneer equally at each, and have you to understand that the only reasonable ceremonial was that which took place at his mosque.

Whether right or wrong in point of ceremony, it was evident the heart of devotion was there: the immense dense crowd moaned and swayed, and you heard a hum of all sorts of wild ejaculations, each man praying seemingly for himself, while the service went on at the altar. The altar candles flickered red in the dark, steaming place, and every now and then from the choir you heard a sweet female voice chanting Mozart's music, which swept over the heads of the people a great deal more pure and delicious than the best incense that ever smoked out of pot.

On the chapel-floor, just at the entry, lay several people moaning, and tossing, and telling their beads. Behind the old woman was a font of holy water, up to which little children were clambering; and in the chapel-yard were several old women, with tin cans full of the same sacred fluid, with which the people, as they entered, aspersed themselves with all their might, flicking a great quantity into their faces, and making a curtsy and a prayer at the same time. "A pretty prayer, truly!" says the parson's wife. "What sad, sad, benighted superstition!" says the Independent minister's lady. Ah! ladies, great as your intelligence is, yet think, when compared with the Supreme One, what a little difference there is after all between your husbands' very best extempore oration and the poor Popish creatures'! One is just as far off Infinite Wisdom as the other: and so let us read the story of the woman and her pot of ointment, that most noble and charming of histories; which equalizes the great and the small, the wise and the poor in spirit, and shows that their merit before heaven lies *in doing their best*.

When I came out of the chapel, the old fellow on the point of death was still howling and groaning in so vehement a manner, that I heartily trust he was an impostor. and that on receiving a sixpence he went home tolerably comfortable, having secured a maintenance for that day. But it will be long before I can forget the strange, wild scene, so entirely different was it from the decent and comfortable observances of our own church.

Three cars set off together from Tralee to Tarbert: three cars full to overflowing. The vehicle before us contained nineteen persons, half a dozen being placed in the receptacle called the well, and one clinging on as if by a miracle at the bar behind. What can people want at Tarbert? I wondered; or anywhere else, indeed, that they rush about from one town to another in this inconceivable way? All the cars in all the towns seem to be thronged: people are perpetually hurrying from one dismal tumble-down town to another; and yet no business is done anywhere that I can see. The chief part of the contents of our three cars was discharged at Listowel, to which, for the greater part of the journey, the road was neither more cheerful nor picturesque than that from Killarney to Tralee. As, however, you reach Listowel, the country becomes better cultivated, the gentlemen's seats are more frequent, and the town itself, as seen from a little distance, lies very prettily on a river, which is crossed by a handsome bridge, which leads to a neat-looking square, which contains a smartish church, which is flanked by a big Roman Catholic chapel, &c. An old castle, gray and ivy-covered, stands hard by. It was one of the strongholds of the Lords of Kerry, whose burying-place (according to the information of the coachman) is seen at about a league from the town.

But pretty as Listowel is from a distance, it has, on a more intimate acquaintance, by no means the prosperous appearance which a first glance gives it. The place seemed like a scene at a country theatre, once smartly painted by the artist; but the paint has cracked in many places, the lines are worn away, and the whole piece only looks more shabby for the flaunting strokes of the brush which remain. And here, of course, came the usual crowd of idlers round the car: the epileptic idiot holding piteously out his empty tin snuff-box; the brutal idiot, in an old soldier's coat, proffering his money-box and grinning and clattering the single halfpenny it contained; the old man with no eyelids, calling upon you in the name of the Lord; the woman with a child at her hideous, wrinkled breast; the children without number. As for trade, there seemed to be none: a great Jeremy-Diddler kind of hotel stood hard by, swaggering and out-at-elbows, and six pretty girls were smiling out of a beggarly straw-bonnet shop, dressed as smartly as any gentleman's daughters of good estate. It was good, among the crowd of bustling, shrieking fellows, who were "jawing" vastly and doing nothing, to see how an English bagman, with scarce any words, laid hold of an ostler, carried him off *vi et armis* in the midst of a speech, in which the latter was going to explain his immense activity and desire to serve, pushed him into a stable, from which he issued in a twinkling, leading the ostler and a horse, and had his bag on the car and his horse off in about two minutes of time, while the natives were still shouting round about other passengers' portmanteaus.

Some time afterwards, away we rattled on our own journey to Tarbert, having a postilion on the leader, and receiving, I must say, some graceful bows from the young bonnet-makeresses. But of all the roads over which human bones were ever jolted, the first part of this from Listowel to Tarbert deserves the palm. It shook us all into headaches; it shook some nails out of the side of a box I had; it shook all the cords loose in a twinkling, and sent the baggage bumping about the passengers' shoulders. The coachman at the call of another English bagman, who was a fellow-traveller, — the postilion at the call of the coachman, descended to re-cord the baggage. The English bagman had the whole mass of trunks and bags stoutly corded and firmly fixed in a few seconds; the coachman helped him as far as his means allowed; the postilion stood by with his hands in his pockets, smoking his pipe, and never offering to stir a finger. I said to him that I was delighted to see in a youth of sixteen that extreme activity and willingness to oblige, and that I would give him a handsome remuneration for his services at the end of the journey: the young rascal grinned with all his might, understanding the satiric nature of the address perfectly well; but he did not take his hands out of his pockets for all that, until it was time to get on his horse again, and then, having carried us over the most difficult part of the journey, removed his horse and pipe, and rode away with a parting grin.

The cabins along the road were not much better than those to be seen south of Tralee, but the people were far better clothed, and indulged in several places in the luxury of pigsties. Near the prettily situated village of Ballylongford, we came in sight of the Shannon mouth; and a huge red round moon, that shone behind an old convent on the banks of the bright river, with dull green meadows between it and us, and white purple flats beyond, would be a good subject for the pencil of any artist whose wrist had not been put out of joint by the previous ten miles' journey.

The town of Tarbert, in the guide-books and topographical dictionaries, flourishes considerably. You read of its port, its corn and provision stores, &c., and of certain good hotels; for which as travellers we were looking with a laudable anxiety. The town, in fact, contains about a dozen of houses, some hundreds of cabins, and two hotels; to one of which we were driven, and a kind landlady, conducting her half-dozen guests into a snug parlor, was for our ordering refreshment immediately, — which I certainly should have done, but for the ominous whisper of a fellow in the crowd as we descended (of course a disinterested patron of the other house), who hissed into my ears, "*Ask to see the beds:*" which proposal, accordingly, I made before coming to any determination regarding supper.

The worthy landlady eluded my question several times with

great skill and good-humor, but it became at length necessary to answer it; which she did by putting on as confident an air as possible, and leading the way up stairs to a bedroom, where there was a good large comfortable bed certainly.

The only objection to the bed, however, was that it contained a sick lady, whom the hostess proposed to eject without any ceremony, saying that she was a great deal better, and going to get up that very evening. However, none of us had the heart to tyrannize over lovely woman in so painful a situation, and the hostess had the grief of seeing four out of her five guests repair across the way to " Brallaghan's " or " Gallagher's Hotel," — the name has fled from my memory, but it is the big hotel in the place; and unless the sick lady has quitted the other inn, which most likely she has done by this time, the English traveller will profit by this advice, and on arrival at Tarbert will have himself transported to " Gallagher's " at once.

The next morning a car carried us to Tarbert Point, where there is a pier not yet completed, and a Preventive station, and where the Shannon steamers touch, that ply between Kilrush and Limerick. Here lay the famous river before us, with low banks and rich pastures on either side.

CHAPTER XIV.

LIMERICK.

A CAPITAL steamer, which on this day was thronged with people, carried us for about four hours down the noble stream and landed us at Limerick quay. The character of the landscape on either side the stream is not particularly picturesque, but large, liberal and prosperous. Gentle sweeps of rich meadows and cornfields cover the banks, and some, though not too many, gentlemen's parks and plantations rise here and there. But the landscape was somehow more pleasing than if it had been merely picturesque; and, especially after coming out of that desolate county of Kerry, it was pleasant for the eye to rest upon this peaceful, rich, and generous scene. The first aspect of Limerick is very smart and pleasing: fine neat quays with considerable liveliness and bustle, a very handsome bridge (the Wellesley Bridge) before the spectator; who, after a walk through two long and flourishing streets, stops at length at one of the best inns in Ireland — the large, neat, and prosperous one kept by Mr. Cruise. Except at Youghal, and the poor fellow whom the Englishman belabored at Glengariff, Mr. Cruise is the only landlord of an inn I have had the honor to see in Ireland. I believe these gentlemen commonly (and very naturally) prefer riding with the hounds, or manly sports, to attendance on their guests; and the landladies, if they prefer to play the piano, or to have a game of cards in the parlor, only show a taste at which no one can wonder: for who can expect a lady to be troubling herself with vulgar chance-customers, or looking after Molly in the bedroom or waiter Tim in the cellar?

Now, beyond this piece of information regarding the excellence of Mr. Cruise's hotel, which every traveller knows, the writer of this doubts very much whether he has anything to say about Limerick that is worth the trouble of saying or reading. I can't attempt to describe the Shannon, only to say that on board the steamboat there was a piper and a bugler, a hundred of genteel persons coming back from donkey-riding and bathing at Kilkee, a couple of heaps of raw hides that smelt very foully, a score of women nursing children, and a lobster-vender, who vowed to me on his honor that he gave eightpence apiece for his fish, and that he had boiled them only the day before; but when I produced the Guide-book, and solemnly told him to swear upon that to the truth of his statement, the lobster-seller turned away quite abashed, and would not be brought to support his previous assertion at all. Well, this is no description of the Shannon, as you have no need to be told, and other travelling cockneys will no doubt meet neither piper nor lobster-seller, nor raw hides; nor, if they come to the inn where this is written, is it probable that they will hear, as I do this present moment, two fellows with red whiskers, and immense pomp and noise and blustering with the waiter, conclude by ordering a pint of ale between them. All that one can hope to do is, to give a sort of notion of the movement and manners of the people; pretending by no means to offer a description of places, but simply an account of what one sees in them.

So that if any traveller after staying two days in Limerick should think fit to present the reader with forty or fifty pages of dissertation upon the antiquities and history of the place, upon the state of commerce, religion, education, the public may be pretty well sure that the traveller has been at work among the guide-books, and filching extracts from the topographical and local works.

They say there are three towns to make one Limerick : there is the Irish Town on the Clare side ; the English Town with its old castle (which has sustained a deal of battering and blows from Danes, from fierce Irish kings, from English warriors who took an interest in the place, Henry Secundians, Elizabethans, Cromwellians, and *vice versâ*, Jacobites, King Williamites, — and nearly escaped being in the hands of the Robert Emmettites) ; and finally the district called Newtown-Pery. In walking through this latter tract, you are at first half led to believe that you are arrived in a second Liverpool, so tall are the warehouses and broad the quays ; so neat and trim a street of near a mile which stretches before you. But even this mile-long street does not, in a few minutes, appear to be so wealthy and prosperous as it shows at first glance ; for of the population that throng the streets, two-fifths are barefooted women, and two-fifths more ragged men : and the most part of the shops which have a grand show with them appear, when looked into, to be no better than they should be, being empty makeshift-looking places with their best goods outside.

Here, in this handsome street too, is a handsome club-house, with plenty of idlers, you may be sure, lolling at the portico ; likewise you see numerous young officers, with very tight waists and absurd brass shell-epaulettes to their little absurd frock-coats, walking the pavement — the dandies of the street. Then you behold whole troops of pear, apple, and plum-women, selling very raw, green-looking fruit, which, indeed, it is a wonder that any one should eat and live. The houses are bright red — the street is full and gay, carriages and cars in plenty go jingling by — dragoons in red are every now and then clattering up the street, and as upon every car which passes with ladies in it you are sure (I don't know how it is) to see a pretty one, the great street of Limerick is altogether a very brilliant and animated sight.

If the ladies of the place are pretty, indeed the vulgar are scarcely less so. I never saw a greater number of kind, pleasing, clever-looking faces among any set of people. There seem, however, to be two sorts of physiognomies which are common : the pleasing and somewhat melancholy one before mentioned, and a square, high-cheeked, flat-nosed physiognomy, not uncommonly accompanied by a hideous staring head of dry red hair. Except, however, in the latter case, the hair flowing loose and long is a pretty characteristic of the women of the country : many a fair one do you see at the door of the cabin, or the poor shop in the town, combing complacently that "greatest ornament of female beauty," as Mr. Rowland justly calls it.

The generality of the women here seem also much better clothed than in Kerry; and I saw many a one going barefoot, whose gown was nevertheless a good one, and whose cloak was of fine cloth. Likewise it must be remarked, that the beggars in Limerick were by no means so numerous as those in Cork, or in many small places through which I have passed. There were but five, strange to say, round the mail-coach as we went away; and, indeed, not a great number in the streets.

The belles lettres seems to be by no means so well cultivated here as in Cork. I looked in vain for a Limerick Guide-book: I saw but one good shop of books, and a little trumpery circulating library, which seemed to be provided with those immortal works of a year old — which, having been sold for half a guinea the volume at first, are suddenly found to be worth only a shilling. Among these, let me mention, with perfect resignation to the decrees of fate, the works of one Titmarsh: they were rather smartly bound by an enterprising publisher, and I looked at them in Bishop Murphy's Library at Cork, in a bookshop in the remote little town of Ennis, and elsewhere, with a melancholy tenderness. Poor flowerets of a season! (and a very short season too), let me be allowed to salute your scattered leaves with a passing sigh! . . . . Besides the bookshops, I observed in the long, best street of Limerick a half-dozen of what are called French shops, with knick-knacks, German-silver chimney-ornaments, and paltry finery. In the windows of these you saw a card with "Cigars;" in the bookshop, "Cigars;" at the grocer's, the whiskey-shop, "Cigars:" everybody sells the noxious weed, or makes believe to sell it, and I know no surer indication of a struggling, uncertain trade than that same placard of "Cigars." I went to buy some of the pretty Limerick gloves (they are chiefly made, as I have since discovered, at Cork). I think the man who sold them had a patent from the Queen, or his Excellency, or both, in his window: but, seeing a friend pass just as I entered the shop, he brushed past, and held his friend in conversation for some minutes in the street, — about the Killarney races no doubt, or the fun going on at Kilkee. I might have swept away a bagful of walnut-shells containing the flimsy gloves; but instead walked out, making him a low bow, and saying I would call next week. He said "wouldn't I wait?" and resumed his conversation; and, no doubt, by this way of doing business, is making a handsome independence. I asked one

of the ten thousand fruit-women the price of her green pears.
" Twopence apiece," she said ; and there were two little ragged
beggars standing by, who were munching the fruit. A book-
shopwoman made me pay threepence for a bottle of ink which
usually costs a penny ; a potato-woman told me that her potatoes cost fourteenpence a stone : and all these ladies treated
the stranger with a leering, wheedling servility which made
me long to box their ears, were it not that the man who lays
his hand upon a woman is an &c., whom 'twere gross flattery
to call a what-d'ye-call-'im? By the way, the man who played
Duke Aranza at Cork delivered the celebrated claptrap above
alluded to as follows : —

> " The man who lays his hand upon a woman,
>   Save in the way of kindness, is a villain,
>   Whom 'twere *a gross piece* of flattery to call a coward ; "

and looked round calmly for the applause, which deservedly
followed his new reading of the passage.

To return to the apple-women : — legions of ladies were
employed through the town upon that traffic ; there were really
thousands of them clustering upon the bridges, squatting down
in doorways and vacant sheds for temporary markets, marching and crying their sour goods in all the crowded lanes of the
city. After you get out of the Main Street the handsome part
of the town is at an end, and you suddenly find yourself in
such a labyrinth of busy swarming poverty and squalid commerce as never was seen — no, not in Saint Giles's, where
Jew and Irishman side by side exhibit their genius for dirt.
Here every house almost was a half ruin, and swarming with
people : in the cellars you looked down and saw a barrel of
herrings, which a merchant was dispensing ; or a sack of meal,
which a poor dirty woman sold to people poorer and dirtier
than herself : above was a tinman, or a shoemaker, or other
craftsman, his battered ensign at the door, and his small wares
peering through the cracked panes of his shop. As for the
ensign, as a matter of course the name is never written in
letters of the same size. You read —

or some similar signboard. High and low, in this country,
they begin things on too large a scale. They begin churches

too big and can't finish them; mills and houses too big, and are ruined before they are done; letters on signboards too big, and are up in a corner before the inscription is finished. There is something quite strange, really, in this general consistency.

Well, over James Hurley, or Pat Hanlahan, you will most likely see another board of another tradesman, with a window to the full as curious. Above Tim Carthy evidently lives another family. There are long-haired girls of fourteen at every one of the windows, and dirty children everywhere. In the cellars, look at them in dingy white nightcaps over a bowl of stirabout; in the shop, paddling up and down the ruined steps, or issuing from beneath the black counter; up above, see the girl of fourteen is tossing and dandling one of them: and a pretty tender sight it is, in the midst of this filth and wretchedness, to see the women and children together. It makes a sunshine in the dark place, and somehow half reconciles one to it. Children are everywhere. Look out of the nasty streets into the still more nasty back lanes: there they are, sprawling at every door and court, paddling in every puddle; and in about a fair proportion to every six children an old woman — a very old, bleareyed, ragged woman — who makes believe to sell something out of a basket, and is perpetually calling upon the name of the Lord. For every three ragged old women you will see two ragged old men, praying and moaning like the females. And there is no lack of young men, either, though I never could make out what they were about: they loll about the street, chiefly conversing in knots; and in every street you will be pretty sure to see a recruiting-sergeant, with gay ribbons in his cap, loitering about with an eye upon the other loiterers there. The buzz and hum and chattering of this crowd is quite inconceivable to us in England, where a crowd is generally silent. As a person with a decent coat passes, they stop in their talk and say, "God bless you for a fine gentleman!" In these crowded streets, where all are beggars, the beggary is but small: only the very old and hideous venture to ask for a penny, otherwise the competition would be too great.

As for the buildings that one lights upon every now and then in the midst of such scenes as this, they are scarce worth the trouble to examine: occasionally you come on a chapel with sham Gothic windows and a little belfry, one of the Catholic places of worship; then, placed in some quiet street, a neat-looking Dissenting meeting-house. Across the river yonder, as you issue out from the street where the preceding sketch was taken, is a handsome hospital; near it the old cathedral,

a barbarous old turreted edifice — of the fourteenth century it is
said : how different to the sumptuous elegance which characterizes the English and continental churches of the same period !
Passing by it, and walking down other streets, — black, ruinous, swarming, dark, hideous, — you come upon the barracks
and the walks of the old castle, and from it on to an old bridge,
from which the view is a fine one. On one side are the gray
bastions of the castle ; beyond them, in the midst of the broad
stream, stands a huge mill that looks like another castle ; further yet is the handsome new Wellesley Bridge, with some little
craft upon the river, and the red warehouses of the New Town
looking prosperous enough. The Irish Town stretches away
to the right ; there are pretty villas beyond it ; and on the
bridge are walking twenty-four young girls, in parties of four
and five, with their arms round each other's waists, swaying
to and fro, and singing or chattering, as happy as if they had
shoes to their feet. Yonder you see a dozen pair of red legs
glittering in the water, their owners being employed in washing their own or other people's rags.

The Guide-book mentions that one of the aboriginal forests
of the country is to be seen at a few miles from Limerick, and
thinking that an aboriginal forest would be a huge discovery,
and form an instructive and delightful feature of the present
work, I hired a car in order to visit the same, and pleased myself with visions of gigantic oaks, Druids, Norma, wildernesses
and awful gloom, which would fill the soul with horror. The
romance of the place was heightened by a fact stated by the
carman, viz. that until late years robberies were very frequent
about the wood ; the inhabitants of the district being a wild,
lawless race. Moreover, there are numerous castles round
about, — and for what can a man wish more than robbers,
castles, and an aboriginal wood?

The way to these wonderful sights lies through the undulating grounds which border the Shannon ; and though the view is
by no means a fine one, I know few that are pleasanter than the
sight of these rich, golden, peaceful plains, with the full harvest
waving on them and just ready for the sickle. The hay harvest
was likewise just being concluded, and the air loaded with the
rich odor of the hay. Above the trees, to your left, you saw
the mast of a ship, perhaps moving along, and every now and
then caught a glimpse of the Shannon, and the low grounds
and plantations of the opposite county of Limerick. Not an
unpleasant addition to the landscape, too, was a sight which I
do not remember to have witnessed often in this country — that

of several small and decent farm-houses, with their stacks and sheds and stables, giving an air of neatness and plenty that the poor cabin with its potato-patch does not present. Is it on account of the small farms that the land seems richer and better cultivated here than in most other parts of the country? Some of the houses in the midst of the warm summer landscape had a strange appearance, for it is often the fashion to whitewash the roofs of the houses, leaving the slates of the walls of their natural color: hence, and in the evening especially, contrasting with the purple sky, the house-tops often looked as if they were covered with snow.

According to the Guide-book's promise, the castles began soon to appear: at one point we could see three of these ancient mansions in a line, each seemingly with its little grove of old trees, in the midst of the bare but fertile country. By this time, too, we had got into a road so abominably bad and rocky, that I began to believe more and more with regard to the splendor of the aboriginal forest, which must be most aboriginal and ferocious indeed when approached by such a savage path. After travelling through a couple of lines of wall with plantations on either side, I at length became impatient as to the forest, and, much to my disappointment, was told this was it. For the fact is, that though the forest has always been there, the trees have not, the proprietors cutting them regularly when grown to no great height, and the monarchs of the woods which I saw round about would scarcely have afforded timber for a bed-post. Nor did any robbers make their appearance in this wilderness: with which disappointment, however, I was more willing to put up than with the former one.

But if the wood and the robbers did not come up to my romantic notions, the old Castle of Bunratty fully answered them, and indeed should be made the scene of a romance, in three volumes at least.

"It is a huge, square tower, with four smaller ones at each angle; and you mount to the entrance by a steep flight of steps, being commanded all the way by the cross-bows of two of the Lord De Clare's retainers, the points of whose weapons may be seen lying upon the ledge of the little narrow *meurtrière* on each side of the gate. A venerable seneschal, with the keys of office, presently opens the little back postern, and you are admitted to the great hall — a noble chamber, *pardi!* some seventy feet in length and thirty high. 'Tis hung round with a thousand trophies of war and chase, — the golden helmet and spear of the Irish king, the long yellow mantle he wore, and the

huge brooch that bound it. Hugo De Clare slew him before
the castle in 1305, when he and his kernes attacked it. Less
successful in 1314, the gallant Hugo saw his village of Bunratty burned round his tower by the son of the slaughtered
O'Neil; and, sallying out to avenge the insult, was brought
back — a corpse! Ah! what was the pang that shot through
the fair bosom of the *Lady Adela* when she knew that 'twas the
hand of *Redmond O'Neil* sped the shaft which slew her sire!

" You listen to this sad story, reposing on an oaken settle
(covered with deer's-skin taken in the aboriginal forest of Carclow hard by) placed at the enormous hall-fire. Here sits
Thonom an Diaoul, ' Dark Thomas,' the blind harper of the
race of De Clare, who loves to tell the deeds of the lordly family.
' Penetrating in disguise,' he continues, ' into the castle, Redmond of the golden locks sought an interview with the Lily of
Bunratty; but she screamed when she saw him under the disguise of the gleeman, and said, " My father's blood is in the
hall! " At this, up started fierce Sir Ranulph. " Ho, Blud-
yer! " he cried to his squire, " call me the hangman and Father
John; seize me, vassals, yon villain in gleeman's guise, and
hang him on the gallows on the tower! " '

" ' Will it please ye walk to the roof of the old castle and see
the beam on which the lords of the place execute the refractory?'
' Nay, marry,' say you, ' by my spurs of knighthood, I have
seen hanging enough in merry England, and care not to see the
gibbets of Irish kernes.' The harper would have taken fire at
this speech reflecting on his country; but luckily here Gulph,
your English squire entered from the pantler (with whom he
had been holding a parley), and brought a manchet of bread,
and bade ye, in the Lord De Clare's name, crush a cup of
Ypocras, well spiced, *pardi*, and by the fair hands of the Lady
Adela.

" ' The Lady Adela! ' say you, starting up in amaze. ' Is
not this the year of grace 1600, and lived she not three hundred
years syne? '

" ' Yes, Sir Knight, but Bunratty tower hath *another Lily*:
will it please you see your chamber? '

" So saying, the seneschal leads you up a winding stair in
one of the turrets, past one little dark chamber and another,
without a fireplace, without rushes (how different from the
stately houses of Nonsuch or Audley End!), and, leading you
through another vast chamber above the baronial hall, similar
in size, but decorated with tapestries and rude carvings, you
pass the little chapel (' Marry,' says the steward, ' many would

it not hold, and many do not come!') until at last you are
located in the little cell appropriated to you. Some rude
attempts have been made to render it fitting for the stranger;
but, though more neatly arranged than the hundred other little
chambers which the castle contains, in sooth 'tis scarce fitted
for the serving-man, much more for Sir Reginald, the English
knight.

"While you are looking at a bouquet of flowers, which lies on
the settle — magnolias, geraniums, the blue flowers of the cactus,
and in the midst of the bouquet, *one lily*; whilst you wonder
whose fair hands could have culled the flowers — hark! the
horns are blowing at the drawbridge and the warder lets the
portcullis down. You rush to your window, a stalwart knight
rides over the gate, the hoofs of his black courser clanging upon
the planks. A host of wild retainers wait round about him:
see, four of them carry a stag, that hath been slain no doubt in
the aboriginal forest of Carclow. 'By my fay!' say you, ''tis
a stag of ten.'

"But who is that yonder on the gray palfrey, conversing so
prettily, and holding the sportive animal with so light a rein?
— a light green riding-habit and ruff, a little hat with a green
plume — sure it must be a lady, and a fair one. She looks up.
O blessed Mother of Heaven, that look! those eyes that smile,
those sunny golden ringlets! It is — *it is* the Lady Adela: the
Lily of Bunrat . . ."

If the reader cannot finish the other two volumes for him or
herself, he or she never deserves to have a novel from a circulating library again: for my part, I will take my affidavit the
English knight will marry the Lily at the end of the third
volume, having previously slain the other suitor at one of the
multifarious sieges of Limerick. And I beg to say that the
historical part of this romance has been extracted carefully
from the Guide-book: the topographical and descriptive portion
being studied on the spot. A policeman shows you over it,
halls, chapels, galleries, gibbets and all. The huge old tower
was, until late years, inhabited by the family of the proprietor,
who built himself a house in the midst of it: but he has since
built another in the park opposite, and half a dozen " Peelers,"
with a commodity of wives and children, now inhabit Bunratty.
On the gate where we entered were numerous placards offering
rewards for the apprehension of various country offenders; and
a turnpike, a bridge, and a quay have sprung up from the place
which Red Redmond (or anybody else) burned.

On our road to Galway the next day, we were carried once more by the old tower, and for a considerable distance along the fertile banks of the Fergus lake, and a river which pours itself into the Shannon. The first town we come to is Castle Clare, which lies conveniently on the river, with a castle, a good bridge, and many quays and warehouses, near which a small ship or two were lying. The place was once the chief town of the county, but is wretched and ruinous now, being made up for the most part of miserable thatched cots, round which you see the usual dusky population. The drive hence to Ennis lies through a country which is by no means so pleasant as that rich one we have passed through, being succeeded " by that craggy, bleak, pastoral district which occupies so large a portion of the limestone district of Clare." Ennis, likewise, stands upon the Fergus — a busy little narrow-streeted, foreign-looking town, approached by half a mile of thatched cots, in which I am not ashamed to confess that I saw some as pretty faces as over any half-mile of country I ever travelled in my life.

A great light of the Catholic Church, who was of late a candlestick in our own communion, was on the coach with us, reading devoutly out of a breviary on many occasions along the road. A crowd of black coats and heads, with that indescribable look which belongs to the Catholic clergy, were evidently on the look-out for the coach; and as it stopped, one of them came up to me with a low bow, and asked if I was the Honorable and Reverend Mr. S——? How I wish I had answered him I was! It would have been a grand scene. The respect paid to this gentleman's descent is quite absurd: the papers bandy his title about with pleased emphasis — the Galway paper calls him the *very* reverend. There is something in the love for rank almost childish: witness the adoration of George IV.; the pompous joy with which John Tuam records his correspondence with a great man; the continual My-Lording of the Bishops, the Right-Honorabling of Mr. O'Connell — which title his party papers delight on all occasions to give him — nay, the delight of that great man himself when first he attained the dignity: he figured in his robes in the most good-humored simple delight at having them, and went to church forthwith in them; as if such a man wanted a title before his name.

At Ennis, as well as everywhere else in Ireland, there were of course the regular number of swaggering-looking buckeens and shabby-genteel idlers to watch the arrival of the mail-coach. A poor old idiot, with his gray hair tied up in bows, and with a ribbon behind, thrust out a very fair soft hand with taper fingers, and told me, nodding his head very wistfully, that he had no father nor mother: upon which score he got a penny. Nor did the other beggars round the carriage who got none seem to grudge the poor fellow's good fortune. I think when one poor wretch has a piece of luck, the others seem glad here: and they promise to pray for you just the same if you give as if you refuse.

The town was swarming with people; the little dark streets, which twist about in all directions, being full of cheap merchandise and its venders. Whether there are many buyers, I can't say. This is written opposite the market-place in Galway, where I have watched a stall a hundred times in the course of the last three hours and seen no money taken: but at every place I come to, I can't help wondering at the numbers; it seems market-day everywhere — apples, pigs, and potatoes being sold all over the kingdom. There seem to be some good shops in those narrow streets; among others, a decent little library, where I bought, for eighteenpence, six volumes of works strictly Irish, that will serve for a half-hour's gossip on the next rainy day.

The road hence to Gort carried us at first by some dismal, lonely-looking, reedy lakes, through a melancholy country; an open village standing here and there, with a big chapel in the midst of it, almost always unfinished in some point or other. Crossing at a bridge near a place called Tubbor, the coachman told us we were in the famous county of Galway, which all readers of novels admire in the warlike works of Maxwell and Lever; and, dismal as the country had been in Clare, I think on the northern side of the bridge it was dismaller still — the stones not only appearing in the character of hedges, but strewing over whole fields, in which sheep were browsing as well as they could.

We rode for miles through this stony, dismal district, seeing more lakes now and anon, with fellows spearing eels in the midst. Then we passed the plantations of Lord Gort's Castle of Loughcooter, and presently came to the town which bears his name, or *vice versâ*. It is a regularly-built little place, with a square and street: but it looked as if it wondered how the deuce it got into the midst of such a desolate country, and seemed to *bore* itself there considerably. It had nothing to do, and no society.

A short time before arriving at Oranmore, one has glimpses of the sea, which comes opportunely to relieve the dulness of the land. Between Gort and that place we passed through little but the most woful country, in the midst of which was a village, where a horse-fair was held, and where (upon the word of the coachman) all the bad horses of the country were to be seen. The man was commissioned, no doubt, to buy for his employers, for two or three merchants were on the look-out for him, and trotted out their cattle by the side of the coach. A very good, neat-looking, smart-trotting chestnut horse, of seven years old, was offered by the owner for 8*l.* ; a neat brown mare for 10*l.*, and a better (as I presume) for 14*l.* ; but all *looked* very respectable, and I have the coachman's word for it that they were good serviceable horses. Oranmore, with an old castle in the midst of the village, woods, and park-plantations round about, and the bay beyond it, has a pretty and romantic look ; and the drive, of about four miles thence to Galway, is the most picturesque part perhaps of the fifty miles' ride from Limerick. The road is tolerably wooded. You see the town itself, with its huge old church-tower, stretching along the bay, " backed by hills linking into the long chain of mountains which stretch across Connemara and the Joyce country." A suburb of cots that seems almost endless has, however, an end at last among the houses of the town ; and a little fleet of a couple of hundred fishing-boats was manœuvring in the bright waters of the bay.

CHAPTER XV.

GALWAY — " KILROY'S HOTEL " — GALWAY NIGHTS' ENTERTAIN-
MENTS — FIRST NIGHT : AN EVENING WITH CAPTAIN FREENY.

WHEN it is stated that, throughout the town of Galway, you cannot get a cigar which costs more than twopence, Londoners may imagine the strangeness and remoteness of the place. The rain poured down for two days after our arrival at " Kilroy's Hotel." An umbrella under such circumstances is a poor resource : self-contemplation is far more amusing ; especially smoking, and a game at cards, if any one will be so good as to play.

But there was no one in the hotel coffee-room who was inclined for the sport. The company there, on the day of our arrival, consisted of two coach-passengers, — a Frenchman

who came from Sligo, and ordered mutton-chops and *fraid
potatoes* for dinner by himself, a turbot which cost two shillings, and in Billingsgate would have been worth a guinea,
and a couple of native or inhabitant bachelors, who frequented
the *table-d'hôte.*

By the way, besides these there were at dinner two turkeys
(so that Mr. Kilroy's two-shilling ordinary was by no means
ill supplied) ; and, as a stranger, I had the honor of carving
these animals, which were dispensed in rather a singular way.
There are, as it is generally known, to two turkeys four wings.
Of the four passengers, one ate no turkey, one had a pinion,
another the remaining part of the wing, and the fourth gentleman took the other three wings for his share.   Does everybody
in Galway eat three wings when there are two turkeys for dinner?   One has heard wonders of the country, — the dashing,
daring, duelling, desperate, rollicking, whiskey-drinking people :
but this wonder beats all.   When I asked the Galway turki-
phagus (there is no other word, for Turkey was invented long
after Greece) " if he would take a third wing?" with a peculiar
satiric accent on the words *third wing*, which cannot be expressed
in writing, but which the occasion fully merited, I thought perhaps that, following the custom of the country, where everybody,
according to Maxwell and Lever, challenges everybody else, —
I thought the Galwagian would call me out ; but no such thing.
He only said, "If you plase, sir," in the blandest way in the
world ; and gobbled up the limb in a twinkling.

As an encouragement, too, for persons meditating that
important change of condition, the gentleman was a teetotal-
er : he took but one glass of water to that intolerable deal of
bubblyjock.   Galway must be very much changed since the
days when Maxwell and Lever knew it.   Three turkey-wings
and a glass of water !   But the man cannot be the representative of a class, that is clear : it is physically and arithmetically
impossible.   They can't *all* eat three wings of two turkeys at
dinner ; the turkeys could not stand it, let alone the men.   These
wings must have been " non usitatæ (nec tenues) pennæ."   But
no more of these flights ; let us come to sober realities.

The fact is, that when the rain is pouring down in the streets
the traveller has little else to remark except these peculiarities
of his fellow-travellers and inn-sojourners ; and, lest one should
be led into further personalities, it is best to quit that water-
drinking gormandizer at once, and retiring to a private apartment, to devote one's self to quiet observation and the acquisition
of knowledge, either by looking out of the window and examin-

ing mankind, or by perusing books, and so living with past heroes and ages.

As for the knowledge to be had by looking out of window, it is this evening not much. A great, wide, blank, bleak, water-whipped square lies before the bedroom window; at the opposite side of which is to be seen the opposition hotel, looking even more bleak and cheerless than that over which Mr. Kilroy presides. Large dismal warehouses and private houses form three sides of the square; and in the midst is a bare pleasure-ground surrounded by a growth of gaunt iron-railings, the only plants seemingly in the place. Three triangular edifices that look somewhat like gibbets stand in the paved part of the square, but the victims that are consigned to their fate under these triangles are only potatoes, which are weighed there; and, in spite of the torrents of rain, a crowd of barefooted, red-pet-ticoated women, and men in gray coats and flower-pot hats, are pursuing their little bargains with the utmost calmness. The rain seems to make no impression on the males; nor do the women guard against it more than by flinging a petticoat over their heads, and so stand bargaining and chattering in Irish, their figures indefinitely reflected in the shining, varnished pave-ment. Donkeys and pony-carts innumerable stand around, similarly reflected; and in the baskets upon these vehicles you see shoals of herrings lying. After a short space this prospect becomes somewhat tedious, and one looks to other sources of consolation.

The eighteenpennyworth of little books purchased at Ennis in the morning came here most agreeably to my aid; and indeed they afford many a pleasant hour's reading. Like the "Biblio-thèque Grise," which one sees in the French cottages in the provinces, and the German "Volksbücher," both of which contain stores of old legends that are still treasured in the country, these yellow-covered books are prepared for the people chiefly; and have been sold for many long years before the march of knowledge began to banish Fancy out of the world, and gave us, in place of the old fairy tales, Penny Magazines and similar wholesome works. Where are the little harlequin-backed story-books that used to be read by children in Eng-land some thirty years ago? Where such authentic narratives as "Captain Bruce's Travels," "The Dreadful Adventures of Sawney Bean," &c., which were commonly supplied to the little boys at school by the same old lady who sold oranges and alycompayne? — they are all gone out of the world, and replaced by such books as "Conversations on Chemistry,"

"The Little Geologist," "Peter Parley's Tales about the Binomial Theorem," and the like. The world will be a dull world some hundreds of years hence, when Fancy shall be dead, and ruthless Science (that has no more bowels than a steam-engine) has killed her.

It is a comfort, meanwhile, to come on occasions on some of the good old stories and biographies. These books were evidently written before the useful had attained its present detestable popularity. There is nothing useful *here*, that's certain: and a man will be puzzled to extract a precise moral out of the "Adventures of Mr. James Freeny;" or out of the legends in the "Hibernian Tales," or out of the lamentable tragedy of the "Battle of Aughrim," writ in most doleful Anglo-Irish verse. But are we to reject all things that have not a moral tacked to them? "Is there any moral shut within the bosom of the rose?" And yet, as the same noble poet sings (giving a smart slap to the utility people the while), "useful applications lie in art and nature," and every man may find a moral suited to his mind in them; or, if not a moral, an occasion for moralizing.

Honest Freeny's adventures (let us begin with history and historic tragedy, and leave fancy for future consideration), if they have a moral, have that dubious one which the poet admits may be elicited from a rose; and which every man may select according to his mind. And surely this is a far better and more comfortable system of moralizing than that in the fable-books, where you are obliged to accept the story with the inevitable moral corollary that *will* stick close to it.

Whereas, in Freeny's life, one man may see the evil of drinking, another the harm of horse-racing, another the danger attendant on early marriage, a fourth the exceeding inconvenience as well as hazard of the heroic highwayman's life — which a certain Ainsworth, in company with a certain Cruikshank, has represented as so poetic and brilliant, so prodigal of delightful adventure, so adorned with champagne, gold-lace, and brocade.

And the best part of worthy Freeny's tale is the noble naïveté and simplicity of the hero as he recounts his own adventures, and the utter unconsciousness that he is narrating anything wonderful. It is the way of all great men, who recite their great actions modestly, and as if they were matters of course; as indeed to them they are. A common tyro, having perpetrated a great deed, would be amazed and flurried at his own action; whereas I make no doubt the Duke of Wellington, after a great victory, took his tea and went to bed just as quietly as he would after a dull debate in the House of Lords. And so with Freeny, — his great and charming characteristic is grave simplicity : he does his work ; he knows his danger as well as another ; but he goes through his fearful duty quite quietly and easily, and not with the least air of bravado, or the smallest notion that he is doing anything uncommon.

It is related of Carter, the Lion-King, that when he was a boy, and exceedingly fond of gingerbread-nuts, a relation gave him a parcel of those delicious cakes, which the child put in his pocket just as he was called on to go into a cage with a very large and roaring lion. He had to put his head into the forest-monarch's jaws, and leave it there for a considerable time, to the delight of thousands : as is even now the case ; and the interest was so much the greater, as the child was exceedingly innocent, rosy-cheeked, and pretty. To have seen that little flaxen head bitten off by the lion would have been a far more pathetic spectacle than that of the decapitation of some gray-bearded old unromantic keeper, who had served out raw meat and stirred up the animals with a pole any time these twenty years : and the interest rose in consequence.

While the little darling's head was thus enjawed, what was the astonishment of everybody to see him put his hand into his little pocket, take out a paper — from the paper a gingerbread-nut — pop that gingerbread-nut into the lion's mouth, then into his own, and so finish at least two-pennyworth of nuts !

The excitement was delirious : the ladies, when he came out of chancery, were for doing what the lion had not done, and eating him up — with kisses. And the only remark the young hero made was, " Uncle, them nuts wasn't so crisp as them I had t'other day." He never thought of the danger, — he only thought of the nuts.

Thus it is with FREENY. It is fine to mark his bravery, and to see how he cracks his simple philosophic nuts in the jaws of innumerable lions.

At the commencement of the last century, honest Freeny's father was house-steward in the family of Joseph Robbins, Esq., of Ballyduff; and, marrying Alice Phelan, a maid-servant in the same family, had issue JAMES, the celebrated Irish hero. At a proper age James was put to school ; but being a nimble, active lad, and his father's mistress taking a fancy to him, he was presently brought to Ballyduff, where she had a private tutor to instruct him during the time which he could spare from his professional duty, which was that of pantry-boy in Mr. Robbins's establishment. At an early age he began to

neglect his duty; and although his father, at the excellent Mrs.
Robbins's suggestion, corrected him very severely, the bent of
his genius was not to be warped by the rod, and he attended
" all the little country dances, diversions and meetings, and
became what is called a good dancer; his own natural inclinations hurrying him" (as he finely says) "into the contrary
diversions."

He was scarce twenty years old when he married (a frightful
proof of the wicked recklessness of his former courses), and
set up in trade in Waterford; where, however, matters went
so ill with him, that he was speedily without money, and 50*l.* in
debt. He had, he says, not any way of paying the debt, except
by selling his furniture or his *riding-mare*, to both of which
measures he was averse: for where is the gentleman in Ireland
that can do without a horse to ride? Mr. Freeny and his
riding-mare became soon famous, insomuch that a thief in gaol
warned the magistrates of Kilkenny to beware of a *one-eyed
man with a mare*.

These unhappy circumstances sent him on the highway to
seek a maintenance, and his first exploit was to rob a gentleman
of fifty pounds; then he attacked another, against whom he
" had *a secret disgust*, because this gentleman had prevented his
former master from giving him a suit of clothes!"

Urged by a noble resentment against this gentleman, Mr.
Freeny, in company with a friend by the name of Reddy, robbed
the gentleman's house, taking therein 70*l.* in money, which was
honorably divided among the captors.

" We then," continues Mr. Freeny, " quitted the house with
the booty, and came to Thomastown; but not knowing how to
dispose of the plate, left it with Reddy, who said he had a friend
from whom he would get cash for it. In some time afterwards I asked him for the dividend of the cash he got for the
plate, but all the satisfaction he gave me was, that it was lost,
which occasioned me *to have my own opinion of him*."

Mr. Freeny then robbed Sir William Fownes' servant of 14*l.*,
in such an artful manner that everybody believed the servant
had himself secreted the money; and no doubt the rascal was
turned adrift, and starved in consequence — a truly comic incident, and one that could be used, so as to provoke a great
deal of laughter, in an historical work of which our champion
should be the hero.

The next enterprise of importance is that against the house
of Colonel Palliser, which Freeny thus picturesquely describes.
Coming with one of his spies close up to the house, Mr. Freeny

watched the Colonel lighted to bed by a servant; and thus, as he cleverly says, could judge " of the room the Colonel lay in."

" Some time afterwards," says Freeny, " I observed a light up stairs, by which I judged the servants were going to bed, and soon after observed that the candles were all quenched, by which I assured myself they were all gone to bed. I then came back to where the men were, and appointed Bulger, Motley, and Commons to go in along with me ; but Commons answered that he never had been in any house before where there were arms : upon which I asked the coward what business he had there, and swore I would as soon shoot him as look at him, and at the same time cocked a pistol to his breast ; but the rest of the men prevailed upon me to leave him at the back of the house, where he might run away when he thought proper.

" I then asked Grace where did he choose to be posted : he answered ' that he would go where I pleased to order him,' for which I thanked him. We then immediately came up to the house, lighted our candles, put Houlahan at the back of the house to prevent any person from coming out that way, and placed Hacket on my mare, well armed, at the front; and I then broke one of the windows with a sledge, whereupon Bulger, Motley, Grace, and I got in ; upon which I ordered Motley and Grace to go up stairs, and Bulger and I would stay below, where we thought the greatest danger would be ; but I immediately, upon second consideration, for fear Motley or Grace should be daunted, desired Bulger to go up with them, and when he had fixed matters above, to come down, as I judged the Colonel lay below. I then went to the room where the Colonel was, and burst open the door ; upon which he said, ' Odds-wounds ! who's there?' to which I answered, ' A friend, sir ;' upon which he said, ' You lie ! by G—d, you are no friend of mine ! ' I then said that I was, and his relation also, and that if he viewed me close he would know me, and begged of him not to be angry : upon which I immediately seized a bullet-gun and case of pistols, which I observed hanging up in his room. I then quitted his room, and walked round the lower part of the house, thinking to meet some of the servants, *whom* I thought would strive to make their escape from the men who were above, and meeting none of them, I immediately returned to the Colonel's room ; where I no sooner entered than he desired me to go out for a villain, and asked why I bred such disturbance in his house at that time of night. At the same time I snatched his breeches from under his head, wherein I got a small purse of gold, and said that abuse was not fit treatment for me who was his relation, and that it would hinder me of calling to see him again. I then demanded the key of his desk which stood in his room; he answered he had no key; upon which I said I had a very good key; at the same time giving it a stroke with the sledge, which burst it open, wherein I got a purse of ninety guineas, a four-pound piece, two moidores, some small gold, and a large glove with twenty-eight guineas in silver.

" By this time Bulger and Motley came down stairs to me, after rifling the house above. We then observed a closet inside his room, which we soon entered, and got therein a basket wherein there was plate to the value of three hundred pounds."

And so they took leave of Colonel Palliser, and rode away with their earnings.

The story, as here narrated, has that simplicity which is beyond the reach of all except the very highest art; and it is not high art certainly which Mr. Freeny can be said to possess, but a noble nature rather, which leads him thus grandly to describe scenes wherein he acted a great part. With what a gallant determination does he inform the coward Commons that he would shoot him " *as soon as look at him ;*" and how dreadful he must have looked (with his one eye) as he uttered that sentiment! But he left him, he says with a grim humor, at the back of the house, " where he might run away when he thought proper." The Duke of Wellington must have read Mr. Freeny's history in his youth (his Grace's birthplace is not far from the scene of the other gallant Irishman's exploit), for the Duke acted in precisely a similar way by a Belgian Colonel at Waterloo.

It must be painful to great and successful commanders to think how their gallant comrades and lieutenants, partners of their toil, their feelings, and their fame, are separated from them by time, by death, by estrangement — nay, sometimes by treason. Commons is off, disappearing noiseless into the deep night, whilst his comrades perform the work of danger; and Bulger, — Bulger, who in the above scene acts so gallant a part, and in whom Mr. Freeny places so much confidence — actually went away to England, carrying off " some plate, some shirts, a gold watch, and a diamond ring " of the Captain's ; and, though he returned to his native country, the valuables did not return with him, on which the Captain swore he would blow his brains out. As for poor Grace, he was hanged, much to his leader's sorrow, who says of him that he was " the faithfullest of his spies." Motley was sent to Naas gaol for the very robbery : and though Captain Freeny does not mention his ultimate fate, 'tis probable he was hanged too. Indeed, the warrior's life is a hard one; and over misfortunes like these the feeling heart cannot but sigh.

But, putting out of the question the conduct and fate of the Captain's associates, let us look to his own behavior as a leader. It is impossible not to admire his serenity, his dexterity, that dashing impetuosity in the moment of action and that aquiline *coup-d'œil* which belong to but few generals. He it is who leads the assault, smashing in the window with a sledge ; he bursts open the Colonel's door, who says (naturally enough), " Odds-wounds ! who's there ? " " A friend, sir," says Freeny. " You lie ! by G–d, you are no friend of mine ! " roars the military blasphemer. " I then said that I was, *and his relation also*, and that if he viewed me close he would know me, and begged of him not to be angry : *upon which I immediately seized* a brace of pistols which I observed hanging up in his room." That is something like presence of mind : none of your brutal braggadocio work, but neat, wary — nay, sportive bearing in the face of danger. And again, on the second visit to the Colonel's room, when the latter bids him " go out for a villain, and not breed a disturbance," what reply makes Freeny ? " *At the same time I snatched his breeches* from under his head." A common man would never have thought of looking for them in such a place at all. The difficulty about the key he resolves in quite an Alexandrian manner ; and from the specimen we already have had of the Colonel's style of speaking, we may fancy how ferociously he lay in bed and swore, after Captain Freeny and his friends had disappeared with the ninety guineas, the moidores, the four-pound piece, and the glove with twenty-eight guineas in silver.

As for the plate, he hid it in a wood : and then, being out of danger, he sat down and paid everybody his deserts. By the way, what a strange difference of opinion is there about a man's *deserts !* Here sits Captain Freeny with a company of gentlemen, and awards them a handsome sum of money for an action which other people would have remunerated with a halter. Which are right? perhaps both : but at any rate it will be admitted that the Captain takes the humane view of the question.

The greatest enemy Captain Freeny had was Counsellor Robbins, a son of his old patron, and one of the most determined thief-pursuers the country ever knew. But though

he was untiring in his efforts to capture (and of course to hang)
Mr. Freeny, and though the latter was strongly urged by his
friends to blow the Counsellor's brains out: yet, to his immortal honor it is said, he refused that temptation, agreeable
as it was, declaring that he had eaten too much of that family's
bread ever to take the life of one of them, and being besides
quite aware that the Counsellor was only acting against him in
a public capacity.   He respected him, in fact, like an honorable though terrible adversary.

How deep a stratagem inventor the Counsellor was may be
gathered from the following narration of one of his plans : —

"Counsellor Robbins finding his brother had not got intelligence that was sufficient to carry any reasonable foundation for
apprehending us, walked out as if merely for exercise, till he
met with a person whom he thought he could confide in, and
desired the person to meet him at a private place appointed for
that purpose, which they did ; and he told that person he had a
very good opinion of him, from the character received from his
father of him, and from his own knowledge of him, and hoped
that the person would then show him that such opinion was not
ill founded.   The person assuring the Counsellor he would do
all in his power to serve and oblige him, the Counsellor told
him how greatly he was concerned to hear the scandalous character that part of the country (which had formerly been an
honest one) had lately fallen into ; that it was said that a gang
of robbers who disturbed the country lived thereabouts.   The
person told him he was afraid what he said was too true ; and,
on being asked whom he suspected, he named the same four
persons Mr. Robbins had, but said he dare not, for fear of being
murdered, be too inquisitive, and therefore could not say anything
material.   The Counsellor asked him if he knew where there was
any private ale to be sold ; and he said Moll Burke, who lived
near the end of Mr. Robbins's avenue, had a barrel or half a
barrel.   The Counsellor then gave the person a moidore, and
desired him to go to Thomastown and buy two or three gallons
of whiskey, and bring it to Moll Burke's, and invite as many as
he suspected to be either principals or accessories to take a
drink, and make them drink very heartily, and when he found
they were fuddled, and not sooner, to tell some of the hastiest
that some other had said some bad things of them, so as to
provoke them to abuse and quarrel with each other ; and then,
probably in their liquor and passion, they might make some
discoveries of each other, as may enable the Counsellor to get
some one of the gang to discover and accuse the rest.

"The person accordingly got the whiskey and invited a good many to drink; but the Counsellor being then at his brother's, a few only went to Moll Burke's, the rest being afraid to venture while the Counsellor was in the neighborhood: among those who met there was one Moll Brophy, the wife of Mr. Robbins's smith, and one Edmund or Edward Stapleton, otherwise Gaul, who lived thereabouts; and when they had drank plentifully, the Counsellor's spy told Moll Brophy that Gaul had said she had gone astray with some persons or other: she then abused Gaul, and told him he was one of Freeny's accomplices, for that he, Gaul, had told her he had seen Colonel Palliser's watch with Freeny, and that Freeny had told him, Gaul, that John Welsh and the two Graces had been with him at the robbery.

"The company on their quarrel broke up, and the next morning the spy met the Counsellor at the place appointed, at a distance from Mr. Robbins's house, to prevent suspicion, and there told the Counsellor what intelligence he had got. The Counsellor not being then a justice of the peace, got his brother to send for Moll Brophy to be examined; but when she came, she refused to be sworn or to give any evidence, and thereupon the Counsellor had her tied and put on a car, in order to be carried to gaol on a mittimus from Mr. Robbins, for refusing to give evidence on behalf of the Crown. When she found she would really be sent to gaol, she submitted to be sworn, and the Counsellor drew from her what she had said the night before, and something further, and desired her not to tell anybody what she had sworn."

But if the Counsellor was acute, were there not others as clever as he? For when, in consequence of the information of Mrs. Brophy, some gentlemen who had been engaged in the burglarious enterprises in which Mr. Freeny obtained so much honor were seized and tried, Freeny came forward with the best of arguments in their favor. Indeed, it is fine to see these two great spirits matched one against the other, — the Counsellor, with all the regular force of the country to back him, — the Highway General, with but the wild resources of his gallant genius, and with cunning and bravery for his chief allies.

"I lay by for a considerable time after, and concluded within myself to do no more mischief till after the assizes, when I would hear how it went with the men who were then in confinement. Some time before the assizes Counsellor Robbins came to Ballyduff, and told his brother that he believed Anderson and Welsh were guilty, and also said he would endeavor to have them both hanged : of which I was informed.

" Soon after, I went to the house of one George Roberts, who asked me if I had any regard for those fellows who were then confined (meaning Anderson and Welsh). I told him I had a regard for one of them : upon which he said he had a friend who was a man of power and interest, — that he would save either of them, provided I would give him five guineas. I told him I would give him ten, and the first gold watch I could get ; whereupon he said that it was of no use to speak to his friend without the money or value, for that he was a mercenary man : on which I told Roberts I had not so much money at that time, but that I would give him my watch as a pledge to give his friend. I then gave him my watch, and desired him to engage that I would pay the money which I promised to pay, or give value for it in plate, in two or three nights after ; upon which he engaged that his friend would act the needful. Then we appointed a night to meet, and we accordingly met ; and Roberts told me that his friend agreed to save Anderson and Welsh from the gallows ; whereupon I gave him a plate tankard, value 10l., a large ladle, value 4l., with some tablespoons. The assizes of Kilkenny, in spring, 1748, coming on soon after, Counsellor Robbins had Welsh transmitted from Naas to Kilkenny, in order to give evidence against Anderson and Welsh ; and they were tried for Mrs. Mounford's robbery, on the evidence of John Welsh and others. The physic working well, six of the jury were for finding them guilty, and six more for acquitting them ; and the other six finding them peremptory, and that they were resolved to starve the others into compliance, as they say they may do by law, were for their own sakes obliged to comply with them, and they were acquitted. On which Counsellor Robbins began to smoke the affair, and suspect the operation of gold dust, which was well applied for my comrades, and thereupon left the court in a rage, and swore he would for ever quit the country, since he found people were not satisfied with protecting and saving the rogues they had under themselves, but must also show that they could and would oblige others to have rogues under them whether they would or no."

Here Counsellor Robbins certainly loses that greatness which has distinguished him in his former attack on Freeny ; the Counsellor is defeated and loses his temper. Like Napoleon, he is unequal to reverses: in adverse fortune his presence of mind deserts him.

But what call had he to be in a passion at all? It may be very well for a man to be in a rage because he is disappointed of his prey: so is the hawk, when the dove escapes, in a rage; but let us reflect that, had Counsellor Robbins had his will, two honest fellows would have been hanged; and so let us be heartily thankful that he was disappointed, and that these men were acquitted by a jury of their countrymen. What right had the Counsellor, forsooth, to interfere with their verdict? Not against Irish juries at least does the old satire apply, "And culprits hang that jurymen may dine?" At Kilkenny, on the contrary, the jurymen starve in order that the culprits might be saved — a noble and humane act of self-denial.

In another case, stern justice, and the law of self-preservation, compelled Mr. Freeny to take a very different course with respect to one of his ex-associates. In the former instance we have seen him pawning his watch, giving up tankard, table-spoons — all, for his suffering friends; here we have his method of dealing with traitors.

One of his friends, by the name of Dooling, was taken prisoner, and condemned to be hanged, which gave Mr. Freeny, he says, "a great shock;" but presently this Dooling's fears were worked upon by some traitors within the gaol, and —

"He then consented to discover; but I had a friend in gaol at the same time, one Patrick Healy, who daily insinuated to him that it was of no use or advantage to him to discover anything, as he received sentence of death; and that, after he had made a discovery, they would leave him as he was, without troubling themselves about a reprieve. But notwithstanding, he told the gentlemen that there was a man *blind of an eye who had a bay-mare*, that lived at the other side of Thomastown bridge, *whom* he assured them would be very troublesome in that neighborhood after his death. When Healy discovered what he told the gentlemen, he one night took an opportunity and made Dooling fuddled, and prevailed upon him to take his oath he never would give the least hint about me any more. He also told him the penalty that attended infringing upon his oath — but more especially as he was at that time near his end — which had the desired effect; for he never mentioned my name, nor even anything relative to me," and so went out of the world repenting of his meditated treason.

What further exploits Mr. Freeny performed may be learned

by the curious in his history : they are all, it need scarcely be said, of a similar nature to that noble action which has already been described. His escapes from his enemies were marvellous ; his courage in facing them equally great. He is attacked by whole " armies," through which he makes his way ; wounded, he lies in the woods for days together with three bullets in his leg, and in this condition manages to escape several " armies " that have been marched against him. He is supposed to be dead, or travelling on the continent, and suddenly makes his appearance in his old haunts, advertising his arrival by robbing ten men on the highway in a single day. And so terrible is his courage, or so popular his manners, that he describes scores of laborers looking on while his exploits were performed, and not affording the least aid to the roadside traveller whom he vanquished.

But numbers always prevail in the end : what could Leonidas himself do against an army? The gallant band of brothers led by Freeny were so pursued by the indefatigable Robbins and his myrmidons, that there was no hope left for them, and the Captain saw that he must succumb.

He reasoned, however, with himself (with his usual keen logic), and said : " My men must fall, — the world is too strong for us, and, to-day, or to-morrow — it matters scarcely when — they must yield. They will be hanged for a certainty, and thus will disappear the noblest company of knights the world has ever seen.

" But as they will certainly be hanged, and no power of mine can save them, is it necessary that I should follow them too to the tree? and will James Bulger's fate be a whit more agreeable to him, because James Freeny dangles at his side? To suppose so, would be to admit that he was actuated by a savage feeling of revenge, which I know belongs not to his generous nature."

In a word, Mr. Freeny resolved to turn king's evidence ; for though he swore (in a communication with the implacable Robbins) that he would rather die than betray Bulger, yet when the Counsellor stated that he must then die, Freeny says, " I promised to submit, and *understood that Bulger should be set.*"

Accordingly some days afterwards (although the Captain carefully avoids mentioning that he had met his friend with any such intentions as those indicated in the last paragraph) he and Mr. Bulger came together : and, strangely enough, it was agreed that the one was to sleep while the other kept watch ;

and, while thus employed, the enemy came upon them. But let Freeny describe for himself the last passages of his history :

"We then went to Welsh's house, with a view not to make any delay there ; but, taking a glass extraordinary after supper, Bulger fell asleep. Welsh, in the meantime, told me his house was the safest place I could get in that neighborhood, and while I remained there I would be very safe, provided that no person knew of my coming there (I had not acquainted him that Breen knew of my coming that way). I told Welsh that, as Bulger was asleep, I would not go to bed till morning : upon which Welsh and I stayed up all night, and in the morning Welsh said that he and his wife had a call to Callen, it being market-day. About nine o'clock I went and awoke Bulger, desiring him to get up and guard me whilst I slept, as I guarded him all night ; he said he would, and then I went to bed charging him to watch close, for fear we should be surprised. I put my blunderbuss and two cases of pistols under my head, and soon fell fast asleep. In two hours after the servant-girl of the house, seeing an enemy coming into the yard, ran up to the room where we were, and said that there were an hundred men coming into the yard ; upon which Bulger immediately awoke me, and, taking up my blunderbuss, he fired a shot towards the door, which wounded Mr. Burgess, one of the sheriffs of Kilkenny, of which wound he died. They concluded to set the house on fire about us, which they accordingly did ; upon which I took my fusee in one hand, and a pistol in the other, and Bulger did the like, and as we came out of the door, we fired on both sides, imagining it to be the best method of dispersing the enemy, who were on both sides of the door. We got through them, but they fired after us, and as Bulger was leaping over a ditch he received a shot in the small of the leg, which rendered him incapable of running ; but, getting into a field, where I had the ditch between me and the enemy, I still walked slowly with Bulger, till I thought the enemy were within shot of the ditch, and then wheeled back to the ditch and presented my fusee at them. They all drew back and went for their horses to ride round, as the field was wide and open, and without cover except the ditch. When I discovered their intention I stood in the middle of the field, and one of the gentlemen's servants (there were fourteen in number) rode foremost towards me ; upon which I told the son of a coward I believed he had no more than five pounds a year from his master, and that I would put him in such a condition that his master would not maintain him afterwards.   To which he answered that he had no view of doing us any harm, but that he was commanded by his master to ride so near us ; and then immediately rode back to the enemy, who were coming towards him.   They rode almost within shot of us, and I observed they intended to surround us in the field, and prevent me from having any recourse to the ditch again.   Bulger was at this time so bad with the wound, that he could not go one step without leaning on my shoulder.   At length, seeing the enemy coming within shot of me, I laid down my fusee and stripped off my coat and waistcoat, and running towards them, cried out, 'You sons of cowards, come on, and I will blow your brains out!'   On which they returned back, and then I walked easy to the place where I left my clothes, and put them on, and Bulger and I walked leisurely some distance further.   The enemy came a second time, and I occasioned them to draw back as before, and then we walked to Lord Dysart's deer-park wall.   I got up the wall and helped Bulger up.   The enemy, who still pursued us, though not within shot, seeing us on the wall, one of them fired a random shot at us to no purpose.   We got safe over the wall, and went from thence into my Lord Dysart's wood, where Bulger said he would remain, thinking it a safe place ; but I told him he would be safer anywhere else, for the army of Kilkenny and Callen would be soon about the wood, and that he would be taken if he stayed there.   Besides, as I was very averse to betraying him at all, I could not bear the thoughts of his being taken in my company by any party but Lord Carrick's. I then brought him about half a mile beyond the wood, and left him there in a brake of briars, and looking towards the wood I saw it surrounded by the army.   There was a cabin near that place where I fixed Bulger : he said he would go to it at night, and he would send for some of his friends to take care of him. It was then almost two o'clock, and we were four hours going to that place, which was about two miles from Welsh's house. Imagining that there were spies fixed on all the fords and by-roads between that place and the mountain, I went towards the bounds of the county Tipperary, where I arrived about nightfall, and going to a cabin, I asked whether there was any drink sold near that place?   The man of the house said there was not ; and as I was very much fatigued, I sat down, and there refreshed myself with what the cabin afforded.   I then begged of the man to sell me a pair of his brogues and stockings, as I was then barefooted, which he accordingly did.   I quitted the house, went through Kinsheenah and Poalacoppal, and having so many thorns in my feet, I was obliged to go barefooted, and went to Sleedelagh, and through the mountains, till I came within four miles of Waterford, and going into a cabin, the man of the house took eighteen thorns out of the soles of my feet, and I remained in and about that place for some time after.

"In the meantime a friend of mine was told that it was impossible for me to escape death, for Bulger had turned against me, and that his friends and Stack were resolved upon my life ; but the person who told my friend so, also said, that if my friend would set Bulger and Breen, I might get a pardon through the Earl of Carrick's means and Counsellor Robbins's interest. My friend said that he *was sure I would not consent to such a thing, but the best way was to do it unknown to me ;* and my friend accordingly set Bulger, who was taken by the Earl of Carrick and his party, and Mr. Fitzgerald, and six of Counsellor Robbins's soldiers, and committed to Kilkenny gaol. He was three days in gaol before I heard he was taken, being at that time twenty miles distant from the neighborhood ; nor did I hear from him or see him since I left him near Lord Dysart's wood, *till a friend* came and told me it was to preserve my life and to fulfil my articles that Bulger was taken."

.   .   .   .

"Finding I was suspected, I withdrew to a neighboring wood and concealed myself there till night, and then went to Ballyduff to Mr. Fitzgerald and surrendered myself to him, till I could write to my Lord Carrick ; which I did immediately, and gave him an account of what I escaped, or that I would have gone to Ballylynch and surrendered myself there to him, and begged his lordship to send a guard for me to conduct me to his house — which he did, and I remained there for a few days.

"He then sent me to Kilkenny gaol ; and at the summer assizes following, James Bulger, Patrick Hacket otherwise Bristeen, Martin Millea, John Stack, Felix Donelly, Edmund Kenny, and James Larrasy were tried, convicted, and executed ; and at spring assizes following, George Roberts was tried for receiving Colonel Palliser's gold watch knowing it to be stolen, but was acquitted on account of exceptions taken to my pardon, which prevented my giving evidence. At the following assizes, when I had got a new pardon, Roberts was again tried for receiving the tankard, ladle, and silver spoons from me knowing them to be stolen, and was convicted and executed. At the same assizes, John Reddy, my instructor, and Martin Millea, were also tried, convicted, and executed."

And so they were all hanged : James Bulger, Patrick Hacket or Bristeen, Martin Millea, John Stack and Felix Donelly, and Edmund Kenny and James Larrasy, with Roberts who received the Colonel's watch, the tankard, ladle, and the silver spoons, were all convicted and executed. Their names drop naturally into blank verse. It is hard upon poor George Roberts too : for the watch he received was no doubt in the very inexpressibles which the Captain himself took from the Colonel's head.

As for the Captain himself, he says that, on going out of gaol, Counsellor Robbins and Lord Carrick proposed a subscription for him — in which, strangely, the gentlemen of the county would not join, and so that scheme came to nothing ; and so he published his memoirs in order to get himself a little money. Many a man has taken up the pen under similar circumstances of necessity.

But what became of Captain Freeny afterwards, does not appear. Was he an honest man ever after? Was he hanged for subsequent misdemeanors? It matters little to him now ; though, perhaps, one cannot help feeling a little wish that the latter fate may have befallen him.

Whatever his death was, however, the history of his life has been one of the most popular books ever known in this country. It formed the class-book in those rustic universities which are now rapidly disappearing from among the hedges of Ireland. And lest any English reader should, on account of its lowness, quarrel with the introduction here of this strange picture of wild courage and daring, let him be reconciled by the moral at the end, which, in the persons of Bulger and the rest, hangs at the beam before Kilkenny gaol.

CHAPTER XVI.

MORE RAIN IN GALWAY — A WALK THERE — AND THE SECOND GALWAY NIGHT'S ENTERTAINMENT.

"Seven hills has Rome, seven mouths has Nilus' stream,
Around the Pole seven burning planets gleam.
Twice equal these is Galway, Connaught's Rome:
Twice seven illustrious tribes here find their home.*
Twice seven fair towers the city's ramparts guard:
Each house within is built of marble hard.
With lofty turret flanked, twice seven the gates,
Through twice seven bridges water permeates.
In the high church are twice seven altars raised,
At each a holy saint and patron's praised.
Twice seven the convents dedicate to heaven, —
Seven for the female sex — for godly fathers seven." †

Having read in Hardiman's History the quaint inscription in Irish Latin, of which the above lines are a version, and looked admiringly at the old plans of Galway which are to be found in the same work, I was in hopes to have seen in the town some considerable remains of its former splendor, in spite of a warning to the contrary which the learned historiographer gives.

The old city certainly has some relics of its former stateliness ; and, indeed, is the only town in Ireland I have seen, where an antiquary can find much subject for study, or a lover of the picturesque an occasion for using his pencil.   It is a wild,

* By the help of an Alexandrine, the names of these famous families may also be accommodated to verse.

"Athey, Blake, Bodkin, Browne, Deane, Dorsey, Frinche,
    Joyce, Morech, Skereth, Fonte, Kirowan, Martin, Lynche."

† If the rude old verses are not very remarkable in quality, in *quantity* they are still more deficient, and take some dire liberties with the laws laid down in the Gradus and the Grammar :

"Septem ornant montes Romam, septem ostia Nilum,
    Tot rutilis stellis splendet in axe Polus.
Galvia, Polo Niloque bis æquas.   Roma Conachtæ,
    Bis septem illustres has colit illa tribus.
Bis urbis septem defendunt mœnia turres,
    Intus et en duro est marmore quæque domus.
Bis septem portæ sunt, castra et culmina circum,
    Per totidem pontûm permeat unda vias.
Principe bis septem fulgent altaria templo,
    Quævis patronæ est ara dicata suo,
Et septem sacrata Deo cœnobia, patrum
    Fœminei et sexus, tot pia tecta tenet."

fierce, and most original old town. Joyce's Castle in one of the principal streets, a huge square gray tower, with many carvings and ornaments, is a gallant relic of its old days of prosperity, and gives one an awful idea of the tenements which the other families inhabited, and which are designed in the interesting plate which Mr. Hardiman gives in his work. The Collegiate Church, too, is still extant, without its fourteen altars, and looks to be something between a church and a castle, and as if it should be served by Templars with sword and helmet in place of mitre and crosier. The old houses in the Main Street are like fortresses : the windows look into a court within ; there is but a small low door, and a few grim windows peering suspiciously into the street.

Then there is Lombard Street, otherwise called Deadman's Lane, with a raw-head and cross-bones and a " memento mori " over the door where the dreadful tragedy of the Lynches was acted in 1493. If Galway is the Rome of Connaught, James Lynch Fitzstephen, the Mayor, may be considered as the Lucius Junius Brutus thereof. Lynch had a son who went to Spain as master of one of his father's ships, and being of an extravagant, wild turn, there contracted debts, and drew bills, and alarmed his father's correspondent, who sent a clerk and nephew of his own back in young Lynch's ship to Galway to settle accounts. On the fifteenth day, young Lynch threw the Spaniard overboard. Coming back to his own country, he reformed his life a little, and was on the point of marrying one of the Blakes, Burkes, Bodkins, or others, when a seaman who had sailed with him, being on the point of death, confessed the murder in which he had been a participator.

Hereon the father, who was chief magistrate of the town, tried his son, and sentenced him to death ; and when the clan Lynch rose in a body to rescue the young man, and avert such a disgrace from their family, it is said that Fitzstephen Lynch hung the culprit with his own hand. A tragedy called " The Warden of Galway " has been written on the subject, and was acted a few nights before my arrival.

The waters of Lough Corrib, which " permeate " under the bridges of the town, go rushing and roaring to the sea with a noise and eagerness only known in Galway ; and along the banks you see all sorts of strange figures washing all sorts of wonderful rags, with red petticoats and redder shanks standing in the stream.   Pigs are in every street : the whole town shrieks with them.   There are numbers of idlers on the bridges, thousands in the streets, humming and swarming in and out of dark old ruinous houses; congregated round numberless apple-stalls, nail-stalls, bottle-stalls, pigsfoot-stalls; in queer old shops, that look to be two centuries old; loitering about warehouses, ruined or not; looking at the washerwomen washing in the river, or at the fish-donkeys, or at the potato-stalls, or at a vessel coming into the quay, or at the boats putting out to sea.

That boat at the quay, by the little old gate, is bound for Arranmore; and one next to it has a freight of passengers for the cliffs of Mohir on the Clare coast; and as the sketch is taken, a hundred of people have stopped in the street to look on, and are buzzing behind in Irish, telling the little boys in that language — who will persist in placing themselves exactly in the front of the designer — to get out of his way: which they do for some time; but at length curiosity is so intense that you are entirely hemmed in and the view rendered quite invisible. A sailor's wife comes up — who speaks English — with a very wistful face, and begins to hint that them black pictures are very bad likenesses, and very dear too for a poor woman, and how much would a painted one cost does his honor think? And she has her husband that is going to sea to the West Indies to-morrow, and she'd give anything to have a picture of him. So I made bold to offer to take his likeness for nothing. But he never came, except one day at dinner, and not at all on the next day, though I stayed on purpose to accommodate him. It is true that it was pouring with rain; and as English water-proof cloaks are not waterproof in *Ireland*, the traveller who has but one coat must of necessity respect it, and had better stay where he is, unless he prefers to go to bed while he has his clothes dried at the next stage.

The houses in the fashionable street where the club-house stands (a strong building, with an agreeable Old Bailey look), have the appearance of so many little Newgates. The Catholic chapels are numerous, unfinished, and ugly. Great warehouses and mills rise up by the stream, or in the midst of unfinished streets here and there; and handsome convents with their gardens, justice-houses, barracks, and hospitals adorn the large, poor, bustling, rough-and-ready-looking town. A man who sells hunting-whips, gunpowder, guns, fishing-tackle, and brass and iron ware, has a few books on his counter; and a lady in a by-street, who carries on the profession of a milliner, ekes out her stock in a similar way. But there were no regular book-shops that I saw, and when it came on to rain I had no resource but the hedge-school volumes again. They, like Patrick Spelman's sign (which was faithfully copied in the

town), present some very rude flowers of poetry and "entertainment" of an exceedingly humble sort; but such shelter is
not to be despised when no better is to be had: nay, possibly
its novelty may be piquant to some readers, as an admirer of
Shakspeare will occasionally condescend to listen to Mr. Punch,
or an epicure to content himself with a homely dish of beans
and bacon.

When Mr. Kilroy's waiter has drawn the window curtains,
brought the hot-water for the whiskey-negus, a pipe and a
"screw" of tobacco, and two huge old candlesticks that were
plated once, the audience may be said to be assembled, and
after a little overture performed on the pipe, the second night's
entertainment begins with the historical tragedy of the "Battle
of Aughrim."

Though it has found its way to the West of Ireland, the
"Battle of Aughrim" is evidently by a Protestant author, a
great enemy of popery and wooden shoes: both of which principles incarnate in the person of Saint Ruth, the French General commanding the troops sent by Louis XIV. to the aid of
James II., meet with a woful downfall at the conclusion of the
piece. It must have been written in the reign of Queen Anne,
judging from some loyal compliments which are paid to that
sovereign in the play; which is also modelled upon "Cato."

The "Battle of Aughrim" is written from beginning to end
in decasyllabic verse of the richest sort; and introduces us to
the chiefs of William's and James's armies. On the English
side we have Baron Ginkell, three Generals, and two Colonels;
on the Irish, Monsieur Saint Ruth, two Generals, two Colonels,
and an English gentleman of fortune, a volunteer, and son of
no less a person than Sir Edmundbury Godfrey.

There are two ladies — Jemima, the Irish Colonel Talbot's
daughter, in love with Godfrey; and Lucinda, lady of Colonel
Herbert, in love with her lord. And the deep nature of the
tragedy may be imagined when it is stated that Colonel Talbot is killed, Colonel Herbert is killed, Sir Charles Godfrey is
killed, and Jemima commits suicide, as resolved not to survive
her adorer. St. Ruth is also killed, and the remaining Irish
heroes are taken prisoners or run away. Among the super-
numeraries there is likewise a dreadful slaughter.

The author, however, though a Protestant is an Irishman
(there are peculiarities in his pronunciation which belong only
to that nation), and as far as courage goes, he allows the two
parties to be pretty equal. The scene opens with a martial
sound of kettle-drums and trumpets in the Irish camp, near

Athlone. That town is besieged by Ginkell, and Monsieur St. Ruth (despising his enemy with a confidence often fatal to Generals) meditates an attack on the besiegers' lines, if, by any chance, the besieged garrison be not in a condition to drive them off. After discoursing on the posture of affairs, and letting General Sarsfield and Colonel O'Neil know his hearty contempt of the English and their General, all parties, after protestations of patriotism, indulge in hopes of the downfall of William. St. Ruth says he will drive the wolves and lions' cubs away. O'Neil declares he scorns the revolution, and, like great Cato, smiles at persecution. Sarsfield longs for the day " when our Monks and Jesuits shall return, and holy incense on our altars burn." When

" *Enter* a Post.

" *Post.* With important news I from Athlone am sent,
Be pleased to lead me to the General's tent.
" *Sars.* Behold the General there. Your message tell.
" *St. Ruth.* Declare your message. Are our friends all **well** ?
" *Post.* Pardon me, sir, the fatal news I bring
Like vulture's poison every heart shall sting.
Athlone is lost without your timely aid.
At six this morning an assault was made,
When, under shelter of the British cannon,
Their grenadiers in armor took the Shannon,
Led by brave Captain Sandys, who *with fame
Plunged to his middle in the rapid stream.*
He led them through, and with undaunted ire
He gained the bank in spite of all our fire ;
Being bravely followed by his grenadiers
Though bullets flew like hail about their ears,
And by this time they enter uncontrolled.
" *St. Ruth.* Dare all the force of England be so **bold**
T' attempt to storm so brave a town, when I
With all Hibernia's sons of war am nigh ?
Return : and if the Britons dare pursue,
Tell them St. Ruth is near, and *that will do.*
" *Post.* Your aid would do much better than your name.
" *St. Ruth.* Bear back this answer, friend, from whence you came.
[*Exit* Post."

The picture of brave Sandys, " who with fame plunged to his middle in the rapid strame," is not a bad image on the part of the Post ; and St. Ruth's reply, " Tell them St. Ruth is near, and *that will do*," characteristic of the vanity of his nation. But Sarsfield knows Britons better, and pays a merited compliment to their valor :

" *Sars.* Send speedy succors and their fate prevent,
You know not yet what Britons dare attempt.

I know the English fortitude is such,
To boast of nothing, though they hazard much.
No force on earth their fury can repel,
Nor would they fly from all the devils in hell.

Another officer arrives : Athlone is really taken, St. Ruth gives orders to retreat to Aughrim, and Sarsfield, in a rage, first challenges him, and then vows he will quit the army. " A *gleam* of horror does my vitals *damp*," says the Frenchman (in a figure of speech more remarkable for vigor than logic) : " I fear Lord Lucan has forsook the camp ! " But not so : after a momentary indignation, Sarsfield returns to his duty, and ere long is reconciled with his vain and vacillating chief.

And now the love-intrigue begins. Godfrey enters, and states Sir Charles Godfrey is his lawful name : he is an Englishman, and was on his way to join Ginckle's camp, when Jemima's beauty overcame him : he asks Colonel Talbot to bestow on him the lady's hand. The Colonel consents, and in Act II., on the plain of Aughrim, at 5 o'clock in the morning, Jemima enters and proclaims her love. The lovers have an interview, which concludes by a mutual confession of attachment, and Jemima says, " Here, take my hand. 'Tis true the gift is small, but when I can I'll give you heart and all." The lines show finely the agitation of the young person. She meant to say, Take *my heart*, but she is longing to be married to him, and the words slip out as it were unawares. Godfrey cries in raptures —

" Thanks to the gods ! who such a present gave :
Such radiant graces ne'er could man *receive* (*resave*) ;
For who on earth has e'er such transports known ?
What is the Turkish monarch on his throne,
Hemmed round *with rusty swords* in pompous state ?
Amidst his court no joys can be so great.
Retire with me, my soul, no longer stay
In public view ! the General moves this way."

'Tis, indeed, the General ; who, reconciled with Sarsfield, straightway, according to his custom, begins to boast about what he will do :

" Thrice welcome to my heart, thou best of friends !
The rock on which our holy faith depends !
May this our meeting as a tempest make
The vast foundations of Britannia shake,
Tear up their orange plant, and overwhelm
The strongest bulwarks of the British realm !
Then shall the Dutch and Hanoverian fall,
And James shall ride in triumph to Whitehall ;

Then to protect our faith he will maintain
An inquisition here like that in Spain.
" *Sars.*   Most bravely urged, my lord ! your skill, I own,
Would be *unparalleled* — had you saved Athlone."

— "Had you saved Athlone ! " Sarsfield has him there.
And the contest of words might have provoked quarrels still
more fatal, but alarms are heard : the battle begins, and St.
Ruth (still confident) goes to meet the enemy, exclaiming,
" Athlone was sweet, but Aughrim shall be sour." The fury
of the Irish is redoubled on hearing of Talbot's heroic death :
the Colonel's corpse is presently brought in, and to it enters
Jemima, who bewails her loss in the following pathetic terms : —

" *Jemima.*   Oh ! — he is dead ! — my soul is all on fire,
Witness ye gods ! — he did with fame expire.
For Liberty a sacrifice was made,
And fell, like Pompey, by some *villain's* blade.
There lies a breathless corse, whose soul ne'er knew
A thought but what was always just and true ;
Look down from heaven, God of peace and love,
Waft him with triumph to the throne above ;
And, O ye winged guardians of the skies !
Tune your sweet harps and sing his obsequies !
Good friends, stand off — whilst I embrace the ground
Whereon he lies — and bathe each mortal wound
With brinish tears, that like to torrents run
From these sad eyes.   O heavens ! I'm undone.
                                        [*Falls down on the body.*
          " *Enter* Sir CHARLES GODFREY.   *He raises her.*
" *Sir Char.*   Why do these precious eyes like fountains flow,
To drown the radiant heaven that lies below ?
Dry up your tears, I trust his soul ere this
Has reached the mansions of eternal bliss.
Soldiers ! bear hence the body out of sight.
                                        [*They bear him off.*
" *Jem.*   Oh, stay — ye murderers, cease to kill me quite :
See how he glares ! — and see again he flies !
The crowds fly open, and he mounts the skies.
Oh ! see his blood, it shines refulgent bright,   )
I see him yet — I cannot lose him quite,   }
But still pursue him on — and — *lose my sight.*")

The gradual disappearance of the Colonel's soul is now finely
indicated, and so is her grief : when showing the body to Sir
Charles, she says, " Behold the mangled cause of all my
woes."   The sorrow of youth, however, is but transitory ; and
when her lover bids her dry her *gushish* tears, she takes out her
pocket-handkerchief with the elasticity of youth, and consoles
herself for the father in the husband.

Act III. represents the English camp : Ginckle and his Generals discourse ; the armies are engaged. In Act IV. the English are worsted in spite of their valor, which Sarsfield greatly describes. " View," says he —

> " View how the foe like an impetuous flood
> Breaks through the smoke, the water, and — the mud !'

It becomes exceedingly hot.   Colonel Earles says —

> " In vain Jove's lightnings issue from the sky,
> For death more sure from British *ensigns* fly.
> Their messengers of death much blood have spilled,
> And full three hundred of the Irish killed."

A description of war (Herbert) : —

> " Now bloody colors wave in all their pride,
> *And each proud hero does his beast bestride.*"

General Dorrington's description of the fight is, if possible, still more noble :

> " *Dor.*   Haste, noble friends, and save your lives by flight,
> For 'tis but madness if you stand to fight.
> Our cavalry the battle have forsook,
> And death appears in each dejected look ;
> Nothing but dread confusion can be seen,
> For severed heads and trunks o'erspread the green ;
> The fields, the vales, the hills, and vanquished plain,
> For five miles round are covered with the slain.
> Death in each quarter does the eye alarm,
> Here lies a leg, and there a shattered arm.
> There heads appear, which, cloven by mighty bangs,
> And severed quite, on either shoulder hangs :
> This is the awful scene, my lords !   Oh, fly
> The impending danger, for your fate is nigh."

Which party, however, is to win — the Irish or English ? Their heroism is equal, and young Godfrey especially, on the Irish side, is carrying all before him — when he is interrupted in the slaughter by *the ghost of his father :* of old Sir Edmundbury, whose monument we may see in Westminster Abbey. Sir Charles, at first, doubts about the genuineness of this venerable old apparition : and thus puts a case to the ghost : —

> " Were ghosts in heaven, in heaven they there would stay,
> Or if in hell, *they could not get away.*"

A clincher, certainly, as one would imagine ; but the ghost jumps over the horns of the fancied dilemma, by saying that he is not at liberty to state where he comes from.

" *Ghost.* Where visions rest, or souls imprisoned dwell,
By heaven's command, we are forbid to tell;
But in the obscure grave — where corpse decay,
Moulder in dust and putrefy away, —
No rest is there; for the immortal soul
Takes its full flight and flutters round the Pole;
Sometimes I hover over the Euxine sea —
From Pole to Sphere, until the judgment day —
Over the Thracian Bosphorus do I float,
And pass the Stygian lake in Charon's boat,
O'er Vulcan's fiery court and sulph'rous cave,
And ride like Neptune on a briny wave;
List to the blowing noise of Etna's flames,
And court the shades of Amazonian dames;
Then take my flight up to the gleamy moon:
Thus do I wander till the day of doom.
Proceed I dare not, or I would unfold
A horrid tale would make your blood run cold,
Chill all your nerves and sinews in a trice
Like whispering rivulets congealed to ice.
" *Sir Char.* Ere you depart me, ghost, I here demand
You'd let me know your last divine command!"

The ghost says that the young man must die in the battle; that
it will go ill for him if he die in the wrong cause; and, therefore, that he had best go over to the Protestants — which poor
Sir Charles (not without many sighs for Jemima) consents to
do. He goes off then, saying —

" I'll join my countrymen, and yet proclaim
Nassau's great title to the *crimson plain.*"

In Act V., that desertion turns the fate of the day. Sarsfield enters with his sword drawn, and acknowledges his fate.
" Aughrim," exclaims Lord Lucan,

" Aughrim is now no more, St. Ruth is dead,
And all his guards are from the battle fled.
As he rode down the hill he met his fall,
And died a victim to a cannon ball."

And he bids the Frenchman's body to

" ——— lie like Pompey in his gore,
Whose hero's blood encircles the Egyptian shore."

" Four hundred Irish prisoners we have got," exclaims an
English General, " and seven thousand lyeth on the spot." In
fact, they are entirely discomfited, and retreat off the stage
altogether; while, in the moment of victory, poor Sir Charles
Godfrey enters, wounded to death, according to the old gentleman's prophecy. He is racked by bitter remorse: he tells his
11

love of his treachery, and declares " no crocodile was ever more unjust." His agony increases, the " optic nerves grow dim and lose their sight, and all his veins are now exhausted quite ; " and he dies in the arms of his Jemima, who stabs herself in the usual way.

And so every one being disposed of, the drums and trumpets give a great peal, the audience huzzas, and the curtain falls on Ginckle and his friends exclaiming —

> " May all the gods th' auspicious evening bless,
> Who crowns Great Britain's *arrums* with success ! "

And questioning the prosody, what Englishman will not join in the sentiment?

In the interlude the band (the pipe) performs a favorite air. Jack the waiter and candle-snuffer looks to see that all is ready ; and after the dire business of the tragedy, comes in to sprinkle the stage with water (and perhaps a little whiskey in it). Thus all things being arranged, the audience takes its seat again and the afterpiece begins.

Two of the little yellow volumes purchased at Ennis are entitled " The Irish and Hibernian Tales." The former are modern, and the latter of an ancient sort ; and so great is the superiority of the old stories over the new, in fancy, dramatic interest, and humor, that one can't help fancying Hibernia must have been a very superior country to Ireland.

These Hibernian novels, too, are evidently intended for the hedge-school universities. They have the old tricks and some of the old plots that one has read in many popular legends of almost all countries, European and Eastern : successful cunning is the great virtue applauded ; and the heroes pass through a thousand wild extravagant dangers, such as could only have been invented when art was young and faith was large. And as the honest old author of the tales says " they are suited to the meanest as well as the highest capacity, tending both to improve the fancy and enrich the mind," let us conclude the night's entertainment by reading one or two of them, and reposing after the doleful tragedy which has been represented. The " Black Thief " is worthy of the Arabian Nights, I think, — as wild and odd as an Eastern tale.

It begins, as usual, with a King and Queen who lived once on a time in the South of Ireland, and had three sons ; but the Queen being on her death-bed, and fancying her husband might marry again, and unwilling that her children should be under the jurisdiction of any other woman, besought his Majesty to place them in a tower at her death, and keep them there safe until the young Princes should come of age.

The Queen dies : the King of course marries again, and the new Queen, who bears a son too, hates the offspring of the former marriage, and looks about for means to destroy them.

"At length the Queen, *having got some business with the hen-wife*, went herself to her, and after a long conference passed, was taking leave of her, when the hen-wife prayed that if ever she should come back to her again she might break her neck. The Queen, greatly incensed at such a daring insult from one of her meanest subjects, to make such a prayer on her, demanded immediately the reason, or she would have her put to death. 'It was worth your while, madam,' says the hen-wife, ' to pay me well for it, for the reason I prayed so on you concerns you much.' ' What must I pay you?' asked the Queen. ' You must give me,' says she, ' the full of a pack of wool ; and I have an ancient crock which you must fill with butter ; likewise a barrel which you must fill for me full of wheat.' ' How much wool will it take to the pack?' says the Queen. ' It will take seven herds of sheep,' said she, ' and their increase for seven years.' ' How much butter will it take to fill your crock?' ' Seven dairies,' said she, ' and the increase for seven years.' ' And how much will it take to fill the barrel you have?' says the Queen. ' It will take the increase of seven barrels of wheat for seven years.' ' That is a great quantity,' says the Queen, ' but the reason must be extraordinary, and before I want it I will give you all you demand.' "

The hen-wife acquaints the Queen with the existence of the three sons, and giving her Majesty an enchanted pack of cards, bids her to get the young men to play with her with these cards, and on their losing, to inflict upon them such a task as must infallibly end in their ruin. All young princes are set upon such tasks, and it is a sort of opening of the pantomime, before the tricks and activity begin. The Queen went home, and "got speaking" to the King "in regard of his children, and *she broke it off* to him in a very polite and engaging manner, so that he could see no muster or design in it." The King agreed to bring his sons to court, and at night, when the royal party "began to sport, and play at all kinds of diversions," the Queen cunningly challenged the three Princes to play cards. They lose, and she sends them in consequence to bring her back the Knight of the Glen's wild steed of bells.

On their road (as wandering young princes, Indian or Irish,

always do) they meet with the Black Thief of Sloan, who tells
them what they must do. But they are caught in the attempt,
and brought "into that dismal part of the palace where the
Knight kept a furnace always boiling, in which he threw all
offenders that ever came in his way, which in a few minutes
would entirely consume them. 'Audacious villains!' says the
Knight of the Glen, ' how dare you attempt so bold an action as
to steal my steed? see now the reward of your folly ; for your
greater punishment, I will not boil you all together, but one
after the other, so that he that survives may witness the dire
afflictions of his unfortunate companions.' So saying, he
ordered his servants to stir up the fire. 'We will boil the
eldest-looking of these young men first,' says he, ' and so on
to the last, which will be this *old champion* with the black cap.
He seems to be the captain, and looks as if he had come
through many toils.' — ' I was as near death once as this Prince
is yet,' says the Black Thief, ' and escaped : and so will he
too.' 'No, you never were,' said the Knight, ' for he is within
two or three minutes of his latter end.' ' But,' says the Black
Thief, ' I was within one moment of my death, and I am here
yet.' ' How was that?' says the Knight. ' I would be glad to
hear it, for it seems to be impossible.' 'If you think, Sir
Knight,' says the Black Thief, ' that the danger I was in surpassed that of this young man, will you pardon him his crime?'
' I will,' says the Knight, 'so go on with your story.'

   " ' I was, sir,' says he, ' a very wild boy in my youth, and
came through many distresses : once in particular, as I was on
my rambling, I was benighted, and could find no lodging. At
length I came to an old kiln, and being much fatigued, I went
up and lay on the ribs. I had not been long there, when I saw
three witches coming in with three bags of gold. Each put her
bag of gold under her head as if to sleep. I heard the one say
to the other that if the Black Thief came on them while they
slept he would not leave them a penny. I found by their discourse that everybody had got my name into their mouth,
though I kept silent as death during their discourse. At
length they fell fast asleep, and then I stole softly down, and
seeing some turf *convenient*, I placed one under each of their
heads, and off I went with their gold as fast as I could.

   " ' I had not gone far,' continued the Thief of Sloan, ' until I
saw a greyhound, a hare, and a hawk in pursuit of me, and began
to think it must be the witches that had taken that metamorphosis, in order that I might not escape them unseen either by
land or water. Seeing they did not appear in any formidable

shape, I was more than once resolved to attack them, thinking that with my broad sword I could easily destroy them. But considering again that it was perhaps still in their power to become so, I gave over the attempt, and climbed with difficulty up a tree, bringing my sword in my hand, and all the gold along with me. However, when they came to the tree they found what I had done, and, making further use of their hellish art, one of them was changed into a smith's anvil, and another into a piece of iron, of which the third one soon made a hatchet. Having the hatchet made, she fell to cutting down the tree, and in course of an hour it began to shake with me.'"

This is very good and original. The "boiling" is in the first fee-faw-fum style, and the old allusion to "the old champion in the black cap" has the real Ogresque humor. Nor is that simple contrivance of the honest witches without its charm : for if, instead of wasting their time, the one in turning herself into an anvil, the other into a piece of iron, and so hammering out a hatchet at considerable labor and expense — if either of them had turned herself into a hatchet at once, they might have chopped down the Black Thief before cock-crow, when they were obliged to fly off and leave him in possession of the bags of gold.

The eldest Prince is ransomed by the Knight of the Glen in consequence of this story ; and the second Prince escapes on account of the merit of a second story ; but the great story of all is of course reserved for the youngest Prince.

"I was one day on my travels," says the Black Thief, "and I came into a large forest, where I wandered a long time and could not get out of it. At length I came to a large castle, and fatigue obliged me to call into the same, where I found a young woman, and a child sitting on her knee, and she crying. I asked her what made her cry, and where the lord of the castle was, for I wondered greatly that I saw no stir of servants or any person about the place. 'It is well for you,' says the young woman, 'that the lord of this castle is not at home at present ; for he is a monstrous giant, with but one eye on his forehead, who lives on human flesh. He brought me this child,' says she — 'I do not know where he got it — and ordered me to make it into a pie, and I cannot help crying at the command.' I told her that if she knew of any place convenient that I could leave the child safely, I would do it, rather than that it should be buried in the bowels of such a monster. She told of a house a distance off, where I would get a woman who would take care of it. 'But what will I do in regard of the pie?' 'Cut a

finger off it,' said I, ' and I will bring you in a young wild pig
out of the forest, which you may dress as if it was the child,
and put the finger in a certain place, that if the giant doubts
anything about it, you may know where to turn it over at first,
and when he sees it he will be fully satisfied that it is made of
the child.' She agreed to the plan I proposed ; and, cutting off
the child's finger, by her direction I soon had it at the house
she told me of and brought her the little pig in the place of it.
She then made ready the pie ; and, after eating and drinking
heartily myself, I was just taking my leave of the young woman
when we observed the giant coming through the castle-gates.
' Lord bless me ! ' said she, ' what will you do now ? run away
and lie down among the dead bodies that he has in the room '
(showing me the place), ' and strip off your clothes that he may
not know you from the rest if he has occasion to go that way.'
I took her advice, and laid myself down among the rest, as if
dead, to see how he would behave. The first thing I heard
was him calling for his pie. When she set it down before him,
he swore it smelt like swine's flesh ; but, knowing where to find
the finger, she immediately turned it up — which fairly convinced him of the contrary. The pie only served to sharpen
his appetite, and I heard him sharpen his knife, and saying he
must have a collop or two, for he was not near satisfied. But
what was my terror when I heard the giant groping among the
bodies, and, fancying myself, cut the half of my hip off, and
took it with him to be roasted. You may be certain I was in
great pain ; but the fear of being killed prevented me from
making any complaint. However, when he had eat all, he began to drink hot liquors in great abundance, so that in a short
time he could not hold up his head, but threw himself on a
large creel he had made for the purpose, and fell fast asleep.
When ever I heard him snoring, bad as I was, I went up and
caused the woman to bind my wound with a handkerchief ; and
taking the giant's spit, I reddened it in the fire, and ran it
through the eye, but was not able to kill him. However, I left
the spit sticking in his head and took to my heels ; but I soon
found he was in pursuit of me, although blind ; and, having an
enchanted ring, he threw it at me, and it fell on my big toe
and remained fastened to it. The giant then called to the ring,
' Where it was ? ' and to my great surprise it made him answer,
' On my foot,' and he, guided by the same, made a leap at me
— which I had the good luck to observe, and fortunately escaped
the danger. However, I found running was of no use in saving
me as long as I had the ring on my foot ; so I took my sword

and cut off the toe it was fastened on, and threw both into a large fish-pond that was convenient. The giant called again to the ring, which, by the power of enchantment, always made answer; but he, not knowing what I had done, imagined it was still on some part of me, and made a violent leap to seize me — when he went into the pond over head and ears and was drowned. Now, Sir Knight," said the Thief of Sloan, " you see what dangers I came through and always escaped; but indeed I am lame for want of my toe ever since."

And now remains but one question to be answered, viz. How is the Black Thief himself to come off? This difficulty is solved in a very dramatic way and with a sudden turn in the narrative that is very wild and curious.

" My lord and master," says an old woman that was listening all the time, " that story is but too true, as I well know: *for I am the very woman that was in the giant's castle, and you, my lord, the child that I was to make into a pie;* and this is the very man that saved your life, which you may know by the want of your finger that was taken off, as you have heard, to deceive the giant."

That fantastical way of bearing testimony to the previous tale, by producing an old woman who says the tale is not only true, but she was the very old woman who lived in the giant's castle, is almost a stroke of genius. It is fine to think that the simple chronicler found it necessary to have a proof for his story, and he was no doubt perfectly contented with the proof found.

" The Knight of the Glen, greatly surprised at what he had heard the old woman tell, and knowing he wanted his finger from his childhood, began to understand that the story was true enough. ' And is this my dear deliverer?' says he. ' O brave fellow, I not only pardon you all, but I will keep you with myself while you live; where you shall feast like princes and have every attendance that I have myself.' They all returned thanks on their knees, and the Black Thief told him the reason they attempted to steal the steed of bells, and the necessity they were under of going home. ' Well,' says the Knight of the Glen, ' if that's the case, I bestow you my steed rather than this brave fellow should die: so you may go when you please: only remember to call and see me betimes, that we may know each other well.' They promised they would, and with great joy they set off for the King their father's palace, and the Black Thief along with them. The wicked Queen was standing all this time on the tower, and hearing the bells ringing at a

great distance off, knew very well it was the Princes coming
home, and the steed with them, and through spite and vex-
ation precipitated herself from the tower and was shattered to
pieces. The three Princes lived happy and well during their
father's reign, always keeping the Black Thief along with them ;
but how they did after the old King's death is not known."

Then we come upon a story that exists in many a European
language — of the man cheating Death ; then to the history of
the Apprentice Thief, who of course cheated his masters : which,
too, is an old tale, and may have been told very likely among
those Phœnicians who were the fathers of the Hibernians, for
whom these tales were devised. A very curious tale is there
concerning Manus O'Malaghan and the Fairies : — " In the
parish of Ahoghill lived Manus O'Malaghan. *As he was searching for a calf that had strayed*, he heard many people talking.
Drawing near, he distinctly heard them repeating, one after the
other, ' Get me a horse, get me a horse ; ' and ' Get me a horse
too,' says Manus. Manus was instantly mounted on a steed,
surrounded with a vast crowd, who galloped off, taking poor
Manus with them. In a short time they suddenly stopped in
a large wide street, asking Manus if he knew where he was ?
' Faith,' says he, ' I do not.' ' You are *in Spain*,' said they."

Here we have again the wild mixture of the positive and
the fanciful. The chronicler is careful to tell us why Manus
went out searching for a calf, and this positiveness prodigiously
increases the reader's wonder at the subsequent events. And
the question and answer of the mysterious horseman is fine :
" Don't you know where you are ? *In Spain.*" A vague solution, such as one has of occurrences in dreams sometimes.

The history of Robin the Blacksmith is full of these strange
flights of poetry. He is followed about " by a little boy in a
green jacket," who performs the most wondrous feats of the
blacksmith's art, as follows : —

" Robin was asked to do something, who wisely shifted it,
saying he would be very sorry not to give the honor of the first
trick to his lordship's smith — at which the latter was called
forth to the bellows. When the fire was well kindled, to the
great surprise of all present, he blew a great shower of wheat
out of the fire, which fell through all the shop. They then demanded of Robin to try what he could do. ' Pho ! ' said Robin,
as if he thought nothing of what was done. ' Come,' said he
to the boy, ' I think I showed you something like that.' The
boy goes then to the bellows and blew out a great flock of
pigeons, who soon devoured all the grain and then disappeared.

"The Dublin smith, sorely vexed that such a boy should outdo him, goes a second time to the bellows and blew a fine trout out of the hearth, who jumped into a little river that was running by the shop-door and was seen no more at that time.

"Robin then said to the boy, 'Come, you must bring us yon trout back again, to let the gentlemen see we can do something.' Away the boy goes and blew a large otter out of the hearth, who immediately leaped into the river and in a short time returned with the trout in his mouth, and then disappeared. All present allowed that it was a folly to attempt a competition any further."

The boy in the green jacket was one "of a kind of small beings called fairies;" and not a little does it add to the charm of these wild tales to feel, as one reads them, that the writer must have believed in his heart a great deal of what he told. You see the tremor as it were, and a wild look of the eyes, as the story-teller sits in his nook and recites, and peers wistfully round lest the beings he talks of be really at hand.

Let us give a couple of the little tales entire. They are not so fanciful as those before mentioned, but of the comic sort, and suited to the first kind of capacity mentioned by the author in his preface.

DONALD AND HIS NEIGHBORS.

"HUDDEN and Dudden and Donald O'Neary were near neighbors in the barony of Ballinconlig, and ploughed with three bullocks; but the two former, envying the present prosperity of the latter, determined to kill his bullock to prevent his farm being properly cultivated and labored — that, going back in the world, he might be induced to sell his lands, which they meant to get possession of. Poor Donald, finding his bullock killed, immediately skinned it, and throwing the skin over his shoulder, with the fleshy side out, set off to the next town with it, to dispose of it to the best advantage. Going along the road a magpie flew on the top of the hide, and began picking it, chattering all the time. This bird had been taught to speak and imitate the human voice, and Donald, thinking he understood some words it was saying, put round his hand and caught hold of it. Having got possession of it, he put it under his great-coat, and so went on to the town. Having sold the hide, he went into an inn to take a dram; and, following the landlady into the cellar, he gave the bird a squeeze, which caused it to chatter some broken accents that surprised her very much.

' What is that I hear?' said she to Donald : ' I think it is talk,
and yet I do not understand.' 'Indeed,' said Donald, ' it is a
bird I have that tells me everything, and I always carry it with
me to know when there is any danger. Faith,' says he, ' it
says you have far better liquor than you are giving me.' 'That
is strange,' said she, going to another cask of better quality,
and asking him if he would sell the bird. ' I will,' said Donald,
' if I get enough for it.' ' I will fill your hat with silver if you
will leave it with me.' Donald was glad to hear the news,
and, taking the silver, set off, rejoicing at his good luck. He
had not been long home when he met with Hudden and Dudden. ' Ha!' said he, ' you thought you did me a bad turn,
but you could not have done me a better : for look here what
I have got for the hide,' showing them the hatful of silver.
' You never saw such a demand for hides in your life as there
is at present.' Hudden and Dudden that very night killed their
bullocks, and set out the next morning to sell their hides. On
coming to the place they went to all the merchants, but could
only get a trifle for them. At last they had to take what they
could get, and came home in a great rage and vowing revenge
on poor Donald. He had a pretty good guess how matters
would turn out, and his bed being under the kitchen-window,
he was afraid they would rob him, or perhaps kill him when
asleep ; and on that account, when he was going to bed, he left
his old mother in his bed, and lay down in her place, which
was in the other side of the house, and they, taking the old
woman for Donald, choked her in the bed ; but he making some
noise, they had to retreat and leave the money behind them,
which grieved them very much. However, by daybreak, Donald got his mother on his back, and carried her to town. Stopping at a well, he fixed his mother with her staff as if she was
stooping for a drink, and then went into a public-house convenient and called for a dram. ' I wish,' said he to a woman
that stood near him, ' you would tell my mother to come in.
She is at yon well trying to get a drink, and she is hard in
hearing : if she does not observe you, give her a little shake,
and tell her that I want her.' The woman called her several
times, but she seemed to take no notice : at length she went
to her and shook her by the arm ; but when she let her go
again, she tumbled on her head into the well, and, as the
woman thought, was drowned. She, in great fear and surprise
at the accident, told Donald what had happened. ' O mercy,'
said he, ' what is this?' He ran and pulled her out of the well,
weeping and lamenting all the time, and acting in such a man-

ner that you would imagine that he had lost his senses. The woman, on the other hand, was far worse than Donald : for his grief was only feigned, but she imagined herself to be the cause of the old woman's death. The inhabitants of the town, hearing what had happened, agreed to make Donald up a good sum of money for his loss, as the accident happened in their place ; and Donald brought a greater sum home with him than he got for the magpie. They buried Donald's mother ; and as soon as he saw Hudden and Dudden, he showed them the last purse of money he had got. 'You thought to kill me last night,' said he ; ' but it was good for me it happened on my mother, for I got all that purse for her to make gunpowder.'

" That very night Hudden and Dudden killed their mothers, and the next morning set off with them to town. On coming to the town with their burden on their backs, they went up and down crying, ' Who will buy old wives for gunpowder?' so that every one laughed at them, and the boys at last clodded them out of the place. They then saw the cheat, and vowing revenge on Donald, buried the old women and set off in pursuit of him. Coming to his house, they found him sitting at his breakfast, and seizing him, put him in a sack, and went to drown him in a river at some distance. As they were going along the highway they raised a hare, which they saw had but three feet, and, throwing off the sack, ran after her, thinking by appearance she would be easily taken. In their absence there came a drover that way, and hearing Donald singing in the sack, wondered greatly what could be the matter. ' What is the reason,' said he, ' that you are singing, and you confined?' ' Oh, I am going to heaven,' said Donald : ' and in a short time I expect to be free from trouble.' ' Oh, dear,' said the drover, ' what will I give you if you let me to your place?' ' Indeed I do not know,' said he : ' it would take a good sum.' ' I have not much money,' said the drover ; ' but I have twenty head of fine cattle, which I will give you to exchange places with me.' ' Well, well,' says Donald, ' I don't care if I should : loose the sack and I will come out.' In a moment the drover liberated him, and went into the sack himself : and Donald drove home the fine heifers and left them in his pasture.

" Hudden and Dudden having caught the hare, returned, and getting the sack on one of their backs, carried Donald, as they thought, to the river, and threw him in, where he immediately sank. They then marched home, intending to take immediate possession of Donald's property ; but how great was their surprise, when they found him safe at home before them, with such a fine herd of cattle, whereas they knew he had none before? 'Donald,' said they, 'what is all this! We thought you were drowned, and yet you are here before us?' 'Ah!' said he, 'if I had but help along with me when you threw me in, it would have been the best job ever I met with; for of all the sight of cattle and gold that ever was seen, is there, and no one to own them; but I was not able to manage more than what you see, and I could show you the spot where you might get hundreds.' They both swore they would be his friends, and Donald accordingly led them to a very deep part of the river, and lifting up a stone, 'Now,' said he, 'watch this,' throwing it into the stream. 'There is the very place, and go in, one of you, first, and if you want help you have nothing to do but call.' Hudden jumping in, and sinking to the bottom, rose up again, and making a bubbling noise as those do that are drowning, seemed trying to speak but could not. 'What is that he is saying now?' says Dudden. 'Faith,' says Donald, 'he is calling for help — don't you hear him? Stand about,' continued he, running back, 'till I leap in. I know how to do better than any of you.' Dudden, to have the advantage of him, jumped in off the bank, and was drowned along with Hudden. And this was the end of Hudden and Dudden."

THE SPAEMAN.

"A POOR man in the North of Ireland was under the necessity of selling his cow to help to support his family. Having sold his cow, he went into an inn and called for some liquor. Having drunk pretty heartily, he fell asleep, and when he awoke he found he had been robbed of his money. Poor Roger was at a loss to know how to act; and, as is often the case, when the landlord found that his money was gone, he turned him out of doors. The night was extremely dark, and the poor man was compelled to take up his lodging in an old uninhabited house at the end of the town.

"Roger had not remained long here until he was surprised by the noise of three men, whom he observed making a hole, and, having deposited something therein, closing it carefully up again and then going away. The next morning, as Roger was walking towards the town, he heard that a cloth-shop had been robbed to a great amount, and that a reward of thirty pounds was offered to any person who could discover the thieves. This was joyful news to Roger, who recollected what he had been witness to the night before. He accordingly went to the shop and told the gentleman that for the reward he would recover the goods, and secure the robbers, provided he got six stout men to attend him. All which was thankfully granted him.

" At night Roger and his men concealed themselves in the old house, and in a short time after the robbers came to the spot for the purpose of removing their booty; but they were instantly seized and carried into the town prisoners, with the goods. Roger received the reward and returned home, well satisfied with his good luck. Not many days after, it was noised over the country that this robbery was discovered by the help of one of the best Spaemen to be found — insomuch that it reached the ears of a worthy gentleman of the county of Derry, who made strict inquiry to find him out. Having at length discovered his abode, he sent for Roger, and told him he was every day losing some valuable article, and as he was famed for discovering lost things, if he could find out the same, he should be handsomely rewarded. Poor Roger was put to a stand, not knowing what answer to make, as he had not the smallest knowledge of the like. But recovering himself a little, he resolved to humor the joke ; and, thinking he would make a good dinner and some drink of it, told the gentleman he would try what he could do, but that he must have a room to himself for three hours, during which time he must have three bottles of strong ale and his dinner. All which the gentleman told him he should have. No sooner was it made known that the Spaeman was in the house than the servants were all in confusion, wishing to know what would be said.

" As soon as Roger had taken his dinner, he was shown into an elegant room, where the gentleman sent him a quart of ale by the butler. No sooner had he set down the ale than Roger said, ' There comes one of them ' (intimating the bargain he had made with the gentleman for the three quarts), which the butler took in a wrong light and imagined it was himself. He went away in great confusion and told his wife. ' Poor fool,' said she, ' the fear makes you think it is you he means ; but I will attend in your place, and hear what he will say to me.' Accordingly she carried the second quart: but no sooner had she opened the door than Roger cried, ' There comes two of them.' The woman, no less surprised than her husband, told him the Spaeman knew her too. ' And what will we do?' said he. ' We will be hanged.' ' I will tell you what we must do,' said she : ' we must send the groom the next time ; and if he is known, we must offer him a good sum not to discover on us.' The butler went to William and told him the whole story, and that he must go next to see what the Spaeman would say to him, telling him at the same time what to do in case he was known also. When the hour was expired, William was sent with the third quart of ale — which when Roger observed, he cried out, ' There is the third and last of them ! ' At which the groom changed color, and told him ' that if he would not discover on them, they would show him where the goods were all concealed and give him five pounds besides.' Roger, not a little surprised at the discovery he had made, told him ' if he recovered the goods, he would follow them no further.'

" By this time the gentleman called Roger to know how he had succeeded. He told him ' he could find the goods, but that the thief was gone.' ' I will be well satisfied,' said he, ' with the goods, for some of them are very valuable.' ' Let the butler come along with me, and the whole shall be recovered.' Roger was accordingly conducted to the back of the stables, where the articles were concealed, — such as silver cups, spoons, bowls, knives, forks, and a variety of other articles of great value.

" When the supposed Spaeman brought back the stolen goods, the gentleman was so highly pleased with Roger that he insisted on his remaining with him always, as he supposed he would be perfectly safe as long as he was about his house. Roger gladly embraced the offer, and in a few days took possession of a piece of land which the gentleman had given to him in consideration of his great abilities.

" Some time after this the gentleman was relating to a large company the discovery Roger had made, and that he could tell anything. One of the gentlemen said he would dress a dish of meat, and bet fifty pounds that he could not tell what was in it, though he would allow him to taste it. The bet being taken and the dish dressed, the gentleman sent for Roger and told him the bet that was depending on him. Poor Roger did not know what to do ; but at last he consented to the trial. The dish being produced, he tasted it, but could not tell what it was. At last, seeing he was fairly beat, he said, ' Gentlemen, it is folly to talk : the fox may run a while, but he is caught at last,' — allowing with himself that he was found out. The gentleman that had made the bet then confessed that it was a fox he had dressed in the dish : at which they all shouted out in favor of the Spaeman, — particularly his master, who had more confidence in him than ever.

Roger then went home, and so famous did he become, that no one dared take anything but what belonged to them, fearing that the Spaeman would discover on them.

And so we shut up the Hedge-school Library, and close the Galway Nights' Entertainments. They are not quite so genteel as Almack's to be sure; but many a lady who has her opera-box in London has listened to a piper in Ireland.

Apropos of pipers, here is a young one that I caught and copied to-day. He was paddling in the mud, shining in the sun careless of his rays, and playing his little tin music as happy as Mr. Cooke with his oboe.

Perhaps the above verses and tales are not unlike my little Galway musician. They are grotesque and rugged; but they are pretty and innocent hearted too; and as such, polite persons may deign to look at them for once in a way. While we have Signor Costa in a white neck-cloth ordering opera-bands to play for us the music of Donizetti, which is not only sublime but genteel: of course such poor little operatives as he who plays the wind instrument yonder cannot expect to be heard often. But is not this Galway? and how far is Galway from the Haymarket?

CHAPTER XVII.

FROM GALWAY TO BALLINAHINCH.

THE Clifden car, which carries the Dublin letters into the heart of Connemara, conducts the passenger over one of the most wild and beautiful districts that it is ever the fortune of a traveller to examine; and I could not help thinking, as we passed through it, at how much pains and expense honest English cockneys are to go and look after natural beauties far inferior, in countries which, though more distant, are not a whit more strange than this one. No doubt, ere long, when people know how easy the task is, the rush of London tourism will come this way : and I shall be very happy if these pages shall be able to awaken in one bosom beating in Tooley Street or the Temple the desire to travel towards Ireland next year.

After leaving the quaint old town behind us, and ascending one or two small eminences to the north-westward, the traveller, from the car, gets a view of the wide sheet of Lough Corrib shining in the sun, as we saw it, with its low dark banks stretching round it. If the view is gloomy, at least it is characteristic : nor are we delayed by it very long ; for though the lake stretches northwards into the very midst of the Joyce country, (and is there in the close neighborhood of another huge lake, Lough Mask, which again is near to another sheet of water,) yet from this road henceforth, after keeping company with it for some five miles, we only get occasional views of it, passing over hills and through trees, by many rivers and smaller lakes, which are dependent upon that of Corrib. Gentlemen's seats, on the road from Galway to Moycullen, are scattered in great profusion. Perhaps there is grass growing on the gravel-walk, and the iron gates of the tumble-down old lodges are rather rickety ; but, for all that, the places look comfortable, hospitable, and spacious. As for the shabbiness and want of finish here and there, the English eye grows quite accustomed to it in a month : and I find the bad condition of the Galway houses by no means so painful as that of the places near Dublin. At some of the lodges, as we pass, the mail-carman, with a warning shout, flings a bag of letters. I saw a little party looking at one which lay there in the road crying, "Come, take me!" but nobody cares to steal a bag of letters in this country, I suppose, and the carman drove on without any alarm. Two days afterwards a gentleman with whom I was in company left on a rock his book of fishing-flies ; and I can assure you there was a very different feeling expressed about the safety of *that*.

In the first part of the journey, the neighborhood of the road seemed to be as populous as in other parts of the country : troops of red-petticoated peasantry peering from their stone-cabins ; yelling children following the car, and crying, "Lash, lash!" It was Sunday, and you would see many a white chapel among the green bare plains to the right of the road, the court-yard blackened with a swarm of cloaks. The service seems to continue (on the part of the people) all day. Troops of people issuing from the chapel met us at Moycullen ; and ten miles further on, at Oughterard, their devotions did not yet seem to be concluded.

A more beautiful village can scarcely be seen than this. It stands upon Lough Corrib, the banks of which are here, for once at least, picturesque and romantic : and a pretty river, the Feogh, comes rushing over rocks and by woods until it passes the town and meets the lake. Some pretty buildings in the village stand on each bank of this stream : a Roman Catholic chapel with a curate's neat lodge ; a little church on one side of it, a fine court-house of gray stone on the other. And here it is that we get into the famous district of Connemara, so celebrated in Irish stories, so mysterious to the London tourist. " It presents itself," says the Guide-book, " under every possible combination of heathy moor, bog, lake, and mountain. Extensive mossy plains and wild pastoral valleys lie embosomed among the mountains, and support numerous herds of cattle and horses, for which the district has been long celebrated. These wild solitudes, which occupy by far the greater part of the centre of the country, are held by a hardy and ancient race of grazing farmers, who live in a very primitive state, and, generally speaking, till little beyond what supplies their immediate wants. For the first ten miles the country is comparatively open ; and the mountains on the left, which are not of great elevation, can be distinctly traced as they rise along the edge of the heathy plain.

" Our road continues along the Feogh river, which expands itself into several considerable lakes, and at five miles from Oughterard we reach Lough Bofin, which the road also skirts. Passing in succession Lough-a-Preaghan, the lakes of Anderran and Shindella, at ten miles from Oughterard we reach Slyme and Lynn's Inn, or Half-way House, which is near the shore of Loughonard. Now, as we advance towards the group of Binabola, or the Twelve Pins, the most gigantic scenery is displayed."

But the best guide-book that ever was written cannot set the view before the mind's eye of the reader, and I won't attempt to pile up big words in place of these wild mountains, over which the clouds as they passed, or the sunshine as it went and came, cast every variety of tint, light, and shadow ; nor can it be expected that long, level sentences, however smooth and shining, can be made to pass as representations of those calm lakes by which we took our way. All one can do is to lay down the pen and ruminate, and cry, " Beautiful !" once more ; and to the reader say, " Come and see ! "

Wild and wide as the prospect around us is, it has somehow a kindly, friendly look ; differing in this from the fierce lone-

12

liness of some similar scenes in Wales that I have viewed.
Ragged women and children come out of rude stone-huts to see
the car as it passes.   But it is impossible for the pencil to give
due raggedness to the rags, or to convey a certain picturesque
mellowness of color that the garments assume. The sexes, with
regard to raiment, do not seem to be particular.   There were
many boys on the road in the national red petticoat, having no
other covering for their lean brown legs.   As for shoes, the
women eschew them almost entirely ; and I saw a peasant
trudging from mass in a handsome scarlet cloak, a fine blue-
cloth gown, turned up to show a new lining of the same color,
and a petticoat quite white and neat — in a dress of which the
cost must have been at least 16⅄. ; and her husband walked in
front carrying her shoes and stockings.

The road had conducted us for miles through the vast property
of the gentleman to whose house I was bound, Mr. Martin, the
Member for the county ; and the last and prettiest part of the
journey was round the Lake of Ballinahinch, with tall mountains
rising immediately above us on the right, pleasant woody hills
on the opposite side of the lake, with the roofs of the houses
rising above the trees ; and in an island in the midst of the
water a ruined old castle cast a long white reflection into the
blue waters where it lay.   A land-pirate used to live in that
castle, one of the peasants told me, in the time of " Oliver
Cromwell."   And a fine fastness it was for a robber, truly ; for
there was no road through these wild countries in his time —
nay, only thirty years since, this lake was at three days' distance of Galway.   Then comes the question, What, in a country
where there were no roads and no travellers, and where the inhabitants have been wretchedly poor from time immemorial, —
what was there for the land-pirate to rob?   But let us not be
too curious about times so early as those of Oliver Cromwell.
I have heard the name many times from the Irish peasant, who
still has an awe of the grim, resolute Protector.

The builder of Ballinahinch House has placed it to command
a view of a pretty melancholy river that runs by it, through
many green flats and picturesque rocky grounds ; but from the
lake it is scarcely visible.   And so, in like manner, I fear it
must remain invisible to the reader too, with all its kind inmates, and frank, cordial hospitality ; unless he may take a
fancy to visit Galway himself, when, as I can vouch, a very small
pretext will make him enjoy both.

It will, however, be only a small breach of confidence to say
that the major-domo of the establishment (who has adopted ac-

curately the voice and manner of his master, with a severe dignity of his own which is quite original,) ordered me on going to bed " not to move in the morning till he called me," at the same time expressing a hearty hope that I should " want nothing more that evening." Who would dare, after such peremptory orders, not to fall asleep immediately, and in this way disturb the repose of Mr. J——n M–ll–y?

There may be many comparisons drawn between English and Irish gentlemen's houses; but perhaps the most striking point of difference between the two is the immense following of the Irish house, such as would make an English housekeeper crazy almost. Three comfortable, well-clothed, good-humored fellows walked down with me from the car, persisting in carrying one a bag, another a sketching-stool, and so on. Walking about the premises in the morning, sundry others were visible in the court-yard and near the kitchen-door. In the grounds a gentleman, by name Mr. Marcus C–rr, began discoursing to me regarding the place, the planting, the fish, the grouse, and the Master; being himself, doubtless, one of the irregulars of the house. As for maids, there were half a score of them skurrying about the house; and I am not ashamed to confess that some of them were exceedingly good-looking. And if I might venture to say a word more, it would be respecting Connemara breakfasts; but this would be an entire and flagrant breach of confidence, and, to be sure, the dinners were just as good.

One of the days of my three days' visit was to be devoted to the lakes; and, as a party had been arranged for the second day after my arrival, I was glad to take advantage of the society of a gentleman staying in the house, and ride with him to the neighboring town of Clifden.

The ride thither from Ballinahinch is surprisingly beautiful; and as you ascend the high ground from the two or three rude stone huts which face the entrance-gates of the house, there are views of the lakes and the surrounding country which the best parts of Killarney do not surpass, I think; although the Connemara lakes do not possess the advantage of wood which belongs to the famous Kerry landscape.

But the cultivation of the country is only in its infancy as yet, and it is easy to see how vast its resources are, and what capital and cultivation may do for it. In the green patches among the rocks, and on the mountain-sides, wherever crops were grown, they flourished; plenty of natural wood is springing up in various places; and there is no end to what the planter may do, and to what time and care may effect. The carriage-road

to Clifden is but ten years old : as it has brought the means of
communication into the country, the commerce will doubtless
follow it ; and in fact, in going through the whole kingdom,
one can't but be struck with the idea that not one hundredth
part of its capabilities are yet brought into action, or even
known perhaps, and that, by the easy and certain progress of
time, Ireland will be poor Ireland no longer.

For instance, we rode by a vast green plain, skirting a lake
and river, which is now useless almost for pasture, and which
a little draining will convert into thousands of acres of rich
productive land. Streams and falls of water dash by every
where — they have only to utilize this water-power for mills and
factories — and hard by are some of the finest bays in the world,
where ships can deliver and receive foreign and home produce.
At Roundstone especially, where a little town has been erected,
the bay is said to be unexampled for size, depth, and shelter ;
and the Government is now, through the rocks and hills on their
wild shore, cutting a coast-road to Bunown, the most westerly
part of Connemara, whence there is another good road to Clifden.   Among the charges which the " Repealers " bring against
the Union, they should include at least this : they would never
have had these roads but for the Union : roads which are as
much at the charge of the London tax-payer as of the most ill-
used Milesian in Connaught.

A string of small lakes follow the road to Clifden, with
mountains on the right of the traveller for the chief part of the
way.   A few figures at work in the bog-lands, a red petticoat
passing here and there, a goat or two browsing among the
stones, or a troop of ragged whity-brown children who came
out to gaze at the car, form the chief society on the road.   The
first house at the entrance to Clifden is a gigantic poor-house —
tall, large, ugly, comfortable ; it commands the town, and looks
almost as big as every one of the houses therein. The town itself
is but of a few years' date, and seems to thrive in its small way.
Clifden Castle is a fine château in the neighborhood, and belongs
to another owner of immense lands in Galway — Mr. D'Arcy.

Here a drive was proposed along the coast to Bunown, and
I was glad to see some more of the country, and its character.
Nothing can be wilder.   We passed little lake after lake, lying
a few furlongs inwards from the shore.   There were rocks everywhere, some patches of cultivated land here and there, nor was
there any want of inhabitants along this savage coast.   There
were numerous cottages, if cottages they may be called, and
women, and above all, children in plenty.   Here is one of the

GAZING AT THE CAR.

former — her attitude as she stood gazing at the car. To depict the multiplicity of her rags would require a month's study.

At length we came in sight of a half-built edifice which is approached by a rocky, dismal, gray road, guarded by two or three broken gates, against which rocks and stones were piled, which had to be removed to give an entrance to our car. The gates were closed so laboriously, I presume, to prevent the egress of a single black consumptive pig, far gone in the family-way — a teeming skeleton — that was cropping the thin, dry grass that grew upon a round hill which rises behind this most dismal castle of Bunown.

If the traveller only seeks for strange sights, this place will repay his curiosity. Such a dismal house is not to be seen in all England : or, perhaps, such a dismal situation. The sea lies before and behind ; and on each side, likewise, are rocks and copper-colored meadows, by which a few trees have made an attempt to grow. The owner of the house had, however, begun to add to it ; and there, unfinished, is a whole apparatus of turrets, and staring raw stone and mortar, and fresh ruinous carpenters' work. And then the court-yard ! — tumbled-down out-houses, staring empty pointed windows, and new-smeared plaster cracking from the walls — a black heap of turf, a mouldy pump, a wretched old coal-scuttle, emptily sunning itself in the midst of this cheerful scene ! There was an old Gorgon who kept the place, and who was in perfect unison with it : Venus herself would become bearded, blear-eyed, and haggard, if left to be the housekeeper of this dreary place.

In the house was a comfortable parlor, inhabited by the priest, who has the painful charge of the district. Here were his books and his breviaries, his reading-desk with the cross engraved upon it, and his portrait of Daniel O'Connell the Liberator to grace the walls of his lonely cell. There was a dead crane hanging at the door on a gaff : his red fish-like eyes were staring open, and his eager grinning bill. A rifle-ball had passed through his body. And this was doubtless the only game about the place ; for we saw the sportsman who had killed the bird hunting vainly up the round hill for other food for powder. This gentleman had had good sport, he said, shooting seals upon a neighboring island, four of which animals he had slain.

Mounting up the round hill, we had a view of the Sline Lights — the most westerly point in Ireland.

Here too was a ruined sort of summer-house, dedicated " DEO

HIBERNIÆ LIBERATORI." When these lights were put up, I am told the proprietor of Bunown was recommended to apply for compensation to Parliament, inasmuch as there would be no more *wrecks* on the coast : from which branch of commerce the inhabitants of the district used formerly to derive a considerable profit. Between these Sline Lights and America nothing lies but the Atlantic. It was beautifully blue and bright on this day, and the sky almost cloudless ; but I think the brightness only made the scene more dismal, it being of that order of beauties which cannot bear the full light, but require a cloud or a curtain to set them off to advantage. A pretty story was told me by the gentleman who had killed the seals. The place where he had been staying for sport was almost as lonely as this Bunown, and inhabited by a priest too — a young, lively, well-educated man. " When I came here first," the priest said, " *I cried for two days :* " but afterwards he grew to like the place exceedingly, his whole heart being directed towards it, his chapel, and his cure. Who would not honor such missionaries — the virtue they silently practise, and the doctrines they preach? After hearing that story, I think Bunown looked not quite so dismal, as it is inhabited, they say, by such another character. What a pity it is that John Tuam, in the next county of Mayo, could not find such another hermitage to learn modesty in, and forget his Graceship, his Lordship, and the sham titles by which he sets such store.

A moon as round and bright as any moon that ever shone, and riding in a sky perfectly cloudless, gave us a good promise of a fine day for the morrow, which was to be devoted to the lakes in the neighborhood of Ballinahinch : one of which, Lough Ina, is said to be of exceeding beauty. But no man can speculate upon Irish weather. I have seen a day beginning with torrents of rain that looked as if a deluge was at hand, clear up in a few minutes, without any reason, and against the prognostications of the glass and all other weather-prophets. So in like manner, after the astonishingly fine night, there came a villanous dark day : which, however, did not set in fairly for rain, until we were an hour on our journey, with a couple of stout boatmen rowing us over Ballinahinch Lake. Being, however, thus fairly started, the water began to come down, not in torrents certainly, but in that steady, creeping, insinuating mist, of which we scarce know the luxury in England ; and which, I am bound to say, will wet a man's jacket as satisfactorily as a cataract would do.

It was just such another day as that of the famous stag-hunt

at Killarney, in a word ; and as, in the first instance, we went
to see the deer killed, and saw nothing thereof, so, in the second
case, we went to see the landscape with precisely the same good
fortune. The mountains covered their modest beauties in impenetrable veils of clouds ; and the only consolation to the
boat's crew was, that it was a remarkably good day for trout-
fishing — which amusement some people are said to prefer to
the examination of landscapes, however beautiful.

O you who laboriously throw flies in English rivers, and
catch, at the expiration of a hard day's walking, casting, and
wading, two or three feeble little brown trouts of two or three
ounces in weight, how would you rejoice to have but an hour's
sport in Derryclear or Ballinahinch ; where you have but to
cast, and lo ! a big trout springs at your fly, and, after making
a vain struggling, splashing, and plunging for a while, is infallibly landed in the net and thence into the boat. The single
rod in the boat caught enough fish in an hour to feast the
crew, consisting of five persons, and the family of a herd of
Mr. Martin's, who has a pretty cottage on Derryclear Lake,
inhabited by a cow and its calf, a score of fowls, and I don't
know how many sons and daughters.

Having caught enough trout to satisfy any moderate appetite, like true sportsmen the gentlemen on board our boat
became eager to hook a salmon. Had they hooked a few
salmon, no doubt they would have trolled for whales, or for a
mermaid ; one of which finny beauties the waterman swore he
had seen on the shore of Derryclear — he with Jim Mullen
being above on a rock, the mermaid on the shore directly
beneath them, visible to the middle, and as usual " racking
her hair." It was fair hair, the boatman said ; and he appeared as convinced of the existence of the mermaid as he was
of the trout just landed in the boat.

In regard of mermaids, there is a gentleman living near
Killala Bay, whose name was mentioned to me, and who declares solemnly that one day, shooting on the sands there, he
saw a mermaid, and determined to try her with a shot. So he
drew the small charge from his gun and loaded it with ball —
that he always had by him for seal-shooting — fired, and hit
the mermaid through the breast. The screams and moans of
the creature — whose person he describes most accurately —
were the most horrible, heart-rending noises that he ever, he
said, heard ; and not only were they heard by him, but by the
fishermen along the coast, who were furiously angry against
Mr. A——n, because, they said, the injury done to the mer-

maid would cause her to drive all the fish away from the bay for years to come.

But we did not, to my disappointment, catch a glimpse of one of these interesting beings, nor of the great sea-horse which is said to inhabit these waters, nor of any fairies (of whom the stroke-oar, Mr. Marcus, told us not to speak, for they didn't like bein' spoken of) ; nor even of a salmon, though the fishermen produced the most tempting flies. The only animal of any size that was visible we saw while lying by a swift black river that comes jumping with innumerable little waves into Derry-clear, and where the salmon are especially suffered to " stand : " this animal was an eagle — a real wild eagle, with gray wings and a white head and belly : it swept round us, within gunshot reach, once or twice, through the leaden sky, and then settled on a gray rock and began to scream its shrill, ghastly aquiline note.

The attempts on the salmon having failed, the rain continuing to fall steadily, the herd's cottage before named was resorted to : when Marcus, the boatman, commenced forthwith to gut the fish, and taking down some charred turf-ashes from the blazing fire, on which about a hundredweight of potatoes were boiling, he — Marcus — proceeded to grill on the floor some of the trout, which we afterwards ate with immeasurable satisfaction. They were such trouts as, when once tasted, remain for ever in the recollection of a commonly grateful mind — rich, flaky, creamy, full of flavor. A Parisian *gourmand* would have paid ten francs for the smallest *cooleen* among them ; and, when transported to his capital, how different in flavor would they have been ! — how inferior to what they were as we devoured them, fresh from the fresh waters of the lake, and jerked as it were from the water to the gridiron ! The world had not had time to spoil those innocent beings before they were gobbled up with pepper and salt, and missed, no doubt, by their friends. I should like to know more of their " *set*." But enough of this : my feelings overpower me : suffice it to say, they were red or salmon trouts — none of your white-fleshed brown-skinned river fellows.

When the gentlemen had finished their repast, the boatmen and the family set to work upon the ton of potatoes, a number of the remaining fish, and a store of other good things ; then we all sat round the turf-fire in the dark cottage, the rain coming down steadily outside, and veiling everything except the shrubs and verdure immediately about the cottage. The herd, the herd's wife, and a nondescript female friend, two healthy young herdsmen in corduroy rags, the herdsman's daughter paddling about with bare feet, a stout black-eyed wench with her gown over her head and a red petticoat not quite so good as new, the two boatmen, a badger just killed and turned inside out, the gentlemen, some hens cackling and flapping about among the rafters, a calf in a corner cropping green meat and occasionally visited by the cow her mamma, formed the society of the place. It was rather a strange picture ; but as for about two hours we sat there, and maintained an almost unbroken silence, and as there was no other amusement but to look at the rain, I began, after the enthusiasm of the first half-hour, to think that after all London was a bearable place, and that for want of a turf-fire and a bench in Connemara, one *might* put up with a sofa and a newspaper in Pall Mall.

This, however, is according to tastes ; and I must say that Mr. Marcus betrayed a most bitter contempt for all cockney tastes, awkwardness, and ignorance : and very right too. The night, on our return home, all of a sudden cleared ; but though the fishermen, much to my disgust — at the expression of which, however, the rascals only laughed — persisted in making more casts for trout, and trying back in the dark upon the spots which we had visited in the morning, it appeared the fish had been frightened off by the rain ; and the sportsmen met with such indifferent success that at about ten o'clock we found ourselves at Ballinahinch. Dinner was served at eleven, and, I believe, there was some whiskey-punch afterwards, recommended medicinally and to prevent the ill effects of the wetting : but that is neither here nor there.

The next day the petty sessions were to be held at Roundstone, a little town which has lately sprung up near the noble bay of that name. I was glad to see some specimens of Connemara litigation, as also to behold at least one thousand beautiful views that lie on the five miles of road between the town and Ballinahinch. Rivers and rocks, mountains and sea, green plains and bright skies, how (for the hundred-and-fiftieth time) can pen-and-ink set you down? But if Berghem could have seen those blue mountains, and Karel Dujardin could have copied some of these green, airy plains, with their brilliant little colored groups of peasants, beggars, horsemen, many an Englishman would know Connemara upon canvas as he does Italy or Flanders now.

CHAPTER XVIII.

ROUNDSTONE PETTY SESSIONS.

"THE temple of august Themis," as a Frenchman would call the sessions-room at Roundstone, is an apartment of some twelve feet square, with a deal table and a couple of chairs for the accommodation of the magistrates, and a Testament with a paper cross pasted on it to be kissed by the witnesses and complainants who frequent the court. The law-papers, warrants, &c., are kept on the sessions-clerk's bed in an adjoining apartment, which commands a fine view of the court-yard — where there is a stack of turf, a pig, and a shed beneath which the magistrates' horses were sheltered during the sitting. The sessions-clerk is a gentleman " having," as the phrase is here, both the English and Irish languages, and interpreting for the benefit of the worshipful bench.

And if the cockney reader supposes that in this remote country spot, so wild, so beautiful, so distant from the hum and vice of cities, quarrelling is not, and litigation never shows her snaky head, he is very much mistaken. From what I saw, I would recommend any ingenious young attorney whose merits are not appreciated in the metropolis, to make an attempt upon the village of Roundstone ; where as yet, I believe, there is no solicitor, and where an immense and increasing practice might speedily be secured. Mr. O'Connell, who is always crying out " Justice for Ireland," finds strong supporters among the Roundstonians, whose love of justice for themselves is inordinate. I took down the plots of the five first little litigious dramas which were played before Mr. Martin and the stipendiary magistrate.

Case I. — A boy summoned a young man for beating him so severely that he kept his bed for a week, thereby breaking an engagement with his master, and losing a quarter's wages.

The defendant stated in reply, that the plaintiff was engaged — in a field through which defendant passed with another person — setting two little boys to fight ; on which defendant took plaintiff by the collar and turned him out of the field. A witness who was present swore that defendant never struck plaintiff at all, nor kicked him, nor ill-used him, further than by pushing him out of the field.

As to the loss of his quarter's wages, the plaintiff ingeniously proved that he had afterwards returned to his master, that he had worked out his time, and that he had in fact received already the greater part of his hire. Upon which the case was dismissed, the defendant quitting court without a stain upon his honor.

Case 2 was a most piteous and lamentable case of killing a cow. The plaintiff stepped forward with many tears and much gesticulation to state the fact, and also to declare that she was in danger of her life from the defendant's family.

It appeared on the evidence that a portion of the defendant's respectable family are at present undergoing the rewards which the law assigns to those who make mistakes in fields with regard to the ownership of sheep which sometimes graze there. The defendant's father, O'Damon, for having appropriated one of the fleecy bleaters of O'Meliboeus, was at present passed beyond sea to a country where wool, and consequently mutton, is so plentiful, that he will have the less temptation. Defendant's brothers tread the Ixionic wheel for the same offence. Plaintiff's son had been the informer in the case : hence the feud between the families, the threats on the part of the defendant, the murder of the innocent cow.

But upon investigation of the business, it was discovered, and on the plaintiff's own testimony, that the cow had not been killed, nor even been injured ; but that the defendant had flung two stones at it, which *might* have inflicted great injury had they hit the animal with greater force in the eye or in any delicate place.

Defendant admitted flinging the stones, but alleged as a reason that the cow was trespassing on his grounds ; which plaintiff did not seem inclined to deny. Case dismissed. — Defendant retires with unblemished honor ; on which his mother steps forward, and lifting up her hands with tears and shrieks, calls upon God to witness that the defendant's own brother-in-law had sold to her husband the very sheep on account of which he had been transported.

Not wishing probably to doubt the justice of the verdict of an Irish jury, the magistrate abruptly put an end to the lamentation and oaths of the injured woman by causing her to be sent out of court, and called the third cause on.

This was a case of thrilling interest and a complicated nature, involving two actions, which ought each perhaps to have been gone into separately, but were taken together. In the first place Timothy Horgan brought an action against Patrick Dolan for breach of contract in not remaining with him for the whole of six months during which Dolan had agreed to serve Horgan. Then Dolan brought an action against Horgan for not paying him his wages for six months' labor done — the wages being two guineas.

Horgan at once, and with much candor, withdrew his charge against Dolan, that the latter had not remained with him for six months : nor can I understand to this day why in the first place he swore to the charge, and why afterwards he withdrew it. But immediately advancing another charge against his late servant he pleaded that he had given him a suit of clothes, which should be considered as a set-off against part of the money claimed.

Now such a suit of clothes as poor Dolan had was never seen — I will not say merely on an English scarecrow, but on an Irish beggar. Strips of rags fell over the honest fellow's great brawny chest, and the covering on his big brown legs hung on by a wonder. He held out his arms with a grim smile, and told his worship to look at the clothes ! The argument was irresistible : Horgan was ordered to pay forthwith. He ought to have been made to pay another guinea for clothing a fellow-creature in rags so abominable.

And now came a case of trespass, in which there was nothing interesting but the attitude of the poor woman who trespassed, and who meekly acknowledged the fact. She stated, however, that she only got over the wall as a short cut home ; but the wall was eight feet high, with a ditch too ; and I fear there were cabbages or potatoes in the inclosure. They fined her a sixpence, and she could not pay it, and went to gaol for three days — where she and her baby at any rate will get a meal.

Last on the list which I took down came a man who will make the fortune of the London attorney that I hope is on his way hither : a rather old, curly-headed man, with a sly smile perpetually lying on his face (the reader may give whatever interpretation he please to the " lying "). He comes before the court almost every fortnight, they say, with a complaint of one kind or other. His present charge was against a man for breaking into his court-yard, and wishing to take possession of the same. It appeared that he, the defendant, and another lived in a row of houses : the plaintiff's house was, however, first built ; and as his agreement specified that the plot of ground behind his house should be his likewise, he chose to imagine that the plot of ground behind all the three houses was his, and built his turf-stack against his neighbor's window. The magistrates of course pronounced against this ingenious

discoverer of wrongs, and he left the court still smiling and
twisting round his little wicked eyes, and declaring solemnly
that he would put in an *appale*. If one could have purchased
a kicking at a moderate price off that fellow's back, it would
have been a pleasant little piece of self-indulgence, and I confess
I longed to ask him the price of the article.

And so, after a few more such great cases, the court rose,
and I had leisure to make moral reflections, if so minded :
sighing to think that cruelty and falsehood, selfishness and
rapacity, dwell not in crowds alone, but flourish all the world
over — sweet flowers of human nature, they bloom in all
climates and seasons, and are just as much at home in a hot-
house in Thavies' Inn as on a lone mountain or a rocky sea-coast
in Ireland, where never a tree will grow !

We walked along this coast, after the judicial proceedings
were over, to see the country, and the new road that the Board
of Works is forming. Such a wilderness of rocks I never
saw ! The district for miles is covered with huge stones, shining
white in patches of green, with the Binabola on one side of the
spectator, and the Atlantic running in and out of a thousand
little bays on the other. The country is very hilly, or wavy
rather, being a sort of ocean petrified ; and the engineers have
hard work with these numerous abrupt little ascents and de-
scents, which they equalize as best they may — by blasting, cutting, filling cavities, and levelling eminences. Some hundreds
of men were employed at this work, busy with their hand-bar-
rows, their picking and boring. Their pay is eighteenpence a
day.

There is little to see in the town of Roundstone, except a
Presbyterian chapel in process of erection — that seems big
enough to accommodate the Presbyterians of the county — and
a sort of lay convent, being a community of brothers of the
third order of Saint Francis. They are all artisans and workmen, taking no vows, but living together in common, and undergoing a certain religious regimen. Their work is said to be very
good, and all are employed upon some labor or other. On the
front of this unpretending little dwelling is an inscription with
a great deal of pretence, stating that the establishment was
founded with the approbation of " His Grace the Most Reverend the Lord Archbishop of Tuam."

The Most Reverend Dr. MacHale is a clergyman of great
learning, talents, and honesty, but his Grace the Lord Archbishop of Tuam strikes me as being no better than a mountebank ; and some day I hope even his own party will laugh

this humbug down. It is bad enough to be awed by big titles
at all; but to respect sham ones! — O stars and garters!
We shall have his Grace the Lord Chief Rabbi next, or his
Lordship the Arch-Imaum!

CHAPTER XIX.

CLIFDEN TO WESTPORT.

ON leaving Ballinahinch (with sincere regret, as any lonely
tourist may imagine, who is called upon to quit the hospitable
friendliness of such a place and society), my way lay back to
Clifden again, and thence through the Joyce country, by the
Killery mountains, to Westport in Mayo. The road, amount-
ing in all to four-and-forty Irish miles, is performed in cars in
different periods of time, according to your horse and your
luck. Sometimes, both being bad, the traveller is two days
on the road; sometimes a dozen hours will suffice for the journey — which was the case with me, though I confess to having
found the twelve hours long enough. After leaving Clifden,
the friendly look of the country seemed to vanish; and though
picturesque enough, was a thought too wild and dismal for eyes
accustomed to admire a hop-garden in Kent, or a view of rich
meadows in Surrey, with a clump of trees and a comfortable
village spire. "Inglis," the Guide-book says, "compares the
scenes to the Norwegian Fiords." Well, the Norwegian Fiords
must, in this case, be very dismal sights! and I own that the
wildness of Hampstead Heath (with the imposing walls of
"Jack Straw's Castle" rising stern in the midst of the green
wilderness) is more to my taste than the general views of yesterday.

We skirted by lake after lake, lying lonely in the midst of
lonely boglands, or bathing the sides of mountains robed in
sombre rifle green. Two or three men, and as many huts,
you see in the course of each mile perhaps, as toiling up the
bleak hills, or jingling more rapidly down them, you pass
through this sad region. In the midst of the wilderness a
chapel stands here and there, solitary, on the hillside; or a
ruinous, useless school-house, its pale walls contrasting with
the general surrounding hue of sombre purple and green.
But though the country looks more dismal than Connemara,

it is clearly more fertile : we passed miles of ground that evidently wanted but little cultivation to make them profitable ; and along the mountain-sides, in many places, and over a great extent of Mr. Blake's country especially, the hills were covered with a thick natural plantation, that may yield a little brushwood now, but might in fifty years' time bring thousands of pounds of revenue to the descendants of the Blakes. This spectacle of a country going to waste is enough to make the cheerfullest landscape look dismal : it gives this wild district a woful look indeed. The names of the lakes by which we came I noted down in a pocket-book as we passed along ; but the names were Irish, the car was rattling, and the only name readable in the catalogue is Letterfrack.

The little hamlet of Leenane is at twenty miles' distance from Clifden ; and to arrive at it, you skirt the mountain along one side of a vast pass, through which the ocean runs from Killery Bay, separating the mountains of Mayo from the mountains of Galway. Nothing can be more grand and gloomy than this pass ; and as for the character of the scenery, it must, as the Guide-book says, " be seen to be understood." Meanwhile, let the reader imagine huge dark mountains in their accustomed livery of purple and green, a dull gray sky above them, an estuary silver-bright below : in the water lies a fisherman's boat or two ; a pair of seagulls undulating with the little waves of the water ; a pair of curlews wheeling overhead and piping on the wing ; and on the hillside a jingling car, with a cockney in it, oppressed by and yet admiring all these things. Many a sketcher and tourist, as I found, has visited this picturesque spot : for the hostess of the inn had stories of English and American painters, and of illustrious book-writers too, travelling in the service of our Lords of Paternoster Row.

The landlord's son of Clifden, a very intelligent young fellow, was here exchanged for a new carman in the person of a raw Irisher of twenty years of age, " having" little English, and dressed in that very pair of pantaloons which Humphrey Clinker was compelled to cast off some years since on account of the offence which they gave to Mrs. Tabitha Bramble. This fellow, emerging from among the boats, went off to a field to seek for the black horse, which the landlady assured me was quite fresh and had not been out all day, and would carry me to Westport in three hours. Meanwhile I was lodged in a neat little parlor, surveying the Mayo side of the water, with some cultivated fields and a show of a village at the spot where the estuary ends, and above them lodges and fine dark plantations climbing over the dark hills that lead to Lord Sligo's seat of Delphi.   Presently, with a curtsy, came a young woman who sold worsted socks at a shilling a pair, and whose portrait is here given.

It required no small pains to entice this rustic beauty to stand while a sketch should be made of her.   Nor did any compliments or cajolements, on my part or the landlady's, bring about the matter : it was not until money was offered that the lovely creature consented.   I offered (such is the ardor of the real artist) either to give her sixpence, or to purchase two pairs of her socks, if she would stand still for five minutes.   On which she said she would prefer selling the socks.   Then she stood still for a moment in the corner of the room ; then she turned her face towards the corner and the other part of her person towards the artist, and exclaimed in that attitude, " I must have a shilling more."   Then I told her to go to the deuce.   Then she made a proposition, involving the stockings and sixpence, which was similarly rejected ; and, finally, the above splendid design was completed at the price first stated.

However, as we went off, this timid little dove barred the door for a moment, and said that " I ought to give her another shilling ; that a gentleman would give her another shilling," and so on.   She might have trod the London streets for ten years and not have been more impudent and more greedy.

By this time the famous fresh horse was produced and the driver, by means of a wraprascal, had covered a great part of the rags of his lower garment.   He carried a whip and a stick, the former lying across his knees ornamentally, the latter being for service ; and as his feet were directly under the horse's tail, he had full command of the brute's back, and belabored it for six hours without ceasing.

What little English the fellow knew he uttered with a howl, roaring into my ear answers — which, for the most part, were wrong — to various questions put to him. The lad's voice was so hideous, that I asked him if he could sing ; on which forthwith he began yelling a most horrible Irish ditty — of which he told me the title, that I have forgotten. He sang three stanzas, certainly keeping a kind of tune, and the latter lines of each verse were in rhyme ; but when I asked him the meaning of the song, he only roared out its Irish title.

On questioning the driver further, it turned out that the horse, warranted fresh, had already performed a journey of eighteen miles that morning, and the consequence was that I had full leisure to survey the country through which we passed. There were more lakes, more mountains, more bog, and an excellent road through this lonely district, though few only of the human race enlivened it. At ten miles from Leenane, we stopped at a roadside hut, where the driver pulled out a bag of oats, and borrowing an iron pot from the good people, half filled it with corn, which the poor tired, galled, bewhipped black horse began eagerly to devour. The young charioteer himself hinted very broadly his desire for a glass of whiskey, which was the only kind of refreshment that this remote house of entertainment supplied.

In the various cabins I have entered, I have found talking a vain matter : the people are suspicious of the stranger within their wretched gates, and are shy, sly, and silent. I have, commonly, only been able to get half-answers in reply to my questions, given in a manner that seemed plainly to intimate that the visit was unwelcome. In this rude hostel, however, the landlord was a little less reserved, offered a seat at the turf-fire, where a painter might have had a good subject for his skill. There was no chimney, but a hole in the roof, up which a small portion of the smoke ascended (the rest preferring an egress by the door, or else to remain in the apartment altogether) ; and this light from above lighted up as rude a set of figures as ever were seen. There were two brown women with black eyes and locks, the one knitting stockings on the floor, the other " racking " (with that natural comb which five horny fingers supply) the elf-locks of a dirty urchin between her knees. An idle fellow was smoking his pipe by the fire ; and by his side sat a stranger, who had been made welcome to the shelter of the place — a sickly, well-looking man, whom I mistook for a deserter at first, for he had evidently been a soldier.

But there was nothing so romantic as desertion in his history. He had been in the Dragoons, but his mother had purchased his

discharge : he was married, and had lived comfortably in Cork
for some time, in the glass-blowing business.   Trade failing at
Cork, he had gone to Belfast to seek for work.   There was no
work at Belfast ; and he was so far on his road home again :
sick, without a penny in the world, a hundred and fifty miles
to travel, and a starving wife and children to receive him at
his journey's end.   He had been thrown off a caravan that day,
and had almost broken his back in the fall.   Here was a cheer-·
ing story !   I wonder where he is now : how far has the poor
starving lonely man advanced over that weary desolate road,
that in good health, and with a horse to carry me, I thought it
a penalty to cross?   What would one do under such circumstances, with solitude and hunger for present company, despair
and starvation at ·the end of the vista?   There are a score of
lonely lakes along the road which he has to pass : would it be
well to stop at one of them, and fling into it the wretched load
of cares which that poor broken back has to carry?   Would
the world he would light on *then* be worse for him than that
he is pining in now?   Heaven help us ! and on this very day,
throughout the three kingdoms, there are a million such stories
to be told.   Who dare doubt of heaven after that? of a place
where there is at last a welcome to the heart-stricken prodigal
and a happy home to the wretched?

The crumbs of oats which fell from the mouth of the feasting
Dives of a horse were battled for outside the door by a dozen
Lazaruses in the shape of fowls ; and a lanky young pig, who
had been grunting in an old chest in the cabin, or in a miserable
recess of huddled rags and straw which formed the couch of the
family, presently came out and drove the poultry away, picking
up, with great accuracy, the solitary grains lying about, and
more than once trying to shove his snout into the corn-pot, and
share with the wretched old galled horse.   Whether it was that
he was refreshed by his meal, or that the car-boy was invigorated
by his glass of whiskey, or inflamed by the sight of eighteenpence — which munificent sum was tendered to the soldier — I
don't know ; but the remaining eight miles of the journey were
got over in much quicker time, although the road was exceedingly bad and hilly for the greatest part of the way to Westport.   However, by running up the hills at the pony's side, the
animal, fired with emulation, trotted up them too — descending
them with the proverbial surefootedness of his race, the car and
he bouncing over the rocks and stones at the rate of at least
four Irish miles an hour.

At about five miles from Westport the cultivation became

much more frequent. There were plantations upon the hills, yellow corn and potatoes in plenty in the fields, and houses thickly scattered. We had the satisfaction, too, of knowing that future tourists will have an excellent road to travel over in this district: for by the side of the old road, which runs up and down a hundred little rocky steeps, according to the ancient plan, you see a new one running for several miles, — the latter way being conducted, not over the hills, but around them, and, considering the circumstances of the country, extremely broad and even. The car-boy presently yelled out " REEK, REEK ! " with a shriek perfectly appalling. This howl was to signify that we were in sight of that famous conical mountain so named, and from which St. Patrick, after inveigling thither all the venomous reptiles in Ireland, precipitated the whole noisome race into Clew Bay. The road also for several miles was covered with people, who were flocking in hundreds from Westport market, in cars and carts, on horseback single and double, and on foot.

And presently, from an eminence, I caught sight not only of a fine view, but of the most beautiful view I ever saw in the world, I think ; and to enjoy the splendor of which I would travel a hundred miles in that car with that very horse and driver. The sun was just about to set, and the country round about and to the east was almost in twilight. The mountains were tumbled about in a thousand fantastic ways, and swarming with people. Trees, cornfields, cottages, made the scene indescribably cheerful ; noble woods stretched towards the sea, and abutting on them, between two highlands, lay the smoking town. Hard by was a large Gothic building — it is but a poor-house ; but it looked like a grand castle in the gray evening. But the Bay — and the Reek which sweeps down to the sea — and a hundred islands in it, were dressed up in gold and purple and crimson, with the whole cloudy west in a flame. Wonderful, wonderful ! . . . The valleys in the road to Leenane have lost all glimpses of the sun ere this ; and I suppose there is not a soul to be seen in the black landscape, or by the shores of the ghastly lakes, where the poor glass-blower from the whiskey-shop is faintly travelling now.

CHAPTER XX.

WESTPORT.

NATURE has done much for this pretty town of Westport; and after nature, the traveller ought to be thankful to Lord Sligo, who has done a great deal too. In the first place, he has established one of the prettiest, comfortablest inns in Ireland, in the best part of his little town, stocking the cellars with good wines, filling the house with neat furniture, and lending, it is said, the whole to a landlord gratis, on condition that he should keep the house warm, and furnish the larder, and entertain the traveller. Secondly, Lord Sligo has given up for the use of the townspeople, a beautiful little pleasure-ground about his house. "You may depend upon it," said a Scotchman at the inn, "that they've right of pathway through the groonds, and that the marquess couldn't shut them oot." Which is a pretty fair specimen of charity in this world — this kind world, that is always ready to encourage and applaud good actions, and find good motives for the same. I wonder how much would induce that Scotchman to allow poor people to walk in *his* park, if he had one!

In the midst of this pleasure-ground, and surrounded by a thousand fine trees, dressed up in all sorts of verdure, stands a pretty little church; paths through the wood lead pleasantly down to the bay; and, as we walked down to it on the day after our arrival, one of the green fields was suddenly black with rooks, making a huge cawing and clanging as they settled down to feed. The house, a handsome massive structure, must command noble views of the bay, over which all the colors of Titian were spread as the sun set behind its purple islands.

Printer's ink will not give these wonderful hues; and the reader will make his picture at his leisure. That conical mountain to the left is Croaghpatrick: it is clothed in the most magnificent violet-color, and a couple of round clouds were exploding as it were from the summit, that part of them towards the sea lighted up with the most delicate gold and rose color. In the centre is the Clare Island, of which the edges were bright cobalt, whilst the middle was lighted up with a brilliant scarlet tinge, such as I would have laughed at in a picture, never having seen in nature before, but looked at now with wonder and pleasure

until the hue disappeared as the sun went away.   The islands
in the bay (which was of a gold color) looked like so many
dolphins and whales basking there.   The rich park-woods
stretched down to the shore; and the immediate foreground
consisted of a yellow cornfield, whereon stood innumerable
shocks of corn, casting immense long purple shadows over the
stubble.   The farmer, with some little ones about him, was
superintending his reapers; and I heard him say to a little girl,
" Norey, I love you the best of all my children!"   Presently,
one of the reapers coming up, says, " It's always the custom in
these parts to ask strange gentlemen to give something to drink
the first day of reaping; and we'd like to drink your honor's
health in a bowl of coffee."   O fortunatos nimium!   The cockney
takes out sixpence, and thinks that he never passed such a
pleasant half-hour in all his life as in that cornfield, looking at
that wonderful bay.

   A car which I had ordered presently joined me from the
town, and going down a green lane very like England, and
across a causeway near a building where the carman proposed
to show me " me lard's caffin that he brought from Rome, and
a mighty big caffin entirely," we came close upon the water
and the port.   There was a long handsome pier (which, no
doubt, remains at this present minute), and one solitary cutter
lying alongside it; which may or may not be there now.   There
were about three boats lying near the cutter, and six sailors,
with long shadows, lolling about the pier.   As for the warehouses, they are enormous; and might accommodate, I should
think, not only the trade of Westport, but of Manchester too.
There are huge streets of these houses, ten stories high, with
cranes, owners' names, &c., marked Wine Stores, Flour Stores,
Bonded Tobacco Warehouses, and so forth.   The six sailors
that were singing on the pier no doubt are each admirals of
as many fleets of a hundred sail that bring wines and tobacco
from all quarters of the world to fill these enormous warehouses.
These dismal mausoleums, as vast as pyramids, are the places
where the dead trade of Westport lies buried — a trade that, in
its lifetime, probably was about as big as a mouse.   Nor is this
the first nor the hundredth place to be seen in this country,
which sanguine builders have erected to accommodate an imaginary commerce.   Mill-owners over-mill themselves, merchants
over-warehouse themselves, squires over-castle themselves, little tradesmen about Dublin and the cities over-villa and over-gig
themselves, and we hear sad tales about hereditary bondage and
the accursed tyranny of England.

Passing out of this dreary, pseudo-commercial port, the road lay along the beautiful shores of Clew Bay, adorned with many a rickety villa and pleasure-house, from the cracked windows of which may be seen one of the noblest views in the world. One of the villas the guide pointed out with peculiar exultation : it is called by a grand name — Waterloo Park, and has a lodge, and a gate, and a field of a couple of acres, and belongs to a young gentleman who, being able to write Waterloo Park on his card, succeeded in carrying off a young London heiress with a hundred thousand pounds. The young couple had just arrived, and one of them must have been rather astonished, no doubt, at the " park." But what will not love do? With love and a hundred thousand pounds, a cottage may be made to look like a castle, and a park of two acres may be brought to extend for a mile. The night began now to fall, wrapping up in a sober gray livery the bay and mountains, which had just been so gorgeous in sunset ; and we turned our backs presently upon the bay, and the villas with the cracked windows, and scaling a road of perpetual ups and downs, went back to Westport. On the way was a pretty cemetery, lying on each side of the road, with a ruined chapel for the ornament of one division, a holy well for the other. In the holy well lives a sacred trout, whom sick people come to consult, and who operates great cures in the neighborhood. If the patient sees the trout float-ing on his back, he dies ; if on his belly, he lives ; or *vice versâ*. The little spot is old, ivy-grown, and picturesque, and I can't fancy a better place for a pilgrim to kneel and say his beads at.

But considering the whole country goes to mass, and that the priests can govern it as they will, teaching what shall be believed and what shall be not credited, would it not be well for their reverences, in the year eighteen hundred and forty-two, to discourage these absurd lies and superstitions, and teach some simple truths to their flock? Leave such figments to magazine-writers and ballad-makers ; but, corbleu! it makes one indignant to think that people in the United Kingdom, where a press is at work and good sense is abroad, and clergy-men are eager to educate the people, should countenance such savage superstitions and silly, grovelling heathenisms.

The chapel is before the inn where I resided, and on Sunday, from a very early hour, the side of the street was thronged with worshippers, who came to attend the various services. Nor are the Catholics the only devout people of this remote district. There is a large Presbyterian church very well attended, as was the Established Church service in the pretty church in the park.

There was no organ, but the clerk and a choir of children sang hymns sweetly and truly ; and a charity sermon being preached for the benefit of the diocesan schools, I saw many pound-notes in the plate, showing that the Protestants here were as ardent as their Roman Catholic brethren. The sermon was extempore, as usual, according to the prevailing taste here. The preacher by putting aside his sermon-book may gain in warmth, which we don't want, but lose in reason, which we do. If I were Defender of the Faith, I would issue an order to all priests and deacons to take to the book again ; weighing well, before they uttered it, every word they proposed to say upon so great a subject as that of religion ; and mistrusting that dangerous facility given by active jaws and a hot imagination. Reverend divines have adopted this habit, and keep us for an hour listening to what might well be told in ten minutes. They are wondrously fluent, considering all things ; and though I have heard many a sentence begun whereof the speaker did not evidently know the conclusion, yet, somehow or other, he has always managed to get through the paragraph without any hiatus, except perhaps in the sense. And as far as I can remark, it is not calm, plain, downright preachers who preserve the extemporaneous system for the most part, but pompous orators, indulging in all the cheap graces of rhetoric — exaggerating words and feelings to make effect, and dealing in pious caricature. Church-goers become excited by this loud talk and captivating manner, and can't go back afterwards to a sober discourse read out of a grave old sermon-book, appealing to the reason and the gentle feelings, instead of to the passions and the imagination. Beware of too much talk, O parsons ! If a man is to give an account of every idle word he utters, for what a number of such loud nothings, windy emphatic tropes and metaphors, spoken, not for God's glory, but the preacher's, will many a cushion-thumper have to answer ! And this rebuke may properly find a place here, because the clergyman by whose discourse it was elicited is not of the eloquent dramatic sort, but a gentleman, it is said, remarkable for old-fashioned learning and quiet habits, that do not seem to be to the taste of the many boisterous young clergy of the present day.

The Catholic chapel was built before their graces the most reverend lord archbishops came into fashion. It is large and gloomy, with one or two attempts at ornament by way of pictures at the altars, and a good inscription warning the in-comer, in a few bold words, of the sacredness of the place he stands in. Bare feet bore away thousands of people who came to pray there : there were numbers of smart equipages for the richer Protestant congregation. Strolling about the town in the balmy summer evening, I heard the sweet tones of a hymn from the people in the Presbyterian praying-house. Indeed, the country is full of piety, and a warm, sincere, undoubting devotion.

On week-days the street before the chapel is scarcely less crowded than on the Sabbath : but it is with women and children merely ; for a stream bordered with lime-trees runs pleasantly down the street, and hither come innumerable girls to wash, while the children make dirt-pies and look on. Wilkie was here some years since, and the place affords a great deal of amusement to the painter of character. Sketching, *tant bien que mal*, the bridge and the trees, and some of the nymphs engaged in the stream, the writer became an object of no small attention ; and at least a score of dirty brats left their dirt-pies to look on, the barelegged washing-girls grinning from the water.

One, a regular rustic beauty, whose face and figure would have made the fortune of a frontispiece, seemed particularly amused and *agaçante ;* and I walked round to get a drawing of her fresh jolly face : but directly I came near she pulled her gown over her head, and resolutely turned round her back ; and, as that part of her person did not seem to differ in character from the backs of the rest of Europe, there is no need of taking its likeness.

CHAPTER XXI.

THE PATTERN AT CROAGHPATRICK.

On the Pattern day, however, the washerwomen and children had all disappeared — nay, the stream, too, seemed to be gone out of town. There was a report current, also, that on the occasion of the Pattern, six hundred teetotalers had sworn to revolt ; and I fear that it was the hope of witnessing this awful rebellion which induced me to stay a couple of days at Westport. The Pattern was commenced on the Sunday, and the priests going up to the mountain took care that there should be no sports nor dancing on that day ; but that the people should only content themselves with the performance of what are called religious duties. Religious duties ! Heaven help us ! - If these reverend gentlemen were worshippers of Moloch or Baal, or any deity whose honor demanded bloodshed, and savage rites, and degradation, and torture, one might fancy them encouraging the people to the disgusting penances the poor things here perform. But it's too hard to think that in our days any priests of any religion should be found superintending such a hideous series of self-sacrifices as are, it appears, performed on this hill.

A friend who ascended the hill brought down the following account of it. The ascent is a very steep and hard one, he says; but it was performed in company of thousands of people who were making their way barefoot to the several "stations" upon the hill.

"The first station consists of one heap of stones, round which they must walk seven times, casting a stone on the heap each time, and before and after every stone's throw saying a prayer.

"The second station is on the top of the mountain. Here there is a great altar — a shapeless heap of stones. The poor wretches crawl *on their knees* into this place, say fifteen prayers, and after going round the entire top of the mountain fifteen times, say fifteen prayers again.

"The third station is near the bottom of the mountain at the further side from Westport. It consists of three heaps. The penitents must go seven times round these collectively, and seven times afterwards round each individually, saying a prayer before and after each progress."

My informant describes the people as coming away from this "frightful exhibition suffering severe pain, wounded and bleeding in the knees and feet, and some of the women shrieking with the pain of their wounds." Fancy thousands of these bent upon their work, and priests standing by to encourage them! — For shame, for shame. If all the popes, cardinals, bishops, hermits, priests, and deacons that ever lived were to come forward and preach this as a truth — that to please God you must macerate your body, that the sight of your agonies is welcome to Him, and that your blood, groans, and degradation find favor in His eyes, I would not believe them. Better have over a company of Fakeers at once, and set the Suttee going.

Of these tortures, however, I had not the fortune to witness a sight: for going towards the mountain for the first four miles, the only conveyance I could find was half the pony of an honest sailor, who said, when applied to, "I tell you what I do wid

you : I give you a spell about." But, as it turned out we were
going different ways, this help was but a small one. A car
with a spare seat, however, (there were hundreds of others
quite full, and scores of rattling country-carts covered with
people, and thousands of bare legs trudging along the road,) —
a car with a spare seat passed by at two miles from the Pattern, and that just in time to get comfortably wet through on
arriving there. The whole mountain was enveloped in mist;
and we could nowhere see thirty yards before us. The women
walked forward, with their gowns over their heads ; the men
sauntered on in the rain, with the utmost indifference to it.
The car presently came to a cottage, the court in front of which
was black with two hundred horses, and where as many drivers
were jangling and bawling ; and here we were told to descend.
You had to go over a wall and across a brook, and behold
the Pattern.

The pleasures of the poor people — for after the business on
the mountain came the dancing and love-making at its foot —
were wofully spoiled by the rain, which rendered dancing on
the grass impossible ; nor were the tents big enough for that
exercise. Indeed, the whole sight was as dismal and half-sav-
age a one as I have seen. There may have been fifty of these
tents squatted round a plain of the most brilliant green grass,
behind which the mist-curtains seemed to rise immediately;
for you could not even see the mountain-side beyond them.
Here was a great crowd of men and women, all ugly, as the
fortune of the day would have it (for the sagacious reader has,
no doubt, remarked that there are ugly and pretty days in life).
Stalls were spread about, whereof the owners were shrieking
out the praises of their wares — great coarse damp-looking
bannocks of bread for the most part, or, mayhap, a dirty collection of pigsfeet and such refreshments. Several of the
booths professed to belong to " confectioners " from Westport
or Castlebar, the confectionery consisting of huge biscuits and
doubtful-looking ginger-beer — ginger-ale or gingeretta it is
called in this country, by a fanciful people who love the finest
titles. Add to these, caldrons containing water for " tay " at
the doors of the booths, other pots full of masses of pale legs
of mutton (the owner " prodding," every now and then, for a
bit, and holding it up and asking the passenger to buy). In
the booths it was impossible to stand upright, or to see much,
on account of smoke. Men and women were crowded in these
rude tents, huddled together, and disappearing in the darkness.
Owners came bustling out to replenish the empty water-jugs :

and landladies stood outside in the rain calling strenuously upon all passers-by to enter. Here is a design taken from one of the booths, presenting ingeniously an outside and an inside view of the same place — an artifice seldom practised in pictures.

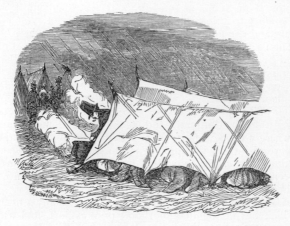

Meanwhile, high up on the invisible mountain, the people were dragging their bleeding knees from altar to altar, flinging stones, and muttering some endless litanies, with the priests standing by. I think I was not sorry that the rain, and the care of my precious health, prevented me from mounting a severe hill to witness a sight that could only have caused one to be shocked and ashamed that servants of God should encourage it. The road home was very pleasant; everybody was wet through, but everybody was happy, and by some miracle we were seven on the car. There was the honest Englishman in the military cap, who sang "The sea, the hopen sea's my 'ome," although not any one of the company called upon him for that air. Then the music was taken up by a good-natured lass from Castlebar; then the Englishman again, "With burnished brand and musketoon;" and there was no end of pushing, pinching, squeezing, and laughing. The Englishman, especially, had a favorite yell, with which he saluted and astonished all cottagers, passengers, cars, that we met or overtook. Presently came prancing by two dandies, who were especially frightened by the noise. "Thim's two tailors from Westport," said the carman, grinning with all his might. "Come, gat out

of the way there, gat along!" piped a small English voice from
above somewhere. I looked up, and saw a little creature
perched on the top of a tandem, which he was driving with the
most knowing air — a dreadful young hero, with a white hat,
and a white face, and a blue bird's-eye neck-cloth. He was five
feet high, if an inch, an ensign, and sixteen; and it was a
great comfort to think, in case of danger or riot, that one of
his years and personal strength was at hand to give help.

"Thim's the afficers," said the carman, as the tandem
wheeled by, a small groom quivering on behind — and the carman spoke with the greatest respect this time. Two days
before, on arriving at Westport, I had seen the same equipage
at the door of the inn — where for a moment there happened
to be no waiter to receive me. So, shouldering a carpet-bag,
I walked into the inn-hall, and asked a gentleman standing
there where was the coffee-room? It was the military tandem-
driving youth, who with much grace looked up in my face, and
said calmly, " *I dawnt knaw.*" I believe the little creature had
just been dining in the very room — and so present my best
compliments to him.

The Guide-book will inform the traveller of many a beautiful
spot which lies in the neighborhood of Westport, and which I
had not the time to visit; but I must not take leave of the
excellent little inn without speaking once more of its extreme
comfort; nor of the place itself, without another parting word
regarding its beauty. It forms an event in one's life to have
seen that place, so beautiful is it, and so unlike all other
beauties that I know of. Were such beauties lying upon English shores it would be a world's wonder: perhaps, if it were
on the Mediterranean, or the Baltic, English travellers would
flock to it by hundreds; why not come and see it in Ireland!
Remote as the spot is, Westport is only two days' journey
from London now, and lies in a country far more strange to
most travellers than France or Germany can be.

CHAPTER XXII.

FROM WESTPORT TO BALLINASLOE.

THE mail-coach took us next day by Castlebar and Tuam to Ballinasloe, a journey of near eighty miles. The country is interspersed with innumerable seats belonging to the Blakes, the Browns, and the Lynches; and we passed many large domains belonging to bankrupt lords and fugitive squires, with fine lodges adorned with moss and battered windows, and parks where, if the grass was growing on the roads, on the other hand the trees had been weeded out of the grass. About these seats and their owners the guard — an honest, shrewd fellow — had all the gossip to tell. The jolly guard himself was a ruin, it turned out: he told me his grandfather was a man of large property; his father, he said, kept a pack of hounds, and had spent everything by the time he, the guard, was sixteen: so the lad made interest to get a mail-car to drive, whence he had been promoted to the guard's seat, and now for forty years had occupied it, travelling eighty miles, and earning seven-and-twopence every day of his life. He had been once ill, he said, for three days; and if a man may be judged by ten hours' talk with him, there were few more shrewd, resolute, simple-minded men to be found on the outside of any coaches or the inside of any houses in Ireland.

During the first five-and-twenty miles of the journey, — for the day was very sunny and bright, — Croaghpatrick kept us company; and, seated with your back to the horses, you could see, " on the left, that vast aggregation of mountains which stretches southwards to the Bay of Galway; on the right, that gigantic assemblage which sweeps in circular outline northward to Killule." Somewhere amongst those hills the great John Tuam was born, whose mansion and cathedral are to be seen in Tuam town, but whose fame is spread everywhere. To arrive at Castlebar, we go over the undulating valley which lies between the mountain of Joyce country and Erris; and the first object which you see on entering the town is a stately Gothic castle that stands at a short distance from it.

On the gate of the stately Gothic castle was written an inscription not very hospitable: " WITHOUT BEWARE, WITHIN AMEND;" just beneath which is an iron crane of neat construction. The castle is the county gaol, and the iron crane is the gallows of the district. The town seems neat and lively : there is a fine church, a grand barracks (celebrated as the residence of the young fellow with the bird's-eye neck-cloth), a club, and a Whig and Tory newspaper. The road hence to Tuam is very pretty and lively, from the number of country seats along the way, giving comfortable shelter to more Blakes, Browns, and Lynches.

In the cottages, the inhabitants looked healthy and rosy in their rags, and the cots themselves in the sunshine almost comfortable. After a couple of months in the country, the stranger's eye grows somewhat accustomed to the rags : they do not frighten him as at first ; the people who wear them look for the most part healthy enough : especially the small children — those who can scarcely totter, and are sitting shading their eyes at the door, and leaving the unfinished dirt-pie to shout as the coach passes by — are as healthy a looking race as one will often see. Nor can any one pass through the land without being touched by the extreme love of children among the people : they swarm everywhere, and the whole country rings with cries of affection towards the children, with the songs of young ragged nurses dandling babies on their knees, and warnings of mothers to Patsey to come out of the mud, or Norey to get off the pig's back.

At Tuam the coach stopped exactly for fourteen minutes and a half, during which time those who wished might dine : but instead, I had the pleasure of inspecting a very mouldy, dirty town, and made my way to the Catholic cathedral — a very handsome edifice indeed ; handsome without and within, and of the Gothic sort. Over the door is a huge coat of arms surmounted by a cardinal's hat — the arms of the see, no doubt, quartered with John Tuam's own patrimonial coat ; and that was a frieze coat, from all accounts, passably ragged at the elbows. Well, he must be a poor wag who could sneer at an old coat, because it was old and poor ; but if a man changes it for a tawdry gimcrack suit bedizened with twopenny tinsel, and struts about calling himself his grace and my lord, when may we laugh if not then ? There is something simple in the way in which these good people belord their clergymen, and respect titles real or sham. Take any Dublin paper, — a couple of columns of it are sure to be filled with movements of the small great men of the world. Accounts from Derrynane state that the " Right Honorable the Lord Mayor is in good health — his lordship went out with his beagles yester-

day;" or "his Grace the Most Reverend the Lord Archbishop
of Ballywhack, assisted by the Right Reverend the Lord
Bishops of Trincomalee and Hippopotamus, assisted," &c.;
or "Colonel Tims, of Castle Tims, and lady, have quitted the
'Shelburne Hotel,' with a party for Kilballybathershins, where
the *august** party propose to enjoy a few days' shrimp-fish-
ing," — and so on.   Our people are not witty and keen of per-
ceiving the ridiculous, like the Irish; but the bluntness and
honesty of the English have wellnigh kicked the fashionable
humbug down; and except perhaps among footmen and about
Baker Street, this curiosity about the aristocracy is wearing
fast away.   Have the Irish so much reason to respect their
lords that they should so chronicle all their movements; and
not only admire real lords, but make sham ones of their own
to admire *them?*

There is no object of special mark upon the road from Tuam
to Ballinasloe — the country being flat for the most part, and
the noble Galway and Mayo mountains having disappeared at
length — until you come to a glimpse of Old England in the
pretty village of Ahascragh.   An old oak-tree grows in the
neat street, the houses are as trim and white as eye can desire,
and about the church and the town are handsome plantations,
forming on the whole such a picture of comfort and plenty as
is rarely to be seen in the part of Ireland I have traversed.
All these wonders have been wrought by the activity of an
excellent resident agent.   There was a countryman on the
coach deploring that, through family circumstances, this gentleman should have been dispossessed of his agency, and declaring that the village had already begun to deteriorate in consequence.   The marks of such decay were not, however, visible
— at least to a new comer; and, being reminded of it, I indulged in many patriotic longings for England: as every Englishman does when he is travelling out of the country which he
is always so willing to quit.

That a place should instantly begin to deteriorate because
a certain individual was removed from it — that cottagers
should become thriftless, and houses dirty, and house-windows
cracked, — all these are points which public economists may
ruminate over, and can't fail to give the carelessest traveller
much matter for painful reflection.   How is it that the presence
of one man more or less should affect a set of people come to
years of manhood, and knowing that they have their duty to

* This epithet is applied to the party of a Colonel somebody, in a
Dublin paper.

do? Why should a man at Ahascragh let his home go to ruin, and stuff his windows with ragged breeches instead of glass, because Mr. Smith is agent in place of Mr. Jones? Is he a child that won't work unless the schoolmaster be at hand? or are we to suppose with the "Repealers," that the cause of all this degradation and misery is the intolerable tyranny of the sister country, and the pain which poor Ireland has been made to endure? This is very well at the Corn Exchange, and among patriots after dinner; but, after all granting the grievance of the franchise (though it may not be unfair to presume that a man who has not strength of mind enough to mend his own breeches or his own windows will always be the tool of one party or another), there is no Inquisition set up in the country: the law tries to defend the people as much as they will allow; the odious tithe has even been whisked off from their shoulders to the landlords'; they may live pretty much as they like. Is it not too monstrous to howl about English tyranny and suffering Ireland, and call for a Stephen's Green Parliament to make the country quiet and the people industrious? The people are not politically worse treated than their neighbors in England. The priests and landlords, if they chose to co-operate, might do more for the country now than any kings or laws could. What you want here is not a Catholic or Protestant party, but an Irish party.

In the midst of these reflections, and by what the reader will doubtless think a blessed interruption, we came in sight of the town of Ballinasloe and its "gash lamps," which a fellow-passenger did not fail to point out with admiration. The road-menders, however, did not appear to think that light was by any means necessary; for, having been occupied, in the morning, in digging a fine hole upon the highway, previous to some alterations to be effected there, they had left their work at sundown, without any lamp to warn coming travellers of the hole — which we only escaped by a wonder. The papers have much such another story. In the Galway and Ballinasloe coach a horse on the road suddenly fell down and died; the coachman drove his coach unicorn-fashion into town; and, as for the dead horse, of course he left it on the road, at the place where it fell, and where another coach coming up was upset over it, bones broken, passengers maimed, coach smashed. By heavens! the tyranny of England is unendurable; and I have no doubt it had a hand in upsetting that coach.

CHAPTER XXIII.

BALLINASLOE TO DUBLIN.

DURING the cattle-fair the celebrated town of Ballinasloe is thronged with farmers from all parts of the kingdom — the cattle being picturesquely exhibited in the park of the noble proprietor of the town, Lord Clancarty. As it was not fair-time the town did not seem particularly busy, nor was there much to remark in it, except a church, and a magnificent lunatic asylum, that lies outside the town on the Dublin road, and is as handsome and stately as a palace. I think the beggars were more plenteous and more loathsome here than almost anywhere. To one hideous wretch I was obliged to give money to go away, which he did for a moment, only to obtrude his horrible face directly afterwards half eaten away with disease. "A penny for the sake of poor little Mery," said another woman, who had a baby sleeping on her withered breast; and how can any one who has a little Mery at home resist such an appeal? "Pity the poor blind man!" roared a respectably dressed grenadier of a fellow. I told him to go to the gentleman with a red neck-cloth and fur cap (a young buck from Trinity College) — to whom the blind man with much simplicity immediately stepped over; and as for the rest of the beggars, what pen or pencil could describe their hideous leering flattery, their cringing, swindling humor!

The inn, like the town, being made to accommodate the periodical crowds of visitors who attended the fair, presented in their absence rather a faded and desolate look; and in spite of the live-stock for which the place is famous, the only portion of their produce which I could get to my share, after twelve hours' fasting and an hour's bell-ringing and scolding, was one very lean mutton-chop and one very small damp kidney, brought in by an old tottering waiter to a table spread in a huge black coffee-room, dimly lighted by one little jet of gas.

As this only served very faintly to light up the above banquet, the waiter, upon remonstrance, proceeded to light the other *bec;* but the lamp was sulky, and upon this attempt to force it, as it were, refused to act altogether, and went out. The big room was then accommodated with a couple of yellow mutton-candles. There was a neat, handsome, correct young

English officer warming his slippers at the fire, and opposite him sat a worthy gentleman, with a glass of "mingled materials," discoursing to him in a very friendly and confidential way.

As I don't know the gentleman's name, and as it is not at all improbable, from the situation in which he was, that he has quite forgotten the night's conversation, I hope there will be no breach of confidence in recalling some part of it. The speaker was dressed in deep black — worn, however, with that *dégagé* air peculiar to the votaries of Bacchus, or that nameless god, offspring of Bacchus and Ceres, who may have invented the noble liquor called whiskey. It was fine to see the easy folds in which his neck-cloth confined a shirt-collar moist with the generous drops that trickled from the chin above, — its little percentage upon the punch. There was a fine dashing black satin waistcoat that called for its share, and generously disdained to be buttoned. I think this is the only specimen I have seen yet of the personage still so frequently described in the Irish novels — the careless drinking squire — the Irish Will Whimble.

"Sir," says he, "as I was telling you before this gentleman came in (from Westport, I preshume, sir, by the mail? and my service to you!), the butchers in Tchume (Tuam) — where I live, and shall be happy to see you and give you a shakedown, a cut of mutton, and the use of as good a brace of pointers as ever you shot over — the butchers say to me, whenever I look in at their shops and ask for a joint of meat — they say : ' Take down that quarther o' mutton, boy ; IT'S NO USE WEIGHING IT for Mr. Bodkin. He can tell with an eye what's the weight of it to an ounce ! ' And so, sir, I can ; and I'd make a bet to go into any market in Dublin, Tchume, Ballinasloe, where you please, and just by looking at the meat decide its weight."

At the pause, during which the gentleman here designated Bodkin drank off his "materials," the young officer said gravely that this was a very rare and valuable accomplishment, and thanked him for the invitation to Tchume.

The honest gentleman proceeded with his personal memoirs ; and (with a charming modesty that authenticated his tale, while it interested his hearers for the teller) he called for a fresh tumbler, and began discoursing about horses. "Them I don't know," says he, confessing the fact at once ; "or, if I do, I've been always so unlucky with them that it's as good as if I didn't.

" To give you an idea of my ill-fortune : Me brother-'n-law

Burke once sent me three colts of his to sell at this very fair of Ballinasloe, and for all I could do I could only get a bid for one of 'em, and sold her for sixteen pounds. And d'ye know what that mare was, sir?" says Mr. Bodkin, giving a thump that made the spoon jump out of the punch-glass for fright. "D'ye know who she was? she was Water-Wagtail, sir, — WATER-WAGTAIL! She won fourteen cups and plates in Ireland before she went to Liverpool; and you know what she did *there?*" (We said, "O! of course.") "Well, sir, the man who bought her from me sold her for four hunder' guineas; and in England she fetched eight hunder' pounds.

"Another of them very horses, gentlemen (Tim, some hot wather — screeching hot, you divil — and a sthroke of the limin) — another of them horses that I was refused fifteen pound for, me brother-in-law sould to Sir Rufford Bufford for a hunder'-and-fifty guineas. Wasn't *that* luck?

"Well, sir, Sir Rufford gives Burke his bill at six months, and don't pay it when it come jue. A pretty pickle Tom Burke was in, as I leave ye to fancy, for he'd paid away the bill, which he thought as good as goold; and sure it ought to be, for Sir Rufford had come of age since the bill was drawn, and before it was due, and, as I needn't tell you, had slipped into a very handsome property.

"On the protest of the bill, Burke goes in a fury to Gresham's in Sackville Street, where the baronet was living, and (would ye believe it?) the latter says he doesn't intend to meet the bill, on the score that he was a minor when he gave it. On which Burke was in such a rage that he took a horsewhip and vowed he'd beat the baronet to a jelly, and post him in every club in Dublin, and publish every circumstance of the transaction."

"It *does* seem rather a queer one," says one of Mr. Bodkin's hearers.

"Queer indeed: but that's not it, you see; for Sir Rufford is as honorable a man as ever lived; and after this quarrel he paid Burke his money, and they've been warm friends ever since. But what I want to show ye is our infernal luck. *Three months before, Sir Rufford had sold that very horse for three hunder' guineas.*"

The worthy gentleman had just ordered in a fresh tumbler of his favorite liquor, when we wished him good-night, and slept by no means the worse, because the bedroom candle was carried by one of the prettiest young chambermaids possible.

Next morning, surrounded by a crowd of beggars more filthy, hideous, and importunate than any I think in the most favored towns of the south, we set off, a coach-load, for Dublin. A clergyman, a guard, a Scotch farmer, a butcher, a bookseller's hack, a lad bound for Maynooth and another for Trinity, made a varied, pleasant party enough, where each, according to his lights, had something to say.

I have seldom seen a more dismal and uninteresting road than that which we now took, and which brought us through the "old, inconvenient, ill-built, and ugly town of Athlone." The painter would find here, however, some good subjects for his sketch-book, in spite of the commination of the Guide-book. Here, too, great improvements are taking place for the Shannon navigation, which will render the town not so inconvenient as at present it is stated to be; and hard by lies a little village that is known and loved by all the world where English is spoken. It is called Lishoy, but its real name is Auburn, and it gave birth to one Noll Goldsmith, whom Mr. Boswell was in the habit of despising very heartily. At the Quaker town of Moate, the butcher and the farmer dropped off, the clergyman went inside, and their places were filled by four Maynoothians, whose vacation was just at an end. One of them, a freshman, was inside the coach with the clergyman, and told him, with rather a long face, of the dismal discipline of his college. They are not allowed to quit the gates (except on general walks); they are expelled if they read a newspaper; and they begin term with "a retreat" of a week, which time they are made to devote to silence, and, as it is supposed, to devotion and meditation.

I must say the young fellows drank plenty of whiskey on the road, to prepare them for their year's abstinence; and, when at length arrived in the miserable village of Maynooth, determined not to go into college that night, but to devote the evening to a "lark." They were simple, kind-hearted young men, sons of farmers or tradesmen seemingly; and, as is always the case here, except among some of the gentry, very gentlemanlike and pleasing in manners. Their talk was of this companion and that; how one was in rhetoric, and another in logic, and a third had got his curacy. Wait for a while; and with the happy system pursued within the walls of their college, those smiling, good-humored faces will come out with a scowl, and downcast eyes that seem afraid to look the world in the face. When the time comes for them to take leave of yonder dismal-looking barracks, they will be men no longer, but bound over to the church, body and soul: their free thoughts chained down and kept in darkness, their honest affections mutilated. Well, I hope they will be happy to-night at any rate, and talk and laugh to their hearts' content. The poor freshman, whose big chest is carried off by the porter yonder to the inn, has but twelve hours more of hearty, natural, human life. To-morrow, they will begin their work upon him; cramping his mind, and biting his tongue, and firing and cutting at his heart, — breaking him to pull the church chariot. Ah! why didn't he stop at home, and dig potatoes and get children?

Part of the drive from Maynooth to Dublin is exceedingly pretty: you are carried through Leixlip, Lucan, Chapelizod, and by scores of parks and villas, until the gas-lamps come in sight. Was there ever a cockney that was not glad to see them; and did not prefer the sight of them, in his heart, to the best lake or mountain ever invented? Pat the waiter comes jumping down to the car and says, "Welcome back, sir!" and bustles the trunk into the queer little bedroom, with all the cordial hospitality imaginable.

CHAPTER XXIV.

TWO DAYS IN WICKLOW.

THE little tour we have just been taking has been performed, not only by myriads of the "car-drivingest, tay-drinkingest, say-bathingest people in the world," the inhabitants of the city of Dublin, but also by all the tourists who have come to discover this country for the benefit of the English nation. "Look here!" says the ragged, bearded genius of a guide at the Seven Churches. "This is the spot which Mr. Henry Inglis particularly admired, and said it was exactly like Norway. Many's the song I've heard Mr. Sam Lover sing here — a pleasant gentleman entirely. Have you seen my picture that's taken off in Mrs. Hall's book? All the strangers know me by it, though it makes me much cleverer than I am." Similar tales has he of Mr. Barrow, and the Transatlantic Willis, and of Crofton Croker, who has been everywhere.

The guide's remarks concerning the works of these gentlemen inspired me, I must confess, with considerable disgust and jealousy. A plague take them! what remains for me to discover after the gallant adventurers in the service of Paternoster Row have examined every rock, lake, and ruin of the district, exhausted it of all its legends, and "invented new" most likely, as their daring genius prompted? Hence it follows that the description of the two days' jaunt must of necessity be short; lest persons who have read former accounts should be led to refer to the same, and make comparisons which might possibly be unfavorable to the present humble pages.

Is there anything new to be said regarding the journey? In the first place, there's the railroad: it's no longer than the railroad to Greenwich, to be sure, and almost as well known; but has it been *done?* that's the question; or has anybody discovered the dandies on the railroad?

After wondering at the beggars and carmen of Dublin, the stranger can't help admiring another vast and numerous class of inhabitants of the city — namely, the dandies. Such a number of smartly-dressed young fellows I don't think any town possesses: no, not Paris, where the young shopmen, with spurs and stays, may be remarked strutting abroad on fête-days; nor London, where on Sundays, in the Park, you see thousands of this cheap kind of aristocracy parading; nor Liverpool, famous for the breed of commercial dandies, desk and counter D'Orsays and cotton and sugar-barrel Brummels, and whom one remarks pushing on to business with a brisk determined air. All the above races are only to be encountered on holidays, except by those persons whose affairs take them to shops, docks, or counting-houses, where these fascinating young fellows labor during the week.

But the Dublin breed of dandies is quite distinct from those of the various cities above named, and altogether superior: for they appear every day, and all day long, not once a week merely, and have an original and splendid character and appearance of their own, very hard to describe, though no doubt every traveller, as well as myself, has admired and observed it. They assume a sort of military and ferocious look, not observable in other cheap dandies, except in Paris perhaps now and then; and are to be remarked not so much for the splendor of their ornaments as for the profusion of them. Thus, for instance, a hat which is worn straight over the two eyes costs very likely more than one which hangs upon one ear; a great oily bush of hair to balance the hat (otherwise the head no doubt would fall hopelessly on one side) is even more economical than a crop which requires the barber's scissors oft-times; also a tuft on the chin may be had at a small expense of bear's-grease by persons of a proper age; and although big pins are the fashion, I am bound to say I have never seen so many or

so big as here. Large agate marbles or " taws," globes terres-
trial and celestial, pawnbrokers' balls, — I cannot find comparisons large enough for these wonderful ornaments of the
person. Canes also should be mentioned, which are sold very
splendid, with gold or silver heads, for a shilling on the Quays ;
and the dandy not uncommonly finishes off with a horn quizzing-
glass, which being stuck in one eye contracts the brows and
gives a fierce determined look to the whole countenance.

In idleness at least these young men can compete with the
greatest lords ; and the wonder is, how the city can support so
many of them, or they themselves ; how they manage to spend
their time : who gives them money to ride hacks in the " Phaynix" on field and race days ; to have boats at Kingstown
during the summer ; and to be crowding the railway-coaches
all the day long? Cars go whirling about all day, bearing
squads of them. You see them sauntering at all the railway-
stations in vast numbers, and jumping out of the carriages as
the trains come up, and greeting other dandies with that rich
large brogue which some actor ought to make known to the
English public : it being the biggest, richest, and coarsest of
all the brogues of Ireland.

I think these dandies are the chief objects which arrest the
stranger's attention as he travels on the Kingstown railroad,
and I have always been so much occupied in watching and
wondering at them as scarcely to have leisure to look at anything else during the pretty little ride of twenty minutes so
beloved by every Dublin cockney. The waters of the bay wash
in many places the piers on which the railway is built, and you
see the calm stretch of water beyond, and the big purple hill of
Howth, and the light-houses, and the jetties, and the shipping.
Yesterday was a boat-race, (I don't know how many scores of
such take place during the season,) and you may be sure there
were tens of thousands of the dandies to look on. There had
been boat-races the two days previous : before that, had been
a field-day — before that, three days of garrison races — to-
day, to-morrow, and the day after, there are races at Howth.
There seems some sameness in the sports, but everybody goes ;
everybody is never tired ; and then, I suppose, comes the
punch-party, and the song in the evening — the same old
pleasures, and the same old songs the next day, and so on
to the end. As for the boat-race, I saw two little boats in the
distance tugging away for dear life — the beach and piers
swarming with spectators, the bay full of small yachts and
innumerable row-boats, and in the midst of the assemblage a

convict-ship lying ready for sail, with a black mass of poor wretches on her deck — who, too, were eager for pleasure.

Who is not, in this country? Walking away from the pier and King George's column, you arrive upon rows after rows of pleasure-houses, whither all Dublin flocks during the summer-time — for every one must have his sea-bathing; and they say that the country houses to the west of the town are empty, or to be had for very small prices, while for those on the coast, especially towards Kingstown, there is the readiest sale at large prices. I have paid frequent visits to one, of which the rent is as great as that of a tolerable London house; and there seem to be others suited to all purses: for instance, there are long lines of two-roomed houses, stretching far back and away from the sea, accommodating, doubtless, small commercial men, or small families, or some of those travelling dandies we have just been talking about, and whose costume is so cheap and so splendid.

A two-horse car, which will accommodate twelve, or will condescend to receive twenty passengers, starts from the railway-station for Bray, running along the coast for the chief part of the journey, though you have but few views of the sea, on account of intervening woods and hills. The whole of this country is covered with handsome villas and their gardens, and pleasure-grounds. There are round many of the houses parks of some extent, and always of considerable beauty, among the trees of which the road winds. New churches are likewise to be seen in various places; built like the poor-houses, that are likewise everywhere springing up, pretty much upon one plan — a sort of bastard or Vauxhall Gothic — resembling no architecture of any age previous to that when Horace Walpole invented the Castle of Otranto and the other monstrosity upon Strawberry Hill: though it must be confessed that those on the Bray line are by no means so imaginative. Well, what matters, say you, that the churches be ugly, if the truth is preached within? Is it not fair, however, to say that Beauty is the truth too, of its kind? and why should it not be cultivated as well as other truth? Why build these hideous barbaric temples, when at the expense of a little study and taste beautiful structures might be raised?

After leaving Bray, with its pleasant bay, and pleasant river, and pleasant inn, the little Wicklow tour may be said to commence properly; and, as that romantic and beautiful country has been described many times in familiar terms, our only chance is to speak thereof in romantic and beautiful language such as no other writer can possibly have employed.

We rang at the gate of the steward's lodge and said, " Grant us a pass, we pray, to see the parks of Powerscourt, and to behold the brown deer upon the grass, and the cool shadows under the whispering trees."

But the steward's son answered, " You may not see the parks of Powerscourt, for the lord of the castle comes home, and we expect him daily." So, wondering at this reply, but not understanding the same, we took leave of the son of the steward and said, " No doubt Powerscourt is not fit to see. Have we not seen parks in England, my brother, and shall we break our hearts that this Irish one hath its gates closed to us? '

Then the car-boy said, " My lords, the park is shut, but the waterfall runs for every man ; will it please you to see the waterfall?" " Boy," we replied, " we have seen many waterfalls ; nevertheless, lead on ! " And the boy took his pipe out of his mouth and belabored the ribs of his beast.

And the horse made believe, as it were, to trot, and jolted the ardent travellers ; and we passed the green trees of Tinnehinch, which the grateful Irish nation bought and consecrated to the race of Grattan ; and we said, " What nation will spend fifty thousand pounds for our benefit? " and we wished we might get it ; and we passed on. The birds were, meanwhile, chanting concerts in the woods ; and the sun was double-gilding the golden corn.

And we came to a hill, which was steep and long of descent ; and the car-boy said, " My lords, I may never descend this hill with safety to your honors' bones : for my horse is not sure of foot, and loves to kneel in the highway. Descend therefore, and I will await your return here on the top of the hill."

So we descended, and one grumbled greatly ; but the other said, " Sir, be of good heart! the way is pleasant, and the footman will not weary as he travels it." And we went through the swinging gates of a park, where the harvest-men sate at their potatoes — a mealy meal.

The way was not short, as the companion said, but still it was a pleasant way to walk. Green stretches of grass were there, and a forest nigh at hand. It was but September : yet the autumn had already begun to turn the green trees into red ; and the ferns that were waving underneath the trees were reddened and fading too. And as Dr. Jones's boys of a Saturday disport in the meadows after school-hours, so did the little clouds run races over the waving grass. And as grave ushers who look on smiling at the sports of these little ones, so stood the old trees around the green, whispering and nodding to one another.

Purple mountains rose before us in front, and we began presently to hear a noise and roaring afar off — not a fierce roaring, but one deep and calm, like to the respiration of the great sea, as he lies basking on the sands in the sunshine.

As we came soon to a little hillock of green, which was standing before a huge mountain of purple black, and there were white clouds over the mountains, and some trees waving on the hillock, and between the trunks of them we saw the waters of the waterfall descending; and there was a snob on a rock, who stood and examined the same.

Then we approached the water, passing the clump of oak-trees. The waters were white, and the cliffs which they varnished were purple. But those round about were gray, tall, and gay with blue shadows, and ferns, heath, and rusty-colored funguses sprouting here and there in the same. But in the ravine where the waters fell, roaring as it were with the fall, the rocks were dark, and the foam of the cataract was of a yellow color. And we stood, and were silent, and wondered. And still the trees continued to wave, and the waters to roar and tumble, and the sun to shine, and the fresh wind to blow.

And we stood and looked : and said in our hearts it was beautiful, and bethought us how shall all this be set down in types and ink? (for our trade is to write books and sell the same — a chapter for a guinea, a line for a penny) ; and the waterfall roared in answer, "For shame, O vain man! think not of thy books and of thy pence now ; but look on, and wonder, and be silent. Can types or ink describe my beauty, though aided by thy small wit? I am made for thee to praise and wonder at : be content, and cherish thy wonder. It is enough that thou hast seen a great thing : is it needful that thou shouldst prate of all thou hast seen?"

So we came away silently, and walked through the park without looking back. And there was a man at the gate, who opened it and seemed to say, "Give me a little sixpence." But we gave nothing, and walked up the hill, which was sore to climb ; and on the summit found the car-boy, who was lolling on his cushions and smoking, as happy as a lord.

Quitting the waterfall at Powerscourt (the grand style in which it has been described was adopted in order that the reader, who has probably read other descriptions of the spot, might have at least *something* new in this account of it), we speedily left behind us the rich and wooded tract of country about Powerscourt, and came to a bleak tract, which, perhaps by way of contrast with so much natural wealth, is not unpleasing, and began ascending what is very properly called the Long Hill. Here you see, in the midst of the loneliness, a grim-looking barrack, that was erected when, after the Rebellion, it was necessary for some time to occupy this most rebellious country ; and a church looking equally dismal, a lean-looking sham-Gothic building, in the midst of this green desert. The road to Luggala, whither we were bound, turns off the Long Hill, up another hill, which seems still longer and steeper, inasmuch as it was ascended perforce on foot, and over lonely boggy moorlands, enlivened by a huge gray boulder plumped here and there, and comes, one wonders how, to the spot. Close to this hill of Slievebuck, is marked in the maps a district called " the uninhabited country," and these stones probably fell at a period of time when not only this district, but all the world was uninhabited, — and in some convulsion of the neighboring mountains this and other enormous rocks were cast abroad.

From behind one of them, or out of the ground somehow, as we went up the hill, sprang little ragged guides, who are always lurking about in search of stray pence from tourists ; and we had three or four of such at our back by the time we were at the top of the hill. Almost the first sight we saw was a smart coach-and-four, with a loving wedding-party within, and a genteel valet and lady's-maid without. I wondered had they been burying their modest loves in the uninhabited district? But presently, from the top of the hill, I saw the place in which their honeymoon had been passed : nor could any pair of lovers, nor a pious hermit bent on retirement from the world, have selected a more sequestered spot.

Standing by a big shining granite stone on the hill-top, we looked immediately down upon Lough Tay — a little round lake of half a mile in length, which lay beneath us as black as a pool of ink — a high, crumbling, white-sided mountain falling abruptly into it on the side opposite to us, with a huge ruin of shattered rocks at its base. Northwards, we could see between mountains a portion of the neighboring lake of Lough Dan — which, too, was dark, though the Annamoe river, which connects the two lakes, lay coursing through the greenest possible flats and shining as bright as silver. Brilliant green shores, too, come gently down to the southern side of Lough Tay ;

through these runs another river, with a small rapid or fall, which makes a music for the lake, and here, amidst beautiful woods, lies a villa, where the four horses, the groom and valet, the postilions, and the young couple had, no doubt, been hiding themselves.

Hereabouts, the owner of the villa, Mr. Latouche, has a great grazing establishment; and some herd-boys, no doubt seeing strangers on the hill, thought proper that the cattle should stray that way, that they might drive them back again, and parenthetically ask the travellers for money, — everybody asks travellers for money, as it seems. Next day, admiring in a laborer's arms a little child — his master's son, who could not speak — the laborer, his he-nurse, spoke for him, and demanded a little sixpence to buy the child apples. One grows not a little callous to this sort of beggary : and the only one of our numerous young guides who got a reward was the raggedest of them. He and his companions had just come from school, he said, — not a Government school, but a private one, where they paid. I asked how much, — "Was it a penny a week?" "No; not a penny a week, but so much at the end of the year." "Was it a barrel of meal, or a few stone of potatoes, or something of that sort?" "Yes; something of that sort."

The something must, however, have been a very small something on the poor lad's part. He was one of four young ones, who lived with their mother, a widow. He had no work; he could get no work; nobody had work. His mother had a cabin with no land — not a perch of land, no potatoes — nothing but the cabin. How did they live? — the mother knitted stockings. I asked had she any stockings at home? — the boy said, "No." How did he live? — he lived how he could ; and we gave him threepence, with which, in delight, he went bounding off to the poor mother. Gracious heavens! what a history to hear, told by a child looking quite cheerful as he told it, and as if the story was quite a common one. And a common one, too, it is : and God forgive us.

Here is another, and of a similar low kind, but rather pleasanter. We asked the car-boy how much he earned. He said, "Seven shillings a week, and his chances" — which, in the summer season, from the number of tourists who are jolted in his car, must be tolerably good — eight or nine shillings a week more, probably. But, he said, in winter his master did not hire him for the car ; and he was obliged to look for work elsewhere : as for saving, he never had saved a shilling in his life.

We asked him was he married? and he said, No, but he was *as good as married;* for he had an old mother and four little brothers to keep, and six mouths to feed, and to dress himself decent to drive the gentlemen. Was not the " as good as married " a pretty expression? and might not some of what are called their betters learn a little good from these simple poor creatures? There's many a young fellow who sets up in the world would think it rather hard to have four brothers to support; and I have heard more than one genteel Christian pining over five hundred a year. A few such may read this, perhaps: let them think of the Irish widow with the four children and *nothing,* and at least be more contented with their port and sherry and their leg of mutton.

This brings us at once to the subject of dinner and the little village, Roundwood, which was reached by this time, lying a few miles off from the lakes, and reached by a road not particularly remarkable for any picturesqueness in beauty; though you pass through a simple, pleasing landscape, always agreeable as a repose, I think, after viewing a sight so beautiful as those mountain lakes we have just quitted. All the hills up which we had panted had imparted a fierce sensation of hunger; and it was nobly decreed that we should stop in the middle of the street of Roundwood, impartially between the two hotels, and solemnly decide upon a resting-place after having inspected the larders and bedrooms of each.

And here, as an impartial writer, I must say that the hotel of Mr. Wheatly possesses attractions which few men can resist, in the shape of two very handsome young ladies his daughters; whose faces were they but painted on his signboard, instead of the mysterious piece which ornaments it, would infallibly draw tourists into the house, thereby giving the opposition inn of Murphy not the least chance of custom.

A landlord's daughters in England, inhabiting a little country inn, would be apt to lay the cloth for the traveller, and their respected father would bring in the first dish of the dinner; but this arrangement is never known in Ireland: we scarcely ever see the cheering countenance of my landlord. And as for the young ladies of Roundwood, I am bound to say that no young persons in Baker Street could be more genteel; and that our bill, when it was brought the next morning, was written in as pretty and fashionable a lady's hand as ever was formed in the most elegant finishing school at Pimlico.

Of the dozen houses of the little village, the half seem to be houses of entertainment. A green common stretches before these, with its rural accompaniments of geese, pigs, and idlers; a park and plantation at the end of the village, and plenty of trees round about it, give it a happy, comfortable, English look; which is, to my notion, the best compliment that can be paid to a hamlet: for where, after all, are villages so pretty?

Here, rather to one's wonder — for the district was not thickly enough populated to encourage dramatic exhibitions — a sort of theatre was erected on the common, a ragged cloth covering the spectators and the actors, and the former (if there were any) obtaining admittance through two doors on the stage in front, marked "PIT & GALERY." Why should the word not be spelt with one L as with two?

The entrance to the "pit" was stated to be threepence, and to the "galery" twopence. We heard the drums and pipes of the orchestra as we sat at dinner: it seemed to be a good opportunity to examine Irish humor of a peculiar sort, and we promised ourselves a pleasant evening in the pit.

But although the drums began to beat at half-past six, and a crowd of young people formed round the ladder at that hour, to whom the manager of the troop addressed the most vehement invitations to enter, nobody seemed to be inclined to mount the steps: for the fact most likely was, that not one of the poor fellows possessed the requisite twopence which would induce the fat old lady who sat by it to fling open the gallery door. At one time I thought of offering a half-crown for a purchase of tickets for twenty, and so at once benefiting the manager and the crowd of ragged urchins who stood wistfully without his pavilion; but it seemed ostentatious, and we had not the courage to face the tall man in the great-coat gesticulating and shouting in front of the stage, and make the proposition.

Why not? It would have given the company potatoes at least for supper, and made a score of children happy. They would have seen "the learned pig who spells your name, the feats of manly activity, the wonderful Italian vaulting;" and they would have heard the comic songs by "your humble servant."

"Your humble servant" was the head of the troop: a long man, with a broad accent, a yellow top-coat, and a piteous lean face. What a speculation was this poor fellow's! he must have a company of at least a dozen to keep. There were three girls in trousers, who danced in front of the stage, in Polish caps, tossing their arms about to the tunes of three musicianers; there was a page, two young tragedy-actors, and a clown; there was the fat old woman at the gallery-door waiting for the twopences; there was the Jack Pudding; and it was evident that there must have been some one within, or else who would take care of the learned pig?

The poor manager stood in front, and shouted to the little Irishry beneath; but no one seemed to move. Then he brought forward Jack Pudding, and had a dialogue with him; the jocularity of which, by heavens! made the heart ache to hear. We had determined, at least, to go to the play before that, but the dialogue was too much: we were obliged to walk away, unable to face that dreadful Jack Pudding, and heard the poor manager shouting still for many hours through the night, and the drums thumping vain invitations to the people. O unhappy children of the Hibernian Thespis! it is my belief that they must have eaten the learned pig that night for supper.

It was Sunday morning when we left the little inn at Roundwood: the people were flocking in numbers to church, on cars, and pillions, neat, comfortable, and well dressed. We saw in this country more health, more beauty, and more shoes than I have remarked in any quarter. That famous resort of sightseers, the Devil's Glen, lies at a few miles' distance from the little village; and, having gone on the car as near to the spot as the road permitted, we made across the fields — boggy, stony, illtilled fields they were — for about a mile, at the end of which walk we found ourselves on the brow of the ravine that has received so ugly a name.

Is there a legend about the place? No doubt for this, as for almost every other natural curiosity in Ireland, there is some tale of monk, saint, fairy, or devil; but our guide on the present day was a barrister from Dublin, who did not deal in fictions by any means so romantic, and the history, whatever it was, remained untold. Perhaps the little breechesless cicerone who offered himself would have given us the story, but we dismissed the urchin with scorn, and had to find our own way through bush and bramble down to the entrance of the gully.

Here we came on a cataract, which looks very big in Messrs. Curry's pretty little Guide-book (that every traveller to Wicklow will be sure to have in his pocket); but the waterfall, on this shining Sabbath morning, was disposed to labor as little as possible, and indeed is a spirit of a very humble, ordinary sort.

But there is a ravine of a mile and a half, through which a river runs roaring (a lady who keeps the gate will not object to receive a gratuity) — there is a ravine, or Devil's glen, which forms a delightful wild walk, and where a Methuselah of a landscape-painter might find studies for all his life long. All sorts of foliage and color, all sorts of delightful caprices of light and shadow — the river tumbling and frothing amidst the boulders —" raucum per lævia murmur saxa ciens," and a chorus of 150,000 birds (there might be more), hopping, twittering, singing under the clear cloudless Sabbath scene, make this walk one of the most delightful that can be taken; and indeed I hope there is no harm in saying that you may get as much out of an hour's walk there as out of the best hour's extempore preaching. But this was as a salvo to our conscience for not being at church.

Here, however, was a long aisle, arched gothically overhead, in a much better taste than is seen in some of those dismal new churches; and, by way of painted glass, the sun lighting up multitudes of various-colored leaves, and the birds for choristers, and the river by way of organ, and in it stones enough to make a whole library of sermons. No man can walk in such a place without feeling grateful, and grave, and humble; and without thanking heaven for it as he comes away. And, walking and musing in this free, happy place, one could not help thinking of a million and a half of brother cockneys shut up in their huge prison (the treadmill for the day being idle), and told by some legislators that relaxation is sinful, that works of art are abominations except on week-days, and that their proper place of resort is a dingy tabernacle, where a loud-voiced man is howling about hell-fire in bad grammar. Is not this beautiful world, too, a part of our religion? Yes, truly, in whatever way my Lord John Russell may vote; and it is to be learned without having recourse to any professor at any Bethesda, Ebenezer, or Jerusalem: there can be no mistake about it; no terror, no bigoted dealing of damnation to one's neighbor: it is taught without false emphasis or vain spouting on the preacher's part — how should there be such with such a preacher?

This wild onslaught upon sermons and preachers needs perhaps an explanation: for which purpose we must whisk back out of the Devil's Glen (improperly so named) to Dublin, and to this day week, when, at this very time, I heard one of the first preachers of the city deliver a sermon that lasted for an hour and twenty minutes — time enough to walk up the Glen and back, and remark a thousand delightful things by the way.

Mr. G——'s church (though there would be no harm in mentioning the gentleman's name, for a more conscientious and excellent man, as it is said, cannot be) is close by the Custom

House in Dublin, and crowded morning and evening with his admirers. The service was beautifully read by him, and the audience joined in the responses, and in the psalms and hymns,* with a fervor which is very unusual in England. Then came the sermon; and what more can be said of it than that it was extempore, and lasted for an hour and twenty minutes? The orator never failed once for a word, so amazing is his practice; though, as a stranger to this kind of exercise, I could not help trembling for the performer, as one has for Madame Saqui on the slack rope, in the midst of a blaze of rockets and squibs, expecting every minute she must go over. But the artist was too skilled for that; and after some tremendous bound of a metaphor, in the midst of which you expect he must tumble neck and heels, and be engulfed in the dark abyss of nonsense, down he was sure to come, in a most graceful attitude too, in the midst of a fluttering "Ah!" from a thousand wondering people.

But I declare solemnly that when I came to try and recollect of what the exhibition consisted, and give an account of the sermon at dinner that evening, it was quite impossible to remember a word of it; although, to do the orator justice, he repeated many of his opinions a great number of times over. Thus, if he had to discourse of death to us, it was, "At the approach of the Dark Angel of the Grave," "At the coming of the grim King of Terrors," "At the warning of that awful Power to whom all of us must bow down," "At the summons of that Pallid Spectre whose equal foot knocks at the monarch's tower or the poor man's cabin"—and so forth. There is an examiner of plays, and indeed there ought to be an examiner of sermons, by which audiences are to be fully as much injured or misguided as by the other named exhibitions. What call have reverend gentlemen to repeat their dicta half a dozen times over, like Sir Robert Peel when he says anything that he fancies to be witty? Why are men to be kept for an hour and twenty minutes listening to that which may be more effectually said in twenty?

* Here is an extract from one of the latter —

"Hasten to some distant isle,
In the bosom of the deep,
Where the skies for ever smile,
And the blacks for ever weep."

Is it not a shame that such nonsensical false twaddle should be sung in a house of the Church of England, and by people assembled for grave and decent worship?

15

And it need not be said here that a church is not a sermon-house — that it is devoted to a purpose much more lofty and sacred, for which has been set apart the noblest service, every single word of which latter has been previously weighed with the most scrupulous and thoughtful reverence. And after this sublime work of genius, learning, and piety is concluded, is it not a shame that a man should mount a desk, who has not taken the trouble to arrange his words beforehand, and speak thence his crude opinions in his doubtful grammar? It will be answered that the extempore preacher does not deliver crude opinions, but that he arranges his discourse beforehand : to all which it may be replied that Mr. —— contradicted himself more than once in the course of the above oration, and repeated himself a half-dozen of times. A man in that place has no right to say a word too much or too little.

And it comes to this, — it is the preacher the people follow, not the prayers ; or why is this church more frequented than any other? It is that warm emphasis, and word-mouthing, and vulgar imagery, and glib rotundity of phrase, which brings them together and keeps them happy and breathless. Some of this class call the Cathedral Service *Paddy's Opera ;* they say it is Popish — downright scarlet — they won't go to it. They will have none but their own hymns — and pretty they are — no ornaments but those of their own minister, his rank incense and tawdry rhetoric. Coming out of the church, on the Custom House steps hard by, there was a fellow with a bald large forehead, a new black coat, a little Bible, spouting — spouting " in omne volubilis ævum " — the very counterpart of the reverend gentleman hard by. It was just the same thing, just as well done : the eloquence quite as easy and round, the amplifications as ready, the big words rolling round the tongue just as within doors. But we are out of the Devil's Glen by this time ; and perhaps, instead of delivering a sermon there, we had better have been at church hearing one.

The country people, however, are far more pious ; and the road along which we went to Glendalough was thronged with happy figures of people plodding to or from mass. A chapel yard was covered with gray cloaks ; and at a little inn hard by, stood numerous carts, cars, shandrydans, and pillioned horses, awaiting the end of the prayers. The aspect of the country is wild, and beautiful of course ; but why try to describe it? I think the Irish scenery just like the Irish melodies — sweet, wild, and sad even in the sunshine. You can neither represent one nor the other by words ; but I am sure if one could translate "The Meeting of the Waters" into form and colors, it would fall into the exact shape of a tender Irish landscape. So take and play that tune upon your fiddle, and shut your eyes, and muse a little, and you have the whole scene before you.

I don't know if there is any tune about Glendalough ; but if there be, it must be the most delicate, fantastic, fairy melody that ever was played. Only fancy can describe the charms of that delightful place. Directly you see it, it smiles at you as innocent and friendly as a little child ; and once seen, it becomes your friend forever, and you are always happy when you think of it. Here is a little lake, and little fords across it, surrounded by little mountains, and which lead you now to little islands where there are all sorts of fantastic little old chapels and grave-yards ; or, again, into little brakes and shrubberies where small rivers are crossing over little rocks, plashing and jumping, and singing as loud as ever they can. Thomas Moore has written rather an awful description of it ; and it may indeed appear big to *him*, and to the fairies who must have inhabited the place in old days, that's clear. For who could be accommodated in it except the little people?

There are seven churches, whereof the clergy must have been the smallest persons, and have had the smallest benefices and the littlest congregations ever known. As for the cathe-dral, what a bishoplet it must have been that presided there. The place would hardly hold the Bishop of London, or Mr. Sydney Smith — two full-sized clergymen of these days — who would be sure to quarrel there for want of room, or for any other reason. There must have been a dean no bigger than Mr. Moore before mentioned, and a chapter no bigger than that chapter in "Tristram Shandy" which does not contain a single word, and mere popguns of canons, and a beadle about as tall as Crofton Croker, to whip the little boys who were play-ing at taw (with peas) in the yard.

They say there was a university, too, in the place, with I don't know how many thousand scholars ; but for accounts of this there is an excellent guide on the spot, who, for a shilling or two, will tell all he knows, and a great deal more too.

There are numerous legends, too, concerning St. Kevin, and Fin MacCoul and the Devil, and the deuce knows what. But these stories are, I am bound to say, abominably stupid and stale ; and some guide * ought to be seized upon and choked,

---

* It must be said, for the worthy fellow who accompanied us, and who acted as cicerone previously to the great Willis, the great Hall, the great

and flung into the lake, by way of warning to the others to stop their interminable prate. This is the curse attending curiosity, for visitors to almost all the show-places in the country : you have not only the guide — who himself talks too much — but a string of ragged amateurs, starting from bush and briar, ready to carry his honor's umbrella or my lady's cloak, or to help either up a bank or across a stream. And all the while they look wistfully in your face, saying, "Give me sixpence !" as clear as looks can speak. The unconscionable rogues ! how dare they, for the sake of a little starvation or so, interrupt gentlefolks in their pleasure !

A long tract of wild country, with a park or two here and there, a police-barrack perched on a hill, a half-starved-looking church stretching its long scraggy steeple over a wide plain, mountains whose base is richly cultivated while their tops are purple and lonely, warm cottages and farms nestling at the foot of the hills, and humble cabins here and there on the wayside, accompany the car, that jingles back over fifteen miles of ground through Inniskerry to Bray. You pass by wild gaps and Greater and Lesser Sugar Loaves ; and about eight o'clock, when the sky is quite red with sunset, and the long shadows are of such a purple as (they may say what they like) Claude could no more paint than I can, you catch a glimpse of the sea beyond Bray, and crying out, " Θάλαττα, θάλαττα !" affect to be wondrously delighted by the sight of that element.

The fact is, however, that at Bray is one of the best inns in Ireland ; and there you may be perfectly sure is a good dinner ready, five minutes after the honest car-boy, with innumerable hurroos and smacks of his whip, has brought up his passengers to the door with a gallop.

As for the Vale of Avoca, I have not described that : because (as has been before occasionally remarked) it is vain to attempt to describe natural beauties ; and because, secondly (though this is a minor consideration), we did not go thither. But we went on another day to the Dargle, and to Shanganah, and the city of Cabinteely, and to the Scalp — that wild pass : and I have no more to say about them than about the Vale of Avoca. The Dublin Cockney, who has these places at his door,

Barrow, that though he wears a ragged coat his manners are those of a gentleman, and his conversation evinces no small talent, taste, and scholarship.

knows them quite well ; and as for the Londoner, who is meditating a trip to the Rhine for the summer, or to Brittany or
Normandy, let us beseech him to see his *own country first* (if
Lord Lyndhurst will allow us to call this a part of it) ; and
if, after twenty-four hours of an easy journey from London,
the Cockney be not placed in the midst of a country as beautiful, as strange to him, as romantic as the most imaginative
man on 'Change can desire, — may this work be praised by the
critics all round and never reach a second edition !

CHAPTER XXV.

COUNTRY MEETINGS IN KILDARE — MEATH — DROGHEDA.

An agricultural show was to be held at the town of Naas,
and I was glad, after having seen the grand exhibition at Cork,
to be present at a more homely, unpretending country festival,
where the eyes of Europe, as the orators say, did not happen
to be looking on. Perhaps men are apt, under the idea of
this sort of inspection, to assume an air somewhat more pompous and magnificent than that which they wear every day.
The Naas meeting was conducted without the slightest attempt
at splendor or display — a hearty, modest, matter-of-fact country meeting.

Market-day was fixed upon of course, and the town, as we
drove into it, was thronged with frieze-coats, the market-place
bright with a great number of apple-stalls, and the street filled
with carts and vans of numerous small tradesmen, vending
cheeses, or cheap crockeries, or ready-made clothes and such
goods. A clothier, with a great crowd round him, had arrayed
himself in a staring new waistcoat of his stock, and was turning slowly round to exhibit the garment, spouting all the
while to his audience, and informing them that he could fit out
any person, in one minute, "in a complete new shuit from
head to fut." There seemed to be a crowd of gossips at
every shop door, and, of course, a number of gentlemen waiting at the inn-steps, criticising the cars and carriages as they
drove up. Only those who live in small towns know what an
object of interest the street becomes, and the carriages and
horses which pass therein. Most of the gentlemen had sent

stock to compete for the prizes. The shepherds were tending the stock. The judges were making their award, and until their sentence was given, no competitors could enter the show-yard. The entrance to that, meanwhile, was thronged by a great posse of people, and as the gate abutted upon an old gray tower, a number of people had scaled that, and were looking at the beasts in the court below. Likewise, there was a tall hay-stack, which possessed similar advantages of situation, and was equally thronged with men and boys. The rain had fallen heavily all night, the heavens were still black with it, and the coats of the men, and the red feet of many ragged female spectators, were liberally spattered with mud.

The first object of interest we were called upon to see was a famous stallion; and passing through the little by-streets (dirty and small, but not so small and dirty as other by-streets to be seen in Irish towns), we came to a porte-cochère, lead-ing into a yard filled with wet fresh hay, sinking juicily under the feet; and here in a shed was the famous stallion. His sire must have been a French diligence-horse; he was of a roan color, with a broad chest, and short, clean legs. His forehead was ornamented with a blue ribbon, on which his name and prizes were painted, and on his chest hung a couple of medals by a chain — a silver one awarded to him at Cork, a gold one carried off by superior merit from other stallions assembled to contend at Dublin. When the points of the ani-mal were sufficiently discussed, a mare, his sister, was pro-duced, and admired still more than himself. Any man who has witnessed the performance of the French horses in the Havre diligence, must admire the vast strength and the extraordinary swiftness of the breed; and it was agreed on all hands, that such horses would prove valuable in this country, where it is hard now to get a stout horse for the road, so much has the fashion for blood, and nothing but blood, prevailed of late.

By the time the stallion was seen, the judges had done their arbitration; and we went to the yard, where broad-backed sheep were resting peaceably in their pens; bulls were led about by the nose; enormous turnips, both Swedes and Aberdeens, reposed in the mud; little cribs of geese, hens, and peafowl were come to try for the prize; and pigs might be seen — some encumbered with enormous families, others with fat merely. They poked up one brute to walk for us: he made, after many futile attempts, a desperate rush forward, his leg almost lost in fat, his immense sides quivering and shaking with the exercise; he was then allowed to return to his straw, into which he sank panting. Let us hope that he went home with a pink ribbon round his tail that night, and got a prize for his obesity.

I think the pink ribbon was, at least to a Cockney, the pleasantest sight of all: for on the evening after the show we saw many carts going away so adorned, having carried off prizes on the occasion. First came a great bull stepping along, he and his driver having each a bit of pink on their heads; then a cart full of sheep; then a car of good-natured-looking people, having a churn in the midst of them that sported a pink favor. When all the prizes were distributed, a select company sat down to dinner at Macavoy's Hotel; and no doubt a reporter who was present has given in the county paper an account of all the good things eaten and said. At our end of the table we had saddle-of-mutton, and I remarked a boiled leg of the same delicacy, with turnips, at the opposite extremity. Before the vice I observed a large piece of roast-beef, which I could not observe at the end of dinner, because it was all swallowed. After the mutton we had cheese, and were just beginning to think that we had dined very sufficiently, when a squadron of apple-pies came smoking in, and convinced us that, in such a glorious cause, Britons are never at fault. We ate up the apple-pies, and then the punch was called for by those who preferred that beverage to wine, and the speeches began.

The chairman gave "The Queen," nine times nine and one cheer more; "Prince Albert and the rest of the Royal Family," great cheering; "The Lord-Lieutenant" — his Excellency's health was received rather coolly, I thought. And then began the real business of the night: health of the Naas Society, health of the Agricultural Society, and healths all round; not forgetting the Sallymount Beagles, and the Kildare Foxhounds — which toasts were received with loud cheers and halloos by most of the gentlemen present, and elicited brief speeches from the masters of the respective hounds, promising good sport next season. After the Kildare Foxhounds, an old farmer in a gray coat got gravely up, and without being requested to do so in the least, sang a song, stating that

> "At seven in the morning by most of the clocks
> We rode to Kilruddery in search of a fox;"

and at the conclusion of his song challenged a friend to give another song. Another old farmer, on this, rose and sang one of Morris's songs with a great deal of queer humor; and no doubt many more songs were sung during the evening, for plenty of hot-water jugs were blocking the door as we went out.

The jolly frieze-coated songster who celebrated the Kilruddery fox, sang, it must be confessed, most wofully out of tune ; but still it was pleasant to hear him, and I think the meeting was the most agreeable one I have seen in Ireland : there was more good-humor, more cordial union of classes, more frankness and manliness, than one is accustomed to find in Irish meetings. All the speeches were kind-hearted, straightforward speeches, without a word of politics or an attempt at oratory : it was impossible to say whether the gentlemen present were Protestant or Catholic, — each one had a hearty word of encouragement for his tenant, and a kind welcome for his neighbor. There were forty stout, well-to-do farmers in the room, renters of fifty, seventy, a hundred acres of land. There were no clergymen present ; though it would have been pleasant to have seen one of each persuasion to say grace for the meeting and the meat.

At a similar meeting at Ballytore the next day, I had an opportunity of seeing a still finer collection of stock than had been brought to Naas, and at the same time one of the most beautiful flourishing villages in Ireland. The road to it from H—— town, if not remarkable for its rural beauty, is pleasant to travel, for evidences of neat and prosperous husbandry are around you everywhere : rich crops in the fields and neat cottages by the roadside, accompanying us as far as Ballytore — a white, straggling village, surrounding green fields of some five furlongs square, with a river running in the midst of them, and numerous fine cattle in the green. Here is a large windmill, fitted up like a castle, with battlements and towers : the castellan thereof is a good-natured old Quaker gentleman, and numbers more of his following inhabit the town.

The consequence was that the shops of the village were the neatest possible, though by no means grand or portentous. Why should Quaker shops be neater than other shops ? They suffer to the full as much oppression as the rest of the hereditary bondsmen ; and yet, in spite of their tyrants, they prosper.

I must not attempt to pass an opinion upon the stock exhibited at Ballytore ; but, in the opinion of some large agricultural proprietors present, it might have figured with advantage in any show in England, and certainly was finer than the exhibition at Naas ; which, however, is a very young society. The best part of the show, however, to everybody's thinking, (and it is pleasant to observe the manly fairplay spirit which characterizes the society), was, that the prizes of the Irish Agricultural Society were awarded to two men — one a laborer, the other a very small holder, both having reared the best stock exhibited on the occasion. At the dinner, which took place in a barn of the inn, smartly decorated with laurels for the purpose, there was as good and stout a body of yeomen as at Naas the day previous, but only two landlords; and here, too, as at Naas, neither priest nor parson. Cattle-feeding of course formed the principal theme of the after-dinner discourse — not, however, altogether to the exclusion of tillage; and there was a good and useful prize for those who could not afford to rear fat oxen — for the best kept cottage and garden, namely — which was won by a poor man with a large family and scanty precarious earnings, but who yet found means to make the most of his small resources and to keep his little cottage neat and cleanly. The tariff and the plentiful harvest together had helped to bring down prices severely; and we heard from the farmers much desponding talk. I saw hay sold for 2l. the ton, and oats for 8s. 3d. the barrel.

In the little village I remarked scarcely a single beggar, and very few bare feet indeed among the crowds who came to see the show. Here the Quaker village had the advantage of the town of Naas, in spite of its poor-house, which was only half full when we went to see it; but the people prefer beggary and starvation abroad to comfort and neatness in the union-house.

A neater establishment cannot be seen than this; and liberty must be very sweet indeed, when people prefer it and starvation to the certainty of comfort in the union-house. We went to see it after the show at Naas.

The first persons we saw at the gate of the place were four buxom lasses in blue jackets and petticoats, who were giggling and laughing as gayly as so many young heiresses of a thousand a year, and who had a color in their cheeks that any lady of Almack's might envy. They were cleaning pails and carrying in water from a green court or playground in front of the house, which some of the able-bodied men of the place were busy in inclosing. Passing through the large entrance of the house, a nondescript Gothic building, we came to a court divided by a road and two low walls: the right inclosure is devoted to the boys of the establishment, of whom there were about fifty at play: boys more healthy or happy it is impossible to see. Separated from them is the nursery; and here were seventy or eighty young children, a shrill clack of happy voices leading the way to the door where they were to be found. Boys and children had a comfortable little uniform, and shoes were furnished for all; though the authorities did not seem particularly severe in enforcing the wearing of the shoes, which most of the young persons left behind them.

In spite of all *The Times's* in the world, the place was a happy one. It is kept with a neatness and comfort to which, until his entrance into the union-house, the Irish peasant must perforce have been a stranger. All the rooms and passages are white, well scoured, and airy; all the windows are glazed; all the beds have a good store of blankets and sheets. In the women's dormitories there lay several infirm persons, not ill enough for the infirmary, and glad of the society of the common room: in one of the men's sleeping-rooms we found a score of old gray-coated men sitting round another who was reading prayers to them. And outside the place we found a woman starving in rags, as she had been ragged and starving for years: her husband was wounded, and lay in his house upon straw; her children were ill with a fever; she had neither meat, nor physic, nor clothing, nor fresh air, nor warmth for them; — and she preferred to starve on rather than enter the house!

The last of our agricultural excursions was to the fair of Castledermot, celebrated for the show of cattle to be seen there, and attended by the farmers and gentry of the neighboring counties. Long before reaching the place we met troops of cattle coming from it — stock of a beautiful kind, for the most part large, sleek, white, long-backed, most of the larger animals being bound for England. There was very near as fine a show in the pastures along the road — which lies across a light green country with plenty of trees to ornament the landscape, and some neat cottages along the roadside.

At the turnpike of Castledermot the droves of cattle met us by scores no longer, but by hundreds, and the long street of the place was thronged with oxen, sheep, and horses, and with those who wished to see, to sell, or to buy. The squires were all together in a cluster at the police-house; the owners of the horses rode up and down, showing the best paces of their brutes: among whom you might see Paddy, in his ragged frieze-coat, seated on his donkey's bare rump, and proposing him for sale. I think I saw a score of this humble though useful breed that were brought for sale to the fair. "I can sell him," says one fellow, with a pompous air, "wid his tackle or widout." He was looking as grave over the negotiation as if it had been for a thousand pounds. Besides the donkeys, of course there was plenty of poultry, and there were pigs without number, shrieking and struggling and pushing hither and thither among the crowd, rebellious to the straw-rope. It was a fine thing to see one huge grunter and the manner in which he was landed into a cart. The cart was let down on an easy inclined plane to tempt him : two men ascending, urged him by the forelegs, other two entreated him by the tail. At length, when more than half of his body had been coaxed upon the cart, it was suddenly whisked up, causing the animal thereby to fall forward ; a parting shove sent him altogether into the cart ; the two gentlemen inside jumped out, and the monster was left to ride home.

The farmers, as usual, were talking of the tariff, predicting ruin to themselves, as farmers will, on account of the decreasing price of stock and the consequent fall of grain. Perhaps the person most to be pitied is the poor pig-proprietor yonder : it is his rent which he is carrying through the market squeaking at the end of the straw-rope, and Sir Robert's bill adds insolvency to that poor fellow's misery.

This was the last of the sights which the kind owner of H—— town had invited me into his country to see ; and I think they were among the most pleasing I witnessed in Ireland. Rich and poor were working friendlily together ; priest and parson were alike interested in these honest, homely, agricultural festivals ; not a word was said about hereditary bondage and English tyranny ; and one did not much regret the absence of those patriotic topics of conversation. If but for the sake of the change, it was pleasant to pass a few days with people among whom there was no quarrelling : no furious denunciations against Popery on the part of the Protestants, and no tirades against the parsons from their bitter and scornful opponents of the other creed.

Next Sunday, in the county Meath, in a quiet old church lying amongst meadows and fine old stately avenues of trees, and for the benefit of a congregation of some thirty persons, I heard for the space of an hour and twenty minutes some thorough Protestant doctrine, and the Popish superstitions properly belabored. Does it strengthen a man in his own creed to hear his neighbor's belief abused? One would imagine so : for though abuse converts nobody, yet many of our pastors think they are not doing their duty by their own fold unless they fling stones at the flock in the next field, and have, for the honor of the service, a match at cudgelling with the shepherd. Our shepherd to-day was of this pugnacious sort.

The Meath landscape, if not varied and picturesque, is extremely rich and pleasant; and we took some drives along the banks of the Boyne — to the noble park of Slane (still sacred to the memory of George IV., who actually condescended to pass some days there), and to Trim — of which the name occurs so often in Swift's Journals, and where stands an enormous old castle that was inhabited by Prince John. It was taken from him by an Irish chief, our guide said; and from the Irish chief it was taken by Oliver Cromwell. O'Thuselah was the Irish chief's name no doubt.

Here too stands, in the midst of one of the most wretched towns in Ireland, a pillar erected in honor of the Duke of Wellington by the gentry of his native county. His birthplace, Dangan, lies not far off. And as we saw the hero's statue, a flight of birds had hovered about it: there was one on each epaulette and two on his marshal's staff. Besides these wonders, we saw a certain number of beggars; and a madman, who was walking round a mound and preaching a sermon on grace; and a little child's funeral came passing through the dismal town, the only stirring thing in it (the coffin was laid on a one-horse country car — a little deal box, in which the poor child lay — and a great troop of people followed the humble procession); and the inn-keeper, who had caught a few stray gentlefolk in a town where travellers must be rare; and in his inn — which is more gaunt and miserable than the town itself, and which is by no means rendered more cheerful because sundry theological works are left for the rare frequenters in the coffee-room — the inn-keeper brought in a bill which would have been worthy of Long's, and which was paid with much grumbling on both sides.

It would not be a bad rule for the traveller in Ireland to avoid those inns where theological works are left in the coffee-room. He is pretty sure to be made to pay very dearly for these religious privileges.

We waited for the coach at the beautiful lodge and gate of Annsbrook; and one of the sons of the house coming up, invited us to look at the domain, which is as pretty and neatly ordered as — as any in England. It is hard to use this comparison so often, and must make Irish hearers angry. Can't one see a neat house and grounds without instantly thinking that they are worthy of the sister country; and implying, in our cool way, its superiority to everywhere else? Walking in this gentleman's grounds, I told him, in the simplicity of my heart, that the neighboring country was like Warwickshire, and the grounds as good as any English park. Is it the fact that English grounds *are* superior, or only that Englishmen are disposed to consider them so?

A pretty little twining river, called the Nanny's Water, runs through the park : there is a legend about that, as about other places. Once upon a time (ten thousand years ago), Saint Patrick being thirsty as he passed by this country, came to the house of an old woman, of whom he asked a drink of milk. The old woman brought it to his reverence with the best of welcomes, and . . . . here it is a great mercy that the Belfast mail comes up, whereby the reader is spared the rest of the history.

The Belfast mail had only to carry us five miles to Drogheda, but, in revenge, it made us pay three shillings for the five miles ; and again, by way of compensation, it carried us over five miles of a country that was worth at least five shillings to see — not romantic or especially beautiful, but having the best of all beauty — a quiet, smiling, prosperous, unassuming *work-day* look, that in views and landscapes most good judges admire. Hard by Nanny's Water, we came to Duleek Bridge, where, I was told, stands an old residence of the De Dath family, who were, moreover, builders of the picturesque old bridge.

The road leads over a wide green common, which puts one in mind of Eng— (a plague on it, there is the comparison again !), and at the end of the common lies the village among trees : a beautiful and peaceful sight. In the background there was a tall ivy-covered old tower, looking noble and imposing, but a ruin and useless ; then there was a church, and next to it a chapel — the very same sun was shining upon both. The chapel and church were connected by a farm-yard, and a score of golden ricks were in the background, the churches in unison, and the people (typified by the corn-ricks) flourishing at the feet of both. May one ever hope to see the day in Ireland when this little landscape allegory shall find a general application?

For some way after leaving Duleek the road and the country round continued to wear the agreeable, cheerful look just now lauded. You pass by a house where James II. is said to have slept the night before the battle of the Boyne (he took care to sleep far enough off on the night after), and also by an old red-brick hall standing at the end of an old chace or terrace-avenue, that runs for about a mile down to the house, and finishes at a moat towards the road. But as the coach arrives near Drogheda, and in the boulevards of that town, all resemblance to England is lost. Up hill and down, we pass low rows of filthy cabins in dirty undulations. Parents are at the cabin-doors dressing the hair of ragged children; shock-heads of girls peer out from the black circumference of smoke, and children inconceivably filthy yell wildly and vociferously as the coach passes by. One little ragged savage rushed furiously up the hill, speculating upon permission to put on the drag-chain at descending, and hoping for a halfpenny reward. He put on the chain, but the guard did not give a halfpenny. I flung him one, and the boy rushed wildly after the carriage, holding it up with joy. "The man inside has given me one," says he, holding it up exultingly to the guard. I flung out another (by-the-by, and without any prejudice, the halfpence in Ireland *are* smaller than those of England), but when the child got this halfpenny, small as it was, it seemed to overpower him: the little man's look of gratitude was worth a great deal more than the biggest penny ever struck.

The town itself, which I had three-quarters of an hour to ramble through, is smoky, dirty, and lively. There was a great bustle in the black Main Street, and several good shops, though some of the houses were in a half state of ruin, and battered shutters closed many of the windows where formerly had been "emporiums," "repositories," and other grandly-titled abodes of small commerce. Exhortations to "repeal" were liberally plastered on the blackened walls, proclaiming some past or promised visit of the "great agitator." From the bridge is a good bustling spectacle of the river and the craft; the quays were grimy with the discharge of the coal-vessels that lay along-side them; the warehouses were not less black; the seamen and porters loitering on the quay were as swarthy as those of Puddledock; numerous factories and chimneys were vomiting huge clouds of black smoke: the commerce of the town is stated by the Guide-book to be considerable, and increasing of late years. Of one part of its manufactures every traveller must speak with gratitude — of the ale namely, which is as good as the best brewed in the sister kingdom. Drogheda ale is to be drunk all over Ireland in the bottled state: candor calls for the acknowledgment that it is equally praiseworthy in draught. And while satisfying himself of this fact, the philosophic observer cannot but ask why ale should not be as good elsewhere as at Drogheda: is the water of the Boyne the only water in Ireland whereof ale can be made?

Above the river and craft, and the smoky quays of the town, the hills rise abruptly, up which innumerable cabins clamber. On one of them, by a church, is a round tower, or fort, with a flag: the church is the successor of one battered down by Cromwell in 1649, in his frightful siege of the place. The place of one of his batteries is still marked outside the town, and known as "Cromwell's Mount:" here he "made the breach assaultable, and, by the help of God, stormed it." He chose the strongest point of the defence for his attack.

After being twice beaten back, by the divine assistance he was enabled to succeed in a third assault: he "knocked on the head" all the officers of the garrison; he gave orders that none of the men should be spared. "I think," says he, "that night we put to the sword two thousand men; and one hundred of them having taken possession of St. Peter's steeple and a round tower next the gate, called St. Sunday's, I ordered the steeple of St. Peter's to be fired, when one in the flames was heard to say, 'God confound me, I burn, I burn!'" The Lord General's history of "this great mercy vouchsafed to us" concludes with appropriate religious reflections: and prays Mr. Speaker of the House of Commons to remember that "it is good that God alone have all the glory." Is not the recollection of this butchery almost enough to make an Irishman turn rebel?

When troops marched over the bridge, a young friend of mine (whom I shrewdly suspected to be an Orangeman in his heart) told me that their bands played the "Boyne Water." Here is another legend of defeat for the Irishman to muse upon; and here it was, too, that King Richard II. received the homage of four Irish kings, who flung their skenes or daggers at his feet and knelt to him, and were wonder-stricken by the riches of his tents and the garments of his knights and ladies. I think it is in Lingard that the story is told; and the antiquarian has no doubt seen that beautiful old manuscript at the British Museum where these yellow-mantled warriors are seen riding down to the King, splendid in his forked beard, and peaked shoes, and long dangling scolloped sleeves and embroidered gown.

The Boyne winds picturesquely round two sides of the town, and following it, we came to the Linen Hall, — in the days of the linen manufacture a place of note, now the place where Mr. O'Connell harangues the people; but all the windows of the house were barricaded when we passed it, and of linen or any other sort of merchandise there seemed to be none. Three boys were running past it with a mouse tied to a string and a dog galloping after; two little children were paddling down the street, one saying to the other, "*Once I had a halfpenny*, and bought apples with it." The barges were lying lazily on the river, on the opposite side of which was a wood of a gentleman's domain, over which the rooks were cawing; and by the shore were some ruins — "where Mr. Ball once had his kennel of hounds" — touching reminiscence of former prosperity!

There is a very large and ugly Roman Catholic chapel in the town, and a smaller one of better construction: it was so crowded, however, although on a week-day, that we could not pass beyond the chapel-yard — where were great crowds of people, some praying, some talking, some buying and selling. There were two or three stalls in the yard, such as one sees near continental churches, presided over by old women, with a store of little brass crucifixes, beads, books, and bénitiers for the faithful to purchase. The church is large and commodious within, and looks (not like all other churches in Ireland) as if it were frequented. There is a hideous stone monument in the churchyard representing two corpses half rotted away: time or neglect had battered away the inscription, nor could we see the dates of some older tombstones in the ground, which were mouldering away in the midst of nettles and rank grass on the wall.

By a large public school of some reputation, where a hundred boys were educated (my young guide the Orangeman was one of them: he related with much glee how, on one of the Liberator's visits, a schoolfellow had waved a blue and orange flag from the window and cried, "King William for ever, and to hell with the Pope!"), there is a fine old gate leading to the river, and in excellent preservation, in spite of time and Oliver Cromwell. It is a good specimen of Irish architecture. By this time that exceedingly slow coach the "Newry Lark" had arrived at that exceedingly filthy inn where the mail had dropped us an hour before. An enormous Englishman was holding a vain combat of wit with a brawny, grinning beggar-woman at the door. "There's a *clever* gentleman," says the beggar-woman. "Sure he'll give me something." "How much should you like?" says the Englishman, with playful jocularity. "Musha," says she, "many a *littler* man nor you has given me a shilling." The coach drives away; the lady had clearly the best of the joking-match; but I did not see, for all that, that the Englishman gave her a single farthing.

From Castle Bellingham — as famous for ale as Drogheda,

and remarkable likewise for a still better thing than ale, an excellent resident proprietress, whose fine park lies by the road, and by whose care and taste the village has been rendered one of the most neat and elegant I have yet seen in Ireland — the road to Dundalk is exceedingly picturesque, and the traveller has the pleasure of feasting his eyes with the noble line of Mourne Mountains, which rise before him while he journeys over a level country for several miles. The "Newry Lark," to be sure, disdained to take advantage of the easy roads to accelerate its movements in any way; but the aspect of the country is so pleasant that one can afford to loiter over it. The fields were yellow with the stubble of the corn — which in this, one of the chief corn counties of Ireland, had just been cut down; and a long straggling line of neat farm-houses and cottages runs almost the whole way from Castle Bellingham to Dundalk. For nearly a couple of miles of the distance, the road runs along the picturesque flat called Lurgan Green; and gentlemen's residences and parks are numerous along the road, and one seems to have come amongst a new race of people, so trim are the cottages, so neat the gates and hedges, in this peaceful, smiling district. The people, too, show signs of the general prosperity. A national school has just dismissed its female scholars as we pass through Dunlar; and though the children had most of them bare feet, their clothes were good and clean, their faces rosy and bright, and their long hair as shiny and as nicely combed as young ladies' need to be. Numerous old castles and towers stand on the road here and there; and long before we entered Dundalk we had a sight of a huge factory-chimney in the town, and of the dazzling white walls of the Roman Catholic church lately erected there. The cabin-suburb is not great, and the entrance to the town is much adorned by the hospital — a handsome Elizabethan building — and a row of houses of a similar architectural style which lie on the left of the traveller.

CHAPTER XXVI.

DUNDALK.

THE stranger can't fail to be struck with the look of Dundalk,
as he has been with the villages and country leading to it, when
contrasted with places in the South and West of Ireland. The
coach stopped at a cheerful-looking *Place*, of which almost the
only dilapidated mansion was the old inn at which it discharged
us, and which did not hold out much prospect of comfort. But
in justice to the "King's Arms" it must be said that good
beds and dinners are to be obtained there by voyagers; and if
they choose to arrive on days when his Grace the Most Reverend the Lord Archbishop of Armagh and Primate of Ireland,
is dining with his clergy, the house of course is crowded, and
the waiters, and the boy who carries in the potatoes, a little
hurried and flustered. When their reverences were gone, the
laity were served; and I have no doubt, from the leg of a duck
which I got, that the breast and wings must have been very
tender.

Meanwhile the walk was pleasant through the bustling little
town. A grave old church with a tall copper spire defends
one end of the Main Street; and a little way from the inn
is the superb new chapel, which the architect, Mr. Duff,
has copied from King's College Chapel in Cambridge. The
ornamental part of the interior is not yet completed; but the
area of the chapel is spacious and noble, and three handsome
altars of scagliola (or some composition resembling marble)
have been erected, of handsome and suitable form. When by
the aid of further subscriptions the church shall be completed,
it will be one of the handsomest places of worship the Roman
Catholics possess in this country. Opposite the chapel stands
a neat low black building — the gaol: in the middle of the
building, and over the doorway, is an ominous balcony and
window, with an iron beam overhead. Each end of the beam
is ornamented with a grinning iron skull! Is this the hanging-
place? and do these grinning cast-iron skulls facetiously explain
the business for which the beam is there? For shame! for
shame! Such disgusting emblems ought no longer to disgrace a Christian land. If kill we must, let us do so with
as much despatch and decency as possible, — not brazen

out our misdeeds and perpetuate them in this frightful satiric
way.

A far better cast-iron emblem stands over a handsome shop
in the " Place " hard by — a plough namely, which figures over
the factory of Mr. Shekelton, whose industry and skill seem to
have brought the greatest benefit to his fellow-townsmen — of
whom he employs numbers in his foundries and workshops.
This gentleman was kind enough to show me through his manufactories, where all sorts of iron-works are made, from a steam-
engine to a door-key; and I saw everything to admire, and a
vast deal more than I could understand, in the busy, cheerful,
orderly, bustling, clanging place. Steam-boilers were ham-
mered here, and pins made by a hundred busy hands in a manufactory above. There was the engine-room, where the monster
was whirring his ceaseless wheels and directing the whole
operations of the factory, fanning the forges, turning the drills,
blasting into the pipes of the smelting-houses : he had a house
to himself, from which his orders issued to the different establishments round about. One machine was quite awful to me,
a gentle cockney, not used to such things : it was an iron-
devourer, a wretch with huge jaws and a narrow mouth, ever
opening and shutting — opening and shutting. You put a
half-inch iron plate between his jaws, and they shut not a
whit slower or quicker than before, and bit through the iron as
if it were a sheet of paper. Below the monster's mouth was a
punch that performed its duties with similar dreadful calmness,
going on its rising and falling.

I was so lucky as to have an introduction to the Vicar of
Dundalk, which that gentleman's kind and generous nature
interpreted into a claim for unlimited hospitality; and he was
good enough to consider himself bound not only to receive me,
but to give up previous engagements abroad in order to do so.
I need not say that it afforded me sincere pleasure to witness,
for a couple of days, his labors among his people ; and indeed
it was a delightful occupation to watch both flock and pastor.
The world is a wicked, selfish, abominable place, as the parson
tells us ; but his reverence comes out of his pulpit and gives
the flattest contradiction to his doctrine : busying himself with
kind actions from morning till night, denying to himself, generous to others, preaching the truth to young and old, clothing
the naked, feeding the hungry, consoling the wretched, and
giving hope to the sick ; — and I do not mean to say that this
sort of life is led by the Vicar of Dundalk merely, but do firmly
believe that it is the life of the great majority of the Protestant

and Roman Catholic clergy of the country. There will be no breach of confidence, I hope, in publishing here the journal of a couple of days spent with one of these reverend gentlemen, and telling some readers, as idle and profitless as the writer, what the clergyman's peaceful labors are.

In the first place, we set out to visit the church — the comfortable copper-spired old edifice that was noticed two pages back. It stands in a green churchyard of its own, very neat and trimly kept, with an old row of trees that were dropping their red leaves upon a flock of vaults and tombstones below. The building being much injured by flame and time, some hundred years back was repaired, enlarged, and ornamented — as churches in those days were ornamented — and has consequently lost a good deal of its Gothic character. There is a great mixture, therefore, of old style and new style and no style : but, with all this, the church is one of the most commodious and best appointed I have seen in Ireland. The vicar held a council with a builder regarding some ornaments for the roof of the church, which is, as it should be, a great object of his care and architectural taste, and on which he has spent a very large sum of money. To these expenses he is in a manner bound, for the living is a considerable one, its income being no less than two hundred and fifty pounds a year ; out of which he has merely to maintain a couple of curates and a clerk and sexton, to contribute largely towards schools and hospitals, and relieve a few scores of pensioners of his own, who are fitting objects of private bounty.

We went from the church to a school, which has been long a favorite resort of the good vicar's : indeed, to judge from the schoolmaster's books, his attendance there is almost daily, and the number of the scholars some two hundred. The number was considerably greater until the schools of the Educational Board were established, when the Roman Catholic clergymen withdrew many of their young people from Mr. Thackeray's establishment.

We found a large room with sixty or seventy boys at work ; in an upper chamber were a considerable number of girls, with their teachers, two modest and pretty young women ; but the favorite resort of the vicar was evidently the Infant-School, — and no wonder : it is impossible to witness a more beautiful or touching sight.

Eighty of these little people, healthy, clean, and rosy — some in smart gowns and shoes and stockings, some with patched pinafores and little bare pink feet — sat upon a half-dozen low benches, and were singing, at the top of their four-score fresh voices, a song when we entered. All the voices were hushed as the vicar came in, and a great bobbing and curtsying took place; whilst a hundred and sixty innocent eyes turned awfully towards the clergyman, who tried to look as unconcerned as possible, and began to make his little ones a speech. "I have brought," says he, "a gentleman from England, who has heard of my little children and their school, and hopes he will carry away a good account of it. Now, you know, we must all do our best to be kind and civil to strangers: what can we do here for this gentleman that he would like? — do you think he would like a song?"

(*All the children.*) — "We'll sing to him!"

Then the schoolmistress, coming forward, sang the first words of a hymn, which at once eighty little voices took up, or near eighty — for some of the little things were too young to sing yet, and all they could do was to beat the measure with little red hands as the others sang. It was a hymn about heaven, with a chorus of "Oh that will be joyful, joyful," and one of the verses beginning, "Little children will be there." Some of my fair readers (if I have the honor to find such) who have been present at similar tender, charming concerts, know the hymn, no doubt. It was the first time I had ever heard it; and I do not care to own that it brought tears to my eyes, though it is ill to parade such kind of sentiment in print. But I think I will never, while I live, forget that little chorus, nor would any man who has ever loved a child or lost one. God bless you, O little happy singers! What a noble and useful life is his, who, in place of seeking wealth or honor, devotes his life to such a service as this! And all through our country, thank God! in quiet humble corners, that busy citizens and men of the world never hear of, there are thousands of such men employed in such holy pursuits, with no reward beyond that which the fulfilment of duty brings them. Most of these children were Roman Catholics. At this tender age the priests do not care to separate them from their little Protestant brethren: and no wonder. He must be a child-murdering Herod who would find the heart to do so.

After the hymn, the children went through a little Scripture catechism, answering very correctly, and all in a breath, as the mistress put the questions. Some of them were, of course, too young to understand the words they uttered; but the answers are so simple that they cannot fail to understand them before long; and they learn in spite of themselves.

The catechism being ended, another song was sung; and now the vicar (who had been humming the chorus along with his young singers, and, in spite of an awful and grave countenance, could not help showing his extreme happiness) made another oration, in which he stated that the gentleman from England was perfectly satisfied; that he would have a good report of the Dundalk children to carry home with him; that the day was very fine, and the schoolmistress would probably like to take a walk; and, finally, would the young people give her a holiday? "As many," concluded he, " as will give the schoolmistress a holiday, hold up their hands!" This question was carried unanimously.

But I am bound to say, when the little people were told that as many as *wouldn't like* a holiday were to hold up *their* hands, all the little hands went up again exactly as before: by which it may be concluded either that the infants did not understand his reverence's speech, or that they were just as happy to stay at school as to go and play; and the reader may adopt whichever of the reasons he inclines to. It is probable that both are correct.

The little things are so fond of the school, the vicar told me as we walked away from it, that on returning home they like nothing better than to get a number of their companions who don't go to school, and to play at infant-school.

They may be heard singing their hymns in the narrow alleys and humble houses in which they dwell: and I was told of one dying who sang his song of " Oh that will be joyful, joyful," to his poor mother weeping at his bedside, and promising her that they should meet where no parting should be.

" There was a child in the school," said the vicar, " whose father, a Roman Catholic, was a carpenter by trade, a good workman, and earning a considerable weekly sum, but neglecting his wife and children and spending his earnings in drink. We have a song against drunkenness that the infants sing; and one evening, going home, the child found her father excited with liquor and ill-treating his wife. The little thing forthwith interposed between them, told her father what she had heard at school regarding the criminality of drunkenness and quarrelling, and finished her little sermon with the hymn. The father was first amused, then touched; and the end of it was that he kissed his wife and asked her to forgive him, hugged his child, and from that day would always have her in his bed, made her sing to him morning and night, and forsook his old haunts for the sake of his little companion."

He was quite sober and prosperous for eight months; but the vicar at the end of that time began to remark that the child looked ragged at school, and passing by her mother's house, saw the poor woman with a black eye. "If it was any one but your husband, Mrs. C——, who gave you that black eye," says the vicar, "tell me; but if he did it, don't say a word." The woman was silent, and soon after, meeting her husband, the vicar took him to task. "You were sober for eight months. Now tell me fairly, C——," says he, "were you happier when you lived at home with your wife and child, or are you more happy now?" The man owned that he was much happier formerly, and the end of the conversation was that he promised to go home once more and try the sober life again, and he went home and succeeded.

The vicar continued to hear good accounts of him; but passing one day by his house he saw the wife there looking very sad. "Had her husband relapsed?"—"No, he was dead," she said—"dead of the cholera;·but he had been sober ever since his last conversation with the clergyman, and had done his duty to his family up to the time of his death." "I said to the woman," said the good old clergyman, in a grave low voice, "'Your husband is gone now to the place where, according to his conduct here, his eternal reward will be assigned him; and let us be thankful to think what a different position he occupies now to that which he must have held had not his little girl been the means under God of converting him.'"

Our next walk was to the County Hospital, the handsome edifice which ornaments the Drogheda entrance of the town, and which I had remarked on my arrival. Concerning this hospital, the governors were, when I passed through Dundalk, in a state of no small agitation: for a gentleman by the name of ——, who, from being an apothecary's assistant in the place, had gone forth as a sort of amateur inspector of hospitals throughout Ireland, had thought fit to censure their extravagance in erecting the new building, stating that the old one was fully sufficient to hold fifty patients, and that the public money might consequently have been spared. Mr. ——'s plan for the better maintenance of them in general is, that commissioners should be appointed to direct them, and not county gentlemen as heretofore; the discussion of which question does not need to be carried on in this humble work.

My guide, who is one of the governors of the new hospital, conducted me in the first place to the old one — a small dirty

house in a damp and low situation, with but three rooms to
accommodate patients, and these evidently not fit to hold fifty,
or even fifteen patients. The new hospital is one of the handsomest buildings of the size and kind in Ireland — an ornament
to the town, as the angry commissioner stated, but not after all
a building of undue cost, for the expense of its erection was but
3,000*l.* ; and the sick of the county are far better accommodated
in it than in the damp and unwholesome tenement regretted by
the eccentric commissioner.

An English architect, Mr. Smith of Hertford, designed and
completed the edifice ; strange to say, only exceeding his estimates by the sum of three-and-sixpence, as the worthy governor
of the hospital with great triumph told me. The building is
certainly a wonder of cheapness, and, what is more, so complete for the purpose for which it was intended, and so handsome in appearance, that the architect's name deserves to be
published by all who hear it ; and if any country-newspaper
editors should notice this volume, they are requested to make
the fact known. The house is provided with every convenience
for men and women, with all the appurtenances of baths, water,
gas, airy wards, and a garden for convalescents ; and, below,
a dispensary, a handsome board-room, kitchen, and matron's
apartments, &c. Indeed, a noble requiring a house for a large
establishment need not desire a handsomer one than this, at its
moderate price of 3,000*l.* The beauty of this building has, as
is almost always the case, created emulation, and a terrace
in the same taste has been raised in the neighborhood of the
hospital.

From the hospital we bent our steps to the Institution ; of
which place I give below the rules, and a copy of the course
of study, and the dietary : leaving English parents to consider
the fact, that their children can be educated at this place for
thirteen pounds a year. Nor is there anything in the establishment savoring of the Dotheboys Hall.* I never saw, in any

* " Boarders are received from the age of eight to fourteen at 12*l.* per
annum, and 1*l.* for washing, paid quarterly in advance.
" Day scholars are received from the age of ten to twelve at 2*l.*, paid
quarterly in advance.
" The Incorporated Society have abundant cause for believing that the
introduction of Boarders into their Establishments has produced far more
advantageous results to the public than they could, at so early a period,
have anticipated ; and that the election of boys to their Foundations *only*
after a fair competition with others of a given district, has had the effect
of stimulating masters and scholars to exertion and study, and promises to
operate most beneficially for the advancement of religious and general
knowledge.

public school in England, sixty cleaner, smarter, more gentle-manlike boys than were here at work. The upper class had been at work on Euclid as we came in, and were set, by way

"The districts for eligible Candidates are as follow : —

"Dundalk Institution embraces the counties of Louth and Down, be-cause the properties which support it lie in this district.

"The Pococke Institution, Kilkenny, embraces the counties of Kilkenny and Waterford, for the same cause.

"The Ranelagh Institution, the towns of Athlone and Roscommon, and three districts in the counties of Galway and Roscommon, which the In-corporated Society hold in fee, or from which they receive impropriate tithes.

(*Signed*) "CÆSAR OTWAY, *Secretary.*"

Arrangement of School Business in Dundalk Institution.

Hours.	Monday, Wednesday, and Friday.	Tuesday and Thursday.	Saturday.
3 to 7	Rise, wash, &c.	Rise, wash, &c.	Rise, wash, &c.
7 " 7½	Scripture by the Mas-ter, and prayer.	Scripture by the Mas-ter, and prayer.	Scripture by the Mas-ter, and prayer.
7½ " 8½	Reading, History, &c.	Reading, History, &c.	Reading, History, &c.
8½ " 9	Breakfast.	Breakfast.	Breakfast.
9 " 10	Play.	Play.	Play.
10 " 10½	English Grammar.	Geography.	10 to 11, Repetition.
10½ " 11¼	Algebra.	Euclid.	11 to 12, Use of Globes.
11¼ " 12	Scripture.	Lecture on principles of Arithmetic.	
12 " 12¾	Writing.	Writing.	12 to 1, Catechism and Scripture by the Catechist.
12¾ " 2	Arithmetic at Desks, and Book-keeping.	Mensuration.	
2 " 2½	Dinner.	Dinner.	Dinner.
2½ " 5	Play.	Play.	The remainder of this day is devoted to ex-ercise till the hour of Supper, after which the Boys assemble in the School-room and hear a portion of Scripture read and explained by the Mas-ter, as on other days, and conclude with prayer.
5 " 7½	Spelling, Mental Arith-metic, and Euclid.	Spelling, Mental Arith-metic, and Euclid.	
7½ " 8	Supper.	Supper.	
8 " 8½	Exercise.	Exercise.	
8½ " 9	Scripture by the Mas-ter, and prayer in School-room.	Scripture by the Mas-ter, and prayer in School-room.	
9	Retire to bed.	Retire to bed.	

The sciences of Navigation and practical Surveying are taught in the Establishment, also a selection of the Pupils, who have a taste for it, are instructed in the art of Drawing.

Dietary.

BREAKFAST. – Stirabout and Milk, every Morning.

DINNER. — On Sunday and Wednesday, Potatoes and Beef; 10 ounces of the latter to each boy. On Monday and Thursday, Bread and Broth ; ½lb. of the former to each boy. On Tuesday, Friday, and Saturday, Potatoes and Milk ; 2lbs. of the former to each boy.

SUPPER. — ½lb. of Bread with Milk, uniformly, except on Monday and Thursday : on these days, Potatoes and Milk.

of amusing the stranger, to perform a sum of compound inter-est of diabolical complication, which, with its algebraic and arithmetic solution, was handed up to me by three or four of the pupils ; and I strove to look as wise as I possibly could. Then they went through questions of mental arithmetic with astonishing correctness and facility ; and finding from the master that classics were not taught in the school, I took oc-casion to lament this circumstance, saying, with a knowing air, that I would like to have examined the lads in a Greek play.

Classics, then, these young fellows do not get. Meat they get but twice a week. Let English parents bear this fact in mind ; but that the lads are healthy and happy, anybody who sees them can have no question ; furthermore, they are well instructed in a sound practical education — history, geography, mathematics, religion. What a place to know of would this be for many a poor half-pay officer, where he may put his chil-dren in all confidence that they will be well cared for and soundly educated ! Why have we not State schools in Eng-land, where, for the prime cost — for a sum which never need exceed for a young boy's maintenance 25*l.* a year — our chil-dren might be brought up? We are establishing national schools for the laborer : why not give education to the sons of the poor gentry — the clergyman whose pittance is small, and would still give his son the benefit of a public education ; the artist, the officer, the merchant's office-clerk, the literary man? What a benefit might be conferred upon all of us if honest charter-schools could be established for our children, and where it would be impossible for Squeers to make a profit ! *

Our next day's journey led us, by half-past ten o'clock, to the ancient town of Louth, a little poor village now, but a great seat of learning and piety, it is said, formerly, where there stood a university and abbeys, and where Saint Patrick worked wonders. Here my kind friend the rector was called upon to marry a smart sergeant of police to a pretty lass, one of the few Protestants who attend his church ; and, the ceremony over, we were invited to the house of the bride's father hard by, where the clergyman was bound to cut the cake and drink a glass of wine to the health of the new-married couple.

---

* The Proprietary Schools of late established have gone far to protect the interests of parents and children ; but the masters of these schools take boarders, and of course draw profits from them. Why make the learned man a beef-and-mutton contractor ? It would be easy to arrange the economy of a school so that there should be no possibility of a want of confidence, or of peculation, to the detriment of the pupil.

There was evidently to be a dance and some merriment in the course of the evening; for the good mother of the bride (oh, blessed is he who has a good mother-in-law!) was busy at a huge fire in the little kitchen, and along the road we met various parties of neatly-dressed people, and several of the sergeant's comrades, who were hastening to the wedding. The mistress of the rector's darling Infant-School was one of the bridesmaids: consequently the little ones had a holiday.

But he was not to be disappointed of his Infant-School in this manner: so, mounting the car again, with a fresh horse, we went a very pretty drive of three miles to the snug lone school-house of Glyde Farm — near a handsome park, I believe of the same name, where the proprietor is building a mansion of the Tudor order.

The pretty scene of Dundalk was here played over again: the children sang their little hymns, the good old clergyman joined delighted in the chorus, the holiday was given, and the little hands held up, and I looked at more clean bright faces and little rosy feet. The scene need not be repeated in print, but I can understand what pleasure a man must take in the daily witnessing of it, and in the growth of these little plants, which are set and tended by his care. As we returned to Louth, a woman met us with a curtsy and expressed her sorrow that she had been obliged to withdraw her daughter from one of the rector's schools, which the child was vexed at leaving too. But the orders of the priest were peremptory; and who can say they were unjust? The priest, on his side, was only enforcing the rule which the parson maintains as his: — the latter will not permit his young flock to be educated except upon certain principles and by certain teachers; the former has his own scruples unfortunately also — and so that noble and brotherly scheme of National Education falls to the ground. In Louth, the national school was standing by the side of the priest's chapel: it is so almost everywhere throughout Ireland: the Protestants have rejected, on very good motives doubtless, the chance of union which the Education Board gave them. Be it so! if the children of either sect be educated apart, so that they *be* educated, the education scheme will have produced its good, and the union will come afterwards.

The church at Louth stands boldly upon a hill looking down on the village, and has nothing remarkable in it but neatness, except the monument of a former rector, Dr. Little, which attracts the spectator's attention from the extreme inappropriateness of the motto on the coat-of-arms of the reverend defunct. It looks rather unorthodox to read in a Christian temple, where a man's bones have the honor to lie — and where, if anywhere, humility is requisite — that there is *multum in Parvo:* "a great deal in Little." O Little, in life you were not much, and lo! you are less now; why should filial piety engrave that pert pun upon your monument, to cause people to laugh in a place where they ought to be grave? The defunct doctor built a very handsome rectory-house, with a set of stables that would be useful to a nobleman, but are rather too commodious for a peaceful rector who does not ride to hounds; and it was in Little's time, I believe, that the church was removed from the old abbey, where it formerly stood, to its present proud position on the hill.

The abbey is a fine ruin, the windows of a good style, the tracings of carvings on many of them; but a great number of stones and ornaments were removed formerly to build farm-buildings withal, and the place is now as rank and ruinous as the generality of Irish burying-places seem to be. Skulls lie in clusters amongst nettle-beds by the abbey walls; graves are only partially covered with rude stones; a fresh coffin was lying broken in pieces within the abbey; and the surgeon of the dispensary hard by might procure subjects here almost without grave-breaking. Hard by the abbey is a building of which I beg leave to offer the following interesting sketch.* The legend in the country goes that the place was built for the accommodation of "Saint Murtogh," who lying down to sleep here in the open fields, not having any place to house under, found to his surprise, on waking in the morning, the above edifice, which the angels had built. The angelic architecture, it will be seen, is of rather a rude kind; and the village antiquary, who takes a pride in showing the place, says that the building was erected *two thousand years ago.* In the handsome grounds of the rectory is another spot visited by popular tradition — a fairy's ring: a regular mound of some thirty feet in height, flat and even on the top, and provided with a winding path for the foot-passengers to ascend. Some trees grew on the mound, one of which was removed in order to make the walk. But the country-people cried out loudly at this desecration, and vowed that the "little people" had quitted the countryside for ever in consequence.

While walking in the town, a woman meets the rector with a number of curtsies and compliments, and vows that "'tis your reverence is the friend of the poor, and may the Lord pre-

* This refers to an illustrated edition of the work.

serve you to us and lady;" and having poured out blessings
innumerable, concludes by producing a paper for her son
that's in throuble in England. The paper ran to the effect that
"We, the undersigned, inhabitants of the parish of Louth,
have known Daniel Horgan ever since his youth, and can speak
confidently as to his integrity, piety, and good conduct." In
fact, the paper stated that Daniel Horgan was an honor to his
country, and consequently quite incapable of the crime of —
sack-stealing I think — with which at present he was charged,
and lay in prison in Durham Castle. The paper had, I should
think, come down to the poor mother from Durham, with a
direction ready written to despatch it back again when signed,
and was evidently the work of one of those benevolent individuals in assize-towns, who, following the profession of the law,
delight to extricate unhappy young men of whose innocence
(from various six-and-eightpenny motives) they feel convinced.
There stood the poor mother, as the rector examined the document, with a huge wafer in her hand, ready to forward it so
soon as it was signed: for the truth is that "We, the undersigned," were as yet merely imaginary.

"You don't come to church," says the rector. "I know
nothing of you or your son : why don't you go to the priest?"

"Oh, your reverence, my son's to be tried next Tuesday,"
whimpered the woman. She then said the priest was not in
the way, but, as we had seen him a few minutes before, recalled
the assertion, and confessed that she *had* been to the priest
and that he would not sign; and fell to prayers, tears, and
unbounded supplications to induce the rector to give his signature. But that hard-hearted divine, stating that he had *not*
known Daniel Horgan from his youth upwards, that he could
not certify as to his honesty or dishonesty, enjoined the woman
to make an attempt upon the R. C. curate, to whose hand-
writing he would certify if need were.

The upshot of the matter was that the woman returned with
a certificate from the R. C. curate as to her son's good behavior
while in the village, and the rector certified that the hand-
writing was that of the R. C. clergyman in question, and the
woman popped her big red wafer into the letter and went her
way.

Tuesday is passed long ere this : Mr. Horgan's guilt or
innocence is long since clearly proved, and he celebrates the
latter in freedom, or expiates the former at the mill. Indeed,
I don't know that there was any call to introduce his adventures to the public, except perhaps it may be good to see

how in this little distant Irish village the blood of life is running.
Here goes a happy party to a marriage, and the parson prays
a "God bless you!" upon them, and the world begins for
them. Yonder lies a stall-fed rector in his tomb, flaunting
over his nothingness his pompous heraldic motto : and yonder
lie the fresh fragments of a nameless deal coffin, which any foot
may kick over. Presently you hear the clear voices of little
children praising God ; and here comes a mother wringing her
hands and asking for succor for her lad, who was a child but
the other day. Such *motus animorum atque hæc certamina tanta*
are going on in an hour of an October day in a little pinch of
clay in the county Louth.

Perhaps being in the moralizing strain, the honest surgeon
at the dispensary might come in as an illustration. He inhabits a neat humble house, a story higher than his neighbors',
but with a thatched roof. He relieves a thousand patients
yearly at the dispensary, he visits seven hundred in the parish,
he supplies the medicines gratis ; and receiving for these services the sum of about one hundred pounds yearly, some county
economists and calculators are loud against the extravagance
of his salary, and threaten his removal. All these individuals
and their histories we presently turn our backs upon, for, after
all, dinner is at five o'clock, and we have to see the new road
to Dundalk, which the county has lately been making.

Of this undertaking, which shows some skilful engineering
— some gallant cutting of rocks and hills, and filling of valleys,
with a tall and handsome stone bridge thrown across the river,
and connecting the high embankments on which the new road
at that place is formed — I can say little, except that it is a
vast convenience to the county, and a great credit to the sur-
veyor and contractor too ; for the latter, though a poor man,
and losing heavily by his bargain, has yet refused to mulct his
laborers of their wages ; and, as cheerfully as he can, still pays
them their shilling a day.

CHAPTER XXVII.

NEWRY, ARMAGH, BELFAST — FROM DUNDALK TO NEWRY.

My kind host gave orders to the small ragged boy that drove the car to take "particular care of the little gentleman;" and the car-boy, grinning in appreciation of the joke, drove off at his best pace, and landed his cargo at Newry after a pleasant two hours' drive. The country for the most part is wild, but not gloomy; the mountains round about are adorned with woods and gentlemen's seats; and the car-boy pointed out one hill — that of Slievegullion, which kept us company all the way — as the highest hill in Ireland. Ignorant or deceiving car-boy! I have seen a dozen hills, each the highest in Ireland, in my way through the country, of which the inexorable Guide-book gives the measurement and destroys the claim. Well, it was the tallest hill, in the estimation of the car-boy; and, in this respect, the world is full of car-boys. Has not every mother of a family a Slievegullion of a son, who, according to her measurement, towers above all other sons? Is not the patriot, who believes himself equal to three Frenchmen, a car-boy in heart? There was a kind young creature, with a child in her lap, that evidently held this notion. She paid the child a series of compliments, which would have led one to fancy he was an angel from heaven at the least; and her husband sat gravely by, very silent, with his arms round a barometer.

Beyond these there were no incidents or characters of note, except an old hostler that they said was ninety years old, and watered the horse at a lone inn on the road. "Stop!" cried this wonder of years and rags, as the car, after considerable parley, got under weigh. The car-boy pulled up, thinking a fresh passenger was coming out of the inn.

"*Stop, till one of the gentlemen gives me something,*" says the old man, coming slowly up with us: which speech created a laugh, and got him a penny: he received it without the least thankfulness, and went away grumbling to his pail.

Newry is remarkable as being the only town I have seen which had no cabin suburb: strange to say, the houses begin all at once, handsomely coated and hatted with stone and slate; and if Dundalk was prosperous, Newry is better still. Such a

sight of neatness and comfort is exceedingly welcome to an
English traveller, who, moreover, finds himself, after driving
through a plain bustling clean street, landed at a large plain
comfortable inn, where business seems to be done, where there
are smart waiters to receive him, and a comfortable warm coffee-
room that bears no traces of dilapidation.

What the merits of the *cuisine* may be I can't say for the
information of travellers; a gentleman to whom I had brought
a letter from Dundalk taking care to provide me at his own
table, accompanying me previously to visit the lions of the
town.   A river divides it, and the counties of Armagh and
Down: the river runs into the sea at Carlingford Bay, and is
connected by a canal with Lough Neagh, and thus with the
North of Ireland.   Steamers to Liverpool and Glasgow sail
continually.   There are mills, foundries, and manufactories, of
which the Guide-book will give particulars; and the town of
13,000 inhabitants is the busiest and most thriving that I have
yet seen in Ireland.

Our first walk was to the church: a large and handsome
building, although built in the unlucky period when the Gothic
style was coming into vogue.   Hence one must question the
propriety of many of the ornaments, though the whole is massive, well-finished, and stately.   Near the church stands the
Roman Catholic chapel, a very fine building, the work of the
same architect, Mr. Duff, who erected the chapel at Dundalk;
but, like almost all other edifices of the kind in Ireland that I
have seen, the interior is quite unfinished, and already so dirty
and ruinous, that one would think a sort of genius for dilapidation must have been exercised in order to bring it to its present
condition.   There are tattered green-baize doors to enter at, a
dirty clay floor, and cracked plaster walls, with an injunction
to the public not to spit on the floor.   Maynooth itself is
scarcely more dreary.   The architect's work, however, does
him the highest credit: the interior of the church is noble
and simple in style; and one can't but grieve to see a fine
work of art, that might have done good to the country, so
defaced and ruined as this is.

The Newry poor-house is as neatly ordered and comfortable
as any house, public or private, in Ireland: the same look of
health which was so pleasant to see among the Naas children
of the union-house was to be remarked here: the same care and
comfort for the old people.   Of able-bodied there were but few
in the house: it is in winter that there are most applicants for
this kind of relief; the sunshine attracts the women out of the

place, and the harvest relieves it of the men. Cleanliness, the matron said, is more intolerable to most of the inmates than any other regulation of the house; and instantly on quitting the house they relapse into their darling dirt, and of course at their periodical return are subject to the unavoidable initiatory lustration.

Newry has many comfortable and handsome public buildings: the streets have a business-like look, the shops and people are not too poor, and the southern grandiloquence is not shown here in the shape of fine words for small wares. Even the beggars are not so numerous, I fancy, or so coaxing and wheedling in their talk. Perhaps, too, among the gentry, the same moral change may be remarked, and they seem more downright and plain in their manner; but one must not pretend to speak of national characteristic from such a small experience as a couple of evenings' intercourse may give.

Although not equal in natural beauty to a hundred other routes which the traveller takes in the South, the ride from Newry to Armagh is an extremely pleasant one, on account of the undeniable increase of prosperity which is visible through the country. Well-tilled fields, neat farm-houses, well-dressed people, meet one everywhere, and people and landscape alike have a plain, hearty, flourishing look.

The greater part of Armagh has the aspect of a good stout old English town, although round about the steep on which the cathedral stands (the Roman Catholics have taken possession of another hill, and are building an opposition cathedral on this eminence) there are some decidedly Irish streets, and that dismal combination of house and pigsty which is so common in Munster and Connaught.

But the main streets, though not fine, are bustling, substantial, and prosperous; and a fine green has some old trees and some good houses, and even handsome stately public buildings, round about it, that remind one of a comfortable cathedral city across the water.

The cathedral service is more completely performed here than in any English town, I think. The church is small, but extremely neat, fresh and handsome — almost too handsome; covered with spick-and-span gilding and carved-work in the style of the thirteenth century: every pew as smart and well-cushioned as my lord's own seat in the country church; and for the clergy and their chief, stalls and thrones quite curious for their ornament and splendor. The Primate with his blue ribbon and badge (to whom the two clergymen bow reverently as, pass-

17

ing between them, he enters at the gate of the altar rail) looks like a noble Prince of the Church; and I had heard enough of his magnificent charity and kindness to look with reverence at his lofty handsome features.

Will it be believed that the sermon lasted only for twenty minutes? Can this be Ireland? I think this wonderful circumstance impressed me more than any other with the difference between North and South, and, having the Primate's own countenance for the opinion, may confess a great admiration for orthodoxy in this particular.

A beautiful monument to Archbishop Stuart, by Chantrey; a magnificent stained window, containing the arms of the clergy of the diocese (in the very midst of which I was glad to recognize the sober old family coat of the kind and venerable rector of Louth), and numberless carvings and decorations, will please the lover of church architecture here. I must confess, however, that in my idea the cathedral is quite too complete. It is of the twelfth century, but not the least venerable. It is as neat and trim as a lady's drawing-room. It wants a hundred years at least to cool the raw colors of the stones, and to dull the brightness of the gilding: all which benefits, no doubt, time will bring to pass, and future Cockneys setting off from London Bridge after breakfast in an aërial machine may come to hear the morning service here, and not remark the faults which have struck a too susceptible tourist of the nineteenth century.

Strolling round the town after service, I saw more decided signs that Protestantism was there in the ascendant. I saw no less than three different ladies on the prowl, dropping religious tracts at various doors; and felt not a little ashamed to be seen by one of them getting into a car with bag and baggage, being bound for Belfast.

The ride of ten miles from Armagh to Portadown was not the prettiest, but one of the pleasantest drives I have had in Ireland, for the country is well cultivated along the whole of the road, the trees in plenty, and villages and neat houses always in sight. The little farms, with their orchards and comfortable buildings, were as clean and trim as could be wished: they are mostly of one story, with long thatched roofs and shining windows, such as those that may be seen in Normandy and Picardy. As it was Sunday evening, all the people seemed to be abroad, some sauntering quietly down the roads, a pair of girls here and there pacing leisurely in a field, a little group seated under the trees of an orchard, which pretty adjunct to the farm is very common in this district; and the crop of apples seemed this year to be extremely plenty. The physiognomy of the people too has quite changed: the girls have their hair neatly braided up, not loose over their faces as in the south; and not only are bare feet very rare, and stockings extremely neat and white, but I am sure I saw at least a dozen good silk gowns upon the women along the road, and scarcely one which was not clean and in good order. The men for the most part figured in jackets, caps, and trousers, eschewing the old well of a hat which covers the popular head at the other end of the island, the breeches, and the long ill-made tail-coat. The people's faces are sharp and neat, not broad, lazy, knowing-looking, like that of many a shambling Diogenes who may be seen lounging before his cabin in Cork or Kerry. As for the cabins, they have disappeared; and the houses of the people may rank decidedly as cottages. The accent, too, is quite different; but this is hard to describe in print. The people speak with a Scotch twang, and, as I fancied, much more simply and to the point. A man gives you a downright answer, without any grin or joke, or attempt at flattery. To be sure, these are rather early days to begin to judge of national characteristics; and very likely the above distinctions have been drawn after profoundly studying a Northern and a Southern waiter at the inn at Armagh.

At any rate, it is clear that the towns are vastly improved, the cottages and villages no less so; the people look active and well-dressed; a sort of weight seems all at once to be taken from the Englishman's mind on entering the province, when he finds himself once more looking upon comfort and activity, and resolution. What is the cause of this improvement? *Protestantism* is, more than one Church-of-England man said to me; but, for Protestantism, would it not be as well to read Scotchism? — meaning thrift, prudence, perseverance, boldness, and common-sense: with which qualities any body of men, of any Christian denomination, would no doubt prosper.

The little brisk town of Portadown, with its comfortable unpretending houses, its squares and market-place, its pretty quay, with craft along the river, — a steamer building on the dock, close to mills and warehouses that look in a full state of prosperity, — was a pleasant conclusion to this ten miles' drive, that ended at the newly opened railway-station. The distance hence to Belfast is twenty-five miles; Lough Neagh may be seen at one point of the line, and the Guide-book says that the station-towns of Lurgan and Lisburn are extremely picturesque;

but it was night when I passed by them, and after a journey of an hour and a quarter reached Belfast.

That city has been discovered by another eminent Cockney traveller (for though born in America, the dear old Bow-bell blood must run in the veins of Mr. N. P. Willis), and I have met, in the periodical works of the country, with repeated angry allusions to his description of Belfast, the pink heels of the chamber-maid who conducted him to bed (what business had he to be looking at the young woman's legs at all?) and his wrath at the beggary of the town and the laziness of the inhabitants, as marked by a line of dirt running along the walls, and showing where they were in the habit of lolling.

These observations struck me as rather hard when applied to Belfast, though possibly pink heels and beggary might be remarked in other cities of the kingdom; but the town of Belfast seemed to me really to be as neat, prosperous, and handsome a city as need be seen; and, with respect to the inn, that in which I stayed, "Kearn's," was as comfortable and well-ordered an establishment as the most fastidious Cockney can desire, and with an advantage which some people perhaps do not care for, that the dinners which cost seven shillings at London taverns are here served for half a crown; but, I must repeat here, in justice to the public, what I stated to Mr. William the waiter, viz. that half a pint of port wine *does* contain more than two glasses — at least it does in happy, happy England. . . . Only, to be sure, here the wine is good, whereas the port-wine in England is not port, but for the most part an abominable drink of which it would be a mercy only to give us two glasses: which, however, is clearly wandering from the subject in hand.

They call Belfast the Irish Liverpool. If people are for calling names, it would be better to call it the Irish London at once — the chief city of the kingdom at any rate. It looks hearty, thriving, and prosperous, as if it had money in its pockets and roast-beef for dinner: it has no pretensions to fashion, but looks mayhap better in its honest broadcloth than *some people* in their shabby brocade. The houses are as handsome as at Dublin, with this advantage, that the people seem to live in them. They have no attempt at ornament for the most part, but are grave, stout, red-brick edifices, laid out at four angles in orderly streets and squares.

The stranger cannot fail to be struck (and haply a little frightened) by the great number of meeting-houses that decorate the town, and give evidence of great sermonizing on Sundays. These buildings do not affect the Gothic, like many of the meagre edifices of the Established and the Roman Catholic churches, but have a physiognomy of their own — a thick-set citizen look. Porticos have they, to be sure, and ornaments Doric, Ionic, and what not? but the meeting-house peeps through all these classical friezes and entablatures; and though one reads of "Imitations of the Ionic Temple of Ilissus, near Athens," the classic temple is made to assume a bluff, downright, Presbyterian air, which would astonish the original builder, doubtless. The churches of the Establishment are handsome and stately. The Catholics are building a brick cathedral, no doubt of the Tudor style: — the present chapel, flanked by the national schools, is an exceedingly unprepossessing building of the Strawberry Hill or Castle of Otranto Gothic: the keys and mitre figuring in the centre — "The cross-keys and nightcap," as a hard-hearted Presbyterian called them to me, with his blunt humor.

The three churches are here pretty equally balanced: Presbyterians 25,000, Catholics 20,000, Episcopalians 17,000. Each party has two or more newspaper organs; and the wars between them are dire and unceasing, as the reader may imagine. For whereas in other parts of Ireland where Catholics and Episcopalians prevail, and the Presbyterian body is too small, each party has but one opponent to belabor: here the Ulster politician, whatever may be his way of thinking, has the great advantage of possessing two enemies on whom he may exercise his eloquence; and in this triangular duel all do their duty nobly. Then there are subdivisions of hostility. For the Church there is a High Church and a Low Church journal; for the Liberals there is a "Repeal" journal and a "No-Repeal" journal; for the Presbyterians there are yet more varieties of journalistic opinion, on which it does not become a stranger to pass a judgment. If the *Northern Whig* says that the *Banner of Ulster* "is a polluted rag," which has hoisted the red banner of falsehood" (which elegant words may be found in the first-named journal of the 13th October), let us be sure the *Banner* has a compliment for the *Northern Whig* in return; if the "Repeal" *Vindicator* and the priests attack the Presbyterian journals and the "home missions," the reverend gentlemen of Geneva are quite as ready with the pen as their brethren of Rome, and not much more scrupulous in their language than the laity. When I was in Belfast, violent disputes were raging between Presbyterian and Episcopalian Conservatives with regard to the Marriage Bill; between Presbyterians and Catholics on the subject of the "home missions;" between the Liberals and Conservatives, of course. "Thank God," for instance, writes a "Repeal" journal, "that the honor and power *of Ireland* are not involved in the disgraceful Afghan war!" — a sentiment insinuating Repeal and something more; disowning, not merely this or that Ministry, but the sovereign and her jurisdiction altogether. But details of these quarrels, religious or political, can tend to edify but few readers out of the country. Even in it, as there are some nine shades of politico-religious differences, an observer pretending to impartiality must necessarily displease eight parties, and almost certainly the whole nine; and the reader who desires to judge the politics of Belfast must study for himself. Nine journals, publishing four hundred numbers in a year, each number containing about as much as an octavo volume: these, and the back numbers of former years, sedulously read, will give the student a notion of the subject in question. And then, after having read the statements on either side, he must ascertain the truth of them, by which time more labor of the same kind will have grown upon him, and he will have attained a good old age.

Amongst the poor, the Catholics and Presbyterians are said to go in a pretty friendly manner to the national schools; but among the Presbyterians themselves it appears there are great differences and quarrels, by which a fine institution, the Belfast Academy, seems to have suffered considerably. It is almost the only building in this large and substantial place, that bears, to the stranger's eye, an unprosperous air. A vast building, standing fairly in the midst of a handsome green and place, and with snug, comfortable red-brick streets stretching away at neat right angles all around, the Presbyterian College looks handsome enough at a short distance, but on a nearer view is found in a woful state of dilapidation. It does not possess the supreme dirt and filth of Maynooth — *that* can but belong to one place, even in Ireland; but the building is in a dismal state of unrepair, steps and windows broken, doors and stairs battered. Of scholars I saw but a few, and these were in the drawing academy. The fine arts do not appear as yet to flourish in Belfast. The models from which the lads were copying were not good: one was copying a bad copy of a drawing by Prout; one was coloring a print. The ragged children in a German national school have better models before them, and are made acquainted with truer principles of art and beauty.

Hard by is the Belfast Museum, where an exhibition of pictures was in preparation, under the patronage of the Belfast Ar

Union. Artists in all parts of the kingdom had been invited to send their works, of which the Union pays the carriage ; and the porters and secretary were busy unpacking cases, in which I recognized some of the works which had before figured on the walls of the London Exhibition rooms.

The book-shops which I saw in this thriving town said much for the religious disposition of the Belfast public : there were numerous portraits of reverend gentlemen, and their works of every variety : — " The Sinner's Friend," " The Watchman on the Tower," " The Peep of Day," " Sermons delivered at Bethesda Chapel," by so-and-so ; with hundreds of the neat little gilt books with bad prints, scriptural titles, and gilt edges, that come from one or two serious publishing houses in London, and in considerable numbers from the neighboring Scotch shores. As for the theatre, with such a public the drama can be expected to find but little favor ; and the gentleman who accompanied me in my walk, and to whom I am indebted for many kindnesses during my stay, said not only that he had never been in the playhouse, but that he never heard of any one going thither. I found out the place where the poor neglected Dramatic Muse of Ulster hid herself ; and was of a party of six in the boxes, the benches of the pit being dotted over with about a score more. Well, it was a comfort to see that the gallery was quite full, and exceedingly happy and noisy : they stamped, and stormed, and shouted, and clapped in a way that was pleasant to hear. One young god, between the acts, favored the public with a song — extremely ill sung certainly, but the intention was everything ; and his brethren above stamped in chorus with roars of delight.

As for the piece performed, it was a good old melodrama of the British sort, inculcating a thorough detestation of vice and a warm sympathy with suffering virtue. The serious are surely too hard upon poor play-goers. We never for a moment allow rascality to triumph beyond a certain part of the third act : we sympathize with the woes of young lovers — her in ringlets and a Polish cap, him in tights and a Vandyke collar ; we abhor avarice or tyranny in the person of " the first old man " with the white wig and red stockings, or of the villain with the roaring voice and black whiskers ; we applaud the honest wag (he is a good fellow in spite of his cowardice) in his hearty jests at the tyrant before mentioned ; and feel a kindly sympathy with all mankind as the curtain falls over all the characters in a group, of which successful love is the happy centre. Reverend gentlemen in meeting-house and church, who shout against the im-

moralities of this poor stage, and threaten all play-goers with
the fate which is awarded to unsuccessful plays, should try and
bear less hardly upon us.

An artist — who, in spite of the Art Union, can scarcely, I
should think, flourish in a place that seems devoted to preaching, politics, and trade — has somehow found his way to this
humble little theatre, and decorated it with some exceedingly
pretty scenery — almost the only indication of a taste for the
fine arts which I have found as yet in the country.

A fine night-exhibition in the town is that of the huge
spinning-mills which surround it, and of which the thousand
windows are lighted up at nightfall, and may be seen from
almost all quarters of the city.

A gentleman to whom I had brought an introduction, good-
naturedly left his work to walk with me to one of these mills,
and stated by whom he had been introduced to me to the mill-
proprietor, Mr. Mulholland. "*That* recommendation," said
Mr. Mulholland, gallantly, "is welcome anywhere." It was
from my kind friend Mr. Lever. What a privilege some men
have, who can sit quietly in their studies and make friends all
the world over!

Here is the figure of a
girl sketched in the place:
there are nearly five hundred girls employed in it.
They work in huge long
chambers, lighted by num-
bers of windows, hot with
steam, buzzing and hum-
ming with hundreds of
thousands of whirling
wheels, that all take their
motion from a steam-engine
which lives apart in a hot
cast-iron temple of its own,
from which it communi-
cates with the innumerable
machines that the five hundred girls preside over.
They have seemingly but
to take away the work
when done — the enormous
monster in the cast-iron
room does it all. He cards

the flax, and combs it, and spins it, and beats it, and twists it : the five hundred girls stand by to feed him, or take the material from him, when he has had his will of it.   There is something frightful in the vastness as in the minuteness of this power. Every thread writhes and twirls as the steam-fate orders it, — every thread, of which it would take a hundred to make the thickness of a hair.

I have seldom, I think, seen more good looks than amongst the young women employed in this place.   They work for twelve hours daily, in rooms of which the heat is intolerable to a stranger ; but in spite of it they looked gay, stout, and healthy ; nor were their forms much concealed by the very simple clothes they wear while in the mill.

The stranger will be struck by the good looks not only of these spinsters, but of almost all the young women in the streets.   I never saw a town where so many women are to be met — so many and so pretty — with and without bonnets, with good figures, in neat homely shawls and dresses.   The grisettes of Belfast are among the handsomest ornaments of it ; and as good, no doubt, and irreproachable in morals as their sisters in the rest of Ireland.

Many of the merchants' counting-houses are crowded in little old-fashioned " entries," or courts, such as one sees about the Bank in London.   In and about these, and in the principal streets in the daytime, is a great activity, and homely unpretending bustle.   The men have a business look, too ; and one sees very few flaunting dandies, as in Dublin.   The shopkeepers do not brag upon their signboards, or keep " emporiums," as elsewhere, — their places of business being for the most part homely ; though one may see some splendid shops, which are not to be surpassed by London.   The docks and quays are busy with their craft and shipping, upon the beautiful borders of the Lough ; — the large red warehouses stretching along the shores, with ships loading, or unloading, or building, hammers clanging, pitch pots flaming and boiling, seamen cheering in the ships, or lolling lazily on the shore.   The life and movement of a port here give the stranger plenty to admire and observe.   And nature has likewise done everything for the place — surrounding it with picturesque hills and water ; — for which latter I must confess I was not very sorry to leave the town behind me, and its mills, and its meeting-houses, and its commerce, and its theologians, and its politicians.

CHAPTER XXVIII.

BELFAST TO THE CAUSEWAY.

THE Lough of Belfast has a reputation for beauty almost as great as that of the Bay of Dublin ; but though, on the day I left Belfast for Larne, the morning was fine, and the sky clear and blue above, an envious mist lay on the water, which hid all its beauties from the dozen of passengers on the Larne coach. All we could see were ghostly-looking silhouettes of ships gliding here and there through the clouds ; and I am sure the coachman's remark was quite correct, that it was a pity the day was so misty. I found myself, before I was aware, entrapped into a theological controversy with two grave gentlemen outside the coach — another fog, which did not subside much before we reached Carrickfergus. The road from the Ulster capital to that little town seemed meanwhile to be extremely lively : cars and omnibuses passed thickly peopled. For some miles along the road is a string of handsome country-houses, belonging to the rich citizens of the town ; and we passed by neat-looking churches and chapels, factories and rows of cottages clustered round them, like villages of old at the foot of feudal castles. Furthermore it was hard to see, for the mist which lay on the water had enveloped the mountains too, and we only had a glimpse or two of smiling comfortable fields and gardens.

Carrickfergus rejoices in a real romantic-looking castle, jutting bravely into the sea, and famous as a background for a picture. It is of use for little else now, luckily ; nor has it been put to any real warlike purposes since the day when honest Thurot stormed, took, and evacuated it. Let any romancer who is in want of a hero peruse the second volume, or it may be the third, of the " Annual Register," where the adventures of that gallant fellow are related. He was a gentleman, a genius, and, to crown all, a smuggler. He lived for some time in Ireland, and in England, in disguise ; he had love-passages and romantic adventures ; he landed a body of his countrymen on these shores, and died in the third volume, after a battle gallantly fought on both sides, but in which victory rested with the British arms. What can a novelist want more? William III. also landed here ; and as for the rest, " M'Skimin, the accurate and laborious historian of the town, informs us

that the founding of the castle is lost in the depths of antiquity."
It is pleasant to give a little historic glance at a place as one
passes through. The above facts may be relied on as coming
from Messrs. Curry's excellent new Guide-book; with the exception of the history of Mons. Thurot, which is "private
information," drawn years ago from the scarce work previously
mentioned. By the way, another excellent companion to the
traveller in Ireland is the collection of the "Irish Penny Magazine," which may be purchased for a guinea, and contains a
mass of information regarding the customs and places of the
country. Willis's work is amusing, as everything is, written
by that lively author, and the engravings accompanying it as
unfaithful as any ever made.

Meanwhile, asking pardon for this double digression, which
has been made while the guard-coachman is delivering his mail-
bags — while the landlady stands looking on in the sun, her
hands folded a little below the waist — while a company of tall
burly troops from the castle has passed by, "surrounded" by
a very mean, mealy-faced, uneasy-looking little subaltern —
while the poor epileptic idiot of the town, wallowing and
grinning in the road, and snorting out supplications for a
halfpenny, has tottered away in possession of the coin: —
meanwhile, fresh horses are brought out, and the small boy
who acts behind the coach makes an unequal and disagreeable
tootooing on a horn kept to warn sleepy carmen and celebrate
triumphal entries into and exits from cities. As the mist
clears up, the country shows round about wild but friendly: at
one place we passed a village where a crowd of well dressed
people were collected at an auction of farm-furniture, and many
more figures might be seen coming over the fields and issuing
from the mist. The owner of the carts and machines is going
to emigrate to America. Presently we come to the demesne of
Red Hall, "through which is a pretty drive of upwards of a
mile in length: it contains a rocky glen, the bed of a mountain
stream — which is perfectly dry, except in winter — and the
woods about it are picturesque, and it is occasionally the resort
of summer-parties of pleasure." Nothing can be more just
than the first part of the description, and there is very little
doubt that the latter paragraph is equally faithful; — with which
we come to Larne, a "most thriving town," the same authority
says, but a most dirty and narrow-streeted and ill-built one.
Some of the houses reminded one of the south. A benevolent
fellow-passenger said that the window was "a convanience."
And here, after a drive of nineteen miles upon a comfortable

coach, we were transferred with the mail-bags to a comfortable car that makes the journey to Ballycastle. There is no harm in saying that there was a very pretty smiling buxom young lass for a travelling companion; and somehow, to a lonely person, the landscape always looks prettier in such society. The "Antrim coast-road," which we now, after a few miles, begin to follow, besides being one of the most noble and gallant works of art that is to be seen in any country, is likewise a route highly picturesque and romantic; the sea spreading wide before the spectator's eyes upon one side of the route, the tall cliffs of limestone rising abruptly above him on the other. There are in the map of Curry's Guide-book points indicating castles and abbey ruins in the vicinity of Glenarm; and the little place looked so comfortable, as we abruptly came upon it, round a rock, that I was glad to have an excuse for staying, and felt an extreme curiosity with regard to the abbey and the castle.

The abbey only exists in the unromantic shape of a wall; the castle, however, far from being a ruin, is an antique in the most complete order — an old castle repaired so as to look like new, and increased by modern wings, towers, gables, and terraces, so extremely old that the whole forms a grand and imposing-looking baronial edifice, towering above the little town which it seems to protect, and with which it is connected by a bridge and a severe-looking armed tower and gate. In the town is a town-house, with a campanile in the Italian taste, and a school or chapel opposite in the early English; so that the inhabitants can enjoy a considerable architectural variety. A grave-looking church, with a beautiful steeple, stands amid some trees hard by a second handsome bridge and the little quay; and here, too, was perched a poor little wandering theatre (gallery 1*d*., pit 2*d*.), and proposing that night to play "Bombastes Furioso, and the Comic Bally of Glenarm in an Uproar." I heard the thumping of the drum in the evening; but, as at Roundwood, nobody patronized the poor players. At nine o'clock there was not a single taper lighted under their awning, and my heart (perhaps it is too susceptible) bled for Fusbos.

The severe gate of the castle was opened by a kind, good-natured old porteress, instead of a rough gallowglass with a battle-axe and yellow shirt (more fitting guardian of so stern a postern), and the old dame insisted upon my making an application to see the grounds of the castle, which request was very kindly granted, and afforded a delightful half-hour's walk.

The grounds are beautiful, and excellently kept; the trees in their autumn livery of red, yellow, and brown, except some stout ones that keep to their green summer clothes, and the laurels and their like, who wear pretty much the same dress all the year round. The birds were singing with the most astonishing vehemence in the dark glistening shrubberies; but the only sound in the walks was that of the rakes pulling together the falling leaves. There was of these walks one especially, flanked towards the river by a turreted wall covered with ivy, and having on the one side a row of lime-trees that had turned quite yellow, while opposite them was a green slope, and a quaint terrace-stair, and a long range of fantastic gables, towers, and chimneys; — there was, I say, one of these walks which Mr. Cattermole would hit off with a few strokes of his gallant pencil, and which I could fancy to be frequented by some of those long-trained, tender, gentle-looking young beauties whom Mr. Stone loves to design. Here they come, talking of love in a tone that is between a sigh and a whisper, and gliding in rustling shot silks over the fallen leaves.

There seemed to be a good deal of stir in the little port, where, says the Guide-book, a couple of hundred vessels take in cargoes annually of the produce of the district. Stone and lime are the chief articles exported, of which the cliffs for miles give an unfailing supply; and, as one travels the mountains at night, the kilns may be seen lighted up in the lonely places, and flaring red in the darkness.

If the road from Larne to Glenarm is beautiful, the coast route from the latter place to Cushendall is still more so; and, except peerless Westport, I have seen nothing in Ireland so picturesque as this noble line of coast scenery. The new road, luckily, is not yet completed, and the lover of natural beauties had better hasten to the spot in time, ere, by flattening and improving the road, and leading it along the sea-shore, half the magnificent prospects are shut out, now visible from along the mountainous old road; which, according to the good old fashion, gallantly takes all the hills in its course, disdaining to turn them. At three miles' distance, near the village of Cairlough, Glenarm looks more beautiful than when you are close upon it; and, as the car travels on to the stupendous Garron Head, the traveller, looking back, has a view of the whole line of coast southward as far as Isle Magee, with its bays and white villages, and tall precipitous cliffs, green, white, and gray. Eyes left, you may look with wonder at the mountains rising above, or presently at the pretty park and grounds of Drumnasole.

Here, near the woods of Nappan, which are dressed in ten thousand colors — ash-leaves turned yellow, nut-trees red, birch-leaves brown, lime-leaves speckled over with black spots (marks of a disease which they will never get over) — stands a school-house that looks like a French château, having probably been a villa in former days, and discharges as we pass a cluster of fair-haired children, that begin running madly down the hill, their fair hair streaming behind them. Down the hill goes the car, madly too, and you wonder and bless your stars that the horse does not fall, or crush the children that are running before, or you that are sitting behind. Every now and then, at a trip of the horse, a disguised lady's-maid, with a canary-bird in her lap and a vast anxiety about her best bonnet in the band-box, begins to scream : at which the car-boy grins, and rattles down the hill only the quicker. The road, which almost always skirts the hillside, has been torn sheer through the rock here and there : an immense work of levelling, shovelling, picking, blasting, filling, is going on along the whole line. As I was looking up a vast cliff, decorated with patches of green here and there at its summit, and at its base, where the sea had beaten until now, with long, thin, waving grass, that I told a grocer, my neighbor, was like mermaid's hair (though he did not in the least coincide in the simile) — as I was looking up the hill, admiring two goats that were browsing on a little patch of green, and two sheep perched yet higher (I had never seen such agility in mutton) — as, I say once more, I was looking at these phenomena, the grocer nudges me and says, " *Look on to this side — that's Scotland yon.*" If ever this book reaches a second edition, a sonnet shall be inserted in this place, describing the author's feelings on HIS FIRST VIEW OF SCOTLAND. Meanwhile, the Scotch mountains remain undisturbed, looking blue and solemn, far away in the placid sea.

Rounding Garron Head, we come upon the inlet which is called Red Bay, the shores and sides of which are of red clay, that has taken the place of limestone, and towards which, between two noble ranges of mountains, stretches a long green plain, forming, together with the hills that protect it and the sea that washes it, one of the most beautiful landscapes of this most beautiful country. A fair writer, whom the Guide-book quotes, breaks out into strains of admiration in speaking of this district ; calls it " Switzerland in miniature," celebrates its mountains of Glenariff and Lurgethan, and lauds, in terms of equal admiration, the rivers, waterfalls, and other natural beauties that lie within the glen.

The writer's enthusiasm regarding this tract of country is quite warranted, nor can any praise in admiration of it be too high; but alas! in calling a place "Switzerland in miniature," do we describe it? In joining together cataracts, valleys, rushing streams, and blue mountains, with all the emphasis and picturesqueness of which type is capable, we cannot get near to a copy of Nature's sublime countenance; and the writer can't hope to describe such grand sights so as to make them visible to the fireside reader, but can only, to the best of his taste and experience, warn the future traveller where he may look out for objects to admire. I think this sentiment has been repeated a score of times in this journal; but it comes upon one at every new display of beauty and magnificence, such as here the Almighty in his bounty has set before us; and every such scene seems to warn one, that it is not made to talk about too much, but to think of and love, and be grateful for.

Rounding this beautiful bay and valley, we passed by some caves that penetrate deep into the red rock, and are inhabited — one by a blacksmith, whose forge was blazing in the dark; one by cattle; and one by an old woman that has sold whiskey here for time out of mind. The road then passes under an arch cut in the rock by the same spirited individual who has cleared away many of the difficulties in the route to Glenarm, and beside a conical hill, where for some time previous have been visible the ruins of the "ancient ould castle" of Red Bay. At a distance, it looks very grand upon its height; but on coming close it has dwindled down to a mere wall, and not a high one. Hence quickly we reached Cushendall, where the grocer's family are on the look-out for him: the driver begins to blow his little bugle, and the disguised lady's-maid begins to smooth her bonnet and hair.

At this place a good dinner of fresh whiting, broiled bacon, and small beer was served up to me for the sum of eightpence, while the lady's-maid in question took her tea. "This town is full of Papists," said her ladyship, with an extremely genteel air; and, either in consequence of this, or because she ate up one of the fish, which she had clearly no right to, a disagreement arose between us, and we did not exchange another word for the rest of the journey. The road led us for fourteen miles by wild mountains, and across a fine aqueduct to Ballycastle; but it was dark as we left Cushendall, and it was difficult to see more in the gray evening but that the country was savage and lonely, except where the kilns were lighted up here and there in the hills, and a shining river might be seen winding in the dark ravines. Not far from Ballycastle lies a little old ruin, called the Abbey of Bonamargy : by it the Margy river runs into the sea, upon which you come suddenly ; and on the shore are some tall buildings and factories, that looked as well in the moonlight as if they had not been in ruins : and hence a fine avenue of limes leads to Ballycastle. They must have been planted at the time recorded in the Guide-book, when a mine was discovered near the town, and the works and warehouses on the quay erected. At present, the place has little trade, and half a dozen carts with apples, potatoes, dried fish, and turf, seem to contain the commerce of the market.

The picturesque sort of vehicle designed on the next page* is said to be going much out of fashion in the country, the solid wheels giving place to those common to the rest of Europe. A fine and edifying conversation took place between the designer and the owner of the vehicle. "Stand still for a minute, you and the car, and I will give you twopence!" "What do you want to do with it?" says the latter. "To draw it." "To *draw* it!" says he, with a wild look of surprise. "And is it *you'll* draw it?" "I mean I want to take a picture of it : you know what a picture is!" "No, I don't." "Here's one," says I, showing him a book. "Oh, faith, sir," says the carman, drawing back rather alarmed, "I'm no scholar!" And he concluded by saying, "*Will you buy the turf, or will you not?*" By which straightforward question he showed himself to be a real practical man of sense ; and, as he got an unsatisfactory reply to this query, he forthwith gave a lash to his pony and declined to wait a minute longer. As for the twopence, he certainly accepted that handsome sum, and put it into his pocket, but with an air of extreme wonder at the transaction, and of contempt for the giver ; which very likely was perfectly justifiable. I have seen men despised in genteel companies with not half so good a cause.

In respect to the fine arts, I am bound to say that the people in the South and West showed much more curiosity and interest with regard to a sketch and its progress than has been shown by the *badauds* of the North ; the former looking on by dozens and exclaiming, "That's Frank Mahony's house!" or "Look at Biddy Mullins and the child!" or "He's taking off the chimney now!" as the case may be ; whereas, sketching in the North, I have collected no such spectators, the people not taking the slightest notice of the transaction.

* This refers to an illustrated edition of the work.

The little town of Ballycastle does not contain much to occupy the traveller; behind the church stands a ruined old mansion with round turrets, that must have been a stately tower in former days. The town is more modern, but almost as dismal as the tower. A little street behind it slides off into a potato-field — the peaceful barrier of the place; and hence I could see the tall rock of Bengore, with the sea beyond it, and a pleasing landscape stretching towards it.

Dr. Hamilton's elegant and learned book has an awful picture of yonder head of Bengore; and hard by it the Guide-book says is a coal-mine, where Mr. Barrow found a globular stone hammer, which, he infers, was used in the coal-mine before weapons of iron were invented. The former writer insinuates that the mine must have been worked more than a thousand years ago, "before the turbulent chaos of events that succeeded the eighth century." Shall I go and see a coal-mine that may have been worked a thousand years since? Why go see it? says idleness. To be able to say that I have seen it. Sheridan's advice to his son here came into my mind; * and I shall reserve a description of the mine, and an antiquarian dissertation regarding it, for publication elsewhere.

Ballycastle must not be left without recording the fact that one of the snuggest inns in the country is kept by the post-master there; who has also a stable full of good horses for travellers who take his little inn on the way to the Giant's Causeway.

The road to the Causeway is bleak, wild, and hilly. The cabins along the road are scarcely better than those of Kerry, the inmates as ragged, and more fierce and dark-looking. I never was so pestered by juvenile beggars as in the dismal village of Ballintoy. A crowd of them rushed after the car, calling for money in a fierce manner, as if it was their right: dogs as fierce as the children came yelling after the vehicle; and the faces which scowled out of the black cabins were not a whit more good-humored. We passed by one or two more clumps of cabins, with their turf and corn-stacks lying together at the foot of the hills; placed there for the convenience of the children, doubtless, who can thus accompany the car either way, and shriek out their "Bonny gantleman, gi'e us a ha'p'ny." A couple of churches, one with a pair of its pinnacles blown off, stood in the dismal open country, and a gentleman's house here and there: there were no trees about them, but a brown

* "I want to go into a coal-mine," says Tom Sheridan, "in order to say I have been there." "Well, then, say so," replied the admirable father.

18

grass round about—hills rising and falling in front, and the sea beyond. The occasional view of the coast was noble ; wild Bengore towering eastwards as we went along ; Raghery Island before us, in the steep rocks and caves of which Bruce took shelter when driven from yonder Scottish coast, that one sees stretching blue in the north-east.

I think this wild gloomy tract through which one passes is a good prelude for what is to be the great sight of the day, and got my mind to a proper state of awe by the time we were near the journey's end. Turning away shorewards by the fine house of Sir Francis Macnaghten, I went towards a lone handsome inn, that stands close to the Causeway. The landlord at Bally-castle had lent me Hamilton's book to read on the road ; but I had not time then to read more than half a dozen pages of it. They described how the author, a clergyman distinguished as a man of science, had been thrust out of a friend's house by the frightened servants one wild night, and butchered by some Whiteboys who were waiting outside and called for his blood. I had been told at Belfast that there was a corpse in the inn : was it there now ? It had driven off, the car-boy said, " in a handsome hearse and four to Dublin the whole way." It was gone, but I thought the house looked as if the ghost was there. See, yonder are the black rocks stretching to Portrush : how leaden and gray the sea looks ! how gray and leaden the sky ! You hear the waters roaring evermore, as they have done since the beginning of the world. The car drives up with a dismal grinding noise of the wheels to the big lone house : there's no smoke in the chimneys ; the doors are locked. Three savage-looking men rush after the car : are they the men who took out Mr. Hamilton — took him out and butchered him in the moon-light? Is everybody, I wonder, dead in that big house? Will they let us in before those men are up? Out comes a pretty smiling girl, with a curtsy, just as the savages are at the car, and you are ushered into a very comfortable room ; and the men turn out to be guides. Well, thank heaven it's no worse ! I had fifteen pounds still left ; and, when desperate, have no doubt should fight like a lion.

CHAPTER XXIX.

THE GIANT'S CAUSEWAY — COLERAINE — PORTRUSH.

THE traveller no sooner issues from the inn by a back door, which he is informed will lead him straight to the Causeway, than the guides pounce upon him, with a dozen rough boatmen who are likewise lying in wait; and a crew of shrill beggar-boys, with boxes of spars, ready to tear him and each other to pieces seemingly, yell and bawl incessantly round him. "I'm the guide Miss Henry recommends," shouts one. "I'm Mr. Macdonald's guide," pushes in another. "This way," roars a third, and drags his prey down a precipice; the rest of them clambering and quarrelling after. I had no friends: I was perfectly helpless. I wanted to walk down to the shore by myself, but they would not let me, and I had nothing for it but to yield myself into the hands of the guide who had seized me, who hurried me down the steep to a little wild bay, flanked on each side by rugged cliffs and rocks, against which the waters came tumbling, frothing, and roaring furiously. Upon some of these black rocks two or three boats were lying: four men seized a boat, pushed it shouting into the water, and ravished me into it. We had slid between two rocks, where the channel came gurgling in: we were up one swelling wave that came in a huge advancing body ten feet above us, and were plunging madly down another, (the descent causes a sensation in the lower regions of the stomach which it is not at all necessary here to describe,) before I had leisure to ask myself why the deuce I was in that boat, with four rowers hurrooing and bounding madly from one huge liquid mountain to another — four rowers whom I was bound to pay. I say, the query came qualmishly across me why the devil I was there, and why not walking calmly on the shore.

The guide began pouring his professional jargon into my ears. "Every one of them bays," says he, "has a name (take my place, and the spray won't come over you): that is Port Noffer, and the next, Port na Gange; them rocks is the Stook-awns (for every rock has its name as well as every bay); and yonder — give way, my boys, — hurray, we're over it now: has it wet you much, sir? — that's the little cave: it goes five hundred feet under ground, and the boats goes into it easy of a calm day."

"Is it a fine day or a rough one now?" said I; the internal disturbance going on with more severity than ever.

"It's betwixt and between; or, I may say, neither one nor the other. Sit up, sir. Look at the entrance of the cave. Don't be afraid, sir: never has an accident happened in any of these boats, and the most delicate ladies has rode in them on rougher days than this. Now, boys, pull to the big cave. That, sir, is six hundred and sixty yards in length, though some say it goes for miles inland, where the people sleeping in their houses hear the waters roaring under them."

The water was tossing and tumbling into the mouth of the little cave. I looked, — for the guide would not let me alone till I did, — and saw what might be expected: a black hole of some forty feet high, into which it was no more possible to see than into a millstone. "For heaven's sake, sir," says I, "if you've no particular wish to see the mouth of the big cave, put about and let us see the Causeway and get ashore." This was done, the guide meanwhile telling some story of a ship of the Spanish Armada having fired her guns at two peaks of rock, then visible, which the crew mistook for chimney-pots — what benighted fools these Spanish Armadilloes must have been: it is easier to see a rock than a chimney-pot; it is easy to know that chimney-pots do not grow on rocks. — "But where, it you please, is the Causeway?"

"That's the Causeway before you," says the guide.

"Which?"

"That pier which you see jutting out into the bay, right a-head."

"Mon Dieu! and have I travelled a hundred and fifty miles to see *that*?"

I declare, upon my conscience, the barge moored at Hungerford market is a more majestic object, and seems to occupy as much space. As for telling a man that the Causeway is merely a part of the sight; that he is there for the purpose of examining the surrounding scenery; that if he looks to the westward he will see Portrush and Donegal Head before him; that the cliffs immediately in his front are green in some places, black in others, interspersed with blotches of brown and streaks of verdure; — what is all this to a lonely individual lying sick in a boat, between two immense waves that only give him momentary glimpses of the land in question, to show that it is frightfully near, and yet you are an hour from it?

They won't let you go away — that cursed guide *will* tell out his stock of legends and stories. The boatmen insist upon your looking at boxes of "specimens," which you must buy of them; they laugh as you grow paler and paler; they offer you more and more "specimens;" even the dirty lad who pulls number three, and is not allowed by his comrades to speak, puts in *his* oar, and hands you over a piece of Irish diamond (it looks like half-sucked alicompayne), and scorns you. "Hurray, lads, now for it, give way!" how the oars do hurtle in the rowlocks, as the boat goes up an aqueous mountain, and then down into one of those cursed maritime valleys where there is no rest as on shore!

At last, after they had pulled me enough about, and sold me all the boxes of specimens, I was permitted to land at the spot whence we set out, and whence, though we had been rowing for an hour, we had never been above five hundred yards distant. Let all Cockneys take warning from this; let the solitary one caught issuing from the back door of the hotel, shout at once to the boatmen to be gone — that he will have none of them. Let him, at any rate, go first down to the water to determine whether it be smooth enough to allow him to take any decent pleasure by riding on its surface. For after all, it must be remembered that it *is* pleasure we come for — that we are not *obliged* to take those boats. — Well, well! I paid ten shillings for mine, and ten minutes before would cheerfully have paid five pounds to be allowed to quit it: it was no hard bargain after all. As for the boxes of spar and specimens, I at once, being on terra firma, broke my promise, and said I would see them all —— first. It is wrong to swear, I know; but sometimes it relieves one *so* much!

The first act on shore was to make a sacrifice to Sanctissima Tellus; offering up to her a neat and becoming Taglioni coat, bought for a guinea in Covent Garden only three months back. I sprawled on my back on the smoothest of rocks that is, and tore the elbows to pieces: the guide picked me up; the boatmen did not stir, for they had had their will of me; the guide alone picked me up, I say, and bade me follow him. We went across a boggy ground in one of the little bays, round which rise the green walls of the cliff, terminated on either side by a black crag, and the line of the shore washed by the poluphloisboiotic, nay, the poluphloisboiotatotic sea. Two beggars stepped over the bog after us howling for money, and each holding up a cursed box of specimens. No oaths, threats, entreaties, would drive these vermin away; for some time the whole scene had

been spoilt by the incessant and abominable jargon of them,
the boatmen, and the guides. I was obliged to give them
money to be left in quiet, and if, as no doubt will be the case,
the Giant's Causeway shall be a still greater resort of travellers than ever, the county must put policemen on the rocks to
keep the beggars away, or fling them in the water when they
appear.

And now, by force of money, having got rid of the sea and
land beggars, you are at liberty to examine at your leisure the
wonders of the place. There is not the least need for a guide
to attend the stranger, unless the latter have a mind to listen
to a parcel of legends, which may be well from the mouth of a
wild simple peasant who believes in his tales, but are odious
from a dullard who narrates them at the rate of sixpence a lie.
Fee him and the other beggars, and at last you are left tranquil
to look at the strange scene with your own eyes, and enjoy
your own thoughts at leisure.

That is, if the thoughts awakened by such a scene may be
called enjoyment; but for me, I confess, they are too near akin
to fear to be pleasant; and I don't know that I would desire to
change that sensation of awe and terror which the hour's walk
occasioned, for a greater familiarity with this wild, sad, lonely
place. The solitude is awful. I can't understand how those
chattering guides dare to lift up their voices here, and cry for
money.

It looks like the beginning of the world, somehow: the sea
looks older than in other places, the hills and rocks strange, and
formed differently from other rocks and hills — as those vast
dubious monsters were formed who possessed the earth before
man. The hill-tops are shattered into a thousand cragged fantastical shapes; the water comes swelling into scores of little
strange creeks, or goes off with a leap, roaring into those mysterious caves yonder, which penetrate who knows how far into
our common world? The savage rock-sides are painted of a
hundred colors. Does the sun ever shine here? When the
world was moulded and fashioned out of formless chaos, this
must have been the *bit over* — a remnant of chaos! Think of
that! — it is a tailor's simile. Well, I am a Cockney: I wish
I were in Pall Mall! Yonder is a kelp-burner: a lurid smoke
from his burning kelp rises up to the leaden sky, and he looks
as naked and fierce as Cain. Bubbling up out of the rocks at
the very brim of the sea rises a little crystal spring: how comes
it there? and there is an old gray hag beside, who has been
there for hundreds and hundreds of years, and there sits and

sells whiskey at the extremity of creation! How do you dare
to sell whiskey there, old woman? Did you serve old Saturn
with a glass when he lay along the Causeway here? In reply,
she says, she has no change for a shilling : she never has ; but
her whiskey is good.

This is not a description of the Giant's Causeway (as some
clever critic will remark), but of a Londoner there, who is by
no means so interesting an object as the natural curiosity in
question. That single hint is sufficient; I have not a word
more to say. "If," says he, "you cannot describe the scene
lying before us — if you cannot state from your personal observation that the number of basaltic pillars composing the
Causeway has been computed at about forty thousand, which
vary in diameter, their surface presenting the appearance of a
tessellated pavement of polygonal stones — that each pillar is
formed of several distinct joints, the convex end of the one
being accurately fitted in the concave of the next, and the
length of the joints varying from five feet to four inches — that
although the pillars are polygonal, there is but one of three
sides in the whole forty thousand (think of that!), but three of
nine sides, and that it may be safely computed that ninety-nine
out of one hundred pillars have either five, six, or seven sides ;
if you cannot state something useful, you had much better, sir,
retire and get your dinner."

Never was summons more gladly obeyed. The dinner must
be ready by this time ; so, remain you, and look on at the awful
scene, and copy it down in words if you can. If at the end of
the trial you are dissatisfied with your skill as a painter, and
find that the biggest of your words cannot render the hues
and vastness of that tremendous swelling sea — of those lean
solitary crags standing rigid along the shore, where they have
been watching the ocean ever since it was made — of those gray
towers of Dunluce standing upon a leaden rock, and looking as
if some old, old princess, of old, old fairy times, were dragon-
guarded within — of yon flat stretches of sand where the Scotch
and Irish mermaids hold conference — come away too, and
prate no more about the scene ! There is that in nature, dear
Jenkins, which passes even our powers. We can feel the beauty
of a magnificent landscape, perhaps : but we can describe a
leg of mutton and turnips better. Come, then, this scene is for
our betters to depict. If Mr. Tennyson were to come hither for
a month, and brood over the place, he might, in some of those
lofty heroic lines which the author of the " Morte d'Arthur"
knows how to pile up, convey to the reader a sense of this gigan-

tic desolate scene. What! you, too, are a poet? Well, then, Jenkins, stay! but believe me, you had best take my advice, and come off.

The worthy landlady made her appearance with the politest of bows and an apology, — for what does the reader think a lady should apologize in the most lonely rude spot in the world? — because a plain servant-woman was about to bring in the dinner, the waiter being absent on leave at Coleraine! O heaven and earth! where will the genteel end? I replied philosophically that I did not care twopence for the plainness or beauty of the waiter, but that it was the dinner I looked to, the frying whereof made a great noise in the huge lonely house; and it must be said, that though the lady *was* plain, the repast was exceedingly good. "I have expended my little all," says the landlady, stepping in with a speech after dinner, "in the building of this establishment; and though to a man its profits may appear small, to such a *being* as I am it will bring, I trust, a sufficient return;" and on my asking her why she took the place, she replied that she had always, from her earliest youth, a fancy to dwell in that spot, and had accordingly realized her wish by building this hotel — this mausoleum. In spite of the bright fire, and the good dinner, and the good wine, it was impossible to feel comfortable in the place; and when the car wheels were heard, I jumped up with joy to take my departure and forget the awful lonely shore, and that wild, dismal, genteel inn. A ride over a wide gusty country, in a gray, misty, half-moonlight, the loss of a wheel at Bushmills, and the escape from a tumble, were the delightful varieties after the late awful occurrences. "Such a being" as I am, would die of loneliness in that hotel; and so let all brother Cockneys be warned.

Some time before we came to it, we saw the long line of mist that lay above the Bann, and coming through a dirty suburb of low cottages, passed down a broad street with gas and lamps in it (thank heaven, there are people once more!), and at length drove up in state, across a gas-pipe, in a market-place, before an hotel in the town of Coleraine, famous for linen and for Beautiful Kitty, who must be old and ugly now, for it's a good five-and-thirty years since she broke her pitcher, according to Mr. Moore's account of her. The scene as we entered the Diamond was rather a lively one — a score of little stalls were brilliant with lights; the people were thronging in the place making their Saturday bargains; the town clock began to toll nine; and hark! faithful to a minute, the horn of the Derry mail was heard tootooing, and four commercial gentlemen, with Scotch accents, rushed into the hotel at the same time with myself.

Among the beauties of Coleraine may be mentioned the price of beef, which a gentleman told me may be had for fourpence a pound; and I saw him purchase an excellent codfish for a shilling. I am bound, too, to state for the benefit of aspiring Radicals, what two Conservative citizens of the place stated to me, viz.; — that though there were two Conservative candidates then canvassing the town, on account of a vacancy in the representation, the voters were so truly liberal that they would elect any person of any other political creed, who would simply bring money enough to purchase their votes. There are 220 voters, it appears; of whom it is not, however, necessary to "argue" with more than fifty, who alone are open to conviction; but as parties are pretty equally balanced, the votes of the quinquagint, of course, carry an immense weight with them. Well, this is all discussed calmly standing on an inn-steps, with a jolly landlord and a professional man of the town to give the information. So, heaven bless us, the ways of London are beginning to be known even here. Gentility has already taken up her seat in the Giant's Causeway, where she apologizes for the plainness of her look: and, lo! here is bribery, as bold as in the most civilized places — hundreds and hundreds of miles away from St. Stephen's and Pall Mall. I wonder, in that little island of Raghery, so wild and lonely, whether civilization is beginning to dawn upon them? — whether they bribe and are genteel? But for the rough sea of yesterday, I think I would have fled thither to make the trial.

The town of Coleraine, with a number of cabin suburbs belonging to it, lies picturesquely grouped on the Bann river: and the whole of the little city was echoing with psalms as I walked through it on the Sunday morning. The piety of the people seems remarkable; some of the inns even will not receive travellers on Sunday; and this is written in an hotel, of which every room is provided with a Testament, containing an injunction on the part of the landlord to consider this world itself as only a passing abode. Is it well that Boniface should furnish his guest with Bibles as well as bills, and sometimes shut his door on a traveller, who has no other choice but to read it on a Sunday? I heard of a gentleman arriving from ship-board at Kilrush on a Sunday, when the pious hotel-keeper refused him admittance; and some more tales, which to go into would re quire the introduction of private names and circumstances, but would tend to show that the Protestant of the North is as much priest-ridden as the Catholic of the South : — priest and old-woman ridden, for there are certain expounders of doctrine in our church, who are not, I believe, to be found in the church of Rome ; and woe betide the stranger who comes in to settle in these parts, if his " seriousness " be not satisfactory to the heads (with false fronts to most of them) of the congregations.

Look at that little snug harbor of Portrush ! a hideous new castle standing on a rock protects it on one side, a snug row of gentlemen's cottages curves round the shore facing northward, a bath-house, an hotel, more smart houses, face the beach westward, defended by another mound of rocks. In the centre of the little town stands a new-built church ; and the whole place has an air of comfort and neatness which is seldom seen in Ireland. One would fancy that all the tenants of these pretty snug habitations, sheltered in this nook far away from the world, have nothing to do but to be happy, and spend their little comfortable means in snug little hospitalities among one another, and kind little charities among the poor. What does a man in active life ask for more than to retire to such a competence, to such a snug nook of the world ; and there repose with a stock of healthy children round the fireside, a friend within call, and the means of decent hospitality wherewith to treat him ?

Let any one meditating this pleasant sort of retreat, and charmed with the look of this or that place as peculiarly suited to his purpose, take a special care to understand his neighborhood first, before he commit himself, by lease-signing or house-buying. It is not sufficient that you should be honest, kind-hearted, hospitable, of good family — what are your opinions upon religious subjects ? Are they such as agree with the notions of old Lady This, or Mrs. That, who are the patronesses of the village ? If not, woe betide you ! you will be shunned by the rest of the society, thwarted in your attempts to do good, whispered against over evangelical bohea and serious muffins. Lady This will inform every new arrival that you are a reprobate, and lost, and Mrs. That will consign you and your daughters, and your wife (a worthy woman, but, alas ! united to that sad worldly man !) to damnation. The clergyman who partakes of the muffins and bohea before mentioned, will very possibly preach sermons against you from the pulpit : this was not done at Portstewart to my knowledge, but

I have had the pleasure of sitting under a minister in Ireland who insulted the very patron who gave him his living, discoursing upon the sinfulness of partridge-shooting, and threatening hell-fire as the last "meet" for fox-hunters; until the squire, one of the best and most charitable resident landlords in Ireland, was absolutely driven out of the church where his fathers had worshipped for hundreds of years, by the insults of this howling evangelical inquisitor.

So much as this I did not hear at Portstewart; but I was told that at yonder neat-looking bath-house *a dying woman* was denied a bath on a Sunday. By a clause of the lease by which the bath-owner rents his establishment, he is forbidden to give baths to any one on the Sunday. The landlord of the inn, forsooth, shuts his gates on the same day, and his conscience on week-days will not allow him to supply his guests with whiskey or ardent spirits. I was told by my friend, that because he refused to subscribe for some fancy charity, he received a letter to state that "he spent more in one dinner than in charity in the course of the year." My worthy friend did not care to contradict the statement, as why should a man deign to meddle with such a lie? But think how all the fishes, and all the pieces of meat, and all the people who went in and out of his snug cottage by the sea-side must have been watched by the serious round about! The sea is not more constant roaring there, than scandal is whispering. How happy I felt, while hearing these histories (demure heads in crimped caps peeping over the blinds at us as we walked on the beach), to think I am a Cockney, and don't know the name of the man who lives next door to me!

I have heard various stories, of course from persons of various ways of thinking, charging their opponents with hypocrisy, and proving the charge by statements clearly showing that the priests, the preachers, or the professing religionists in question, belied their professions wofully by their practice. But in matters of religion, hypocrisy is so awful a charge to make against a man, that I think it is almost unfair to mention even the cases in which it is proven, and which, — as, pray God, they are but exceptional, — a person should be very careful of mentioning, lest they be considered to apply generally. *Tartuffe* has been always a disgusting play to me to see, in spite of its sense and its wit; and so, instead of printing, here or elsewhere, a few stories of the Tartuffe kind which I have heard in Ireland, the best way will be to try and forget them. It is an awful thing to say of any man walking under God's sun by the

side of us, " You are a hypocrite, lying as you use the Most
Sacred Name, knowing that you lie while you use it." Let it
be the privilege of any sect that is so minded, to imagine that
there is perdition in store for all the rest of God's creatures
who do not think with them: but the easy countercharge of
hypocrisy, which the world has been in the habit of making in
its turn, is surely just as fatal and bigoted an accusation as any
that the sects make against the world.

What has this disquisition to do àpropos of a walk on the
beach at Portstewart? Why, it may be made here as well as
in other parts of Ireland, or elsewhere as well, perhaps, as here.
It is the most priest-ridden of countries; Catholic clergymen
lord it over their ragged flocks, as Protestant preachers, lay
and clerical, over their more genteel co-religionists. Bound to
inculcate peace and good-will, their whole life is one of emnity
and distrust.

Walking away from the little bay and the disquisition which
has somehow been raging there, we went across some wild dreary
highlands to the neighboring little town of Portrush, where is a
neat town and houses, and a harbor, and a new church too, so
like the last-named place that I thought for a moment we had
only made a round, and were back again at Portstewart. Some
gentlemen of the place, and my guide, who had a neighborly
liking for it, showed me the new church, and seemed to be well
pleased with the edifice; which is, indeed, a neat and convenient
one, of a rather irregular Gothic. The best thing about the
church, I think, was the history of it. The old church had
lain some miles off, in the most inconvenient part of the parish, whereupon the clergyman and some of the gentry had
raised a subscription in order to build the present church.
The expenses had exceeded the estimates, or the subscriptions
had fallen short of the sums necessary; and the church, in consequence, was opened with a debt on it, which the rector and
two more of the gentry had taken on their shoulders. The living is a small one, the other two gentlemen going bail for the
edifice not so rich as to think light of the payment of a couple
of hundred pounds beyond their previous subscriptions — the
lists are therefore still open; and the clergyman expressed himself perfectly satisfied either that he would be reimbursed one
day or other, or that he would be able to make out the payment of the money for which he stood engaged. Most of the
Roman Catholic churches that I have seen through the country
have been built in this way, — begun when money enough was
levied for constructing the foundation, elevated by degrees as

fresh subscriptions came in, and finished — by the way, I don't think I *have* seen one finished; but there is something noble in the spirit (however certain economists may cavil at it) that leads people to commence these pious undertakings with the firm trust that " Heaven will provide."

Eastward from Portrush, we came upon a beautiful level sand which leads to the White Rocks, a famous place of resort for the frequenters of the neighboring watering-places. Here are caves, and for a considerable distance a view of the wild and gloomy Antrim coast as far as Bengore. Midway, jutting into the sea, (and I was glad it was so far off,) was the Causeway; and nearer, the gray towers of Dunluce.

Looking north, were the blue Scotch hills and the neighboring Raghery Island. Nearer Portrush were two rocky islands, called the Skerries, of which a sportsman of our party vaunted the capabilities, regretting that my stay was not longer, so that I might land and shoot a few ducks there. This unlucky lateness of the season struck me also as a most afflicting circumstance. He said also that fish were caught off the island — not fish good to eat, but very strong at pulling, eager of biting, and affording a great deal of sport. And so we turned our backs once more upon the Giant's Causeway, and the grim coast on which it lies; and as my taste in life leads me to prefer looking at the smiling fresh face of a young cheerful beauty, rather than at the fierce countenance and high features of a dishevelled Meg Merrilies, I must say again that I was glad to turn my back on this severe part of the Antrim coast, and my steps towards Derry.

CHAPTER XXX.

PEG OF LIMAVADDY.

BETWEEN Coleraine and Derry there is a daily car (besides one or two occasional queer-looking coaches), and I had this vehicle, with an intelligent driver, and a horse with a hideous raw on his shoulder, entirely to myself for the five-and-twenty miles of our journey. The cabins of Coleraine are not parted with in a hurry, and we crossed the bridge, and went up and down the hills of one of the suburban streets, the Bann flowing picturesquely to our left; a large Catholic chapel, the before-mentioned cabins, and farther on, some neat-looking houses and plantations, to our right. Then we began ascending wide lonely hills, pools of bog shining here and there amongst them, with birds, both black and white, both geese and crows, on the hunt. Some of the stubble was already ploughed up, but by the side of most cottages you saw a black potato-field that it was time to dig now, for the weather was changing and the winds beginning to roar. Woods, whenever we passed them, were flinging round eddies of mustard-colored leaves; the white trunks of lime and ash trees beginning to look very bare.

Then we stopped to give the raw-backed horse water; then we trotted down a hill with a noble bleak prospect of Lough Foyle and the surrounding mountains before us, until we reached the town of Newtown Limavaddy, where the raw-backed horse was exchanged for another not much more agreeable in his appearance, though, like his comrade, not slow on the road.

Newtown Limavaddy is the third town in the county of Londonderry. It comprises three well-built streets, the others are inferior; it is, however, respectably inhabited: all this may be true, as the well-informed Guide-book avers, but I am bound to say that I was thinking of something else as we drove through the town, having fallen eternally in love during the ten minutes of our stay.

Yes, Peggy of Limavaddy, if Barrow and Inglis have gone to Connemara to fall in love with the Misses Flynn, let us be allowed to come to Ulster and offer a tribute of praise at your feet — at your stockingless feet, O Margaret! Do you remember the October day ('twas the first day of the hard weather), when the way-worn traveller entered your inn? But the circumstances of this passion had better be chronicled in deathless verse.

PEG OF LIMAVADDY.

Riding from Coleraine
  (Famed for lovely Kitty),
Came a Cockney bound
  Unto Derry city;

Weary was his soul,
  Shivering and sad he
Bumped along the road
  Leads to Limavaddy.

Mountains stretch'd around,
  Gloomy was their tinting,
And the horse's hoofs
  Made a dismal clinting;
Wind upon the heath
  Howling was and piping,
On the heath and bog,
  Black with many a snipe in;
Mid the bogs of black,
  Silver pools were flashing,
Crows upon their sides
  Picking were and splashing.
Cockney on the car
  Closer folds his plaidy,
Grumbling at the road
  Leads to Limavaddy.

Through the crashing woods
  Autumn brawl'd and bluster'd,
Tossing round about
  Leaves the hue of mustard;
Yonder lay Lough Foyle,
  Which a storm was whipping,
Covering with mist
  Lake, and shores, and shipping.
Up and down the hill
  (Nothing could be bolder),
Horse went with a raw,
  Bleeding on his shoulder.
" Where are horses change 1 ? "
  Said I to the laddy
Driving on the box:
  " Sir, at Limavaddy."
Limavaddy inn's
  But a humble baithouse,
Where you may procure
  Whiskey and potatoes;
Landlord at the door
  Gives a smiling welcome
To the shivering wights
  Who to his hotel come.
Landlady within
  Sits and knits a stocking,
With a wary foot
  Baby's cradle rocking.

To the chimney nook,
  Having found admittance,
There I watch a pup
  Playing with two kittens;
(Playing round the fire,
  Which of blazing turf is,
Roaring to the pot
  Which bubbles with the marphies;)

And the cradled babe
  Fond the mother nursed it!
Singing it a song
  As she twists the worsted!

Up and down the stair
  Two more young ones patter
(Twins were never seen
  Dirtier nor fatter);
Both have mottled legs,
  Both have snubby noses,
Both have — Here the Host
  Kindly interposes:
" Sure you must be froze
  With the sleet and hail, sir,
So will you have some punch,
  Or will you have some ale, sir ? "

Presently a maid
  Enters with the liquor,
(Half a pint of ale
  Frothing in a beaker).
Gods! I didn't know
  What my beating heart meant,
Hebe's self I thought
  Enter'd the apartment.
As she came she smiled,
  And the smile bewitching,
On my word and honor,
  Lighted all the kitchen!

With a curtsy neat
  Greeting the new comer,
Lovely, smiling Peg
  Offers me the rummer;
But my trembling hand
  Up the beaker tilted,
And the glass of ale
  Every drop I spilt it:
Spilt it every drop
  (Dames, who read my volumes
Pardon such a word,)
  On my whatd'ycall'ems!

Witnessing the sight
  Of that dire disaster,
Out began to laugh
  Missis, maid, and master;
Such a merry peal,
  'Specially Miss Peg's was.
(As the glass of ale
  Trickling down my legs was),
That the joyful sound
  Of that ringing laughter
Echoed in my ears
  Many a long day after.

Such a silver peal!
  In the meadows listening,
You who've heard the bells
  Ringing to a christening;
You who ever heard
  Caradori pretty,
Smiling like an angel
  Singing "Giovinetti,"
Fancy Peggy's laugh,
  Sweet, and clear and cheerful,
At my pantaloons
  With half a pint of beer full!

When the laugh was done,
  Peg, the pretty hussy,
Moved about the room
  Wonderfully busy;
Now she looks to see
  If the kettle keep hot,
Now she rubs the spoons,
  Now she cleans the teapot;
Now she sets the cups
  Trimly and secure,
Now she scours a pot
  And so it was I drew her.

Thus it was I drew her
  Scouring of a kettle.*
(Faith! her blushing cheeks
  Redden'd on the metal!)
Ah! but 'tis in vain
  That I try to sketch it;
The pot perhaps is like,
  But Peggy's face is wretched.
No: the best of lead,
  And of Indian-rubber,
Never could depict
  That sweet kettle-scrubber!

See her as she moves!
  Scarce the ground she touches,
Airy as a fay,
  Graceful as a duchess;
Bare her rounded arm,
  Bare her little leg is,
Vestris never show'd
  Ankles like to Peggy's:
Braided is her hair,
  Soft her look and modest,
Slim her little waist
  Comfortably bodiced.

This I do declare,
  Happy is the laddy
Who the heart can share
  Of Peg of Limavaddy;
Married if she were,
  Blest would be the daddy
Of the children fair
  Of Peg of Limavaddy;
Beauty is not rare
  In the land of Paddy,
Fair beyond compare
  Is Peg of Limavaddy.

Citizen or squire,
  Tory, Whig, or Radi-
cal would all desire
  Peg of Limavaddy.
Had I Homer's fire,
  Or that of Sergeant Taddy,
Meetly I'd admire
  Peg of Limavaddy.
And till I expire,
  Or till I grow mad, I
Will sing unto my lyre
  Peg of Limavaddy!

* The late Mr. Pope represents Camilla as "*scouring the plain*," an absurd and useless task. Peggy's occupation with the kettle is much more simple and noble. The second line of this verse (whereof the author scorns to deny an obligation) is from the celebrated "Frithiof" of Esaias Tigner. A maiden is serving warriors to drink, and is standing by a shield — "Und die Runde des Schildes ward wie das Mägdelein roth," — perhaps the above is the best thing in both poems.

CHAPTER XXXI.

TEMPLEMOYLE — DERRY.

FROM Newtown Limavaddy to Derry the traveller has many
wild and noble prospects of Lough Foyle and the plains and
mountains round it, and of scenes which may possibly in this
country be still more agreeable to him — of smiling cultivation,
and comfortable well-built villages, such as are only too rare in
Ireland. Of a great part of this district the London Companies are landlords — the best of landlords, too, according to
the report I could gather; and their good stewardship shows
itself especially in the neat villages of Muff and Ballikelly,
through both of which I passed. In Ballikelly, besides numerous simple, stout, brick-built dwellings for the peasantry, with
their shining windows and trim garden-plots, is a Presbyterian
meeting-house, so well-built, substantial, and handsome, so
different from the lean, pretentious, sham-Gothic ecclesiastical
edifices which have been erected of late years in Ireland, that
it can't fail to strike the tourist who has made architecture his
study or his pleasure. The gentlemen's seats in the district are
numerous and handsome; and the whole movement along the
road betokened cheerfulness and prosperous activity.

As the carman had no other passengers but myself, he made
no objection to carry me a couple of miles out of his way,
through the village of Muff, belonging to the Grocers of London (and so handsomely and comfortably built by them as to
cause all Cockneys to exclaim, "Well done our side!") and
thence to a very interesting institution, which was established
some fifteen years since in the neighborhood — the Agricultural
Seminary of Templemoyle. It lies on a hill in a pretty wooded
country, and is most curiously secluded from the world by the
tortuousness of the road which approaches it.

Of course it is not my business to report upon the agricultural system practised there, or to discourse on the state of the
land or the crops; the best testimony on this subject is the fact,
that the Institution hired, at a small rental, a tract of land,
which was reclaimed and farmed, and that of this farm the
landlord has now taken possession, leaving the young farmers
to labor on a new tract of land, for which they pay five times
as much rent as for their former holding. But though a person

19

versed in agriculture could give a far more satisfactory account
of the place than one to whom such pursuits are quite unfamiliar, there is a great deal about the establishment which
any citizen can remark on; and he must be a very difficult
Cockney indeed who won't be pleased here.

After winding in and out, and up and down, and round
about the eminence on which the house stands, we at last found
an entrance to it, by a court-yard, neat, well-built, and spacious,
where are the stables and numerous offices of the farm.   The
scholars were at dinner off a comfortable meal of boiled beef,
potatoes, and cabbages, when I arrived; a master was reading
a book of history to them; and silence, it appears, is preserved
during the dinner.   Seventy scholars were here assembled,
some young, and some expanded into six feet and whiskers —
all, however, are made to maintain exactly the same discipline,
whether whiskered or not.

The "head farmer" of the school, Mr. Campbell, a very
intelligent Scotch gentleman, was good enough to conduct me
over the place and the farm, and to give a history of the establishment and the course pursued there.   The Seminary was
founded in 1827, by the North-west of Ireland Society, by
members of which and others about three thousand pounds were
subscribed, and the buildings of the school erected.   These are
spacious, simple, and comfortable; there is a good stone house,
with airy dormitories, school-rooms, &c., and large and convenient offices.   The establishment had, at first, some difficulties to contend with, and for some time did not number
more than thirty pupils.   At present, there are seventy scholars, paying *ten pounds* a year, with which sum, and the labor
of the pupils on the farm, and the produce of it, the school is
entirely supported.   The reader will, perhaps, like to see an
extract from the Report of the school, which contains more
details regarding it.

"TEMPLEMOYLE WORK AND SCHOOL TABLE.

" *From 20th March to 23rd September.*

" Boys divided into two classes, A and B.

Hours.		At work.	At school.
5½—	All rise.		
6—8	....	A	B
8—9	Breakfast.		
9—1	....	A	B
1—2	Dinner and recreation.		
2—6	....	B	A
6—7	Recreation.		
7—9	Prepare lessons for next day.		
9—	To bed.		

"On Tuesday B commences work in the morning and A at school, and so on alternate days.

"Each class is again subdivided into three divisions, over each of which is placed a monitor, selected from the steadiest and best-informed boys ; he receives the Head Farmer's directions as to the work to be done, and superintends his party while performing it.

"In winter the time of labor is shortened according to the length of the day, and the hours at school increased.

"In wet days, when the boys cannot work out, all are required to attend school.

"Dietary.

"*Breakfast.*— Eleven ounces of oatmeal made in stirabout, one pint of sweet milk.

"*Dinner.*— Sunday — Three-quarters of a pound of beef stewed with pepper and onions, or one half-pound of corned beef with cabbage, and three and a half pounds of potatoes.

"Monday — One half-pound of pickled beef, three and a half pounds of potatoes, one pint of buttermilk.

"Tuesday — Broth made of one half-pound of beef, with leeks, cabbages, and parsley, and three and a half pounds of potatoes.

"Wednesday — Two ounces of butter, eight ounces of oatmeal made into bread, three and a half pounds of potatoes, and one pint of sweet milk.

"Thursday — Half a pound of pickled pork, with cabbage or turnips, and three and a half pounds of potatoes.

"Friday — Two ounces of butter, eight ounces wheat meal made into bread, one pint of sweet milk or fresh buttermilk, three and a half pounds of potatoes.

"Saturday — Two ounces of butter, one pound of potatoes mashed, eight ounces of wheat meal made into bread, two and a half pounds of potatoes, one pint of buttermilk.

"*Supper.* — In summer, flummery made of one pound of oatmeal seeds, and one pint of sweet milk. In winter, three and a half pounds of potatoes, and one pint of buttermilk or sweet milk.

"Rules for the Templemoyle School.

"1. The pupils are required to say their prayers in the morning, before leaving the dormitory, and at night, before retiring to rest, each separately, and after the manner to which he has been habituated.

"2. The pupils are requested to wash their hands and faces before the commencement of business in the morning, on returning from agricultural labor, and after dinner.

"3. The pupils are required to pay the strictest attention to their instructors, both during the hours of agricultural and literary occupation.

"4. Strife, disobedience, inattention, or any description of riotous or disorderly conduct, is punishable by extra labor or confinement, as directed by the Committee, according to circumstances.

"5. Diligent and respectful behavior, continued for a considerable time, will be rewarded by occasional permission for the pupil so distinguished to visit his home.

"6. No pupil, on obtaining leave of absence, shall presume to continue it for a longer period than that prescribed to him on leaving the Seminary.

"7. During their rural labor, the pupils are to consider themselves amenable to the authority of their Agricultural Instructor alone, and during their attendance in the school-room, to that of their Literary Instructor alone.

"8. Non-attendance during any part of the time allotted either for literary or agricultural employment, will be punished as a serious offence.

"9. During the hours of recreation the pupils are to be under the superintendence of their Instructors, and not suffered to pass beyond the limits of the farm, except under their guidance, or with a written permission from one of them.

"10. The pupils are required to make up their beds, and keep those clothes not in immediate use neatly folded up in their trunks, and to be particular in never suffering any garment, book, implement, or other article belonging to or used by them, to lie about in a slovenly or disorderly manner.

"11. Respect to superiors, and gentleness of demeanor, both among the pupils themselves and towards the servants and laborers of the establishment, are particularly insisted upon, and will be considered a prominent ground of approbation and reward.

"12. On Sundays the pupils are required to attend their respective places of worship, accompanied by their Instructors or Monitors ; and it is earnestly recommended to them to employ a part of the remainder of the day in sincerely reading the Word of God, and in such other devotional exercises as their respective ministers may point out."

At certain periods of the year, when all hands are required, such as harvest, &c., the literary labors of the scholars are stopped, and they are all in the field. On the present occasion we followed them into a potato-field, where an army of them were employed digging out the potatoes ; while another regiment were trenching-in elsewhere for the winter : the boys were leading the carts to and fro. To reach the potatoes we had to pass a field, part of which was newly ploughed : the ploughing was the work of the boys, too ; one of them being left with an experienced ploughman for a fortnight at a time, in which space the lad can acquire some practice in the art. Amongst the potatoes and the boys digging them, I observed a number of girls, taking them up as dug and removing the soil from the roots. Such a society for seventy young men would, in any other country in the world, be not a little dangerous ; but Mr. Campbell said that no instance of harm had ever occurred in consequence, and I believe his statement may be fully relied on : the whole country bears testimony to this noble purity of morals. Is there any other in Europe which in this point can compare with it?

In winter the farm works do not occupy the pupils so much, and they give more time to their literary studies. They get a good English education ; they are grounded in arithmetic and mathematics ; and I saw a good map of an adjacent farm, made from actual survey by one of the pupils. Some of them are good draughtsmen likewise, but of their performances I could see no specimen, the artists being abroad, occupied wisely in digging the potatoes.

And here, àpropos, not of the school but of potatoes, let me tell a potato story, which is, I think, to the purpose, wherever it is told. In the county of Mayo a gentleman by the name of Crofton is a landed proprietor, in whose neighborhood great distress prevailed among the peasantry during the spring and summer, when the potatoes of the last year were consumed, and before those of the present season were up. Mr. Crofton, by liberal donations on his own part, and by a subscription which was set on foot among his friends in England as well as in Ireland, was enabled to collect a sum of money sufficient to purchase meal for the people, which was given to them, or sold at very low prices, until the pressure of want was withdrawn, and the blessed potato-crop came in. Some time in October, a smart night's frost made Mr. Crofton think that it was time to take in and pit his own potatoes, and he told his steward to get laborers accordingly.

Next day, on going to the potato-grounds, he found the whole fields swarming with people; the whole crop was out of the ground, and again under it, pitted and covered, and the people gone, in a few hours. It was as if the fairies that we read of in the Irish legends, as coming to the aid of good people and helping them in their labors, had taken a liking to this good landlord, and taken in his harvest for him. Mr. Crofton, who knew who his helpers had been, sent the steward to pay them their day's wages, and to thank them at the same time for having come to help him at a time when their labor was so useful to him. One and all refused a penny; and their spokesman said, " They wished they could do more for the likes of him or his family." I have heard of many conspiracies in this country; is not this one as worthy to be told as any of them?

Round the house of Templemoyle is a pretty garden, which the pupils take pleasure in cultivating, filled not with fruit (for this, though there are seventy gardeners, the superintendent said somehow seldom reached a ripe state), but with kitchen herbs, and a few beds of pretty flowers, such as are best suited to cottage horticulture. Such simple carpenters' and masons' work as the young men can do is likewise confided to them; and though the dietary may appear to the Englishman as rather a scanty one, and though the English lads certainly make at first very wry faces at the stirabout porridge (as they naturally will when first put in the presence of that abominable mixture), yet, after a time, strange to say, they begin to find it actually palatable ; and the best proof of the excellence of the diet is, that nobody is ever ill in the institution ; colds and fevers and the ailments of lazy, gluttonous gentility, are unknown ; and the doctor's bill for the last year, for seventy pupils, amounted to thirty-five shillings. *O beati agricoliculæ!* You do not know what it is to feel a little uneasy after half a crown's worth of raspberry-tarts, as lads do at the best public schools ; you don't know in what majestic polished hexameters the Roman poet has described your pursuits ; you are not fagged and flogged into Latin and Greek at the cost of two hundred pounds a year. Let these be the privileges of your youthful betters ; meanwhile content yourselves with thinking that you *are* preparing for a profession, while they are *not ;* that you are learning something useful, while they, for the most part, are not : for after all, as a man grows old in the world, old and fat, cricket is discovered not to be any longer very advantageous to him — even to have pulled in the Trinity boat does not in old age amount to a substantial advantage ; and though to read a Greek play be an immense pleasure, yet it must be confessed few enjoy it. In the first place, of the race of Etonians, and Harrovians, and Carthusians that one meets in the world, very few *can* read the Greek ; of those few — there are not, as I believe, any considerable majority of poets. Stout men in the bow-windows of clubs (for such young Etonians by time become) are not generally remarkable for a taste for Æschylus.* You do not hear much poetry in Westminster Hall, or I believe at the bar-tables afterwards ; and if occasionally, in the House of Commons, Sir Robert Peel lets off a quotation — a pocket-pistol wadded with a leaf torn out of Horace — depend on it it is only to astonish the country gentlemen who don't understand him : and it is my firm conviction that Sir Robert no more cares for poetry than you or I do.

Such thoughts would suggest themselves to a man who has had the benefit of what is called an education at a public school in England, when he sees seventy lads from all parts of the empire learning what his Latin poets and philosophers have informed him is the best of all pursuits, — finds them educated at one-twentieth part of the cost which has been bestowed on his own precious person ; orderly without the necessity of submitting to degrading personal punishment ; young, and full of

---

* And then, how much Latin and Greek does the public school-boy know ? Also, does he know anything else, and what ? Is it history, or geography, or mathematics, or divinity ?

health and blood, though vice is unknown among them; and brought up decently and honestly to know the things which it is good for them in their profession to know. So it is, however; all the world is improving except the gentlemen. There are at this present writing five hundred boys at Eton, kicked, and licked, and bullied, by another hundred — scrubbing shoes, running errands, making false concords, and (as if that were a natural consequence!) putting their posteriors on a block for Dr. Hawtrey to lash at; and still calling it education. They are proud of it — good heavens! — absolutely vain of it; as what dull barbarians are not proud of their dulness and barbarism? They call it the good old English system: nothing like classics, says Sir John, to give a boy a taste, you know, and a habit of reading — (Sir John, who reads the "Racing Calendar," and belongs to a race of men of all the world the least given to reading,) — it's the good old English system; every boy fights for himself — hardens 'em, eh, Jack? Jack grins, and helps himself to another glass of claret, and presently tells you how Tibbs and Miller fought for an hour and twenty minutes "like good uns." . . . Let us come to an end, however, of this moralizing; the car-driver has brought the old raw-shouldered horse out of the stable, and says it is time to be off again.

Before quitting Templemoyle, one thing more may be said in its favor. It is one of the very few public establishments in Ireland where pupils of the two religious denominations are received, and where no religious disputes have taken place. The pupils are called upon, morning and evening, to say their prayers privately. On Sunday, each division, Presbyterian, Roman Catholic, and Episcopalian, is marched to its proper place of worship. The pastors of each sect may visit their young flock when so inclined; and the lads devote the Sabbath evening to reading the books pointed out to them by their clergymen.

Would not the Agricultural Society of Ireland, of the success of whose peaceful labors for the national prosperity every Irish newspaper I read brings some new indication, do well to show some mark of its sympathy for this excellent institution of Templemoyle? A silver medal given by the Society to the most deserving pupil of the year, would be a great object of emulation amongst the young men educated at the place, and would be almost a certain passport for the winner in seeking for a situation in after life. I do not know if similar seminaries exist in England. Other seminaries of a like nature have been tried in this country, and have failed: but English country gentlemen cannot, I should think, find a better object of their attention than this school; and our farmers would surely find such establishments of great benefit to them: where their children might procure a sound literary education at a small charge, and at the same time be made acquainted with the latest improvements in their profession. I can't help saying here, once more, what I have said àpropos of the excellent school at Dundalk, and begging the English middle classes to think of the subject. If Government will not act (upon what never can be effectual, perhaps, until it become a national measure), let small communities act for themselves, and tradesmen and the middle classes set up CHEAP PROPRIETARY SCHOOLS. Will country newspaper editors, into whose hands this book may fall, be kind enough to speak upon this hint, and extract the tables of the Templemoyle and Dundalk establishments, to show how, and with what small means, boys may be well, soundly, and humanely educated — not brutally, as some of us have been, under the bitter fagging and the shameful rod. It is no plea for the barbarity that use has made us accustomed to it; and in seeing these institutions for humble lads, where the system taught is at once useful, manly, and kindly, and thinking of what I had undergone in my own youth, — of the frivolous monkish trifling in which it was wasted, of the brutal tyranny to which it was subjected, — I could not look at the lads but with a sort of envy: please God, their lot will be shared by thousands of their equals and their betters before long!

It was a proud day for Dundalk, Mr. Thackeray well said, when, at the end of one of the vacations there, fourteen English boys, and an Englishman with his little son in his hand, landed from the Liverpool packet, and, walking through the streets of the town, went into the school-house quite happy. That *was* a proud day in truth for a distant Irish town, and I can't help saying that I grudge them the cause of their pride somewhat. Why should there not be schools in England as good, and as cheap, and as happy?

With this, shaking Mr. Campbell gratefully by the hand, and begging all English tourists to go and visit his establishment, we trotted off for Londonderry, leaving at about a mile's distance from the town, and at the pretty lodge of Saint Columb's, a letter, which was the cause of much delightful hospitality.

Saint Columb's Chapel, the walls of which still stand picturesquely in Sir George Hill's park, and from which that gentleman's seat takes its name, was here since the sixth century. It is but fair to give precedence to the mention of the old abbey, which was the father, as it would seem, of the town. The approach to the latter from three quarters, certainly, by which various avenues I had occasion to see it, is always noble. We had seen the spire of the cathedral peering over the hills for four miles on our way; it stands, a stalwart and handsome building, upon an eminence, round which the old-fashioned stout red houses of the town cluster, girt in with the ramparts and walls that kept out James's soldiers of old. Quays, factories, huge red warehouses, have grown round this famous old barrier, and now stretch along the river. A couple of large steamers and other craft lay within the bridge; and, as we passed over that stout wooden edifice, stretching eleven hundred feet across the noble expanse of the Foyle, we heard along the quays a great thundering and clattering of iron-work in an enormous steam frigate which has been built in Derry, and seems to lie alongside a whole street of houses. The suburb, too, through which we passed was bustling and comfortable; and the view was not only pleasing from its natural beauties, but has a manly, thriving, honest air of prosperity, which is no bad feature, surely, for a landscape.

Nor does the town itself, as one enters it, belie, as many other Irish towns do, its first flourishing look. It is not splendid, but comfortable; a brisk movement in the streets: good downright shops, without particularly grand titles; few beggars. Nor have the common people, as they address you, that eager ̤ile, — that manner of compound fawning and swaggering, ̤ch an Englishman finds in the townspeople of the West and ̤th. As in the North of England, too, when compared with ̤cts, the people are greatly more familiar, though by ̤srespectful to the stranger.

̤her hand, after such a commerce as a traveller has ̤ race of waiters, postboys, porters, and the like (and ̤ be that the vast race of postboys, &c., whom I did not ̤the North, are quite unlike those unlucky specimens ̤hom I came in contact), I was struck by their excessive ̤ess after the traveller's gratuities, and their fierce dis-̤isfaction if not sufficiently rewarded. To the gentleman who brushed my clothes at the comfortable hotel at Belfast, and carried my bags to the coach, I tendered the sum of two shillings, which seemed to me quite a sufficient reward for his services: he battled and brawled with me for more, and got it too; for a street-dispute with a porter calls together a number of delighted bystanders, whose remarks and company are by no means agreeable to a solitary gentleman. Then, again, there was the famous case of Boots of Ballycastle, which, being upon the subject, I may as well mention here: Boots of Ballycastle, that romantic little village near the Giant's Causeway, had cleaned a pair of shoes for me certainly, but declined either to brush my clothes, or to carry down my two carpet-bags to the car; leaving me to perform those offices for myself, which I did: and indeed they were not very difficult. But immediately I was seated on the car, Mr. Boots stepped forward and wrapped a mackintosh very considerately round me, and begged me at the same time to "remember him."

There was an old beggar-woman standing by, to whom I had a desire to present a penny; and having no coin of that value, I begged Mr. Boots, out of a sixpence which I tendered to him, to subtract a penny, and present it to the old lady in question. Mr. Boots took the money, looked at me, and his countenance, not naturally good-humored, assumed an expression of the most indignant contempt and hatred as he said, "I'm thinking I've no call to give my money away. Sixpence is my right for what I've done."

"Sir," says I, "you must remember that you did but black one pair of shoes, and that you blacked them very badly too."

"Sixpence is my right," says Boots; "a gentleman would give me sixpence!" and though I represented   him that a pair of shoes might be blacked in a minute — tha.   pence a minute was not usual wages in the country — tl.   y gentlemen, half-pay officers, briefless barristers, unf   literary gentlemen, would gladly black twelve pairs of shoe diem if rewarded with five shillings for so doing   w means of convincing Mr. Boots. I then den   sixpence, which proposal, however, he decline   struggle, he would give the money, but a   have given sixpence: and so left me with furio   contempt.

As for the city of Derry, a carman who drove me out to dinner at a gentleman's house, where he hi   provided with a comfortable meal, was dissatisfied   teenpence, vowing that a "dinner job" was always   crown, and not only asserted this, but continued to assert it for a quarter of an hour with the most noble though unsuccessful perseverance. A second car-boy, to whom I gave a shilling fo a drive of two miles altogether, attacked me because I gave the

other boy eighteenpence ; and the porter who brought my bags
fifty yards from the coach, entertained me with a dialogue that
lasted at least a couple of minutes, and said, ' I should have had
sixpence for carrying one of 'em."

For the car which carried me two miles the landlord of the
inn made me pay the sum of five shillings. He is a godly landlord, has Bibles in the coffee-room, the drawing-room, and every
bedroom in the house, with this inscription —

UT MIGRATURUS HABITA.

THE TRAVELLER'S TRUE REFUGE.

Jones's Hotel, Londonderry.

This pious double or triple entendre, the reader will, no
doubt, admire — the first simile establishing the resemblance
between this life and an inn ; the second allegory showing that
the inn and the Bible are both the traveller's refuge.

In life we are in death — the hotel in question is about as
gay as a family vault : a severe figure of a landlord, in seedy
black, is occasionally seen in the dark passages or on the
creaking old stairs of the black inn. He does not bow to you
— very few landlords in Ireland condescend to acknowledge
their guests — he only warns you : — a silent solemn gentleman
who looks to be something between a clergyman and a sexton
— "ut migraturus habita ! " — the " migraturus " was a vast
comfort in the clause.

It must, however, be said, for the consolation of future travellers, that when at evening, in the old lonely parlor of the
which the great gaunt fireplace is filled with coals, two dreary
South-sea candles, and sticks glimmering upon the old fashioned
other district, rain pattering fiercely without, the wind roar-
no means dying in the streets, this worthy gentleman can pro-

On the other, port-wine for the use of his migratory guest,
with the latter to be almost reconciled to the cemetery
it may be he is resting himself, and he finds himself, to his sur-
see in most cheerful. There is a mouldy-looking old kitchen,
with which strange to say, sends out an excellent comfortable
greeting, that the sensation of fear gradually wears off.

At Chester, the ramparts of the town form a pleasant
promenade ; and the batteries, with a few of the cannon, are
preserved, with which the stout 'prentice boys of Derry beat off
King James in '88. The guns bear the names of the London
Companies — venerable Cockney titles ! It is pleasant for a

Londoner to read them, and see how, at a pinch, the sturdy citizens can do their work.

The public buildings of Derry are, I think, among the best I have seen in Ireland; and the Lunatic Asylum, especially, is to be pointed out as a model of neatness and comfort. When will the middle classes be allowed to send their own afflicted relatives to public institutions of this excellent kind, where violence is never practised — where it is never to the interest of the keeper of the asylum to exaggerate his patient's malady, or to retain him in durance, for the sake of the enormous sums which the sufferer's relatives are made to pay! The gentry of three counties which contribute to the Asylum have no such resource for members of their own body, should any be so afflicted — the condition of entering this admirable asylum is, that the patient must be a pauper, and on this account he is supplied with every comfort and the best curative means, and his relations are in perfect security. Are the rich in any way so lucky? — and if not, why not?

The rest of the occurrences at Derry belong, unhappily, to the domain of private life, and though very pleasant to recall, are not honestly to be printed. Otherwise, what popular descriptions might be written of the hospitalities of St. Columb's, of the jovialities of the mess of the —th Regiment, of the speeches made and the songs sung, and the devilled turkey at twelve o'clock, and the headache afterwards; all which events could be described in an exceedingly facetious manner. But these amusements are to be met with in every other part of her Majesty's dominions; and the only point which may be mentioned here as peculiar to this part of Ireland, is the difference of the manner of the gentry to that in the South. The Northern manner is far more *English* than that of the other provinces of Ireland — whether it is *better* for being English is a question of taste, of which an Englishman can scarcely be a fair judge.

CHAPTER XXXII.

DUBLIN AT LAST.

A WEDDING-PARTY that went across Derry Bridge to the sound of bell and cannon, had to flounder through a thick coat of frozen snow, that covered the slippery planks, and the hills round about were whitened over by the same inclement material. Nor was the weather, implacable towards young lovers and unhappy buckskin postilions shivering in white favors, at all more polite towards the passengers of her Majesty's mail that runs from Derry to Ballyshannon.

Hence the aspect of the country between those two places can only be described at the rate of nine miles an hour, and from such points of observation as may be had through a coach window, starred with ice and mud. While horses were changed we saw a very dirty town, called Strabane ; and had to visit the old house of the O'Donnel's in Donegal during a quarter of an hour's pause that the coach made there — and with an umbrella overhead. The pursuit of the picturesque under umbrellas let us leave to more venturesome souls : the fine weather of the finest season known for many long years in Ireland was over, and I thought with a great deal of yearning of Pat the waiter, at the "Shelburne Hotel," Stephen's Green, Dublin, and the gas-lamps, and the covered cars, and the good dinners to which they take you.

Farewell, then, O wild Donegal! and ye stern passes through which the astonished traveller windeth! Farewell, Ballyshannon, and thy salmon-leap, and thy bar of sand, over which the white head of the troubled Atlantic was peeping! Likewise, adieu to Lough Erne, and its numberless green islands, and winding river-lake, and wavy fir-clad hills! Goodby, moreover, neat Enniskillen, over the bridge and churches whereof the sun peepeth as the coach starteth from the inn! See, how he shines now on Lord Belmore's stately palace and park, with gleaming porticos and brilliant grassy chases : now, behold he is yet higher in the heavens, as the twanging horn proclaims the approach to beggarly Cavan, where a beggarly breakfast awaits the hungry voyager.

Snatching up a roll wherewith to satisfy the pangs of hunger, sharpened by the mockery of breakfast, the tourist now

hastens in his arduous course, through Virginia, Kells, Na-
van, by Tara's threadbare mountain, and Skreen's green
hill; day darkens, and a hundred thousand lamps twinkle in
the gray horizon — see above the darkling trees a stumpy column rise, see on its base the name of Wellington (though this,
because 'tis night, thou canst not see), and cry, "It is the
Phaynix!" — On and on, across the iron bridge, and through
the streets, (dear streets, though dirty, to the citizen's heart
how dear you be!) and lo, now, with a bump, the dirty coach
stops at the seedy inn, six ragged porters battle for the bags,
six wheedling carmen recommend their cars, and (giving first
the coachman eighteenpence) the Cockney says, "Drive, car-
boy, to the 'Shelburne.'"

And so having reached Dublin, it becomes necessary to curtail the observations which were to be made upon that city;
which surely ought to have a volume to itself: the humors of
Dublin at least require so much space. For instance, there
was the dinner at the Kildare Street Club, or the Hotel opposite, — the dinner in Trinity College Hall, — that at Mr. ——,
the publisher's, where a dozen of the literary men of Ireland
were assembled, — and those (say fifty) with Harry Lorrequer
himself, at his mansion of Templeogue. What a favorable opportunity to discourse upon the peculiarities of Irish character!
to describe men of letters, of fashion, and university dons!

Sketches of these personages may be prepared, and sent
over, perhaps, in confidence to Mrs. Sigourney in America —
(who will of course not print them) — but the English habit
does not allow of these happy communications between writers
and the public; and the author who wishes to dine again at his
friend's cost, must needs have a care how he puts him in print.

Suffice it to say, that at Kildare Street we had white neck-
cloths, black waiters, wax-candles, and some of the best wine
in Europe; at Mr. ——, the publisher's, wax-candles, and some
of the best wine in Europe; at Mr. Lever's, wax-candles, and
some of the best wine in Europe; at Trinity College — but
there is no need to mention what took place at Trinity College;
for on returning to London, and recounting the circumstances
of the repast, my friend B——, a Master of Arts of that university, solemnly declared the thing was impossible: — no
stranger *could* dine at Trinity College; it was too great a privilege — in a word, he would not believe the story, nor will he to
this day; and why, therefore, tell it in vain?

I am sure if the Fellows of Colleges in Oxford and Cambridge were told that the Fellows of T. C. D. only drink beer

at dinner, they would not believe *that*. Such, however, was the fact : or may be it was a dream, which was followed by another dream of about four-and-twenty gentlemen seated round a common-room table after dinner ; and, by a subsequent vision of a tray of oysters in the apartments of a tutor of the university, sometime before midnight. Did we swallow them or not? — the oysters are an open question.

Of the Catholic College of Maynooth, I must likewise speak briefly, for the reason that an accurate description of that establishment would be of necessity so disagreeable, that it is best to pass it over in a few words. An Irish union-house is a palace to it. Ruin so needless, filth so disgusting, such a look of lazy squalor, no Englishman who has not seen can conceive. Lecture-room and dining-hall, kitchen and students'-room, were all the same. I shall never forget the sight of scores of shoulders of mutton lying on the filthy floor in the former, or the view of a bed and dressing-table that I saw in the other. Let the next Maynooth grant include a few shillings'-worth of whitewash and a few hundredweights of soap ; and if to this be added a half-score of drill-sergeants, to see that the students appear clean at lecture, and to teach them to keep their heads up and to look people in the face, Parliament will introduce some cheap reforms into the seminary, which were never needed more than here. Why should the place be so shamefully ruinous and foully dirty? Lime is cheap, and water plenty at the canal hard by. Why should a stranger, after a week's stay in the country, be able to discover a priest by the scowl on his face, and his doubtful downcast manner? Is it a point of discipline that his reverence should be made to look as ill-humored as possible? And I hope these words will not be taken hostilely. It would have been quite as easy, and more pleasant, to say the contrary, had the contrary seemed to me to have been the fact ; and to have declared that the priests were remarkable for their expression of candor, and their college for its extreme neatness and cleanliness.

This complaint of neglect applies to other public institutions besides Maynooth. The Mansion-house, when I saw it, was a very dingy abode for the Right Honorable Lord Mayor, and that Lord Mayor Mr. O'Connell. I saw him in full council, in a brilliant robe of crimson velvet, ornamented with white satin bows and sable collar, in an enormous cocked-hat, like a slice of an eclipsed moon.

The Aldermen and Common Council, in a black oak parlor, and at a dingy green table, were assembled around him, and a debate of thrilling interest to the town ensued. It related, I think, to water-pipes; the great man did not speak publicly, but was occupied chiefly at the end of the table, giving audiences to at least a score of clients and petitioners.

The next day I saw him in the famous Corn Exchange. The building without has a substantial look, but the hall within is rude, dirty, and ill-kept. Hundreds of persons were assembled in the black, steaming place; no inconsiderable share of frieze-coats were among them; and many small Repealers, who could but lately have assumed their breeches, ragged as they were. These kept up a great chorus of shouting, and "hear, hear!" at every pause in the great Repealer's address. Mr. O'Connell was reading a report from his Repeal-wardens; which proved that when Repeal took place, commerce and prosperity would instantly flow into the country; its innumerable harbors would be filled with countless ships, its immense water-power would be directed to the turning of myriads of mills; its vast energies and resources brought into full action. At the end of the report, three cheers were given for Repeal, and in the midst of a great shouting Mr. O'Connell leaves the room.

"Mr. Quiglan, Mr. Quiglan!" roars an active aide-de-camp to the door-keeper, "a covered kyar for the Lard Mayre." The covered car came; I saw his lordship get into it. Next day he was Lord Mayor no longer; but Alderman O'Connell in his state-coach, with the handsome grays whose manes were tied up with green ribbon, following the new Lord Mayor to the right honorable inauguration. Javelin men, city marshals (looking like military undertakers), private carriages, glass coaches, cars, covered and uncovered, and thousands of yelling ragamuffins, formed the civic procession of that faded, worn-out, insolvent old Dublin Corporation.

The walls of this city had been placarded with huge notices to the public, that O'Connell's rent-day was at hand; and I went round to all the chapels in town on that Sunday (not a little to the scandal of some Protestant friends), to see the popular behavior. Every door was barred, of course, with plate-holders; and heaps of pence at the humble entrances, and bank-notes at the front gates, told the willingness of the people to reward their champion. The car-boy who drove me had paid his little tribute of fourpence at morning mass; the waiter who brought my breakfast had added to the national subscription with his humble shilling; and the Catholic gentleman with whom I dined, and between whom and Mr. O'Connell there is no great love lost, pays his annual donation, out of gratitude for old services, and to the man who won Catholic Emancipation for Ireland. The piety of the people at the chapels is a sight, too, always well worthy to behold. Nor indeed is this religious fervor less in the Protestant places of worship: the warmth and attention of the congregation, the enthusiasm with which hymns are sung and responses uttered, contrasts curiously with the cool formality of worshippers at home.

The service at St. Patrick's is finely sung; and the shameless English custom of retreating after the anthem, is properly prevented by locking the gates, and having the music after the sermon. The interior of the cathedral itself, however, to an Englishman who has seen the neat and beautiful edifices of his own country, will be anything but an object of admiration. The greater part of the huge old building is suffered to remain in gaunt decay, and with its stalls of sham Gothic, and the tawdry old rags and gimcracks of the " most illustrious order of Saint Patrick," (whose pasteboard helmets, and calico banners, and lath swords, well characterize the humbug of chivalry which they are made to represent,) looks like a theatre behind the scenes. " Paddy's Opera," however, is a noble performance; and the Englishman may here listen to a half-hour sermon, and in the anthem to a bass singer whose voice is one of the finest ever heard.

The Drama does not flourish much more in Dublin than in any other part of the country. Operatic stars make their appearance occasionally, and managers lose money. I was at a fine concert, at which Lablache and others performed, where there were not a hundred people in the pit of the pretty theatre, and where the only encore given was to a young woman in ringlets and yellow satin, who stepped forward and sang, " Coming through the rye," or some other scientific composition, in an exceedingly small voice. On the nights when the regular drama was enacted, the audience was still smaller. The theatre of Fishamble Street was given up to the performances of the Rev. Mr. Gregg and his Protestant company, whose soirées I did not attend; and, at the Abbey Street Theatre, whither I went in order to see, if possible, some specimens of the national humor, I found a company of English people ranting through a melodrama, the tragedy whereof was the only laughable thing to be witnessed.

Humbler popular recreations may be seen by the curious. One night I paid twopence to see a puppet-show — such an entertainment as may have been popular a hundred and thirty years ago, and is described in the *Spectator*. But the company here assembled were not, it scarcely need be said, of the genteel sort. There were a score of boys, however, and a dozen of laboring men, who were quite happy and contented with the piece performed, and loudly applauded. Then in passing homewards of a night, you hear, at the humble public-houses, the sound of many a fiddle, and the stamp of feet dancing the good old jig, which is still maintaining a struggle with teetotalism, and, though vanquished now, may rally some day and overcome the enemy. At Kingstown, especially, the old " fire-worshippers" yet seem to muster pretty strongly ; loud is the music to be heard in the taverns there, and the cries of encouragement to the dancers.

Of the numberless amusements that take place in the *Phaynix*, it is not very necessary to speak. Here you may behold garrison races, and reviews ; lord-lieutenants in brown great-coats ; aides-de-camp scampering about like mad in blue ; fat colonels roaring " charge " to immense heavy dragoons ; dark riflemen lining woods and firing ; galloping cannoneers banging and blazing right and left. Here comes his Excellency the Commander-in-Chief, with his huge feathers, and white hair, and hooked nose ; and yonder sits his Excellency the Ambassador from the republic of Topinambo in a glass coach, smoking a cigar. The honest Dublinites make a great deal of such small dignitaries as his Excellency of the glass coach ; you hear everybody talking of him, and asking which is he ; and when presently one of Sir Robert Peel's sons makes his appearance on the course, the public rush delighted to look at him.

They love great folks, those honest Emerald Islanders, more intensely than any people I ever heard of, except the Americans. They still cherish the memory of the sacred George IV. They chronicle genteel small beer with never-failing assiduity. They go in long trains to a sham court — simpering in tights and bags, with swords between their legs. O heaven and earth, what joy ! Why are the Irish noblemen absentees? If their lordships like respect, where would they get it so well as in their own country?

The Irish noblemen are very likely going through the same delightful routine of duty before their real sovereign — in *real* tights and bag-wigs, as it were, performing their graceful and lofty duties, and celebrating the august service of the throne. These, of course, the truly loyal heart can only respect : and I think a drawing-room at St. James's the grandest spectacle that ever feasted the eye or exercised the intellect. The crown, surrounded by its knights and nobles, its priests, its sages, and their respective ladies; illustrious foreigners, men learned in the law, heroes of land and sea, beef-eaters, gold-sticks, gentlemen-at-arms, rallying round the throne and defending it with those swords which never knew defeat (and would surely, if tried, secure victory) : these are sights and characters which every man must look upon with a thrill of respectful awe, and count amongst the glories of his country. What lady that sees this will not confess that she reads every one of the drawing-room costumes, from Majesty down to Miss Ann Maria Smith; and all the names of the presentations, from Prince Baccabocksky (by the Russian ambassador) to Ensign Stubbs on his appointment?

We are bound to read these accounts. It is our pride, our duty as Britons. But though one may honor the respect of the aristocracy of the land for the sovereign, yet there is no reason why those who are not of the aristocracy should be aping their betters : and the Dublin Castle business has, I cannot but think, a very high-life-below-stairs look. There is no aristocracy in Dublin. Its magnates are tradesmen — Sir Fiat Haustus, Sir Blacker Dosy, Mr. Serjeant Bluebag, or Mr. Counsellor O'Fee. Brass plates are their titles of honor, and they live by their boluses or their briefs. What call have these worthy people to be dangling and grinning at lord-lieutenants' levées, and playing sham aristocracy before a sham sovereign? Oh, that old humbug of a Castle! It is the greatest sham of all the shams in Ireland.

Although the season may be said to have begun, for the Courts are opened, and the *noblesse de la robe* have assembled, I do not think the genteel quarters of the town look much more cheerful. They still, for the most part, wear their faded appearance and lean, half-pay look. There is the beggar still dawdling here and there. Sounds of carriages or footmen do not deaden the clink of the burly policeman's boot-heels. You may see, possibly, a smutty-faced nursemaid leading out her little charges to walk ; or the observer may catch a glimpse of Mick the footman lolling at the door, and grinning as he talks to some dubious tradesman. MICK and JOHN are very different characters externally and inwardly ; — profound essays (involving the histories of the two countries for a thousand years) might be written regarding Mick and John, and the moral and political influences which have developed the flunkies of the two nations. The friend, too, with whom Mick talks at the door is a puzzle to a Londoner. I have hardly ever entered a Dublin house without meeting with some such character on my way in or out. He looks too shabby for a dun, and not exactly ragged enough for a beggar — a doubtful, lazy, dirty family vassal — a guerilla footman. I think it is he who makes a great noise, and whispering, and clattering, handing in the dishes to Mick from outside of the dining-room door. When an Irishman comes to London he brings Erin with him ; and ten to one you will find one of these queer retainers about his place.

London one can only take leave of by degrees : the great town melts away into suburbs, which soften, as it were, the parting between the Cockney and his darling birthplace. But you pass from some of the stately fine Dublin streets straight into the country. After No. 46, Eccles Street, for instance, potatoes begin at once. You are on a wide green plain, diversified by occasional cabbage-plots, by drying-grounds white with chemises, in the midst of which the chartered wind is revelling ; and though in the map some fanciful engineer has laid down streets and squares, they exist but on paper ; nor, indeed, can there be any need of them at present, in a quarter where houses are not wanted so much as people to dwell in the same.

If the genteel portions of the town look to the full as melancholy as they did, the downright poverty ceases, I fear, to make so strong an impression as it made four months ago. Going over the same ground again, places appear to have quite a different aspect ; and, with their strangeness, poverty and misery have lost much of their terror. The people, though dirtier and more ragged, seem certainly happier than those in London.

Near to the King's Court, for instance (a noble building, as are almost all the public edifices of the city), is a straggling green suburb, containing numberless little shabby, patched, broken-windowed huts, with rickety gardens dotted with rags that have been washed, and children that have not ; and thronged with all sorts of ragged inhabitants. Near to the suburb in the town, is a dingy old mysterious district, called Stoneybatter, where some houses have been allowed to reach an old age, extraordinary in this country of premature ruin, and look as if they had been built some sixscore years since. In these and the neighboring tenements, not so old, but equally ruinous and mouldy, there is a sort of vermin swarm of humanity ; dirty faces at all the dirty windows ; children on all the broken steps ; smutty slipshod women clacking and bustling about, and old men dawdling. Well, only paint and prop the tumbling gates and huts in the suburb, and fancy the Stoneybatterites clean, and you would have rather a gay and agreeable picture of

human life — of work-people and their families reposing after
their labors. They are all happy, and sober, and kind-hearted,
— they seem kind, and play with the children — the young
women having a gay good-natured joke for the passer-by; the
old seemingly contented, and buzzing to one another. It is
only the costume, as it were, that has frightened the stranger,
and made him fancy that people so ragged must be unhappy.
Observation grows used to the rags as much as the people do,
and my impression of the walk through this district, on a sunshiny, clear, autumn evening, is that of a fête. I am almost
ashamed it should be so.

Near to Stoneybatter lies a group of huge gloomy edifices —
an hospital, a penitentiary, a mad-house, and a poor-house. I
visited the latter of these, the North Dublin Union-house, an
enormous establishment, which accommodates two thousand
beggars. Like all the public institutions of the country, it
seems to be well conducted, and is a vast, orderly, and cleanly
place, wherein the prisoners are better clothed, better fed, and
better housed than they can hope to be when at liberty. We
were taken into all the wards in due order: the schools and
nursery for the children; the dining-rooms, day-rooms, &c., of
the men and women. Each division is so accommodated, as
also with a large court or ground to walk and exercise in.

Among the men, there are very few able-bodied: the most
of them, the keeper said, having gone out for the harvest-time,
or as soon as the potatoes came in. If they go out, they cannot return before the expiration of a month: the guardians
have been obliged to establish this prohibition, lest the persons
requiring relief should go in and out too frequently. The old
men were assembled in considerable numbers in a long day-
room that is comfortable and warm. Some of them were picking oakum by way of employment, but most of them were past
work; all such inmates of the house as are able-bodied being
occupied upon the premises. Their hall was airy and as clean
as brush and water could make it: the men equally clean, and
their gray jackets and Scotch caps stout and warm. Thence
we were led, with a sort of satisfaction, by the guardian, to
the kitchen — a large room, at the end of which might be seen
certain coppers, emitting, it must be owned, a very faint inhospitable smell. It was Friday, and rice-milk is the food on
that day, each man being served with a pint-canful, of which
cans a great number stood smoking upon stretchers — the
platters were laid, each with its portion of salt, in the large
clean dining-room hard by. "Look at that rice," said the

keeper, taking up a bit; " try it, sir, it's delicious." I'm sure
I hope it is.

The old women's room was crowded with, I should think,
at least four hundred old ladies — neat and nice, in white
clothes and caps — sitting demurely on benches, doing nothing
for the most part; but some employed, like the old men, in
fiddling with the oakum. " There's tobacco here," says the
guardian in a loud voice; " who's smoking tobacco?" " Faith,
and I wish dere *was* some tabaccy here," says one old lady,
" and my service to you, Mr. Leary, and I hope one of the
gentlemen has a snuff-box, and a pinch for a poor old woman."
But we had no boxes; and if any person who reads this visit,
goes to a poor-house or a lunatic asylum, let him carry a box,
if for that day only — a pinch is like Dives's drop of water to
those poor limboed souls. Some of the poor old creatures began to stand up as we came in — I can't say how painful such
an honor seemed to me.

There was a separate room for the able-bodied females; and
the place and courts were full of stout, red-cheeked, bouncing
women. If the old ladies looked respectable, I cannot say the
young ones were particularly good-looking; there were some
Hogarthian faces amongst them — sly, leering, and hideous. I
fancied I could see only too well what these girls had been. Is
it charitable or not to hope that such bad faces could only belong to bad women?

" Here, sir, is the nursery," said the guide, flinging open
the door of a long room. There may have been eighty
babies in it, with as many nurses and mothers. Close to the
door sat one with as beautiful a face as I almost ever saw: she
had at her breast a very sickly and puny child, and looked up,
as we entered, with a pair of angelical eyes, and a face that
Mr. Eastlake could paint — a face that *had* been angelical that
is; for there was the snow still, as it were, but with the foot-
mark on it. I asked her how old she was — she did not know.
She could not have been more than fifteen years, the poor child.
She said she had been a servant — and there was no need of
asking anything more about her story. I saw her grinning at
one of her comrades as we went out of the room; her face did
not look angelical then. Ah, young master or old, young or
old villain, who did this! — have you not enough wickedness
of your own to answer for, that you must take another's sins
upon your shoulders; and be this wretched child's sponsor in
crime? . . . .

But this chapter must be made as short as possible: and so

I will not say how much prouder Mr. Leary, the keeper, was of his fat pigs than of his paupers — how he pointed us out the burial-ground of the family of the poor — their coffins were quite visible through the niggardly mould; and the children might peep at their fathers over the burial-ground-play-ground-wall — nor how we went to see the Linen Hall of Dublin — that huge, useless, lonely, decayed place, in the vast windy solitudes of which stands the simpering statue of George IV., pointing to some bales of shirting, over which he is supposed to extend his august protection.

The cheers of the rabble hailing the new Lord Mayor were the last sounds that I heard in Dublin : and I quitted the kind friends I had made there with the sincerest regret. As for forming " an opinion of Ireland," such as is occasionally asked from a traveller on his return — that is as difficult an opinion to form as to express ; and the puzzle which has perplexed the gravest and wisest, may be confessed by a humble writer of light literature, whose aim it only was to look at the manners and the scenery of the country, and who does not venture to meddle with questions of more serious import.

To have " an opinion about Ireland," one must begin by getting at the truth ; and where is it to be had in the country? Or rather, there are two truths, the Catholic truth and the Protestant truth. The two parties do not see things with the same eyes. I recollect, for instance, a Catholic gentleman telling me that the Primate had forty-three thousand *five hundred* a year ; a Protestant clergyman gave me, chapter and verse, the history of a shameful perjury and malversation of money on the part of a Catholic priest : nor was one tale more true than the other. But belief is made a party business ; and the receiving of the archbishop's income would probably not convince the Catholic, any more than the clearest evidence to the contrary altered the Protestant's opinion. Ask about an estate : you may be sure almost that people will make misstatements, or volunteer them if not asked. Ask a cottager about his rent, or his landlord : you cannot trust him. I shall never forget the glee with which a gentleman in Munster told me how he had sent off MM. Tocqueville and Beaumont " with *such* a set of stories." Inglis was seized, as I am told, and mystified in the same way. In the midst of all these truths, attested with " I give ye my sacred honor and word," which is the stranger to select? And how are we to trust philosophers who make theories upon such data?

Meanwhile it is satisfactory to know, upon testimony so

general as to be equivalent almost to fact, that, wretched as it
is, the country is steadily advancing, nor nearly so wretched
now as it was a score of years since; and let us hope that the
middle class, which this increase of prosperity must generate
(and of which our laws have hitherto forbidden the existence
in Ireland, making there a population of Protestant aristocracy
and Catholic peasantry), will exercise the greatest and most
beneficial influence over the country.   Too independent to be
bullied by priest or squire — having their interest in quiet, and
alike indisposed to servility or to rebellion; may not as much
be hoped from the gradual formation of such a class, as from
any legislative meddling.   It is the want of the middle class
that has rendered the squire so arrogant, and the clerical or
political demagogue so powerful; and I think Mr. O'Connell
himself would say that the existence of such a body would do
more for the steady acquirement of orderly freedom, than the
occasional outbreak of any crowd, influenced by any eloquence
from altar or tribune.

CHARACTER SKETCHES.

CAPTAIN ROOK AND MR. PIGEON.

THE statistic-mongers and dealers in geography have calculated to a nicety how many quartern loaves, bars of iron, pigs
of lead, sacks of wool, Turks, Quakers, Methodists, Jews,
Catholics, and Church-of-England men are consumed or produced in the different countries of this wicked world : I should
like to see an accurate table showing the rogues and dupes of
each nation ; the calculation would form a pretty matter for a
philosopher to speculate upon. The mind loves to repose and
broods benevolently over this expanded theme. What thieves
are there in Paris, O heavens ! and what a power of rogues
with pigtails and mandarin buttons at Pekin ! Crowds of
swindlers are there at this very moment pursuing their trade at
St. Petersburg : how many scoundrels are saying their prayers
alongside of Don Carlos ! how many scores are jobbing under
the pretty nose of Queen Christina ! what an inordinate number
of rascals is there, to be sure, puffing tobacco and drinking flat
small-beer in all the capitals of Germany ; or else, without a
rag to their ebony backs, swigging quass out of calabashes,
and smeared over with palm-oil, lolling at the doors of clay
huts in the sunny city of Timbuctoo ! It is not necessary to
make any more topographical allusions, or, for illustrating the
above position, to go through the whole Gazetteer ; but he is a
bad philosopher who has not all these things in mind, and does
not in his speculations or his estimate of mankind duly consider and weigh them. And it is fine and consolatory to think
that thoughtful Nature, which has provided sweet flowers for
the humming bee ; fair running streams for glittering fish ;
store of kids, deer, goats, and other fresh meat for roaring
lions ; for active cats, mice ; for mice, cheese, and so on ;

establishing throughout the whole of her realm the great doctrine that where a demand is, there will be a supply (see the romances of Adam Smith, Malthus, and Ricardo, and the philosophical works of Miss Martineau) : I say it is consolatory to think that, as Nature has provided flies for the food of fishes, and flowers for bees, so she has created fools for rogues ; and thus the scheme is consistent throughout. Yes, observation, with extensive view, will discover Captain Rooks all over the world, and Mr. Pigeons made for their benefit. Wherever shines the sun, you are sure to find Folly basking in it ; and knavery is the shadow at Folly's heels.

It is not, however, necessary to go to St. Petersburg or Pekin for rogues (and in truth I don't know whether the Timbuctoo Captain Rooks prefer cribbage or billiards). " We are not birds," as the Irishman says, " to be in half a dozen places at once ; " so let us pretermit all considerations of rogues in other countries, examining only those who flourish under our very noses. I have travelled much, and seen many men and cities ; and, in truth, I think that our country of England produces the best soldiers, sailors, razors, tailors, brewers, hatters, and rogues, of all. Especially there is no cheat like an English cheat. Our society produces them in the greatest numbers as well as of the greatest excellence. We supply all Europe with them. I defy you to point out a great city of the Continent where half a dozen of them are not to be found : proofs of our enterprise and samples of our home manufacture. Try Rome, Cheltenham, Baden, Toeplitz, Madrid, or Tzarskoselo : I have been in every one of them, and give you my honor that the Englishman is the best rascal to be found in all ; better than your eager Frenchman ; your swaggering Irishman, with a red velvet waistcoat and red whiskers ; your grave Spaniard, with horrid goggle eyes and profuse diamond shirt-pins ; your tallow-faced German baron, with white moustache and double chin, fat, pudgy, dirty fingers, and great gold thumb-ring ; better even than your nondescript Russian — swindler and spy as he is by loyalty and education — the most dangerous antagonist we have. Who has the best coat even at Vienna? who has the neatest britzska at Baden? who drinks the best champagne at Paris? Captain Rook, to be sure, of her Britannic Majesty's service : — he *has* been of the service, that is to say, but often finds it convenient to sell out.

The life of a blackleg, which is the name contemptuously applied to Captain Rook in his own country, is such an easy, comfortable, careless, merry one, that I can't conceive why all the world do not turn Captain Rooks; unless, may be, there are some mysteries and difficulties in it which the vulgar know nothing of, and which only men of real genius can overcome. Call on Captain Rook in the day (in London, he lives about St. James's; abroad, he has the very best rooms in the very best hotels), and you will find him at one o'clock dressed in the very finest *robe-de-chambre*, before a breakfast-table covered with the prettiest patties and delicacies possible; smoking, perhaps, one of the biggest Meerschaum pipes you ever saw; reading, possibly, *The Morning Post*, or a novel (he has only one volume in his whole room, and that from a circulating library); or having his hair dressed; or talking to a tailor about waistcoat patterns; or drinking soda-water with a glass of sherry; all this he does every morning, and it does not seem very difficult, and lasts until three. At three, he goes to a horse-dealer's, and lounges there for half an hour; at four he is to be seen at the window of his Club; at five, he is cantering and curveting in Hyde Park with one or two more (he does not know any ladies, but has many male acquaintances: some, stout old gentlemen riding cobs, who knew his family, and give him a surly grunt of recognition; some, very young lads with pale dissolute faces, little moustaches perhaps, or at least little tufts on their chin, who hail him eagerly as a man of fashion): at seven, he has a dinner at " Long's " or at the " Clarendon ; " and so to bed very likely at five in the morning, after a quiet game of whist, broiled bones, and punch.

Perhaps he dines early at a tavern in Covent Garden; after which, you will see him at the theatre in a private box (Captain Rook affects the Olympic a good deal). In the box, beside himself, you will remark a young man — very young — one of the lads who spoke to him in the Park this morning, and a couple of ladies: one shabby, melancholy, raw-boned, with numberless small white ringlets, large hands and feet, and a faded light blue silk gown; she has a large cap, trimmed with yellow, and all sorts of crumpled flowers and greasy blond lace; she wears large gilt ear-rings, and sits back, and nobody speaks to her, and she to nobody, except to say, " Law, Maria, how well you *do* look to-night; there's a man opposite has been staring at you this three hours; I'm blest if it isn't him as we saw in the Park, dear! "

" I wish, Hanna, you'd 'old your tongue, and not bother me about the men. You don't believe Miss 'Ickman, Freddy, do you? " says Maria, smiling fondly on Freddy. Maria is sitting in front: she says she is twenty-three, though Miss Hickman knows very well she is thirty-one (Freddy is just of age). She wears a purple-velvet gown, three different gold bracelets on each arm, as many rings on each finger of each hand; to one is hooked a gold smelling-bottle: she has an enormous fan, a laced pocket-handkerchief, a cashmere shawl, which is continually falling off, and exposing, very unnecessarily, a pair of very white shoulders: she talks loud, always lets her playbill drop into the pit, and smells most pungently of Mr. Delcroix's shop. After this description it is not at all necessary to say who Maria is: Miss Hickman is her companion, and they live together in a very snug little house in Mayfair, which has just been new-furnished *à la Louis Quatorze* by Freddy, as we are positively informed. It is even said that the little carriage, with two little white ponies, which Maria drives herself in such a fascinating way through the Park, was purchased for her by Freddy too; ay, and that Captain Rook got it for him — a great bargain of course.

Such is Captain Rook's life. Can anything be more easy? Suppose Maria says, "Come home, Rook, and heat a cold chicken with us, and a glass of hiced champagne;" and suppose he goes, and after chicken — just for fun — Maria proposes a little chicken-hazard; — she only plays for shillings, while Freddy, a little bolder, won't mind half-pound stakes himself. Is there any great harm in all this? Well, after half an hour, Maria grows tired, and Miss Hickman has been nodding asleep in the corner long ago; so off the two ladies set, candle in hand.

"D—n it, Fred," says Captain Rook, pouring out for that young gentleman his fifteenth glass of champagne, "what luck you are in, if you did but know how to back it!"

What more natural, and even kind, of Rook than to say this? Fred is evidently an inexperienced player; and every experienced player knows that there is nothing like backing your luck. Freddy does. Well; fortune is proverbially variable; and it is not at all surprising that Freddy, after having had so much luck at the commencement of the evening, should have the tables turned on him at some time or other. — Freddy loses.

It is deuced unlucky, to be sure, that he should have won all the little *coups* and lost all the great ones; but there is a plan which the commonest play-man knows, an infallible means of retrieving yourself at play: it is simply doubling your stake. Say, you lose a guinea: you bet two guineas, which if you win, you win a guinea and your original stake: if you lose, you have but to bet four guineas on the third stake, eight on the fourth, sixteen on the fifth, thirty-two on the sixth, and so on. It stands to reason that you cannot lose *always*, and the very first time you win, all your losings are made up to you. There is but one drawback to this infallible process; if you begin at a guinea, double every time you lose, and lose fifteen times, you will have lost exactly sixteen thousand three hundred and eighty-four guineas; a sum which probably exceeds the amount of your yearly income: — mine is considerably under that figure.

Freddy does not play this game then, yet; but being a poor-spirited creature, as we have seen he must be by being afraid to win, he is equally poor-spirited when he begins to lose: he is frightened; that is, increases his stakes, and backs his ill-luck: when a man does this, it is all over with him.

When Captain Rook goes home (the sun is peering through the shutters of the little drawing-room in Curzon Street, and the ghastly footboy — oh, how bleared his eyes look as he opens the door!) — when Captain Rook goes home, he has Freddy's I O U's in his pocket to the amount, say, of three hundred pounds. Some people say that Maria has half of the money when it is paid; but this I don't believe: is Captain Rook the kind of fellow to give up a purse when his hand has once clawed hold of it?

Be this, however, true or not, it concerns us very little. The Captain goes home to King Street, plunges into bed much too tired to say his prayers, and wakes the next morning at twelve to go over such another day as we have just chalked out for him. As for Freddy, not poppy, nor mandragora, nor all the soda-water at the chemist's, can ever medicine him to that sweet sleep which he might have had but for his loss. "*If* I had but played my king of hearts," sighed Fred, "and kept back my trump; but there's no standing against a fellow who turns up a king seven times running: if I *had* even but pulled up when Thomas (curse him!) brought up that infernal Curaçoa punch, I should have saved a couple of hundred," and so on go Freddy's lamentations. O luckless Freddy! dismal Freddy! silly gaby of a Freddy! you are hit now, and there is no cure for you but bleeding you almost to death's door. The homœopathic maxim of *similia similibus* — which means, I believe, that you are to be cured " by a hair of the dog that bit you " — must be put in practice with regard to Freddy — only not in homœopathic infinitesimal doses; no hair of the dog that bit him; but, *vice versâ*, the dog of the hair that tickled him. Freddy has begun to play; — a mere trifle at first, but he must play it out; he must go the whole dog now, or there is no chance for him. He must play until he can play no more; he *will* play until he has not a shilling left to play with, when, perhaps, he may turn out an honest man, though the odds are against him : the betting is in favor of his being a swindler always ; a rich or a poor one, as the case may be. I need not tell Freddy's name, I think, now ; it stands on this card : —

> MR. FREDERICK PIGEON,
>
> LONG'S HOTEL.

I have said the chances are that Frederick Pigeon, Esq., will become a rich or a poor swindler, though the first chance, it must be confessed, is very remote. I once heard an actor, who could not write, speak, or even read English ; who was not fit for any trade in the world, and had not the " nous " to keep an applestall, and scarcely even enough sense to make a Member of Parliament : I once, I say, heard an actor, — whose only qualifications were a large pair of legs, a large voice, and a very large neck, — curse his fate and his profession, by which, do what he would, he could only make eight guineas a week. " No men," said he, with a great deal of justice, " were so ill paid as ' dramatic artists ; ' they labored for nothing all their youths, and had no provision for old age." With this, he sighed, and called for (it was on a Saturday night) the forty-ninth glass of brandy-and-water which he had drunk in the course of the week.

The excitement of his profession, I make no doubt, caused my friend Claptrap to consume this quantity of spirit-and-water, besides beer in the morning, after rehearsal ; and I could not help musing over his fate. It is a hard one. To eat, drink, work a little, and be jolly ; to be paid twice as much as you are worth, and then to go to ruin ; to drop off the tree when you are swelled out, seedy, and over-ripe ; and to lie rotting in the mud underneath, until at last you mingle with it.

Now, badly as the actor is paid, (and the reader will the more readily pardon the above episode, because, in reality, it has nothing to do with the subject in hand,) and luckless as his fate is, the lot of the poor blackleg is cast lower still. You never hear of a rich gambler ; or of one who wins in the end. Where does all the money go to which is lost among them?

Did you ever play a game at loo for sixpences? At the end of the night a great many of those small coins have been lost, and in consequence, won : but ask the table all round ; one man has won three shillings ; two have neither lost nor won ; one rather thinks he has lost ; and the three others have lost two pounds each. Is not this the fact, known to everybody who indulges in round games, and especially the noble game of loo? I often think that the devil's books, as cards are called, are let out to us from Old Nick's circulating library, and that he lays his paw upon a certain part of the winnings, and carries it off privily : else, what becomes of all the money?

For instance, there is the gentleman whom the newspapers call " a noble earl of sporting celebrity ; " — if he has lost a shilling, according to the newspaper accounts, he has lost fifty millions : he drops fifty thousand pounds at the Derby, just as you and I would lay down twopence-halfpenny for half an ounce of Macabaw. Who has won these millions? Is it Mr. Crockford, or Mr. Bond, or Mr. Salon-des-Etrangers? (I do not call these latter gentlemen gamblers, for their speculation is a certainty) ; but who wins his money, and everybody else's money who plays and loses? Much money is staked in the absence of Mr. Crockford ; many notes are given without the interference of the Bonds ; there are hundreds of thousands of gamblers who are *étrangers* even to the *Salon-des-Etrangers.*

No, my dear sir, it is not in the public gambling-houses that the money is lost ; it is not in them that your virtue is chiefly in danger. Better by half lose your income, your fortune, or your master's money, in a decent public hell, than in the private society of such men as my friend Captain Rook ; but we are again and again digressing ; the point is, is the Captain's trade a good one, and does it yield tolerably good interest for outlay and capital?

To the latter question first : — at this very season of May, when the Rooks are very young, have you not, my dear friend, often tasted them in pies? — they are then so tender that you cannot tell the difference between them and pigeons. So, in like manner, our Rook has been in his youth undistinguishable from a pigeon. He does as he has been done by : yea, he has been plucked as even now he plucks his friend Mr. Frederick Pigeon. Say that he began the world with ten thousand pounds : every maravedi of this is gone ; and may be considered as the capital which he has sacrificed to learn his trade. Having spent 10,000*l.*, then, on an annuity of 650*l.*, he must look to a larger interest for his money — say fifteen hundred, two thousand, or

21

three thousand pounds, decently to repay his risk and labor. Besides the money sunk in the first place, his profession requires continual annual outlays, as thus —

Horses, carriages (including Epsom, Goodwood, Ascot, &c.) . .	£500 0 0
Lodgings, servants, and board	350 0 0
Watering-places, and touring	300 0 0
Dinners to give	150 0 0
Pocket-money	150 0 0
Gloves, handkerchiefs, perfumery, and tobacco (very moderate) .	150 0 0
Tailor's bills (£100 say, never paid)	0 0 0
TOTAL	£1,600 0 0

I defy any man to carry on the profession in a decent way under the above sum: ten thousand sunk, and sixteen hundred annual expenses; no, it is *not* a good profession: it is *not* good interest for one's money: it is *not* a fair remuneration for a gentleman of birth, industry, and genius: and my friend Clap-trap, who growls about *his* pay, may bless his eyes that he was not born a gentleman and bred up to such an unprofitable calling as this. Considering his trouble, his outlay, his birth, and breeding, the Captain is most wickedly and basely rewarded. And when he is obliged to retreat, when his hand trembles, his credit is fallen, his bills laughed at by every money-lender in Europe, his tailors rampant and inexorable — in fact, when the *coup* of life will *sauter* for him no more — who will help the play-worn veteran? As Mitchel sings after Aristophanes —

> " In glory he was seen, when his years as yet *were green;*
> But now when his dotage is on him,
> God help him ; — for no eye of those who pass him by,
> Throws a look of compassion upon him."

Who indeed will help him? — not his family, for he has bled his father, his uncle, his old grandmother; he has had slices out of his sisters' portions, and quarrelled with his brothers-in-law; the old people are dead; the young ones hate him, and will give him nothing. Who will help him? — not his friends; in the first place, my dear sir, a man's friends very seldom do: in the second place, it is Captain Rook's business not to keep, but to give up his friends. His acquaintances do not last more than a year; the time, namely, during which he is employed in plucking them; then they part. Pigeon has not a single feather left to his tail, and how should he help Rook, whom, *au reste*, he has learned to detest most cordially, and has found out to be a rascal? When Rook's ill day comes, it is simply because he has no more friends; he has exhausted them all, plucked every one as clean as the palm of your hand. And to arrive at this conclusion, Rook has been spending sixteen hundred a year, and the prime of his life, and has moreover sunk ten thousand pounds! *Is* this a proper reward for a gentleman? I say it is a sin and a shame that an English gentleman should be allowed thus to drop down the stream without a single hand to help him.

The moral of the above remarks I take to be this; that blacklegging is as bad a trade as can be; and so let parents and guardians look to it, and not apprentice their children to such a villanous, scurvy way of living.

It must be confessed, however, that there are some individuals who have for the profession such a natural genius, that no entreaties or example of parents will keep them from it, and no restraint or occupation occasioned by another calling. They do what Christians do not do; they leave all to follow their master the Devil; they cut friends, families, and good, thriving, profitable trades to put up with this one, that is both unthrifty and unprofitable. They are in regiments: ugly whispers about certain midnight games at blind-hookey, and a few odd bargains in horseflesh, are borne abroad, and Cornet Rook receives the gentlest hint in the world that he had better sell out. They are in counting-houses, with a promise of partnership, for which papa is to lay down a handsome premium; but the firm of Hobbs, Bobbs and Higgory can never admit a young gentleman who is a notorious gambler, is much oftener at the races than his desk, and has bills daily falling due at his private banker's. The father, that excellent old man, Sam Rook, so well known on 'Change in the war-time, discovers, at the end of five years, that his son has spent rather more than the four thousand pounds intended for his partnership, and cannot, in common justice to his other thirteen children, give him a shilling more. A pretty pass for flash young Tom Rook, with four horses in stable, a protemporaneous Mrs. Rook, very likely, in an establishment near the Regent's Park, and a bill for three hundred and seventy-five pounds coming due on the fifth of next month.

Sometimes young Rook is destined to the bar: and I am glad to introduce one of these gentlemen and his history to the notice of the reader. He was the son of an amiable gentleman, the Reverend Athanasius Rook, who took high honors at Cambridge in the year 1: was a fellow of Trinity in the year 2: and so continued a fellow and tutor of the College until a living fell vacant, on which he seized. It was only two hundred and fifty pounds a year; but the fact is, Athanasius was in love. Miss Gregory, a pretty, demure, simple governess at Miss Mickle's establishment for young ladies in Cambridge (where the reverend gentleman used often of late to take his tea), had caught the eye of the honest college tutor : and in Trinity walks, and up and down the Trumpington Road, he walked with her (and another young lady of course), talked with her, and told his love.

Miss Gregory had not a rap, as might be imagined ; but she loved Athanasius with her whole soul and strength, and was the most orderly, cheerful, tender, smiling, bustling little wife that ever a country parson was blessed withal. Athanasius took a couple of pupils at a couple of hundred guineas each, and so made out a snug income ; ay, and laid by for a rainy day — a little portion for Harriet, when she should grow up and marry, and a help for Tom at college and at the bar. For you must know there were two little Rooks now growing in the rookery ; and very happy were father and mother, I can tell you, to put meat down their tender little throats. Oh, if ever a man was good and happy, it was Athanasius ; if ever a woman was happy and good, it was his wife : not the whole parish, not the whole county, not the whole kingdom, could produce such a snug rectory, or such a pleasant *ménage*.

Athanasius's fame as a scholar, too, was great; and as his charges were very high, and as he received but two pupils, there was, of course, much anxiety among wealthy parents to place their children under his care. Future squires, bankers, yea, lords and dukes, came to profit by his instructions, and were led by him gracefully over the " Asses' bridge " into the sublime regions of mathematics, or through the syntax into the pleasant paths of classic lore.

In the midst of these companions, Tom Rook grew up ; more fondled and petted, of course, than they ; cleverer than they ; as handsome, dashing, well-instructed a lad for his years as ever went to college to be a senior wrangler, and went down without any such honor.

Fancy, then, our young gentleman installed at college, whither his father has taken him, and with fond veteran recollections has surveyed hall and grass-plots, and the old porter, and the old fountain, and the old rooms in which he used to live. Fancy the sobs of good little Mrs. Rook, as she parted with her boy ; and the tears of sweet pale Harriet, as she clung round his neck, and brought him (in a silver paper, slobbered with many tears) a little crimson silk purse (with two guineas of her own in it, poor thing!). Fancy all this, and fancy young Tom, sorry too, but yet restless and glad, panting for the new life opening upon him; the freedom, the joy of the manly struggle for fame, which he vows he will win. Tom Rook, in other words, is installed at Trinity College, attends lectures, reads at home, goes to chapel, uses wine-parties moderately, and bids fair to be one of the topmost men of his year.

Tom goes down for the Christmas vacation. (What a man he is grown, and how his sister and mother quarrel which shall walk with him down the village; and what stories the old gentleman lugs out with his old port, and how he quotes Æschylus, to be sure!) The pupils are away too, and the three have Tom in quiet. Alas! I fear the place has grown a little too quiet for Tom: however, he reads very stoutly of mornings; and sister Harriet peeps with a great deal of wonder into huge books of scribbling-paper, containing many strange diagrams, and complicated arrangements of x's and y's.

May comes, and the college examinations: the delighted parent receives at breakfast, on the 10th of that month, two letters, as follows: —

FROM THE REV. SOLOMON SNORTER TO THE REV. ATHANASIUS ROOK.

"TRINITY, May 10.

"DEAR CREDO *—I wish you joy. Your lad is the best man of his year, and I hope in four more to see him at our table. In classics he is, my dear friend, *facile princeps*; in mathematics he was run hard (*entre nous*) by a lad of the name of Snick, a Westmoreland man and a sizer. We must keep up Thomas to his mathematics, and I have no doubt we shall make a fellow and a wrangler of him.

"I send you his college bill, 105*l*. 10*s*.; rather heavy, but this is the first term, and that you know is expensive: I shall be glad to give you a receipt for it. By the way, the young man is *rather* too fond of amusement, and lives with a very expensive set. Give him a lecture on this score.

"Yours,
"SOL. SNORTER."

Next comes Mr. Tom Rook's own letter: it is long, modest: we only give the postscript: —

"P.S. — Dear father, I forgot to say that, as I live in the very best set in the University, (Lord Bagwig, the Duke's eldest son you know, vows he will give me a living,) I have been led into one or two expenses which will

---

* This is most probably a joke on the Christian name of Mr. Rook.

frighten you : I lost £30 to the honorable Mr. Deuceace (a son of Lord Crabs) at Bagwig's, the other day at dinner ; and owe £54 more for desserts and hiring horses, which I can't send into Snorter's bill.* Hiring horses is so deuced expensive ; next term I must have a nag of my own, that's positive."

The Rev. Athanasius read the postscript with much less gusto than the letter : however, Tom has done his duty, and the old gentleman won't balk his pleasure ; so he sends him 100*l.*, with a " God bless you !" and mamma adds, in a postscript, that " he must always keep well with his aristocratic friends, for he was made only for the best society."

A year or two passes on : Tom comes home for the vacations ; but Tom has sadly changed ; he has grown haggard and pale. At second year's examination (owing to an unlucky illness) Tom was not classed at all ; and Snick, the Westmoreland man, has carried everything before him. Tom drinks more after dinner than his father likes ; he is always riding about and dining in the neighborhood, and coming home, quite odd, his mother says — ill-humored, unsteady on his feet, and husky in his talk. The Reverend Athanasius begins to grow very, very grave : they have high words, even the father and son ; and oh ! how Harriet and her mother tremble and listen at the study-door when these disputes are going on !

The last term of Tom's undergraduateship arrives ; he is in ill health, but he will make a mighty effort to retrieve himself for his degree ; and early in the cold winter's morning — late, late at night — he toils over his books : and the end is that, a month before the examination, Thomas Rook, Esquire, has a brain fever, and Mrs. Rook, and Miss Rook, and the Reverend Athanasius Rook, are all lodging at the " Hoop," an inn in Cambridge town, and day and night round the couch of poor Tom.

. . . .

O sin, woe, repentance ! O touching reconciliation and burst of tears on the part of son and father, when one morning at the parsonage, after Tom's recovery, the old gentleman produces a bundle of receipts, and says, with a broken voice, " There, boy, don't be vexed about your debts. Boys will be boys, I know, and I have paid all demands." Everybody cries in the house at this news ; the mother and daughter most

---

* It is, or was, the custom for young gentlemen at Cambridge to have unlimited credit with tradesmen, whom the college tutors paid, and then sent the bills to the parents of the young men.

profusely, even Mrs. Stokes the old housekeeper, who shakes master's hand, and actually kisses Mr. Tom.

Well, Tom begins to read a little for his fellowship, but in vain; he is beaten by Mr. Snick, the Westmoreland man. He has no hopes of a living; Lord Bagwig's promises were all moonshine. Tom must go to the bar; and his father, who has long left off taking pupils, must take them again, to support his son in London.

Why tell you what happens when there? Tom lives at the west end of the town, and never goes near the Temple: Tom goes to Ascot and Epsom along with his great friends; Tom has a long bill with Mr. Rymell, another long bill with Mr. Nugee; he gets into the hands of the Jews — and his father rushes up to London on the outside of the coach to find Tom in a spunging-house in Cursitor Street — the nearest approach he has made to the Temple during his three years' residence in London.

I don't like to tell you the rest of the history. The Reverend Athanasius was not immortal, and he died a year after his visit to the spunging-house, leaving his son exactly one farthing, and his wife one hundred pounds a year, with remainder to his daughter. But, heaven bless you! The poor things would never allow Tom to want while they had plenty, and they sold out and sold out the three thousand pounds, until, at the end of three years, there did not remain one single stiver of them; and now Miss Harriet is a governess, with sixty pounds a year, supporting her mother, who lives upon fifty.

As for Tom, he is a regular *leg* now — leading the life already described. When I met him last it was at Baden, where he was on a professional tour, with a carriage, a courier, a valet, a confederate, and a case of pistols. He has been in five duels, he has killed a man who spoke lightly about his honor; and at French or English hazard, at billiards, at whist, at loo, écarté, blind hookey, drawing straws, or beggar-my-neighbor, he will cheat you — cheat you for a hundred pounds or for a guinea, and murder you afterwards if you like.

Abroad, our friend takes military rank, and calls himself Captain Rook; when asked of what service, he says he was with Don Carlos or Queen Christina; and certain it is that he was absent for a couple of years nobody knows where; he may have been with General Evans, or he may have been at the Sainte Pélagie in Paris, as some people vow he was.

We must wind up this paper with some remarks concerning poor little Pigeon. Vanity has been little Pigeon's failing through life. He is a linendraper's son, and has been left with money : and the silly fashionable works that he has read, and the silly female relatives that he has — (N.B. All young men with money have silly, flattering she-relatives) — and the silly trips that he has made to watering-places, where he has scraped acquaintance with the Honorable Tom Mountcoffeehouse, Lord Ballyhooly, the celebrated German Prince, Sweller Mobskau, and their like (all Captain Rooks in their way), have been the ruin of him.

I have not the slightest pity in the world for little Pigeon. Look at him ! See in what absurd finery the little prig is dressed. Wine makes his poor little head ache, but he will drink because it is manly. In mortal fear he puts himself behind a curveting cameleopard of a cab-horse ; or perched on the top of a prancing dromedary, is borne through Rotten Row, when he would give the world to be on his own sofa, or with his own mamma and sisters, over a quiet pool of commerce and a cup of tea. How riding does scarify his poor little legs, and shake his poor little sides ! Smoking, how it does turn his little stomach inside out ; and yet smoke he will : Sweller Mobskau smokes ; Mountcoffeehouse don't mind a cigar ; and as for Ballyhooly, he will puff you a dozen in a day, and says very truly that Pontet won't supply *him* with near such good ones as he sells Pigeon. The fact is, that Pontet vowed seven years ago not to give his lordship a sixpence more credit ; and so the good-natured nobleman always helps himself out of Pigeon's box.

On the shoulders of these aristocratic individuals, Mr. Pigeon is carried into certain clubs, or perhaps we should say he walks into them by the aid of these " legs." But they keep him always to themselves. Captain Rooks must rob in companies ; but of course, the greater the profits, the fewer the partners must be. Three are positively requisite, however, as every reader must know who has played a game at whist : number one to be Pigeon's partner, and curse his stars at losing, and propose higher play, and " settle " with number two ; number three to transact business with Pigeon, and drive him down to the city to sell out. We have known an instance or two where, after a very good night's work, number three has bolted with the winnings altogether, but the practice is dangerous ; not only disgraceful to the profession, but it cuts up your own chance afterwards, as no one will act with you. There is only one occasion on which such a manœuvre is allowable. Many are sick of the profession, and desirous to turn honest men : in this case, when you can get a good coup, five thousand say. bolt without scruple. One thing is clear, the other men *must* be mum, and you can live at Vienna comfortably on the interest of five thousand pounds.

Well, then, in the society of these amiable confederates little Pigeon goes through that period of time which is necessary for the purpose of plucking him. To do this, you must not, in most cases, tug at the feathers so as to hurt him, else he may be frightened, and hop away to somebody else: nor, generally speaking, will the feathers come out so easily at first as they will when he is used to it, and then they drop in handfuls. Nor need you have the least scruple in so causing the little creature to moult artificially: if you don't, somebody else will: a Pigeon goes into the world fated, as Chateaubriand says —

"Pigeon, il va subir le sort de tout pigeon."

He *must* be plucked, it is the purpose for which nature has formed him: if you, Captain Rook, do not perform the operation on a green table lighted by two wax-candles, and with two packs of cards to operate with, some other Rook will: are there not railroads, and Spanish bonds, and bituminous companies, and Cornish tin-mines, and old dowagers with daughters to marry? If you leave him, Rook of Birchin Lane will have him as sure as fate: if Rook of Birchin Lane don't hit him, Rook of the Stock Exchange will blaze away both barrels at him, which if the poor trembling flutterer escape, he will fly over and drop into the rookery, where dear old swindling Lady Rook and her daughters will find him and nestle him in their bosoms, and in that soft place pluck him until he turns out as naked as a cannon-ball.

Be not thou scrupulous, O Captain! Seize on Pigeon; pluck him gently but boldly; but, above all, never let him go. If he is a stout cautious bird, of course *you* must be more cautious; if he is excessively silly and scared, perhaps the best way is just to take him round the neck at once, and strip the whole stock of plumage from his back.

The feathers of the human pigeon being thus violently abstracted from him, no others supply their place: and yet I do not pity him. He is now only undergoing the destiny of pigeons, and is, I do believe, as happy in his plucked as in his feathered state. He cannot purse out his breast, and bury his head, and fan his tail, and strut in the sun as if he were a turkey-cock. Under all those fine airs and feathers, he was but what he is now, a poor little meek, silly, cowardly bird, and his state of pride is not a whit more natural to him than his fallen condition. He soon grows used to it. He is too great a coward to despair; much too mean to be frightened because he must live by doing meanness. He is sure, if he cannot fly, to fall somehow or other on his little miserable legs: on these he hops about, and manages to live somewhere in his own mean way. He has but a small stomach, and doesn't mind what food he puts into it. He spunges on his relatives; or else just before his utter ruin he marries and has nine children (and such a family *always* lives); he turns bully most likely, takes to drinking, and beats his wife, who supports him, or takes to drinking too; or he gets a little place, a very little place: you hear he has some tide-waitership, or is clerk to some new milk company, or is lurking about a newspaper. He dies, and a subscription is raised for the Widow Pigeon, and we look no more to find a likeness of him in his children, who are as a new race. Blessed are ye little ones, for ye are born in poverty, and may bear it, or surmount it and die rich. But woe to the pigeons of this earth, for they are born rich that they may die poor.

The end of Captain Rook — for we must bring both him and the paper to an end — is not more agreeable, but somewhat more manly and majestic than the conclusion of Mr. Pigeon. If you walk over to the Queen's Bench Prison, I would lay a wager that a dozen such are to be found there in a moment. They have a kind of Lucifer look with them, and stare at you with fierce, twinkling, crow-footed eyes; or grin from under huge grizzly moustaches, as they walk up and down in their tattered brocades. What a dreadful activity is that of a mad-house, or a prison! — a dreary flagged court-yard, a long dark room, and the inmates of it, like the inmates of the ménagerie cages, ceaselessly walking up and down! Mary Queen of Scots says very touchingly: —

> "Pour mon mal estranger
> Je ne m'arreste en place;
> Mais, j'en ay beau changer
> Si ma douleur n'efface!"

Up and down, up and down — the inward woe seems to spur the body onwards; and I think in both madhouse and prison you will find plenty of specimens of our Captain Rook. It is fine to mark him under the pressure of this woe, and see how fierce he looks when stirred up by the long pole of memory. In these asylums the Rooks end their lives; or, more happy, they die miserably in a miserable provincial town abroad, and for the benefit of coming Rooks they commonly die early; you as seldom hear of an old Rook (practising his trade) as of a rich one. It is a short-lived trade; not merry, for the gains are most precarious, and perpetual doubt and dread are not pleasant accompaniments of a profession: — not agreeable either, for though Captain Rook does not mind *being* a scoundrel, no man likes to be considered as such, and as such, he knows very well, does the world consider Captain Rook: not profitable, for the expenses of the trade swallow up all the profits of it, and in addition leave the bankrupt with certain habits that have become as nature to him, and which, to live, he must gratify. I know no more miserable wretch than our Rook in his autumn days, at dismal Calais or Boulogne, or at the Bench yonder, with a whole load of diseases and wants, that have come to him in the course of his profession; the diseases and wants of sensuality, always pampered, and now agonizing for lack of its unnatural food; the mind, which *must* think now, and has only bitter recollections, mortified ambitions, and unavailing scoundrelisms to con over! Oh, Captain Rook! what nice " chums " do you take with you into prison; what pleasant companions of exile follow you over the *fines patriæ*, or attend, the only watchers, round your miserable death-bed!

My son, be not a Pigeon in thy dealings with the world: — but it is better to be a Pigeon than a Rook.

THE FASHIONABLE AUTHORESS.

PAYING a visit the other day to my friend Timson, who, I need not tell the public, is editor of that famous evening paper, the . . . . (and let it be said that there is no more profitable acquaintance than a gentleman in Timson's situation, in whose office, at three o'clock daily, you are sure to find new books, lunch, magazines, and innumerable tickets for concerts and plays): going, I say, into Timson's office, I saw on the table an immense paper cone or funnel, containing a bouquet of such a size, that it might be called a bosquet, wherein all sorts of rare geraniums, luscious magnolias, stately dahlias, and other floral produce were gathered together — a regular flower-stack.

Timson was for a brief space invisible, and I was left alone in the room with the odors of this tremendous bow-pot, which filled the whole of the inky, smutty, dingy apartment with an agreeable incense. "O rus! quando te aspiciam?" exclaimed I, out of the Latin grammar, for imagination had carried me away to the country, and I was about to make another excellent and useful quotation (from the 14th book of the Iliad, Madam), concerning "ruddy lotuses, and crocuses, and hyacinths," when all of a sudden Timson appeared. His head and shoulders had, in fact, been engulfed in the flowers, among which he might be compared to any Cupid, butterfly, or bee. His little face was screwed up into such an expression of comical delight and triumph, that a Methodist parson would have laughed at it in the midst of a funeral sermon.

"What are you giggling at?" said Mr. Timson, assuming a high, aristocratic air.

"Has the goddess Flora made you a present of that bower, wrapped up in white paper ; or did it come by the vulgar hands

of yonder gorgeous footman, at whom all the little printer's
devils are staring in the passage?"

"Stuff!" said Timson, picking to pieces some rare exotic,
worth at the very least fifteenpence; "a friend, who knows
that Mrs. Timson and I are fond of these things, has sent us
a nosegay, that's all."

I saw how it was. "Augustus Timson," exclaimed I,
sternly, "the Pimlicoes have been with you; if that footman
did not wear the Pimlico plush, ring the bell and order me out:
if that three-cornered billet lying in your snuff-box has not the
Pimlico seal to it, never ask me to dinner again."

"Well, if it *does*," says Mr. Timson, who flushed as red as
a peony, "what is the harm? Lady Fanny Flummery may
send flowers to her friends, I suppose? The conservatories at
Pimlico House are famous all the world over, and the Countess
promised me a nosegay the very last time I dined there."

"Was that the day when she gave you a box of bonbons for
your darling little Ferdinand?"

"No, another day."

"Or the day when she promised you her carriage for Epsom
Races?"

"No."

"Or the day when she hoped that her Lucy and your Barbara-Jane might be acquainted, and sent to the latter from the
former a new French doll and tea-things?"

"Fiddlestick!" roared out Augustus Timson, Esquire: "I
wish you wouldn't come bothering here. I tell you that Lady
Pimlico is my friend — my friend, mark you, and I will allow
no man to abuse her in my presence; I say again *no man;*"
wherewith Mr. Timson plunged both his hands violently into his
breeches-pockets, looked me in the face sternly, and began
jingling his keys and shillings about.

At this juncture (it being about half-past three o'clock in the
afternoon), a one-horse chaise drove up to the . . . . office (Timson lives at Clapham, and comes in and out in this machine) —
a one-horse chaise drove up; and amidst a scuffling and crying
of small voices, good-humored Mrs. Timson bounced into the
room.

"Here we are, deary," said she, "we'll walk to the Mery-
weathers; and I've told Sam to be in Charles Street at twelve
with the chaise: it wouldn't do, you know, to come out of the
Pimlico box and have the people cry, ' Mrs. Timson's carriage!'
for old Sam and the chaise."

Timson, to this loving and voluble address of his lady, gave a peevish, puzzled look towards the stranger. as much as to say, "*He's* here."

"La, Mr. Smith! and how *do* you do? — So rude — I didn't see you: but the fact is, we are all in *such* a bustle! Augustus has got Lady Pimlico's box for the *Puritani* to-night, and I vowed I'd take the children."

Those young persons were evidently from their costume prepared for some extraordinary festival. Miss Barbara-Jane, a young lady of six years old, in a pretty pink slip and white muslin, her dear little poll bristling over with papers, to be removed previous to the play; while Master Ferdinand had a pair of nankeens (I can recollect Timson in them in the year 1825 — a great buck), and white silk stockings, which belonged to his mamma. His frill was very large and very clean, and he was fumbling perpetually at a pair of white kid gloves, which his mamma forbade him to assume before the opera.

And "Look here!" and "Oh, precious!" and "Oh, my!" were uttered by these worthy people as they severally beheld the vast bouquet, into which Mrs. Timson's head flounced, just as her husband's had done before.

"I must have a green-house at the Snuggery, that's positive, Timson, for I'm passionately fond of flowers — and how kind of Lady Fanny! Do you know her ladyship, Mr. Smith?"

"Indeed, Madam, I don't remember having ever spoken to a lord or a lady in my life."

Timson smiled in a supercilious way. Mrs. Timson exclaimed, "La, how odd! Augustus knows ever so many. Let's see, there's the Countess of Pimlico and Lady Fanny Flummery; Lord Doldrum (Timson touched up his travels, you know); Lord Gasterton, Lord Guttlebury's eldest son: Lady Pawpaw (they say she ought not to be visited, though); Baron Strum — Strom — Strumpf——"

What the baron's name was I have never been able to learn; for here Timson burst out with a "Hold your tongue, Bessy!" which stopped honest Mrs. Timson's harmless prattle altogether, and obliged that worthy woman to say meekly, "Well, Gus, I did not think there was any harm in mentioning your acquaintance." Good soul! it was only because she took pride in her Timson that she loved to enumerate the great names of the persons who did him honor. My friend the editor was, in fact, in a cruel position, looking foolish before his old acquaintance, stricken in that unfortunate sore point in his honest, good-humored character. The man adored the aristocracy, and had that wonderful respect for a lord which, perhaps the observant reader may have remarked, especially characterizes men of Timson's way of thinking.

In old days at the club (we held it in a small public-house near the Coburg Theatre, some of us having free admissions to that place of amusement, and some of us living for convenience in the immediate neighborhood of one of his Majesty's prisons in that quarter) — in old days, I say, at our spouting and toasted-cheese club, called "The Forum," Timson was called Brutus Timson, and not Augustus, in consequence of the ferocious republicanism which characterized him, and his utter scorn and hatred of a bloated, do-nothing aristocracy. His letters in *The Weekly Sentinel*, signed "Lictor," must be remembered by all our readers : he advocated the repeal of the corn laws, the burning of machines, the rights of labor, &c. &c., wrote some pretty defences of Robespierre, and used seriously to avow, when at all in liquor, that, in consequence of those "Lictor" letters, Lord Castlereagh had tried to have him murdered, and thrown over Blackfriars Bridge.

By what means Augustus Timson rose to his present exalted position it is needless here to state ; suffice it, that in two years he was completely bound over neck-and-heels to the bloodthirsty aristocrats, hereditary tyrants, &c. One evening he was asked to dine with a secretary of the Treasury (the . . . . is Ministerial, and has been so these forty-nine years) ; at the house of that secretary of the Treasury he met a lord's son : walking with Mrs. Timson in the Park next Sunday, that lord's son saluted him. Timson was from that moment a slave, had his coats made at the west end, cut his wife's relations (they are dealers in marine-stores, and live at Wapping), and had his name put down at two Clubs.

Who was the lord's son? Lord Pimlico's son, to be sure, the Honorable Frederick Flummery, who married Lady Fanny Foxy, daughter of Pitt Castlereagh, second Earl of Reynard, Kilbrush Castle, county Kildare. The earl had been ambassador in '14 : Mr. Flummery, his attaché : he was twenty-one at that time, with the sweetest tuft on his chin in the world. Lady Fanny was only four-and-twenty, just jilted by Prince Scoronconcolo, the horrid man who had married Miss Solomonson with a plum. Fanny had nothing — Frederick had about seven thousand pounds less. What better could the young things do than marry? Marry they did, and in the most delicious secrecy. Old Reynard was charmed to have an opportunity of breaking with one of his daughters for ever, and only longed for an occasion never to forgive the other nine.

A wit of the Prince's time, who inherited and transmitted to his children a vast fortune in genius, was cautioned on his marriage to be very economical. "Economical!" said he; "my wife has nothing, and I have nothing: I suppose a man can't live under *that!*" Our interesting pair, by judiciously employing the same capital, managed, year after year, to live very comfortably, until, at last, they were received into Pimlico House by the dowager (who has it for her life), where they live very magnificently. Lady Fanny gives the most magnificent entertainment in London, has the most magnificent equipage, and a very fine husband; who has his equipage as fine as her ladyship's; his seat in the omnibus, while her ladyship is in the second tier. They say he plays a good deal — ay, and pays, too, when he loses.

And how, pr'ythee? Her ladyship is a FASHIONABLE AUTHORESS. She has been at this game for fifteen years; during which period she has published forty-five novels, edited twenty-seven new magazines, and I don't know how many annuals, besides publishing poems, plays, desultory thoughts, memoirs, recollections of travel, and pamphlets without number. Going one day to church, a lady, whom I knew by her Leghorn bonnet and red ribbons, *ruche* with poppies and marigolds, brass ferronière, great red hands, black silk gown, thick shoes, and black silk stockings; a lady, whom I knew, I say, to be a devotional cook, made a bob to me just as the psalm struck up, and offered me a share of her hymn-book. It was, —

HEAVENLY CHORDS;

A COLLECTION OF

SACRED STRAINS,

SELECTED, COMPOSED, AND EDITED, BY THE

LADY FRANCES JULIANA FLUMMERY.

— Being simply a collection of heavenly chords robbed from the lyres of Watts, Wesley, Brady and Tate, &c.; and of sacred strains from the rare collection of Sternhold and Hopkins. Out of this, cook and I sang; and it is amazing how much our fervor was increased by thinking that our devotions were directed by a lady whose name was in the Red Book.

The thousands of pages that Lady Fanny Flummery has covered with ink exceed all belief. You must have remarked, Madam, in respect of this literary fecundity, that your amiable sex possesses vastly greater capabilities than we do; and that while a man is painfully laboring over a letter of two sides, a lady will produce a dozen pages, crossed, dashed, and so beautifully neat and close, as to be wellnigh invisible. The readiest of ready pens has Lady Fanny; her Pegasus gallops over hot-pressed satin so as to distance all gentlemen riders: like Camilla, it scours the plain — of Bath, and never seems punished or fatigued; only it runs so fast that it often leaves all sense behind it; and there it goes on, on, scribble, scribble, scribble, never flagging until it arrives at that fair winning-post on which is written " FINIS," or, " THE END ; " and shows that the course, whether it be of novel, annual, poem, or what not, is complete.

Now, the author of these pages doth not pretend to describe the inward thoughts, ways, and manner of being, of my Lady Fanny, having made before that humiliating confession, that lords and ladies are personally unknown to him; so that all milliners, butchers' ladies, dashing young clerks, and apprentices, or other persons who are anxious to cultivate a knowledge of the aristocracy, had better skip over this article altogether. But he hath heard it whispered, from pretty good authority, that the manners and customs of these men and women resemble, in no inconsiderable degree, the habits and usages of other men and women, whose names are unrecorded by Debrett. Granting this, and that Lady Fanny is a woman pretty much like another, the philosophical reader will be content that we rather consider her ladyship in her public capacity, and examine her influence upon mankind in general.

Her person, then, being thus put out of the way, her works, too, need not be very carefully sifted and criticised; for what is the use of peering into a millstone, or making calculations about the figure 0? The woman has not, in fact, the slightest influence upon literature for good or for evil: there are a certain number of fools whom she catches in her flimsy traps; and why not? They are made to be humbugged, or how should we live? Lady Flummery writes everything; that is, nothing. Her poetry is mere wind; her novels, stark nought; her philosophy, sheer vacancy: how should she do any better than she does? how could she succeed if she *did* do any better? If she did write well, she would not be Lady Flummery; she would not be praised by Timson and the critics, because she would be an honest woman, and would not bribe them. Nay, she would probably be written down by Timson and Co., because, being an honest woman, she utterly despised them and their craft.

We have said what she writes for the most part. Individ⁕

ually, she will throw off any number of novels that Messrs. Soap and Diddle will pay for; and collectively, by the aid of self and friends, scores of "Lyrics of Loveliness," "Beams of Beauty," "Pearls of Purity," &c. Who does not recollect the success which her "Pearls of the Peerage" had? She is going to do the "Beauties of the Baronetage;" then we shall have the "Daughters of the Dustmen," or some such other collection of portraits. Lady Flummery has around her a score of literary gentlemen, who are bound to her, body and soul: give them a dinner, a smile from an opera-box, a wave of the hand in Rotten Row, and they are hers, neck and heels. *Vides, mi fili,* &c. See, my son, with what a very small dose of humbug men are to be bought. I know many of these individuals: there is my friend M'Lather, an immense, pudgy man: I saw him one day walking through Bond Street in company with an enormous ruby breastpin. "Mac!" shouted your humble servant, "that is a Flummery ruby;" and Mac hated and cursed us ever after. Presently came little Fitch, the artist; he was rigged out in an illuminated velvet waistcoat — Flummery again — "There's only one like it in town," whispered Fitch to me confidentially, "and Flummery has that." To be sure, Fitch had given, in return, half a dozen of the prettiest drawings in the world. "I wouldn't charge for them, you know," he says: "for, hang it, Lady Flummery is my friend." Oh, Fitch, Fitch!

Fifty more instances could be adduced of her ladyship's ways of bribery. She bribes the critics to praise her, and the writers to write for her; and the public flocks to her as it will to any other tradesman who is properly puffed. Out comes the book; as for its merits, we may allow, cheerfully, that Lady Flummery has no lack of that natural *esprit* which every woman possesses; but here praise stops. For the style, she does not know her own language; but, in revenge, has a smattering of half a dozen others. She interlards her works with fearful quotations from the French, fiddle-faddle extracts from Italian operas, German phrases fiercely mutilated, and a scrap or two of bad Spanish: and upon the strength of these murders, she calls herself an authoress. To be sure there is no such word as authoress. If any young nobleman or gentleman of Eton College, when called upon to indite a copy of verses in praise of Sappho, or the Countess of Dash, or Lady Charlotte What-d'ye-call-'em, or the Honorable Mrs. Somebody, should fondly imagine that he might apply to those fair creatures the title of *auctrix* — I pity that young nobleman's or gentleman's case. Doctor Wordsworth and assistants would swish that error out of him in a way that need not here be mentioned. Remember it henceforth, ye writeresses — there is no such word as authoress. *Auctor*, Madam, is the word. *"Optima tu proprii nominis auctor eris;"* which, of course, means that you are, by your proper name, an author, not an authoress: the line is in Ainsworth's Dictionary, where anybody may see it.

This point is settled then: there is no such word as authoress. But what of that? Are authoresses to be bound by the rules of grammar? The supposition is absurd. We don't expect them to know their own language; we prefer rather the little graceful pranks and liberties they take with it. When, for instance, a celebrated authoress, who wrote a Diaress, calls somebody the prototype of his own father, we feel an obligation to her ladyship; the language feels an obligation; it has a charm and a privilege with which it was never before endowed: and it is manifest, that if we can call ourselves antetypes of our grandmothers — can prophesy what we had for dinner yesterday, and so on, we get into a new range of thought, and discover sweet regions of fancy and poetry, of which the mind hath never even had a notion until now.

It may be then considered as certain that an authoress *ought* not to know her own tongue. Literature and politics have this privilege in common, that any ignoramus may excel in both. No apprenticeship is required, that is certain; and if any gentleman doubts, let us refer him to the popular works of the present day, where, if he find a particle of scholarship, or any acquaintance with any books in any language, or if he be disgusted by any absurd, stiff, old-fashioned notions of grammatical propriety, we are ready to qualify our assertion. A friend of ours came to us the other day in great trouble. His dear little boy, who had been for some months attaché to the stables of Mr. Tilbury's establishment, took a fancy to the corduroy breeches of some other gentleman employed in the same emporium — appropriated them, and afterwards disposed of them for a trifling sum to a relation — I believe his uncle. For this harmless freak, poor Sam was absolutely seized, tried at Clerkenwell Sessions, and condemned to six months' useless rotatory labor at the House of Correction. "The poor fellow was bad enough before, sir," said his father, confiding in our philanthropy: "he picked up such a deal of slang among the stable-boys: but if you could hear him since he came from the mill! he knocks you down with it, sir. I am afraid, sir, of his becoming a regular prig: for though he's a 'cute chap, can read and write, and is mighty smart and handy, yet no one will take him into service, on account of that business of the breeches!"

"What, sir!" exclaimed we, amazed at the man's simplicity; "*such* a son, and you don't know what to do with him! a 'cute fellow, who can write, who has been educated in a stable-yard, and has had six months' polish in a university — I mean a prison — and you don't know what to do with him? Make a *fashionable novelist* of him, and be hanged to you!" And proud am I to say that that young man, every evening, after he comes home from his work (he has taken to street-sweeping in the day, and I don't advise him to relinquish a certainty) — proud am I to say that he devotes every evening to literary composition, and is coming out with a novel, in numbers, of the most fashionable kind.

This little episode is only given for the sake of example; *par exemple*, as our authoress would say, who delights in French of the very worst kind. The public likes only the extremes of society, and votes mediocrity vulgar. From the Author they will take nothing but Fleet Ditch; from the Authoress, only the very finest of rose-water. I have read so many of her ladyship's novels, that, egad! now I don't care for anything under a marquis. Why the deuce should we listen to the intrigues, the misfortunes, the virtues, and conversations of a couple of countesses, for instance, when we can have duchesses for our money? What's a baronet? pish! pish! that great coarse red fist in his scutcheon turns me sick! What's a baron? a fellow with only one more ball than a pawnbroker; and, upon my conscience, just as common. Dear Lady Flummery, in your next novel, give us no more of these low people; nothing under strawberry leaves, for the mercy of heaven! Suppose, now, you write us

ALBERT;

OR,

WHISPERINGS AT WINDSOR.

BY THE LADY FRANCES FLUMMERY.

There is a subject — fashionable circles, curious revelations, exclusive excitement, &c. To be sure, you *must* here introduce a viscount, and that is sadly vulgar; but we will pass him for the sake of the ministerial *portefeuille*, which is genteel. Then you might do "Leopold; or, the Bride of Neuilly;" "The

Victim of Würtemberg;" "Olga; or, the Autocrat's Daughter" (a capital title); "Henri; or, Rome in the Nineteenth Century;" we can fancy the book, and a sweet paragraph about it in Timson's paper.

"HENRI, by Lady Frances Flummery — Henri! Who can he be? a little bird whispers in our ear, that the gifted and talented Sappho of our hemisphere has discovered some curious particulars in the life of *a certain young chevalier*, whose appearance at Rome has so frightened the court of the Tu-l-ries. Henri de B-rd—ux is of an age when the *young god* can shoot his darts into the bosom with fatal accuracy; and if the Marchesina degli Spinachi (whose portrait our lovely authoress has sung with a *kindred hand*) be as beauteous as she is represented (and as all who have visited in the exclusive circles of the Eternal City say she is), no wonder at her effect upon the Pr-nce. *Verbum sap.* We hear that a few copies are still remaining. The enterprising publishers, Messrs. Soap and Diddle, have announced, we see, several other works by the same accomplished pen."

This paragraph makes its appearance, in small type, in the . . . . by the side, perhaps, of a disinterested recommendation of bears'-grease, or some remarks on the extraordinary cheapness of plate in Cornhill. Well, two or three days after, my dear Timson, who has been asked to dinner, writes in his own hand, and causes to be printed in the largest type, an article to the following effect : —

"HENRI.

"BY LADY F. FLUMMERY.

" This is another of the graceful evergreens which the fair fingers of Lady Fanny Flummery are continually strewing upon our path. At once profound and caustic, truthful and passionate, we are at a loss whether most to admire the manly grandeur of her ladyship's mind, or the exquisite nymph-like delicacy of it. Strange power of fancy! Sweet enchantress, that rules the mind at will : stirring up the utmost depths of it into passion and storm, or wreathing and dimpling its calm surface with countless summer smiles. As a great Bard of old Time has expressed it, what do we not owe to woman?

"What do we not owe her? More love, more happiness, more calm of vexed spirit, more truthful aid, and pleasant counsel; in joy, more delicate sympathy; in sorrow, more kind companionship. We look into her cheery eyes, and, in those wells of love, care drowns; we listen to her siren voice, and, in that balmy music, banished hopes come winging to the breast again."

This goes on for about three-quarters of a column: I don't pretend to understand it; but with flowers, angels, Wordsworth's poems, and the old dramatists, one can never be wrong, I think; and though I have written the above paragraphs myself, and don't understand a word of them, I can't, upon my conscience, help thinking that they are mighty pretty writing. After, then, this has gone on for about three-quarters of a column (Timson does it in spare minutes, and fits it to any book that Lady Fanny brings out), he proceeds to particularize, thus:—

" The griding excitement which thrills through every fibre of the soul as we peruse these passionate pages, is almost too painful to bear. Nevertheless, one drains the draughts of poesy to the dregs, so deliciously intoxicating is its nature. We defy any man who begins these volumes to quit them ere he has perused each line. The plot may be briefly told as thus:— Henri, an exiled prince of Franconia (it is easy to understand the flimsy allegory), arrives at Rome, and is presented to the sovereign Pontiff. At a feast, given in his honor at the Vatican, a dancing girl (the loveliest creation that ever issued from poet's brain) is introduced, and exhibits some specimens of her art. The young prince is instantaneously smitten with the charms of the Saltatrice; he breathes into her ear the accents of his love, and is listened to with favor. He has, however, a rival, and a powerful one. The POPE has already cast his eye upon the Apulian maid, and burns with lawless passion. One of the grandest scenes ever writ, occurs between the rivals. The Pope offers to Castanetta every temptation; he will even resign his crown and marry her; but she refuses. The prince can make no such offers; he cannot wed her: 'The blood of Borbone,' he says, ' may not be thus misallied.' He determines to avoid her. In despair, she throws herself off the Tarpeian rock; and the Pope becomes a maniac. Such is an outline of this tragic tale.

" Besides this fabulous and melancholy part of the narrative, which is unsurpassed, much is written in the gay and sparkling

style for which our lovely author is unrivalled. The sketch of
the Marchesina degli Spinachi and her lover, the Duca di Gam-
moni, is delicious; and the intrigue between the beautiful
Princess Kalbsbraten and Count Bouterbrod is exquisitely
painted: everybody, of course, knows who these characters are.
The discovery of the manner in which Kartoffeln, the Saxon
envoy, poisons the princess's dishes, is only a graceful and real
repetition of a story which was agitated throughout all the
diplomatic circles last year. Schinken, the Westphalian, must
not be forgotten; nor Olla, the Spanish Spy. How does Lady
Fanny Flummery, poet as she is, possess a sense of the ridiculous and a keenness of perception which would do honor to a
Rabelais or a Rochefoucauld? To those who ask this question,
we have one reply, and that an example: — Not among women,
'tis true; for till the Lady Fanny came among us, woman never
soared so high. Not among women, indeed! — but in comparing her to that great spirit for whom our veneration is highest
and holiest, we offer no dishonor to his shrine: — in saying that
he who wrote of *Romeo* and *Desdemona* might have drawn
Castanetta and Enrico, we utter but the truthful expressions of
our hearts; in asserting that so long as SHAKSPEARE lives, so
long will FLUMMERY endure; in declaring that he who rules in
all hearts, and over all spirits and all climes, has found a con-
genial spirit, we do but justice to Lady Fanny — justice to him
who sleeps by Avon!"

With which we had better, perhaps, conclude. Our object
has been, in descanting upon the Fashionable Authoress, to
point out the influence which her writing possesses over society,
rather than to criticise her life. The former is quite harmless;
and we don't pretend to be curious about the latter. The
woman herself is not so blamable; it is the silly people who
cringe at her feet that do the mischief, and, gulled themselves,
gull the most gullible of publics. Think you, O Timson, that
her ladyship asks you for your *beaux yeux* or your wit? Fool!
you do think so, or try and think so; and yet you know she loves
not you, but the . . . . newspaper. Think, little Fitch, in your
fine waistcoat, how dearly you have paid for it! Think,
M'Lather, how many smirks, and lies, and columns of good
three-halfpence-a-line matter that big garnet pin has cost you!
the woman laughs at you, man! you, who fancy that she is
smitten with you — laughs at your absurd pretensions, your
way of eating fish at dinner, your great hands, your eyes, your
whiskers, your coat, and your strange north-country twang.

Down with this Delilah! Avaunt, O Circe! giver of poisonous feeds. To your natural haunts, ye gentlemen of the press! if bachelors, frequent your taverns, and be content. Better is Sally the waiter, and the first cut of the joint, than a dinner of four courses, and humbug therewith. Ye who are married, go to your homes; dine not with those persons who scorn your wives. Go not forth to parties, that ye may act Tom Fool for the amusement of my lord and my lady; but play your natural follies among your natural friends. Do this for a few years, and the Fashionable Authoress is extinct. O Jove, what a prospect! She, too, has retreated to her own natural calling, being as much out of place in a book as you, my dear M·Lather, in a drawing-room. Let milliners look up to her; let Howell and James swear by her; let simpering dandies caper about her car; let her write poetry if she likes, but only for the most exclusive circles; let mantua-makers puff her — but not men: let such things be, and the Fashionable Authoress is no more! Blessed, blessed thought! No more fiddle-faddle novels! no more namby-pamby poetry! no more fribble "Blossoms of Loveliness!" When will you arrive, O happy Golden Age?

THE ARTISTS.

It is confidently stated that there was once a time when the quarter of Soho was thronged by the fashion of London. Many wide streets are there in the neighborhood, stretching cheerfully towards Middlesex Hospital in the north, bounded by Dean Street in the west, where the lords and ladies of William's time used to dwell, — till in Queen Anne's time, Bloomsbury put Soho out of fashion, and Great Russell Street became the pink of the mode.

Both these quarters of the town have submitted to the awful rule of nature, and are now to be seen undergoing the dire process of decay. Fashion has deserted Soho, and left her in her gaunt, lonely old age. The houses have a vast, dingy, mouldy, dowager look. No more beaux, in mighty periwigs, ride by in gilded clattering coaches ; no more lackeys accompany them, bearing torches, and shouting for precedence. A solitary policeman paces these solitary streets, — the only dandy in the neighborhood. You hear the milkman yelling his milk with a startling distinctness, and the clack of a servant-girl's pattens sets people a-staring from the windows.

With Bloomsbury we have here nothing to do ; but as genteel stock-brokers inhabit the neighborhood of Regent's Park, — as lawyers have taken possession of Russell Square, — so Artists have seized upon the desolate quarter of Soho. They are to be found in great numbers in Berners Street. Up to the present time, naturalists have never been able to account for this mystery of their residence. What has a painter to do with Middlesex Hospital? He is to be found in Charlotte Street, Fitzroy Square. And why? Philosophy cannot tell, any more than why milk is found in a cocoa-nut.

Look at Newman Street. Has earth, in any dismal corner of her great round face, a spot more desperately gloomy? The windows are spotted with wafers, holding up ghastly bills, that tell you the house is "To Let." Nobody walks there — not even an old-clothes-man; the first inhabited house has bars to the windows, and bears the name of " Ahasuerus, officer to the Sheriff of Middlesex;" and here, above all places, must painters take up their quarters, — day by day must these reckless people pass Ahasuerus's treble gate. There was my poor friend, Tom Tickner (who did those sweet things for " The Book of Beauty"). Tom, who could not pay his washerwoman, lived opposite the bailiff's; and could see every miserable debtor, or greasy Jew writ-bearer that went in or out of his door. The street begins with a bailiff's, and ends with a hospital. I wonder how men live in it, and are decently cheerful, with this gloomy, double-barrelled moral pushed perpetually into their faces. Here, however, they persist in living, no one knows why; owls may still be found roosting in Netley Abbey, and a few Arabs are to be seen at the present minute in Palmyra.

The ground-floors of the houses where painters live are mostly make-believe shops, black empty warehouses, containing fabulous goods. There is a sedan-chair opposite a house in Rathbone Place, that I have myself seen every day for forty-three years. The house has commonly a huge india-rubber-colored door, with a couple of glistening brass-plates and bells. A portrait-painter lives on the first floor; a great historical genius inhabits the second. Remark the first-floor's middle drawing-room window; it is four feet higher than its two companions, and has taken a fancy to peep into the second-floor front. So much for the outward appearance of their habitations, and for the quarters in which they commonly dwell. They seem to love solitude, and their mighty spirits rejoice in vastness and gloomy ruin.

I don't say a word here about those geniuses who frequent the thoroughfares of the town, and have picture-frames containing a little gallery of miniature peers, beauties, and general officers, in the Quadrant, the passages about St. Martin's Lane, the Strand, and Cheapside. Lord Lyndhurst is to be seen in many of these gratis exhibitions — Lord Lyndhurst cribbed from Chalon; Lady Peel from Sir Thomas; Miss Croker from the same; *the* Duke, from ditto; an original officer in the Spanish Legion; a colonel or so, of the Bunhill-Row Fencibles; a lady on a yellow sofa, with four children in little caps and blue ribbons. We have all of us seen these pretty pictures, and are aware that our own features may be "done in this style." Then there is the man on the chain-pier at Brighton, who pares out your likeness in sticking-plaster; there is Miss Croke, or Miss Runt, who gives lessons in Poonah-painting, japanning, or mezzotinting; Miss Stump, who attends ladies' schools with large chalk heads from Le Brun or the Cartoons; Rubbery, who instructs young gentlemen's establishments in pencil; and Sepio, of the Water-Color Society, who paints before eight pupils daily, at a guinea an hour, keeping his own drawings for himself.

All these persons, as the most indifferent reader must see, equally belong to the tribe of Artists (the last not more than the first), and in an article like this should be mentioned properly. But though this paper has been extended from eight pages to sixteen, not a volume would suffice to do justice to the biographies of the persons above mentioned. Think of the superb Sepio, in a light-blue satin cravat, and a light-brown coat, and yellow kids, tripping daintily from Grosvenor Square to Gloucester Place, a small sugar-loaf boy following, who carries his morocco portfolio. Sepio scents his handkerchief, curls his hair, and wears, on a great coarse fist a large emerald ring that one of his pupils gave him. He would not smoke a cigar for the world; he is always to be found at the Opera; and, gods! how he grins, and waggles his head about, as Lady Flummery nods to him from her box.

He goes to at least six great parties in the season. At the houses where he teaches, he has a faint hope that he is received as an equal, and propitiates scornful footmen by absurd donations of sovereigns. The rogue has plenty of them. He has a stock-broker, and a power of guinea-lessons stowed away in the Consols. There are a number of young ladies of genius in the aristocracy, who admire him hugely; he begs you to contradict the report about him and Lady Smigsmag; every now and then he gets a present of game from a marquis; the city ladies die to have lessons of him; he prances about the Park on a high-bred cock-tail, with lacquered boots and enormous high heels; and he has a mother and sisters somewhere — washerwomen, it is said, in Pimlico.

How different is his fate to that of poor Rubbery, the school drawing-master! Highgate, Homerton, Putney, Hackney, Hornsey, Turnham Green, are his resorts; he has a select seminary to attend at every one of these places; and if, from all these nurseries of youth, he obtains a sufficient number of half-crowns to pay his week's bills, what a happy man is he!

He lives most likely in a third floor in Howland Street, and has commonly five children, who have all a marvellous talent for drawing — all save one, perhaps, that is an idiot, which a poor, sick mother is ever carefully tending. Sepio's great aim and battle in life is to be considered one of the aristocracy; honest Rubbery would fain be thought a gentleman, too; but, indeed, he does not know whether he is so or not. Why be a gentleman? — a gentleman Artist does not obtain the wages of a tailor; Rubbery's butcher looks down upon him with a royal scorn; and his wife, poor gentle soul (a clergyman's daughter, who married him in the firm belief that her John would be knighted, and make an immense fortune), — his wife, I say, has many fierce looks to suffer from Mrs. Butcher, and many meek excuses or prayers to proffer, when she cannot pay her bill, — or when, worst of all, she has humbly to beg for a little scrap of meat upon credit, against John's coming home. He has five-and-twenty miles to walk that day, and must have something nourishing when he comes in — he is killing himself, poor fellow, she knows he is: and Miss Crick has promised to pay him his quarter's charge on the very next Saturday. "Gentlefolks, indeed," says Mrs. Butcher; "pretty gentlefolks these, as can't pay for half a pound of steak!" Let us thank heaven that the Artist's wife has her meat, however, — there is good in that shrill, fat, mottle-faced Mrs. Brisket, after all.

Think of the labors of that poor Rubbery. He was up at four in the morning, and toiled till nine upon a huge damp icy lithographic stone; on which he has drawn the "Star of the Wave," or the "Queen of the Tourney," or, "She met at Almack's," for Lady Flummery's last new song. This done, at half-past nine, he is to be seen striding across Kensington Gardens, to wait upon the before-named Miss Crick, at Lamont House. Transport yourself in imagination to the Misses Kittle's seminary, Potzdam Villa, Upper Homerton, four miles from Shoreditch: and at half-past two, Professor Rubbery is to be seen swinging along towards the gate. Somebody is on the look-out for him; indeed it is his eldest daughter, Marianne, who has been pacing the shrubbery, and peering over the green railings this half-hour past. She is with the Misses Kittle on the "mutual system," a thousand times more despised than the butchers' and the grocers' daughters, who are educated on the same terms, and whose papas are warm men in Aldgate. Wednesday is the happiest day of Marianne's week · and this the happiest hour of Wednesday. Behold! Professor Rubbery wipes his hot brows and kisses the poor thing, and they go in together out of the rain, and he tells her that the twins are well out of the measles, thank God! and that Tom has just done the Antinous, in a way that must make him sure of the Academy prize, and that mother is better of her rheumatism now. He has brought her a letter, in large round-hand, from Polly; a famous soldier, drawn by little Frank; and when, after his two hours' lesson, Rubbery is off again, our dear Marianne cons over the letter and picture a hundred times with soft tearful smiles, and stows them away in an old writing-desk, amidst a heap more of precious home relics, wretched trumpery scraps and baubles, that you and I, Madam, would sneer at; but that in the poor child's eyes (and, I think, in the eyes of One who knows how to value widows' mites and humble sinners' offerings) are better than bank-notes and Pitt diamonds. O kind heaven, that has given these treasures to the poor! Many and many an hour does Marianne lie awake with full eyes, and yearn for that wretched old lodging in Howland Street, where mother and brothers lie sleeping; and, gods! what a fête it is, when twice or thrice in the year she comes home!

I forget how many hundred millions of miles, for how many billions of centuries, how many thousands of decillions of angels, peris, houris, demons, afreets, and the like, Mahomet travelled, lived, and counted, during the time that some water was falling from a bucket to the ground; but have we not been wandering most egregiously away from Rubbery, during the minute in which his daughter is changing his shoes, and taking off his reeking mackintosh in the hall of Potzdam Villa? She thinks him the finest artist that ever cut an H. B.; that's positive: and as a drawing-master, his merits are wonderful; for at the Misses Kittle's annual vacation festival, when the young ladies' drawings are exhibited to their mammas and relatives (Rubbery attending in a clean shirt, with his wife's large brooch stuck in it, and drinking negus along with the very best) ; — at the annual festival, I say, it will be found that the sixty-four drawings exhibited — " Tintern Abbey," " Kenilworth Castle," " Horse — from Carl Vernet," " Head — from West," or what not (say sixteen of each sort) — are the one exactly as good as the other ; so that, although Miss Slamcoe gets the prize, there is really no reason why Miss Timson, who is only four years old, should not have it; her design being accurately stroke for stroke, tree for tree, curl for curl, the same as Miss Slamcoe's, who is eighteen. The fact is, that of these drawings, Rubbery, in the course of the year, has done every single stroke, although the girls and their parents are ready to take their affidavits (or, as I heard once a great female grammarian say, their *affies davit*) that the drawing-master has never been near the sketches. This is the way with them ; but mark !— when young ladies come home, are settled in life, and mammas of families, — can they design so much as a horse, or a dog, or a " moo-cow " for little Jack who bawls out for them? Not they ! Rubbery's pupils have no more notion of drawing, any more than Sepio's of painting, when that eminent artist is away.

Between these two gentlemen, lie a whole class of teachers of drawing, who resemble them more or less. I am ashamed to say that Rubbery takes his pipe in the parlor of an hotel, of which the largest room is devoted to the convenience of poor people, amateurs of British gin : whilst Sepio trips down to the Club, and has a pint of the smallest claret : but of course the tastes of men vary ; and you find them simple or presuming, careless or prudent, natural and vulgar, or false and atrociously genteel, in all ranks and stations of life.

As for the other persons mentioned at the beginning of this discourse, viz. the cheap portrait-painter, the portrait-cutter in sticking-plaster, and Miss Croke, the teacher of mezzotint and Poonah-painting, — nothing need be said of them in this place, as we have to speak of matters more important. Only about Miss Croke, or about other professors of cheap art, let the reader most sedulously avoid them. Mezzotinto is a take-in, Poonah-painting a rank, villanous deception. So is " Grecian art without brush or pencils." These are only small mechanical contrivances, over which young ladies are made to lose time. And now, having disposed of these small skirmishers who hover round the great body of Artists, we are arrived in presence of the main force, that we must begin to attack in form. In the " partition of the earth," as it has been described by Schiller, the reader will remember that the poet, finding himself at the end of a general scramble without a single morsel of plunder, applied passionately to Jove, who pitied the poor fellow's condition, and complimented him with a seat in the Empyrean. " The strong and the cunning," says Jupiter, " have seized upon the inheritance of the world, whilst thou wert star-gazing and rhyming : not one single acre remains wherewith I can endow thee ; but, in revenge, if thou art disposed to visit me in my own heaven, come when thou wilt, it is always open to thee."

The cunning and strong have scrambled and struggled more on our own little native spot of earth than in any other place on the world's surface; and the English poet (whether he handles a pen or a pencil (has little other refuge than that windy, unsubstantial one which Jove has vouchsafed to him. Such airy board and lodging is, however, distasteful to many; who prefer, therefore, to give up their poetical calling, and, in a vulgar beef-eating world, to feed upon and fight for vulgar beef.

For such persons (among the class of painters), it may be asserted that portrait-painting was invented. It is the Artist's compromise with heaven; "the light of common day," in which, after a certain quantity of "travel from the East," the genius fades at last. Abbé Barthelemy (who sent Le Jeune Anacharsis travelling through Greece in the time of Plato, — travelling through ancient Greece in lace ruffles, red heels, and a pigtail), — Abbé Barthelemy, I say, declares that somebody was once standing against a wall in the sun, and that somebody else traced the outline of somebody's shadow; and so painting was "invented." Angelica Kauffmann has made a neat picture of this neat subject; and very well worthy she was of handling it. Her painting *might* grow out of a wall and a piece of charcoal; and honest Barthelemy might be satisfied that he had here traced the true origin of the art. What a base pedigree have these abominable Greek, French, and High-Dutch heathens invented for that which is divine! — a wall, ye gods, to be represented as the father of that which came down radiant from you! The man who invented such a blasphemy, ought to be impaled upon broken bottles, or shot off pitilessly by spring-guns, nailed to the bricks like a dead owl or a weasel, or tied up — a kind of vulgar Prometheus — and baited forever by the house-dog.

But let not our indignation carry us too far. Lack of genius in some, of bread in others, of patronage in a shop-keeping world, that thinks only of the useful, and is little inclined to study the sublime, has turned thousands of persons calling themselves, and wishing to be, Artists, into so many common face-painters, who must look out for the "kalon" in the fat features of a red-gilled Alderman, or, at best, in a pretty, simpering, white-necked beauty from "Almack's." The dangerous charms of these latter, especially, have seduced away many painters; and we often think that this very physical superiority which English ladies possess, this tempting brilliancy of health and complexion, which belongs to them more than to any others, has operated upon our Artists as a serious disadvantage, and kept them from better things. The French call such beauty " *La Beauté du Diable ;*" and a devilish power it has truly ; before our Armidas and Helens how many Rinaldos and Parises have fallen, who are content to forget their glorious calling, and slumber away their energies in the laps of these soft tempters. O ye British enchantresses! I never see a gilded annual-book, without likening it to a small island near Cape Pelorus, in Sicily, whither, by twanging of harps, singing of ravishing melodies, glancing of voluptuous eyes, and the most beautiful fashionable undress in the world, the naughty sirens lured the passing seaman. Steer clear of them, ye Artists! pull, pull for your lives, ye crews of Suffolk Street and the Water-Color gallery! stop your ears, bury your eyes, tie yourselves to the mast, and away with you from the gaudy, smiling " Books of Beauty." Land, and you are ruined! Look well among the flowers on yonder beach — it is whitened with the bones of painters.

For my part, I never have a model under seventy, and her with several shawls and a cloak on. By these means the imagination gets fair play, and the morals remain unendangered.

Personalities are odious ; but let the British public look at the pictures of the celebrated Mr. Shalloon — the moral British public — and say whether our grandchildren (or the grandchildren of the exalted personages whom Mr. Shalloon paints) will not have a queer idea of the manners of their grandmammas, as they are represented in the most beautiful, dexterous, captivating water-color drawings that ever were? Heavenly powers, how they simper and ogle! with what gimcracks of lace, ribbons, ferronières, smelling-bottles, and what not, is every one of them overloaded! What shoulders, what ringlets, what funny little pug-dogs do they most of them exhibit to us! The days of Lancret and Watteau are lived over again, and the court ladies of the time of Queen Victoria look as moral as the immaculate countesses of the days of Louis Quinze. The last President of the Royal Academy * is answerable for many sins, and many imitators ; especially for that gay, simpering, meretricious look which he managed to give to every lady who sat to him for her portrait ; and I do not know a more curious contrast than that which may be perceived by any one who will examine a collection of his portraits by the side of some by Sir Joshua Reynolds. They seem to have painted different races of people ; and when one hears very old gentlemen talking of the superior beauty that existed in their early days (as very

* Sir Thomas Lawrence.

old gentlemen, from Nestor downwards, have and will), one is inclined to believe that there is some truth in what they say; at least, that the men and women under George the Third were far superior to their descendants in the time of George the Fourth. Whither has it fled — that calm matronly grace, or beautiful virgin innocence, which belonged to the happy women who sat to Sir Joshua? Sir Thomas's ladies are ogling out of their gilt frames, and asking us for admiration; Sir Joshua's sit quiet, in maiden meditation fancy free, not anxious for applause, but sure to command it; a thousand times more lovely in their sedate serenity than Sir Thomas's ladies in their smiles, and their satin ball-dresses.

But this is not the general notion, and the ladies prefer the manner of the modern Artist. Of course, such being the case, the painters must follow the fashion. One could point out half a dozen Artists who, at Sir Thomas's death, have seized upon a shred of his somewhat tawdry mantle. There is Carmine, for instance, a man of no small repute, who will stand as the representative of his class.

Carmine has had the usual education of a painter in this country; he can read and write — that is, has spent years drawing the figure — and has made his foreign tour. It may be that he had original talent once, but he has learned to forget this, as the great bar to his success; and must imitate, in order to live. He is among Artists what a dentist is among surgeons — a man who is employed to decorate the human head, and who is paid enormously for so doing. You know one of Carmine's beauties at any exhibition, and see the process by which they are manufactured. He lengthens the noses, widens the foreheads, opens the eyes, and gives them the proper languishing leer; diminishes the mouth, and infallibly tips the ends of it with a pretty smile of his favorite color. He is a personable, white-handed, bald-headed, middle-aged man now, with that grave blandness of look which one sees in so many prosperous empty-headed people. He has a collection of little stories and court gossip about Lady This, and " my particular friend, Lord So-and-so," which he lets off in succession to every sitter: indeed, a most bland, irreproachable, gentlemanlike man. He gives most patronizing advice to young Artists, and makes a point of praising all — not certainly too much, but in a gentlemanlike, indifferent, simpering way. This should be the maxim with prosperous persons, who have had to make their way, and wish to keep what they have made. They praise everybody, and are called good-natured, benevolent men.

Surely no benevolence is so easy; it simply consists in lying, and smiling, and wishing everybody well. You will get to do so quite naturally at last, and at no expense of truth. At first, when a man has feelings of his own — feelings of love or of anger — this perpetual grin and good-humor is hard to maintain. I used to imagine, when I first knew Carmine, that there were some particular springs in his wig (that glossy, oily, curly crop of chestnut hair) that pulled up his features into a smile, and kept the muscles so fixed for the day. I don't think so now, and should say he grinned, even when he was asleep and his teeth were out; the smile does not lie in the manufacture of the wig, but in the construction of the brain. Claude Carmine has the organ of *don't-care-a-damn-ativeness* wonderfully developed; not that reckless don't-care-a-damn-ativeness which leads a man to disregard all the world, and himself into the bargain. Claude stops before he comes to himself; but beyond that individual member of the Royal Academy, has not a single sympathy for a single human creature. The account of his friends' deaths, woes, misfortunes, or good luck, he receives with equal good-nature; he gives three splendid dinners per annum, Gunter, Dukes, Fortnum, and Mason, everything; he dines out the other three hundred and sixty-two days in the year, and was never known to give away a shilling, or to advance, for one half-hour, the forty pounds per quarter wages that he gives to Mr. Scumble, who works the backgrounds, limbs, and draperies of his portraits.

He is not a good painter: how should he be; whose painting as it were never goes beyond a whisper, and who would make a general simpering as he looked at an advancing cannon-ball? — but he is not a bad painter, being a keen respectable man of the world, who has a cool head, and knows what is what. In France, where tigerism used to be the fashion among the painters, I make no doubt Carmine would have let his beard and wig grow, and looked the fiercest of the fierce; but with us a man must be genteel; the perfection of style (in writing and in drawing-rooms) being "*de ne pas en avoir*," Carmine of course is agreeably vapid. His conversation has accordingly the flavor and briskness of a clear, brilliant, stale bottle of soda-water, — once in five minutes or so, you see rising up to the surface a little bubble — a little tiny shining point of wit, — it rises and explodes feebly, and then dies. With regard to wit, people of fashion (as we are given to understand) are satisfied with a mere *soupçon* of it. Anything more were indecorous; a genteel stomach could not bear it:

Carmine knows the exact proportions of the dose, and would not venture to administer to his sitters anything beyond the requisite quantity.

There is a great deal more said here about Carmine — the man, than Carmine — the Artist; but what can be written about the latter? New ladies in white satin, new Generals in red, new Peers in scarlet and ermine, and stout Members of Parliament pointing to inkstands and sheets of letter-paper, with a Turkey-carpet beneath them, a red curtain above them, a Doric pillar supporting them, and a tremendous storm of thunder and lightning lowering and flashing in the background, spring up every year, and take their due positions " upon the line " in the Academy, and send their compliments of hundreds to swell Carmine's heap of Consols. If he paints Lady Flummery for the tenth time, in the character of the tenth Muse, what need have we to say anything about it? The man is a good workman, and will manufacture a decent article at the best price; but we should no more think of noticing each, than of writing fresh critiques upon every new coat that Nugee or Stultz turned out. The papers say, in reference to his picture " No 591. ' Full-length portrait of her Grace the Duchess of Doldrum. Carmine, R. A.' Mr. Carmine never fails; this work, like all others, by the same artist, is excellent: " — or, " No. 591, &c. The lovely Duchess of Doldrum has received from Mr. Carmine's pencil ample justice; the *chiar' oscuro* of the picture is perfect; the likeness admirable; the keeping and coloring have the true Titianesque gusto; if we might hint a fault, it has the left ear of the lap-dog a ' little ' out of drawing."

Then, perhaps, comes a criticism which says : — " The Duchess of Doldrum's picture by Mr. Carmine is neither better nor worse than five hundred other performances of the same artist. It would be very unjust to say that these portraits are bad, for they have really a considerable cleverness; but to say that they were good, would be quite as false; nothing in our eyes was ever further from being so. Every ten years Mr. Carmine exhibits what is called an original picture of three inches square, but beyond this, nothing original is to be found in him : as a lad, he copied Reynolds, then Opie, then Lawrence; then having made a sort of style of his own, he has copied himself ever since," &c.

And then the critic goes on to consider the various parts of Carmine's pictures. In speaking of critics, their peculiar relationship with painters ought not to be forgotten; and as in a former paper we have seen how a fashionable authoress has her

critical toadies, in like manner has the painter his enemies and
friends in the press; with this difference, probably, that the
writer can bear a fair quantity of abuse without wincing, while
the artist not uncommonly grows mad at such strictures, considers them as personal matters, inspired by a private feeling
of hostility, and hates the critic for life who has ventured to
question his judgment in any way. We have said before, poor
Academicians, for how many conspiracies are you made to
answer! We may add now, poor critics, what black personal
animosities are discovered for you, when you happen (right or
wrong, but according to your best ideas) to speak the truth!
Say that Snooks's picture is badly colored. — " O heavens ! "
shrieks Snooks, " what can I have done to offend this fellow?"
Hint that such a figure is badly drawn — and Snooks instantly
declares you to be his personal enemy, actuated only by envy
and vile pique. My friend Pebbler, himself a famous Artist,
is of opinion that the critic should *never* abuse the painter's
performances, because, says he, the painter knows much better
than any one else what his own faults are, and because you
never do him any good. Are men of the brush so obstinate? —
very likely : but the public — the public? are we not to do our
duty by it too ; and, aided by our superior knowledge and
genius for the fine arts, point out to it the way it should go?
Yes, surely ; and as by the efforts of dull or interested critics
many bad painters have been palmed off upon the nation as
geniuses of the first degree ; in like manner, the sagacious and
disinterested (like some we could name) have endeavored to
provide this British nation with pure principles of taste, — or
at least, to prevent them from adopting such as are impure.

Carmine, to be sure, comes in for very little abuse; and,
indeed, he deserves but little. He is a fashionable painter,
and preserves the golden mediocrity which is necessary for the
fashion. Let us bid him good-by. He lives in a house all to
himself, most likely, — has a footman, sometimes a carriage ;
is apt to belong to the " Athenæum ; " and dies universally
respected ; that is, not one single soul cares for him dead, as
he, living, did not care for one single soul.

Then, perhaps, we should mention M'Gilp, or Blather, rising young men, who will fill Carmine's place one of these days,
and occupy his house in ——, when the fulness of time shall
come, and (he borne to a narrow grave in the Harrow Road
by the whole mourning Royal Academy,) they shall leave their
present first floor in Newman Street, and step into his very
house and shoes.

There is little difference between the juniors and the seniors; they grin when they are talking of him together, and express a perfect confidence that they can paint a head against Carmine any day — as very likely they can. But until his demise, they are occupied with painting people about the Regent's Park and Russell Square; are very glad to have the chance of a popular clergyman, or a college tutor, or a mayor of Stoke Poges after the Reform Bill. Such characters are commonly mezzotinted afterwards; and the portrait of our esteemed townsman So-and-so, by that talented artist Mr. M'Gilp, of London, is favorably noticed by the provincial press, and is to be found over the sideboards of many country gentlemen. If they come up to town, to whom do they go? To M'Gilp, to be sure; and thus, slowly, his practice and his prices increase.

The Academy student is a personage that should not be omitted here; he resembles very much, outwardly, the medical student, and has many of the latter's habits and pleasures. He very often wears a broad-brimmed hat and a fine dirty crimson velvet waistcoat, his hair commonly grows long, and he has braiding to his pantaloons. He works leisurely at the Academy, he loves theatres, billiards, and novels, and has his house-of-call somewhere in the neighborhood of Saint Martin's Lane, where he and his brethren meet and sneer at Royal Academicians. If you ask him what line of art he pursues, he answers with a smile exceedingly supercilious, " Sir, I am an historical painter; " meaning that he will only condescend to take subjects from Hume, or Robertson, or from the classics — which he knows nothing about. This stage of an historical painter is only preparatory, lasting perhaps from eighteen to five-and-twenty, when the gentleman's madness begins to disappear, and he comes to look at life sternly in the face, and to learn that man shall not live by historical painting alone. Then our friend falls to portrait-painting, or annual-painting, or makes some other such sad compromise with necessity.

He has probably a small patrimony, which defrays the charge of his studies and cheap pleasures during his period of apprenticeship. He makes the *obligé* tour to France and Italy, and returns from those countries with a multitude of spoiled canvases, and a large pair of moustaches, with which he establishes himself in one of the dingy streets of Soho before mentioned. There is poor Pipson, a man of indomitable patience, and undying enthusiasm for his profession. He could paper Exeter Hall with his studies from the life, and with portraits in chalk and oil of French *sapeurs* and Italians brigands, that kindly descend from their mountain-caverns, and quit their murderous occupations, in order to sit to young gentlemen at Rome, at the rate of tenpence an hour. Pipson returns from abroad, establishes himself, has his cards printed, and waits and waits for commissions for great historical pictures. Meanwhile, night after night, he is to be found at his old place in the Academy, copying the old life-guardsman — working, working away — and never advancing one jot. At eighteen, Pipson copied statues and life-guardsmen to admiration ; at five-and-thirty he can make admirable drawings of life-guardsmen and statues. Beyond this he never goes ; year after year his historical picture is returned to him by the envious Academicians, and he grows old, and his little patrimony is long since spent ; and he earns nothing himself. How does he support hope and life ? — that is the wonder. No one knows until he tries (which God forbid he should !) upon what a small matter hope and life can be supported. Our poor fellow lives on from year to year in a miraculous way ; tolerably cheerful in the midst of his semi-starvation, and wonderfully confident about next year, in spite of the failures of the last twenty-five. Let us thank God for imparting to us, poor weak mortals, the inestimable blessing of *vanity*. How many half-witted votaries of the arts — poets, painters, actors, musicians — live upon this food, and scarcely any other ! If the delusion were to drop from Pipson's eyes, and he should see himself as he is, — if some malevolent genius were to mingle with his feeble brains one fatal particle of common sense, — he would just walk off Waterloo Bridge, and abjure poverty, incapacity, cold lodgings, unpaid baker's bills, ragged elbows, and deferred hopes, at once and for ever.

We do not mean to depreciate the profession of historical painting, but simply to warn youth against it as dangerous and unprofitable. It is as if a young fellow should say, " I will be a Raffaelle or a Titian, — a Milton or a Shakspeare," and if he will count up how many people have lived since the world began, and how many there have been of the Raffaelle or Shakspeare sort, he can calculate to a nicety what are the chances in his favor. Even successful historical painters, what are they ? — in a worldly point of view, they mostly inhabit the second floor, or have great desolate studios in back premises, whither life-guardsmen, old-clothesmen, blackamoors, and other " properties " are conducted, to figure at full length as Roman conquerors, Jewish high-priests, or Othellos on canvas. Then there are gay, smart, water-color painters, — a flourishing and pleasant trade. Then there are shabby, fierce-looking geniuses, in ringlets, and all but rags, who paint, and whose pictures are never sold, and who vow they are the objects of some general and scoundrelly conspiracy.　There are landscape-painters, who travel to the uttermost ends of the earth and brave heat and cold, to bring to the greedy British public views of Cairo, Calcutta, St. Petersburg, Timbuctoo.　You see English artists under the shadow of the Pyramids, making sketches of the Copts, perched on the backs of dromedaries, accompanying a caravan across the desert, or getting materials for an annual in Iceland or Siberia.　What genius and what energy do not they all exhibit — these men, whose profession, in this wise country of ours, is scarcely considered as liberal!

If we read the works of the Reverend Dr. Lempriere, Monsieur Winckelmann, Professor Plato, and others who have written concerning the musty old Grecians, we shall find that the Artists of those barbarous times meddled with all sorts of trades besides their own, and dabbled in fighting, philosophy, metaphysics, both Scotch and German, politics, music, and the deuce knows what.　A rambling sculptor, who used to go about giving lectures in those days, Socrates by name, declared that the wisest of men in his time were artists.　This Plato, before mentioned, went through a regular course of drawing, figure and landscape, black-lead, chalk, with or without stump, sepia, water-color, and oils.　Was there ever such absurdity known? Among these benighted heathens, painters were the most accomplished gentlemen, — and the most accomplished gentlemen were painters; the former would make you a speech, or read you a dissertation on Kant, or lead you a regiment, — with the very best statesman, philosopher, or soldier in Athens.　And they had the folly to say, that by thus busying and accomplishing themselves in all manly studies, they were advancing eminently in their own peculiar one.　What was the consequence?　Why, that fellow Socrates not only made a miserable fifth-rate sculptor, but was actually hanged for treason.

And serve him right.　Do *our* young artists study anything beyond the proper way of cutting a pencil, or drawing a model? Do you hear of *them* hard at work over books, and bothering their brains with musty learning?　Not they, forsooth: we understand the doctrine of division of labor, and each man sticks to his trade.　Artists do not meddle with the pursuits of the rest of the world; and, in revenge, the rest of the world does not meddle with Artists.　Fancy an Artist being a senior wrangler or a politician; and on the other hand, fancy a real gentleman turned painter!　No, no; ranks are defined.　A real gentleman may get money by the law, or by wearing a red coat and fighting, or a black one and preaching; but that he should sell himself to *Art* — forbid it, heaven! And do not let your ladyship on reading this cry, " Stuff! — stupid envy, rank republicanism, — an artist *is* a gentleman." Madam, would you like to see your son, the Honorable Fitzroy Plantagenet, a painter? You would die sooner; the escutcheon of the Smigsmags would be blotted for ever, if Plantagenet ever ventured to make a mercantile use of a bladder of paint.

Time was — some hundred years back — when writers lived in Grub Street, and poor ragged Johnson shrunk behind a screen in Cave's parlor — that the author's trade was considered a very mean one; which a gentleman of family could not take up but as an amateur. This absurdity is pretty nearly worn out now, and I do humbly hope and pray for the day when the other shall likewise disappear. If there be any nobleman with a talent that way, why — why don't we see him among the R.A.'s?

501.	The Schoolmaster. Sketch taken abroad	Brum, Henry, Lord, *R. A. F.R S. S.A.* *of the National Institute of France*
502.	View of the Artist's residence at Windsor	Maconkey, Right Honorable T. B.
503.	Murder of the Babes in the Tower	Rustle, Lord J. Pill, Right Honorable Sir Robert.
504.	A little Agitation	O'Carrol, Daniel, M.R.I.A.

Fancy, I say, such names as these figuring in the catalogue of the Academy: and why should they not? The real glorious days of the art (which wants equality and not patronage) will revive then. Patronage — a plague on the word! — it implies inferiority; and in the name of all that is sensible, why is a respectable country gentleman, or a city attorney's lady, or any person of any rank, however exalted, to " patronize" an Artist!

There are some who sigh for the past times, when magnificent, swaggering Peter Paul Rubens (who himself patronized a queen) rode abroad with a score of gentlemen in his train, and a purse-bearer to scatter ducats; and who love to think how he was made an English knight and a Spanish grandee, and went of embassies as if he had been a born marquis. Sweet it is to remember, too, that Sir Antony Vandyck, K.B., actually married out of the peerage: and that when Titian dropped his mahlstick, the Emperor Charles V. picked it up (O gods! what heroic self-devotion) — picked it up, saying, " I can make fifty dukes, but not one Titian." Nay, was not the Pope of Rome going to make Raffaelle a Cardinal, — and were not these golden days?

Let us say at once " No." The very fuss made about certain painters in the sixteenth and seventeenth centuries shows that the body of artists had no rank or position in the world. They hung upon single patrons : and every man who holds his place by such a tenure, must feel himself an inferior, more or less. The times are changing now, and as authors are no longer compelled to send their works abroad under the guardianship of a great man and a slavish dedication, painters, too, are beginning to deal directly with the public. Who are the great picture-buyers now? — the engravers and their employers, the people, — " the only source of legitimate power," as they say after dinner. A fig then for Cardinals' hats ! were Mr. O'Connell in power to-morrow, let us hope he would not give one, not even a paltry bishopric *in partibus*, to the best painter in the Academy. What need have they of honors out of the profession? Why are they to be be-knighted like a parcel of aldermen? — for my part, I solemnly declare, that I will take nothing under a peerage, after the exhibition of my great picture, and don't see, if painters *must* have titles conferred upon them for eminent services, why the Marquis of Mulready or the Earl of Landseer should not sit in the house as well as any law or soldier lord.

The truth to be elicited from this little digressive dissertation is this painful one, — that young Artists are not generally as well instructed as they should be ; and let the Royal Academy look to it, and give some sound courses of lectures to their pupils on literature and history, as well as on anatomy, or light and shade.

THE END.